UNDERSTANDING

THE

VOICE-ENABLED

INTERNET

Covering Web-Enabled Call Centers and Help Desks, Web-To-IVR Links, Text-To-Speech Web Browsing, FAX-On-Demand, Personal AIN (incl. One Number Calling and Call Re-routing), Multimedia Gateways, Collaborative Distance Computing, Interactive Gaming, Unified Messaging and, of course, Toll-Free Phone Calls.

by Edwin Margulies

A Telecom Library, Inc. Book
Published by Flatiron Publishing, Inc.
Copyright © 1996 by Edwin K. Margulies

ISBN 0-936648-91-0

Manufactured in the United States of America

First Edition, August, 1996
Cover Designed by Mara Leonardi
Printed at BookCrafters, Chelsea, MI.

Acknowledgments

The brightest and most creative minds are making *The Voice-Enabled Internet* flourish. This book tells the story in full. There are so many to thank, I put more acknowledgments at the end of each chapter. The response to my *call for papers* was phenomenal. There are one hundred organizations represented here. My thanks to all of you:

Active Voice Corporation, Advantage KBS, American International, American Network Systems, Inc., Applied Voice Technology, Inc., Aspect Telecommunications, Aum Tech, Inc., Automated Management Software, Black Ice Software, Inc., Boardwatch Magazine, Bonzi Software, Brooktrout Technology, Call Center Magazine, CallWare Technologies, Inc., Camelot, Centigram Communications Corporation, Computer Telephony Magazine, Connectix, Cyber Radio 1, DataBeam Corporation, Davidson Consulting, Dialogic Corporation, Digital Sound Corporation, Edify Corporation, Enhanced Systems, Inc., FaxSav, Inc., FreeTel Communications, Inc., G & R Data Group, Inc., GMD Fokus, HTI Voice Solutions, Ibex Technologies, Inc., IBM Corp., Inference, Intel Corporation, iNTELiTRAK Technologies, Inc., Intelligent Visual Computing, International Data Corporation, International Multimedia, International Telecommunications Union, IPC Peripherals, Inc., Jabra Corporation, KnowledgeBroker, Inc., Lansys Ltd., Latitude Communications, LINKON Corporation, Logicom, Inc., Lucent Technologies, Marin Software Partners, MediaGate, Microsoft, MIT, Natural MicroSystems, NetCall Technologies Limited, NetPhonic Communications, Netspeak Corporation, NetWatch, Inc., NetXchange Communications Ltd., Nice Systems, Inc., Novell, Octel Communications Corporation, Periphonics Corporation, Precept Software, Inc., Precision Systems, Inc., Professional Help Desk, Progressive Networks, Prospect Software, Inc., Quarterdeck Corporation, Quest Interactive Media, Inc., Remedy Corporation,

Rockwell Switching Systems, Securicor Telecoms, ShadowTel Communications Corporation, Siemens Rolm Communications, Inc., Silversoft, Smith Micro Software, Inc., SoftLinx, Inc., Spanlink Communications, Stardust Technologies, Inc., Stylus Product Group, Sun Microsystems, Syntellect Inc., TAC Systems, Inc., Teknekron Infoswitch Corporation, TELE-CONNECT Magazine, Telescape Communications, Telinet, Tribal Voice, Trumpet Software International, UNISYS Corporation, University of Illinois, University of North Carolina, VDONet, Venturian Software, Virtuosity, VocalTec, Inc., Vosaic Corporation, Voxware, Inc., White Pine Software, Inc. and Xing Technology Corp.

All the contact information for editorial contributors is in Appendix C. It's a treasure chest of the greatest Voice-Enabled Internet experts in the world. Enjoy their knowledge.

Ed Margulies
New York City, August 1996
EdMargulies@mcimail.com
www.computertelephony.com

FOREWORD

TELEPHONY ON THE INTERNET

THE NEXT BIG FRONTIER

by Harry Newton

"John," I ask, "what do you think of my design?"

"Not bad," he replies, "let me move this column a little over here. See the difference?"

"Yup. The perfect touch. Let's send it to Production. Joe, Ron and Bert?"

Click.

"They have it."

"John," I say happily, "I'd love to celebrate with you. But I don't have the six hours it takes to get to you physically. Here's some electronic money. Use it for a beer."

What wonderful deck of hands we've been dealt. Just when physical travel has become so painful -- today two friends had four hour airline delays -- we have an explosion of cheap, powerful, rich ways to communicate with each other.

These ways will immeasurably improve the quality of our lives -- from the way we run our businesses to the way seek medical help. We'll live longer.

The Internet is key. The invention of the Internet is an important as the invention of the Gutenberg press in 1453. To produce a book then took one monk one year. He wrote it by hand. There were 30,000 books on the continent of Europe. By the year 1500, 50 years later, there were nine million. No one knew then how the Gutenberg press would change the world. In 1996, no one has any idea of the profound changes the Internet, and now, its new partnership with the phone, will bring.

In 1994, some savvy Israelis wrote software that let them make voice phone calls over the Internet. The motivation wasn't the "climb it because it's there" you hear from mountain climbers. There was real motivation. The Israeli phone company, Bezek, charged $2.50 a minute to call New York. The Internet was free. Who cared if the new Internet phone calls sounded scratchy, had a half second delay (worse than a satellite circuit) and crashed regularly. So what! It was that or Bezek and its outrageous prices. Everyone hated Bezek.

The Israelis sold a bunch of Internet "phones" to Americans, who always enjoyed trying something new, but were not motivated by saving long distance phone calls at 10 cents a minute -- the price Sprint was widely advertising. Pain is endurable when you're saving $2.50 a minute, or more. But not to save a dime. Internet phoning in 1996 in the United States was a gimmick.

But voice is not the only medium of communications, nor necessarily the most important. For example, combine real-time speaking with real-time messaging -- fax, email, voice, video, images, presentations, white boarding, collaborative computing -- and you get a double whammy. Look at my example above. My drawing is the focus of our joint long distance venture. We're concentrating on the drawing, on improving it.

Our voices are the glue that focuses and coordinates our efforts to improve the drawing. Our voices are not the focus. It matters not that our voices are scratchy, break up and suffer a half second delay. So long as the voice conversation is mildly understandable. We're glued to the picture.

There are 1001 variations on this theme. Today's biggest use of the Internet is for electronic mail -- what we call non-real time messaging. I like email. Written words are my lifeblood. But two days ago I received my first video mail. It was a one minute video-with-audio clip of a plump engineer, called David Glass, demonstrating his new video product, called AudioVision, and holding up his packaging. He reminded me of the man on late night TV who peddles a product that cleans your toilet bowl with blue gunk every time you flush.

As a movie, Dave's audio clip was awful. It showed up as a two inch square frame on my screen. But it was positively engrossing. I've played it several times. I've showed it to my friends. It's my first video mail. David Glass did more to sell me, a reporter, on his new product, AudioVision, than he could ever have done with an old-fashioned voice mail, email, or God forbid, a press kit.

Non-real-time messaging -- today's biggest Internet application -- suddenly came alive for me. All it took was one video mail. Non-real-time multimedia messaging suddenly begins to make enormous sense when today's standard email is enhanced with fax, voice, video and image messaging.

As we craft The New Internet Communications, we find we have enormous flexibility. I love shopping. But I hate going to shops. I catalog shop. But paper catalogs never have enough information to answer all my questions. I love Web shopping. I visit a Web site. It's bursting with information on the company's products. I mouse click. Suddenly I'm speaking to an operator. Not just any operator. I clicked the "Expert" button and now I'm speaking to someone trained on that product. What's even better is that person, the product expert, is seeing on their computer screen exactly what I'm seeing on mine.

As I move around, their screen moves around. And vice versa. They are able to guide me around, taking me to the information I'm seeking. Imagine how powerful such a tool would be for a customer support center, or a help desk.

As I write this, I remember the time at 1:00 AM my wife, Susan, insisted I repair our dishwasher. I called GE on their 800 number. I was hoping GE would be closed and I could go sleep. No such luck. A nice man insisted on helping me. In 15 minutes he'd walked me through the dishwasher fix. It wasn't difficult. But it might have been. Picture: I call. He says, "Hang up. Go into our Web site. I'll meet you there. I'll throw up a couple of exploded diagrams of your dishwasher and walk you through them. Then, with my diagrams up on your PC, you can try and fix your dishwasher. If not, I'll include part numbers of the offending parts. You can order them through the Web or click. I'll come back on line and take the order personally."

Two days ago I visited a Web site and joined a space shoot-em-up game. This was no ordinary computer game -- me against the computer. It was me against an ever-changing number of players -- those who entered the game through their Web site. I could hear the sounds of my space ship being shot down by other players, from all parts of the world. It was exhilarating. I am hooked.

I love one-number phone calling. In 1996 MCI introduced a service called MCI One. MCI gave my an 800 number. You could call it and it would call my office, wait four rings, call my home, wait four rings and call my cell phone. And if that didn't answer, it would ask my caller to leave a message on my voice mail. I could also call my own 800 number, punch in some numbers and change the routing. It's a good service. But it's limited and it's not easy changing the routing numbers on purely voice call and I'd really like some more options. For example, at some times and for some people, I'd like MCI to call me simultaneously on five numbers -- not wait four rings between numbers and limit itself to only four numbers. All this is possible.

The problem is simply that programming it over the phone gets hideously complicated. It's a snap to program it over the web.

The good news about the Internet and your company's Intranet (a private version of the public Internet) is that the Internet and the Intranet might just provide us the flexibility that today's phone service so miserably fails at.

Making voice calls today is trivial and easy. Pick up the handset. Dial a number. Ring. Ring. Someone's there. If they're not, leave a message. Nothing could be easier. Yet, today's phone service is increasingly letting us down. 75% of my business calls end in voice mail. Half my calls begin, "Did you get my fax?" I answer, "Which fax? When?" They hang up, send the fax and call back. If my fax machine is nearby and if it's got paper, if it's got toner in it, and if, IF, I-F, we might get a conversation going on the fax that he sent me. It's usually painful and time-consuming. Worse: To change the fax, I have to retype it, or resort to White-Out. Yuch.

The phone system hasn't extended its definition of a "conversation." But the Internet has.

The new words are "Internet Telephony." Ed Margulies, the author of this book, calls it "The Voice-Enabled Internet." What is The Voice-Enabled Web? What is Internet telephony? Remember the old story about describing an elephant wearing a blindfold and touching one small part of it. Internet telephony is like that: unexplored and undiscovered. But very large.

Conventional telephoning, in contrast, is fairly simple. It is point-to-point and just audio. Point-to-point means I call Grandma. Audio means it's just voice. The new "Internet Telephony" is about extending the phone call into data and ultimately video.

This promises to give us a richer and more effective call since it harnesses the computer's CPU power, rich user interface, and personal information found in the PC. Microsoft is calling it Internet conferencing.

Imagine, I call someone from my Internet phone to their Internet phone. I use a bonded ISDN channel, i.e. 128 Kbps. I call them. We talk. They want a 20-page fax from me. I click on my "send fax" button. It shoots the fax at 128 Kbps. That's 13 times as fast as if I sent them the regular way -- Group III fax machine at 9.6 Kbps. (Or 8.8 times as fast if I have 14.4 Kbps fax machines on either end.)

Once it's shot them, I'm back on the Internet phone, asking "if they understood my brilliance?" Perhaps I send more. Or maybe I send the faxes on one of the two B channels (still four to six times faster) and keep talking on the other B channel. That's simultaneous voice and data. None of today's idiocy, "When you get my fax, call me and we'll go through it..."

There are variations. I can send the faxes not as "dead" faxes, but as live binary file transfers. I can send them as word processed documents. They look exactly like faxes, but you can edit them at the other end. No more irksome re-typing. No more White-Out.

I like the idea of flipping slides on my Internet phone connection while I'm talking the presentation through on a separate analog line. I have that choice. Devote the Internet channel to only data and a separate dial-up phone channel to decent quality voice. No more traveling two days for a 30 minute presentation. No more half-ounce bags of pretzels for a four hour airline flight. I can get fat in the quietude of my own office.

What's nice is that I can use my PowerPoint presentation over a real-time Internet connection. Perhaps 50 people could be watching and listening -- some on Internet voice. Some on switched voice. Setting up a 50-person conference on the Internet is trivial. Setting up a 50-person conference on today's cumbersome phone network is difficult and very expensive.

The Internet (and the Intranet) is great for all forms of messaging. Imagine a company with offices in London, New York, Tokyo and Sydney. You could have a voice mail box in four cities. Your clients can call you locally.

Their "messages" (voice, video, data, faxes, images, etc.) could flow back and forth across the Internet at odd times, allowing you to pick them up wherever you are. And you could pick the messages up in several ways -- from your phone, from your laptop, from your fax machine, etc.

Today I sit on planes, on trains, in hotels, in remote offices answering email. I can't answer my voice mail messages on my laptop on the plane because I can't drag my messages out of my dumb voice mail system. As a result, I can't enhance my voice mail messages with text, diagrams, images, video, etc. And I can't send a voice mail message directly into your voice mail machine or into your email messaging system.

The analog phone system is one paradigm -- circuit switched, full-time, 3 Khz switching fast in either direction. That's it. One idea. Unchanged for 120 years.

The Internet is much more flexible. It's packet switched. But the packets, depending on how fast you get them and what type of compression power you bring to the party, can be made to appear real-time or can be made to be messaging. Or somewhere in between. Fast packet switching is real-time. Slow packet switching is messaging.

It's all coming very quickly. In mid-1996, Microsoft announced NetMeeting. It's a 100% software product that lets a sound-equipped PC do collaborative computing with audio over the Internet. Microsoft describes NetMeeting as enabling real-time voice and data communications over the Internet. It lets two or more people share applications, transfer files, view and illustrate a shared whiteboard and chat. And do it all over standard Internet connections.

NetMeeting opens your eyes. Ed and I logged on to the Internet and used the NetMeeting server to get a directory of who was "on line." You get "on line" by logging into the Internet with NetMeeting. Your ID is automatically dropped into the directory. While you're on line, you're available to "speak" to anyone else who logs on.

Which means you can call (on the phone) your nearest and dearest and ask them to log on now. Or send them a fax or email telling them when to log on. Or simply schedule a time when everyone will be on line. The possibilities on your own Intranet are great. With your own high-speed (more predictable) system (say one using T-1 lines), you can have a voice connection over the office phone system and a data connection / multipoint data conferencing over the LAN.

Microsoft's listing of NetMeeting's features makes interesting reading:

- Application Sharing lets you share a program running on one computer with other people in a conference. Because Microsoft NetMeeting handles this feature transparently, it works with existing Windows-based programs. You can share a Microsoft Word document with three co-workers. Each person now sees an image of your program on his or her computer. You can review the document together and each can take turns editing. Your colleagues do not need a copy of the program or the file. But they do need a copy of NetMeeting.

- Real-time Voice enables you to talk to another person over the Internet. It can be used in with the other data and conferencing features.

- Whiteboard is a multi-page, multi-user drawing program. Use it to sketch an organization chart, draw a diagram and type action items. You can point out your co-workers' errors using a remote pointer or highlighting tool. You can take a "snapshot" of a window and then paste the graphic on a page. You can drop stuff from clipboard onto it and take stuff off it.

- File Transfer lets you to send a file to all conference participants. Just drag the file into the NetMeeting window. File transfer occurs in the background as everyone continues sharing programs, using the whiteboard, and chatting.

- Chat lets you type and record meeting minutes and action items. You can carry on a conversation with fellow conference participants. Chat is like real-time email. It's more disciplined than talking.

- The User Location Service provides a way to find other people to communicate with on the Internet. You can find out who is currently logged in.

Ed and I tested NetMeeting. Microsoft's description is accurate, with a couple of caveats: Voice quality is not smashing. But then no one's is. And the thing was not a speed demon. It needs a bigger pipe than 28,800 bits per second, which is all we had. Our office ISDN lines at 128,000 bits per second, run four times faster. They should be a lot more fun.

Microsoft is very proud of the fact that NetMeeting is "standards based." To me, this is very critical also. With standards come what the industry calls interoperability (connect to other packages and equipment) and extensibility (it becomes a platform on which you and I can build on and add things to). Extensibility is important because Microsoft will shortly join NetMeeting to Exchange. At NetMeeting's public introduction, Microsoft had 20+ companies announce products and services that are interoperable with NetMeeting. These included bridges (VideoServer, Accord), conferencing services (MCI), interactive white boards (Liveworks) and videoconferencing (Intel, PictureTel and Creative Labs).

NetMeeting is based on two new international standards -- T.120 (ratified and accepted) for multipoint data conferencing, and H.323 (ratified and accepted) voice, data, video over packet networks. T.120 is the most important transmission protocol standard for document conferencing over transmission media ranging from analog phone lines to the Internet. T.120 is the International Telecommunications Union (ITU-T) standards suite for document conferencing. Virtually all major players in the document conferencing industry have announced support for this new standard. Document conferencing adds a visual dimension to voice-only conference calls by allowing groups of people to share computer documents.

All this in real-time while participating in a standard voice conference call. Whatever materials would normally be distributed in a face-to-face meeting -- graphs, spreadsheets, diagrams, or documents -- can be shared on-line, in real-time. Participants can easily connect to a conference anywhere in the world, with the only requirements being a Windows PC, a modem and a document conferencing software program. T.120 series standards provide a framework to enable multi-point data conferencing across LANs and WANs and the Internet. The T.120 architecture relies on a multilayered approach with defined protocols and service definitions between layers. Each layer presumes the existence of all layers below. The lower level layers (T.122, T.123, T.124 and T.125) specify an application-independent mechanism for providing multi-point data communications services to any application that can use these facilities. The upper level layers (T.126 and T.127) define protocols for specific conferencing applications, such as shared whiteboarding and binary file transfer.

H.320 is the most common family of ITU-T videoconferencing standards. These standards allow dissimilar videoconferencing systems and videophones to communicate with each other. "H.320 compatible videoconferencing systems" are now the most common videoconferencing systems. They work on ISDN BRI circuits, one dial-up phone lines and on the Internet. H.320 is like T.120 in that there are a whole bunch of layered and allied standards here, including T.121, T.122, T.123, T.124, T.125, T.126 and T.127.

The Voice-Enabled Internet is an exciting journey. In the next few years, as our "conversations" are immensely enriched by this new technology, our business and personal lives will take on profound new directions. This book is the beginning of that journey. I am pleased Ed asked me to write the Foreword.

Harry Newton
New York City, August 1996
harrynewton@mcimail.com
www.computertelephony.com

Table of Contents

Chapter 4

Chapter 5

Chapter 6

Chapter 7
Fax and the Internet

Chapter 11

Chapter 12

Voice-Enabled Internet Standards

Chapter 1

Internet Primer

Computer Telephony and it's impact on the Internet is creating an explosion of good products and services. There's a rush of activity at the meeting place between CT and the 'Net. The number of projects going on in this area is nothing short of amazing. Literally dozens of companies are involved. No, hundreds. This book shows you what many of them are doing.

You'll learn how to save thousands by re-thinking your information delivery model. You see how the Voice-Enabled Internet will supercharge your call center with Web links and what vendors to partner with and buy from. The pages ahead contain some of the best work from the brightest market-makers the communications industry. But where to start?

It's only fitting to begin with a thorough explanation of what the Internet is, where it came from and where it's going. And who better to ask than Jack Rickard, editor and publisher of *Boardwatch Magazine* and a leading authority on the subject.

His publication is hailed as the authoritative source for the goings on throughout the Internet community. The rest of the book concentrates on how new service models and applications are forcing computer telephony into a great partnership with the Internet.

The Internet - What Is It?

The Internet is a complicated matrix of connections in a constant state of upgrade with 2300 vendors making changes on a daily basis. But it is a legitimate question. Connections do vary, sometimes dramatically. All T-1 links are not created equal, all backbones are not created equal and all Internet Service Providers are simply not created equal. Pricing and performance are total chaos, with no connection between the two.

And after talking with our readers at some length, what we found is that they were really struggling to form a mental picture or map of the Internet in an attempt to locate themselves on it. It's a psychological bit of a geography exercise -- "Where am I?" And the corollary, "Where do I want to be?"

It is helpful, in dealing with the Internet, to form some working mental image of what it is, how it works, and where the walls are. Since a great deal of its operation is logical rather than physical, this can be a bit of a challenge. Physically, it is a series of equipment rooms scattered across the globe with rackmounted routers in them and few if any people nearby most of the time. That mental picture has little utility.

Picturing what is connected and where it is connected on the map is somewhat more useful. It is not perfectly accurate. All backbone maps are logical and symbolic simplifications of often extremely complex connections. But they can be useful. Figure 1.1 is one such map. It shows all the major interconnect point to the backbone in the U.S.

Figure 1.1 – Major U.S. Peer Interconnect Points

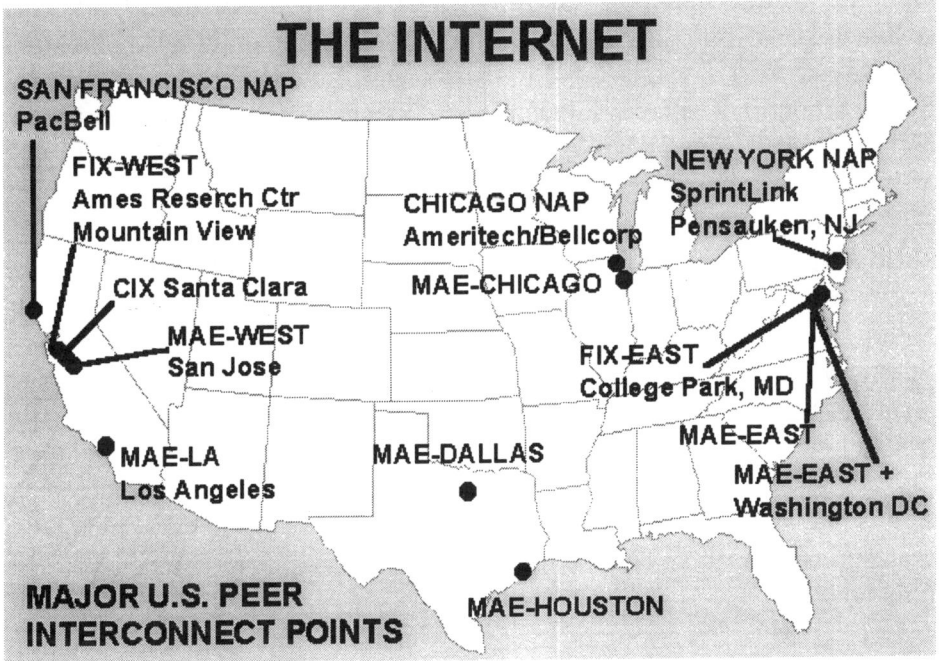

Internet History Lesson

Historically, the Internet began with packet switching projects in the late 1960's, most notably the Advanced Research Project Agency's ARPANET. During the '70's this network grew to support many organizations in the US Department of Defense, other government agencies, and it began to support university and research organizations. The Transmission Control Protocol/Internet Protocol (TCP/IP) was developed as a packet protocol that would allow connections across a variety of physical mediums including satellite connections, wireless packet radio, telephone links, etc. It was included in a popular release of the Berkeley Standard UNIX which was freely distributed through the university community. This was a rather loose development of technology and in no clear sense a network of any kind.

In 1985, the National Science Foundation funded several national super-computer centers including the Cornell Theory Center at Cornell University in Ithaca, New York; The National Center for Supercomputing Applications (NCSA) at the University of Illinois, Urbana, Champaign; The Pittsburgh Supercomputing Center in Pittsburgh; the San Diego Supercomputer Center at the University of California, San Diego; and the Jon von Neumann Center at Princeton University.

The NSF desired to make these supercomputer centers available to the research community in universities across the country. Many state and regional universities had already developed some basic TCP/IP networks linking various university computer sites using leased 56 kbps lines. The National Science Foundation funded a 56 kbps network linking these five original supercomputer centers, and offered to let any of the regional and university computer centers that could reach this network physically connect to it. This was the "seed" of the Internet network as we know it today and the original reason to connect to it was to access supercomputer facilities remotely.

A number of universities did link to the NSF network to gain access to the supercomputers. But beyond research, they found that the network was useful for other things such as electronic mail, file transfer and newsgroups. The traffic on the network rose fairly dramatically.

In November, 1987, the National Science Foundation awarded a contract to Merit Network, Inc. in partnership with IBM, MCI and the State of Michigan, to upgrade and operate the NSFNET backbone using 1.544 Mbps T-1 leased lines connecting six regional networks: the National Center for Atmospheric Research (NCAR) in Boulder, Colorado, the five existing supercomputer centers, and Merit at the Computer Center in the University of Michigan.

No one had ever attempted a data networking project of this scale. Barely eight months after the award, the T-1 backbone was completed on July 1, 1988.

It linked thirteen sites and carried 152 million data packets in its first month. Merit, IBM, and MCI also developed a state of the art Network Operation Center at the Merit site in Ann Arbor Michigan and staffed it 24 hours per day. The new NSFNet T-1 backbone started life with a total of 170 local area networks from the supercomputer centers and regional networks, served. On July 24, 1988, the old 56 kbps NSF network was shut off. The original thirteen sites include:

Merit University of Michigan Computing Center in Ann Arbor Michigan.

National Center for Atmospheric Research in Boulder, Colorado

Cornell Theory center at Cornell University in Ithaca, New York

The National Center for Supercomputing Applications (NCSA) at the University of Illinois, Urbana, Champaign

The Pittsburgh Supercomputing Center in Pittsburgh

San Diego Supercomputer Center at the University of California, San Diego

Jon von Neumann Center at Princeton University

BARRNet - Palo Alto, California

MIDnet - Lincoln, Nebraska

Westnet - Salt Lake City, Utah

NorthWestNet - Seattle, Washington

SESQUINET - Rice University, Houston, Texas

SURANET - Georgia Tech, Atlanta Georgia

It is worth noting that the NSFnet backbone was not the first, and indeed it's purpose by this time was to LINK and interconnect the growing "regional" networks setup by various university systems.

In January of 1989, the Merit/IBM/MCI team presented a plan to upgrade the network to higher speed using T3 lines to handle the rapidly increasing network traffic. IBM developed the first router capable of handling T3 speeds using their RS/6000 workstations running a subset of UNIX. These were eventually capable of routing some 100,000 packets per second.

In September 1990, Merit, IBM and NICI spun off a new independent non-profit organization known as Advanced Network and Services, Inc. (ANS) to operate this NSFNET backbone and tackle the challenges of moving to 45 Mbps backbone speeds. IBM and MCI each contributed $4 million and ANS acted as subcontractor to Merit. The backbone was expanded to 16 sites and the final T3 router was installed in November of 1991. The new 45 Mbps T3 backbone now connected some 3500 networks.

This then was the National Science Foundation Network backbone. It reached such a critical mass of participation /population, that it became itself a thing to connect your private network to. The more smaller networks that connected to it, the more attractive it became. The term "Internet" was first used in 1983 to describe this concept of interconnecting networks. And ten years later, *the* Internet was largely defined as having connectivity to the NSFNet national backbone.

There was a great deal of discussion regarding the commercialization and privatization of the NSFNet backbone. The issues centered around whether the government should fund and operate a communications structure that competed with private companies such as MCI, AT&T, Sprint, and others -- particularly when a growing amount of NSFNet traffic was becoming largely commercial in nature. To address this issue, a number of private commercial backbone operators joined to establish a separate point for the exchange of Internet traffic. The Commercial Internet Exchange was formed and a router was set up in the Willtel equipment room in Santa Clara California.

In theory, the private companies were "connected" through this CIX router. As a practical matter, most traffic still transited the NSFNet backbone. But it was a first step in addressing the issue.

Figure 1.2 – Internet Growth Statistics

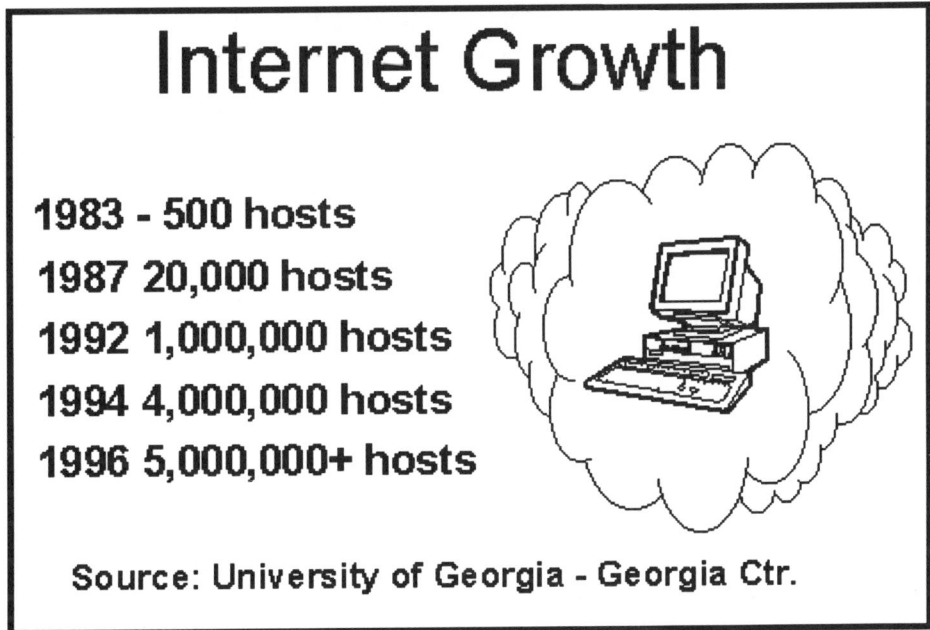

Internet Growth

1983 - 500 hosts
1987 20,000 hosts
1992 1,000,000 hosts
1994 4,000,000 hosts
1996 5,000,000+ hosts

Source: University of Georgia - Georgia Ctr.

The New Internet

In May, 1993, the National Science Foundation issued a solicitation for bids [NSF 93-52] that would radically alter the architecture of the Internet. They were getting out of the backbone business. In its place, they designated a series of Network Access Points (NAPs), really quite similar to the CIX concept, where private commercial backbone operators could "interconnect" much as they had using the NSFNet backbone. But rather than connecting to different points on an intermediary backbone, they would directly connect at a series of single points.

In this way, anyone could develop a national backbone for the connection of LANs, sell connectivity to it, and use the NAP as the physical point where they interconnected and exchanged traffic with all the other service providers. The naps would be based on a high speed switch or LAN technology. This is increasingly moving toward Asynchronous Transfer Mode (ATM) switches. No content or usage restrictions would be placed on traffic. The naps would serve to connect multiple providers, to allow the set of providers to suffice as a replacement for the current NSFNET service.

In February, 1994, NSF announced that three NAPS would be built. One would be located in San Francisco, under the operation of PacBell. The second was in Chicago, operated by Bellcore and Ameritech. And the third would be in New York, operated by SprintLink. Sprint had already been coordinating international connections to the Internet for NSF. The New York NAP is actually located in Pennsauken New Jersey across the river from Philadelphia. Merit was awarded a contract as routing Arbiter to maintain a database of information regarding the issues of interconnection. On April 30, 1995, the NSFNet backbone was essentially shut down, and the NAP architecture became the Internet.

NAPs Are A Good Idea

Currently, the heart of the Internet remains the three "official" network access points or naps in San Francisco, Chicago, and Pennsauken. They establish the concept that interconnection is good, and that at least these three points, anyone can in theory interconnect with the rest of the Internet. This is a bit of a key concept. Private backbone operators are not inherently inclined to "share" their customers by connecting them with someone else's customers.

But the demand to be connected to The Internet quite outgrew their own inclinations. If the NSF said that by connecting to what were essentially three "rings in the sand" you were connected to the Internet, then you were. Once that resistance to interconnection is overcome via three official naps, the concept of interconnecting becomes increasingly attractive.

Why should an e-mail message traveling from one office in Washington DC to another across the street have to transit through Chicago just because one of the correspondents uses SprintLink and the other user internetMCl? The more interconnections you have across the country, if it is physically convenient to cross connect, the more you can shortcut or shunt traffic and avoid bottlenecks. This concept is called "hot potato routing" in that as backbone, you should offload packets destined for a site on another backbone at the nearest connection rather than hauling it across country and then delivering it. The destination site backbone should be responsible for cross country transit.

As it so happens, Metropolitian Fiber Systems, Inc. operates a series of Metropolitan Area Ethernet (MAE) systems in largish metropolitan areas such as Washington DC. This is a basically a fiber-optic data ring around the city where they can inexpensively connect companies and offices to this citywide network. MFS had been quite successful with this in Washington DC, and their facilities made a natural point to interconnect private back-bones. MAE-EAST, located in Washington DC, was actually doing inter-connections on a fairly significant scale before the three official naps were really off the ground. It is some what unofficially the *fourth NAP*.

Today, MFS operates MAE's in San Jose (MAE-WEST), Los Angeles (MAE-LA), Dallas (MAE-DALLAS), and Chicago (MAE-CHICAGO). And they actually have two in Washington DC, the existing 10 Mbps Ethernet MAE-EAST, and a higher speed 100 Mbps Ethernet usually termed MAE-EAST+. They currently plan two additional MAEs in unspecified cities during 1996. The two MAE-EAST NAPs and MAE WEST are essentially defacto NAPS, with the other MAEs potentially serving as defacto NAPs. MFS has even gone so far as to redefine the MAE acronym as Metropolitan Area Exchanges rather than Metropolitan Area Ethernets.

Finally, there are two Federal Internet Exchange points: FIX-EAST at the University of Maryland in College Park Maryland, and FIX-WEST at the NASA Ames Research Center at Moffet Field between Sunnyvale and Mountain View California.

These FIXs largely exist to interconnect MILNET and NASA Science Net and some other federal government networks. Since this represents a large population of federal workers, we don't really have an Internet with them totally disconnected. So there has been some interconnection through Metropolitan Fiber Systems largely to these FIX locations, and a largish volume of data traffic still goes through the FIX points. The current aim is to decrease this by moving more of the Interconnect to the official naps as they become more operational and of course the MAEs. The CIX router is still up in Santa Clara, but is somewhat salutory at this point. CIX also has a router in Herndon, Virginia, but with few actual interconnects there. The CIX and FIX NAPs can be thought of as historical legacy NAPs.

So we currently have approximately eleven major interconnection points -- three official NAPs, three historical NAPs (CIX, FIX-EAST, FIX-WEST), and five defacto NAPs (MAE). Any national backbone operator that has a peer connection at one or more of these interconnects has some connectivity to the Internet. Most of the national service providers are connected to all three official NAPs and often to most of the MAEs as well. This series of NAPs could be considered the top of the Internet or the heart of the Internet. That said, at this point most backbone operators are cross connecting with other backbones at virtually any location of convenience.

A Typical NAP

All the NAPs perform a similar function -- providing interconnections between service providers. But each does it in a different way architecturally. Pacific Bell's San Francisco NAP would serve as an example in Figure 1.3. Pacific Bell's NAP is based on their FasTrak ATM Cell Relay Service, a full featured ATM service. NAP access is specifically designed to allow Service Providers to interconnect and exchange traffic amongst themselves. ATM technology allows NAP customers to pass TCP/IP traffic across the NAP backbone at broadband speeds up to 36Mbps (for DS3 access) and up t 139Mbps (for OC3 access). ATM service is being rolled out in phases, with the first phase utilizing Permanent Virtual Circuits (PVC's) between customer sites and a later phase utilizing Switched Virtual Connections (SVCs).

The difference between PVC's and SVCs is that: PVC's appear as point-to-point or point-to-multipoint, and must be set up a head of time through a provisioning process, whereas SVCs are dynamic and established as easily as making a phone call.

Figure 1.3 – Network Access Point Topology

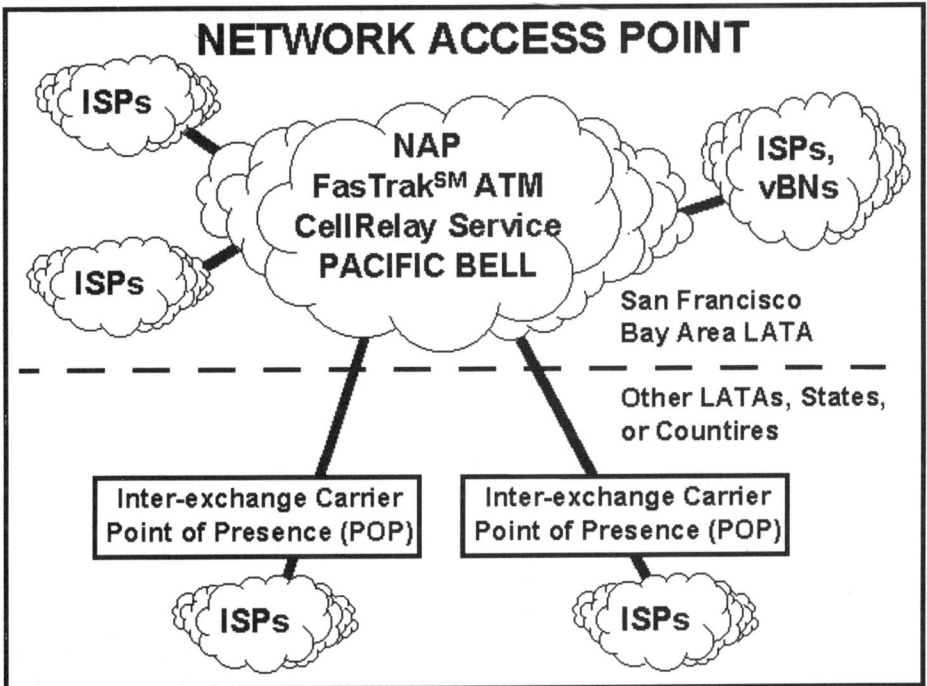

Currently, customers can connect speeds up to 36.8 Mbps (DS-3 rates) using the combination of a Cisco DS-3 rates HSSI card and the Kentrox ADSU. They can also connect to the NAP at speeds up to 139 Mbps (OC-3c SONET) utilizing the Cisco OC3c AIP board. NAP clients must make bilateral agreements with other NAP clients for the exchange of TCP/IP routing information and TCP/IP traffic. In addition, the NSF sponsors a Routing Arbiter service at each NAP.

Clients may make arrangements with the Routing Arbiter for dissemination of routing information among participants in the service. Upon the mutual consent of customers, Pacific Bell will establish a PVC between customer sites reflecting the peering agreement, as well as a PVC from the customer site to the Routing Arbiter.

Operational targets include 99.92% availability, or no more than 7 hours/year of unavailable time with less than 225 service outages per year. The mean time to restore service is 2.5 hours. In order to meet these targets, Pacific Bell's Network Data Products Service Center (NDPSC) is dedicated to their FasTrak data product line, monitoring the NAP architecture. The NDPSC is staffed 24 hours a day, 7 days a week, and provides a single-point-of contact for NAP customers requiring network support. It is responsible for the provisioning, surveillance, and maintenance of Pacific Bell's ATM network. The NDPSC can be reached at 1-800-870-9007.

The San Francisco Bay Area (LATA 1) is the hub for NAP traffic. Customer sites outside of this area must establish inter LATA service through an interexchange carrier from the PacBell NAP connection, to the customer's service area (LATA), to one of the connection points in the San Francisco Area. Pacific Bell will work with whichever inter-exchange carrier is providing the long distance portion of the customer's data transport.

NAP access is priced as follows: DS-3 (36.8 Mbps) $5,000 (installation), $4,850 (monthly service). OC-3c (139 Mbps) $8,500 (installation), $7,900 (monthly service). To order NAP, contact your Pacific Bell Account Representative or call 1-800-PACBELL and ask for information on a NAP attachment to their FasTrakSM ATM Cell Relay Service.

Warren Williams is the NAP project manager at (510)867-9065 or wkwilli@ pacbell.com. They maintain a NAP mailing list at ca-nap@pacbell.com. More information on NAPS is available through the World Wide Web site associated with each NAP.

  • SAN FRANCISCO NETWORK ACCESS POINT - Pacific Bell -
    www.pacbell.com/Products/NAP/

- CHICAGO NETWORK ACCESS POINT - Ameritech Advanced Data Services and Bellcorp. http://www.ameritech.com/products/data/nap/

- NEW YORK NETWORK ACCESS POINT - SprintLink Actually in Pennsauken New Jersey near Philadelphia www.sprintlink.net

- Metropolitan Area Ethernets- (MAE)http://ext2.mfsdatanet.com/MAE/

- CIX Commercial Internet Exchange - Santa Clara - http://www.cix.org

- FIX - Federal Internet Exchange - Http://www.arc.nasa.gov

Backbones Defined

A brief sidetrip might be in order to describe what we mean by a backbone. Basically, the entire Internet is a logical construct made up of packet routers that can be connected in almost any fashion, including wireless, satellite, landline, or conceivably smoke signals. These routers are connected in a matrix with each router typically connected to two or more others. The router examines packets and based on their "address" sends or "routes" them in various directions intended to get them closer to their ultimate destination.

As a practical matter, land lines of either copper or fiber provide the best performance and allow transmission of the highest data rates. And so most routers are connected using telephone lines from the existing telephone network. These lines can, and often are for small businesses and individuals, simply Plain Old Telephone Service (POTS) analog voice lines with a 28.8 kbps V.34 modem on each end. For higher speeds, the routers are linked by leased permanent lines often with higher data rates.

You can typically lease a Data Service -- 0 (DSO) 56 kbps line from any telephone company linking any two points within their system. Similarly, you can lease, at some- what higher cost, a 1.544 Mbps data line from any telephone company - usually referred to as Data Service-1 (DS1) or T Carrier Level-1 (T-1). And for yet a bit more money, you can lease a 45 Mbps line Data Service 3 line variously referred to as "DS3" or "T3". These are just a few standard, off-the-shelf data line products typically offered by telcos. There are other products such as Frame Relay, etc.

So for any TCP/IP Internet, there is an underlying structure of physical connections -- usually provided by an existing local or long distance telephone company. Additionally, there is the "network" consisting of TCP/IP routers connected by this physical network. We usually refer to these as the physical layer and the logical layer of a backbone.

While leased lines are relatively inexpensive locally, they can be somewhat more expensive when they link distant; cities. When we refer to a "national Internet backbone provider," we are describing a company that has physically located a high-speed TCP/IP router in a number of cities, and then leased high speed data lines from long distance exchange carriers to link the routers thus forming a national "backbone" connecting those cities. By doing so, they can then sell access to many individual: and companies within each backbone city, and the traffic between cities move: over the leased lines of the backbone.

The leased lines can actually be purchased from different long distance companies for each city, and in fact some backbone providers will lease several lines from different carriers to connect two cities so that if one carrier happens to have a backbone incident and the link is lost, they still have a connection through the other carrier - maintaining their backbone at a perhaps reduced data rate. This is termed "redundancy." Currently, backbones are generally formed from 45 Mbps T3 leased lines. But this is a gross over-simplification of any backbone. In addition to a half dozen or a dozen major metropolitan areas that a backbone operator may link using T3 lines, they will likely extend dozens or even hundreds less expensive 1.544 Mbps T-1 lines to surrounding communities from the major backbone cities.

And they may further extend from THOSE points with less expensive yet 56 kbps leased lines. The whole makes up a rather complex network linking often hundreds of cities large and small. Generally, we refer to all the nodes of the network owned by the national service provider as Points of Presence or POPS. Business customers then lease their own telephone line from the telco to this POP and so connect to the Internet. In my Directory of Service Providers publication, we show national backbone providers at the very top high speed T3 backbone level, and list all known POPs at the bottom level. But note that there is often a very complex subnetwork extending this logical top level backbone to those POP locations.

And so generally, when shopping for a high-speed connection, you are looking For a provider with a POP near to you, and you might be interested in the nature of the POP - whether this is a T3 node, a T-1 node, a 56 kbps node, etc. It would make little sense, for example, to lease a T-1 line to a POP that was connected to the backbone network with a 56 kbps line, and in practice, no backbone operator would allow you to. But similarly, the costs of running a leased line 300 miles to connect to a T3 connection when a barely used T-1 POP is down the street is a consideration.

Levels Of Access

To form a rational image of the Internet, we can somewhat arbitrarily divide the topic into five categories or levels. These are depicted in Figure 1.4.

Level 1- Interconnect Level - NAPS

Level 2 - National Backbone Level

Level 3 - Regional Networks

Level 4 - Internet Service Providers

Level 5 - Consumer and Business Market

Figure 1.4 – Levels Of Internet Access

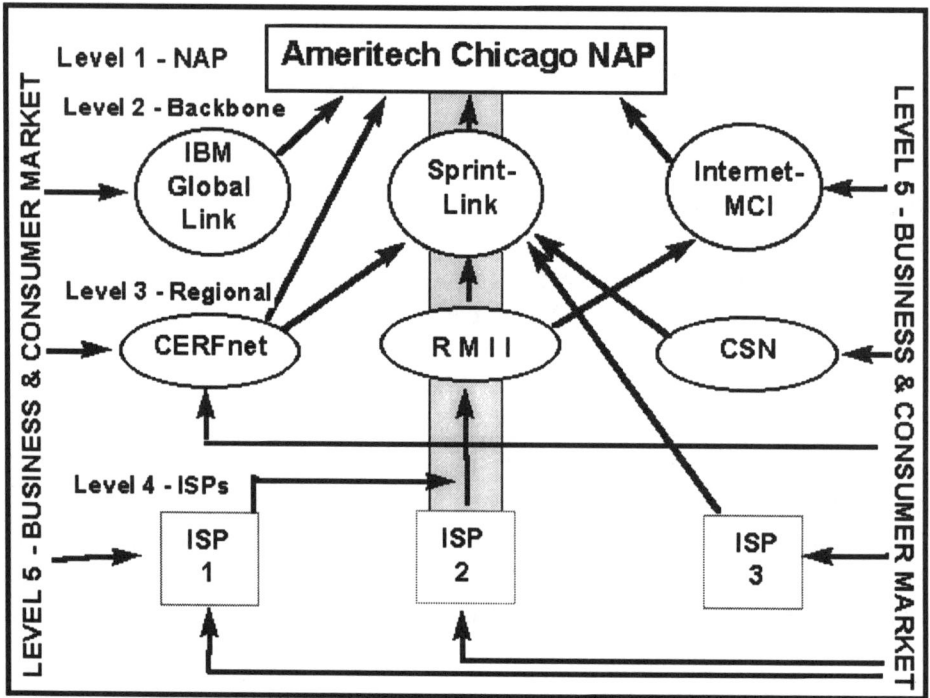

These are not absolute and indeed you will find many entities that operate in two or more of these levels but they broadly hold true. We have already discussed the tip of the iceberg level, so to speak, with the network access points. This is where major backbone operators interconnect to establish the core concept of an Internet. Level two would be the national backbone operators, sometimes referred to as national service providers.

The third level of the Internet we think of as regional network operators. Most of these are remnants from the original NSF regional entities that connected Universities. CERFnet in San Diego, JvnCnet in New Jersey, Colorado Supernet in Colorado are examples of regional networks. Typically, they operate backbones within a state or among several adjoining states much like the national backbone operators. They typically connect to a national backbone operator, or increasingly to SEVERAL national backbone operators to be on the Internet.

Some do in fact have a presence at a NAP, but usually just a single NAP. But then they extend this network to smaller cities and towns in their areas with a combination of 1.544 Mbps T-1 lines, fractional T-1 lines, and 56 kbps leased lines. They connect businesses to those points with direct access connections and usually maintain dialup terminal banks to offer 28.8 kbps dialup SLIP/PPP connections to consumers. In many cases, regional networks are much more extensive than national backbones, just on a smaller geographic scale.

The fourth level of the Internet would be the individual Internet Service Provider. These vary from small two or three person operations up to actually quite largish operations. We know of one with over 100,000 dialup customers. But they don't generally operate a backbone or even regional network of their own. They lease connections to a national backbone provider, or a regional network operator. They might indeed offer service nationally, but using the POPs and backbone structure of their larger backbone operator associate.

Figure 1.5 – Service Use By Provider

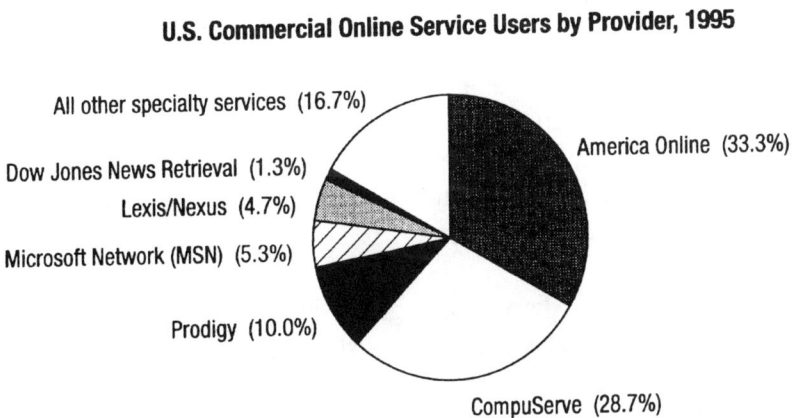

U.S. Commercial Online Service Users by Provider, 1995

All other specialty services (16.7%)

Dow Jones News Retrieval (1.3%)

Lexis/Nexus (4.7%)

Microsoft Network (MSN) (5.3%)

Prodigy (10.0%)

America Online (33.3%)

CompuServe (28.7%)

Total users = 15.0 M
Note: These numbers represent IDC preliminary estimates.
Source: International Data Corporation, 1996

AT&T WorldNet actually operates at this fourth level -- leasing their backbone connection from BBN Planet. Earthlink has a similar arrangement with UUNET as does Microsoft. Pacific Bell links to AGIS. And for that matter, so does George Peace with PAONLINE in Harrisburg Pennsylvania. Generally, they operate an equipment room in a single area code, lease connections to a national backbone provider, and offer dialup connections and leased connections to consumers and businesses in their area. They tend to focus on customer service, configuration, and training and often offer lower prices. Of the 2,272 Internet Service Providers we list, the average number of area codes where they have a point of presence is 1.9 with over half offering service in a single area code.

The fifth level of the Internet is the consumer and business market. Each time a small office leases a line from their office to an Internet Service Provider's point-of- presence, they have in fact extended the Internet by that number of linear feet. With a lot of this happening, we find today that most metropolitan areas of the United States have more linear feet of "Internet" constructed in this fashion than ever did exist in the original NSFnet backbone. Further, many companies- then setup dialup ports at their offices for employees to make the connection from home or on road.

Again, these levels are somewhat arbitrary, but broadly true. There is some cross dressing. Sprint, for example, operates a NAP at level 1. They are also one of the largest National Backbone Operators and in fact provide the connection for the majority of level three and four Internet Service Providers. This summer, they intend to launch consumer access nationwide much like a level three or level four operator.

AT&T on the other hand, with great fanfare and much public relations ado, announced the AT&T WorldNet service this spring. In fact, they lease all backbone operations from BBN Planet Corp, a national backbone provider. And in turn, BBN Planet operates a mixture of their own backbone, and backbone leased in turn from MCI. As a result, MCI is at least in part providing AT&T WorldNet's backbone.

AT&T is in no detectable respect different than George Peace with PAON-LINE and we would consider them a level four Internet Service Provider. But at this writing, they have sent out some 600,000 software packages and signed up over 150,000 end users.

This is not an isolated situation. Deals are cut between operators at and across all levels of the Internet to the point of frenzied confusion. I suspect that some operators are agreeing to buy things from themselves through several third parties in some cases. And there is a fear that somewhere in the Internet there is a single router that all of this hangs on such that one power hiccup and the entire network takes a tumble The point here is that there is an enormous amount of co-mingling of body fluids in the operation of an Internet. And there is a never ending quest to have the largest, best, and most munificent network, made up entirely of the work and investment of somebody else, and offer it for sale to the public.

Further, the Internet service business is growing rapidly. Many of these organizations have gone through an initial public stock offering, or are in the process of doing so. Enormous quantities of cash are being invested in these companies, and they are adding personnel in groups of hundreds and thousands at a time. The number of knowledgeable Internet technicians and engineers available doesn't approach the need.

In attempting to assemble this data into some form of graspable information, we repeatedly encountered marketers and sales people who were enthusiastically and energetically ignorant and confused about their products, the network services they were selling, and just what an Internet was. Some of the conversations and interactions were comical and generally frustrating for both parties. In one case, we have actually omitted a modestly successful backbone operator simply because we were unable to deal with them in real time. As best we can tell, they are almost wholly manned by 24-year-old marketing babes who have successfully navigated the rigors of Marketing 101 at the local junior college, and know nothing about nothing beyond that. But what they lack in comprehension they more than make up for with arrogance.

Figure 1.6 – World Wide Web Users

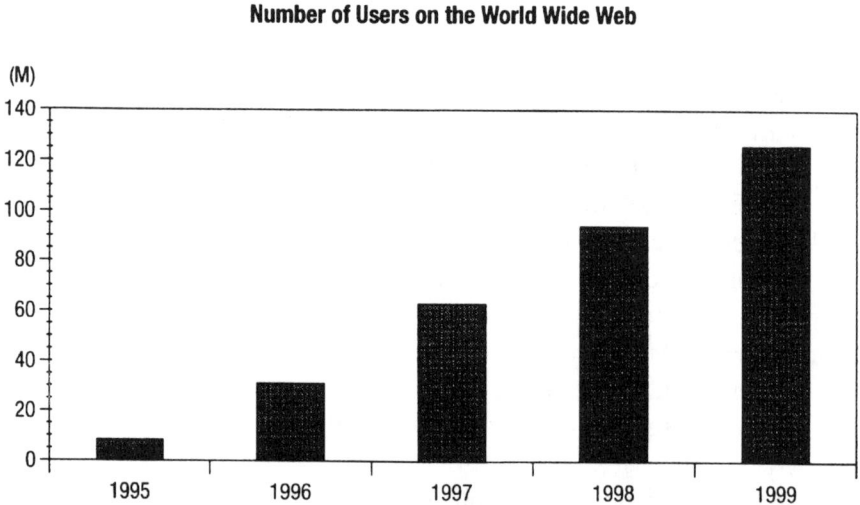

Number of Users on the World Wide Web

(M)

1995	1996	1997	1998	1999

Source: International Data Corporation, 1996

The point here is that you are likely to hear almost anything from an Internet connectivity sales representative. Some of it may be true. Some of it they may honestly believe to be true. In general, the signal to noise level is a little discouraging and you should take most assurances of quality, reliability, and service with a grain of salt.

That said, we did encounter other situations where the salesman at the field level was much more informed and competent than anyone at the management or public relations level.

Quest For A Clear Channel

The very heart of this publication, and particularly this section of it, is to provide networking professionals with some rational presentation of the Internet they are trying to connect to and a basis for comparing the services and connections they are attempting to purchase.

It is a task we are inevitably doomed to fail at, though we hope to fail in somewhat artful fashion. The core of the conundrum is that you want the GOOD connection to the Internet, and don't want to be saddled with the BAD connection to the Internet.

In an ideal world, the GOOD connection would be at the high price, the BAD connection would be at the low price, and you could pick the level of "goodness" based on your ability and willingness to pay. In the chaos of the current market, we have not found a persuasive coefficient of correlation between connectivity quality and price -- all nearly hysterical assurances to the contrary notwithstanding.

Much of the feedback from our first directory seemed to be directed at cutting out all the middlemen and getting closest to the REAL Internet or the CENTER of the Internet, or the HEART of the Internet - in any event, the GOOD connection. Since there is a geographic component to this, we assembled these maps and comparisons in an attempt to provide information you can use relative to your locale.

Figure 1.7 – Geographic Distribution of Web Users

Geographic Distribution of WWW Users

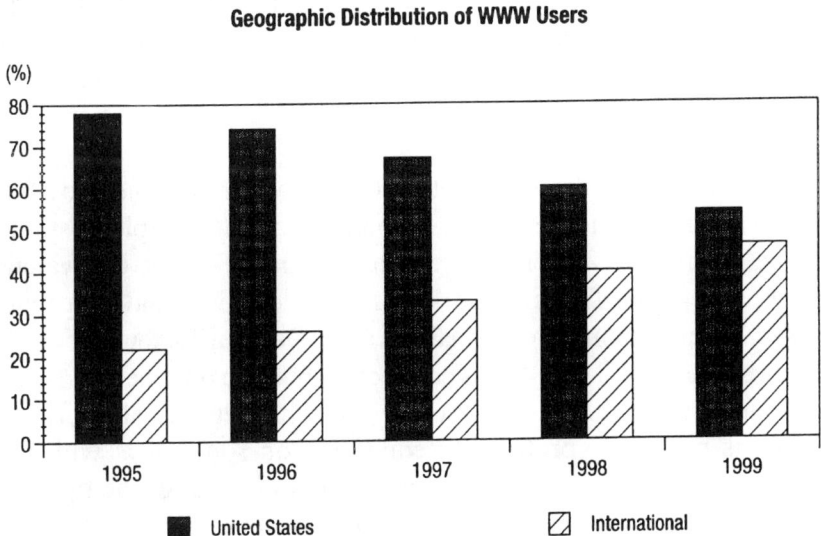

Source: International Data Corporation, 1996

The second element of this is the concept of oversubscription of Internet Services. Networking professionals accustomed to purchasing voice telephone service, leased data lines for networking, etc. are somewhat insistent on assurances from vendors that they will have 100% guaranteed bandwidth as advertised and purchased. "If I buy 1.544 Mbps T-1 pipes I want the full 1.544 Mbps T-1 pipe available at all times."

This seems reasonable enough. But it is actually related to the quest for the heart of the Internet. There is no center to the network. And the entire concept of clear channel capacity is alien to the packet-based TCP/IP networking philosophy and technical operation. In other words, it just doesn't work that way, and without total redesign from top to bottom, it cannot. There is no "clear channel" to the Internet because at its essence, the Internet is a packet switching technology and is not channel based.

In voice and dedicated data connections, a connection is SETUP for the duration of the need for a connection. It exists whether used to capacity or not, and is torn down at the end of the communication. In packet networks, there are no connections at all. All packets are individually addressed and aggregated inherent in the routing function. A single text file might be broken into a hundred individual packets, and each packet take a different route through the Internet to its destination. The software at the two ends keep track of what was sent and received, and retransmits "lost" packets of which there are many.

It is quite common for an Internet Service Provider to connect to a backbone with a single T-1 and yet sell T-1 connections to multiple customers. On average, a single T-1 connects about 14 other T-1s or equivalents. The packet aggregation function works quite as designed, and as a function of statistical multiplexing, this actually works. Data traffic tends to be "bursty" where you need the 1.544 Mbps connection but you only need it for seconds. Someone else can use it when you're not. This actually all works. But the Internet is becoming profoundly congested on some days with relatively high packet losses. We think the problem is not that capacity is oversubscribed from the use end, but rather at the server end.

If you put up a web site offering Rush Limbaugh neckties over the Internet and take over a million connections the first day, there isn't enough bandwidth in the world at your server end to handle the traffic -- even if your server hardware could keep up. If it is connected with a T-1, you might have 300 or 400 users on THAT end o the pipe at one time, making the 14 to 1 ratio at the user end seem generous Most of the "congestion" you will see on the Internet centers on individual sites that just can't deal with it.

If you access a different, less popular site, the "congestion" disappears. This appears inherent in a connectionless network where we could all, in response to some event or advertisement, all land on the same single server at the same time This is analogous to a single McDonalds Restaurant that finds itself faced with. 30,000 starving customers on the same noon hour. There are some traffic problems on the roads, but the roads are basically in good shape. And the McDonalds owner is thrilled. But a lot of people have to wait on hamburgers and in fact, the majority won't get their quarter pounder at all that day. This reminds me of the T-shirt "THE INTERNET IS FULL -- GO HOME."

So if you could get an utterly clear T-1 guaranteed channel directly to the Chicago NAP, you still don't have one. The routes to almost everywhere else FROM the NAP are aggregated in the same fashion. Larger vendors are no help. If they do have a T3 connection in your city, they simply sell more T-1 connections off of it and the same dynamic works on a slightly larger scale. The bottom line is that the Internet works to about the degree the worst part of it works. And if you could gain a BETTER connection to it, you haven't accomplished a whole lot with regards to day to day performance that your users within your company will be able to detect.So if you demand a clear channel to the Internet, you are asking for something that isn't available. If someone sells you a clear channel to the Internet, you've bought something they can't deliver. That is not to say that all vendors are created equal. Any particular vendor will manage the load factor slightly differently. But this is a fluid thing. A vendor who manages this very conservatively in March simply attracts more customers in April and the pressure to hook them up and catch up on the load factor later is enormous.

Largely, the performance and reliability you will ACTUALLY experience with your connection to the Internet is ultimately a function of the technical expertise of those in the equipment room at your service provider.

National Internet Backbone Operators

Since 1993, a number of serious players have entered the Internet service arena, including MCI, Sprint, IBM, ANS, and others. They basically operate their own national backbones -- often larger than that originally operated by the National Science Foundation. As such any TCP/IP connection to a national backbone operator is inherently a connection to the Internet.

Many smaller regional networks get their connection from a national backbone operator. Sprint IP Services, for example, has been quite aggressive in signing up smaller Internet Service Providers for a connection to the Sprint backbone. These smaller ISPs, in turn, offer connections to the public and businesses large and small -- often at attractive prices and usually focused on a particular type of Internet user.

The first issue of Boardwatch Directory of Internet Service Providers (www.boardwatch.com) was intended to empower consumers with information to select an Internet Service Provider in their area. The availability of interconnect connections remains a very regional or even local proposition. But we are somewhat stunned by the amount of response from LAN managers in businesses across the country who were also a bit perplexed by where and how to get the "good" connection to the Internet in their area.

Even at the backbone level, where you are makes a difference. Generally, backbone providers have their BIG backbone, typically operating at T3 or greater speeds-some just now introducing 155 Mbps service. From each "node" on this backbone, other cities are serviced with smaller T-1 or often multiple T-1 lines operating at 1.554 Mbps.

If you are in a specific city that is a MAJOR NODE at T3 speeds for one service provider, but for another, you would probably be attracted to the larger node -- particularly if you yourself were looking for a T3 or fractional T3 connection.

Unfortunately, selecting an ISP is not nearly as simple as finding the big nodes and calling for a connection. Installation times, prices, and services all play a role. Over and over we find much smaller ISPs offering better services at a much better price. But even then, you may need to know who THEY are connected to for THEIR connection. It can make a difference. You may only need an ISDN connection from a small service provider, but if they have multiple T-1 connections to a backbone provider with a T3 in your city, you may have a much better performance than to a national service provider that has a T-1 connection to the entire city.

For larger companies, it my be a balancing act between several city locations where you have offices to find the National Service Provider with the best average connection to all the cities you are trying to connect. That said, it is our hope that by providing a map of the major interconnection points, and then maps and POP lists for each of the national backbone operators along with specifics on where they interconnect, we can provide you a picture of how the Internet is laid out, and how each National Backbone Operator or Internet Service Provider fits into it. In this way, you can locate your own position on the Internet.

Internet Service Provider Shopping Tips

Provisioning Internet Service often entails a number of operations:

The Installation Charge. This is a one time setup fee the provider charges to get you set up with their service. It can vary widely, not only in price, but in what is included. Some operators actually provide all customer premise equipment (CPE) as part of the setup charge.

Others provide nothing in the way of CPE, but use the setup charge to equip THEIR end of the connection to accommodate you.

Customer Premise Equipment. The basic customer premise equipment consists of a Channel Service Unit/Digital Service Unit and a router. The CSU/DSU is the "modem" that connects to the telephone line. The provider will have a similar unit at their end. A variety of brands of CSU/DSU are available and we've found features relatively unimportant They work or they don't. But they do differ by speed. Generally you will use a different CSU/DSU for 56 kbps connections than for TI connections.

The CSU/DSU connects to the router typically using a V.35 cable. The router typically connects to the CSU/DSU on one end, and via Ethernet to your local area network on the other. Generally you are better off selecting a CSU/DSU and router that your provider is familiar with. It is rare to get these installed without some configuration issues. Often the provider will offer a package CSU/DSU and router for a price.

Port Charge. The port charge is typically a monthly recurring charge you pay the service provider for the connection to their router, and thus to the Internet. It varies by bandwidth generally.

Local Loop Costs. In general. providers do NOT include local loop costs in their quoted monthly recurring charge. Typically, you contract with your local telephone company for the necessary line from your office to the provider point of presence. This is not an insignificant additional expense. It will typically be half again as much as the port charge. Since some providers DO include the local loop charges in the port charge, you do need to ascertain whether or not it is included when comparing prices.

Broadly, a 10 mile local loop at T-1 speeds seems to run in the neighborhood of $500-$600 monthly right now. Frame Relay connections tend to be less expensive, but can suffer in efficiency and additional congestion. Often, the ISP will manage the local loop ordering and installation process for you, but it almost always involves a custom quote on the additional cost.

Incidentals. There are a number of small but important items necessary to complete your connection. Domain Name Registration, for example, typically carries a one time fee of $100 to register your company domain name (i.e. Boardwatch.com.) The provider typically maintains a domain name server and forwards e-mail to you. You may want a number of POP e-mail boxes maintained on their server so that you do not have to run your own mail server for example. If you want a USENET news feed, this may or may not incur additional charges. Most providers are now hosting Web pages for customers on provider equipment, usually for a fee and some even offer design services.

Installation Time. Incredibly, in a world of instant networked communication, it can take 3 to 8 weeks to set up a high speed connection to the Internet. Check to see average installation time from date of signed contract.

Network Operations Center. Despite all assurances of reliability you may hear, we've never heard of anyone on the Internet who did not encounter periodic service outages. How you reach your provider and what they do in response in the event of outage is a critical element to consider. A 24-hour network operations center manned and capable of getting your link back up with a simple phone call from you is a huge plus. If you get voice mail and pager procedures when your network is down, you'll not likely be a happy Internet camper.

IP Addresses

The identity of your network and every computer on it depends on Internet Protocol addresses of the form 204.144.169.10. Typically, you will need a Class C IP address block for up to 255 machines - 204.144.169.0 through 204.144.169.254 for example. You can use multiple Class C's for more machines. In theory, these are your addresses and until 1995 you would typically obtain them directly from the InterNIC and they were yours for life. The growth of the net brought on some problems in the speed and design of packet routers.

A router receives packets in one port, opens the packet, examines the header for address information, and sends the packet on its way via one of several routes depending on its ultimate destination and the connections the router has. To do this, it maintains a table of "routes."

As the network has grown, the size of this router table has grown correspondingly - and somewhat alarmingly. To alleviate this, the Internet community developed a concept referred to as Classless Inter Domain Routing or CIDR. In its most basic form, CIDR is a shorthand notation for routers that replaces thousands of addresses with a simple reference to another backbone provider that services those addresses. So all packets destined for any of these *gadzillion* addresses can simply be routed to Sprint for example, and they will know how to route from there.

The problem is that as the routing tables have grown, addresses that do NOT fall into a block of some size somewhere, have been eliminated from some routing tables. Sprint was the first to employ this obnoxious tactic beginning in June of 1995. Their version of the Internet simply didn't include some addresses in the 204.xxx.xxx.xxxx and 206.xxx. xxx.xxxx ranges. So if you were in one of those address ranges, anyone connected to the Sprint backbone couldn't reach you. This has the potential of fracturing the Internet into several networks based on addresses.

In practice, it doesn't quite. It simply strands a few small companies. But it ends the concept of independent Internet addresses. In general, you will have to obtain an IP address from your Internet Service Provider and so exist as part of their CIDR block to be assured of being reachable. The downside to this is that if you change Internet Service Providers later - after they notify you of a 400% price increase, for example, you will have to reconfigure every machine in your network - a tedious, expensive, and error prone process given the current software and operating systems. As a result, Internet Service Providers have a bit of a hold on you as a customer. This makes the initial selection of an Internet Service Provider perhaps more important than it might otherwise be.

Chapter Acknowledgments

My sincere thanks to Jack Rickard. He was gracious enough to share his vast knowledge of the Internet for the opening chapter of this book. Jack is editor and publisher of *Boardwatch Magazine*, a monthly publication covering online information services, the World Wide Web and the Internet. This chapter was based on his Internet Architecture abstract. It was recently published in his quarterly *Directory of Internet Service Providers*. Published monthly since 1987, Boardwatch Magazine is widely hailed as the authoritative print publication covering the online community and the developing technologies for wide area PC communications. Rickard has emerged as one of the leading authorities in the area of grassroots communications issues, the Internet, the World Wide Web, electronic bulletin boards and commercial online services.

Rickard also serves as President of Online Networking Expositions, Inc., promoters of the Online Networking Exposition and Internet Service Provider Convention, an annual trade show and convention of ISPs and online service providers held each August since 1992.

Prior to founding Boardwatch Magazine, Rickard spent twelve years developing communications and electronic technologies for the defense and aerospace industries with McDonnell Aircraft Corporation, Emerson Electric Electronics & Space Division, Martin Marietta Denver Aerospace and Martin Marietta Data Systems as an engineer and systems analyst.

www.boardwatch.com (Boardwatch Magazine)
www.ispcon.com (ONE ISPCON show)
jack.rickard@boardwatch.com (e-mail)

Chapter 2

Computer Telephony and the Internet

The rapid growth and development of the Internet represents tremendous potential and change in all areas of computing. This chapter discusses the impact that the Internet will have on computer and telephone integration (CTI), or computer telephony. This is a high-level overview of subjects discussed in greater detail in the rest of the book.

The people of the Stylus Product Group (Artisoft, Inc.) have a tremendous grasp of this subject. What you read here is based on their collective experience. Stylus sells tools for creating computer telephony solutions. Many of the results are in this book. You can get reprints of this material from Dave Krupinski, Vice President of Marketing (www.stylus.com).

Computer Telephony Market Size

Both the computer telephony industry and the Internet industry are experiencing explosive growth. The size of the telephony industry is currently estimated to be $3.5 billion annually. Some sectors of the industry (such as interactive voice response, fax-on-demand, and voice mail) are growing at a rate of 30% a year. Other sectors are experiencing growth of over 100%. In 1995, the technology sector of the Internet industry was estimated to be just over $1.2 billion. This sector is expected to experience a 12-fold increase by the year 2000. Content-related Internet services, currently estimated at less than $100 million, are expected to exceed $10 billion by the end of the decade. Undoubtedly, computer telephony and the Internet are two of the economy's most active industries.

This high growth represents tremendous business opportunity for individuals in both industries. For readers from the computer telephony industry, this chapter will describe, for example, the architecture of applications that provide "free" long distance phone call services by using the Internet instead of phone lines. For readers from the Internet industry, this chapter will describe, for example, how to create an "instant" IVR or fax-on-demand system using your company's existing Web page. The Internet shares some characteristics of other communication networks, such as the public switched telephone network (PSTN) as shown in Figure 2.1. Unlike the PSTN, the Internet has been optimized for efficient communication between *computers*. The packet switched architecture of the Internet is designed for high-throughput of all communications, including audio and video. The PSTN is optimized for real-time voice communications.

Internet Applications

The devices connected to the Internet are computers capable of running software that supports the communication protocol of the Internet - TCP/IP. Many of these computers can run sophisticated graphical applications designed to access, share, and exchange information across the network. The information that is exchanged can be in a variety of media, including text, graphics, audio and video.

Probably the most common Internet application is electronic mail, or e-mail, for exchanging messages with specified individuals. Recent innovations have focused on enhancing a user's experience when accessing the information resources of the Internet. The World Wide Web (WWW) is a technology for publishing documents of multi-media information that can be accessed from a point-and-click interface. Netscape Communications Corporation has received tremendous attention based on the popularity of its Navigator product for browsing the rich document resources of the WWW.

Figure 2.1-- Internet vs. PSTN. Source: Hambrecht & Quist

Attribute	Internet	PSTN
Ubiquity	Everywhere	Everywhere
Standards-based	Everywhere	Within Countries
Switching Mechanism	Packet	Circuit
Location	Transparent	Within Zones
Voice Capability	Emerging	Best Suited
Computer Capability	Optimized	Moderate
Ownership	Numerous	Small Number
Cost Mechanism	Bandwidth	Distance, Time, and Bandwidth
Cost Per User	Low, fixed	Moderate, Variable
Usage and Content	Multifaceted	Simple, Spontaneous
User Interface	Numerous	Not Applicable

Many Internet users access the Internet using a modem connected to a standard analog telephone line. Standard analog phone service is known as Plain Old Telephone Service, or POTS. Modems used on POTS lines reach their data transfer limit around 30 kilobits per second (kbps) without compression. With compression, data transfer rates can be as great as 60 kbs.

Such bandwidth is adequate for real-time audio communication, but a poor solution for applications requiring higher throughput, such as video. As a result, services such as Integrated Services Digital Network (ISDN) are becoming increasingly popular as users are looking for a higher bandwidth option for Internet connectivity. Figure 2.2 Illustrates the options for connecting to the Internet and the real-time multi-media applications for which they are appropriate.

Figure 2.2 – Bandwidth and Applications of Access Types

Option	Bandwidth	Applications	Typical Users
POTS	28.8 kbps	Audio (FM mono quality)	Home
ISDN BRI	144 kbps	Audio (FM stereo quality), Low-end Video	Home, Small Business
ISDN PRI	1544 kbps	Audio (CD quality), Video	Business
T-1	1544 kbps	Audio (CD quality), Video¤	Business
ATM	Up to 622,000 kbps	Audio (CD quality), Video (broadcast quality), Virtual Reality Applications	Large Business

Internet Telephony Applications

There are four broad categories of computer telephony applications: information access and transaction processing, unified messaging, intelligent call management and real-time voice communication. First, characteristic applications in each of these categories that are *not* Internet-enabled will be presented. Then, Internet-enabled applications in each category will be discussed. Applications in each of these categories can be created using industry standard programming tools such as Microsoft Visual Basic and C++. Many of the Internet-enabled telephony applications discussed below are based on an architecture that includes a WWW server enhanced to support voice processing. Such a server is the basis for integrating computer telephony with the Internet.

Information Access and Transaction Processing

Information access and transaction processing includes applications such as interactive voice response (IVR) (e.g. touch-tone banking) and fax-on-demand systems. IVR and fax-on-demand applications allow organizations to leverage the availability and convenience of the telephone as an input/output mechanism for data as illustrated in Figure 2.3. By entering touch-tones (or even by just speaking), callers can directly update database records or select specific information for retrieval. Retrieved information can be converted to speech and played over the phone or sent to the caller as a facsimile document. A voice processing board in the Computer Telephony Server answers phone calls, plays and records voice files, and retrieves caller input. The Computer Telephony Server may access an organization's complete data resources.

Figure 2.3 – Computer Telephony Server and PSTN

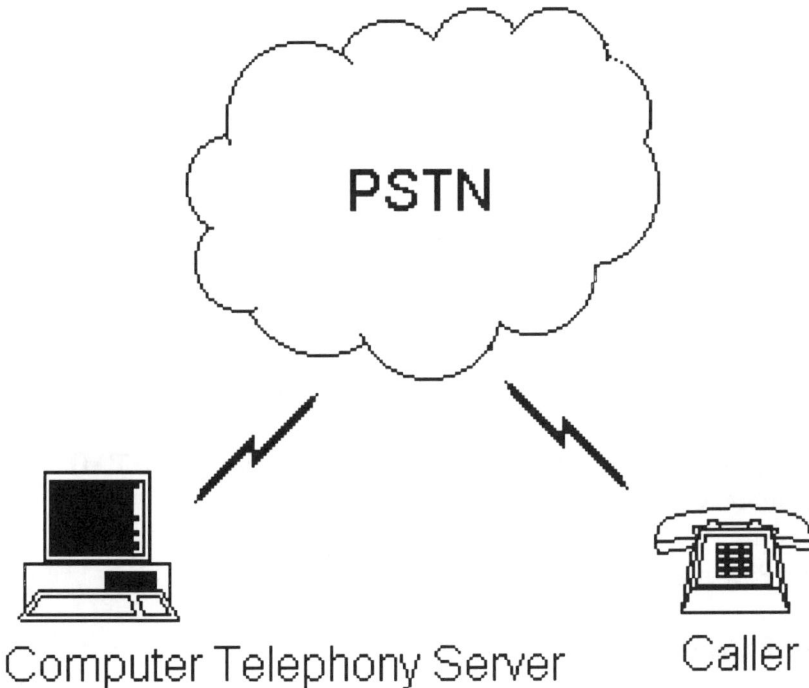

Business Benefits. The business benefits associated with this category of application are significant. Allowing customers to access information or place orders 24 hours a day without waiting for a service representative lowers costs and increases revenues and profits. IVR systems can also increase customer satisfaction by allowing customers to access services at their convenience.

Internet-Enabled IVR

With the emergence of the Internet, more organizations are publishing information on the WWW. The quantity of information on the WWW is increasing rapidly. Many organizations already use the WWW as the primary vehicle for sharing important announcements, technical and marketing information, pre- and post- sales support information, and much more. The language used to create WWW documents is known as Hyper Text Markup Language, or simply HTML. HTML is similar to other "markup" languages that use "tags" to specify how the content of a document is formatted. For instance, the HTML tags to format text in italics are *and* /I. The text between these tags is presented in italics.

Internet-based computer telephony applications allow users calling from any phone to listen to or receive a facsimile document of information published on the WWW. Stylus has developed a collection of *voice response* extensions to HTML that allow authors of WWW documents to easily specify how a WWW document should sound to callers over a telephone. These extensions allow a WWW page author to create an "instant" IVR application. Collectively, the voice response extensions to HTML are referred to in this document as Hyper Voice Markup Language, or HVML:

Language definition for voice response extensions to HTML. Note: All parameters in brackets are optional.

Action: Play a prerecorded voice file.

HVML Extension:

PLAY [NAME=string] FILE=string [TERM=string] [CLEAR=integer]

Notes: NAME is an identifier this tag. FILE is the name of a prerecorded voice file. TERM is a string containing digits that can terminate playing the file. CLEAR can be 0 or 1, 1 will clear the digit buffer before the file is played.

Action: Prompt a caller for touch-tone input.

HVML Extension:

PROMPT [NAME=string] [FILE=string] [MAX=integer] [TERM=string] [TIMEOUT=integer] [SWITCH=string:string, string:string, string]

In this example, NAME is an identifier this tag. FILE is the name of a prerecorded voice file. MAX specifies the maximum number of digits a caller can enter. TERM is a string containing digits that can terminate playing the file. TIMEOUT specifies the length of time to wait for the user to enter digits. The SWITCH parameter contains DIGIT, LABEL pairs that indicate the named label to which the flow of control should pass based on the digits entered. The final unpaired LABEL is the default.

Action: Speak information from a WWW page to a caller.

HVML Extension:

¯SAY [NAME=string] [FORMAT=string] [SUBFORMAT=string] [text] /VOICE SAY

In the example above, speaking information requires a start and an end tag. These tags enclose the text to be spoken to the caller. NAME is an identifier this tag.. FORMAT specifies how the text to be spoken should be interpreted. FORMAT can be one of the following types: MONEY, DATE, NUMBER, PRICE, ORDINAL, TEXT, CHAR. The SUBFORMAT parameter is dependent on the FORMAT parameter and describes how the format should be played (precision, etc.).

Action: Traverse a link to another WWW page

HVML Extension:

LINK [NAME=string]

The VOICE LINK tag must be contained within a set of anchors that specify a location. For example: A HREF="news.htm" LINK NAME=NEWSWhat's New?/A. NAME is an identifier this tag.

The HVML extensions are parsed and understood by an Internet IVR Server application. This application acts as a gateway for telephone callers to access the Internet as depicted in Figure 2.4. The Internet IVR Server can be enhanced to allow callers to request a facsimile copy of any WWW page. Stylus demonstrated an example of an Internet IVR Server at Computer Telephony Expo 96. Callers dial into an Internet IVR Sever. The Internet IVR server allows callers to access WWW pages and interprets HTML voice response extensions. Callers can hear a variety of information from WWW pages including stock quotes, movie reviews, news headlines, etc.

Figure 2.4 – Internet IVR Server

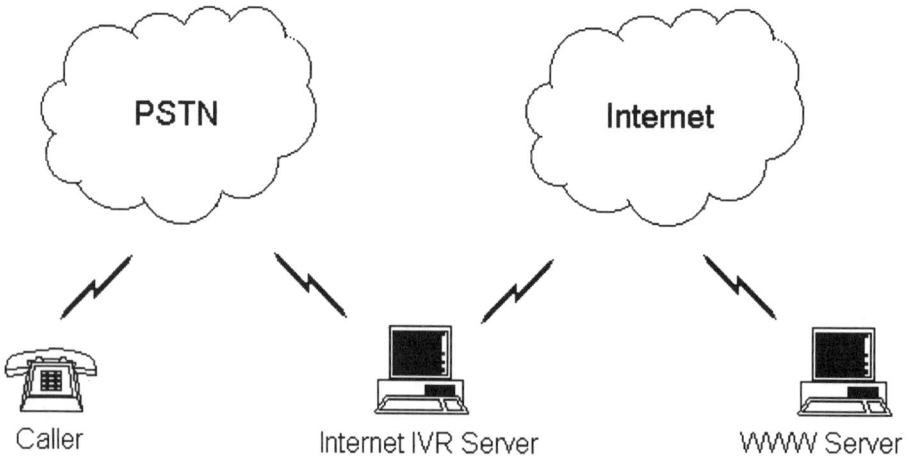

| Caller | Internet IVR Server | WWW Server |

Unified Messaging and The Internet

Unified messaging systems allow users to manage e-mail, voice mail, and fax documents in a single in-box. Most unified messaging applications include both a graphical computer interface and a telephone interface for remote users. For remote users, e-mail messages can be read over the phone by using speech synthesis technology.

Business Benefits. A unified messaging system enhances productivity by reducing the number of systems that a user must become familiar with and check for messages. By consolidating communication points, unified messaging systems allow users to spend less time and effort locating and retrieving messages. Also, a unified messaging system's graphical user interface (GUI) makes it easier to listen to any section of a voice message, forward a message, file a message, etc.

Internet-Based Unified Messaging Systems. The increasing popularity of the Internet and the graphical nature of Internet applications can be leveraged to allow users more convenient and full-featured access to their message in-box. Figure 2.5 shows how the Internet Unified Messaging Server acts as a bridge between the Internet and the PSTN.

Figure 2.5 -- Internet Unified Messaging Server

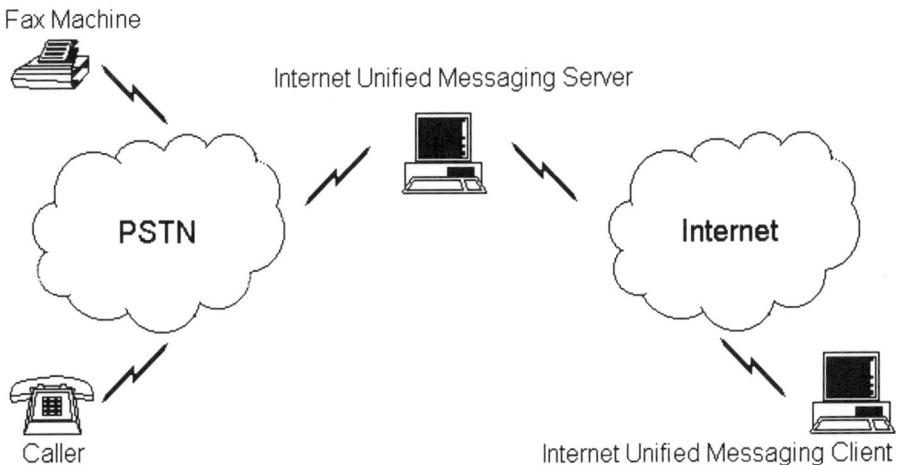

An Internet Unified Messaging Client lets users manage e-mail, voice mail, and fax documents from anywhere on the Internet with a single graphical interface. The Internet Unified Messaging Server receives and stores e-mail, voice, and fax messages. Any computer connected to the Internet can be used to access and manage a unified in-box. For example, a remote user can access the Internet and receive e-mail, voice mail, or fax messages stored on a server at the user's office.

Intelligent Call Management

This category includes numerous applications that add programmed intelligence to the manner in which incoming or outbound calls are managed. This is one of the fastest growing categories of computer telephony applications and includes systems such as:

- Outbound predictive dialers.

- Incoming call routing systems that use Automatic Number Identification/Dialed.

- Number Identification Service (ANI/DNIS) information.

- Applications that identify a caller with Caller ID and provide a "screen-pop" displaying information about the caller on an agent's computer screen.

- International callback systems.

- Systems that automatically dial a series of telephone numbers in an attempt to locate the called party.

- Call scheduling applications and many more.

Business Benefits. Organizations are realizing substantial benefits by being able to easily build systems that make more efficient use of their human, computer, and financial resources. Predictive dialers, for example, eliminate the need for call center agents to manually dial telephone numbers. Numbers are dialed by a predictive dialing application and a call is only connected to an agent when the predictive dialer recognizes that an individual answered. If an answering machine or a busy signal is encountered, the predictive dialer leaves a prerecorded voice message or schedules a callback.

Leveraging the Internet. The Internet adds a new dimension to intelligent call management as it allows an organization to open its call management systems to users of the Internet. For example, imagine an application that allows an Internet user to request an immediate phone call from an organization while viewing that organization's WWW page. The user enters her name and phone number on the WWW page. This information is passed to the organization's predictive dialer and within moments a representative can be talking to the user on the phone. In the meantime, the user is browsing the WWW site and learning more about the organization. As shown in Figure 2.6, an Internet-Enabled Predictive Dialer accepts requests from Internet Users who wish to be contacted by phone. The Internet-Enabled Predictive Dialer calls the Internet User and connects the call to an available Call Center Agent.

Another example of a powerful Internet-based computer telephony application is a distributed inbound call center. A large organization sometimes has customer service agents located in a number of places around the world. Inbound calls are routed to specific agents based on call loads, caller location, etc. Using the Internet, customer history records can be routed to the agent's PC screen at the same time the phone call is being routed.

A final example involves "call pursuit." Before leaving the office, someone using an advanced voice messaging system can specify a series of phone numbers that the auto-attendant will use to connect an incoming call (e.g., car phone, hotel phone, etc.). Using an application written for the Internet, the user can change this series of phone numbers, or other parameters, remotely with a graphical user interface.

Figure 2.6 -- Internet-Enabled Predictive Dialer

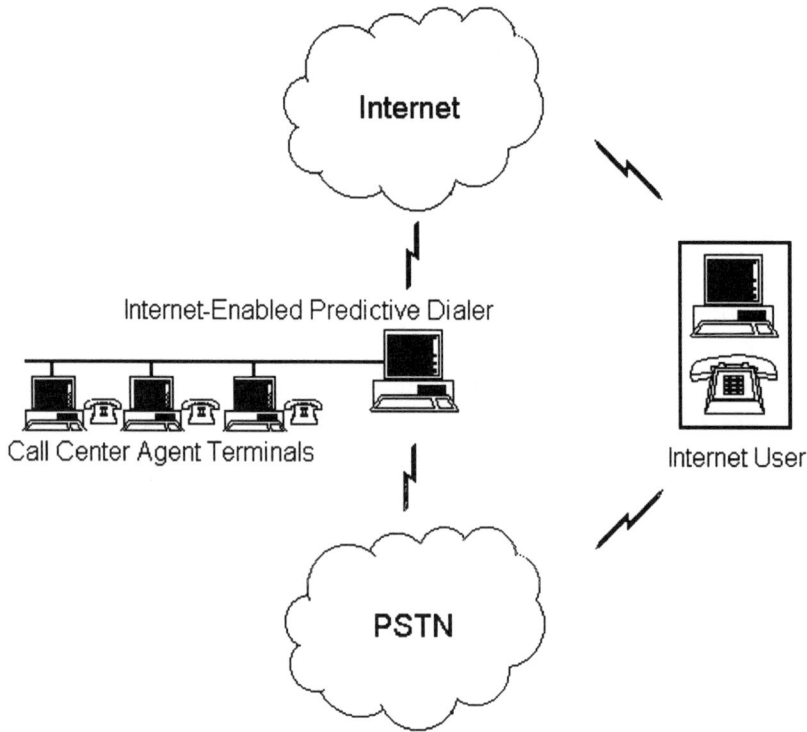

Internet

Internet-Enabled Predictive Dialer

Call Center Agent Terminals

Internet User

PSTN

Real-Time Voice Communication

A well publicized union between the Internet and computer telephony is software that allows users to have real-time voice conversations over the Internet. Often referred to as "Internet Phone," this software transforms a caller's computer into a speaker phone. An extension to the Internet phone concept allows callers to use conventional telephones to place calls that are routed across the Internet. Callers dial into a local server application that provides an interface to real-time Internet-based voice communication.

A second local server application provides the corresponding interface between the Internet and the local phone system used by the called party. Figure 2.7 illustrates how this works: Party 1 places a call to a local Internet Phone Telephony Server. The server provides real-time two way voice communication across the Internet to another Internet Phone Telephony Server located locally relative to Party 2. Party 1 and Party 2 can be located anywhere in the world and communicate for the cost of tow local calls.

Figure 2.7 -- Internet Phone Telephony Server

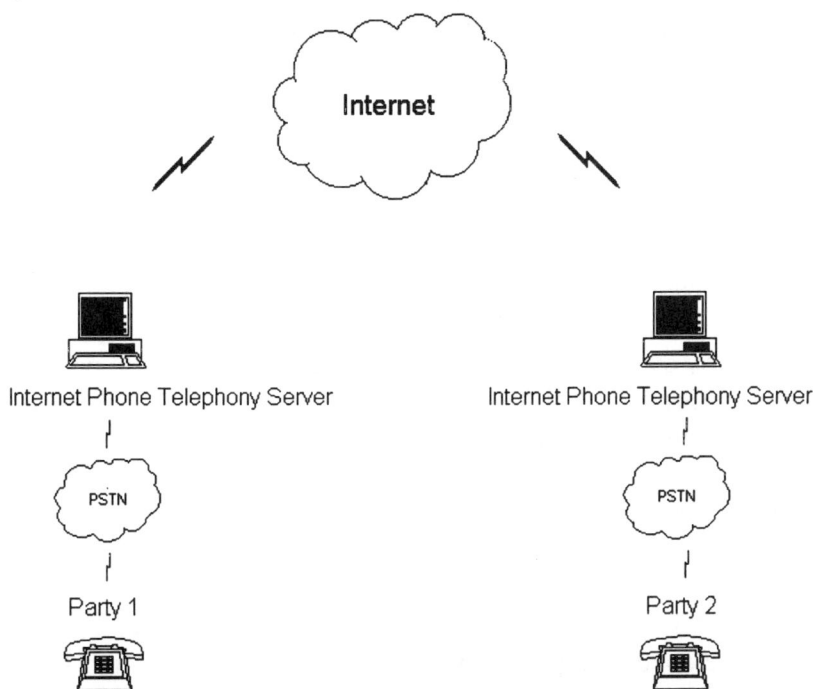

Business Benefits. This category of Internet-based telephony applications has tremendous potential as it takes advantage of the significantly lower cost structure of the Internet for voice communication. Another example of a real-time voice system enhanced by the Internet is document conferencing. This technology allows both (or all) parties on a phone call to *see* a document under discussion on their PC screens.

This document (e.g., a budget) can be edited in real-time while all parties are watching. The voice communication is handled by the PSTN; the document communication is handled by the Internet.

Stylus Visual Voice

Visual Voice is an application developer's toolkit for building telephony and fax applications on all Microsoft Windows platforms (3.x, 95, NT). Many of the applications presented above can easily be created using Visual Voice. Other common examples of telephony and fax applications include; touch-tone banking, 24-hour order entry, product brochure fax-on-demand systems, golf tee reservation systems, outdialing patient reminders, and voice mail/auto-attendant systems.

Visual Voice is an *open architecture* toolkit. It is designed to transform *any* Windows development tool into a toolkit that can build computer telephony applications. The most popular Windows development tool is Microsoft Visual Basic. Visual Basic is an easy-to-learn, non-proprietary language used by over 3 million developers. Visual Voice is also commonly used with Microsoft Visual C++, Powersoft PowerBuilder, and Borland Delphi. Applications developed with Visual Voice can interact with practically every available data source and network because of the extensive third party and built-in support available for these development environments.

Visual Voice allows someone with no telephony experience to develop sophisticated telephony applications. Visual Voice provides high-level interfaces to answer inbound calls, place outbound calls and prompt for and retrieve touch-tone input from callers. In addition, you can play and record voice files and send and receive faxes. More sophisticated call control applications can be built due to support of transferring and conferencing calls. You can hook up to analog, and digital T-1, E-1 and ISDN lines. With Visual Voice, Stylus pioneered the concept of low-cost, open architecture toolkits for telephony and fax applications.

As the Internet's popularity increases, the applications discussed above, and others, will become commonplace. The merger of computer telephony with the Internet presents tremendous business opportunity for individuals and organization from both industries. With tools like Stylus Visual Voice, developers can very easily build sophisticated computer telephony applications that leverage the communication infrastructure of both the PSTN and the Internet.

Chapter Acknowledgments

My sincere thanks to Dave Krupinski, Vice President of Marketing at the Stylus Product Group of Artisoft, Inc. This chapter is based on his white paper: C*omputer Telephony and the Internet.* Reprinted with permission. (c) 1996 Stylus Product Group

Chapter 3

The Confluence Model

The convergence of telecommunications and computing: What are the implications today? This was the burning question answered perhaps best by David G. Messerschmitt, professor in the Department of Electrical Engineering and Computer Sciences at the University of California at Berkeley. He and his colleagues see this convergence as the driving force behind all future means of communication and lifestyle. Computing and telecommunications technologies are converging. This has meant different things at different times. Here we describe the current state of convergence, and speculate about what it may mean in coming years. In particular, we argue that as a result of the horizontal integration of all media (voice, audio, video, animation, data) in a common network and terminal infrastructure, telecommunications and networked-computing applications are no longer distinguishable.

Considering that the old terminology is no longer meaningful, we attempt to codify networked applications in accordance with their functionality and immediacy. Application functionality is increasingly defined in software.

With programmable terminals and means for distribution of applications over the network, we argue that user-to-user applications will be greatly impacted. They will move into the rapid-innovation regime that has characterized user-to-information-server applications in the recent past. Finally, we identify a number of areas where different technical approaches and design philosophies have characterized telecommunications and computing, and discuss how these technical approaches are merging and identify areas of needed research. We do not address complementary forms of convergence at the application or industrial level, such as convergence of the information and content-provider industries, but rather restrict attention to the infrastructure and technology. The terms "telecommunications" and "computing" are losing their relevance as separate identities, and also that these fields will become virtually indistinguishable in the relatively near future.

Why should we care? The convergence has, and will continue to have, profound impact on technology, industry, and the larger society. The traditional fields of telecommunications and computing have already been irreparably changed by the other, and, as we argue below, will be even more substantially recast in the future. We argue that much more profound changes are forthcoming, changes no less weighty than the rapid disintegration of the vertically integrated industrial model (from silicon to applications). Finally, while computing in the absence of communications has led to new applications and made substantive changes to leisure and work life, computing in conjunction with communications will have a profoundly greater impact on society. This is because communications is at the heart of what makes a society and a civilization, and the convergence with computing will revolutionize its nature.

Telecommunications, Computing Defined

The term telecommunications is derived from "tele", meaning at a distance, and "communications", meaning exchanging of information. The dictionary definition of telecommunications is "communication at a distance (as by telephone)," and the term is most commonly applied to the telephone, but also applications like video conferencing. At its origin, the computer was envisioned as a machine to perform massive numerical calculations.

Indeed, this is the origin of the term "computer", as "something that can compute". Later, with the development of large peripheral storage devices, the computer became a repository of large amounts of data that could be modified, manipulated, and queried. This is reflected in the current dictionary definition of the computer, as "a programmable electronic device that can store, retrieve, and process data." These classical views of telecommunications and computing are well differentiated with respect to applications.

Recently, the infrastructure and applications for these technologies have become seriously blurred. In both the network (embodied in the *Internet* and *asynchronous transfer mode*, or ATM) and the desktop computer, data has become integrated with continuous media (audio and video), enabling so-called multimedia applications

Applications are becoming blurred as well. Accessing bank records using a DTMF telephone and voice response unit, or with a networked computer over a computer network, differ as to medium but not basic functionality. Thus, the classical terminology of telecommunications and computing is no longer as useful, and possibly even delusory. In light of this, it is appropriate to define a more transparent classification of networked applications that is media-blind, and focuses on the functionality provided the user.

A Three-Level Architecture

As an aid to understanding, we adopt the three-level model of Figure 3.1. In the traditional terminology of network operators, users have accessed "services" (like telephone, call waiting, voice mail), while computer users have accessed "applications" (like spreadsheets and word processors). The origin of this distinction is undoubtedly the presence of a "service provider" in telecommunications, largely absent in the modern computing industry.

We define an application as a collection of functionality that provides value to a user (a person). In this paper we are concerned with networked applications, implying that they are distributed across a distributed telecommunications and computing environment.

Figure 3.1 -- Three-level Information Network

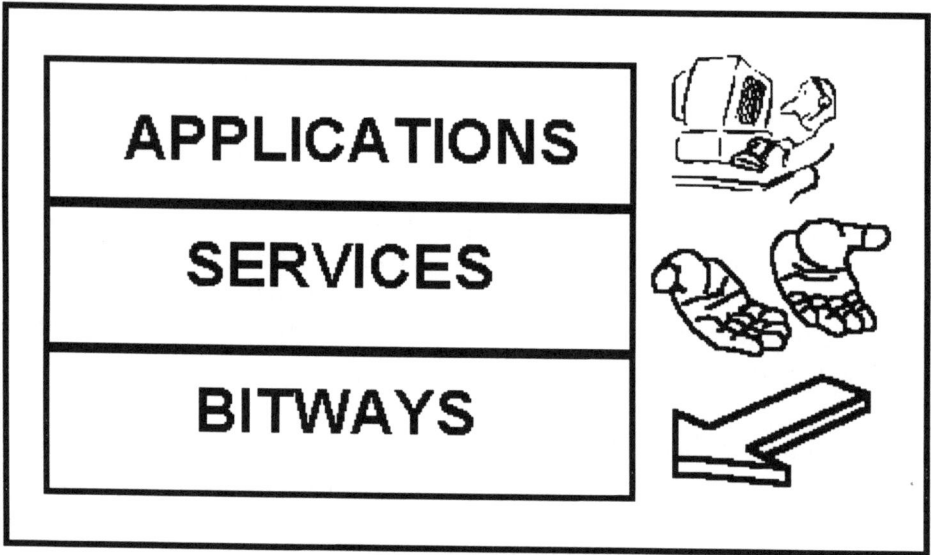

Examples of networked applications are electronic mail, telephony, data-base access, file transfer, World Wide Web browsing, and video conferencing. A service is defined as functionality of a generic or supportive nature, provided as a part of a computing and telecommunications infrastructure, that is available for use in building all applications. Examples of services would be audio or video transport, file-system management, printing, electronic payment mechanisms, encryption and key distribution, and reliable data delivery. Bitways are network mechanisms for transporting bits from one location to another. Examples of bitways with sufficient flexibility for integrated multimedia applications are Asynchronous Transfer Mode (ATM) or internets interfaced with the Internet Protocol (IP).

We can build a taxonomy of networked applications into four categories as shown in Figure 3.2. Two categories relate to the functionality:

User-To-User Applications, in which two (or more) users each participate in some shared functionality.

User-To-Information-Server Applications, in which a user (or sometimes two or more users) interacts with a remote system to access, receive, or interact with information stored on that system.

Each user in a networked application interacts with a local terminal, which communicates in turn with remote computers or terminals across the network.

Figure 3.2 -- Taxonomy of Networked Applications

	IMMEDIATE	DEFERRED
User-to-Information Server	Video On Demand WWW Browsing	File Transfer
User-to-User	Telephony Video Conferencing	E-Mail Voice Mail

We also separate networked applications into two classes with respect to the temporal relationship in the interaction of the user with a server or with another user:

Immediate, meaning a user is interacting with a server or another user in real-time, typically with requirements on the maximum latency or delay.

Deferred, meaning a user is interacting with another user or a server in a manner that implies no fixed temporal relationship and for which the delay is typically not critical.

One useful test is whether the user concentrates solely on the application (immediate) or typically moves to another task in the middle of an interaction (deferred).

Immediate applications would sometimes be called synchronous or real-time, and deferred would sometimes be termed asynchronous or messaging.

Two Architectures For Networked Applications

Networked applications are physically realized by terminal nodes (or just terminals) interconnected by *bitways*. Functionally there are two basic architectures available for networked services, as illustrated in Figure 3.3.

Peer-To-Peer Architecture, in which two (or more) peer terminals, each associated with a local user, communicate over a bitway to provide a user-to-user networked application. The networked communications component between peers is often symmetrical (in terms of both functionality and bitway resources).

Client-Server Architecture, in which a client terminal associated with a user communicates over the bitway with a server computer, which is not associated directly with a user, but rather realizes an information-server function. The functionality is often asymmetric, with the server embodying the primary functionality or database access and the client terminal focusing on the user interface. (As will be described later, this partitioning is rapidly shifting.) The communications component is also often asymmetric, with the server-to-client direction typically requiring much higher bandwidth.

Often the peer or client terminal functions will be realized in software in a desktop computer, or they may be dedicated-function terminals (like a telephone or video conference set). For simplicity, we will refer to "peers," "clients," and "servers" without the associated terms "terminal" or "computer." Note that the terminal vs. bitway is (primarily) a physical partitioning of functionality between a terminal at the edges of the bitway, and the bitway itself. The three-level architecture of Figure 3.1 is a logical separation of functionality, where application functionality will typically physically reside in the terminals, and services functionality may reside in the terminals or somewhere within the bitway.

Figure 3.3. -- Client-Server and Peer-to-Peer

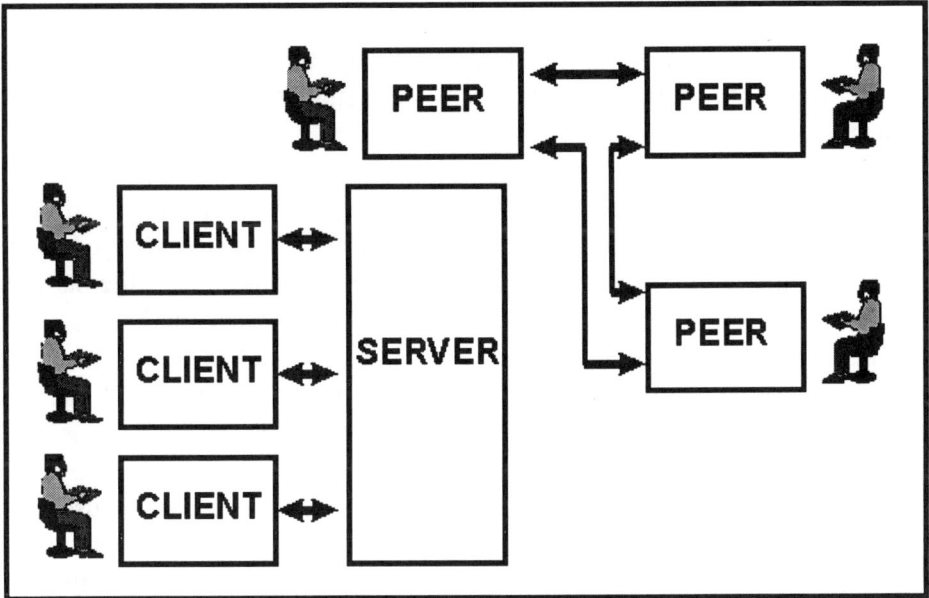

Figure 3.4 -- User-to-User and Peer-to-Peer

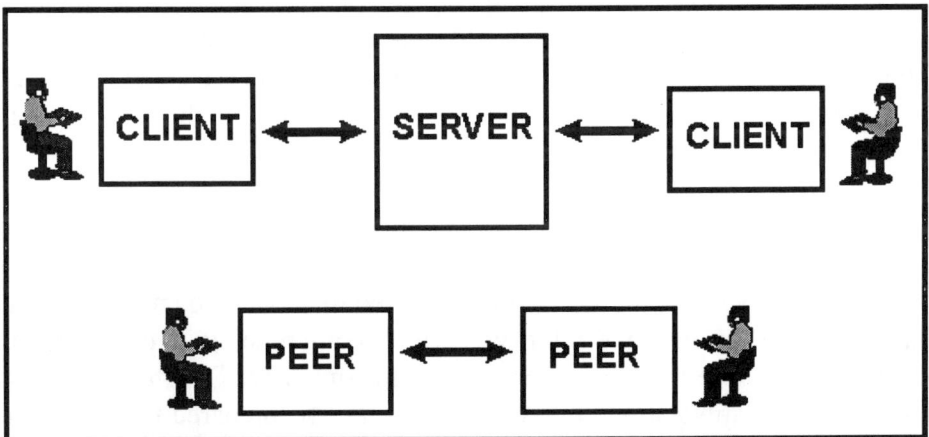

A user-to-information-server application is always realized with the client-server architecture. As shown in Figure 3.3, many clients will typically access a single server, which provides functionally separated but time-shared services to the clients.

On the other hand, a user-to-user application can be realized in either the peer-to-peer or client-server architectures, as illustrated in Figure 3.4 (for two users). In the client-server architecture, the two clients are communicating through the server, which may be realizing additional application or control functionality.

The client-server architecture is particularly appropriate for deferred user-to-user applications, since the server provides a convenient point for the necessary buffering with guaranteed availability regardless of the state of another peer. One such example in Figure 3.2 is voice mail, where the originating user (by way of his or her client telephone) forwards the voice message to a voice mail server, where it is stored to be accessed later by the destination user (by way of his or her client telephone).

From the perspective of the two users, the application is user-to-user and deferred, which is how it is listed in the table. However, the interaction of each user with the voice mail server (at different times) is user-to-information-server and immediate. This example illustrates several points. For one, the server adds functionality not available in the client telephone, such as menu-based control primitives, and is available even when the destination user is unavailable. For another, a terminal can serve as either a peer or a client in the context of different services. The telephone is a client to a voice mail server, but is more commonly a peer to another telephone in a (user-to-user and immediate) telephony application.

Although clients and peers serve a similar user-interface functionality, there are some basic differences. Typically many clients will connect to a single server, whereas a peer must be prepared to connect to any other peer. In some applications, like multi-way video conferencing, a peer may be connected to more than one other peer simultaneously. To establish a new instance of an application, a server must always be prepared to respond to an establishment request from a client (but doesn't originate requests), whereas a client may originate establishment request (but isn't prepared to respond to such requests).

A peer must be able to either originate or respond to establishment requests, and in this sense is a hybrid between a client and a server. A client can rely on the server for some functionality, whereas a peer must be self-contained. The biggest differences are in scalability to large numbers of users, interactive delay, and interoperability.

Convergence - A Short History

We are arriving at a network and terminal/computer environment that seamlessly supports user-to-user and user-to-information-server applications incorporating multimedia datatypes, one where there are no remaining vestiges of telecommunications and computing (in their classical definitions at least). It is helpful to list some of the key developments that has led us to this point, as well as ongoing developments that will have a large identifiable impact. To this end, we identify a number of distinct stages of development on the road to convergence, which we list in approximate chronological order.

Common Technology

The genesis of computer technology was basic technology arising from telephony; namely, the relays used in telephone switches. Subsequently, both computers and telecommunications exploited underlying advances in electronics and optoelectronics (the latter in the case of communications). More to the point, functional as opposed to technological convergence occurred with the advent of stored-program control for telephony switches and the development of digital representation of telephony signals (through quantization and analog-to-digital conversion in the so-called pulse-code modulation) in the 1950's.

These two developments presaged two profound shifts in telecommunications. First, computers became common as control and signaling points in telephony networks, enabling more functionally complex telecommunications services, and second, digital representations of audio, image and video signals allowed them to be stored and manipulated by standard computational hardware.

While the first factor has resulted in a major shift toward the automation of the telephone networks, it has had relatively little influence on the computer industry. The second development has had far wider implications outside communications, such as compact digital audio, digital HDTV, and the extremely flexible manipulation of signals by standard or custom digital hardware (the latter called digital signal processing). Only today is this technology joining the computing mainstream, as enabled by the increasing performance of desktop computers.

Networked Computers

Two seminal developments were the desktop computer as well as networks devoted specifically to the communication among them, first in the "local area network" (LAN) and later the "wide area network" (WAN). Two early examples of WANs are synchronous network architecture (SNA) and AR-PANET (the latter having evolved into the Internet). Early examples of applications enabled specifically by the networked computer include electronic mail, file transfer, concurrent databases, and recently the World Wide Web (WWW). The stand-alone desktop computer had previously enabled its own set of high-value applications, such as desktop publishing, spreadsheets, and other personal-productivity applications. The networked computer provides a ready large-scale market for new applications, thereby reducing the barriers to entry for new applications developers.

Computer networking, like the control computer before it, was widely adopted in the telecommunications industry as the basis of signaling and control. This signaling function was originally realized in-band on the same voice channel, but was replaced by a signaling computer network called common-channel interoffice signaling (CCIS). This enabled the advance from simple circuit-connection functions to much more advanced features (like caller identification), and ultimately will provide terminal-to-terminal signaling capabilities (a basis for dynamic deployment). Up to this point, there remained an infrastructure for computing that emphasized data-oriented media (graphics, animation), and a relatively separate telecommunications infrastructure that focused on continuous-media signals (voice and video).

These converged in a relatively superficial way, at the physical and link layers, where telephone and videoconferencing and computer networks shared a common technology base for the physical layer transport of bits across geographical distances. The telecommunications industry made extensive use of computer and software technologies in the implementation of the configuration and control of the network.

The computer industry made use of the telecommunications infrastructure to network computers, which enable networked applications. However, it is fair so say that the disciplines remained intellectually separate, sharing common hardware and communications media but pursuing distinct agendas and possessing distinct cultures.

Programmability And Adaptability

There are a number of inventions embodied in computing, but arguably the most important is programmability. The expanding importance of programmability flows from extraordinary advances in the cost/performance of the underlying electronics and communications technologies. In the context of any single application (like control, voice, audio, video, etc.), the performance requirements in relationship to the capabilities of the underlying technology passes through three stages:

- Initially, the application is very expensive to implement, and cost effectiveness dictates a customized hardware design. In this stage, efficiency (in metrics like processing power, bandwidth, etc.) is critical to cost-effectiveness, and hence commercial exploitation.

- Next, programmable software-defined implementations become feasible, and eventually cost effective. At this point, efficiency remains a dominant consideration, but the lower design cost and lower time to market afforded by a software definition can often overcome the manufacturing-cost penalties of general-purpose hardware.

- Finally, the technology advances so far that software-defined implementations become the norm. At this point, the greater efficiency of a custom hardware implementation is definitively overcome by its lower volume of manufacture, greater design costs (including especially the cost of tracking advancing technology), and greater time to market.

The final stage -- a software-defined solution -- has an important implication; namely, the basic functionality need not be included or defined at the time of manufacture, but rather can be modified and extended later. This property -- that the basic functionality can change and advance over time -- is the key to the triumph, for example, of the personal computer over the stand-alone word processor.

The advances in underlying technology are such that software-defined implementations are cost effective for audio as well as virtually all data media, and as time passes will become viable as well for video at increasing temporal and spatial resolution. Thus, the programmable implementation can be expected to spread to all corners of the computer and communications world (although there will always remain high-performance functions that are implemented directly in hardware).

The modern trend is toward adaptability, a capability that (usually) builds on programmability and adds the capability to adjust to the environment. For example, in a heterogeneous environment it is helpful for each element to adapt to the capabilities of other system elements (bandwidth, processing, resolution, etc.).

Horizontal Integration

There are two architectural models for provisioning networked applications, as illustrated in Figure 3.5. In the most extreme form of vertical integration, a dedicated infrastructure is used to realize each application. The premier example is the public telephone network, which was originally designed and deployed specifically for voice telephony.

In contrast, the horizontal integration model is characterized by:

- One or more integrated bitways that transport integrated data and stream media like audio and video with configurable quality-of-service (QoS) parameters .

- A set of services, such as middleware services (directory, electronic funds transfer, privacy key management, etc.) and media services (audio, video, etc.) that are made available to all applications.

- A diverse set of applications made available to the user.

We use the terms vertical and horizontal integration as an *architectural* model. These terms are used by economists as well, but in the different context of the partitioning of organization and ownership. Architecture and ownership tend to be coupled, but not completely as illustrated by the Internet where the ownership of a horizontal infrastructure is highly fragmented. A key advantage of the horizontal model is that it allows the integration of different media within each application, as well as different applications within the bitway. (For this reason, this is often called an integrated-services network in the telecommunications industry.)

Figure 3.5 -- Vertical And Horizontal Integration

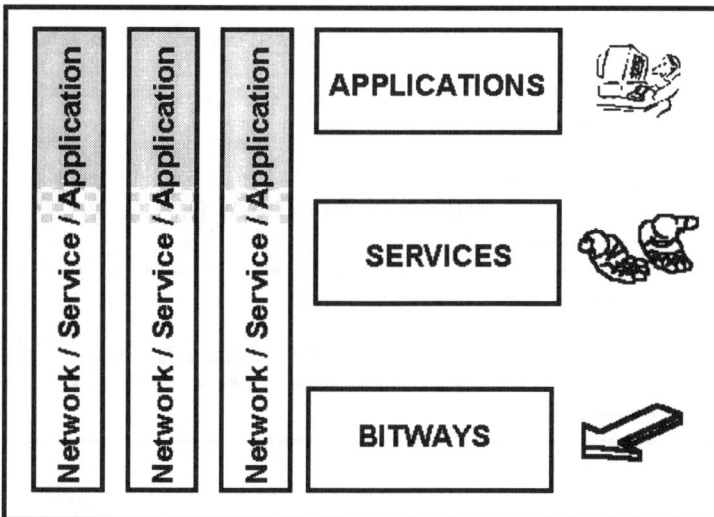

Another useful distinction among networks is whether or not they are *content-aware*, and whether or not they are *application-aware*. Vertically-integrated networks are frequently application-aware, meaning they are cognizant of the applications they are carrying (e.g. videoconferencing vs. file transfer), whereas horizontal bitways are often application-blind (e.g. the current Internet). Vertically-integrated networks are frequently even content-aware (e.g. a video-on-demand network that is cognizant of what movie is requested). A primary source of the rapid innovation in the Internet is the clean separation it forms between bitway, service, and application, making the service and application layers application-blind and thus allowing new applications to be constructed without modification to the bitway. An important feature of horizontal integration is the open interface, which has several properties: It has a freely available specification, wide acceptance, and allows a diversity of implementations that are separated from the specification. Another desirable property is the ability to add new or closed functionality. We define *closed* functionality as not published or extensible by other parties. *Proprietary* functionality may be published and extensible, but is subject to intellectual-property protection.

Figure 3.6 -- Open Horizontal Interfaces

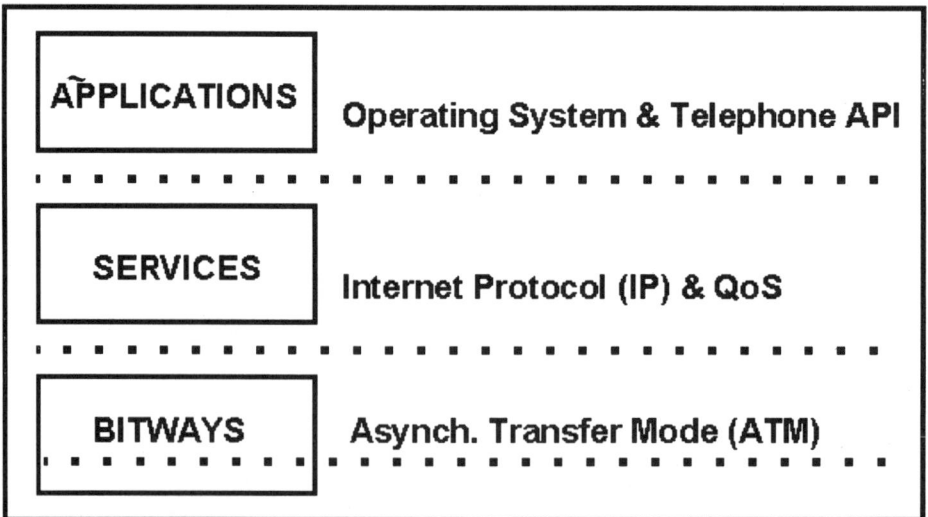

Open interfaces enforce modularity and thus allow a diversity of implementations and approaches to coexist and evolve on both sides of the interface. Some of the most important open horizontal interfaces in the computer industry are illustrated in Figure 3.6. ATM is a protocol designed specifically to accommodate a diverse mix of traffic types.

The Internet Protocol is an open standard for interconnecting bitways below it, where those bitways may incorporate a diverse set of technologies (including ATM). IP also allows for a diverse set of media types and applications to reside above it. Another critical interface is the operating system application program interface, which allows a diverse set of applications to co-exist on the same bitways and services infrastructure, while hiding as much as feasible the details from that infrastructure. Horizontal interfaces also exist for the control and signaling (e.g. control of telephony network features from a desktop computer application in the telephone application-program interface (TAPI), which supports computer-telephony integration.

One critically important consideration is complexity management. One purpose of open horizontal interfaces is to contribute to the modularity by the separation or independence of the definition of the application from the "execution engine" upon which it runs, which we call *platform independence*. Increasingly, applications can be simultaneously developed for multiple target platforms, by generating distinct platform representations from a common functional description, based on appropriate software toolsets. An even more powerful concept that is currently emerging is *middleware*, which is a horizontal layer residing on top of a set of networked computers, providing a set of distributed services with standard programming interfaces and communication protocols even though the underlying hosts and operating systems may be heterogeneous. Open horizontal interfaces are not completely successful at isolating horizontal functional layers. For example, one open interface is dependent on the suite of primitive functions offered by a lower interface, a phenomenon called *protocol dependence*. In his "Interoperation, Open Interfaces, and Protocol Architecture," (draft white paper at NII 2000 Forum, Washington, DC, May 23, 1995), David Clark has defined a special type of open interface called a *spanning layer*, which adds the characteristic that the extent of its adoption is nearly ubiquitous.

A specific spanning layer called the "open data network bearer service" is proposed in *Realizing the Information Future: The Internet and Beyond* (Washington D.C. National Academy Press, 1994). Spanning layers are particularly useful because higher interfaces can presume their existence and the services they provide, thus effectively isolating the design of the horizontal layers above and below. By this we mean a functional isolation. It will always remain performance and coordination issues. The computer industry is well along in the evolution to horizontal integration. The networked desktop computer resulted in the division of the industry into distinct horizontal segments (hardware, network, operating system, and application).

Today, we are in the process of integrating non-data media such as audio and video into this same environment, supported at both the bitway level (LANs and the Internet) and on the desktop. The telecommunications industry was once vertically integrated, with a focus on provisioning a single application with a dedicated network, such as voice telephony, or video conferencing, or cable television. Today this industry is also moving toward architectural horizontal integration at the bitway level with ATM bitways that flexibly mix different media; however, it remains largely vertically integrated at the services and applications layers, as bitway providers aspire to valued-added applications such as video on demand and differentiated terminals such as "set-top boxes."

We hypothesize that powerful economic and technological forces are driving us toward horizontal integration. Advances in technology have already resulted in the integration of different media in both the bitway (such as ATM or the Internet) and in the terminals (such as desktop computers). This level of horizontal integration offers the service provider substantial administrative benefits, relative to the alternatives of separate or overlay bitways, and adds value to the user, since different media can easily be incorporated into *multimedia* applications. The separation of the applications from bitways and services best serves the user by encouraging a diversity of applications, including many defined for specialized as well as widely popular purposes. Vertical integration discourages this diversity because a dedicated infrastructure demands a large market, and because users don't want to deal with multiple providers.

Horizontal integration lowers the barriers to entry for application developers since most of the infrastructure (bitways and services and even programmable terminals) are already available. Applications can be defined in software and coexist in the same programmable terminals with other applications, reducing the distribution cost and the incremental cost of a new application. Finally, it is unlikely that a single company can accumulate the range of expertise required to provide the best solutions across such a wide range of media and technologies.

Open interfaces offer vendors a large and immediate market for new applications. The resulting diversity of applications increases the utility of the open interface to the user. This positive reinforcement leads eventually to a dominant open interface, to be displaced only by a new interface that offers significant functional or performance advantages. The same inherent value of application diversity does not apply to bitways and services. They are generic and widely applicable to different applications, difficult to differentiate except in terms of cost and performance, and are capital intensive and benefit from economies of scale.

The computer industry is far along in the evolution to horizontal integration. The desktop computer freed the user of the constraints from the computer center bureaucracy and lowered the barriers to entry of application developers, which in turn offered greater value to the user. Our speculation is that the telecommunications industry will be pushed by market forces in the same direction, even though many companies would doubtless prefer vertical integration and closed solutions.

Untethered, Nomadic And Mobile Services

Here we use the term "untethered" to refer to *wireless* access to a bitway, "nomadic" to refer to *geographic flexibility* in accessing a bitway, and "mobile" to refer to bitway access while the user is in *motion* (The use of these terms has been inconsistent in the literature). In a sense, these three concepts build upon one another, but not strictly.

While mobile services are necessarily untethered, nomadic services are not. Mobile services are by definition nomadic. These three concepts lead to a different but overlapping set of challenging technological issues.

Nomadic telephony has long been available in the form of extension and pay telephones (Perhaps because there is no computing "service provider", an analogous infrastructure is yet to appear in networked computing.) Untethered telephony has been offered for some time by the cordless phone, and later, mobile telephony arose in the extraordinarily successful deployment of cellular telephone systems.

Computing has remained fixed-location for some time, although one might view networked client-server computing as nomadic in the sense of making an application executed on a server available to a nomadic user, should they be able to find a bitway access point. The laptop computer has supported the nomadic and even mobile computer user (although alas not the *networked* computer user, except to the extent such networking can be accomplished over the telephone). Recently, there is beginning to develop an infrastructure supporting nomadic and mobile networked computers.

Nomadic and mobile services and applications have been so successful because a fixed-location constraint is a mismatch to the roving nature of human activity (indeed, even *within* the office or residence). To the extent services and applications can be provisioned in a cost-effective mobile (or even untethered) fashion, experience has shown that users will choose this option. Thus, it is clear that nomadic and mobile telecommunications and computing are extremely important for the future, while offering many serious technological challenges.

Nomadicity and mobility provide another point of convergence: the issues raised by mobile telecommunications and by mobile networked computing are similar. Both require the dynamic migration of resources (connections, internal state, processes, reserved memory and bandwidth, etc.), and both raise serious issues related to QoS (uninterrupted service, inability to reserve resources in advance without regard to location).

Since telecommunications has addressed these difficult issues for some time, there is an excellent opportunity for cross-fertilization to nomadic and mobile computing.

Network Deployment

Beyond a couple of applications of universal interest -- voice telephony and video conferencing -- user-to-user applications are much fewer in number than user-to-information-server applications (although nevertheless very successful). These universal user-to-user applications have previously used the dedicated telephone network but are migrating to the Internet, for example with CU-SeeMe. A less familiar example is groupware and collaborative computing, where two or more users can performed shared functions on a document or database, as in a collaborative design project. There are also less familiar applications, such as telepresence and telemanipulation, which are important in military, outer space, and dangerous environments, but potentially also of importance in medicine. In contrast, there are a large and expanding number of user-to-information-server applications, such as the World Wide Web (WWW).

Why are user-to-user applications so few in number? This could be inherent, or perhaps this class of applications has been overlooked by the application software industry. Yet another is that the human factor aspects are not sufficiently developed. Another is the requirement for a cumbersome and time-consuming standardization process if two or more vendors are to achieve interoperability in a given application.

There are some notable successes in standardization, such as the V.34 voiceband data modem and MPEG where the standardization process probably speeded technical advance by involving a technical community of many companies. These examples are probably more accurately described as cooperative design combined with standardization. None of these reasons is as important as a fundamental obstacle to the commercial exploitation of user-to-user applications that economists call *direct network externality*.

This property of networked applications, which distinguishes them from most other market goods, is that the value of an application to a particular user grows with the number of other users that have an interoperable application available; that is, the community of interest willing and able to participate in that application. The technical definition of a *positive consumption externality* is "the value of a unit of the good increases with the number of units sold." In contrast, early adopters derive very little value, which is an economic barrier to a vendor attempting to establish such an application. (Who is the first user to buy a video conferencing application if there are no other users with whom to conference?).

User-to-user applications display strong network externalities. In contrast, user-to-information-server applications have an weaker network externality that makes them much easier to establish in the marketplace. This is because, once an information server is made available on the network, the first user derives the same value as later users. There is some externality coming from the larger market resulting from an increasing number of clients, which in turn stimulates more activity from application developers and content providers.

Network externality can be partly overcome by a good mechanism for distribution of application software. If a user-to-user application can be distributed to a large number of users virtually simultaneously, interoperability and a community of available users is guaranteed, even for early adopters. For software-defined applications, this is technically feasible, since an application can be distributed over the network itself. As shown in Figure 3.7, the user obtains a binary executable for a client or peer application over the network itself as a prelude to participating in the application.

Developers of user-to-information-server applications like World-Wide Web browsers, document viewers, and audio and video players are distributing new versions of those applications over the network. In fact, they are bypassing many externality issues by distributing them for free (hoping to derive revenue from the interoperable server software), thus establishing a community of interest quickly.

By bypassing traditional slow distribution channels, the velocity of innovation in these applications has been increased dramatically. Since user-to-user applications have a much stronger network externality, network distribution has the potential to make a much bigger impact on this class of applications.

Figure 3.7 -- Network Distribution Of Applications

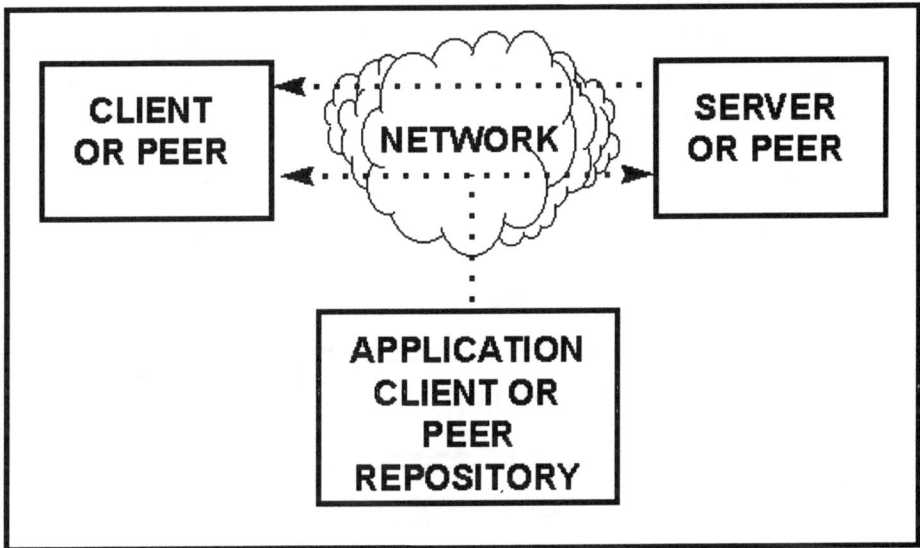

Network distribution in the Internet remains cumbersome, however, since a user has to anticipate the need for an application and execute the relatively sophisticated and manual "network file transfer." Other problems are multiple microprocessor instruction sets and operating systems, and security problems associated with downloading binary executables from untrusted sources. Recently, a technical advance with great promise has appeared that addresses these problems, associated with a new horizontal open interface called the *virtual machine*.

Dynamic Deployment And Transportable Computation

The virtual machine is illustrated in Figure 3.8. A layer of software is inserted between the operating system and the application that separates the application from the specifics of the operating system and hardware platform. The virtual machine open interface defines a general instruction set, as well as API's to resources like network services, all in an OS-independent way. It supports *transportable computation*, meaning that even though the program representing application functionality is stored in one node (typically peer or server), that program can be transported to and executed on another node (typically peer or client).

Figure 3.8 -- Virtual Machine Open Horizontal Interface

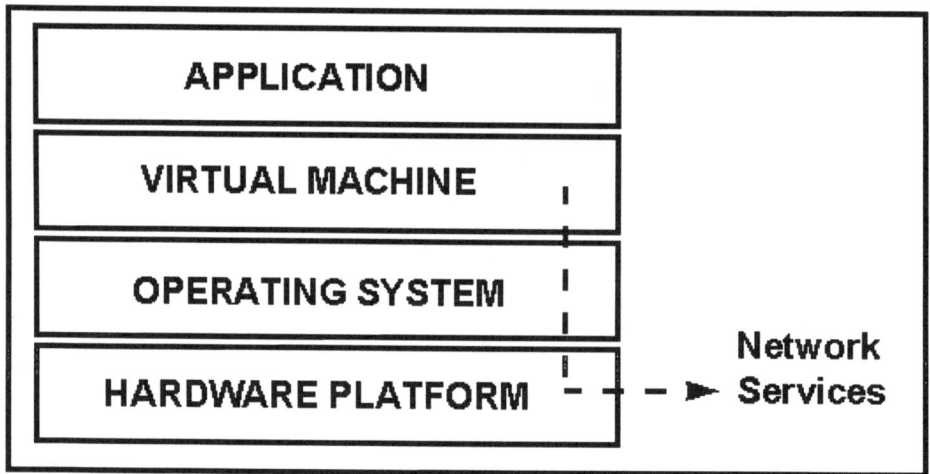

The virtual machine is implemented as an interpreter on various computing platforms or operating systems. Thus, applications can be written in a high-level language and compiled into the virtual machine instruction set, and subsequently run on any computing platform or terminal with an implementation of the virtual machine interpreter.

The process is illustrated in more detail in Figure 3.9, for the special case of the transport of computation from a server to a client. The client portion of an application is written in a high-level language that is compiled into a program composed of instructions for the virtual machine. This executable program is stored permanently in the repository on the server, and on demand is distributed over the network to the client. At the client, the program is run in an interpreter for the virtual machine. Thus far, this approach is embodied in several high-level application-description languages: Safe-Tcl (an embeddable command language), Telescript, and Java. Built into the interpreter are various safeguards against malicious or misbehaving programs (that are inevitable when allowing programs to be loaded from untrusted sources). The program executes more slowly on an interpreter, as compared to a native applications, although "just-in-time compilers" are expected that will compile the virtual machine language into native code on the target processor as it arrives.

Transportable computation offers four important advantages:

Scalability. It allows both memory (transient and persistent) and computation to be located on whatever terminal or computer is most advantageous. For example, in a client-server application it allows computation to be shifted from the server to its clients, thus avoiding overload of the server.

Latency. Executing the program in local peer or client as opposed to a remote host eliminates interactive latencies due to network transport delay.

Interoperability. If the programs associated with a distributed application originate from a common source, it can be assured that they are *interoperable*, meaning that they properly coordinate their operations. The conventional approach to interoperability, standardization (including *de facto* standardization), is by comparison cumbersome and time-consuming. This is doubtless the most important advantage.

Locality of data access. A transportable program can access and modify data stored on any computer to which it can be transported. This has serious security implications, and for that reason may well be prohibited by the virtual machine.

Figure 3.9 -- Dynamic Distribution of Applications

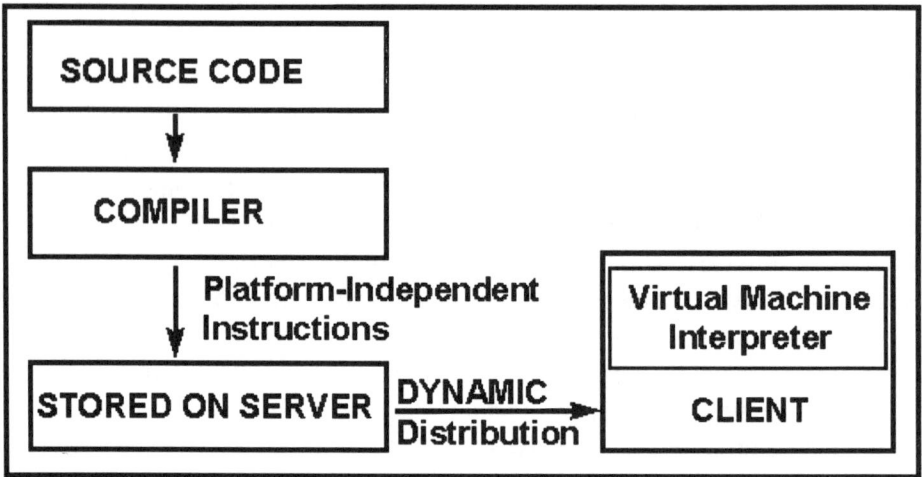

Transportable computation facilitates the *dynamic network deployment* of applications. That is, a distributed application can be copied over the network during establishment, transparently and invisibly to the user, with guaranteed interoperability, as illustrated in Figure 3.10 for a client-server architecture. The client application code is stored in a repository in the server, to be loaded dynamically across the network into the client when the user invokes that application. In contrast to the network distribution in Figure 3.7, the manual intervention of the user is not required: the deployment occurs transparently to the user whenever the corresponding application is invoked at the server. Other problems with network deployment like supporting different operating systems (or versions of those operating systems) are avoided, because the programs in the client repository are written to run on the "universal" virtual machine.

The success of this approach depends on the availability of a support library as a part of the virtual machine that abstracts machine-dependent functions like the graphical-user interface, sound and video input and output, etc. into platform-independent calls by the application. The success of platform independence in this sense is as yet inconclusive.

Figure 3.10 -- Client Applet Repository

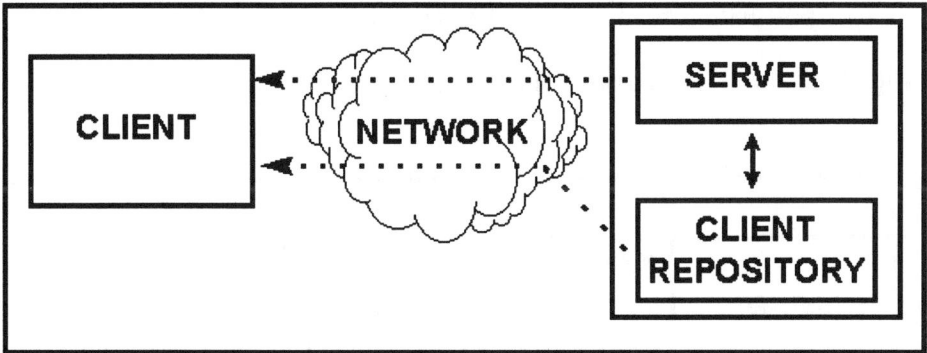

Thus far, dynamic deployment has been applied primarily to user-to-information-server applications (adding functionality to a WWW browser in particular). As shown in Figure 3.11, it has equal applicability to user-to-user applications, in this case in a peer-to-peer architecture.

The peer that initiates the application contains a repository of programs for the other peer, which are dynamically loaded at establishment of an application (Alternatively, a repository of programs for both peers could be obtained from a central server). We have demonstrated this using Tcl as the application-description language and more recently to peers consisting of Java-enabled WWW browsers. Dynamic deployment will have a far greater impact on peer-to-peer applications than client-server applications, because it neatly avoids network externality obstacles.

When a user purchases a user-to-user application for which one peer program is targeted at the virtual machine, he or she can readily participate in that application with any other user with the appropriate virtual machine interpreter (as opposed to the application itself). One can easily imagine a "toolbox" for defining collaborative user-to-user applications that includes standard components like "whiteboard," "shared editor," etc. It is only necessary for one user to possesses the toolbox, and temporary licenses for co-users can be created as necessary.

The application can dynamically add new components, even contributed by different participants. The ability to expand both types of applications will be a powerful force for the proliferation of virtual machine interpreters.

Figure 3.11 -- Interoperable Application Peers

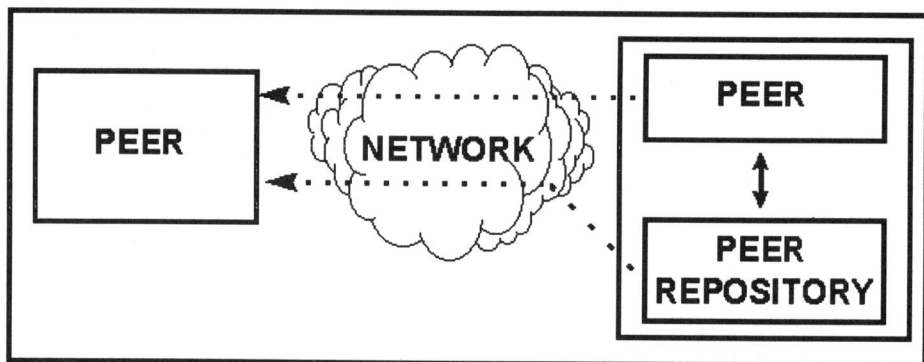

Dynamic deployment benefits from (and may even require) broadband networking, since application executables will sometimes be large. This will be an important driver for broadband access to the bitway, just as low-latency downloading of executables is a primary driver for broadband local-area bitways. This also has impact on the symmetry or asymmetry of the bitrate. Some bitway providers are assuming a much higher bitrate in one direction (server to client) than the other (client to server). Such assumptions do not take into account the peer-to-peer applications, nor the dynamic distribution of peer applications.

Intelligent Agents

Dynamic deployment does not exploit the full power of transportable computation, which is embodied in the more general concept of an intelligent agent. An intelligent agent is a transportable program that includes four attributes and capabilities:

Autonomy. It contains all information necessary for its execution.

Social Ability. It can interact with other agents or its environment.

Reactivity. It can exert actions based on attributes of its environment.

Pro-Active. It can initiate actions by itself.

The capabilities of the intelligent agent open up a number of possibilities. Intelligent agent technology originated in artificial intelligence, where one can imagine sophisticated human-like qualities such as adaptation to the environment and higher-level cognitive functions. Here, we can conceptualize more mundane applications that provide useful generalizations of user-driven information retrieval or even as basic as electronic mail. In this application domain, agents can act as "itinerant assistants" that are not restricted to particular servers, but cruise the network gathering or disseminating information. Such "itinerant agents" represent a different dimension of mobility; rather than the user being mobile, the user is represented by a mobile agent.

Complete Convergence

...The Logical Conclusion

As networked applications become more sophisticated, especially as enabled by the interoperability and scalability benefits of dynamic deployment, we expect the application types and architectural models to become increasingly mixed. Typical collaborative applications will combine user-to-user and user-to-information server functionality, as in a collaborative design involving two or more users and a common information server (storing the design being modified). The compelling performance benefits of the peer-to-peer architecture for the user-to-user interactions suggest that the peer-to-peer messaging will enjoy increasing popularity in such applications.

An example of a resulting mixed architectural model is shown in Figure 3.12 for three users (with associated mixed client and peer functionality) and a single information server. All client/peer and server terminals or hosts can include repositories of applets, yielding the flexibility to locate computation wherever it results in the best responsiveness, lowest latency, and can access the data it needs while insuring interoperability.

Figure 3.12 -- Mixed Peer-To-Peer And Client-Server

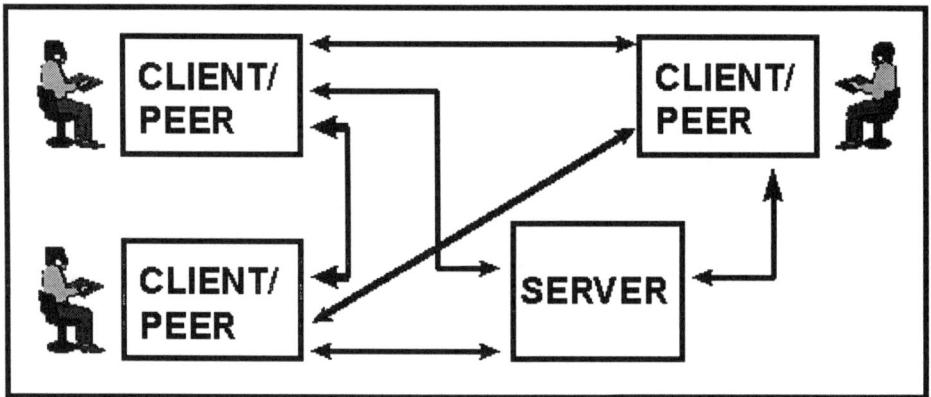

At the beginnings of convergence, telecommunications and computing shared many common technologies, but were distinguished in two primary ways. First, telecommunications focused on immediate user-to-user applications (principally telephony and video conferencing), while computing focused on initially stand-alone, and subsequently deferred user-to-user and immediate user-to-information-server applications, both on their dedicated and separate infrastructures. Second, telecommunications focused on continuous-media like audio and video, while computing focused on information storage, retrieval, and manipulation.

These distinctions are no longer useful, for two reasons. First, all applications and media will share a common horizontally integrated infrastructure for the future. Second, largely as a result of this common infrastructure, networked applications will no longer be neatly segmented.

With dynamic deployment of networked applications, and the removal of traditional network externality obstacles to networked applications (particularly user-to-user applications), we can expect a proliferation of user-to-user collaboratory applications that freely mix user-to-information-management components. The dynamic deployment of interwoven user-to-user and user-to-information-server multimedia applications in a horizontally-integrated terminal and network environment represents the pinnacle of convergence. Networked applications that freely mix the constituent elements traditional to telecommunications and computing will become commonplace. At this point, there no longer exists any technological or intellectual differences that distinguish telecommunications from computing. At this point, the dynamism and rate of progress in user-to-user applications becomes as great as has been recently experienced in user-to-information-server applications. As the availability of appropriate networked terminals is becoming widespread (for example Internet-connected personal computers with multimedia capabilities), this pinnacle of convergence will soon be upon us.

Common Themes In Convergence

The preceding has given a historical perspective on convergence, from the perspective of the users, applications, and industries. Here we discuss some broad technical themes that have distinguished telecommunications and computing and have been at the foundation of the intellectual dissimilitudes. These dissimilitudes represent opportunities, since each field has its own perspectives that suggest new research directions. Understanding how these technical distinctions are disappearing is also another way to appreciate the implications of convergence.

Best-Effort Vs. Quality-Of-Service (QoS)

Arguably the greatest distinction between telecommunications and computing has been in performance metrics. A model of service provided by many computer systems and computer networks is *best-effort*, which can be described as "always strive to achieve better performance though more advanced technology or improvements in architecture, but there is no absolute performance standard; we are never satisfied."

Since best-effort service does not take account of application needs, it is a "resources are cheap" model, in which applications may be provided considerably greater performance than they need, possibly at the expense of other applications that may receive less resources than they need. In fact, in the case of limited resources, most best-effort systems strive to achieve "fairness", attempting to apportion those limited resources according to some equality criteria. An early example of best-effort service (uncharacteristically in telecommunications) is *digital speech interpolation* (DSI), which statistically multiplexes speech sources, apportioning the available bit rate equally among the stochastically varying active sources. Because the speech quality deteriorates gracefully with increasing traffic load, high traffic can be accommodated, at the expense of no guarantee on the quality of speech reproduction for any customer. Best effort is the philosophy of design of the present Internet. For example, *fair queuing* allocates bitway bandwidth in packet networks during periods of congestion equitably among competing sources.

With rare exceptions like DSI, telecommunications has focused on *quality of service* (QoS) guarantees, which can be described as "reliably achieve a level of performance that the user finds acceptable, but no better than that". Thus, QoS is resource-conserving, assuming resources are expensive and must be conserved. Because bitways support a variety of applications, each with a different standard of what the user finds acceptable, it is usually assumed that bitways provide variable QoS (a different QoS to each application). This requires resource-allocation mechanisms that adjust resources (such as bandwidth, buffer space, etc.) to the provisioned QoS. It is inherent in QoS that there have to be pricing mechanisms that distinguish different QoS; otherwise, the application will always choose the highest available QoS. Resource-allocation and pricing and billing mechanisms add a significant level of complexity to the bitway.

Further, provisioning run-time variable QoS adds additional processing mechanisms that may actually slow down the bitway, since switching electronics is a significant bottleneck in today's bitways and there is often an inverse relationship between speed and complexity in electronics.

Another related difference in approach is one of trust. Perhaps because of its QoS objectives and related pricing, telecommunications has placed defenses against hostile users, for example deploying policing policies at network access points. Networked computing has placed more trust in the users, for example building flow control mechanisms into protocol suites but not enforcing them within the bitway.

These different philosophies have been driven by their different applications. In particular, telecommunications has focused on continuous-media like audio and video, where improvements in performance beyond a certain level are not perceived by the user. Further, the focus has been on immediate applications like telephony or broadcast television with broad appeal, rather than high performance applications for smaller customer groups. In computing, on the other hand, there are always technology-driving applications that stress the available technology. Further, networked-computing applications have typically been deferred, and thus have not required performance guarantees. Consistent with horizontal integration, networks of the future will integrate deferred and immediate networked applications. Thus, there has been considerable effort in mixing the QoS and best-effort service models, including into today's premier horizontally integrated bitway technologies, ATM and the Internet IP.

There are, of course, other performance attributes, such as establishment or setup time, outage probability for wireless links, blocking probability for admission control, etc. But three QoS performance attributes of a bitway that we can *consider* guaranteeing are:

The *rate* with which bits are generated, the temporal evolution of that rate, and the duplex symmetry or asymmetry of that rate.

The *latency* between the time information enters the bitway and when it emerges at the destination. Components of the latency include the time required to accumulate a packet at the source (if the information is packetized), the speed-of-light propagation delay, queuing delays in switches, and processing and buffering delays in the computer operating systems.

The *reliability* with which the information is delivered. There are two forms of unreliability: *loss* (packet never arrives) and *corruption* (packet with a valid header arrives, but with bit errors in the payload).

There are significant requirement variations in all three of these performance attributes across different applications, and there are typical divergent assumptions made in telecommunications and network computing. These differing assumptions have resulted in different technological solutions to resolve in horizontal integration. We will now review each of these three performance attributes in turn.

Rate Of Bit Generation

A basic distinction can be made between two basic types of bit streams:

- *Continuous media* like digital audio, video, and animation, are digital representations of analog signals and generate a continuous stream of information bits constrained by the underlying structure of the analog signal being represented. For example, video is composed of a sequence of image frames, which are desirably reconstructed in a reasonable facsimile of their original order and relative timing.

- *Sporadic* media like graphics and data, where information bits are allowed to flow in an unpredictable and unstructured fashion.

In terms of rate characteristics, continuous media can be represented by a continuous stream of bits with variable or constant bitrate, whereas sporadic media may have periods of very high bitrate interspersed with dormant periods.

The telecommunications infrastructure traditionally focused on the continuous-media extreme, fixed bitrate (circuit) transport with no statistical multiplexing, whereas computer networking has focused on sporadic media with extremes of statistical multiplexing advantage.

Circuit switching avoided congestion losses, but is forced to perform admission control in the form of blocking at establishment during traffic overloads. Computer networking has not used admission control, offering service to all comers, but has utilized best-effort techniques to divide the available capacity among all services. As mentioned below, both communities appear to be evolving toward a horizontally integrated bitway infrastructure supporting both service models.

Latency Of Transmission

Quite distinct transport requirements apply to immediate and deferred applications. For immediate applications, interactive latency is often a critical element of subjective quality; thus, transport latencies are often required to be both *short* (tens or hundreds of milliseconds) and *guaranteed*. The desire for low latency in such applications is a key reason for the choice of a short packet size in ATM, as this reduces the time required to accumulate a packet at the bitway access point for a low bitrate service such as voice. Guaranteed latency is particularly important for immediate applications built on continuous-media services, such as voice telephony and video conferencing. These services typically require a synchronous reconstruction with strict temporal requirements, and thus any data arriving with excess latency is not used, just as if it had been lost. This has led to attempts to insure bounded delays in packet networks. Other immediate applications have less critical latency requirements; for example, video on demand may allow multiple-second delays.

A primary advantage of the peer-to-peer architecture (when compared to the client-server architecture in user-to-user applications) is low latency, which is one reason it has been widely applied to immediate user-to-user applications in telecommunications. Client server adds not only server delay, but also possibly excess propagation delay due to more circuitous routing.

Statistical multiplexing accommodates streams with aggregate peak bitrates larger than the available bandwidth, and is therefore extremely efficient for sporadic media. A side effect of statistical multiplexing is latency associated with the buffering required to accommodate high instantaneous bitrates.

In addition, sporadic media often require reliable delivery, which can only be achieved over unreliable transport bitways through multiple transmissions, with the side effect that latency cannot be guaranteed. Fortunately, sporadic media can tolerate the larger latencies imposed by statistical multiplexing and reliability.

For the future, horizontal integration requires a high degree of flexibility in accommodating both continuous and sporadic media. Similar challenges occur in the computer operating system, where additional latency is added though the statistical sharing of processing and memory resources, running counter to the latency requirements of continuous media. These are challenging issues, since the techniques usually associated with statistical speedups (caching, paging, queuing) and often at odds with performance guarantees.

One very attractive feature of transportable computation is the ability to finesse the latency issue by performing application functionality locally, avoiding bitway round-trip delays.

Reliability Of Transport

Reliability in transport is adversely affected by congestion, which may cause *loss* by buffer overflow, and bit errors caused by noise or interference in transmission (which may cause loss if they occur in the packet headers or *corruption* if they occur in the packet payload). The techniques available for improving reliability, including forward error-correction coding, diversity, and acknowledgment and retransmission protocols, have the fundamental side effect of increasing latency.

As in rate and latency, there is a wide gulf in reliability guarantees between the approaches traditionally used in telecommunications and computer networking. Continuous media, since they represent an analog signal, can tolerate reasonable levels of loss and corruption with adequate subjective quality.

On the other hand, these media often have critical latency requirements. Thus, telecommunications has focused on transport techniques like circuit switching that guarantee latency but not reliability. Computer networking, on the other hand, has typically dealt with sporadic media and thus has focused on transport techniques such as packet switching and statistical multiplexing, appending transport protocols (like TCP/IP) that guarantee reliable delivery at the expense of indeterminate delay. Horizontal integration at the bitways level requires an interesting mix of these service models.

Where QoS Is Important

Advocates of best-effort transport argue that mechanisms for controlling QoS will slow the bitrates supported by the bitways, since switching electronics is a bottleneck, and in addition the associated infrastructure required for signaling and billing will add significant costs. Thus, it is argued, a scalable best-effort bitway will provide adequate performance near-term for the lowest cost by simply provisioning adequate resources, possibly accompanied by admission control to insure that those resources are adequate under worst-case traffic conditions. Whether or not this best-effort argument is valid, it is clear that given geometric advances with time in processing, storage, and bandwidth, many performance issues will rapidly disappear. Research should focus on serious fundamental limitations or bottlenecks that are not mitigated by technology advances. We can easily identify two such bottlenecks:

- The total traffic density of wireless (radio and infrared) access links is subject to fundamental limitations that are much more limiting than backbone bitways. These limits on traffic are strongly dependent on the corruption QoS requirement; in fact, corruption is more important than bit rate in determining capacity limits (which is diametrically opposite to backbone bitways). The disparity between traffic capacity of wireless access links and backbone bitways will only widen as backbone bitways get faster. There are emerging millimeter-wave radio technologies that will significantly ease this bottleneck in the indoor environment, but it will likely remain an issue in wide area access technologies.

- The latency is lower bounded by propagation delay. In a global information infrastructure, the propagation delay (several hundred milliseconds round-trip halfway around the world) is already a serious
  problem for interactive applications. Thus, there is little headroom to
  increase delay through compression signal processing, queuing, etc.
  Propagation delay will also increasingly interfere with bitway control
  and coordination as the bandwidth increases.

At the same time, both processing power and bandwidth in backbone
bitways advance geometrically. Disturbingly, the two lasting bottlenecks
are largely ignored, while most attention is focused on bandwidth efficiency
and other less critical issues. For example, video compression research
focuses almost entirely on minimizing bit rate (a resource increasingly
available in fiber bitways and storage systems) while ignoring the resulting
stringent reliability requirements (a scarce resource on interference-dominated wireless access links) and the signal processing delay.

Similarly, a disturbing tendency is to solve interoperability problems in
heterogeneous environments by utilizing conversions or transcoding, operations that can introduce significant delay (as well as interfere with security
and privacy by precluding encryption). Most research in terminal-to-network
coordination is focused on congestion mechanisms in backbone bitways,
while neglecting the more fundamental interference-related impairments in
wireless access links.

Similarly, *information theory* focuses on fidelity, providing fundamental
limitations on the throughput of physical channels with high fidelity and
the maximum fidelity that can be achieved for a given bit rate in a signal's
digital encoding. For the most part, information theory ignores delay (in
many aspects it explicitly allows delay and complexity to be unbounded as
a key assumption, with notable exceptions like error exponent bounds). On
the other hand, queuing theory, which has been applied extensively to both
computer networks and computer systems, focuses on delay and loss due
to congestion, but offers no insights on fidelity.

A key issue in convergence is uniform and unified ways of dealing with delay, loss, and corruption at the practical as well as theoretical levels. Particularly challenging, as mentioned before, is the problem of integration of different media and applications with variable QoS (delay and reliability) requirements.

Associated with QoS are numerous other issues where the traditional signal processing and communications theory communities can make a strong contribution. Among them are the relationship of quantifiable transport impairments on subjective quality, the aggregation of impairments in concatenated transport media, and various optimization questions related to the allocation of end-to-end impairments to individual facilities. Also of great interest are negotiation strategies between network and terminals to arrive at acceptable solutions, and the mechanization of these negotiations.

Scalability Of Architecture

A powerful force underlying both telecommunications and computing are exponential increases with time in the processing of electronics, the bandwidth provided by photonics, and the capacity of storage systems. These advances have a strong tendency to overwhelm performance issues, given the passage of reasonable time. Nevertheless, at any given time, it is important to be able to accommodate whatever performance level or number of users necessary by simply *adding* resources to the system, as opposed to *replacing* the technology for higher performance.

An architecture with this property is *scalable*. A desirable form of scalability is a resource cost that is at most linear in some measure of performance or usage. Scalability and technology advances together represent a powerful force: at any given time we can accommodate any number of users or achieve any performance at a cost roughly constant per user or proportional to performance, and over time the cost-performance (if we are willing to replace the hardware) improves geometrically. Scalability has always been an overriding requirement in telecommunications, because of the desire to serve ever larger numbers of users in a common networked system.

With network externality, the utility to each user increases with the number of users, and there may actually be economies of scale so that the cost per user decreases with the number of users, resulting in extremely favorable economics. (In addition, cross subsidies have also been used to achieve "universal" service in the telephone network.) Pre-networked computing, on the other hand, has focused on the single-user model, where scalability is not an issue.

For networked computers, a strength of the peer-to-peer architecture is its inherent scalability. The server in the client-server architecture, however, represents an obstacle to scalability, both with respect to bitway bandwidth and processing power, unless the server is itself a parallel processor with scalability properties or can be mirrored indefinitely.

An example where scalability is a dominant consideration is communicating a single source simultaneously to multiple sinks, as illustrated in Figure 3.13. An example is multi-party video conferencing (where each user participant wishes to see all the other users) or remote learning (where each student wishes to see a common lecture).

Figure 3.13 -- One Source And Multiple Sinks

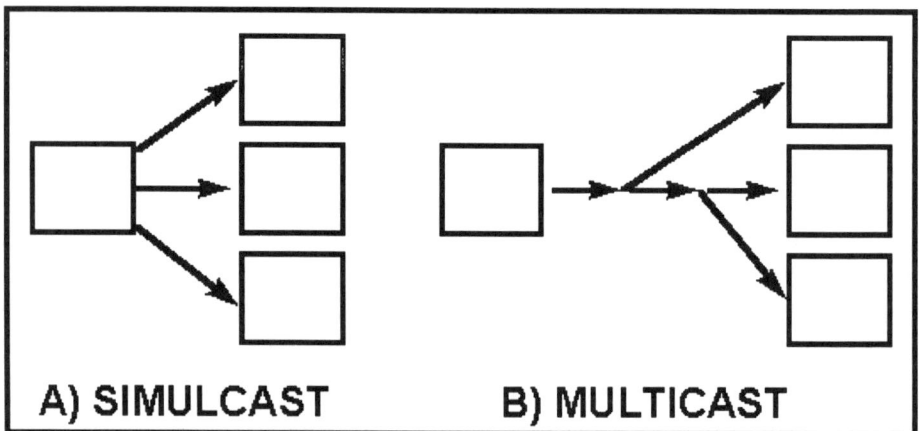

A) SIMULCAST   B) MULTICAST

An obvious approach requiring no special measures in the bitways is for the source to *simulcast* to each of the sinks over separate streams. Simulcast is fine for a small number of sinks, but is not scalable to large number of sinks because, as the number of sinks increases, either the source processing power or access bitway bitrate will eventually be exceeded.

A scalable approach is *multicast*, in which the source generates a single stream common to all sinks, and that stream is appropriately replicated within the bitway. Bitways supporting multicast are fundamentally different from unicast bitways, and a topic of intense research for both the Internet (the Multicast backbone "MBONE"), ATM bitways, and ATM-based internets. An alternative architecture is to add servers to the network which perform the splitting function (as for example the reflectors in CuSeeMe, but this approach is also not scalable.

Transportable computation will play a major role in scalability. For example, the dynamic deployment of application functionality to a client reduces the transport bandwidth during the session and shifts computational cycles from the server to the client. The result can be a considerable increase in the number of clients supported by the server.

Terminal And Network Coordination

All networked applications require some level of coordination among the terminals (peer, clients, and servers) participating in the application, and between those terminals and the network. This coordination can occur during the setup phase, using so-called *establishment protocols* (in computer communications) or *signaling* (in telecommunications). The distinction in terminology arises in part from the tendency to perform signaling functions over the same port and network as is used for data in computer communications (*in-band signaling*), and over a logically separate signaling network (*out-of-band signaling*) in telecommunications (as for example the modern *Signaling System No. 7*).

As telecommunications moves toward horizontally integrated packet networks, there is debate as to whether to employ the in-band or out-of-band model. Signaling is usually applied to the configuration of terminals and network, including the resource reservations that may be required for QoS guarantees and establishing the state in the bitway required to maintain connections. This coordination can also occur dynamically during the execution phase of the application, called a *session* (computer communications) or *call* (telecommunications), through some form of flow control or other control mechanism.

Consider the coordination needed between a terminal originating a bit stream (called the *source*), the network carrying that stream, and the destination of that stream (called the *sink*). Both computer communications and telecommunications have used a *network-reactive signaling* model, in which the source makes a configuration request through the signaling channel and the network reacts to this request to perform the appropriate internal configuration. The network may also decline if it cannot provision the necessary resources, called *admission control* (computer communications) or *blocking* (telecommunications).

Network-reactive signaling is not the only way to perform active establishment configuration; in fact, enhanced mechanisms may be needed in the future. Consider, for example, configuration of the bitrate needed for a given service. Bitways such as ATM will be capable of provisioning a wide range of bitrates, and yet may or may not have wireless access at one or both ends. A broadband bitway with or without wireless access may have quite distinct capabilities, and the source may therefore have to configure in response to the network. This requires either *source-reactive signaling*, or better yet a *two-way negotiation* between source and bitway.

Another important example is pricing. If bitways price their service based on resources consumed, finding the desired trade-off of resources vs. price will require a negotiation, auction, or other two-way interaction. It is also possible to coordinate a source and bitway dynamically during a session using flow control.

This coordination approach is common for best-effort bitways, and is especially natural for reliable delivery protocols (like TCP/IP) since unacknowledged packets are an excellent estimate of traffic excesses. However, as bitway bitrates increase, propagation delay will remain constant, making flow control progressively less effective (due to the delay in receiving feedback from congestion bottlenecks coupled with more rapid variations in congestion). A more subtle problem is lost packets due to high bit error rates on wireless access links, which do not necessarily reflect congestion. For the future, an interesting alternative for continuous media is to use a *scalable* source coding, which presents a set of N *layers* made visible to the bitway.

The convention is that if the sink has available only layers (1,k), it can construct an increasingly accurate and subjectively pleasing representation as k increases. If the granularity of the layers is small and there are a large number of layers, there is no need for flow control since the bitway can simply throw away the highest layers as necessary. Scalable audio coding was used successfully two decades ago for voice transmission, and scalable video coders have recently been proposed.

Coordination issues become much more serious for bitways supporting multicast connections (see Figure 3.13). It is neither scalable nor reasonable to expect a source to deal with a multiplicity of downstream bitway links and sinks, including some dynamically entering or leaving the session. Experimental multicast source coders for continuous media have thus of necessity been scalable. The most interesting approaches to configuration are sink (rather than source) driven. In a typical approach, the sink subscribes to layers (1,k), makes an estimate of the resulting reliability (say by counting lost packets), and chooses to either increase or decrease k based on that estimate.

Terminal to network coordination is an area of great divergence between the traditional approaches of the computing and telecommunications communities. It is also arguably an area of great challenge for the future, with many competing approaches, as well as new requirements such as multicast.

Scalable source coding and reliability measurements will be a profitable area for research.

Connection-Oriented Vs. Connectionless

Telecommunications has traditionally focused on *connection-oriented* transport, where information is constrained to traverse the same route from source to destination. This approach enables resource allocation along that route to actively control QoS. Computer networks sometimes use *connectionless* transport, where information is routed dynamically according to congestion and availability. This approach is a natural outgrowth of the "efficiency by statistical means" orientation, and has many advantages, such as robustness to failure, ability to dynamically route around points of congestion, and the absence of state in the bitway (a tremendous simplification to the software). On the other hand, it makes QoS guarantees difficult to realize.

This distinction is narrowing. The Internet, while considering various forms of QoS guarantees in the future, as well as new services like multicast, add functionality and state information to the bitway, defining what are in effect connections. ATM retains the notion of "virtual circuit", or the fixed route that packets traverse, while not constraining that virtual circuit to be fixed throughout a session. This architecture enables faster routing and reduces the addressing overhead per packet (since only local addressing is required), which is important because of the small packets. There is a desire to realize connectionless IP service on public wide-area ATM networks, which requires a layer of connectionless routers interconnected by ATM virtual circuits.

The notion of connection-oriented TCP transport riding on a connectionless IP network which in turn rides on the connection-oriented ATM network is humorous, although it does offer some robustness to congestion and equipment failure and reduced establishment overhead.

Issues of mobility raise another layer of complications for connection-oriented protocols, since connections must be destroyed and re-established dynamically during a session. The evolving approaches to connections (or lack thereof) can only be described as chaotic at present, although as driven by QoS considerations there is a definite trend toward connection-oriented protocols.

Control Architecture

Telecommunications has come full circle. The earliest electromechanical relay switches relied on a self-routing strategy for telephone calls, but with the advent of stored-program control a more centralized configuration strategy was followed based on an out-of-band signaling network, where the control and knowledge of service semantics resides primarily in the switches. As telephone switch software has suffered from inflexibility and runaway complexity, the problems of centralized control have become evident. More recently, ATM bitways have generally adopted a "command and control" approach, utilizing for example the legacy SS7 signaling network for control of ATM switches, even though ATM could be quite amenable to a distributed control approach similar to the Internet.

The computer communications community has followed a diametrically opposite approach in which the control within the network is consciously minimized. In the Internet, the network typically doesn't store any state of particular TCP connections, but rather distributes that state information into the stream of packets passing through the network.

Routing tables do reside in the network, but they are updated through a distributed adaptive algorithm. This philosophy has been successfully extended to multicast connections in the Mbone. A considerable burden is put on the terminal nodes to retain knowledge of connections, perform flow control, and insure reliability through ARQ protocols, consistent with rapidly declining cost of the required processing. Cognizance of application semantics is strictly reserved for the terminals.

This approach has proven quite effective at containing complexity, and also in maintaining flexibility for ready deployment of new applications since no upgrades to the network itself are needed. Running counter to this is the client-server architecture used to realize user-to-user applications, which can be considered a centralized control at the application layer (with the important distinction that the servers are administered separately from the bitway).

Regardless of the network control, application functionality will migrate to the terminals. This is consistent with the increasing cost effectiveness of terminal intelligence, and offers compelling advantages in flexibility and rapid innovation. This trend will accelerate as network deployment becomes widespread. This raises a number of issues relative to the transition that may occur, especially in the traditional telecommunications infrastructure. One approach is to encapsulate the existing centrally controlled telephone network for interface to computer applications, as in the Telephony Services API and Windows Telephony API. Another approach would be to migrate to ATM bitways, which accommodate more directly a distributed control model.

Interconnection vs. Interoperability

Since telecommunications has traditionally provisioned a small set of functionally simple "universal" applications, it has focused on interconnection as a basic issue. The goal has been to attract as many customers as possible, and fully interconnect them utilizing standardized protocols. Networked computing, on the other hand, focusing on a large number of functionally complex applications, has placed more emphasis on interoperability. How can the distributed pieces of a networked application interact properly in accordance with their shared functionality and communication protocols? Looking to the future, interoperability will be an increasing issue for the converging infrastructure. Approaches to interoperability that avoid cumbersome standardization at the application layer are immature, as there are competing approaches with different strengths and weaknesses.

The distributed operating system attempts to make a distributed collection of processors appear as one entity, whereas distributed object-based programming models explicitly highlights the distributed environment by structuring the distributed application as a set of autonomous interacting agents or objects. The virtual machine follows the object model, but with the twist of transportable computation. All these approaches fall within the category of middleware, although the boundary between operating system and middleware is fluid. It seems that the distributed operating system model is an option only for coordinated "intranets" (internets under control of a single organizational entity), while the strength of the virtual machine is its applicability to the general public network. However, a great deal of research is needed to establish the best approaches, presumably merging the best features of these disparate models and defining new ones.

Embedded vs. General-Purpose Computing

In a software implementation, there are alternative implementation styles that also have significant impact on issues like application deployment. The highest-performance software approach uses *embedded computing*, in which a processor is dedicated to a single function or application is embedded within a larger system, with a minimal operating system, highly optimized special-purpose instruction set, optimized code (perhaps even written in assembly language), etc. Such tuned software implementations have been used extensively for digital signal processing functions in telecommunications.

Where lower performance is acceptable, a software implementation on a general-purpose (often desktop) computer can serve a variety of functions simultaneously. This approach is very flexible, but current desktop operating systems typically do not support resource reservation for a given application to guarantee, for example, real-time performance. (There is no fundamental reason they can't, however.) On the other hand, as the processor speeds increase in relation to the application, a point is reached at which it no longer matters (desktop computers are completely adequate for audio applications today).

Perhaps the role of embedded computing would be reduced in the future with advances in technology. However, once again the role of communications in computing looms large. When a computer is networked at sufficient speed, the need for aggregating within it a variety of functions like memory, storage, etc. becomes less compelling, because some of those functions become available on the network at sufficient levels of performance. Thus, one can envision in the future embedded computers that serve the single function of running dynamically distributed applications with a minimum of local storage and peripherals. In a sense, this is a hybrid of the two models of computing, since the such a computer would be dedicated to running a single interpreter (and hence is embedded) very efficiently, and at the same time is able to serve a variety of applications (represented by the interpreted programs).

Once again, we see technology taking a full circle. At one time there were dedicated computer designs for word processing, computer-aided design, etc. Advances in technology obsoleted this approach, as users preferred a general-purpose machine. In the future, it is possible that dedicated interpreter engines for dynamically distributed network applications will reappear, partially obsoleting the general-purpose computer.

Heterogeneity In Networks

Historically, both computers and communications networks were relatively homogeneous entities. The modern digital telephone network, for example, at its heart provisions a single service, the 64 kb/s connection-oriented bit stream. Likewise, most terminals (telephones) perform a basic analog voiceband channel function. Before networking of computers, the application developer only had to worry about a single homogeneous platform. We are entering a challenging age of heterogeneity. Heterogeneity will occur at several levels:

- There will be *heterogeneity in customer-premise terminals*, with a number of terminal options (telephones, desktop and laptop computers, personal digital assistants, "Dick Tracy" wristwatches, etc.).

- There will be *heterogeneity in transport systems* (packet switching, circuit switching, fiber optics, wireless access, etc.). This is complicated by the many combinations of concatenated transport options that are available for any given connection.

- There will be *heterogeneity in services and applications*, as described earlier, integrated within a common bitway and terminal infrastructure.

Due to network externality, there is a strong economic push toward universal interoperability among terminals, at least for the most common services and applications, irrespective of the details like terminal type or capability, terminal manufacturer, bitway, etc. The user wants applications to operate seamlessly across this infrastructure, configuring themselves to the infrastructure. This problem is most serious for continuous-media services, where the issue is not simply functional interoperability, but also matching resources to achieve QoS guarantees and required processing performance levels.

Historically, the telecommunications industry has pursued an end-to-end application in a vertically integrated architecture, like telephony or video conferencing. Where heterogeneity has existed in telecommunications, the approach has been to partition the subsystems at the service level. For example, wireless cellular telephony is assembled by concatenating a wireless voiceband telephone channel with a wired voiceband channel; in other words, in the base station, a voiceband telephone channel is the assumed application.

Looking ahead to horizontal integration, where there will be many different services co-existing within the same facilities, this approach will not work. It will not be possible to embed within the bitways assumptions about the services being carried, without introducing a large element of complexity and inflexibility. The different path that is necessary for the future is to modularize bitways from the services and applications insofar as possible, with coordinated resource-allocation.

The services and applications will need to adapt to a variety of heterogeneous terminal and transport configurations, as well as resource allocations, and conversely the transport and terminals will need to attempt to accommodate the differing needs of a variety of services and applications. All constituent fields will need to concentrate less on point solutions to narrowly defined problems, and more on coordination to achieve objectives like interoperability and QoS on an end-to-end system-level basis.

Architecture And Complexity Management

Networks of the future will need to satisfy a variety of requirements, which are unfortunately interrelated and interdependent. Among them, we can cite:

- Point-to-point, multicast, and multisource connections.

- Privacy by end-to-end encryption.

- Predictability of and control over subjective quality.

- Negotiation of quality-of-service requirements on an end-to-end basis, and the allocation of impairments on a traffic-dependent fashion to concatenated transport links.

- Application scalability to transport quality-of-service parameters as well as terminal processing and display capabilities.

- Low delay for critical interactive applications.

- High traffic capacity, particularly on bottleneck facilities such as wireless access.

- Interoperability across heterogeneous terminal and transport environments, and integration of heterogeneous services and applications within shared-resource environments.

All of these important objectives interact, and are sometimes at cross purposes. Finding a reasonable compromise among these objectives will require carefully crafted architectural concepts. A key question is what horizontal interfaces should be established. Another question is how we avoid a proliferation of multiple interfaces that have not only different syntactical structure (a minor problem), but also present different semantic models of the underlying functionality. (For example, can we define parameterized QoS models that fit universally across radically different transport media like congestion-dominated backbone bitways and interference-dominated wireless access links?)

Once such architectural concepts are established, there are numerous detailed research issues that are stimulated in areas like compression, error-correction coding and modulation, and encryption. In particular, the nature of the overall network design problem forces much greater attention to architectural issues, and much greater influence of architectural issues on detailed research areas like signal processing and networking. This is a systematic way of coordinating the activities in these detail areas to meet the many interacting objectives mentioned above.

There is inadequate research that bridges the signal processing and networking worlds, and also inadequate research bridging the backbone and wireless access worlds. Today the important constraints introduced by the wireless access bottleneck are largely unrepresented in the design of backbone networks, even though they introduce important constraints.

One impact of the coming heterogeneity at the application, transport, and terminal levels is the critical importance of complexity management. Complexity management has traditionally been a dominant consideration in the design of software systems, but is now also a dominant consideration in the larger context of large-scale systems including hardware, software, and physical channels. A whole host of techniques, many of them developed in the context of software system engineering, become important, such as architecture, modularity, and abstraction.

More than anything, complexity management is a manner of thinking about system design. There is need for the infusion of this complexity management thinking throughout the domain of communications and computing, not just software design.

Economic And Business Models

In the environment of converged telecommunications and computing, the old-style design problem embodied in one organization presenting a complete end-to-end turnkey solution is gone. Rather, many vendors are participating, in effect, in the collective design of the infrastructure of the future. Such designs must take in account numerous external considerations, such as network externality, standards (or lack thereof), interoperability, adaptability and etiquette, etc. The lowered barriers to application development embodied in the migration from vertical to horizontal architectures have and will play an important role in industrial organization. Considerations such as these play a seminal role in the design of products, and should also have a larger presence in research and engineering education.

Applications

New developments like platform independence, network deployment, and dynamic deployment will create an environment in which the innovation in user-to-user applications will have similar characteristics to user-to-information-server applications; namely, an rapidly evolving and fragmented application space. As in client-server computing, this will be a fertile field for research.

Conclusions

An exciting future is at hand. The relentless march of technology has resulted in a de-emphasis of traditional performance metrics and much more focus on functionally complex and heterogeneous systems, as well as on applications.

While this will result in a much richer set of applications to the end user, it also burdens technologists with the strain of relentless change. The rapidly advancing performance of electronics and photonics enables less efficient but functionally more complex software implementations, and hence greater emphasis on functionally complex services realized in a heterogeneous transport and terminal infrastructure.

This implies that the traditional challenges of efficiency and performance are being partially displaced by considerations of architecture, complexity management, and greater focus on the end user and their applications and requirements.

The greatest shift can be expected in user-to-user applications, a traditional focus of telecommunications, where the ability to flexibly deploy new applications is limited only by the imagination of entrepreneurs and designers, as opposed to the constraints of interoperability and standardization.

Chapter Acknowledgments

This chapter based on a paper accepted by IEEE Proceedings, to appear August 1996. Version 5.0 May, 1996. Copyright (c) 1996, Regents of the University of California. Written by David G. Messerschmitt.

The author is indebted to the following colleagues who provided valuable comments on drafts of this paper: G. David Forney, Levent Gun, David Leeper, and John Major of Motorola, Stewart Personick of Bell Communications Research, Bob Rosin of ESPI, Edward Lazowska of the University of Washington, John Godfrey of the National Research Council Computer Science and Telecommunications Board, Carl Strathmeyer of Dialogic, Ken Krechmer of Communications Standards Review, and Wan-teh Chang, Hal Varian, Robert Wilensky, and William Li of the University of California at Berkeley.

David G. Messerschmitt is a Professor in the Department of Electrical Engineering and Computer Sciences at the University of California at Berkeley, and from 1993 to 1996 was Department Chair. Prior to 1977 he was at AT&T Bell Laboratories in Holmdel, N.J. Current research interests include issues overlapping signal processing (especially video and graphics coding) and transport in broadband networks with wireless access, network services and protocols for multimedia, wireless multimedia computing, and the economics of networks. He has served as a consultant to a number of companies, and is a co-founder and member of the Board of Directors of TCSI Corporation (NASDAC). He received a B.S. degree from the University of Colorado, and an M.S. and Ph.D. from the University of Michigan, is a Fellow of the IEEE, a Member of the National Academy of Engineering, and a Member of the Computer Sciences and Telecommunications Board of the National Research Council.

Chapter 4

Gateways and New Services

Beneath the pretty Web pages and slick brochures lurks a rock solid technology not fully exploited by computer telephony. It's the Internet and the World Wide Web. It gives CT developers some instant projects to work on. It gives resellers a shot in the arm for their sales kit. Sprinkling CT on top of the 'Net is good for business. The standards to make it work are here: T120, H.323 and RTP.

Computer telephony is adding intelligence to the Internet and the World Wide Web with a vengeance. As if adding intelligence to phone calls wasn't a big enough hurdle. What really excites is bolting Internet and Web-based transactions into switching environments. Virtual circuit switching and traditional circuit stuff. And hybrids. Computer Telephony and the Internet are creating some of the best couples in the industry. This chapter is dedicated to those unique and robust platforms we call gateways. They are manifestations of great theory. But they are real. And with access to the Web as cheap as it is, you can bet on a flurry of new and innovative services. And these gateways will be running them. The 'Net is Cheap. There's plenty of IPs selling inexpensive and unlimited access.

You can transmit images, text and voice for a flat monthly rate. It's great for traveling employees to stay in touch. They can forward faxes, pick-up their mail and do research from their hotel rooms. Users like the idea of being able to predict talcum expenses. Flat rates are predictable.

There's a number of reasons why companies are investing thousands, even millions into the Internet. It's the "information is power" thing. Bright companies look at the web as a Big Public Disk Drive with a GUI. Now document fulfillment is much easier. You can create HTML-based data sheets, brochure and press releases. Customers, investors and the press can access your materials at any time. You can take orders and share your knowledge easily with a corporate home page. This easy access idea made fax-on-demand and Audiotex popular. Users want more of the same. It's just another way to turn your data stores outward to your customers. The Internet add a whole new meaning to the phrase: "disk drive megs keep dropping in price."

Aum Tech, Inc.

Information Services Platform

Aum Tech, Inc. makes the Aum Tech Information Services Platform (AISP). It's a messaging, call control and IVR platform targeted at telephone companies and enhanced service providers. They also have a national retail chain niche. Their solutions run on Solaris 2.4, SCO, UnixWare and NT RAS. Any Intel-based system will run Aum Tech solutions. They support ISA-bus versions of both Dialogic and Linkon CT boards.

AISP Architecture

AISP is made up of software modules. These provide mixed media trans-action processing, messaging and telephony services. You can configure these platforms to work stand alone or networked. There are three types of modules: Access Services, Information Services and Management Services.

Access Services. These let users access information and services via telephone, fax, PC or workstation. This represents the "front-end" client side of the architecture. Telecom Services support Analog T-1 and E-1 network access with DTMF, Fax, Modem, Speech Recognition and TTS. Workstation Services let PCs access services through a TCP/IP network, direct connect, dial-up or with a WEB Browser. You get support for UNIX Motif and MS-Windows Workstation Clients.

Information Services. This part of AISP represents the "back-end" database access and information retrieval process. With it, you can access legacy systems, foreign database and asynchronous hosts. SNA Services support SNA with 3270 SDLC and SNA LU6.2. TCP/IP Services add Ethernet or RS232 and dial-up access. Database Services give your data a voice with access to relational databases using standard SQL queries.

Management Services. These are the utility and creation parts of the architecture. This includes Service Creation (SCE) and Utilities. The Aum Tech SCE is a high level development tool with a graphical User Interface. It uses a "drag and drop" model for building apps. With it, you can generate executable programs. You can create prompts and package distributable run-times with the SCE. Service Utilities include a resource manger, logging, scheduling and system monitor. The system monitor gives you a near-real time view at system activity on the access services side of transactions.

For a basic platform, retail chain stores can expect to pay $7,000 for a starter system. Software runs about $200/port based a minimum purchase of 5,000 ports. This includes the hardware processor platform, CT boards and basic IVR software.

Service Providers and Telcos can expect to pay $1,000 per port for software only. Add-on service modules CPU run-time based versus port-based. The SCE is $5,000. Add $7,200 for TCP/IP or SNA. $4,800 for a workstation server with 24 concurrent sessions.

Figure 4.1 – AumTech ISP Service Creation Environment

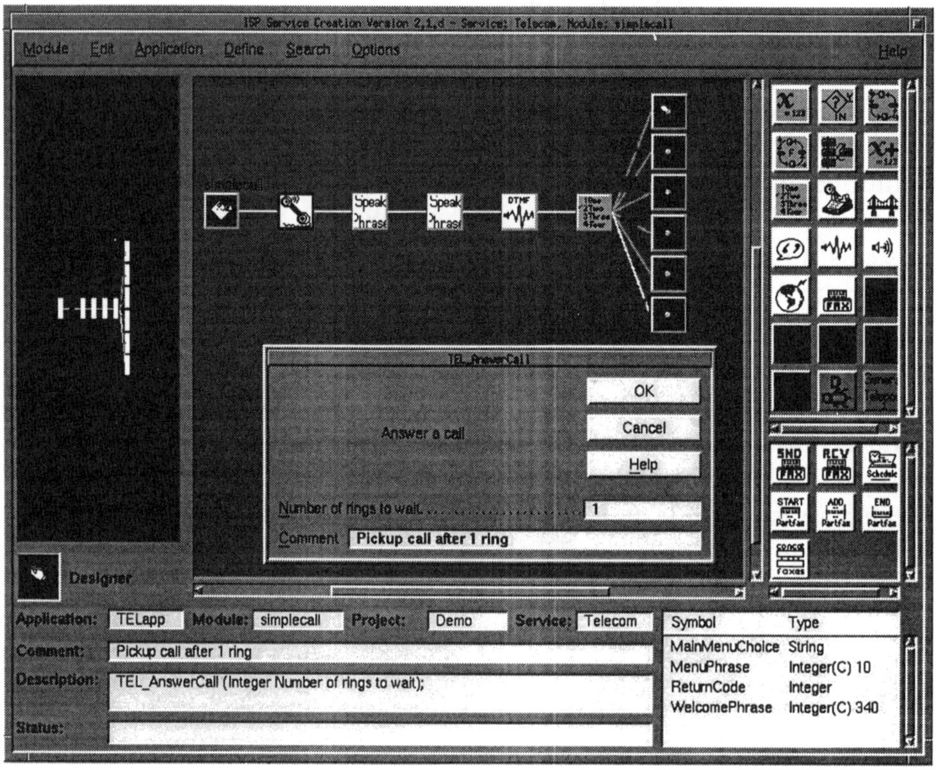

Figure 4.1 is a screen from Aum Tech's Service Creation Environment (SCE). It's a GUI application development tool. There are two levels: Developer and Designer. Developers can construct their own C code and create icons for others to use.

These include applets to access databases, record message strings and send a faxes. Designers don't need to know any C code. You simply link icons to create logic flow. Each icon sports a pop-up window when dragged onto the workspace. The pop-up lets you set parameters for each icon's actions.

Figure 4.2 – AISP Access Services Topology

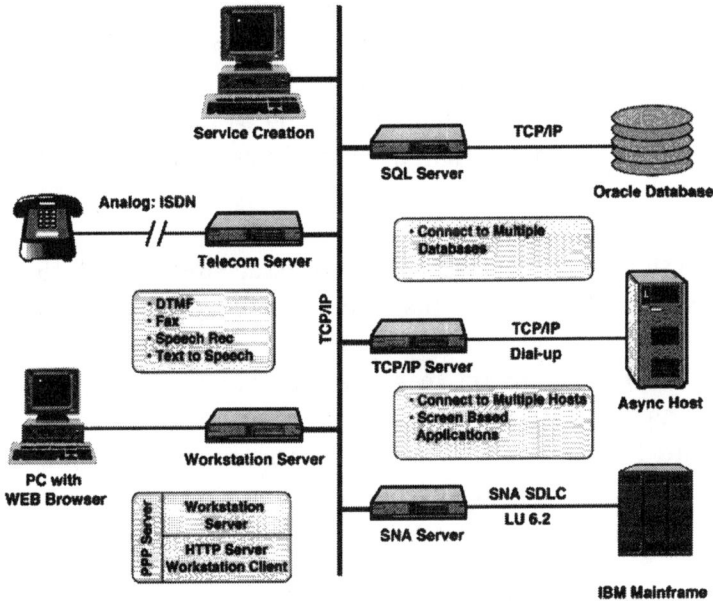

Figure 4.2 illustrates Aum Tech's AISP environment. Access Services clients can be PSTN, Private Network or Internet users. The system doesn't care if you are a telephone caller or a web-browsing PC user. All requests for information are serviced by an Information Services module. Data an reside on a mainframe, asynch host or SQL database. It's all the same to AISP. This modular approach makes it easy for Aum Tech to adapt their product for any telco or service provider.

Intelligent Visual Computing

OmniMail Message Retrieval System

Intelligent Visual Computing (IVC is on the forefront of a new breed of unified messaging. They have been working closely with Linkon Corporation (Fairfield, CT -- 203-319-3123) as a Linkon partner and systems integrator. Linkon manufactures a line of SBus compatible CT products (their flagship offering is the Maestro FS4000 CT card).

IVC designs systems for corporations and service providers including telephone companies, cable networks, and Internet Service Providers. IVC sells an Internet-based messaging service based on Linkon's LinkVox application development tools and Maestro DSP platform. IVC uses Sun's Java computer programming language and Internet browsers from Netscape and others.

The new system is called the OmniMail Message Retrieval System. Michael Clark, president of IVC calls his creation a "Java Linkon Applet." Clark says that by developing the Java applet, he can now quickly deploy and customize the best common message retrieval systems on the Internet. OmniMail lets Internet users browse all types of messages (voice, fax, email) with standard Internet tools. When messages are received on a web site or sent to an email address a message notification icon appears on the desktop and the user retrieves messages via the browser.

With standard audio tools, you can play voice messages or download them to your laptop PC or desktop. The conversion of the audio files are done on the web messaging server or at the desktop. The system eliminates having to access multiple message bins. It integrates all message types via the Internet. The system also supports conventional voice message retrieval via telephone. E-mail messages can be retrieved this way using text to speech. You can redirect faxes to any local fax machine. E-mail can be converted to fax format by the system and delivered the same way. IVC wrote a Java applet for the client side of these transactions. They did this so it's possible to run the software and access the messaging service from any computing platform. The idea here is to leverage the power of the network and network-based applications.

Figure 4.3 illustrates the OmniMail Integrated Messaging Server topology. It's based on Linkon's Maestro and IVC's Java-based OmniApplet. Here, e-mail, faxes and voice messages converge over the Internet and PSTN in the OmniMail server. The system puts a global twist on unified messaging. You can pick up and store messages on your laptop while traveling. Users simply launch the OmniMail applet during any Internet connection.

Figure 4.3 -- OmniMail Topology

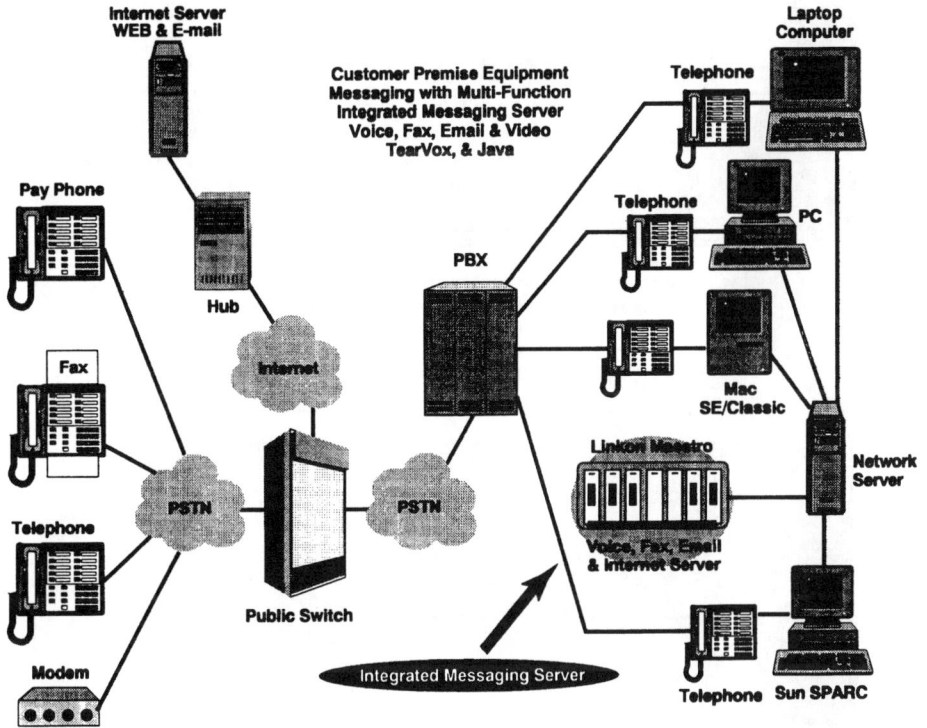

IVC's OmniMail Applet and user interface are illustrated in Figure 4.4. Here's what you see when you pick up messages over the Web with OmniMail. You get time stamps on watch message and an icon indicating the type of media. The Linkon-based Integrated Messaging Server acts as repository for voice messages. You can alternately access your e-mail and faxes with a regular phone. In this case, OmniMail uses text-to-speech to convert your e-mail into the spoken word.

Figure 4.4 -- OmniMail User Interface

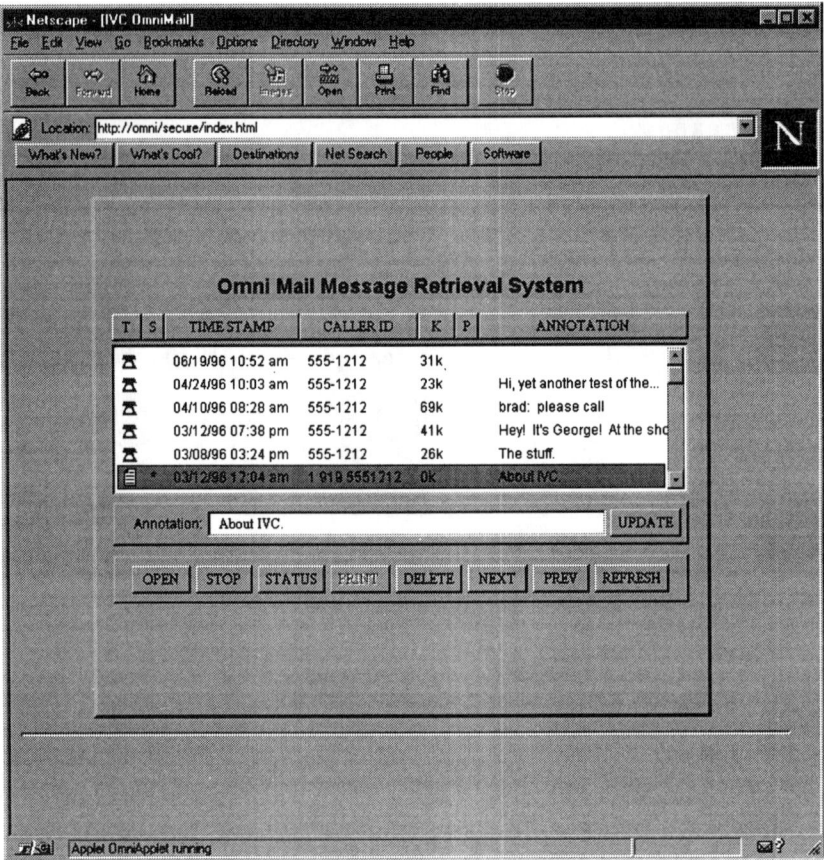

Latitude Communications

MeetingPlace Conference Server

Latitude Communications makes applications to "facilitate more productive business meetings among people working in different locations." This is a mouthful, but their product does a lot. The company developed the industry's first conference server, enabling increasingly dispersed employees to streamline conference calls and meeting process.

The company has received key patents on the MeetingPlace technology and are widely regarded as delivering the first real-world, collaborative work tools. The management team came from Aspect, Octel, VMX, and ROLM. With these firms, Latitude employees were directly responsible for the developing, marketing and selling telecommunication and voice processing solutions. Based upon this experience, the founders of the company conceptualized and built the industry's first conference server. Latitude customers include Credit Suisse, ADP Brokerage Services, Best Buy Corporation, 3Com and Microsoft. They use MeetingPlace to conduct their business meetings.

The company is doing well, having sold over 40 systems -- from $40K to $250K. One of their customers is Microsoft which has created what they call the "Expert Roundtable." These are conferences held as part of their "Premier" support offerings covering topics such as Windows NT, SQL Server, System Management Server. With MeetingPlace, they can create a "library" of meeting topics and post them to their web page.

The MeetingPlace Conference Server lets you set up your telephone voice conferences via the Internet / Intranet. You can hear meeting comments and / or complete recordings of meetings with streaming RealAudio or Microsoft ActiveMovie. You can also see meeting "attachments" -- PowerPoint slides, Word notes, Excel sheets, etc.

The MeetingTime desktop software lets participants connect to the MeetingPlace conference server over a company's internal Local Area Network. The MeetingTime graphical user interface and allows users to schedule, attend and review meetings. Figure 4.5 shows how the folks at Latitude have a sense of humor: If you punch in the wrong password, you get this cool and very retro 1950s screen. Which is curious, since no one at Latitude was alive in the 1950s. When scheduling via MeetingTime, users can schedule recurring meetings, select participant notification options or attach meeting materials (voice and data). When attending via MeetingTime, participants may see meeting participants and current speaker, invoke meeting features (e.g. recording or break out sessions) or review meeting attachments.

Figure 4.5 -- MeetingPlace Network Connection Error Screen

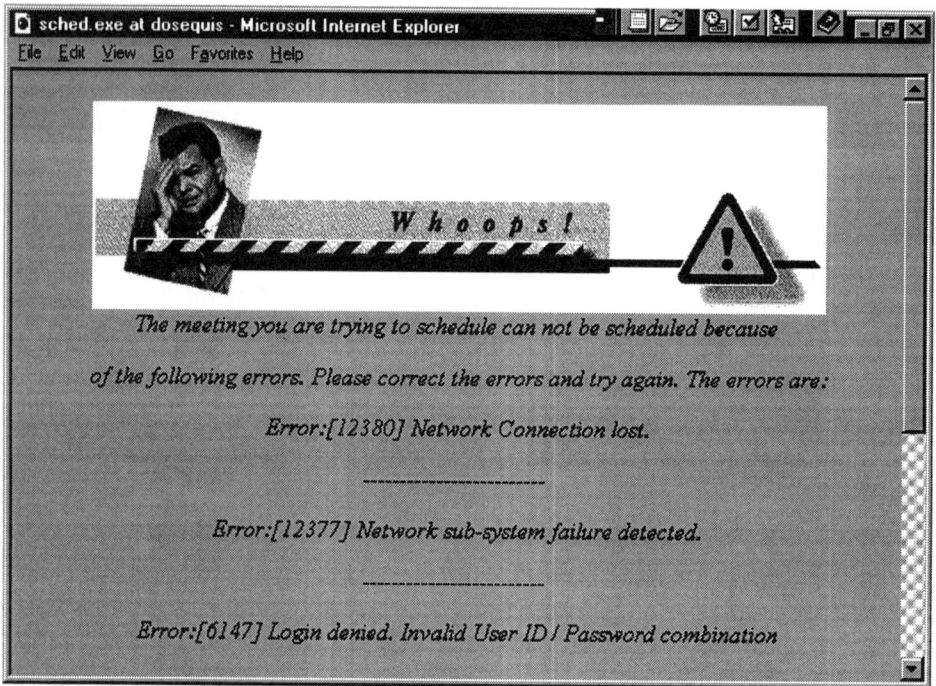

MeetingPlace Conference Server

The MeetingPlace conference server addresses all aspects of the *meeting process*, not just time participants are actually in the meeting. The server creates virtual meeting rooms that are more like face to face meetings. It establishes and coordinates multiple voice connections for a conference call. The platform can support up to 120 ports in any combination of simultaneous conference calls.

Users can schedule meetings, access in-conference features, review previous meetings and attach and retrieve documents from their desktops. The system enables users to "see" who is in the call and provides for breakout sessions (private side conferences).

This ensures a secure meeting environment, facilitates document distribution and allows participants to record all or part of the meeting. These tightly integrated, face to face like features make meetings more productive.

Users can schedule conferences from any location. MeetingPlace will notify all meeting participants of their conference call via e-mail or fax. At the start of the meeting, the system will page or dial out to users to bring them into the meeting. Documents may be distributed with the meeting notification, pulled down from the server in advance of the meeting or retrieved during the meeting. Finally, MeetingPlace makes the meeting available to non participants by storing all meeting materials (documents and recordings) for those who were not able to attend. Latitude points out that a meeting is much more than just the time participants spend in the actual meeting. Meeting organizers and participants are impacted by a meeting before, during and after the actual meeting. Because of this, the company designed MeetingPlace to address five distinct stages of every meeting:

Schedule. Ensure meeting resources are available

Notify. Inform meeting participants

Distribute. Disseminate meeting materials/documents

Attend. Round up participants to start meeting

Follow-up. Provide meeting recording/documents to non participants

MeetingPlace Server Hardware

The MeetingPlace conference server hardware uses standard components such as SCSI disk drives, EISA and MVIP buses, and a Pentium system processor. The system has a distributed processing architecture, multiple buses, DSP/RISC processing and a telephony grade power supply. The MeetingPlace conference server uses T-1 lines, analog POTS lines and Ethernet LANs.

MeetingPlace Server Software

The MeetingPlace Server software is high performance code written in C++. The software is composed of several key modules:

Digital Signal Processing. The system has automatic gain control (AGC) to amplify low level speakers. The DSP algorithms detect and remove touch tones from the conference call as participants invoke MeetingPlace features. These algorithms also remove any call progress tones (e.g. busy and dial-tone) from the call. Finally, the DSP algorithms also identify and remove constant noise sources (e.g. fans) from being injected into the meeting. The instant speaker algorithm recognizes the current speakers and suppresses noise from all other locations.

Notification Agent. Monitors meeting activity and automatically notifies participants of meetings via fax, e-mail, outdial or pager. Participants may be notified in advance of the meeting by fax or e-mail. At the time of the meeting, participants may be notified via pager or outdial. The system will also notify attendees when changes are made to previously scheduled meetings. Figure 4.6 shows how MeetingPlace informs you of requested meetings. You get the time, date and scheduler's name. You can easily send mail to the coordinator of the meeting to confirm you participation.

Conference Scheduler. Manages all of the resources for the system (conference ports, meeting IDs, recording space) such that all meetings can be held without conflict and that ports can be dynamically allocated to meetings. The scheduler is configured by the system manager and determines: how early participants may call into meetings, when participants are warned about meeting end time, how users can extend their call, and when reserved ports are released when no one shows up. Figure 4.7 shows how you set up a voice conference over the Internet / Intranet. The form replicates what you have been seeing up to date when you've set meetings up via your internal LAN using either their MeetingTime software or their e-mail interface.

Figure 4.6 -- MeetingPlace Notification Agent

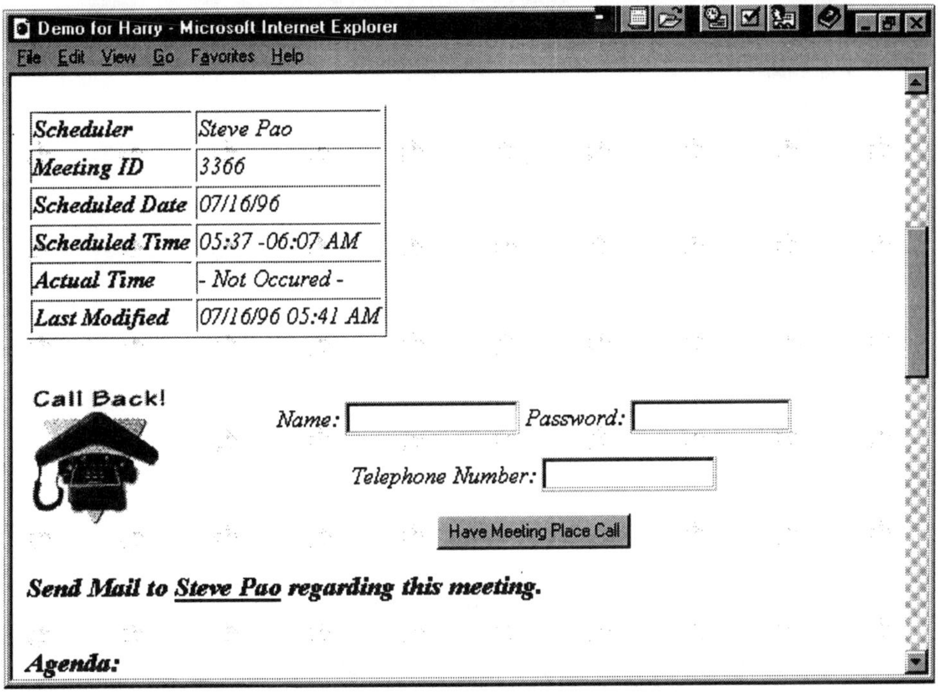
Demo for Harry - Microsoft Internet Explorer
File Edit View Go Favorites Help
Scheduler
Steve Pao
Meeting ID
3366
Scheduled Date
07/16/96
Scheduled Time
05:37 -06:07 AM
Actual Time
- Not Occured -
Last Modified
07/16/96 05:41 AM
Call Back!
Name:
Password:
Telephone Number:
Have Meeting Place Call
Send Mail to Steve Pao regarding this meeting.
Agenda:

MeetingNotes. Allows for the recording and storage of all relevant meeting materials. You can search and review previously held meetings by playing back recordings or viewing attached documents. Figure 4.8 shows you how the MeetingNotes portion of MeetingPlace works. You can browse through a list of today's meeting notes. Click on the meeting's name and see the next screen. There are a number of items you can inspect.

Voice comments lets you record meeting proceedings, record meeting agendas and attach voice comments when participants cannot attend a meeting (390 hours of voice storage). *Electronic Documents* software allows end users to attach files to a meeting for subsequent distribution. These files may include presentation slides, spreadsheets or word processing documents that will be reviewed during the meeting.

Figure 4.7 -- MeetingPlace Conference Scheduler

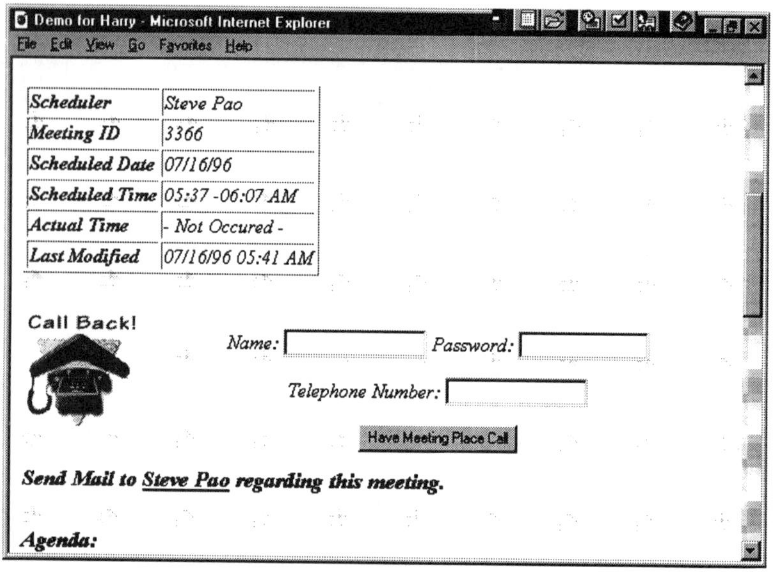

Scheduler	Steve Pao
Meeting ID	3366
Scheduled Date	07/16/96
Scheduled Time	05:37 -06:07 AM
Actual Time	- Not Occured -
Last Modified	07/16/96 05:41 AM

Call Back!

Name: [ ]   Password: [ ]

Telephone Number: [ ]

[Have Meeting Place Call]

Send Mail to Steve Pao regarding this meeting.

Agenda:

Figure 4.8 -- MeetingPlace MeetingNotes

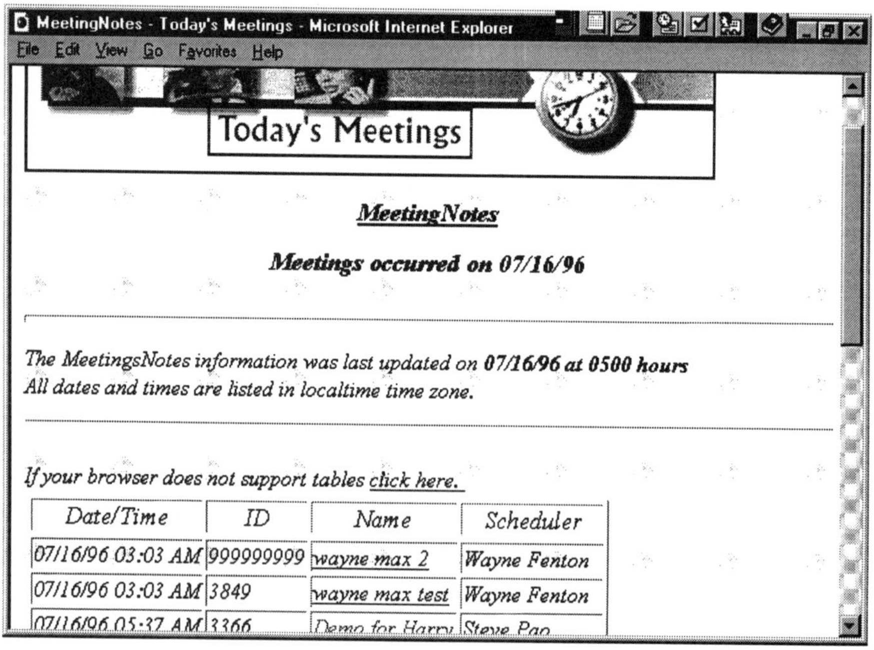

Today's Meetings

MeetingNotes

Meetings occurred on 07/16/96

*The MeetingsNotes information was last updated on 07/16/96 at 0500 hours
All dates and times are listed in localtime time zone.*

If your browser does not support tables click here.

Date/Time	ID	Name	Scheduler
07/16/96 03:03 AM	999999999	wayne max 2	Wayne Fenton
07/16/96 03:03 AM	3849	wayne max test	Wayne Fenton
07/16/96 05:37 AM	3366	Demo for Harry	Steve Pao

Figure 4.9 shows how you can see the meeting's voice files and use Progressive Networks' RealAudio player to browse messages. The files may range from simple comments to a recording of the entire meeting. Click on what you want to hear and bingo, a RealAudio player appears. You start to hear words within a few seconds of clicking -- even over a miserable dial-up voice line at 28.8 Kbps. You can also see the meeting attachments -- which can be everything from DOC to PPT files. You can see them before, during or after the meeting -- in short, the moment they were posted.

Figure 4.9 -- RealAudio Player Applet

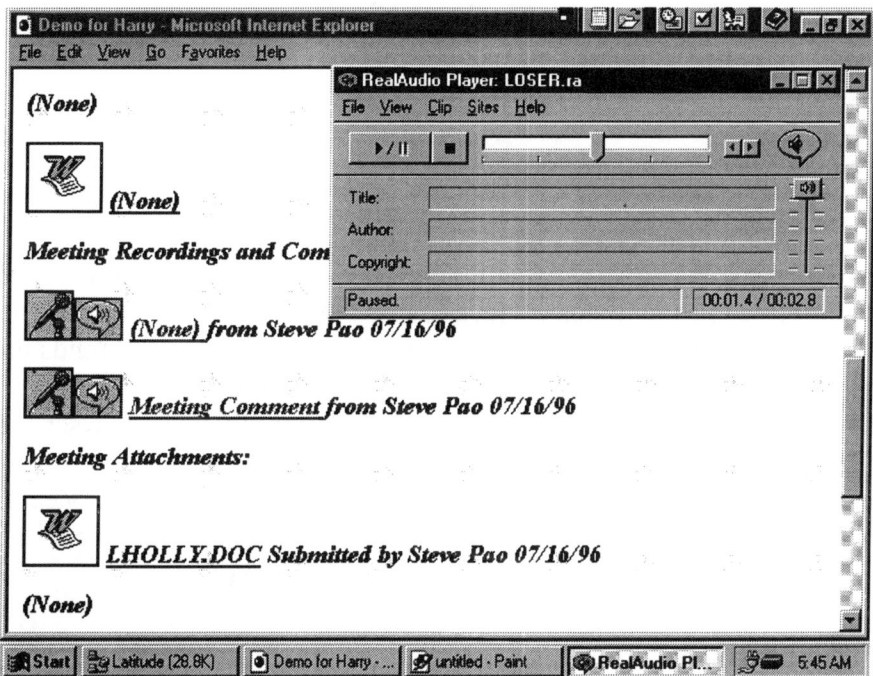

System Services. An integrated SQL Database on a high performance operating system provide all system services. The internal voice file system is optimized for real-time use and fast response time. The built-in license management controls simultaneous MeetingTime client software connections. An SNMP agent provides remote monitoring services compatible with the MIB II specifications.

MeetingPlace Fax Gateway

Since MeetingPlace is a conference server, it attaches both to your internal voice and data network. The MeetingPlace Fax Gateway integrates with fax server technology already deployed on your Local Area Network. This architecture does not require the purchase of multiple fax server platforms. Participants may use the Fax Gateway to proactively send out meeting notifications or meeting attachments to participants. This tells participants to be aware that they have been invited to a meeting and allows them to receive the meeting materials before the meeting begins. If participants are unable to review the materials before the meeting, they may elect to retrieve documents via fax during or after the meeting. Since these meeting participants may be mobile, they can specify the fax number nearest them at the time they elect to receive these documents.

MeetingPlace E-mail Gateway

Since MeetingPlace is a conference server, it attaches both to your internal voice and data network. The MeetingPlace E-mail Gateway software enables MeetingPlace to communicate with existing VIM or SMTP compliant e-mail systems. Participants can schedule meetings, distribute documents and notify participants of upcoming meetings. Users fill out a simple e-mail scheduling form and send this to the conference server. MeetingPlace will then schedule the meeting, notify all participants via e-mail and distribute any attached documents. Alternatively, if users schedule their meetings via the Meeting-Time desktop software, they can specify that invited participants be notified via e-mail or that meeting materials be distributed via e-mail.

MeetingPlace touch tone interface

The MeetingPlace touch tone interface provides an easy to use environment where users can schedule, attend and review any meeting. Voice prompts guide users through MeetingPlace's feature set with little or no training. Latitude's voice processing interface allows users to customize their meeting environments for secure meetings, to determine how participants are announced into and out of meetings and to select vanity meeting IDs.

MeetingPlace Numeric Paging

MeetingPlace integrates numeric paging to notify participants at the start of a meeting. Given today's hectic business environment, it is often not enough to notify participants of a conference call in advance. The pager notification allows the meeting scheduler to "round up" meeting participants at the start of a meeting. This page serves as a last minute reminder that the meeting is starting and results in higher attendance and rapid start times. The paging integration can also be used to support crisis management teams. When an emergency arises, a MeetingPlace conference can be setup and all members of the crisis management team can be paged.

Media Mail

Internet Message Center (IMC)

Media Mail partnered with Telinet to provide unified messaging over the Internet and through corporate Intranets. Media Mail's products are Ebox, Internet Message Center (IMC) and MediaCache Server. Telinet's product is the TelCore server.

Ebox is a service available to businesses and individuals. An Ebox lets you send and receive voice mail, fax messages and email. Access to the Ebox is provided through Internet Message Center on the Web and a TelCore Server on the phone side. For telephone access to the Ebox service an individual 888 tollfree number is assigned to you. People can call you at this number and leave voice messages for you. You pick up your messages by dialing your number and punching in a PIN #.

As part of their IMC account , subscribers receive an email address and their own 800 number for receiving messages. With these, they can retrieve voice, email, and fax messages without incur- ring international telephone charges.

They can retrieve messages either through their Internet browsers (Netscape, Spyglass Mosaic, or Microsoft Internet Explorer right now), or over the phone, via their 800 number. Retrieving them via phone does, however, incur long-distance telephone charges, as they travel through the regular phone network.

Figure 4.10 -- Media Mail IMC Inbox

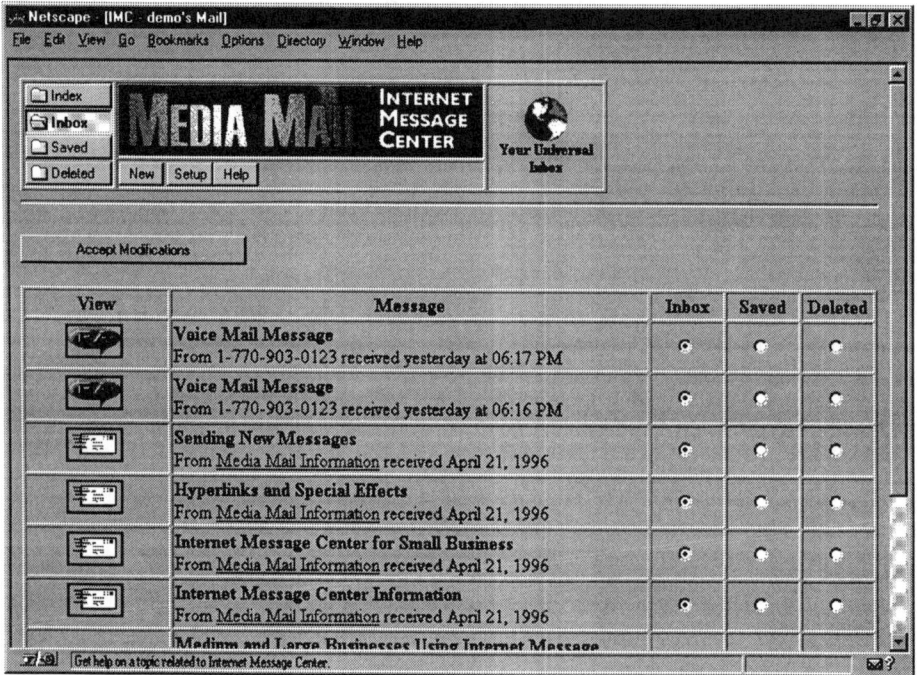

Figure 4.10 shows how you check your messages at the Media Mail Internet Message Center through your Ebox page . This is done using Netscape or some other Web browser. Messages of all types appear in your inbox.

Voice mail messages are played over PC speakers, if retrieved through the web site. Email messages, to date, are not read aloud. The system uses light-duty text-to-speech and simply reports the sender, the time, and the relative urgency of the e-mail message.

The fax option lets subscribers calling for messages via phone to enter fax numbers and receive stored faxes or text-to-fax copies of email. Those retrieving faxes via the web site will have a fax viewer imbedded in the IMC software. Pager notification is up and running, alerting users when a specified number of messages accumulate in their mailboxes. Telinet handles the individual account side of the business on its own server; currently a 48-line system using two Dialogic D/240SC-T1 boards for voice and network interface and a GammaLink 6-port fax board with Scbus connectivity. Using DNIS (Dialed Number Identification Service) via in-band T-1 signaling, Telinet can accommodate 500 different 800 numbers on only 48 trunks. ANI (Automatic Number Identification) is used as well, to give subscribers the number the calling party used to leave messages.

The system runs on Windows NT and was built with Visual Voice 3.0 from Stylus Innovation. The voice engine, first built with Visual Voice 2.0, was ported to Visual Voice 3.0, for both Windows 95 and NT. For audio technology, the system uses Real Audio, by Progressive Networks. This is depicted in figure 4.11.

Figure 4.11 -- Media Mail IMC and RealAudio

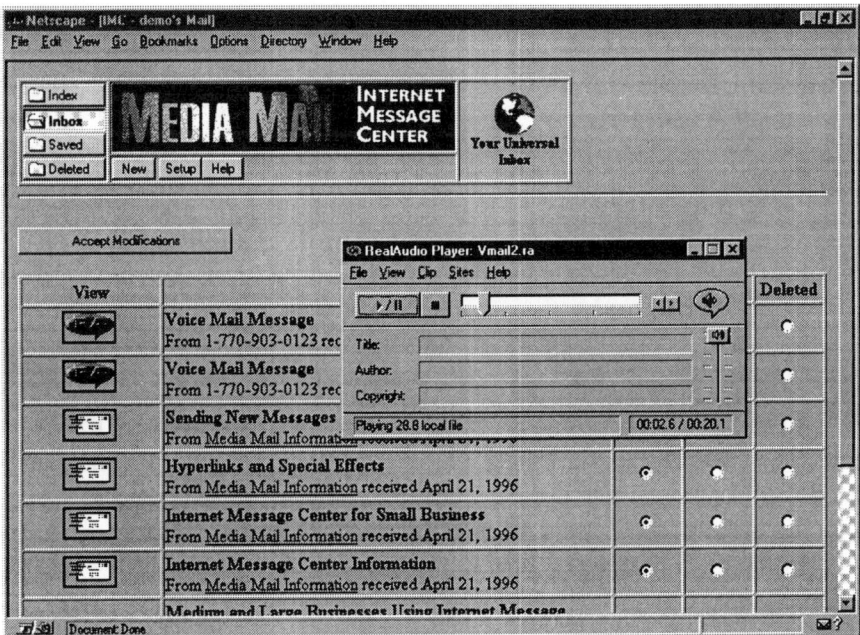

You can listen to your voice mail with the Real Audio Player from Progressive Networks. You can respond to a hyperlink with a Media Mail message. Subscribers are offered downloads of the algorithm (as well as Netscape 2.0) at the web site. RealAudio has superior compression technology that gets voice files down to 2K per second,.

Internet Message Center is server software that provides a Web interface to standard mail systems. It's available for all major Web servers on UNIX and Windows NT platforms. It's compliant with SMTP, POP3, MIME and several other standards. IMC is marketed to organizations needing a Web frontend to their email system.

MediaCache Server is server software required to provide the unified messaging solution. MediaCache integrates and extends the TelCore and IMC servere to provide compatibility with message backends from Microsoft and Lotus. Service Providers (ISPs) and Intranet integrators use MediaCache Server along with TelCore and IMC to provide unified messaging or Ebox service to end users. Ebox accounts start at $76.95 per year. Customized solutions are also available.

NetSpeak Corporation

Business WebPhone System

NetSpeak Corporation makes WebPhone, a commercially available Internet Telephony product. For $49.95, you can turn your PC into a telephone. The WebPhone client looks like a cellular phone on your PC's screen. You call other WebPhone users by their e-mail address or phone number.

NetSpeak has patents pending on their method of establishing virtual circuit connections (point to point) over an IP network. The distinction in their client phone interface and competing (commercial/client) products is their use of this conventional point-to-point paradigm. Other products use the "meet me here" approach, so users have to log-on to a real-time server and call only those folks who are likewise connected.

Although WebPhone is bundled with some Creative Labs (SOHO phone and multimedia) products, NetSpeak designed it and other products for call centers. This quarter marks the launch of their suite of WebPhone-based business products. This stuff is serious.

What's exciting is how the seemingly innocuous WebPhone client package is the basis for an aggressive and comprehensive enterprise-wide telephone system. NetSpeak calls this system the Business WebPhone System (BWS). It uses their virtual circuit switching scheme and a group of specialized servers and WebPhone clients. Together, these elements provide Internet and Intranet based business communication. The entire BWS is made up of these components:

- WebPhone Client

- WebPhone PBX (WPBX)

- WebPhone ACD (WACD)

- WebPhone PSTN Gateway (WGX)

- WebPhone Credit Processing Server (WCPS)

- WebPhone Pager Server (WPS)

- WebPhone Forum Server (WFS)

Each server module can run concurrently on the same machine or in separate machines for better performance and redundancy. By default, these components are CPE. NetSpeak built them so they can run as Intelligent Peripherals in an AIN / SS7 network or as embedded apps for IP / Internet service provisioning. The modules can be used for wireless and cable based services, too. The company's master plan is to make them useable in any high-end service environment.

WPBX, WACD, CPS and WPS are software only. They run on Solaris or Windows NT operating systems (requires Oracle 7.x on Solaris or Microsoft SQL Server 6.x on Windows NT). Any organizations with TCP/IP-based LANs or WANs can make it work. WGX and WFS are software and hardware. They require adapter cards in the server to work.

WebPhone Client

The WebPhone client is what agents and callers see on their screen when using the BWS. If real-time calls are initiated or answered with regular phones, the client is not seen by the user (but it's acting as a proxy for the control of the media stream in the server). Even casual point-to-point callers are actually using NetSpeak's BWS. The idea here is to take the architecture that enables the regular Internet Telephony calls and apply it to commercial/enterprise applications.

The screen-based interface looks like a cellular phone. It runs on PCs under Win 3.x and Win 95. NetSpeak is working on a POSIX compliant X-Windows version to run on Sun platforms. The software behind the WebPhone client is based on a custom operating system. It was written by veteran Unix kernel gurus at NetSpeak. The software uses its own data stream mixer. It can handle dynamic bandwidth allocation. This means real-time media streams (voice and video) can be handled as a priority while non real time streams (e-mail and short message text) work in the background.

The code is tight and highly portable. In the future, it may be possible to run WebPhone clients as firmware in embedded systems. This may be the means to enable a new breed of (hardware) phones to gain user-transparent access to Internet Telephony services.

From a user standpoint, the WebPhone client lets you make calls, leave voice messages and pick up voice messages from other users. They've built-in a lot of additional features not seen by casual users. This same interface, hooked to the appropriate server transforms the client into a Business WebPhone (BWP) or an Agent WebPhone (AWP).

BWPs get selectable directory assistance. This organization-wide directory assistance to obtain WebPhone numbers from fellow workers. BWP users can isolate their own profile so their phone number is "private or non-published." This translates to a form of internal PBX extension. As with regular WebPhone clients, BWS users may be located anywhere an Internet connection exists. You can also get a form of "Follow Me" calling. This all comes with secure transmission of all voice and data via RSA public key encryption.

AWPs are a form of WebPhone client for use with the ACD product. They have all the capabilities of the BWP with some notable additions. These agents communicate with the WACD to provide real-time call statistics. AWP users can also help regular WebPhone users to navigate URLs. Great potential for Help Desk apps here.

WebPhone PBX

NetSpeak's has their own "Master" WebPhone PBX. The primary unit is called the NetSpeak Global Server. It holds the SQL database and servers. The PBX engine is made up of two software-only servers: The Connection Server (CS) and the Information Server (IS). At NetSpeak's corporate office, the CS and IS parts run on separate SUN systems (20s with 4 CPUs now being upgraded to Sun Servers). Another (secondary) NetSpeak Server is running on a DEC Alpha 4100 with four 300 MHz RISC CPUs.

The CS and IS work together to ratify all IP addresses by name and phone number during real-time calls. When you log-on to the Internet with your WebPhone client activated, you are automatically registered as "active" in the CS. This means you can be anywhere in the world and the PBX will know where you are and how to reach you.

Multiple WPBXs scattered across the Internet can form a "virtual private network." For multi-site corporations and traveling workers, this is the foundation for a radical re-think in the way calls are handled and shared.

WebPhone Automatic Call Distributor (WACD)

The WebPhone PBX is a prerequisite. Supervisors on a Control Center (Administrative Server) can define Business WebPhone clients as Agent WebPhones. This is done by moving an icon on the screen from one side to another. You can drag the icon into a department or more than one "agent department." You can even define splits. The agent administration is patterned after the controls of a conventional ACD. The difference is you can do all of this in real time and with drag and drop. The Control Center gives you conventional ACD reporting. You can also do ad hoc reporting with the SQL database.

Call Centers can route inbound calls from WebPhone users to the first available agent in a specified department (i.e. Sales, Technical Support, Customer Service, Reservations). In the event all agents in the department are unavailable, the WACD queues the inbound calls until agents are free. The system periodically plays custom outgoing messages and sends URLs to the queued callers. The queued callers can leave voice mail which in turn is automatically routed to agents in a load distributing manner.

This automation applies to queued outbound calls as well. This based on answer detection criteria. Answered calls can be sent to available agents in specified departments. This is useful for outbound telemarketing, notification and collection applications. Each agent phone can be located anywhere on the Internet. In addition, each phone feeds back stats to the ACD such as DND, time stamping and status on each taken call and other call statistics.

All calls into the ACD are based on a "Caller ID" paradigm. This uses the profile in the caller's WebPhone. Outgoing messages are defined in the Control Center. These messages can be language-specific. The system recognizes the spoken language of the caller found in his WebPhone profile. This means ACD queue messages are played in the language of the caller. Outgoing messages also indicate the number of people in queue ahead of you. In addition, the keypad on the WebPhone also allows "virtual DTMFs" to be sent into the ACD.

This is used for intelligent (interactive routing). This means you don't need voice cards to do auto attendant or IVR functions with this system. Callers who choose to leave a message rather than wait can leave voice mail. The ACD routes the voice mail evenly amongst the agents.

For ACD agent supervision, AWPs can be "tapped." This is useful for agent monitoring and quality assurance. In addition, AWP users can use their WebPhone to record conversations. These messages can be archived, annotated and forwarded to others. This is useful for help desk chain messaging and legal/insurance message archiving.

NetSpeak says the PBX and ACD modules can be used as CPE or can be housed by an ISP and shared by many companies. This shared tenant/service bureau capability is common across all BWS modules.

WebPhone PSTN Gateway (WGX)

The gateway consists of software and a specialized DSP-based voice card. It uses G.723 codecs and has a network interface. Each PSTN interface can handle four or eight ports of analog telephony (two-wire E&M or POTS). On the digital side, you have an option of T-1/PRI or E-1. These come in single, dual or quad densities. The analog version is actually a daughter cards on the base DSP engine.

These come in PCI or ISA versions but you need PCI for the quad digital spans. If you use a DEC Alpha Server 4100, you can get over 500 ports running under NT. Multiple Pentium boxes running Solaris will do the same thing. The WGX can sit behind a PBX or as a tandem on E&M tie trunks. You can do the same thing with T-1. Or you can plug the gateway directly into the PSTN. The gateway is based on the principle that each PSTN-initiated telephone session is handled by its own dedicated virtual WebPhone client (in the Gateway). Each virtual WebPhone is its own traffic and routing cop. Each virtual call first goes to the NetSpeak Global Server to try to resolve where the called party is. There are a number of these on the Internet and their database changes are replicated.

The Global Server returns the IP address of the virtual WebPhone in the closest Gateway to the called party. By using the WGX and PBX/ACD together, you can spawn virtual-to-physical circuit connections from Web-based transactions. This means you can use your existing (conventional circuit-switched) inbound and outbound call centers and link the web cruising buyers right from your home page. Callers can get directory assistance on their own WebPhone. X.500 based directories can be tapped into by the IS on the WPBX as well.

Communication between the Gateway (and all the modules) is based on NetSpeak's WebPhone API (WAPI). A WAPI-driven virtual WebPhone is behind every circuit switch-initiated call. This means DTMFs punched-in by (regular) phone callers can access all the WebPhone features. This because there are DTMF gathering resources in the Gateway's DSPs. These tones are mapped to the ACD using WAPI calls. Or they are mapped to another WebPhone. This allows callers to set-up sophisticated transactions like multi-party conferences and pages right from their DTMF pad.

WebPhone Credit Processing Server (WCPS)

The WCPS enables real-time credit card order processing through VISANet via WAPI-based Order Management software. It uses VISANet POS-port hardware. This software an run on the same box as the PBX and ACD modules. The system uses 950 number access to VISANet using a proprietary protocol. In effect, WCPS turns WebPhone users into a POS credit card terminal.

Generic WCPS client software provides Order Management, Product Management, Agent Management, Customer Management and an ODBC-based Database Server. It supports Perl script for credit card information acquisition and processing on home pages. You also get the WAPI 32 bit DLL and the source code to the generic applications. The apps are written in C++ using the Win32 API. It's really an SDK for NetSpeak's WAPI. This means you can define your products, services, and PIM data. It's all secure because of WAPI' built-in encryption.

WebPhone Pager Server (WPS)

The text board in WebPhone can be used to send and receive alphanumeric pages with paging terminals. You can tell the WebPhone to forward your calls to "party-specific" pagers (Party-Specific call forwarding). The Pager server will inform the calling WebPhone that the called party is set to intercept a page. It pops up the text board on the caller's WebPhone. It will say: "You've reached a pager. Enter your paging text here." This session is managed by the Pager Server (another modified WebPhone), so it will take the two-way response and put it back on the callers text board.

WebPhone Forum Server (WFS)

The WebPhone Forum Server uses a software module and special hardware. The card is a DSP-based multicast unit with codecs. It does mixing, subtraction, summing of timeslots and media streams and compression right on the card. It, too harbors a WebPhone.

With the WFS, users can schedule and participate in full duplex conference calls by subject. Forums can supporting hundreds of simultaneous participants. This is bandwidth limited, so only half-duplex is available for large conferences. Participants may be located anywhere an Internet connection exists. Users can use their WebPhone client or conventional telephones if a WebPhone PSTN Gateway exists.

By using the WFS Perl Script on a home page, you can let Web browser users participate in your company's Forums. In a user's WebPhone directory, a new "Forums" button is being developed. It will bring up a dialogue displaying what forums have been scheduled. You can even schedule your own forum. The possibilities for charging users to participate in a conference is huge. Any WAPI process can send a message or credit card or debit form to a prospective forum participant. The WebPhone credit card processor can be used to automatically bill participants. Or you can use the transaction log in the database to do your own billing.

NetSpeak hopes to make WAPI the generic hook to Internet-based telephone transitions around the globe. It has hooks already to RTP, RTCP and RSVP Internet multimedia transmission standards. The company is working with MIT, IBM, VocalTec and Creative Labs to establish a common communication link between all the different Internet Telephony products.

The company has et to put a price on the BWS modules. NetSpeak says using their products versus conventional switches will cut per seat costs by an order of magnitude on large systems. They are quick to point out how SOHO products will be adapted from this technology.

Figure 4.12 – NetSpeak WebPhone PBX

WebPhone PBX and WebPhone ACD Configuration

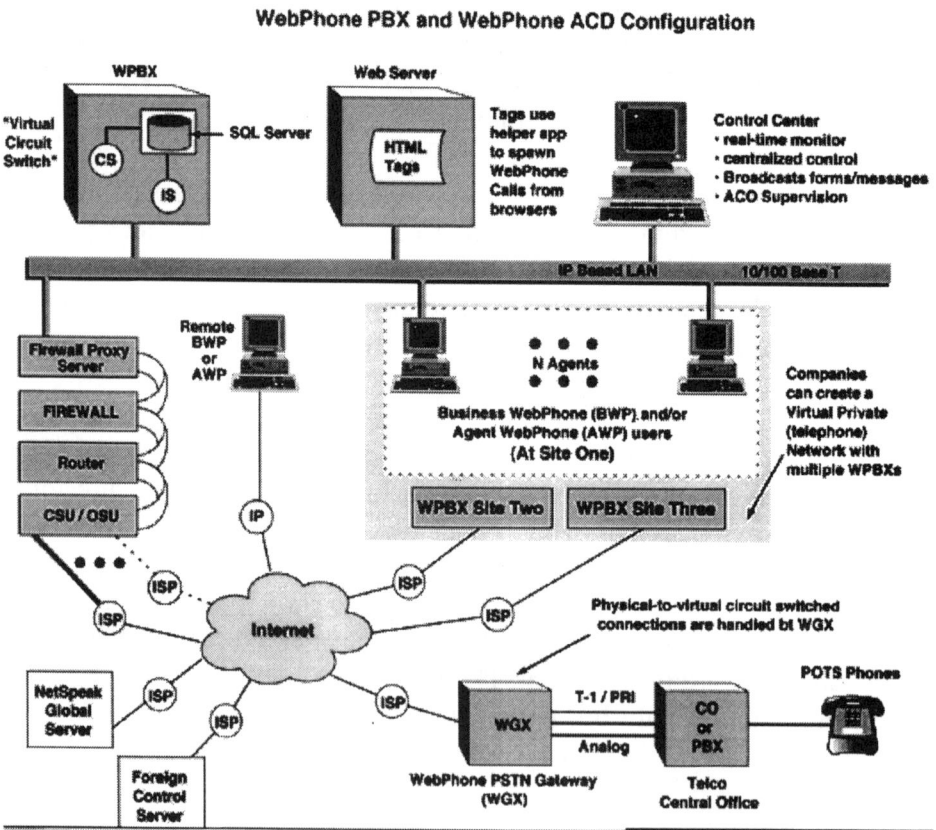

Figure 4.12 illustrates NetSpeak's Incredible WebPhone PBX. It's Sun and Microsoft drenched. It's software only. That means all calls routed through the system use "virtual circuit switch" technology. Callers can get through from their on (Internet Telephony) WebPhone client or from a regular phone. POTS calls are sent through the Internet via a special DSP-loaded gateway. A WebPhone Internet client acts as a proxy for each call initiated from a PSTN-based phone. Once the gateway connection is made, the call is treated like any other WebPhone-based transaction. This is a revolution in call center design. Watch NetSpeak. They've got some great ideas.

NetSpeak belongs to the redundancy school of IP access. They use UUNET, Sprint and MCI as their Internet Service Providers (IPs). T-1s from each IP converge on the NetSpeak corporate LAN (a 100Mbps network). This distributes the load and provides fault tolerance. NetSpeak wrote their own firewall software running on a series of Sun boxes. The WebPhone PBX server itself comes with its own firewall proxy server. NORAD would be proud.

Precision Systems, Inc.

PCA-ATLAS

Harry Newton told me the Internet is great as a control tool for computer telephony applications, like one-number "follow-me" services. He thinks MCI One is a neat service. You give out an 800 number to your friends, family or business people. They call. It tries one number, waits four rings, tries another, waits four rings, tries another and then pages or puts the call into voice mail. You can reprogram MCI One on the fly. But reprogramming is cumbersome over the phone. Easier would be to program it via the Internet and your GUI browser. Also doing it over the Internet would mean you could offer dumb subscribers (like me) more options -- like simultaneously dialing five numbers where I might be. I could reserve this option for my most important clients and my most important loved ones -- all of whom could be identified by Caller ID, ANI, IVR or voice rec.

Precision Systems has such an Internet system for their one number service. It's called Personal Communications Assistant / ATLAS (PCA-ATLAS or ATLAS). It's very impressive. ATLAS is one in a series of voice-centric applications available though UniPort, PSI's high-volume enhanced services platform.

ATLAS is a multi-functional personal telecommunications assistant. Subscribers manage all of their varied communications needs with a single voice-activated interface. With its functional, integrated features, ATLAS is a powerful telecommunications tool.

For telcos and service providers, ATLAS is a means to generate revenue through subscription. ATLAS allows the subscriber to implement a kind of telephonic one-stop-shopping. This includes voice mail, wake-up and reminder calls, call screening and conference calling. Subscribers are totally in charge of activating and deactivating functions so that they can control their own service selections.

Subscribers connect to the application by calling an access number. Through the use of voice recognition technology (which provides additional security), the caller simply identifies him/herself to enter the system. ATLAS responds to requests, constantly monitoring the connection to hear commands, even during calls. And since the application is network-based, the subscriber can use any phone, anywhere. In addition, ATLAS recognizes the ANI and will automatically route preferred calls to that number.

Through the UniPort Enhanced Services Platform, control commands are network-based and simple to use from any phone. Precision Systems also offers integration with customer billing systems with rating and billing software. This allows for the speedy rollout of new features and applications. It also provides billing options and valuable traffic information. Harry Newton got a look at the new Web interface for ATLAS. Figure 4.13 shows how a subscriber can enter phone number so ATLAS can locate you to deliver messages and phone calls. This is a simple way of reprogramming your one number "follow me" service. The graphics on top are all hot buttons. It's a neat way of getting around.

Figure 4.13 – ATLAS Phone Number and Routing Form

set up   phone   caller   help!   paging   call   voice   fax
        numbers   profile   schedules   mail   mail

Phone Numbers

Enter the 10-digit phone numbers that Atlas should use to find you. You may enter up to ten numbers. You must also add a short description for each number, and you must define it as a voice phone, a fax machine, or as a pager.

	Number	Description	Route to
Phone 1:	8135556782	Home	Voice Phone ▼
Phone 2:	8135555426	Mobile	Voice Phone ▼
Phone 3:	8135557814	Work	Voice Phone ▼
Phone 4:	8135739300	Direct	Voice Phone ▼

Figure 4.14 – ATLAS Call Schedule

Call Schedule

Type a descriptive label of up to twenty characters for each schedule. Then show which days of the week you want for each schedule. Do not assign the same day(s) to more than one schedule.

Next, select a terminating phone number for each schedule.

Then click on each schedule to set up its phone numbers and times.

Schedule 1:	Weekday	Sun.	Mon.	Tues.	Wed.	Thur.	Fri.	Sat.
Terminating #	Atlas Voice Mail ▼	□	☑	☑	☑	☑	☑	□

Schedule 2:	Weekend	Sun.	Mon.	Tues.	Wed.	Thur.	Fri.	Sat.
Terminating #	Home ▼	☑	□	□	□	□	□	☑

Schedule 3:	Offsite Meeting	Sun.	Mon.	Tues.	Wed.	Thur.	Fri.	Sat.
Terminating #	Mobile ▼	□	☑	□	□	□	□	□

Schedule 4:	Vacation Day	Sun.	Mon.	Tues.	Wed.	Thur.	Fri.	Sat.
Terminating #	Atlas Voice Mail ▼	□	□	□	□	□	☑	□

Figure 4.14 shows how you can enter your entire schedule so ATLAS knows what phone number to ring depending on where you are. You input phone numbers, time of day, days of the week and locations into this form. ATLAS will route calls, take messages or deliver real-time calls based on the rules you set up here. It's very personalized. To listen to a message, you simply click on the description of your liking. ATLAS uses ANI, so you'll know who called in if they called from an ANI-enabled carrier. Little scroll boxes let you take actions on each message. The interface is easy to look at (see figure 4.15) and easy to understand. Once you use it, you'll become very spoiled.

Figure 4.15 – Atlas Voice Mail Screen

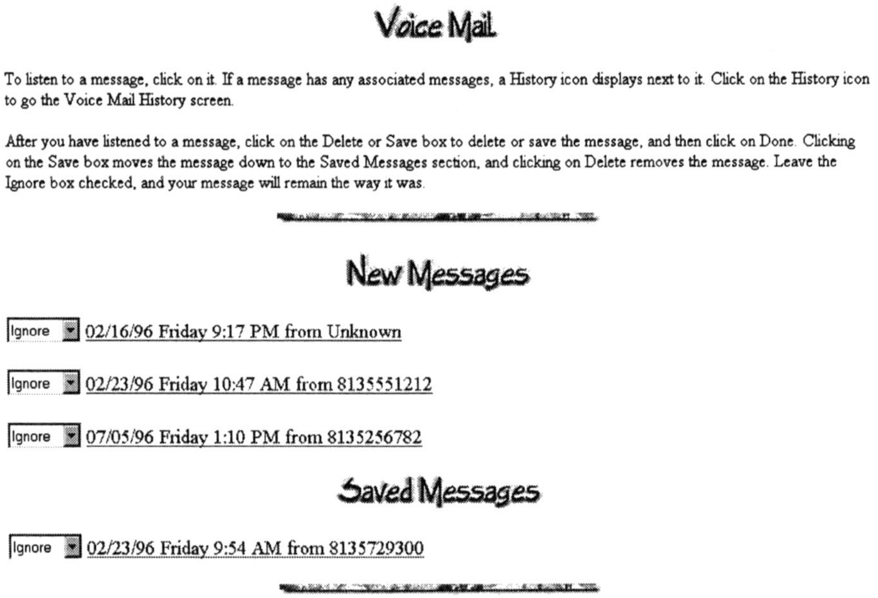

Voice Mail

To listen to a message, click on it. If a message has any associated messages, a History icon displays next to it. Click on the History icon to go the Voice Mail History screen.

After you have listened to a message, click on the Delete or Save box to delete or save the message, and then click on Done. Clicking on the Save box moves the message down to the Saved Messages section, and clicking on Delete removes the message. Leave the Ignore box checked, and your message will remain the way it was.

New Messages

Ignore ▼ 02/16/96 Friday 9:17 PM from Unknown

Ignore ▼ 02/23/96 Friday 10:47 AM from 8135551212

Ignore ▼ 07/05/96 Friday 1:10 PM from 8135256782

Saved Messages

Ignore ▼ 02/23/96 Friday 9:54 AM from 8135729300

Besides ATLAS, PSI sells a suite of apps under the umbrella name of UniPort. PSI has installed Single-Number technology and other enhanced platforms for GTE, Motorola and AirTouch. Their recent acquisition of Vicorp Systems gives them a global reach into a variety of wireless, central office and mission critical environments. Vicorp's BETEX Enhanced Services Platform (BETEX-ESP) supports apps for cellular and Personal Communication Services (PCS) providers.

This includes short message service, voice activated dialing, and IVR. PSI just announced a new SBus-compatible T-1 card. Now systems integrators are added to the list of PSI prospects. UniPort is a service creation and run-time environment for Unix-based platforms.

UniPort runs on Hewlett-Packard, Tandem, Sun, Stratus, and Sequent computers. PSI says you can scale the number of ports from 24 to more than 10,000. You can run many apps at the same time and in different languages, too.

With the UniPort platform, you can buy pre-packaged apps and use an application creation language (with GUI) to create and modify apps. In addition to ATLAS, UniPort-based apps include:

PCA. Atlas Personal Communications Agent named Atlas. Gives telephone subscribers a voice-activated interface.

PrePaid Calling Cards. Card holders can get weather updates, news reports, sports scores, and entertainment news.

Voice Activated Dialing. Hands-free connection for cellular and LD users.

For Developers Only. Evante is the 4GL scripting language included in the UniPort Telephony Middleware. Evante is similar to C but optimized for computer telephony. It is an interpreted, event-driven language optimized for telephony apps.

The middle ware uses native switching and telephony functions. Evante accesses these functions through the API. Programmers are abstracted from the nature and type of device being used in this way. For developers, PSI plans on selling an SDK including the "middleware" for $53,000. This includes one set of AMC boards and 48 port software license. You also get Summa Four DSD and Excel LNX/PCX switch drivers.

ShadowTel Communications

ShadowTel Network

The ShadowTel Network, or The Long Distance Internet Communications (LINC) by ShadowTel Communications was formed to tackle the worldwide problem of high priced long-distance telephone calls by offering an alternative telephony system. The LINC is an Internet based communication service currently being launched in Ontario, Canada. ShadowTel provides fifteen hours of calling over long distances for $20.00 per month from a regular phone without the need for any extra equipment or phone add-ons.

ShadowNet is an interesting hybrid system that enhances the efficiency of conventional phone lines in addition to taking advantage of the Internet: It can increase bandwidth use over existing phone lines (copper or fiber optic) during transmission by compressing the analog voice data of both callers with proprietary hardware built around Digital Signal Processor (DSP) chips.

The transmission analog signal of a regular telephone is converted by ShadowTel hardware in real time to a digital data stream which can be further optimized through multiplexing and routing through existing digital phone lines (ISDN, Centrex).

The call is first validated by Caller ID at the local dial-in ShadowNet site, an electronic validation provides a new dial tone and the caller then enters the number (area code + 7 digits) of the person to call. The ShadowNet site then logs on to the ShadowTel Network Master System Router to get information on the quickest and most available routing path to the local ShadowTel site closest to the exchange of the receiving party.

The ShadowNet site then connects to the remote ShadowNet site in the receiving party's area code and exchange. The receiving ShadowNet site then seizes one of its local lines and dials the receiving party's number. The call is completed normally.

It sounds complex but the whole process takes place during the time you hear the ShadowTel electronic message say "Thank you for using ShadowTel Networks. Your call is being connected now through our site at (destination)." No special equipment at the home or desktop is required for a station to station telephone call. An upgrade ISA card and software is available to convert a desktop or network PC computer to an alternative telephony system. Here's where the Internet comes in. ShadowTel can connect to a suitably equipped and registered computer's Internet address, enabling Internet telephony with normal telephone systems. ShadowTel's protocols for routing can interface with Novell compatible networks. ShadowTel will offer direct connection to its infrastructure for corporate clients.

Each home user will pay an initial activation fee and be activated for universal access. The minimum flat monthly fee for home use is $19.99 per line based on weekly usage of 720 minutes (three hours) or just under three cents a minute. For SOHOs and commercial sites, the usage rate is $49.99 per line per month, a rate still calculated at the base usage rate of under three cents a minute. These users will also benefit from ShadowTel's Internet connectivity: The integration of e-mail, paging, messaging, call-answer and voice mail with full telephony to a desktop computer. The company recently announced an agreement with Vancouver based Telescape Communications Inc. to license Telescape's TS Intercom for Windows. Telescape's TS Intercom allows two users to exchange audio, visual and data files simultaneously through a direct Internet connection. TS Intercom Lite, is available for free download from Telescape's web site (www.telescape.com) and TS Intercom SE (Special Edition), is available from Original Equipment Manufacturers (OEM's).

VocalTec, Inc.

Internet Phone Telephony Gateway

VocalTec, Inc., the Internet Phone Company, is an international provider of audio and voice communication software for the Internet. Its products are used for real time voice communication and audio broadcasting over the Internet.

They are designed to improve productivity, reduce communications costs and maximize investments in computer and network technology. VocalTec's objective is to make its software the de facto standard for realtime voice and audio communications over computer networks. Its core products include:

- **Internet Phone.** (see chapter 11) With Internet Phone, users can conduct unlimited long distance and international conversations for the cost of an Internet connection. Internet Phone incorporates VocalTec-developed voice compression, voice packet reconstruction and delay handling mechanisms.

- **Internet Wave.** or IWave, which gives you a way to broadcast shows, lectures, music in a highquality audio format to Internet users worldwide. IWave has two main components: a server package that includes an encoder and works in conjunction with standard web servers, and the IWave Windowscompatible application that enables users to listen to IWave broadcasts from their Web browsers. Both are available free of charge at VocalTec's Web site.

- **VocalChat WAN.** This lets large corporate telephone users aggregate voice traffic onto highcapacity T1 or switched 56 Kbps data circuits.

- **The CAT**. Compact Audio Technology is highquality audio recording and playback for desktop and portable PCs. It works by connecting to the computer's printer port.

VocalTec has forged relationships with a number of key players in the networking arena, including America Online's Global Network Navigator, Boca Research Inc., Cirrus Logic Inc., Motorola Inc. and Performance Systems International. Motorola's Information Systems Group, Transmission Products Division offers Internet Phone for distribution worldwide with Motorola's Power Class 28.8 desktop modems for business and professional users and computer savvy power users.

Other partners include Connectware, Diamond Multimedia Systems, Inc., JABRA Corporation, US Cyber Inc., and ZOOM Telephonics, Inc.

The Internet Phone Telephony Gateway. Perhaps the most intriguing of all VocalTec's products is a simple yet powerful Internet voice communications solution called the gateway. The product represents an alliance between VocalTec with its software and Dialogic Corporation with its hardware. The system is comprised of a PC running Windows 95 and the Internet Phone Telephony Gateway software, equipped with a Dialogic Corporation computer telephony card linked to the telephone network, and an Internet connection through a 28.8 Kbps modem or a faster connection. If an Internet connection is already available in your company, it can be used simultaneously for data transfer and Gateway communication, assuming adequate bandwidth is available.

The Internet Phone Telephony Gateway provides connections between the Internet and local telephone lines, enabling callers to combine the low cost of Internet connections, the convenience of initiating calls from either PCs or telephones, and the ability to communicate with anybody with a telephone via the public switched telephone network.

Dialogic Corporation is the leading manufacturer of high performance, standardsbased computer telephony (CT) components. Computer telephony systems built with Dialogic products manage more than one third of all telephone, facsimile, and multimedia calls answered by computers over wireless and wired networks worldwide. Dialogic products are used in a multitude of CT applications, including voice, fax, data, voice recognition, speech synthesis and call center management. More than two million ports have been deployed by Dialogic's development and integration partners.

Internet Phone Telephony Gateway enables computertotelephone, telephonetotelephone, and telephonetocomputer calls. Beyond the cost of your Internet connection, the only additional costs incurred are for calls between the Gateway and the telephone network. It's a costefficient way to maximize existing investments in computers, networks and telecommunications systems.

You can incorporate PBXs and voice mail systems into the gateway. You get the low cost of Internet connections, the convenience of initiating calls from either PCs or telephones, and the ability to communicate with anybody with a telephone via the public switched telephone network.

Calls over the Internet mean you can reduce long distance phone charges. This is especially true for corporate "Intranet" and remote/branch of office applications. Internet Phone's audio capabilities enable realtime, twoway, fullduplex conversations. VocalTec has built automatic routing devices into the Gateway. The gateway also handles traffic balancing and sends calls over the least congested routes.

Network Monitoring alerts you to points of failure on the Telephone Network and the Internet, and may also provide alternate routing to the PSTN when the Internet is congested. You can define call restrictions. You can restrict the hours of service, block 900 numbers, and restrict calling to certain area codes. Dialing definitions also keep track of who has access to use the Gateway while password protection prevents unauthorized access. All of the activity on your system is saved in log files so you can keep track of usage and billing.

Internet Phone Gateway Architecture

Bob Heymann, vice president of business development at Dialogic says the Internet Telephony Gateway will enable VARS and systems integrators to offer innovative applications. He names international 'hop off' and Internet-based customer service as the top two. He says VocalTec's gateway (from a hardware perspective) is based on Dialogic telephone interfaces and programmable signal processing products. The platform is compatible with Signal Computing System Architecture (SCSA), Dialogic's open platform. Figure 4.16 shows how Dialogic's off-the-shelf components enable this "Internet Telephony CT Server" architecture. The company has worldwide analog, T1/E1 and ISDN connectivity, so the gateways can be placed in virtually any country. VocalTec has developed software to enable a number of configurations detailed below.

Figure 4.16 -- Internet Telephony CT Server

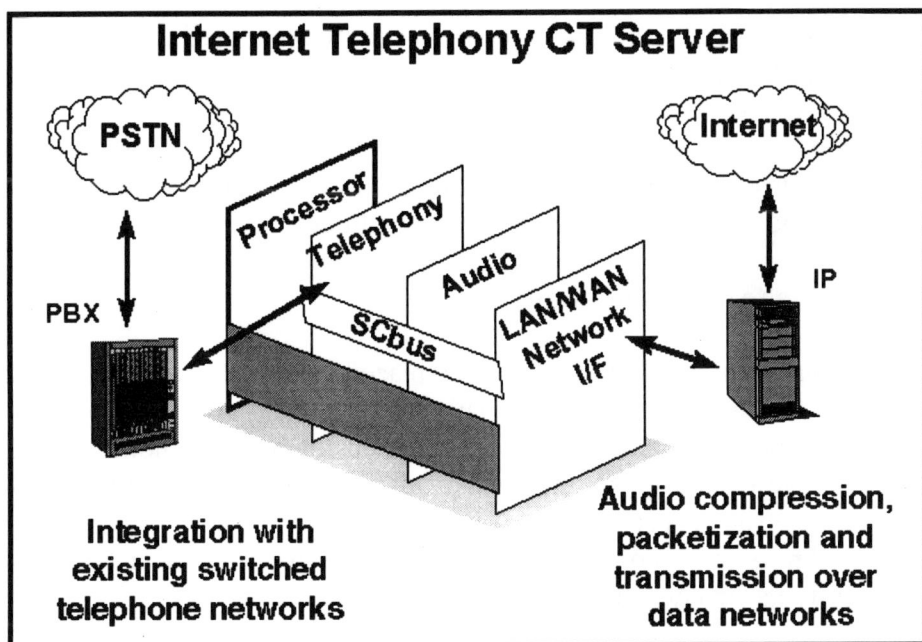

Figure 4.17 -- Computer toTelephone Gateway

Computer toTelephone Gateway

When placing call from a computer, the call travels over the Internet to the Gateway closest to the call destination (automatically determined by the system). At this point, the only charge incurred is the cost of the Internet connection. From the Gateway, the call then travels over a telephone network to its final destination and a charge is incurred for the call time between the Gateway and the call destination. This is pictured in Figure 4.17.

Telephone toTelephone Gateway

As shown in Figure 4.18 a call can be placed from one phone to another. You dial the number of the Gateway closest to your current location. A voice prompt then guides you to enter the destination telephone number. Once you've entered this number, the call travels over the Internet to the second Gateway (chosen by the system for its proximity to the call destination). From the second Gateway, the call is routed over a telephone network to its finaldestination.

Figure 4.18 -- Telephone to Telephone Gateway

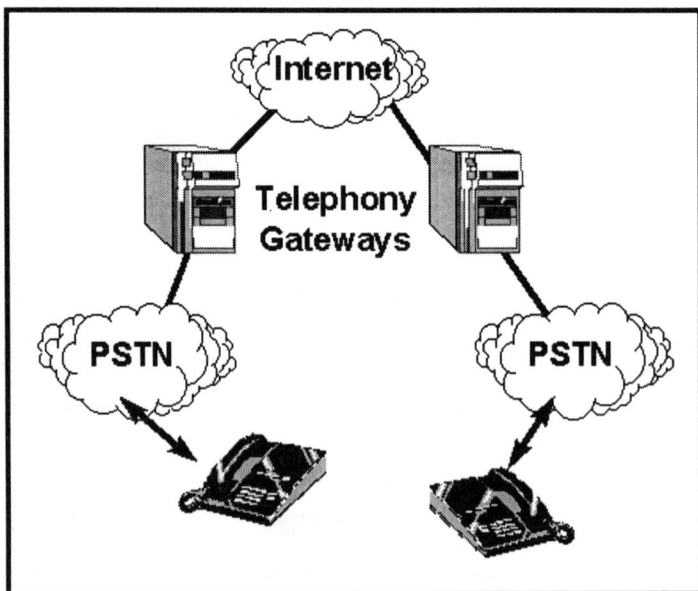

Costs for the call include only applicable charges for the call to the first Gateway, the cost of the Internet connection, and applicable charges for the call from the second Gateway. Calls to wireline and cellular phones are possible, and the cost of a call is limited to the telephone charges incurred when linking to the Internet on either end of the connection plus the standard Internet connectivity charges.

Telephone to Computer Gateway

To call from a phone to a computer, first dial the number of the closest Gateway. When prompted by the voice message, enter the destination Internet address. The call then goes to the Gateway and travels over the Internet directly to the computer you're calling. Costs include the cost of the Internet connection and the call to the Gateway. This is illustrated in Figure 4.19.

Figure 4.19 --- Telephone to Computer Gateway

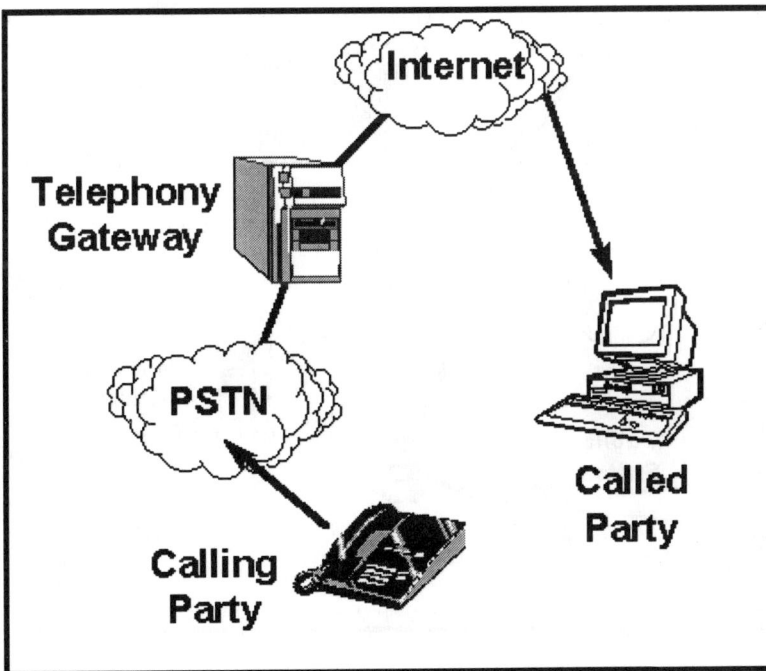

Virtual PBX Network Gateway

The Internet Phone Telephony Gateway is ideal for companies with remote office locations. Using the Gateway, an employee can place a call from the company's US office to an office overseas as pictured in Figure 4.20. The call goes over the local office PBX to the office Gateway. From the Gateway, the call then travels over the Internet to the office Gateway overseas and is routed over the local PBX to the call destination. The resulting charge is the cost of the Internet connection. Essentially, the Gateway becomes a global virtual PBX network, eliminating long distance charges on interoffice calls.

Figure 4.20 -- Virtual PBX Network Gateway

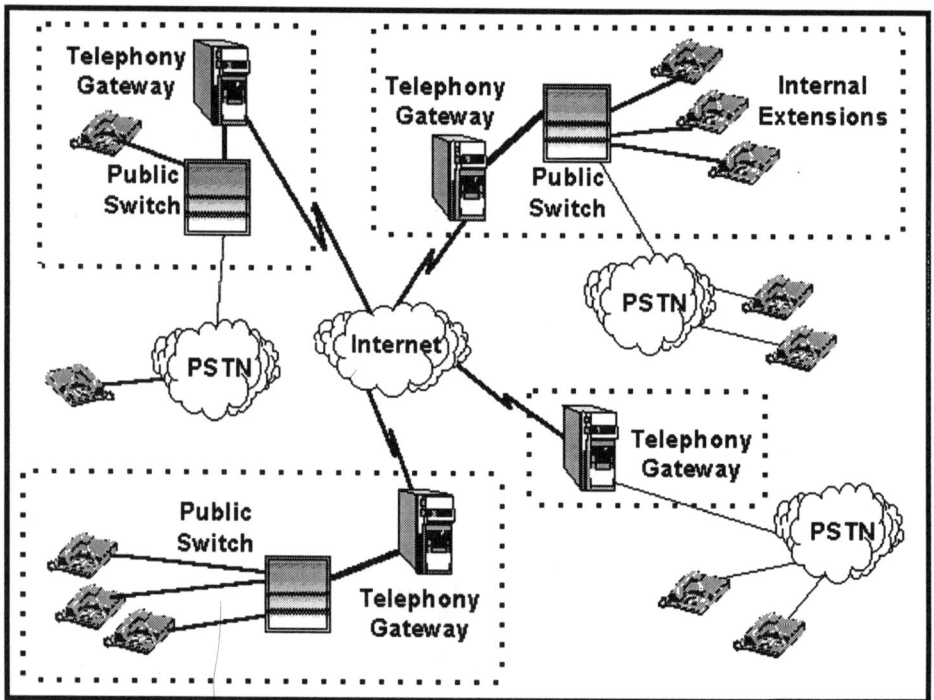

Chapter 5

Mixed Media Messaging

Bright-eyed people with great ideas and investors with deep pockets are rushing to put mixed media messaging services on the Internet. They come from many backgrounds including voice processing, data communications and computer engineering. One thing is certain. An incredible amount of discipline and hard work is being put into the merger of traditional unified messaging and Internet access to its media.

I asked Alan W. Wokas, president and CEO of the new MediaGate company to share his views on how it's all coming together. Mr. Wokas has over 17 years experience in the micro electronics industry, 14 of which are directly related to computer telephony. He founded Vynet and Rhetorex and is well known in the industry as one of its founders. You'll find an overview of his new Multimedia Server in the product roundup. You'll be hearing more about him.

Bandwidth

... The Net's Achilles Heel

The two main functions the Internet provides today are Web site access and E-mail. Much attention has been placed on increasing bandwidth on the Internet for faster Web-Site access. Many feel that a severe deficiency of the Internet is the lack of speed in response to request from users of the Net, and the less than desirable quality of other media's transferred on the Net, such as voice and data.

The cause of the "bogging down" of the Net is a result of two main sources. First, the exponential growth of users on the Internet, and second, the use of new media's, in particular voice and video, that are much more data intensive than standard text and graphics. The combination of these two directions are placing a burden on the Internet that make the uses of voice and video, and the Net itself tedious at best when requesting information.

To solve the problem, many companies are rushing to increase bandwidth by replacing the current infrastructure with newer, faster technologies. Phone companies are improving infrastructure with services such as ISDN and in the future cable modems and ADSL technologies to squeeze more data down the same size wires. Other companies are developing better compression techniques for reducing the size of the data. However, the rate at which these technologies are adopted are effected by two functions:

1) The up-front expense to upgrade an existing network infrastructure

2) The "chicken or the egg" syndrome. In other words, the end user has to change their equipment to adapt to the new infrastructure. However, end users will not buy new equipment if they cannot get service. Service providers will not install new infrastructure unless there is an installed base to sell to.

Regardless of the predictions for increased bandwidth on the Net, one thing is for sure. Ubiquitous instantaneous access to the Net is not here today.

MultiMedia Messaging

...The Net's Killer App

Although bandwidth limitations exist for the Net, there is a "killer application" that addresses the four main drawbacks of the Net:

1) Provides instantaneous response to the user

2) The quality of data intensive media's remains high

3) Can utilize existing, as well as new infrastructure, and

4) Access is ubiquitous for all end user communication technologies

This application is called MultiMedia Messaging. This also can be referred to as MultiMedia store and forward, or MultiMedia mail. To understand MultiMedia Messaging for the Internet, we first have to understand what messaging really is. Messaging is basically the reverse of requesting information. When requesting information, the receiving party is initiating the transaction and requesting content developed by the request. When messaging or delivering information, the sending party develops the content and initiates the transaction. A message is not limited in definition to just a simple phrase or comments. It may consist of all types of content created in all types of media. As in standard snail mail, you can receive more than just written letters.

Color brochures, video tapes, catalogs, advertisements, coupons, etc. are all defined as messaging. One of the most widely uses of mail messaging is advertising, where content is directed to a particular address. The difference between Messaging and requesting as it applies to the Net, is as follows: When initiating a request for information, a user selects a location (i.e. a Web site) by either knowing its URL address or using a search engine to find one.

He then accesses its home page (which contains the content) through a browser; then waits (sometimes painstakingly) for that information to be downloaded into his computer. Requests can only be made with browser software, and the user must be a subscriber to an Internet service.

Messaging on the Net is the reverse corollary of Web site access. The messaging medium is E-mail with the ability to attach files. When initiating a message, the sender develops the content; selects a predefined destination(s) through an E-mail address, and sends the message. When it arrives, the receiving party is notified and the message is available *instantaneously* to the recipient. In this way, messaging reduces the dependency on bandwidth.

Instantaneous Access
...Non Real Time Communication

To understand why message retrieval is instantaneous one first must understand how the Internet treats a message. When a message is initiated on the Internet, it is delivered into the recipients local IP (Internet Provider) server. Every Internet E-mail address has associated with it an IP address that defines which server that E-mail client dials into.

Only until the message has fully completed delivery, is the client notified. This is significant in that the message delivery is subjected to the same delays as Web page access. However, unlike Web page access, the delay occurs at a time when the recipient is not expecting a response, or in effect, not waiting. Once the recipient is notified, the message is already delivered. A typical Information Service Provider (ISP) provides simple access, or "post office services" to Internet users. Figure 5.1 shows how you can access an ISP via analog or ISDN lines. You can get speedy connections to the IP, but once you begin to access other IP servers, things can bog down considerably.

Figure 5.1 -- Typical ISP Access to the Internet

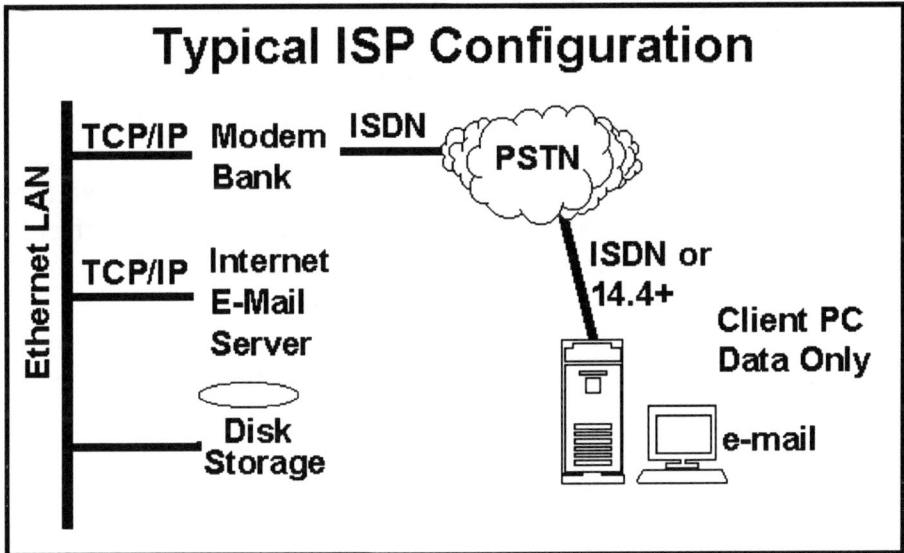

Typical ISP Configuration

This can best be described as non real time communication. In Web page access, the ultimate desire is to in effect have real time communication with someone's home page. You are communicating in real time with that home page in attempt to receive some content. The solution to improving this form of communication is to increase bandwidth. With Internet messaging, the sender is not concerned with real time communication, therefore bandwidth is of little concern. Both parties are not required to be connected simultaneously and continuously, as they are with a Web page. Even if the non real time period is short (in the range of minutes), this is plenty of time in cyberspace to deliver a message.

High Quality MultiMedia on the Internet

Expanding on the concept of non real time communication also leads to improved quality of newer media's such as voice and video. First, a further description on how a message is delivered over the Internet is required. When a message is initiated, the availability of the pipes, or bandwidth of the Internet cannot be guaranteed from point to point.

Therefore the Internet backbone utilizes complex routing protocols that breaks the message into pieces (or packets) and physically routes each packet over the least used and sometimes separate paths. The message is than reassembled in its exact form at the IP destination. This system is referred to as the frame relay system. When accessing a Web page, the content is delivered in this same manner. When dealing with text or graphics, the Web page is transmitted over the frame relay system and is assembled in its exact form at the client . However, since the frame relay system cannot guarantee the bandwidth, (i.e. the bandwidth is variable) delays result that effect the speed at which the Web page is recreated at the client.

However, the problem is further compounded when trying to deliver continuous data, such as voice and video, in real time. Since the packets are routed over different pipes at different speeds, the resulting content will not match the original, and in many cases the quality degradation can be severe. Several audio and video technologies, called streaming technologies, are available to help smooth these transaction deficiencies, but the delivered content is still far from the original.

Messaging on the other hand, delivers all media's in its original form to the local IP server. Even in the case of audio and video, all the data is preserved. The recipient then has two methods to retrieve the message. First, the MultiMedia data can be downloaded to the clients PC. This of course would require the user to wait, but the quality would be preserved. The second method is that the data can also be streamed, therefore the recipient would receive it instantaneously. But the real advantage is that the data is transferred from the local server to the client on a fixed point to point connection, or in other words, outside the frame relay system. This means that the bandwidth between the client and server is fixed. By fixing the bandwidth, the quality is preserved.

Internet Open Network: The Most Effective Messaging

The Internet is by far the most widespread cost effective message delivery system in the world. The open network standards of the Internet are quickly becoming the networking platforms of choice for both consumers and corporate.

For ease of accessibility, lower cost, wider reach, and interoperability, the Internet provides a much better competitive alternative to private networks. The emergence of both the Internet and Intranet has made this a reality.

To understand the importance of the Internet's open network, we must first define what a network is. We define an electronic communications network as the combination of:

1) The carrier

2) The access device

3) The subscriber database or directory

The carrier is the physical medium on which the content is carried. The access device is the human interface to the network, and the directory is the technique that defines how access devices are routed and connected. Any network requires all three of these elements to provide a communication channel. Networks exist as both public and private, depending on the type of service the network provides.

For example, plain old telephone service (POTS), the largest communication network in the world, provides real time audio communication between two parties. The carrier is the phone line, typically controlled by the phone company, the access device is a telephone, and the directory is the list of unique phone numbers (or addresses) of the subscribers to the service.

Initially, in the US, all three aspects of the telephone network were controlled by one company, AT&T. The breakup of AT&T in the early 80's opened up the telecom carriers, allowing other companies to provide telephone service as well as independent access devices. But the telephone companies still controlled the directories. In order for your access device to connect to someone else's access device, a user still has to go through the telephone companies "toll booth", that is, its directory.

Internet - A Totally Open Network

Now, for the first time, the phenomena of the Internet will open up databases or directories to create a truly open network. Since addressing methods are standard and open on the Internet, any one can be a directory provider and communicate with someone else's directory. There are no more proprietary toll booths. Furthermore, distance is no longer a factor. Just as deregulation opened up network access devices, *the Internet has opened up network directories!* This is a major fundamental shift in the basic approach of telecommunication services. Furthermore, corporations can use the same Internet model and therefore take advantage of the multitude of applications and equipment to build Intranets with secured directories.

Internet Ubiquitous Access

As described above, MultiMedia messaging addresses three of the four major drawbacks of the Internet. Mainly:

1) Instantaneous access

2) High quality MultiMedia data

3) Can utilize existing, as well as new infrastructure

The messaging aspects of the Internet can further be exploited by expanding access to other communication devices. The top four two way communication devices in terms of installed base are telephones (1B), PC's with modems (180M), Fax machines (75M) and video conferencing devices (1M). Clearly, the most pervasive interactive communication device in the world today is the telephone. And in most households, the telephone is the only interactive communication device, other than the mail. Most other forms of ubiquitous communication appliances are designed to be one way. Television, Radio, VCR's , CD players all broadcast (i.e. deliver) information to you, but are not designed to deliver information back.

With the advent of the modem enabled PC, this marks for the first time in over 100 years the availability of a new interactive communication device. However, the original intent of the PC was not for communication, and certainly not for real time communication, as is the telephone. It was mainly designed as a productivity tool. The following is a comparison of the intended types of uses for PC's and Telephones.

PC's. The intended class service for PCs are primarily: 1) Productivity Tool (word processing, spreadsheets); 2) Entertainment (computer games); 3) Non Real-time Messaging (e-mail) and 4) Non Real-time Information Retrieval (Data access). PCs were not originally designed for real time communication or real-time information retrieval.

Telephone. The intended class service for telephones are primarily: 1) Real Time Communication (conversation) and 2) Real-time Information Retrieval (request information).

In comparison, the telephone network was designed to provide a very highly reliable class of service that would continue to provide non-blocking real-time connections under tremendous bandwidth loads. The cost of this reliability is of course passed on to the caller. The Internet on the other hand is designed to provide a very highly reliable class of service to provide non-real time communication and data access. The cost of this service is much lower. The types of services intended for the Internet are *non real time*, highly reliable and *inexpensive*. This compared to telephone networks which were designed for *real time*, highly reliable but relatively expensive (long distance) services. Another major difference is that the access devices to each network are radically different in regards to complexity and cost. Obviously, the PC is much higher in cost and complexity relative to the telephone.

Over twenty years ago, practically all communication on the phone system was real time. However, within the last twenty years, a simple device known as the answering machine, and later, the PC, the FAX machine and voice mail, gave rise to a new phenomena, non real time telephone communication.

It is now estimated that almost 70% of all connections on the telephone network are for non real time communication. This leads to an interesting paradox, where you have an overkill of a network designed for real-time communication (the telephone network) but only used 30% of the time for its intended purpose. Conversely, you have a very low cost non real time network (the Internet), but the access devices (PC's) are prohibitively expensive and complicated!

Therefore, the ultimate "killer app" would be to combine the Internet benefits of messaging with low cost easy to use access devices such as telephones, fax machines, and video conferencing devices, resolving the final Internet application roadblock by making Internet access ubiquitous to all communication devices

The opportunities for Multimedia non real-time communication applications(i.e. messaging) for any communication devices for the Internet are tremendous. Below is just a sample of the applications that can be delivered today on the Internet:

Voice Messaging. Storing voice audio, delivering it to another site, and replaying it a another time. Different from VM/AA in that with VM/AA the initial intention of the caller is to speak to someone in real time, while Voice Messaging, the intent is to only deliver a spoken message.

Audiotex. Provides automated information with a spoken menu over the phone, driven by input from the caller, typically with Touch Tones (DTMF). Ex. Press 1 for business hours, 2 for directions, 3 for info on our products, etc.
Interactive Voice Response. IVR. Similar to Audiotex, but also has access to a computer database through a network. Ex. Press 1 for stock quotes, 2 for bank balance, etc.

FAX on Demand. FOD. Also similar to Audiotex, but instead of spoken information, the information is Faxed to you. Ex., the system requests you to enter in your Fax number using touch tones then asks Press 1 for product information, 2 for latest press release, etc.

FAX Messaging. Similar to Voice Mail, but with FAX. The system stores Fax's sent to you whereas you can redirect them to a FAX machine of your choice at your convenience.

Automated Paging. Similar to Automated Attendant, when a caller enters a persons pager code, the system automatically notifies that person they have a call.

Video Conferencing. The ability to view one another on a screen while communicating in real time.

Video Messaging. Storing a video image, delivering it to another site, and replaying it a another time.

Video Text. Provides automated information with a visual menu sent to the video conferencing device, driven by input from the caller, typically with DTMF. Ex. press 1 for map directions, 2 for product demonstration, etc.

Video Advertising. The ability to send video commercials targeted and tailored to a particular audience under computer control. Unlike standard TV commercials which are broadcast only.

Interactive Video Response. Similar to video text, but also has access to a computer data base through a network. (press 1 to view weather information, 2 to view ski resort routes, 3 to view tourist information, etc.)

Remote Video Security Control. One central station controls multiple remote video sites, stores the streams for future evidence and forwards the video streams over the Internet.

Active Voice Corporation

TeLANophy

Active Voice makes open standards compliant, PC-based computer telephony products. These products include automated attendant call routing, voice and fax messaging, and fax-on-demand systems. In 1993, the company introduced TeLANophy, one of the first products to fully integrate voice and fax processing and a wide range of proprietary PBX and key system telephone switching equipment into a standard LAN environment.

TeLANophy is Active Voice's trade name for the client-server architecture incorporated into its Repartee communications server products. TeLANophy provides protocol-independent communications between the Repartee server and a variety of desktop client software. TeLANophy needs little or no hardware or software modifications to the telephone switch. This makes TeLANophy fully compatible with a wide range of current and legacy equipment. The system is supported on over 150 different switches.

Figure 5.2 shows TeLANophy topology on a local area network. Inbound calls are answered by the automated attendant component of the Repartee server. Callers route themselves to a desired destination by dialing an extension number directly. With fax calls, CNG tone is automatically detected and the fax is routed to a fax machine or disk storage for later retrieval. Unanswered calls are typically handled by the voice messaging component of Repartee.

The Repartee platform is an Intel-based computer. The physical link between the switch and Repartee is supported by analog or digital voice board hardware installed within Repartee (typically, Dialogic D/41D or equivalent hardware). Communications between the switch and Repartee are accomplished through a variety of means.

Figure 5.2 - TeLANophy on a Local Area Network

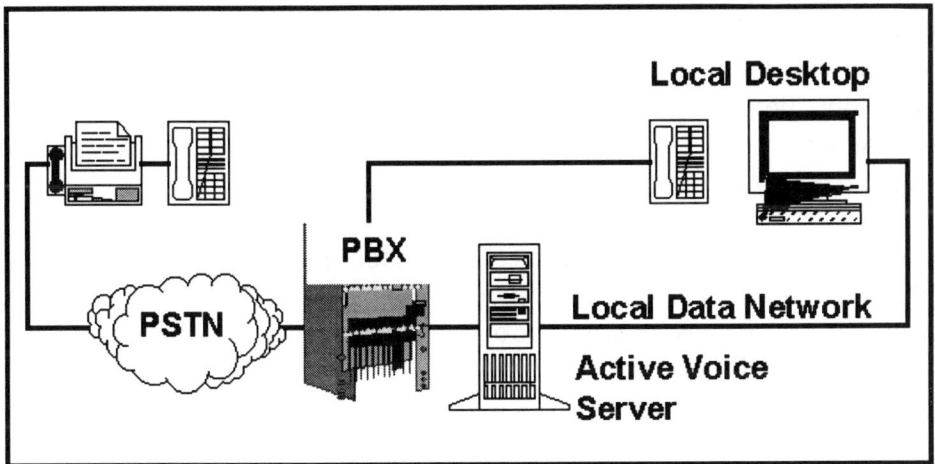

In-band analog signaling, digital telephone set emulation and switch-provided CSTA integration links are also supported. TeLANophy works on a LAN. It integrates voice and fax processing and proprietary PBX and key systems into a standard LAN environment. Active Voice provides analog and digital integration support for over 150 switches. LAN support for TeLANophy includes SPX/IPX and TCP/IP protocols running in Novell, Microsoft, IBM, and other common network environments. TeLANophy adds a standard Ethernet or token ring network connection and the protocol needed for communication between the Repartee server and a variety of desktop client software. Currently, the protocol is a proprietary API. Messaging and telephony functions are based on Microsoft's Messaging API and Telephony API, respectively. Active Voice provides four Windows-based client applications for this environment:

ViewMail provides desktop access to voice messaging. Incoming and outgoing messages are displayed on screen in a typical mailbox interface with controls for addressing, sending, replying, forwarding, and so on. Message header information identifies the sender, date, time, length, and other pertinent information. Users play and record on-screen using an extension phone or a multimedia device.

ViewFax adds fax message handling to ViewMail. Incoming faxes are viewable on screen. The entire fax or selected pages can be printed to any standard printer. The program includes print-to-fax features, as well. Users can print any document to the Repartee server for background faxing. In addition, ViewFax provides direct access to the Repartee server's fax-on-demand features. Users can select and fax standard documents from a centralized company library.

ViewCall provides real time call handling for inbound calls routed through the automated attendant. Caller ID information is displayed along with the call. This may be linked to any one of more than a dozen Personal Information Management (PIM) products to automatically pop up the caller's database record. Then, while the call is ringing, the ViewCall user can play a selected greeting, ask the caller to hold, or transfer the call to another extension. Multiple calls can hold, and the user can talk to them in any order. Other unique features allow a user to monitor a voice message as it is being left, even pulling the caller out of voice mail for a live conversation, if desired.

ViewCall Plus adds outbound call origination and handling to ViewCall. This product combines dialing, conferencing, and other enhanced features available on TSAPI enabled telephone systems or TAPI enabled PCs with TeLANophy. The user has complete inbound and outbound call handling in a single desktop interface. TeLANophy also supports server-to-server communications for telephone access to data stored on other servers. Repartee users can access e-mail by phone using text-to-fax or text-to-speech. In addition, Repartee can redeliver voice and fax messages to an e-mail database. This gives users unified access to e-mail, voice, and fax within third-party client mailbox applications like Microsoft Mail or Exchange, Lotus cc:Mail or Notes Mail, or Novell GroupWise.

TeLANophy Is TeWANophy

TeLANophy is not limited to local area networks. The architecture extends directly to private wide area networks, and is applicable to both switched and non-switch WAN topologies.

A typical switched WAN configuration uses a dial-up data router for remote connection to the LAN. This configuration is suitable for mobile workers or for satellite offices that don't need a continuous connection to the home-office network. Users connect directly to the office network as needed via public analog or ISDN phone lines. Microsoft's Remote Access Software (RAS, provided as part of Windows 95 and NT) or similar products provide a transparent connection to LAN-based data and applications, including ViewMail and ViewCall.

TeLANophy scales transparently from local to wide area networks. Remote workers can connect directly to the office data network via switched or dedicated connections for access to LAN based data and applications, including ViewMail, ViewFax, and ViewCall.

With switched connections, user capacity is equal to the number of modems supported by the router hardware. Bandwidth use is minimal (a few dozen bytes for a message header or inbound call control information). Real time playback of voice messages requires a peak bandwidth of roughly 25Kbs (thousand bits per second), so analog connections require a 28.8Kbs modem. Engineering efforts are underway to apply supplemental compression to voice and fax data with the goal of reducing bandwidth requirements to levels usable with 14.4Kbs modems. Non-switched connections provide full-time connections between two or more office sites. Typically these are leased 56Kbs lines, fractional T1 lines, and so on. Here, bandwidth is shared between users. User capacity is determined by the sum of the peak bandwidth needed by all applications and users. If there were no other network activity, two users could play voice messages on a 56Kbs connection at the same time. In practice, calculating bandwidth required for shared use can be complex.

Figure 5.3 shows how TeLANophy works as well on the Internet as it does on private wide area networks. Since TeLANophy supports TCP/IP, it is compatible with the networking environment of the Internet. This gives mobile workers and satellite offices low-cost, switched access through CompuServe, America Online, the Microsoft Network, and hundreds of other, smaller service providers.

Figure 5.3 -- TeLANophy on the Internet

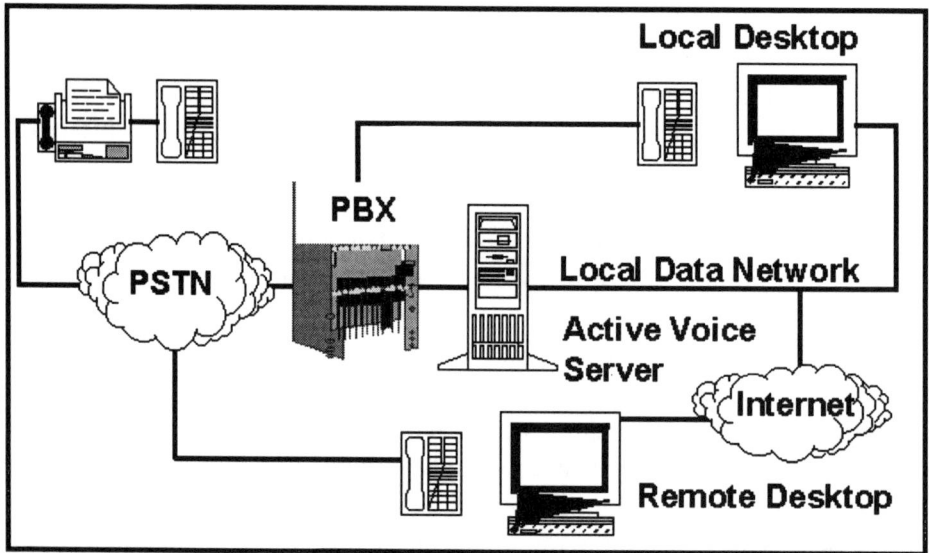

In addition, a remote office requiring a full-time connection to the home office can install a dedicated Internet connection. The topology is effectively the same as a private WAN. The private network access point is replaced by a dedicated connection to the Internet. With a connection in place, using Repartee with the Internet is straightforward: the administrator simply assigns a permanent IP address to the Repartee server. On the client side, users specify TCP protocol and the server IP address (or a registered, resolvable name such as repartee.omnimax.com) when signing in.

Active Voice is currently testing Repartee prototypes that include a fully integrated Web Server. With this architecture, the Repartee server and the attached telephone system can be accessed within any general purpose browser. As shown in figure 5.4, this approach integrates TeLANophy with the World Wide Web. This is a simplified schematic of the Repartee server with an integrated World Wide Web server from an end user's perspective. In addition to accessing server data and functionality by phone and through custom applications, users have access through a browser.

Figure 5.4 - Repartee and Integrated Web Server

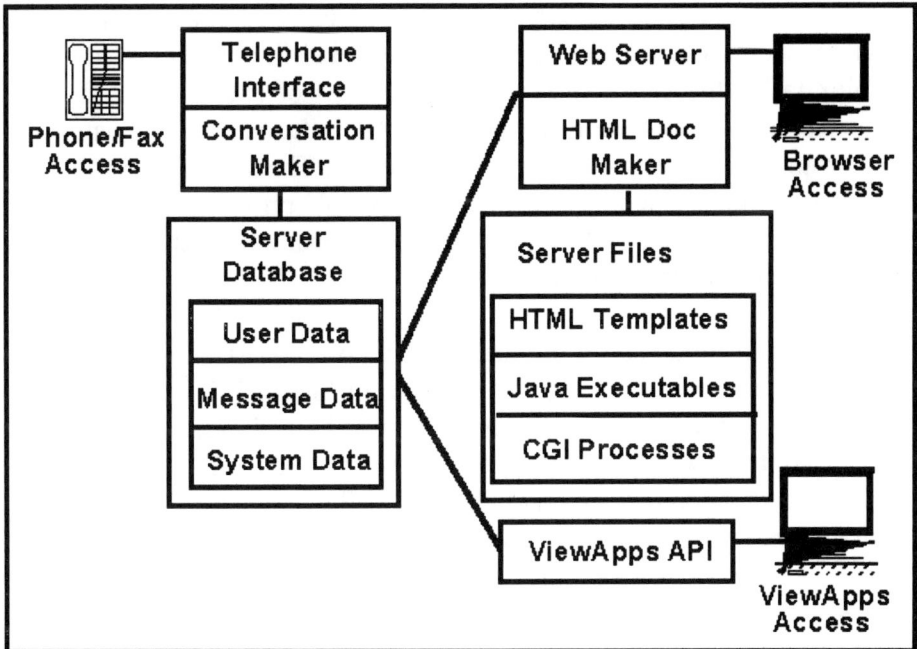

The Web server runs as a separate process within the Repartee server. It has full access to the Repartee server database and specific system functionality, like initiating outbound dialing through the interface to the telephone system. Active Voice created its own Web server rather than adapt a third-party product. This approach provided the best level of integration with TeLANophy while minimizing resource impact on the system as a whole.

The server stores HTML documents and HTML "proto-documents" called templates. Like HTML, templates are plain text documents. Templates are used to make finished HTML documents that contain actual data retrieved from the server on demand. A template contains "tags" that identify database information on a field level. When the template is processed, tags are replaced with actual information.

The resulting document is regulation HTML and compatible with any conventional browser. In addition to tags, templates can contain simple instructions for building lists, testing conditions, and so on. These are interpreted by the Web server. A handful of conventional programming directives yields a surprising range of finished HTML documents. For more complex tasks, the server also stores two forms of executable code. The first, accessible though conventional Web CGI (Common Gateway Interface) protocols, is designed to run on the server. The second form, Java, is executed on client machines, within a compatible browser. The integrated Web server can provide system-level access to Repartee server configuration and administration from any browser.

Another interesting use for an integrated Web server is browser access to voice, fax, and e-mail messages. As shown in Figure 5.5, it is possible to present links to messages using conventional HTML. Users can see or hear message contents with a mouse click. Other expected mailbox functionality is awkward or impossible to provide in HTML. Sun's Java programming language, however, allows custom user interfaces for any compatible browser. Currently, Active Voice has Java prototypes of interface elements for reading and creating text messages, viewing and creating fax messages, and playing and recording voice messages. The results have been encouraging.

Figure 5.5 -- Netscape WebMail for ViewMail

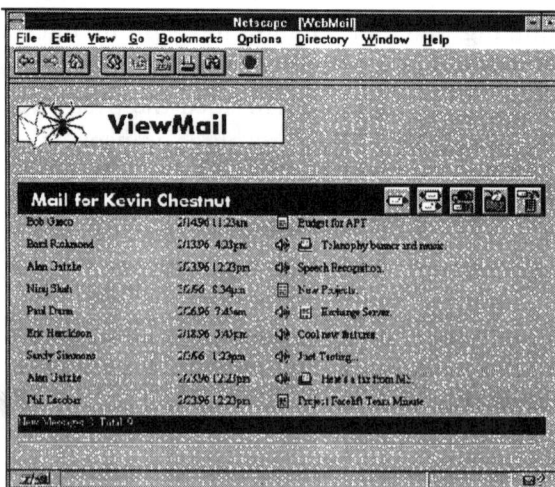

This illustrates that by integrating a Web server with TeLANophy, message information can be served nearly as easily as console information. Voice, fax, and e-mail messages can be unified and presented in a browser rather than in a custom client version of ViewMail. Java makes it possible to provide nearly the same level user interface.

American Network Systems, Inc.

ANSerPhone

ANSerPhone is one of two offerings from American Network Systems, Inc. (Amnet). ANSerPhone includes software (ANSerSoft), and hardware (ANSerCard). It's an integrated system for Internet and computer telephony functions such as Internet voice mail, PIM (Personal Information Manager), auto-answering and message forwarding. ANSerPhone is the first offering from Amnet.

ANSerSoft is the second offering from Amnet. It runs under Win 95 and supports basic e-mail connectivity through SMTP and POP. It also supports connectivity to local phone lines with a TAPI interface. It will work with any TAPI compliant voice I/O device. Both offerings are designed to support three basic functions: Voice mail over Internet, PIM, and auto-answering and message forwarding.

ANSerPhone is a voice mail system that bridges POTS (Plain Old Telephone System) and the Internet. It is targeted to help SOHO (Small Office/Home Office) users be more productive at work by using the personal voice mail system. The ANSerCard hardware is a PC plug-in card that provides the voice I/O. It contains two RJ11 sockets. The connection between PC and ANSerCard and the connection between PC and modem are shown in Figure 5.6. The on-screen dialer PPB will pop up when you lift the phone or when you click the selection of sending voice mail. The dial out number is just one click away.

Figure 5.6 -- ANSerCard Connection to PSTN

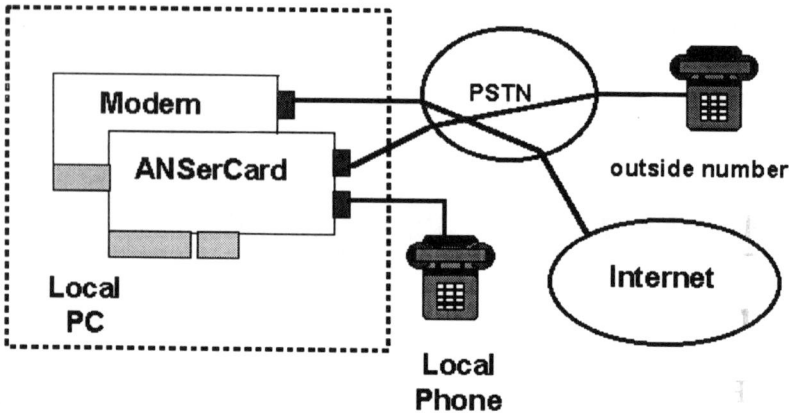

Any outbound call can be scheduled to be automatically dialed at a later time. ANSerPhone guarantees the connection between the phone and the CO line even when the PC is powered off.

ANSerPhone also supports a PIM with caller ID detection. The PIM screen will pop up on the PC screen when you finish dialing or when an incoming call with caller ID information is detected. You are prompted with history information related to the other party. You can also update the record of the history by manually inputting the text description in the note field. You can record the conversation and forward the recorded voice message to anyone with an e-mail address.

ANSerPhone is also an intelligent answering machine. Different messages can be played depending upon the detection of caller ID information. You can retrieve recorded messages from any phone or any Internet terminal with a pass code. It supports a single in-box so all incoming messages can be found in one list. All the incoming messages can be forwarded to either an e-mail address or an outside telephone number. ANSerPhone supports phone-to-phone message forwarding, phone-to-mail message forwarding, mail-to-mail message forwarding and mail-to-phone message forwarding.

The criterion of message forwarding can be either the detected incoming phone number or the incoming mail address.

ANSerSoft Internet Voice Mail

Internet voice mail is the major feature of ANSerPhone. It has an integrated on-screen dialer. This means you can send voice mail as easy as sending Internet e-mail. ANSerPhone will help you select the mail destination with a PPB (Personal Phone Book).

If the receiver of the voice message doesn't have ANSerPhone, there is an option to download the decoding software from Amnet's Web page, so the decoded voice message can be converted to a WAV format and played through any PC audio system.

You have two options of doing voice mail over Internet. You can do voice mail plus e-mail as the first option or voice mail over the Internet only as the second option. Each operation has its own icon and dialog boxes. When you choose the first option, multiple voice messages can be sent through Internet. With the second option, only one voice message which needs to be recorded on the spot can be sent through Internet.

When only voice mail over the Internet is desired, you click onto the *Vmail* icon and either record the voice message or select the mail destination. You then click the SEND button to complete the whole operation. ANSerSoft will prepare the voice mail as any regular e-mail with attachment of a voice file. The software will insert the sentence: *"This is a voice mail"* into the SUBJECT area and it will also insert the help message into the TEXT area of the e-mail to help recipients decode and to listen to the voice message. This takes 5 mouse clicks. When both voice and e-mail is desired, you click the *Vmail* icon. You will need to select the destination mail address and fill the SUBJECT and TEXT areas. ANSerSoft supports multiple attachments, so you can record the voice message or select the voice message from a file. You can also attach multiple files along with the selected voice message. The software supports 50 attachments in one mail message.

ANSerSoft will prepare the mail message after you click the SEND button. It will insert the help message into TEXT area to help the recipient(s) to decode and to listen to the voice message.

Both operations invoke the same 8 kbps voice compression scheme. A voice recording of 2 minutes will result in a voice file of 120 kbytes under this compression scheme. The software uses three different attachment encoding and decoding schemes (MIME-B64, MIME-Quoted Printable and UUENCODE). There is no need to specify the decoding scheme since the software will automatically decide which one to use.

The decompression software is freeware on Amnet's home page. Recipients of message with voice attachments can download the freeware to decode the voice file to WAV. This lets recipients listen to the voice message through any sound card device. Recipients with ANSerPhone or ANSerSoft can decode the voice attachment automatically. A timer is also integrated for voice mail over the Internet. You can schedule the time to send the voice message based on the hour of the day and the time difference between yourself and the receiver.

Figure 5.7 -- PIM Screen

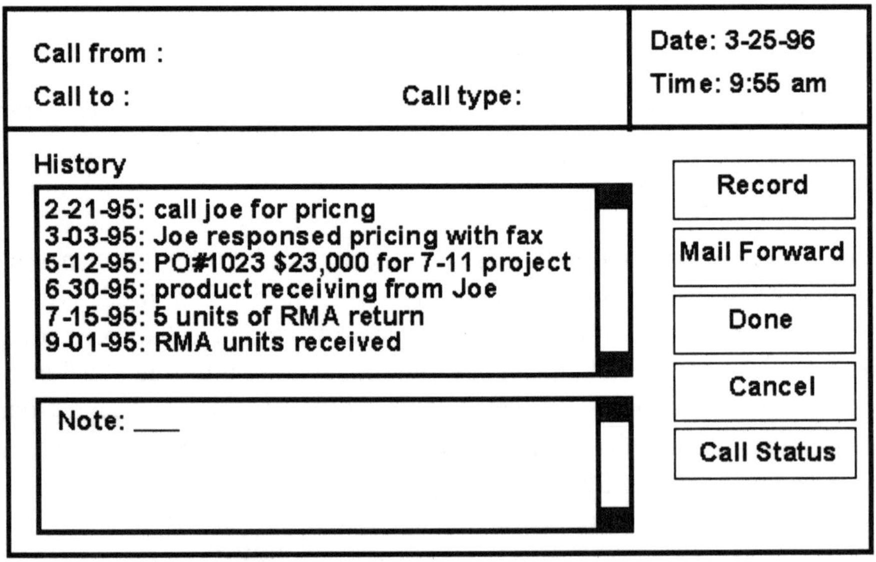

Call from :	Date: 3-25-96
Call to : Call type:	Time: 9:55 am

History

2-21-95: call joe for pricng
3-03-95: Joe responsed pricing with fax
5-12-95: PO#1023 $23,000 for 7-11 project
6-30-95: product receiving from Joe
7-15-95: 5 units of RMA return
9-01-95: RMA units received

Note: ___

Record

Mail Forward

Done

Cancel

Call Status

PIM. Personal Information Manager. ANSerSoft supports a PIM to help maintain contacts as shown in Figure 5.7. The PIM is a database of records you can use while on the phone with a person. The record describes the activity conducted with the other party. The record provides a history of activities with this person. The PIM also lets you record live conversations. You can forward these as part of any regular voice mail. ANSerSoft will invoke the PIM to help you to maintain the records of the contact when the dial-out operation is completed.

PPB. The Personal Phone Book helps users dial out or to send mail. PPB contains the records of contact names, phone numbers, e-mail address, home addresses and special notes. You can divide the phone book into different categories such as friend, client, business or relative. ANSerSoft will pop up PPB each time you pick up the phone or selects phone dial-out from the screen. The PPB provides a selection of the dial-out destination. This can be sorted based on the name or usage of the call. The screen changes over to the PIM after the dialing is completed. PPB is also used to help send mail. ANSerSoft will invoke PPB so you can select the destination mail address. At that time PPB will only show the name and mail address as the main content of the database.

PAB. The Personal Activity Book is another database. It lists all the activities related to each contact including the records of history and individual an InBox. The InBox is the place where incoming messages are stored. It contains incoming voice and mail messages. You can reconcile the history records and incoming messages related to a specific person in the PAB. With it, you can keep track of activities with each contact.

Auto-Answering and Message Forwarding. This is ANSerSoft's software answering machine. It has the ability to answer incoming calls as any upscale answering machine. You configure the number of rings before answering the call, and add the voice as part of the set-up. All incoming messages are stored in the InBox. ANSerSoft sorts all the messages in date and time format.

Incoming mail messages are also stored in InBox. To retrieve the voice messages from InBox, you first configure your own pass code. After entering the pass code, you can pick up and listen to voice messages from outside the office. There are seven phone action templates and three mail action templates that work with caller ID information. You can forward incoming messages to a user-specified destination. All templates will go into the icon of "Action List" as the active actions.

You can make specific voice announcements to someone you anticipate. You can set up multiple actions as long as the caller ID information is not repeated. You can answer phone calls with caller ID detection and forward the incoming message to either a phone number, a pager number or an e-mail address.

You can do similar things without the detection of caller ID. This includes scheduling the time and date for ANSerSoft to forward the messages. It ensures that you will be kept informed with all the incoming messages within a defined period of time. There are three mail action templates for processing incoming mail messages. You can specify a particular mail address or multiple mail addresses so ANSerSoft will match them with incoming mail. Once matched, ANSerSoft can forward the mail message to either another mail address, a phone number (for voice mail only) or a pager number (for voice mail only).

Applied Voice Technology, Inc.

Desktop Message Manager
for Exchange Inbox

Applied Voice Technology, Inc. (AVT) develops, manufactures, markets and supports open systems-based computer-telephony software products and systems. These systems automate call processing and enable a user to manage different types of messages from either a personal computer or telephone. Their product line includes CTI (computer telephone integration) software, basic call answering systems and voice messaging systems.

AVT recently announced major upgrades to its key unified-messaging products, E-Mail Access and Desktop Message Manager, as well as a new unified-messaging module, CallXpress3 Desktop Message Manager for Exchange Inbox. The later is for users of the Microsoft Exchange component of Win 95. The three products allow users of AVT's CallXpress3 systems to retrieve all of their messages -- voice, fax, and e-mail -- from a single user interface and with a single set of commands.

E-Mail Access version 1.1 brings true unified messaging to users who want the ability to retrieve and manage all of their messages (voice, fax, and e-mail) from any touch-tone telephone and within a single call. The new version supports users of the three major groupware e-mail programs, Microsoft Mail, Lotus cc:Mail, and Lotus Notes Mail. Desktop Message Manager version 3.0 and CallXpress3 Desktop for Exchange Inbox are designed for users who want to retrieve and manage multiple types of messages from a personal computer using an intuitive graphical interface.

Telephonic User Interface. TUI is for Unified Messaging. In a CallXpress3 system with voice mail, fax mail, and E-Mail Access, subscribers can make a single call from any touch-tone telephone in the world to: listen to their voice messages; listen to their e-mail messages, which E-Mail Access converts to speech. You can forward any fax or e-mail message to any fax machine. The system provides subscribers a single set of procedures for processing all messages over the telephone. This includes answering, storing, deleting, forwarding to other system subscribers, or changing message ordering or notification options.

Now E Mail Access now supports users of Microsoft Mail, Lotus cc:Mail and Lotus Notes Mail e-mail programs. This provides a telephonic user interface to unified messaging for tens of millions of groupware e-mail users. E-Mail Access also offers two new options in text-to-speech (TTS converts electronic messages to speech). It provides a choice of hardware-based or software-based text-to-speech. The text-to-speech capability in E-Mail Access also supports multiple languages.

GUI for Unified Messaging. With the introduction of E-Mail Access in 1995, AVT said it became the first company to offer true unified messaging over the telephone. They have been careful not to use the word "Internet" or "Intranet" in their literature, but it is clear (what with the announcement of Exchange support) that they are headed for the 'Net. They now offers two options for managing all of their messages from the graphical user interface of a desktop computer: CallXpress3 Desktop Message Manager 3.0 and CallXpress3 Desktop Message Manager for Exchange Inbox. Both options enable subscribers to view, prioritize, review, archive, forward, and store messages of various media types on their PC displays. You can see the length of each message, and use familiar icons such as slider bars and radio buttons to make message handling more efficient.

Desktop Message Manager 3.0. CallXpress3 Desktop Message Manager 3.0 is a major upgrade to the company's LAN-based CallXpress3 Desktop for Windows (unified-messaging product). It includes Caller ID and ANI (automatic number identification) compatibility. Where Caller ID or ANI is available, Desktop Message Manager can display the caller's phone number as part of the message header information. This helps to identify the sender of each voice mail message, and makes it easy to return calls. The Desktop Message Manager for Exchange Inbox is the second most significant upgrade.

Desktop Message Manager for Exchange Inbox. This application is designed for users who want to use the Microsoft Exchange e-mail component of Win 95. Desktop Message Manager for Exchange Inbox lets you view voice, fax and e-mail messages in a single list in the Exchange Inbox. You can manage messages with a single set of commands. You can incorporate voice and fax messaging capabilities with the same e-mail messaging interface. For example, users who are accustomed to the familiar folder system for organizing files can use the same folders for storing voice and fax messages. It will work with either Microsoft Mail or Microsoft Exchange as your message store. AVT claims to be the first manufacturer to offer true unified messaging (meaning access to voice, fax, and e-mail messages from a single list and with a single set of commands) from both graphical and telephonic user interfaces.

To access a message, you double-click on the message indicator in the Inbox. If it's a voice message, the application rings your phone and plays the message. You can listen to the message and then forward, respond, archive or delete the message like you do with touch-tones (but a lot easier). If the message is a fax, you can read it on-screen and then forward it to any fax machine or printer for hard copy. If the message is an e-mail you open it and read it on-screen and reply to it like always. You can voice-annotate any message (voice, fax, or e-mail) when forwarding it to someone else. Annotating it is a simple matter of recording a voice message "in front of" the other message and sending the composite. When your recipient sees the message on his or her screen, icons beside the message indicate what type of message it is. A voice-annotated fax will contain a voice icon and a fax icon. When the recipient opens the message, he can view the fax on his screen and listen to the voice annotation on his telephone.

AVT has 18,000 systems installed worldwide in over 50 countries. That's about 1.5 million users. You can get into a low-end AVT CallServer Model 6 computer telephony hardware platform for $9,900. It has 4 voice ports. If you need 64 ports, try on their CallServer Model 20 for size. It uses a heavy-duty passive backplane with 18 slots, hot swappable power supplies, redundant RAID, a 100Mhz DX4 and 16 Meg 14" monitor. $149,000. Now all you do is add the software. Basic voice mail and automated attendant packages start at $2,700 for 4 ports. Add $7,700 to grow it to 64 ports. If you want to go the unified messaging route, the client-side CallXpress3 Desktop for Windows is $450 for 10 seats -- $3,300 for 100 seats. Generally, unified messaging can be deployed for $100-$250 per user.

Bonzi Software

Voice E-Mail 3.0

Using digital audio, Voice E-Mail 3.0 lets you now send your voice, music, and photos to friends and business contacts all over the world. There's a Voice E-Mail version for WinCIM, America Online, Microsoft Mail/Exchange, Eudora and Netscape.

The Voice E-Mail add-on for Microsoft Mail/Exchange enhances your current versions of Microsoft Mail and Microsoft Exchange. Along with a sound cad and microphone, you can attached voice messages to your Exchange-based transactions. You can send and receive Voice E-Mail exactly like regular e-mail. The only difference is instead of typing your messages, you simply click the "Record" button and speak.

Voice E-Mail requires no editing, spelling, grammar or punctuation, etc. You just record your thoughts as they enter your mind. You can include pictures and photographs in your Voice E-Mail messages (you can see what people look like and hear their voices). Bonzi says this voice messaging capability makes Voice E-Mail more "real," more personal, more intimate and friendly.

Figure 5.8 -- Voice E-Mail for Microsoft Mail/Exchange

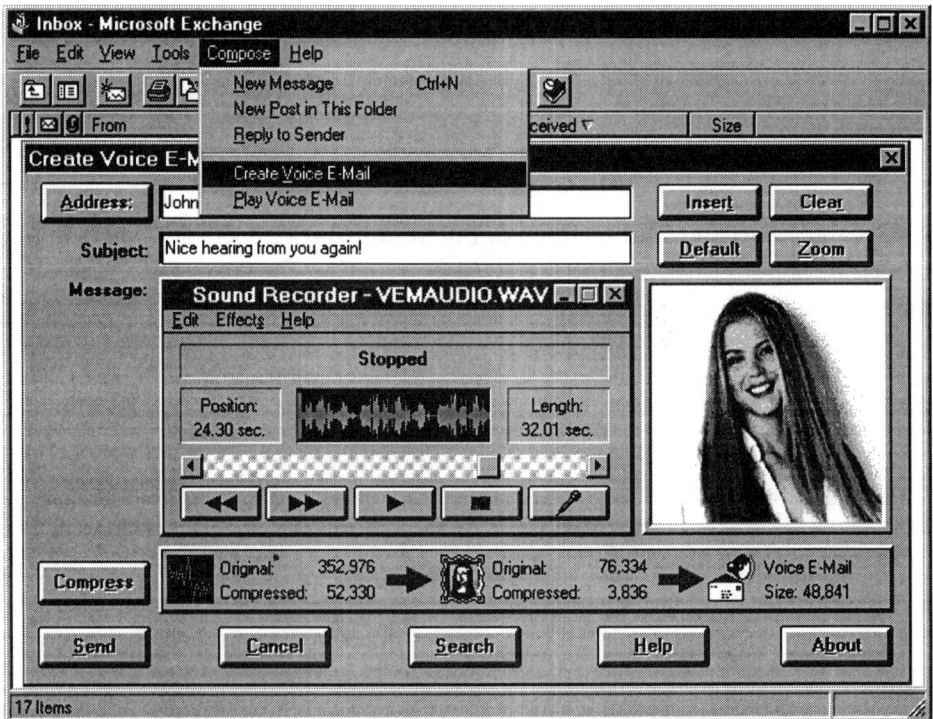

You need a sound card and microphone along with Win 3.x, 95, or Windows NT. The system requires Microsoft Mail or Microsoft Exchange and 4MB of RAM and 2MB of Free Disk Space. Microsoft Exchange users can send and receive Voice E-Mail messages from the Internet, CompuServe, MSN, and Microsoft Mail, and all of the other "Information Services" that Microsoft Exchange supports

The Voice E-Mail add-on for Microsoft Mail/Exchange comes with Online Documentation and Help. The entire package has been compressed into a single file (VMSETUP.EXE), making it easy to download and install. Downloading the Voice E-Mail add-on incurs a onetime user fee of $27.95. After downloading, simply run VMSETUP.EXE from within Windows. www.bonzi.com

CallWare Technologies, Inc.

CallWare Server Clustering

CallWare Technologies, Inc. specializes in call control and unified messaging applications for LANs and WANs. The company has expertise in PBX integration, LAN connectivity and CTI implementations. CallWare is one of the first companies to develop CTI solutions for the Novell Telephony Services (TSAPI) model. The company has extended their LAN model to embrace global interconnection of voice messaging systems. This is called CallWare server clustering.

CallWare server clustering is intended to reduce the cost of exchanging messages between CallWare Voice Mail servers, using the Internet/Intranet as a backbone. Exchanging these messages across the boundaries of a single voice mail server allows organizations to link branch offices and departments together into a voice mail system that may be geographically dispersed or have multiple voice mail servers. This system could belong to a single corporation, a consortium, or a service provider. It allows anyone to access any mail box in the system from any designated location.

This provides the ability to call a local phone number to leave or to retrieve messages from a voice mail system. In the past, the cost associated with this type of interaction between voice mail servers required a phone call along with the usual toll charges and expenses.

Anywhere in the world, where a company maintains a site, CallWare Voice Mail servers are able to connect to each other through the Internet and forward voice messages to other servers in the network. Individuals are able to call local numbers and send voice messages to someone in another country. Figure 5.9 depicts offices in London, New York, San Francisco, and Tokyo. A company is able to broadcast information by forwarding messages originating in London to the Tokyo office.

Figure 5.9 - CallWare Server Clustering Topology

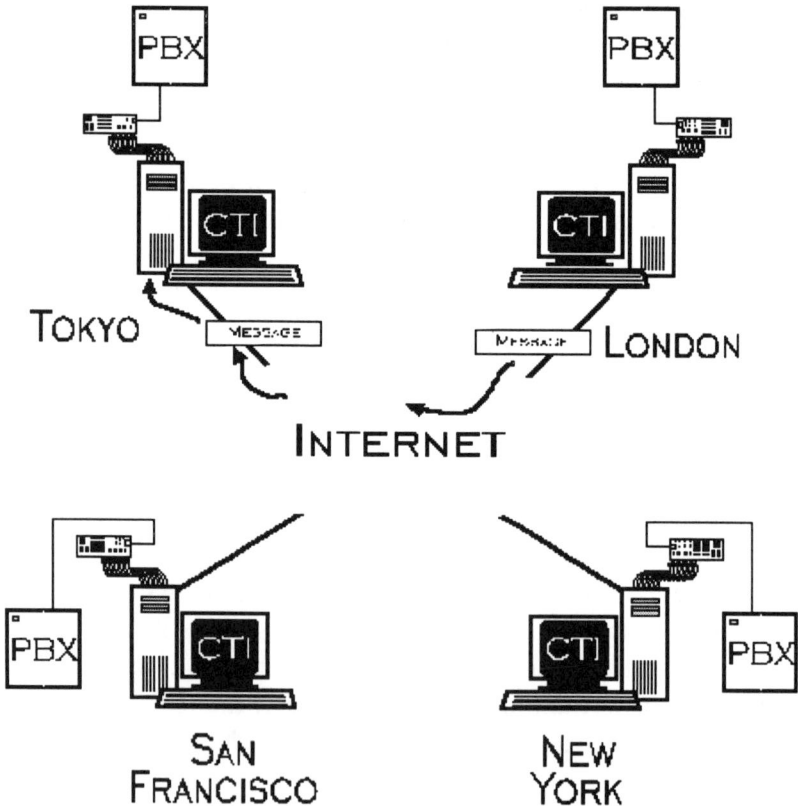

With CallWare server clustering virtual network connections are maintained between individual CallWare servers to coordinate the exchange of messages between servers through the Internet or through an Intranet. The virtual network connection can be a persistent network connection or can be a dial-in connection. The cost savings come even with a dial-in connection, because the dial-in connection is to a local Internet Service Provider (ISP). Persistent network connections occur when an organization has an Intranet, a WAN, or a T-1 type connection to the Internet.

The communication between CallWare servers occurs at a session protocol level and is structured to deliver the necessary information along with the message being forwarded. Server clustering layers are designed to allow protocol independence. Protocol independence allows server clustering to be provided on additional protocols.

Figure 5.10 -- Server Clustering Code Layers

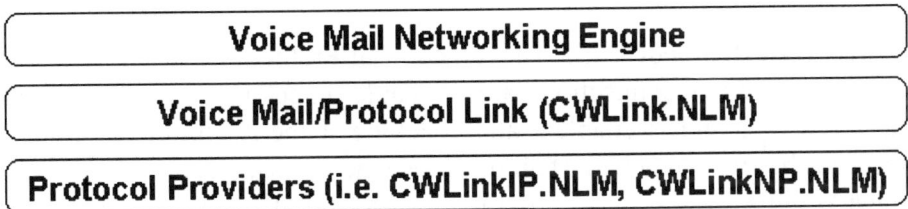

```
┌─────────────────────────────────────────────────────┐
│          Voice Mail Networking Engine                │
└─────────────────────────────────────────────────────┘
┌─────────────────────────────────────────────────────┐
│       Voice Mail/Protocol Link (CWLink.NLM)          │
└─────────────────────────────────────────────────────┘
┌─────────────────────────────────────────────────────┐
│  Protocol Providers (i.e. CWLinkIP.NLM, CWLinkNP.NLM) │
└─────────────────────────────────────────────────────┘
```

The other two server clustering layers are the protocol/voice mail interface provider and the voice mail networking portion. These layers are responsible for directing the messages for forwarding to the network. The voice mail networking engine handles the actual logic for determining whether a message destination is local or remote. When it determines that the message is remote, the engine checks whether the remote site is using AMIS networking or CallWare digital networking. The message is then handed on to the appropriate module for the correct network handler.

The Voice Mail/Protocol Link maintains information as to which sites are configured to use which protocols and then passes the message on to the appropriate protocol for transport to the remote system.

Voice Mail Networking Engine. The voice mail network engine consists of the logic to manage remote site information and exchange the proper messages with the remote site. This module is adapted from the AMIS Analog specification. The point at which the AMIS logic picks up a phone line to connect to the remote site is the point at which the server clustering code branches to use the network to communicate the information. The engine makes a function call to the Voice Mail/Protocol Link layer, submitting the source box number, the destination box number, the message type, and the local path to the message.

The voice mail networking engine will also register a callback function to receive notification of incoming messages from the network. This will allow messages coming in from the network to be integrated into the message processing already in place in the voice mail networking engine.

Voice Mail/Protocol Link. The Voice Mail/Protocol Link is responsible for determining if connections are available, checking if the destination mailbox exists and is enabled, and checking if the maximum number of messages has been reached. If all of these conditions are favorable, then the Voice Mail/Protocol Link will perform the transfer of the message and return success after receipt is acknowledged. In verifying and sending information between the two conversation endpoints, this layer relies on the well-defined interface provided by any of the Protocol Provider layer modules. This layer provides a well-defined interface for the voice mail networking layer to call: CWSendNetworkMessage. For the protocol providers, this layer maintains the routing information necessary to coordinate the destination to the correct protocol. This information is provided through configuration and registration of the protocol provider module with the Voice Mail Protocol Interface. This layer also provides three exported function calls to the protocol providers: VerifyMailbox, VerifyMailboxStatus, and ReceiveMessage.

Protocol Providers. The protocol providers will register with the Voice Mail/Protocol Link layer and provide a well-defined set of function calls for the interface layer to call in order to perform the various necessary operations. These functions are encompassed by the following functions. These functions also contain specific logical steps.

ConnectToRemoteSite. Ping Connection, Create Connection and Negotiate Connection.

SendToRemoteSite. Verify Mailbox and Status, Send Message and Verify Successful Delivery.

DisconnectFromRemoteSite. Terminate connection.

Server Clustering Module Architecture

Figure 5.11 -- Server Clustering Architecture

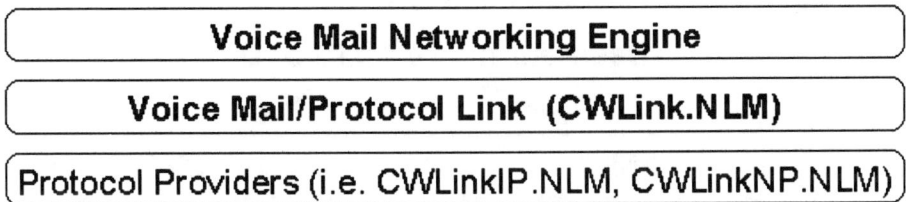

> **Voice Mail Networking Engine**
>
> **Voice Mail/Protocol Link (CWLink.NLM)**
>
> **Protocol Providers (i.e. CWLinkIP.NLM, CWLinkNP.NLM)**

The Server Clustering Architecture consists of three layers, the voice mail networking engine, the voice mail/communication protocol interface and the protocol providers. The first layer is built as part of the CallWare engine. The second layer consists of the CWLINK.NLM. The third layer consists of individual modules that provide the communications protocol control to transport messages across diverse networks and using various standards.

Voice Mail Networking Engine. The Voice Mail Networking Engine is a part of the CallWare Voice Mail Engine. This part of the server clustering architecture consistently handles messages for local, AMIS network, and CW digital network destinations.

When the final location is determined, this module executes the appropriate code for local, AMIS network, or CW digital network transport. When the message goes to a remote site being networked with digital networking, the engine will make the function call to CWLink. When a message is received by a protocol provider, it will pass the information to the Link Layer by calling ReceiveMessage, which calls CWNetworkMessageReceived, provided in the engine. This is illustrated in figure 5.12. This function allows new messages to be integrated into the new message handling logic of the CW voice mail engine.

Figure 5.12 -- Sending a Network Message

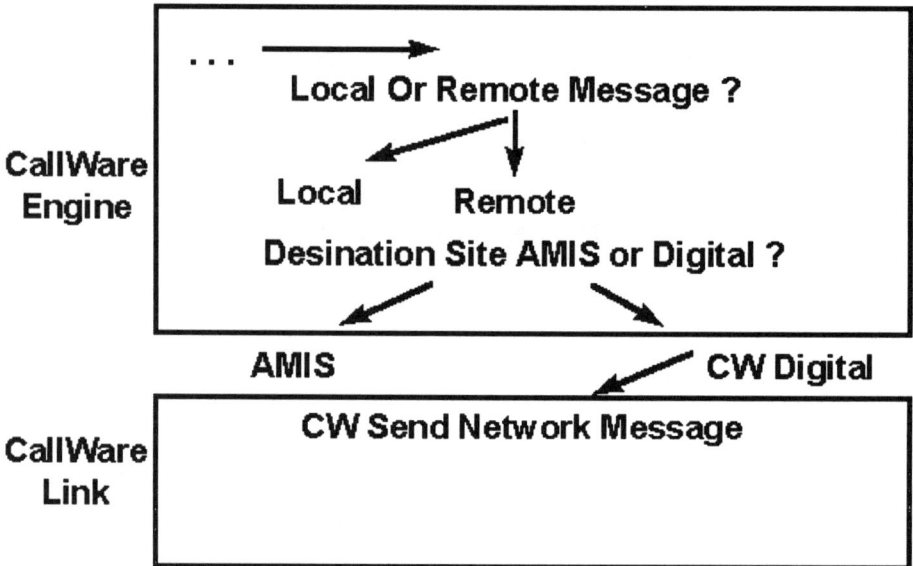

Voice Mail/Protocol Link. The voice mail/protocol link is designed as an abstraction layer to allow the engine a simple interface to multiple protocols. This layer provides a link between the engine layer and the protocol providers through a well-defined application programming interface.

One function is defined for the voice mail engine to communicate to the link layer and several functions are provided by the engine for this interface to communicate to. The controlling logic for the link layer begins on startup. If the CallWare Voice Mail Engine is in place, than the link layer loads with the load dependencies fulfilled.

After the link layer is in place, the protocol providers are loaded and register with the link layer. The protocol provider uses the addressType as a module identifier and registers its entry points for the well known functions. A message is passed through the link layer to the appropriate protocol provider for ConnectToRemoteSite, SendToRemoteSite, and DisconnectFromRemoteSite.

For the protocol providers, the link layer provides functions necessary to communicate information from end-point to end-point of the conversation. These functions include calls such as VerifyMailboxAndStatus and Link-ReceiveMessage. These functions allow a local system to query a remote system before transporting the voice mail message. The data returned by the verify function calls is small enough to cause very little overhead on the connection. When the voice mailbox status is successfully confirmed, then a message can be transported with increased confidence and reliability and decreased performance costs.

Protocol Providers. The protocol providers register with the voice mail/provider link layer. This registration allows multiple network protocols and standards for communicating messages between voice mail servers to function simultaneously. Several well-defined interfaces are provided to the link layer. The protocol provider receives commands or information through these interfaces from the link layer. For each different protocol, the protocol provider translates the command and information provided into the protocol-specific steps necessary to complete the command. Once the command is completed, the protocol provider will return success or failure status to the link layer (which, in turn, is passed on to the engine). When the protocol provider registers with the link layer, it provides two variables. The first variable is the addressType.

This will be used as the module identifier when a message is to be sent through the network. The other variable is a pointer to a structure of function pointers. This structure of function pointers provides the link layer the entry points for each of the required well-defined function calls the link layer uses to transport the message through the network.

All protocols must listen for connections after registering with the link layer. Additionally, all protocol providers must listen for messages once a connection is established.

Ping Connection. Ping Connection verifies that the physical link between sites is available and in a valid state. If the physical connection is available and in working condition, this function returns success. If the physical connection is not available, then the function needs to return the most explicit error code possible for the protocol and NetWare server configuration.

All protocol providers need to listen for connections or use an underlying service to listen for a connection. When the link layer in the local node calls ConnectToRemoteSite, the protocol provider will check for an existing connection. If an existing connection is already in place, that connection can be used and the function would return successfully. If a connection does not exist, the protocol provider is responsible for setting one up. All protocol providers must provide a connection-oriented, reliable delivery virtual connection with handshaking and error checking.

Send Message. The Send Message verb actually moves the message from one network site to another. The protocol will behave much like a message- or stream-based mechanism for the link layer to use for sending the CallWare messages. Individual protocol providers are responsible for scattering/gathering the total data from and into the full file. This is transparent to the link and engine layers.

Verify Successful Delivery. The Message Delivered verb is sent to the remote site on completion of the message moving from one network site to another.

This verb requests acknowledgment from the receiving end to verify that the message successfully arrived at the destination. This verb is only sent for box messages.

Terminate Connection. This function is provided for connection clean up. Best use of this function occurs in error conditions and at shutdown of the networking modules. For the NCP Extension implementation, this verb consists of a call to LogoutFromFileServer and a release of any resources for that connection.

Error Conditions and Error Handling. Several states of error conditions can occur in moving message across the Internet or an Intranet. These states occur most often due to network link status changes and to communication endpoint failures . If an error occurs during or after the file is transported to the remote partner but before successful delivery is acknowledged, the protocol provider must handle the error from two levels.

Centigram Communications Corporation

OneView Web

Centigram solves communication problems by integrating voice, data and facsimile on its Series 6 communications server platform, and by providing access to this multimedia information through a telephone or PC. The Series 6 platform is based on industry- standard hardware and software. The products are used in computer telephony integration (CTI) applications, remote access and one-number services. Centigram also licenses TruVoice, its patented text-to-speech software.

OneView integrates messages on desktop PCs, giving users a simple point-and-click interface for full control of their business communications, including voice, fax and e-mail messages. This allows users to sort through messages quickly and respond to the most important ones first.

With OneView Remote, you can create, play, answer and forward voice, fax and compound messages from a PC regardless of your location. In addition, one-number services allow access through a single telephone number to your office, home or cellular telephone, as well as to voice mail, pagers and facsimile machines. Figure 5.13 shows how all messages are unified in a single InBox.

Figure 5.13 -- OneView Remote InBox

Caller	Subject	Mailbox#	Date/Time	Length
Outside Caller	Computer Telephony Information		10/01/1995 10:23:17	63.3 s
✓ ☎ Outside Caller	Networking Trade Show Info		02/28/1995 16:38:40	55.4 s
✓ 🖹 Unknown	Supercomm Information	5124	02/24/1995 10:45:53	·
☎ Unknown	Supercomm Information	5124	02/24/1995 10:45:53	7.6 s
☎ Thibault,Rene	-	5500	02/24/1995 10:08:08	31.4 s
☎ Maguire,Joy	-	3569	02/23/1995 13:46:23	79.6 s
✓ ☎ Outside Caller	boo		02/23/1995 00:13:58	10.0 s
✓ 🖹 Ferguson, Pam	UMIX	3722	02/21/1995 09:42:22	·
☎ Ferguson, Pam	UMIX	3722	02/21/1995 09:42:22	32.2 s
☎ McMahon,Catherin·	-	3273	02/21/1995 09:30:14	41.3 s
☎ Ferguson, Pam	-	3722	02/21/1995 09:21:54	124.8 s
☎ Cuggino,Peggy	-	3646	02/19/1995 07:19:20	113.5 s
☎ Ferguson, Pam	-	3722	02/17/1995 13:57:46	129.1 s
✓ 🖹 Ferguson, Pam	OneView PR Opportunity	3722	02/18/1995 09:56:11	·
☎ Ferguson, Pam	OneView PR Opportunity	3722	02/18/1995 09:56:11	9.2 s
☎ Weinstein,Dave	-	3509	02/17/1995 19:08:24	8.5 s
☎ Outside Caller			02/17/1995 12:25:10	46.3 s
✓ ☎ Outside Caller	smile		02/02/1995 23:50:32	22.0 s

Total: 21   Urgent: 0   Unread: 0

OneView   Press F1 at any time to get help.   15:39:35

OneView Web is an add-on to the OneView Remote Windows-based messaging product. With it, you can receive your voice and fax messages via the Internet from a Netscape Navigator browser.

OneView Web allows users to see the voice and fax message InBox, open compound messages, and play voice and view fax messages, all through the World Wide Web or private Intranet. Centigram is using a Web host and a Common Gateway Interface (CGI) script to access the Series 6 via the Centigram Messaging Application Program Interface (CMAPI). CMAPI is the same API used to complement OneView.

Series 6 is the name of Centigram's hardware platform. It offers fault tolerance and redundant message storage. Based on Centigram's modular expandable system architecture (MESA), Series can handle up to 240 ports, 2,880 hours of message storage, and more than 300,000 mailboxes in a single system. By adding TCP/IP Ethernet connectivity to Centigram's MESA-Net (digital networking product), customers can now use their existing wide-area networks to digitally exchange messages among as many as 1,500 system nodes at speeds up to 10 megabits per second. The single-platform design provides up to 12 prompt and greeting languages per system for international users. Series 6 uses industry standards, including the Multi-Vendor Industry Protocol (MVIP) bus and Signaling System 7 (SS7)-based protocols. Series 6 is based on Intel Pentium processors and digital signal processor (DSP) technology.

Centigram is also developing a Web optimized, client-server implementation of their TruVoice text-to-speech software. The client part will be an integrated Netscape Plugin or helper app for Netscape Web browsers. The Server will run as CGI server, invoked by the Netscape (and other) Web server.

Traditionally, speech synthesis ran as one process on a single computer. This resulted in a big, CPU- intensive program. The program would convert compact text input into a big output stream of PCM data. For usage on the Web this is far from ideal. If you put the text-to-speech conversion on the Web server you bog down the server with the large PCM stream. If you put the text-to-speech on the client it will not work on slower machines. The client side software will be very large (a pain when downloading). You would need different software for each language.

TruVoice Brain/Mouth Architecture

The new TruVoice Brain/Mouth architecture provides a solution for theses. In this architecture the TruVoice TTS engine is divided into two parts. The "brain" contains the email reading, text normalization rules, letter to sound, allophonic and prosodic rules. The output of this "brain" module is a compact stream of parameters. This stream of parameters is sent over the Net to the client part (part two). The stream consists mainly of the vocal tract. We call this part the "mouth" and it runs on the client side. Here the vocal tract produces the actual PCM output stream which is fed to the sound card driver.

By making this division you get evenly split CPU usage is between client and server. The data stream that is sent over the Net is very small. All improvements in speech quality will be in the Server-side code, The vocal tract almost never changes, so people do not have to download a updated "mouth" every few months. The "mouth" is a relatively small program (less than 100 Kbytes) The "mouth" can handle all languages, only the server needs a different program for each language. The "mouth" can be given away, while the "brain" can be sold to the operators of the Web servers. The user can on the client side change the voice, pitch etc.

By having the "brain" add sentence boundary information to the data stream, the "mouth" can process the data sentence by sentence. This means that if the data transmission rate on your Internet connection is very irregular, the mouth can stop speaking at a sentence boundary and wait until the next complete sentence has arrived before starting to speak again. This result in a much higher intelligibility in bad conditions. Also the "FastForward" and "Rewind" functions of the mouth can jump to the beginning of the next or previous sentence, which is much more natural. By having the brain add phonemes to the data stream, the mouth is able to implement a synchronized animation of the lip movements. Or an API can be provided for JAVA programs to implement the animation. The Brain will initially be implemented as an CGI server on the WIN32 and SUN Solaris platforms. The Mouth will first be implemented as a Netscape Plugin. It will have a tape-recorder like interface and an animated picture of a mouth that will move synchronously with the spoken text.

Text to Speech can be used on the Web in a variety of ways. It can be used for error messages, tips and hints. This is useful if you're filling out forms on a Web page and need help. It can be used as addition to a standard Web page asynchronous alert. This to get people's attention while they are doing something else. You can use it to develop interactive educational programs or add extra dimension to a VRML world, games and avatars.

Digital Sound Corporation

InfoMail

Digital Sound Corporation (DSC) specializes in high-performance messaging solutions for network service providers. The company introduced its first voice messaging platform in 1985. InfoMail is designed as an "information messaging" application capable of supporting multiple message formats (voice, fax and text). DSC's mission is to deliver powerful, easy-to-use messaging solutions by providing the industry's best unified mailbox.

Access to the mailbox can be achieved with a variety of end-user devices over multiple network transports (PSTN, Internet, wireless, etc.). Today, Digital Sound has millions of mailboxes deployed in the networks of telecommunications service providers and large corporations, universities, and other organizations. Digital Sound's unified messaging server provides a single mailbox for all message types, binary files (and eventually video). The mailbox can be accessed from a variety of terminal devices via the PSTN, and from PCs via the Internet or a TCP/IP LAN. This approach is founded on the premise that unified messaging solutions should be media independent, terminal independent, and network independent. You can communicate any time, any where and across any network.

Voice and Fax Integration. Digital Sound launched its first unified messaging product in 1992 by adding fax capability to InfoMail. Subscribers can receive fax messages into the same mailbox that they use for voice messages.

In addition, this capability in InfoMail allows a caller to attach voice comments to a fax message—a "voice cover sheet"—which appears to the user as a single, mixed-media message.

Integrated PC Access to Fax Mailbox. The next step in unified messaging came in 1994 and enabled PC access to the InfoMail mailbox. In the voice processing industry, Digital Sound pioneered the approach of inter-operating with third-party client applications rather than requiring a custom application that works only with voice mail. They claim to be the first to deliver a commercial service integrated with third-party PC software.

The voice/fax mailbox is bundled with Delrina WinFax client software and is sold under the name "Delrina Fax MailBox." The Delrina Fax MailBox enables users of WinFax PRO fax software running on desktop and portable PCs to retrieve fax messages from their personal fax mailboxes residing on a Digital Sound server in the public switched telephone network. Users can download faxes to their PCs wherever and whenever they choose from any standard analog telephone line by simply clicking on the "retrieve from mailbox" command in WinFax PRO.

Integration with Microsoft Exchange Client. Digital Sound's third major step in unified messaging is InfoMail Express 2.0. First demonstrated as part of Microsoft's keynote address at the Computer Telephony Expo 1995, this application provides a single mailbox for voice messages, fax, and SMTP e-mail, and integrates with the Microsoft Exchange MAPI client application connected over the PSTN as pictured in Figure 5.14.

In this implementation, the user will see a mailbox icon on the PC screen after dialing into the server. Clicking on the mailbox icon will display the contents of the in-box (voice messages, fax and e-mail). When the user selects fax and e-mail for review, the messages are downloaded to the PC and displayed on screen. Clicking on a voice message causes the application to instruct the VoiceView modem to switch to "voice mode" and play the message in real-time.

Figure 5.14 -- InfoMail Express Mailbox with Exchange

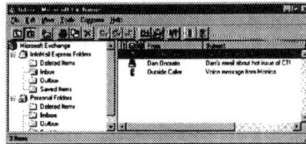

InfoMail Integration with Web Browsers

InfoMail Express 2.0 is designed for mixed-media messaging to PSTN-connected PCs. But this client-server solution will also work over a variety of network transport technologies, including ISDN and TCP/IP Ethernet. At CT Expo 1996, Digital Sound demonstrated Internet access to InfoMail, allowing visual access to voice, fax and e-mail messages from a Web browser on a PC. A typical screen is illustrated in Figure 5.15.

Figure 5.15 -- InfoMail Express from Web Browser

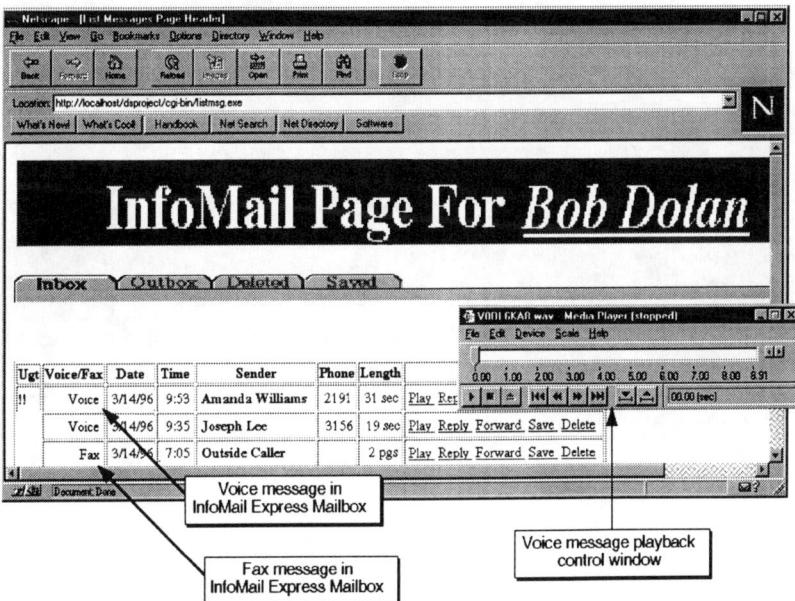

Voice message in
InfoMail Express Mailbox

Fax message in
InfoMail Express Mailbox

Voice message playback
control window

As with the Microsoft Exchange implementation, the Web browser presents a single list of messages on screen for the user. Fax and e-mail messages are displayed on screen when selected by the user. Voice messages are converted to WAV files and played out over the PC speaker. One of the benefits of this approach is that the client side of the solution is "platform independent" — Web browsers operate on PCs running Windows, Unix, and OS/2, and on Macintoshes.

While Digital Sound has focused on delivering unified messaging first across the traditional telephone network, they are extending their solutions to other networks (Internet, wireless, and cable). This is due to a user trend in acquiring new types of two-way client applications and devices (browsers, personal communicators, and set-top boxes). Digital Sound envisions many "points of integration" as client, network, and server vendors work together to develop innovative solutions to address particular end-user needs.

GTE CO-Based Unified Messaging

Figure 5.16 -- GTE FlexMail from Digital Sound

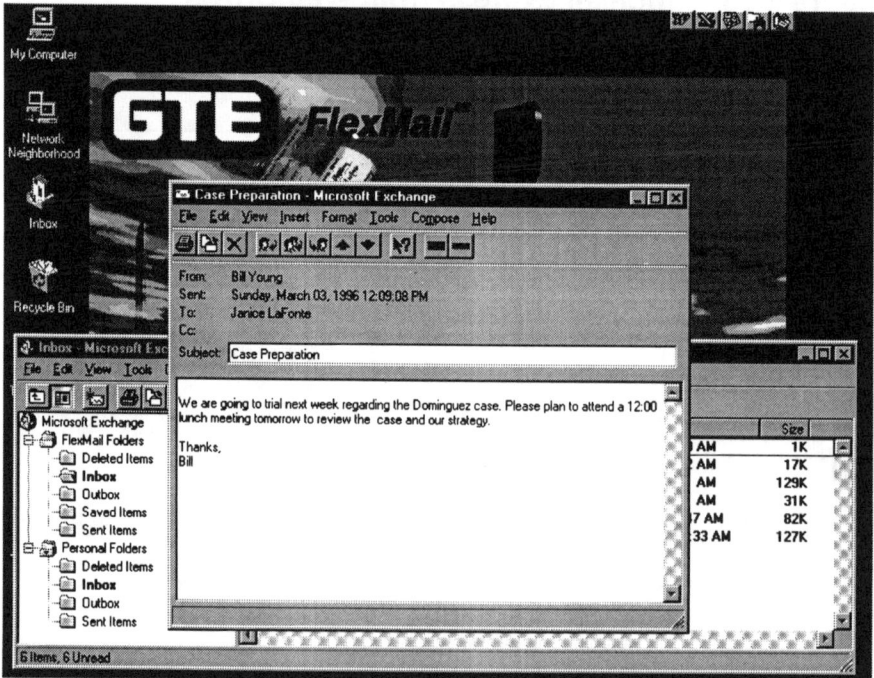

Digital Sound continues to seek partnerships with hardware and software developers and service providers across computing, telecommunications, and broadcasting industries. One notable partnership is with GTE. This one is brilliant. Stick a server in a telephone company central office. Have the phone company sell voice mail, fax mail and Internet email to home and small businesses. The customer will need a VoiceView compatible modem, with handset to listen to the voice mail, Win 95 and Exchange Server client software.

Figure 5.17 -- GTE FlexMail FaxViewer

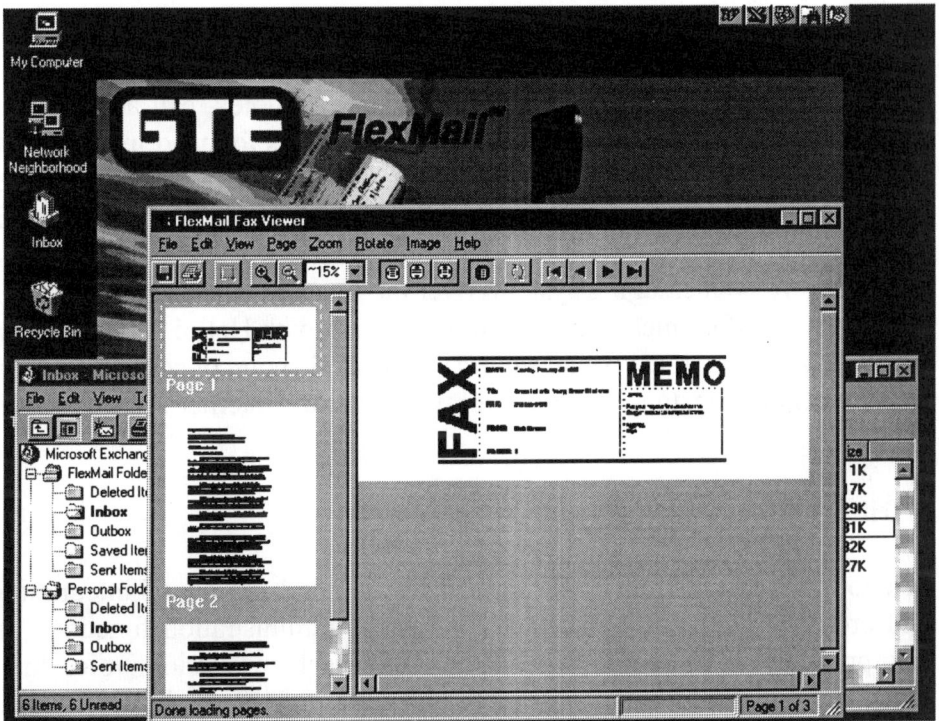

Digital Sound wrote a service provider under MAPI, which connects to the GTE central office unified messaging server. It's clearly a lot nicer way of playing your voice mail messages. You hear the sound via your VoiceView modem.

To get in, a GTE phone customer simply dials a local number—the local voice mail server and bingo, you can see the results in Figure 5.16. This your typical Win95 Exchange Inbox. You can see voice, fax and email messages. Click on a fax message and you get the screen shown in figure 5.17. Note the thumbnails on the left and the pages on the right.

Enhanced Systems, Inc.

Hello! NT and @once

Enhanced Systems, Inc. (ESI) designs, manufactures, and markets PC-based telecommunications products. This includes interactive voice response, voice messaging, automated attendant, Audiotex, call accounting, text messaging and development languages. ESI was founded in 1986 and is a subsidiary of Vodavi Technology, Inc. Two products figure into the company's Internet messaging scheme. The fist is *Hello! NT*, a voice messaging system with traditional capabilities. It can also share messages with other voice messaging systems over the Internet. The second product, *@once*, is a unified messaging server that works with Hello! NT and other messaging servers. It to provides users with a single point of access, through a single connection, to messages of all types over the Internet's World Wide Web.

Hello! NT

Hello! NT supports four to 48 ports, offers in-band and digital integration and provides a graphical interface for system administration functions. It also provides fax store-and forward, text-to-speech conversion, voice activated dialing, multi-lingual prompts and custom IVR applications. The system:

1) Interfaces with other Hello! NT systems over any TCP/IP transport, including the Internet, to create an "intranetwork" of voice mail systems.

2) Operates with @once, ESI's unified messaging server. It lets mailbox owners retrieve e-mail, faxes, voice mail, and pages over the Internet. This is done within a single connection, using a standard Web browser.

Linking Hello! NT with Other Hello! NT Systems. Organizations with multiple locations typically have a separate voice mail system at each site. The customers, suppliers, and other organizations with whom we routinely communicate also have separate voice mail systems. In a world where voice mail has become the predominant message medium, this "separateness" of standalone systems has an inherent shortcoming related to the "closed" nature of these systems.

If a user in a Los Angeles subsidiary receives a voice message from a caller in a New York headquarters, there is typically no way to press a "reply" key and simply respond -- the receiver of the message must instead place a long distance call to the originator (often to simply receive that user's voice mailbox). Similarly, if someone in the New York office receives a message from a customer that needs to be relayed to the Los Angeles office, there is typically no way to forward it; instead, the original receiver must jot down the message, contact the person who needs to receive it, and relay it in a separate communication. And originating a voice message to someone at another system always requires a real-time connection. When these scenarios combine for multiple users within an organization, the result is an increase in communications costs and a limit to the usefulness of voice mail.

Currently, the most popular methods for linking two systems to accomplish system-to-system voice mail are AMIS and digital AMIS, both of which require inefficient transfer of entire messages over landline carriers. Long-distance charges drives up these communications costs. Various manufac-turers have also implemented proprietary methods, which have the disadvantage of locking a customer into a specific brand of voice messaging system or phone system at each site. Hello! NT instead uses ESI's Unified Messaging Protocol (UMP).

It is a set of extensions to existing Internet e-mail protocols developed by ESI. UMP makes possible the transport of voice messages over TCP/IP links, most notably the Internet, for efficient, low-cost information exchange amongst worldwide systems.

This linking of Hello! NT systems enables the sharing of voice messaging resources within Intranet systems. For example, a New York office can share mailbox setups with offices in Los Angeles, Hong Kong, London, or anywhere else in the world that another Hello! NT system is in operation. When a user needs to create a new message, reply to a message, or forward a message to any user on another system, that user simply conducts voice messaging as usual. The message is recorded locally, then sent transparently to the remote Hello! NT system over the Internet, with no quality loss. Transmission costs are limited to each location's costs for dedicated or dial-up Internet access. In a world where long-distance calls typically end up reaching a voice mailbox anyway, the savings represented by store-and-forward transmissions that eliminate long-distance carriers produces superior flexibility at a fraction of the cost.

Because Hello! NT supports fax messaging (with faxes sent to any user's local mailbox for store-and-forward), this capability offers low-cost point-to-point fax transmissions between two Hello! NT systems (the same as voice mail). A fax can be delivered to another Hello! NT system anywhere by sending the fax to the locally established mailbox. It is then forwarded over the Internet to the remote mailbox.

Hello! NT also supports scripting via Enhanced Systems' high-level Application Development Language (ADL). ADL uses simple commands to orchestrate communications, file handling and telephone operations. ADL can be used to write scripts for caller dialogs, file and databases manipulation and host communications. Once written, scripts are compiled into reusable modules. ADL can be used to extract information from a host system and fax it to a server over the Internet. Customers could select the information to be retrieved and faxed by selecting from voice menus during a telephone call, or by making selections from a Web page.

Hello NT! and @once. With Hello! NT's Internet capabilities, any organization can link it with other Hello! NT systems to create an "intranetwork" for global voice messaging and fax store-and-forward. This allows the interconnection of phone systems of strategic partners, customers, suppliers, and anyone else who would benefit from the ability to move voice and fax messages not only within a central site.

Unified Messaging Over the Internet. Hello! NT works with ESI's @once unified messaging server. @once gives users the ability to access e-mail, voice mail, fax messages, and pages, all in a single session and with a visual user interface (standard Web browser). These activities can be conducted from anywhere in the world. @once is a Win NT-based server. It functions as the connection source for servers of various types.

From the central-site perspective, @once provides for unified messaging by managing message resources through a single network connection. @once uses the UMP extensions to SMTP and POP3 protocols to communicate with complementary messaging systems; all servers communicate with @once, not with each other. @once keeps track of each user's messages by type and location.

Complementary servers must support UMP to communicate with @once, or must be connected through a gateway built into @once. Voice mail and fax store-and-forward are provided by @once with its native UMP support. E-mail is provided by a Microsoft Mail gateway built into @once. ESI is currently working with third-party server manufacturers. Additional gateways, such as cc:Mail, will be added to @once in the future.

UMP can be implemented on any operating system. It has been placed in the public domain by ESI. UMP will also allow those third-party products to exchange messages with any other UMP-compliant system, both locally and over the Internet, independent of any ESI-specific products. For a copy of ESI's white paper, "Extending Existing Protocols to Enable Unified Messaging over the Internet," go to www.esisys.com.

From the client (end user) perspective, @once provides for unified messaging. It gives you a single connection and visual interface for the sending,
receiving and management of all message types. You connect to @once via
the host organization's home page. Once you connect and enter the required
mailbox number and password, @once handles connections to the other
clients. It provides listings (grouped by type) of all messages. With @once,
you can manage messages in a single session, from anywhere, through a
visual user interface. This is illustrated in Figure5.18.

Figure 5.18 -- @once Web Browser Interface

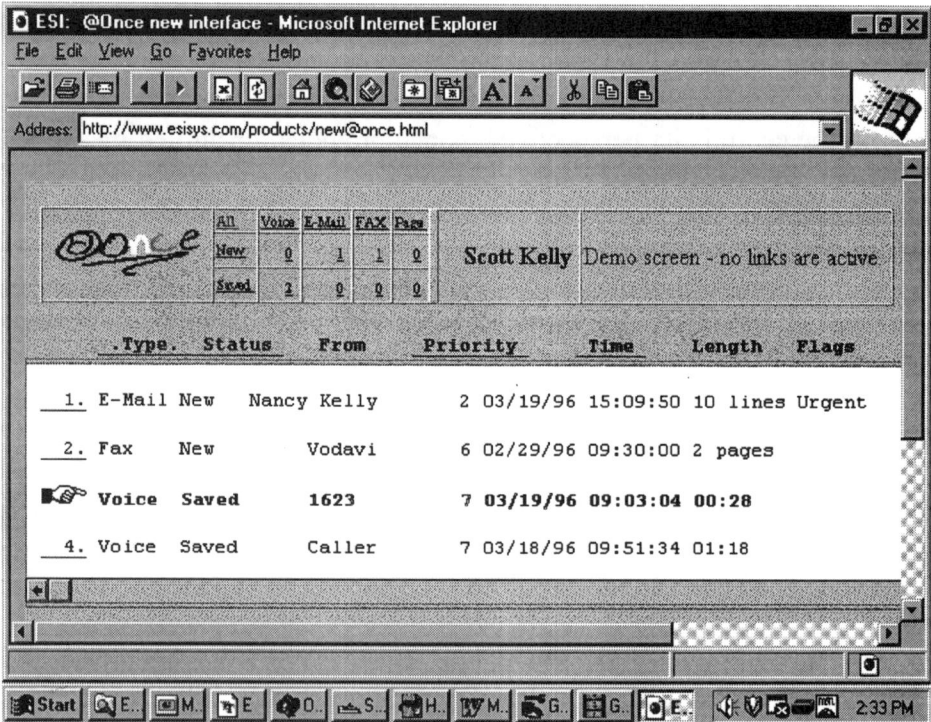

Clicking on a voice message causes the message to be played immediately
over the PC's WAV file player. Clicking on a fax message displays the fax
image on a standard viewer, and clicking on an e-mail message displays the
e-mail using the Web browser's e-mail reader.

Controls at the bottom of the screen provide for message management. Remote and mobile users can log onto the corporate Web server and retrieve messages of any type. This at the cost of a local Internet connection. A user on business in Europe, for example, can retrieve voice messages, fax messages, and e-mail in a single connection, without negotiating through expensive, sometimes unreliable land-line service. The same unified messaging benefits extend to telecommuting professionals and those who perform after-hours work from a home office. Rather than spending time checking with multiple message services, a single connection provides access to all messages, with management through a single user interface. An organization can set up "guest mailboxes" for partners, suppliers, and key customers, and provide access to those users through the Web. You can standardize on any Web browser as the front end to any Intranet (including intra-LAN) messaging infrastructure. Users at the central site will have a single user interface for the management of all messages (versus multiple PC applications plus a telephone).

Future Plans for Hello! NT and @once. ESI is planning on real-time, extension-to-extension connections over the Internet. This will allow the connection of two extensions for conversation, using the Internet as the long-distance carrier. This will require the development of a new transport, like Real Audio, over TCP/IP. Database collaboration between servers is another project. This will identify extension availability as a means to optimize resources (prior to initiating a real-time connection). ESI is also working on the ability to use a telephone (not just a Web browser) to retrieve messages of all types. The company plans to support OCR for faxes and text-to-speech conversion for converted faxes and e-mail messages.

IBM

DirectTalkMail

DirectTalkMail is IBM's voice-messaging product. It's the first to support the new international standard (ISO/IEC 13714) for user interface to voice mail systems and also the first to provide access to your voice-mail messages from your favorite Web browser.

Voice mail users can now listen to, delete and save their messages directly from their computers using Web browsers such as those in the IBM Internet Connection family. With the DirectTalkMail software, it's possible to check phone messages from either a computer or phone providing users with more choice and flexibility. You can be on a phone call while another call comes in, then check to see who has called without interrupting the current call.

While traveling, business executives can use the one available phone line in a hotel room to connect their computers, then check for e-mail and phone messages at the same time. If you who work at your computer most of the day you may find it more convenient to check phone messages from the computer screen. Ditto if you don't want to tie up the phone line for incoming calls, because you can check for new messages directly on the computer screen.

you can try IBM DirectTalkMail software at no cost. Instructions for the trial are on www.hursley.ibm.com/dtmail. As part of the trial, you will be required to make a call and leave a message at the IBM laboratory in the U.K. where the software was developed. The length of your call depends on the length of your message. Within minutes, you can retrieve your own message from the World Wide Web and hear your own voice without having to pick up the telephone.

DirectTalkMail, can send messages to users of another voice messaging system, provided that it supports the Audio Messaging Interface Standard (AMIS).

Voice Messages Access From a Web Browser. Type in your extension number and password, select the sound format and press the DirectTalkMail button. If your personal computer or workstation doesn't have sound capability, your messages can be delivered via the nearest phone. After this, your voice message details are displayed. On the Web page, you can see a list of all your messages at a glance and immediately select the one you want to hear.

Selecting the message downloads and plays it on your personal computer or workstation, or sends it to the phone number you specified, which then rings. You can also save or delete messages by selecting buttons on the Web page.

You don't need any special software on your personal computer or workstation, to get World Wide Web access to your voice messages. All you need is Internet access via a Web browser such as Navigator, Netscape, NCSA Mosaic, or IBM WebExplorer. If you're away from home, you can check your voice mail from anywhere in the world, often at the cost of a local phone call.

The processes you use to access your voice mail over the World Wide Web are only loosely coupled with DirectTalkMail. Response times will vary greatly, as with any other Internet access to data. When checking your voice messages do not backtrack using your browser's "Back" function. If you are working on an old copy of the voice message details you may inadvertently listen to or delete the wrong message. Always use the page most recently presented by DirectTalkMail. If you are using your browser regularly for DirectTalkMail, you may find it advisable to switch caching off so that all pages are refreshed from source when they are reloaded.

When you have listened to a new message it is good practice to save it otherwise it will still appear in the sender's outgoing mail, and the sender still has the capability to delete it. Your Web browser probably doesn't keep an accurate track of hyperlink usage when you are deleting or saving messages. Therefore you should pay no attention to whether a hyperlink appears to have been used or not. Treat all hyperlinks as being the same - whether or not your browser has grayed them out.

Internet Voice with DirectTalkMail. IBM's Internet Connection Phone works with DirectTalkMail. IBM recently showed a technology demonstration of this. The company says it's the first example of a software telephone leaving messages in a conventional voice mail system over the Internet.

MediaGate

Computer Telephony MultiMedia Platform

MediaGate provides total MultiMedia messaging systems for the Internet. MediaGate products enable the Internet to provide MultiMedia applications beyond what is currently offered, and make them accessible to virtually any communications device with a single phone number. MediaGate's product, the Computer Telephony MultiMedia Platform (CTMP), is both a hardware and software open server platform designed to be installed in Internet and Intranet Point of Presence (POP) locations.

Figure 5.19 -- MediaGate Multimedia Server with CTMP

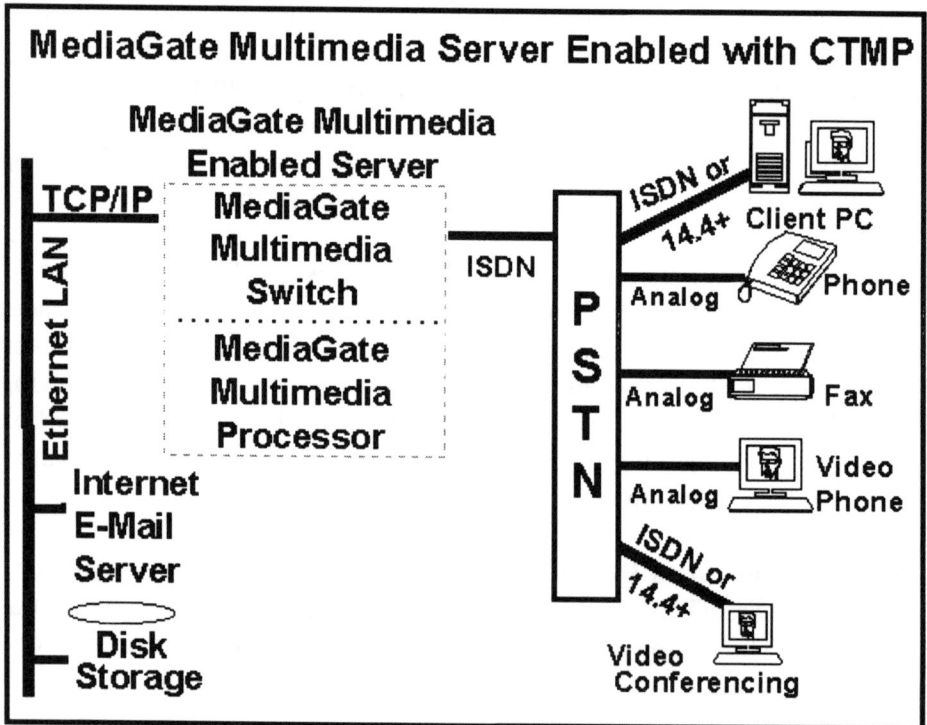

The CTMP interfaces to the standard telephone network and receives incoming calls. The function of the CTMP is twofold. First, the MediaGate MultiMediaSwitch determines whether an incoming call is either voice, fax, or computer modem. Secondly, once the type of call is determined, the call is passed to the MediaGate MultiMedia Processor which notifies the server what application to run, and may store or retrieve MultiMedia data for messaging purposes. The MediaGate CTMP enables access to a multitude of communication devices and applications, as illustrated in Figure 5.19.

Below are examples of the kinds of applications that the CTMP can provide on the Internet, depending on the type of access device:

Telephone as access device. Voice Messaging, AudioWeb Page , Audio E-Mail, Paging and Conference Calling

FAX machine as access device. Fax on Demand (FOD), FAX broadcast and Fax Mail.

PC as access device. E-Mail, WebPage and Internet Telephony.

Video Conferencing as access device. Video Messaging, Video Broadcast, Full Motion Video WebPage, Advertising and Video On Demand. The CTMP will automatically notify the appropriate application for the corresponding access device. Furthermore, the CTMP will work with any existing telephone or PC, without any hardware modifications. This is because all of the MultiMedia functionality is provided by the CTMP and does not need to be downloaded to the local client. For example, a voice message is played by the CTMP directly to the telephone, or it can be packaged in a standard file format to be played on a PC.

CTMP Video Messaging on the Net

Equally as important, MediaGate is developing technology that allows high quality video to be delivered by the CTMP. This to a client PC over a standard modem in real time.

This happens without the need for a large hard disk, memory or special graphics cards in the PC. It will not require the user to download huge imaging files. In other words, the video can be sent to any other server as a video message to be viewed by anyone with *only a standard PC and modem.* This unique technology makes every PC with a modem video enabled. This is made possible by proprietary MediaGate technology that utilizes the Internet server, not the PC, to provide the computing resources.

The applications for this technology are tremendous. An executive can video record a speech or video conference and send it to all its employees for later viewing. Corporations can send out full motion product demo's. Consumers could send video clips of their family to other family members. And unlike broadcast TV, advertisers could target market specific clients with video commercials.

MediaGate Application Overview. The target application for MediaGate is MultiMedia messaging for any real time communication device. Media-Gate will provide message delivery of voice, video, and fax over the Internet through the use of an attached file to E-mail. Message addressing from a PC will be accomplished in the same manner as E-mail, that is by using the recipients E-mail address. Message delivery from a telephone, video phone or fax machine will utilize touch tone input of the recipients phone number that will then be cross referenced by the MediaGate application to the recipients E-mail address. In the case where the recipient is not an E-mail subscriber, the phone number will be cross referenced to the nearest IP address in that area code. The reverse process will occur for receiving a message. If the recipient is receiving from a PC, the message is delivered as a standard E-mail. If it is voice or Fax, the file is downloaded into the PC. If it is video, the video is immediately streamed to the user when selected (no download time). MediaGate anticipates offering audio and fax streaming as well.

If the recipient is receiving from an analog device, such as a telephone, video phone, or fax machine, the recipient verifies themselves as the receiver by dialing in and entering their phone number.

The MediaGate application verifies their number by cross referencing it with the recipients E-mail address and speaks the message if it is voice, streams the video, or initiates a fax.

If the recipient is a non E-mail subscriber, the CTMP will dial out the recipients phone number until someone answers and verifies they want to receive a voice or video message either via a touch tone entry, or fax tone if the message is a fax.

The directory look up is accomplished in three methods. First, MediaGate anticipates that ISP's have extensive internal databases of their subscribers that can be accessed through the MediaGate application. This would allow ISP's to offer MultiMedia messaging services to their client base on an exclusive basis. Second, the MediaGate application will support a common registration method where each user that subscribes to the new service will register their name, E-Mail address, and phone number. In this way the subscribers build up the directory addresses. The third method is to utilize directories of third party services that supply this information on the Internet.

Octel Communications Corporation

Octel Unified Messaging

Octel Communications put a new spin on their messaging strategy way back in June 1994. With the first hint of Microsoft Exchange, they jumped at the chance to bolt their voice / fax messaging systems onto this logical information exchange infrastructure. The company looks at doing Internet-based messaging as a natural extension to their architecture.

Octel is part of the VPIM working group, a standards organization working on Internet-based message passing between disparate voice mail systems. In addition to VPIM, a big part of the company's strategy is interoperability with the Microsoft Exchange Server.

Like other traditional CT voice / fax messaging companies, the next leap is enterprise messaging, unifying disparate messaging types into a single architecture. Together with Microsoft Exchange, Octel wants its users to retrieve, organize and exchange information from a single point of access.

The concept, again, is sublime. Each employee will have a mailbox, similar to their separate voice-mail and e-mail box today, except now there will be only one mailbox. All voice-mail, fax, e-mail and data messages (such as documents or forms) will be stored in this mailbox. Messages in the mailbox can be viewed, heard, stored, faxed or retrieved by personal computer, telephone or fax machine-regardless of the form in which they were created.

Figure 5.20 – Octel's Microsoft Exchange User Interface

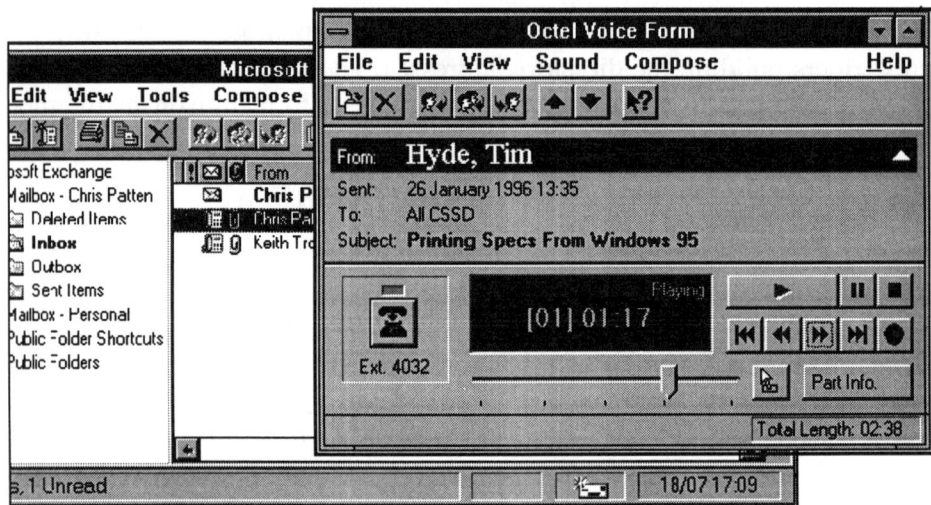

Figure 5.20 shows how users can view all of their messages (e-mail, voice, fax) in a single place. You can view documents or faxes on screen, listen to voice messages, send faxes, create e-mail and manage information in the way that works most productively for them. Network administrators will work from a single screen as well -- setting up e-mail, voice and fax messaging or managing moves, adds and changes in one place.

The Octel plan requires the Microsoft Exchange Server, the Octel Server, LAN and PBX connections, clients and, if desired, gateways to outside networks or the Internet.

The Octel server will be the integral link between the Exchange Server(s) / LAN and PBX / telephone network and will contain the voice, fax, text-to-speech and voice recognition hardware and software. When managing voice messages, its roll is: play and record voice messages; provide telephone answering service for individual subscribers; compress and decompress audio in real-time for storage and retrieval on the Microsoft Exchange Server; interpret DTMF or speech commands for voice messaging navigation; perform text-to-speech conversion for audio playback of text such as e-mail; and send and receive voice or fax messages with subscribers on existing Octel systems.

Figure 5.21 – Octel Server Topology

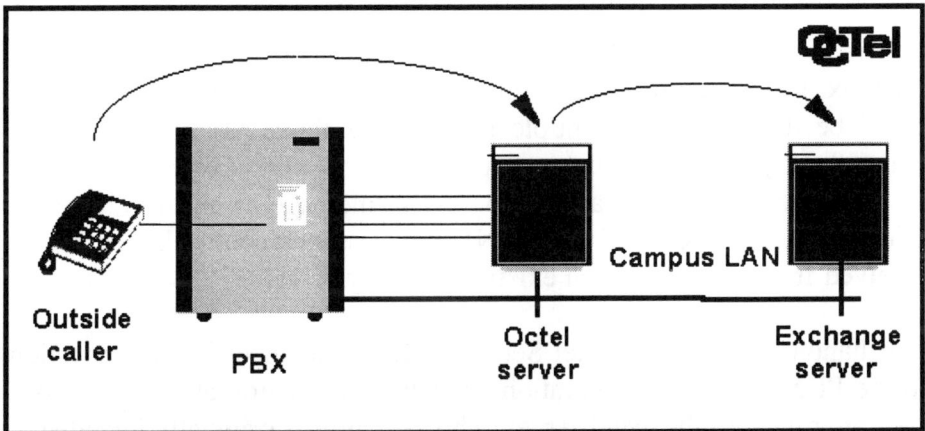

The Octel Server connects the LAN and telephone networks and acts as a bridge to provide transparent management of voice and fax data stored on the Microsoft Exchange Server. The Octel Server records the message, compresses it into a file and sends it to the user's mailbox on the Microsoft Exchange Server. No messages are stored on the Octel Server. This is illustrated in Figure 5.21.

Unified Messaging connections include both LAN interfaces and PBX integrations. Existing Octel systems and "Unified Messaging" systems can "co-exist" to meet enterprise needs. Users are located where they prefer and migration can occur at a customer's pace.

Voice messages will be recorded and compressed into files on the Octel server and then transported to and stored on the user's Microsoft Exchange Server in the proper mailbox. Voice messages will be played back by reversing the process -- retrieving the message file from the subscriber's Microsoft Exchange Server to the Octel Server for playback through a telephone. Playback could also be done through a multimedia PC by retrieving the message from the Microsoft Exchange Server and using the PC's sound system to play the message.

The Octel Server will also provide fax mail services, letting individuals receive faxes in their mailbox, view or send fax messages at their desktops or direct them to be printed to any fax machine or printer.

Users will be notified immediately as faxes arrive directly in an individual's mailbox. Faxes cannot be lost, misplaced or read by someone else. Faxes could be distributed to multiple recipients without having to print and manually send one document multiple times. Incoming fax messages could be forwarded along with a voice or e-mail message as an introduction to other people on the LAN or WAN. Fax messages could also be sent or received from subscribers on existing Octel systems.

To handle all this, the Octel Server will include specialized connections to the PBX. The PBX integration provides information about the calls as they are routed to the Octel server: who the call was originally intended for (called party), who placed the call (calling party) and what caused the call to be routed (no answer, busy). The system was designed to co-exist with existing Octel systems through a telephony networking protocol called OctelNet as shown in Figure 5.22. In this way users will continue to send voice and fax messages regardless of which system their mailbox is located.

Figure 5.22 -- OctelNet Networking Protocol

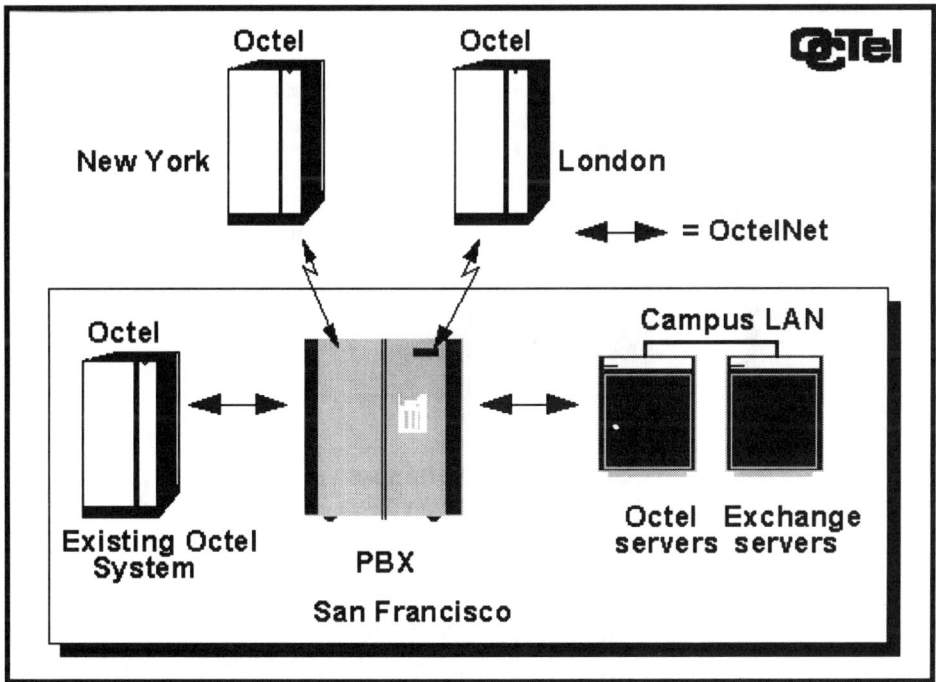

Octel's Unified Messaging operates as an application running on an NT based server on the LAN along with the MS Exchange Server. Unified Messaging stores voice and fax messages along with e-mail messages in a user's single mailbox on the Exchange server as illustrated in Figure 5.23. PC clients access messages via a GUI. The Octel Server allows "telephone clients" to manage the same messages with simple voice or touch-tone commands.

Voice messages are selected from the mailbox window in the same way -- just click on the voice message icon. In the case of voice, the Octel Server will retrieve the message from the user's mailbox on the Microsoft Exchange Server and stages it for playback.

Figure 5.23 – LAN and Telephone Access

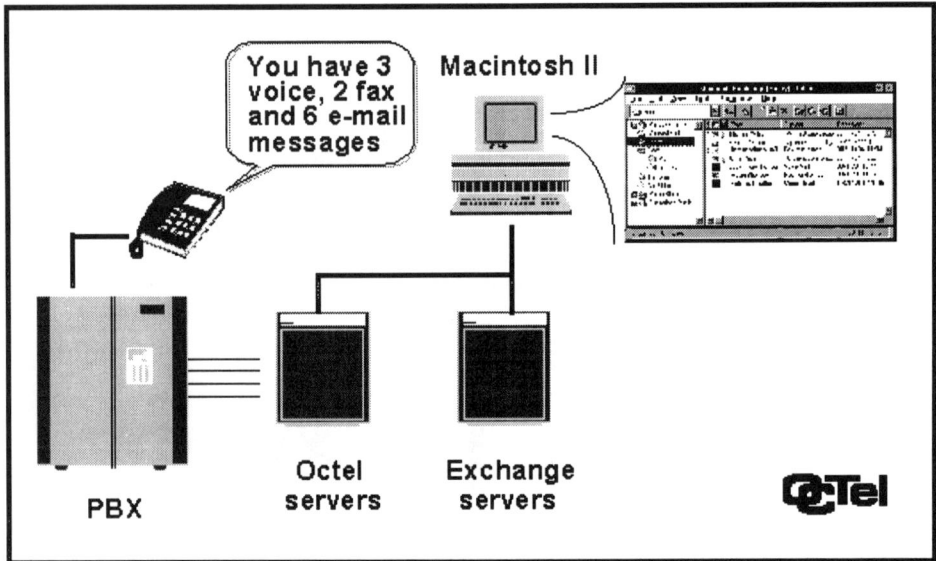

Of course, unlike LAN interfaces, which are based on industry standards, PBX interfaces remain proprietary. But Octel has experience dealing with strange PBXs. With Octel's CTI integration, the telephone becomes a client. It can be used to record and to hear voice and e-mail messages (via TTS). It will also serve as an input device (using the keypad or spoken commands) allowing the user to act on a message -- replying to or forwarding messages, storing them, directing a fax to be printed, deleting messages or directing e-mail to be faxed.

You can also send voice messages just like e-mail. Compose a message, address it and send it. If the message is addressed to another user whose mailbox is on the local Microsoft Exchange Server, it's deposited there. If the recipient's mailbox resides on another network Microsoft Exchange server, the Microsoft Exchange Message Transfer Agent (MTA) sends the message to the correct server according to the address found in the Microsoft Exchange Directory.

If the recipient is at another company or on an existing Octel system, he may still be listed in the Directory and messages will be sent via the Internet or their own OctelNet networking protocol. Faxes are composed right on desktop computers. When you're ready to send, say, a Word file, it will be converted to a fax image format, routed to the Octel server and then faxed to the recipient(s) using the internal fax ports on the Octel server. Octel will provide client software that interacts within the Microsoft Exchange Client to control the recording and playback of voice messages and the viewing and sending of fax messages. Octel intends to support the same PC environments as Microsoft (Windows NT, Windows 95, Windows 3.11, Macintosh and UNIX).

Chapter Acknowledgments

Special thanks to Alan Wokas, president and CEO of MediaGate for his contribution to this chapter. Mr. Wokas was co-founder and president of Rhetorex, a leading worldwide Internet supplier of DSP based CTI components for PC's. Rhetorex was founded in 1988 and invented the first DSP based voice processing board. Under Mr. Wokas' direction, Rhetorex has grown to over 100 employees with a revenue run rate of $30M and has operated profitably with increasing revenue for 22 straight quarters. Rhetorex was acquired by VMX in 1993 which in 1994 was acquired by Octel, the worlds largest voice messaging company. Rhetorex was Octel's most profitable division. Prior to founding Rhetorex, Mr. Wokas was co-founder and president of Vynet Corporation in 1982. Vynet established many firsts in the industry, including the first voice processing products for Apple, IBM/PC/XT and AT computers as well as the first multiline voice processing board, pioneering the technology that is used in the majority of voice processing systems today. Prior to Vynet, Mr. Wokas held various engineering and marketing positions at Fairchild Semiconductor in their microprocessor and telecommunications division. Mr. Wokas holds a BSEE from Michigan State University and finishing an MBA from the University of California.

Chapter 6

IVR Meets the Internet

Computer telephony has revolutionized the way we do business, manage our personal affairs and communicate. This goes for telephone access to bank accounts, automated product registration and voice messaging. With CT, the lowly telephone is the ultimate, ubiquitous access terminal. People not only accept but expect CT apps to save them time and access information. All this with as little human intervention as possible. The attraction of distributing data on the Internet is becoming legend.

Until computer telephony came along, this data was only accessible to those with computer access. By applying the same voice enabling techniques now used by many market segments, you can now get your data on the Internet via text-to-speech, touch-tone response and ASR. The Internet and Intranets are having a profound effect on CT applications in three broad areas:

1) Messaging. Universal terminal access and media translations. Event driven or on demand.

2) Call Control. Voice over data networking. Simultaneous voice / text / graphics / video. Application sharing.

3) Information Access. Instant, remote access. Personalized and intuitive. Ubiquitous, high value info. This is the domain of IVR and other "information on demand" systems like fax and video-on-demand.

In this chapter, we discuss Information Access as it relates to IVR, but the distinctions are often blurred. You can initiate an IVR-based telephone call and still be connected to an operator. The operator transfer or call back is really a call control type of application. An application is an IVR application if the *intent* was to get information automatically. Often, IVR transactions transform into call control applications because the users wants them to. So there is some cross-over.

IVR Impact on the Internet

Companies use IVR to improve customer service. This is done by offering 24 hour service, handling peak traffic overflow calls and providing customers with options for information access. With the ongoing explosion of the Internet and the Web, companies are searching for new ways to offer better service. Linking the IVR system to a Home Page meets these needs in an innovative and affordable way. You can offer around-the-clock order processing, technical support or fax on demand service. All this as an add-on to traditional call centers and IVR systems.

Internet-Aware IVR Examples

On-Line Banking

This includes account Inquiry, funds transfer and mortgage information. Banks are rushing to go on-line with Web-browsing customers.

Financial institutions have always been on the cutting edge of automation. Why? IVR makes doing business easy on their pocketbooks (vaults?) and it delivers around-the-clock service.

Healthcare

Web-browsing patients can view basic service information with their browser. If a "secure page" comes up (prompt for social security number or account code), and IVR front-end can be used to collect sensitive password information. This can be done with touch-tones or voice verification. The IVR system sends a message via CGI script to "unlock" these pages so the patient can continue with the transaction.

Help Desk IVR Alternatives

Most help desk and AI companies are jumping on to the Web. This because help desk client software can be extended globally and with fewer employees. From a home page, users can browse through "intelligent search engines" to solve their problem. This browsing can also be done over the phone (amazing fact – not everyone in the world has a PC, let alone an ISP account).

IVR & Fax-On-Demand

The basic idea here is to use the Internet and the Web as an overgrown, global disk drive for stored documents. You can use the same document source for getting faxes by phone (faxback), Web browsing, or company Intranet. Documents can be centralized, managed and revised much easier this way. It's easier than maintaining disparate image catalogs for each type of access point.

Data Collection and Speedy Input

Phones are ubiquitous. Computers aren't. IVR systems can prompt delivery people and sales agents to enter critical and timely information by phone.

A local call made anywhere in the world can be the front-end to a touch-tone delivery confirmation, sales report, or dispatch request. IVR gateways can send the data over the Internet to a "collection point." The data can be dynamically updated with virtually millions of global entry points (Interactive touch-tone sessions). Back at the "office" dispatchers and sales managers can use their Intra/Internet browsers to view and take action on the data. This is fast.

Alternate Billing And Collection

Smart companies, take Logicom for instance, are using 900-based billing and collection as a means to charge for Web-based services. This is very creative. You're browsing the Web. You see something you like. You don't want to use a credit card (or don't have one). Instead, you call a 900 number to retrieve a "credit" chit. The chit has a number associated with it. You enter the chit number in an order-entry box on the home page in question. You get billed on your phone bill.

Education

UCLA has Edify's Electronic Workforce. They use it for student services. Students can contact the school via Web and telephone. The system took a month design and implementation. UCLA student will se the system for registration, course study and eventually distance learning applications.

Human Resources & Benefits

Employees access their company's Web page through any standard Web browser to change their address or benefits information or to initiate a purchase requisition order. The system updates and requests information automatically. The time consuming steps of filling out paper forms and having to train an employee to type in the data are now eliminated. Users can be given secure access options such as "call me" buttons if they want to talk to a human resources manager or input sensitive data via touch tone.

First Union Corporation offers retirement services via the Web and telephone. The Edify-based system integrates the company's back-office applications and databases.

Call Queue By Proxy

Everyone hates "going into queue" when agents are busy. Now Web-browsing callers can have special software do the waiting for them. This while the customer goes about his business and either makes other calls or visits other Web sites. An IVR software client waits in queue for them. This client provides an IVR system with the customers telephone number. The IVR system will then initiate the call to Web-browsing user. The system can do a traditional IVR session or hand-off the call to a live agent.

Call Me Applications

Web site browsers sometimes wish to speak to a "live" person. Now they can click on a "call me" icon. This initiates a real-time telephone call from the company to the user. Companies like Edify, HTI Voice Solutions, NetCall, Spanlink and Venturian Software are pioneers of this technology.

International Callback Systems

Companies are leveraging the fact that international callback systems have been domestically legalized as part of the Telecom Act of 1996. Even without the WWW, International callback is hot. A real money saver.

Internet Transaction Security

Internet Transaction Security is *the* "killer app" for the IVR-Enabled Web. It's the one common theme in virtually every IVR/Web application discussed here. Now order entry, account status and inquiry can be made secure with the human voice (speech verification gateways). If you don't trust Internet security, touch-toning your credit card numbers feels a whole lot safer.

The attraction and implications of distributing data on the Internet has become legend. According to a report by the University of California at Berkeley, the use of information networks for business is expanding enormously. The average number of electronic point-of-sale transactions in the United States went from 38K per day in 1985 to 1.2 million per day in 1993. An average $800 billion is transferred among partners in international currency markets every day; about $1 trillion is transferred daily among U.S. banks; and an average $2 trillion worth of securities are traded daily in New York markets. Nearly all of these financial transactions pass over information networks.

But until now this data was only accessible to those with computer access. By applying the same voice enabling techniques now used by many market segments, you can now get your data on the Internet via text-to-speech, touch tome response and ASR. In this section Joe Baranauskas, president of iNTELiTRAK Technologies, provides a look at how transaction security can be simplified using speech recognition technology. You'll find a description of his "Citadel GateKeeper" platform in the product roundup in this chapter.

Security Issues
...and Stifled Commerce

Commerce on the Internet has been slowed by security issues. Most companies refrain from distributing vital/sensitive business information over the Internet due to these concerns. Special IVR systems now help the Internet to realize its full commerce potential.

Most companies refrain from distributing vital/sensitive business information over the Internet due in part to security issues. As a result, the full potential of easy access information provided by the WWW has not been utilized to its greatest extent. Most security measures lend themselves to compromise. This remains the only true obstacle to effective use of the Internet for commerce.

Web site browsers sometimes need to communicate sensitive information (credit card numbers, PINs). Now callers visiting financial transaction or secure Web sites can do business with a heightened sense of confidence. After product information has been submitted, users can click a "secure" link icon to initiate an IVR-based transaction. An IVR application or a company representative will automatically call the user back to collect the required information. The user enters data by speaking or uses touch tones to input the secure information. You can get systems like this from HTI Voice Solutions, iNTELiTRAK Technologies and Logicom.

Security Threat Statistics

Michigan State University recently studied 200 businesses and found 93.6% had been victimized by computer criminals. Most of these crimes were committed by employees or contract workers.

Computer theft costs $22.4 million dollars per day says the British Banking Industry. Their studies show average (non-computer) business fraud as amounting to $23,000 per incident. In contrast, computer fraud blows this away at $500,000 per incident.

The federal government says 42% of all criminal computer crimes investigated went unreported. This because the perceived cost of revealing the thefts is perceived as far more damaging than the dollars lost in the crime. Public companies say a loss of confidence by the stockholders and in the market place can destroy their enterprise. "Computer crime is going to get worse!" says Scott Charney, head of the U.S. Justice Department's Computer Crimes Unit.

In its agency audits and evaluations, the General Accounting Office (GAO) identified several recent instances of information-security and privacy problems (to get the UC Berkeley report in full, see http://lucien.sims.berkeley.edu/OTA/info.security/info.security.rpt.txt): In November 1988, a virus caused thousands of computers on the Internet to shut down.

The virus' primary impact was lost processing time on infected computers and lost staff time in putting the computers back on line. Related dollar losses are estimated to be between $100,000 and $10 million. The virus took advantage of UNIX's trusted-host features to propagate among accounts on trusted machines.

Between April 1990 and May 1991, hackers penetrated computer systems at 34 Department of Defense sites by weaving their way through university, government, and commercial systems on the Internet. The hackers exploited a security hole in the Trivial File Transfer Protocol, which allowed users on the Internet to access a file containing encrypted passwords without logging onto the system.

Authorized users of the Federal Bureau of Investigation's National Crime Information Center misused the network's information. Such misuse included using the information to, for example, determine whether friends, neighbors, or relatives had criminal records, or inquire about backgrounds for political purposes.

In October 1992, the Internal Revenue Service's (IRS's) internal auditors identified 368 employees who had used the IRS's Integrated Data Retrieval System without management knowledge, for non-business purposes. Some of these employees had used the system to issue fraudulent refunds or browse taxpayer accounts that were unrelated to their work, including those of friends, neighbors, relatives, and celebrities.

More recent events have continued to spur government and private-sector interest in information security. A series of hacker attacks on military computers connected to the Internet has prompted the Defense Information Systems Agency to tighten security policies and procedures in the defense information infrastructure. The hackers, operating within the United States and abroad, have reportedly penetrated hundreds of sensitive, but unclassified, military and government computer systems.

The break-ins have increased significantly since February 1994, when the Computer Emergency Response Team first warned that unknown intruders were gathering Internet passwords by using what are called sniffer programs. The sniffer programs operate surreptitiously, capturing authorized users' logins and passwords for later use by intruders. The number of captured passwords in this series of attacks has been estimated at a million or more, potentially threatening all the host computers on the Internet--and their users.

Network Security

Given these startling statistics, it's no wonder that companies are cautious when contemplating a move onto the Internet. Some experience an administrator's nightmare when trying to control access on an internal network, but what do you do when your company wants to compete in a global economy? How can we get our vital information to key field personnel in an efficient manner? The Internet. How do we currently secure access to our most private data on the Internet?

Most network operating systems offer a user access table for controlling access to machines, directories, applications and files. The inherent weakness of traditional user access table thinking is the storage of these user-names and passwords, "encrypted key combinations," placed on the server for an indefinite amount of time.

It is this same user access table with the "encrypted key combinations" that a hacker will penetrate. He could download all of the encrypted keys. Once he has done this, he might use brute force methods to attack the encryption scheme in an effort to break the encryption and decode the user-names and passwords. With this accomplishment, he now has the keys and freedom to access your protected information as the key combinations still reside on the server when he/she authenticates using the stolen keys.

To counter this threat, the establishment has determined that they need to make encryption schemes more sophisticated by means of complicated, larger encoding methods.

As encryption grows more sophisticated, so do the hackers and the computers they use. It's a never ending up-grade cycle with no end in sight.

Encryption Problematics

Because encryption deploys mathematical calculations within the algorithm, there are certain patterns or traces that could be predicted or discovered through several "cracking methods." Stored user names and passwords are no longer an effective deterrent to computer crime. With the ever-increasing availability of more powerful computer resources, these traditional ways of thinking are no longer secure.

Easily the most cost effective and accurate solution would be speaker dependent voice verification. With nothing on the client side other than a simple telephone, it proves to be a more efficient and cost effective way of managing authentication / access from a systems administrative stand point.

Secure Key Access

To utterly secure access to that sensitive application, simply do not but the keys out there. Instead, we use tokens. A token is a device to authenticate a user's identity in order to have the keys written to the user access table. These tokens have been traditionally in the form of "credit" type cards, to electronic "crypto" cards. "Cryptos" have passwords beamed into them by wireless communications.

Once the token card has been inserted into the card reader, the server recognizes that specific card and then takes the password from a list on a protected table and writes it and the user name to the user access table.

But confirming the client's right to possess that card is at issue. Authentication methods abound, and each has its own merits and disadvantages. None, however, has the reliability of speaker-dependent voice verification.

Authentication Methods

Physical Token Authentication. Physical, tangible devices used for the purpose of identifying an individual. Examples: Crypto cards, limited use access cards. Problem: easily lost, stolen, loaned or duplicated.

Enter Biometric Technology. Biometric Authentication. A means for positive identification by using unique body characteristics as an identifier, such as fingerprints, retina scans, facial recognition and voice pattern recognition.

Retina Scanning. Retinal scanning technology recognizes an individual's retinal vascular pattern in a short time. Contact lenses do not prevent identification, but glasses must be removed to use the system.

Based on the fact that retinal blood vessel patterns are unique and do not change over a person's lifetime, the system uses the natural reflective and absorption properties of the eye's retina to identify specific data points and create a digital template. When the person is scanned again to verify identity, s/he looks into the equipment at a green dot alignment target. Problem: Expensive, client-side hardware/software solution. Difficult system administration.

Finger Printing. Self explanatory. Problem: Expensive, client-side hardware/software solution. Difficult system administration.

Hand Geometry. The measurement of angular distances from predetermined reference points on an individual's hand. Problem: Expensive, client-side hardware/software solution. Difficult system administration.

Facial Recognition. The measurement of angular distances from predetermined reference points on an individual's face. Problem: Expensive, client-side hardware/software solution. Difficult system administration.

Voice Authentication

Voice recognition and voice verification are quite distinctive from each other. While each must perform well in the presence of background noise, and often over narrow band-width transmission lines, the extracted audio features examined by each technology meet two very different goals. MOSCOM's Votan division researches and develops voice verification and recognition technologies. They say: "In a voice recognition application, the speaker utters a word and the system determines the spoken word by selecting from a pre-defined vocabulary. It makes this determination by comparing the spoken utterance to a reference set of utterances. It compares each match and selects the one that achieved the highest score relative to the scores of the other word matches."

On the other hand, speaker verification (also known as voice authentication) differs from voice recognition in that the match must be *absolute*, not relative. The test utterance is compared to a specific reference utterance and it must match closely enough to provide assurance that the speaker is the authentic original enrollee, not another person imitating the authentic speaker. In summary, recognition chooses the closest match, with small regard to how close the match is, while verification bases its choice entirely on the closeness itself.

HTI Voice Solutions

WebVox

HTI Voice Solutions is a voice, data and image processing company. HTI has delivered Integrated Voice Response (IVR) technology for over ten years. WebVox is a new Web-enabled IVR solution the company just launched. By adding telephony functions to traditional Web sites and applications, users and providers gain another communication avenue (via touch-tone telephone) when the Web action does not satisfy their needs.

Telephony integration can provide a secure link to pass sensitive information that may be required for a Web transaction. WebVox can improve service and communications by giving Web browsers an easy way to speak directly with the company. The traditional benefits of IVR such as increased user satisfaction, reduced expenses and greater productivity still apply.

WebVox Client Server Architecture

WebVox is a distributed application. It allows you to communicate between voice and Internet platforms. It is made up of a client CGI application residing on a Web server, a WebVox server running on the IVR platform and a special voice processing application. The product has been designed around Windows NT and the Internet Information Server from Microsoft. Plans to port WebVox to Sun Solaris, UnixWare and other operating systems are underway.

Internet Front-End For IVR

WebVox provides an Internet front end to existing IVR applications by creating a communication channel between the Web and voice servers. A browsing customer can visit an "IVR-Enabled Web site and go through an order entry application. This is illustrated in Figure 6.1. Here, he or she will select products and fill-out forms for delivery information, etc. The system will prompt the customer for sensitive information such as a credit card number. The user clicks a "secured call" and enters his or her callback number.

The Web Server activates a CGI script. This passes the telephone number back to the IVR system. So far, this is done over the Internet with no real-time circuit switching. Additional information such as the user's order information is also passed to the IVR system. An order number is automatically processed. The IVR system then receives the callback number from the CGI script and enters it into the IVR dialing application program. The IVR system initiate a real-time telephone call to the user. This is a real-time circuit-switched call over the regular telephone network.

Once connected, the IVR system prompts the user for his or her credit card number and confirms his or her desire to complete the transaction. The user inputs the data with touch tones. Figure 6.1 shows the IVR/Internet Loop between the customers' telephone and Web browser.

The IVR system then matches the order number and credit card information and creates a transaction record. It initiates an automatic credit card billing transaction. The system can now confirm the order on the Web page or speak a prompt over the phone to confirm order completion.

Figure 6.1 -- Internet Front-End to IVR

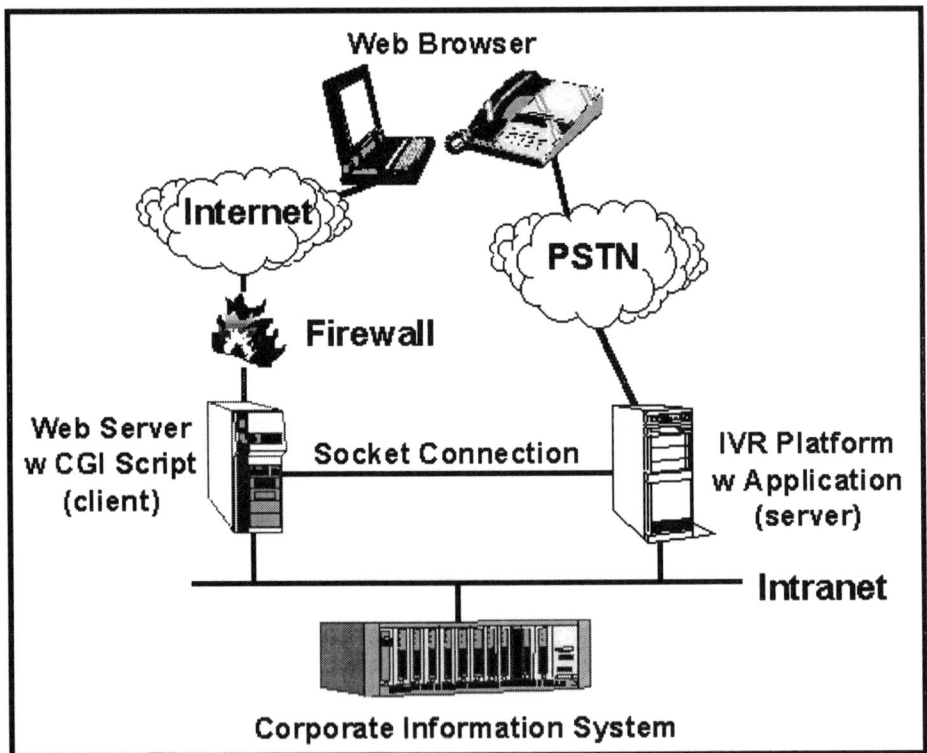

International Callback

...Web-Enabled

In a normal international callback system, a French businessman calling Japan dials a US number, assigned by a service provider, lets it ring once and hangs-up (that's the A-leg of the call). The system calls back with US dial tone (that's the B-leg of the call). The caller dials and seconds later there's a cheap IDDD call, US-to-France conferenced with US to Japan at a 25% savings to the Parisian (the C-leg of the call). International callback systems are now using the Internet to initiate the A-Leg of the call to the US. By skipping the phone system for the A-Leg, you don't need a Direct Inward Dial number.

Figure 6.2 -- Web-Enabled International Callback

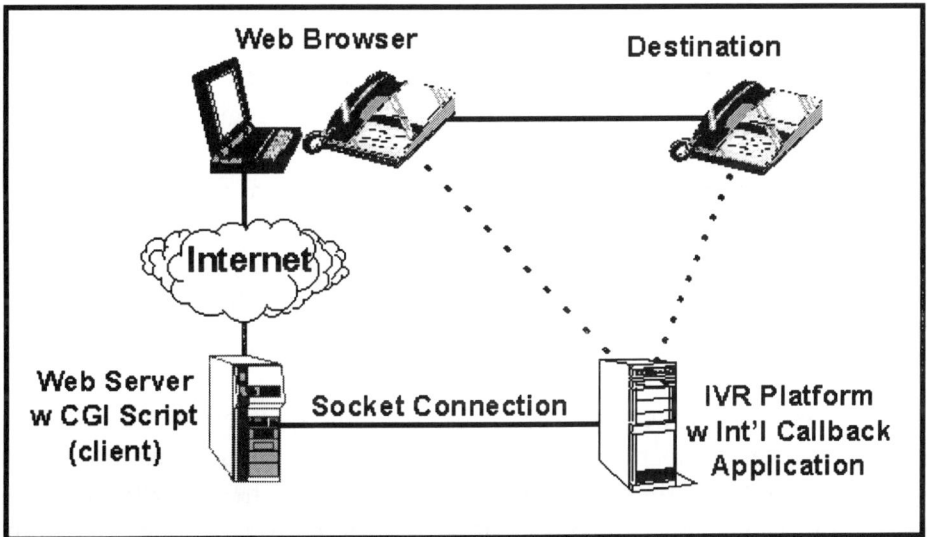

WebVox does this. Users go a service provider's home page, click on the callback icon to enter their account number. This information is sent via a Web Server an IVR system. The system reads the number, looks it up in the database and initiates a callback to the user. Here the called party enters their destination number and the calls are bridged to make the connection.

This is described in more detail below and illustrated in Figure 6.2. Here's the basic steps of a "Web-Initiated" International Call Back transaction:

- A browsing customer can visit a "Call Back-Enabled Web site and click a "call me" icon after entering his or her name and callback number. This is the person wishing to be called, who initiates the callback. He or she is the "first party."

- The Web Server activates a CGI script. This passes the telephone number back to the IVR system. So far, this is done over the Internet with no real-time circuit switching.

- The IVR system then receives the callback number from the CGI script and looks it up in the database.

- The IVR system dials the person who is to initiate the real-time telephone call from the "foreign" end. He or she is the "second party.": This is a real-time circuit-switched call over the regular telephone network. Once connected, the IVR system prompts the second party for a PIN number and confirms his or her desire to complete the call.

- The IVR system then places a (real time circuit switched) call over the regular telephone network to the first party. When the first party is connected, the IVR system bridges the two calls together.

WebVox is a turnkey system for establishing an international callback system. It gives companies complete control over how and when the system is used. It can be configured to meet each company's needs. Large international companies can reduce the cost of calling between offices. WebVox has security password protection, simple system administration and comprehensive accounting reports. The system allows International calling service providers to set-up customer debit or credit cards and set their own phone rates. The system can immediately register charges when the call is complete and it manages billing from within the system.

The instant call rating features allows hotels and cruise ships to set-up a WebVox system their guests can use to call international locations. Travel agents can even offer calling cards so their customers can call home for less. HTI has other IVR-integrated Internet solutions including "call me" applications for Web sites and On-Line Commerce and Banking systems.

iNTELiTRAK Technologies

Citadel GateKeeper

Speaker verification verifies the speaker's presumed identity; the speaker alleges a claimed identity and the application verifies or denies it. A different technology, speaker identification, seeks to identify the speaker based solely on the spoken utterance. Speaker identification is best suited to small groups of users (50 to 100 people). It is rarely used by itself for security. It may be used, however, to tentatively identify a speaker after which verification of a secret pass phrase may be used for confirmation.

Figure 6.3 -- Voice Verification as Security Gatekeeper

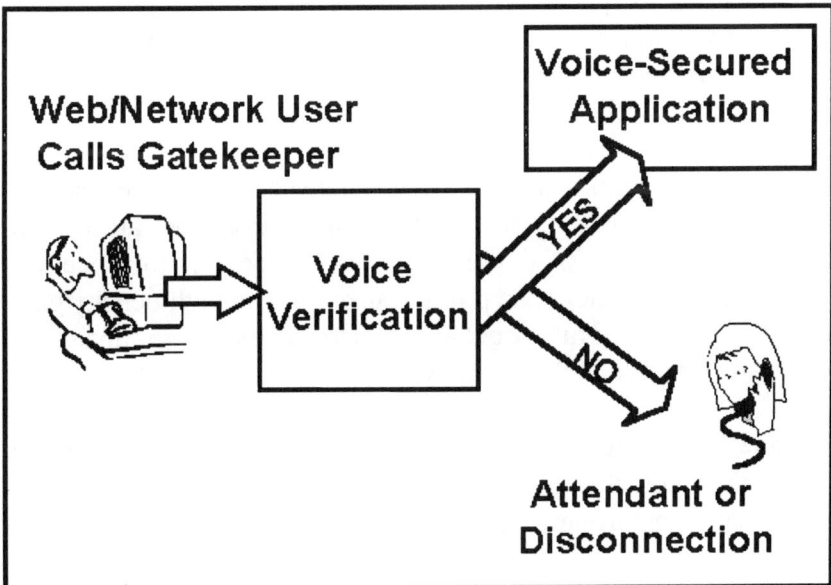

Web/Network User Calls Gatekeeper

Voice Verification

Voice-Secured Application

YES

NO

Attendant or Disconnection

iNTELiTRAK Technologies uses this approach effectively in the Citadel GateKeeper system architecture. Verification makes access to applications, directories or files highly secure. iNTELiTRAK developed the voice verification gateway with Pronexus' VBVoice, an IVR application generator (Ottawa, Ontario Canada - 613-839-0033), and VoiceBuilder for Windows, a voice verification Developer's Kit, and the model VPC2400 voice board from Votan, a division of Moscom Corporation (Pittsford, NY.- 716-381-6000). Figure 6.3 illustrates how a network user can call in to a voice verification gateway to gain secure access for computer transactions. After verifying the person's identity, the user is either allowed to pass or is disconnected or sent to an operator.

The verification architecture consists of feature extraction and pattern matching algorithms. These run on a Texas Instruments TMS320C51 digital signal processing chip (DSP) and a MOSCOM proprietary pattern processing VLSI chip. This chip performs pattern matching between the features of the digitized incoming voice print and those of previously trained reference samples. The pattern processing chip, DSP chip and governing algorithm form the core of the voice verification engine.

The Citadel GateKeeper relies on the MOSCOM VPC2400 voice verification platform. This is an integrated 4-line, board solution that combines an analog telephone-line interface with voice recognition circuitry comprising an efficient and reliable voice-rec engine.

Under current development is a TCP/IP network verification board that would be capable of handling up to 10,000 voice transactions an hour. When this board is ready, the Citadel GateKeeper will be able to process up to 40,000 verifications an hour and provide an extremely high-density gateway for secure Web access. This would allow us to address approximately 1,600 phone lines in a single rack-mount system!

The Citadel GateKeeper has a number of interesting and promising applications for the Internet, Intranet, and Interactive Cable TV in both private and public sector environments.

Security with Random Volatile Gateway

Current network security methods rely upon a stored table of keys to access applications, directories and files. Because of the existence of this table, it lends itself to penetration and acquisition (liberation?) of stored PIN# and password combinations by "unauthorized personnel" for authentication and future access.

The Citadel Architecture uses an empty PIN# and password table as the access "gateway". This table is referred to as a "Random Volatile Gateway", meaning that the PIN# and passwords are generated randomly, encrypted and written to the table on a per use, per client request basis and then destroyed.

Once the "Random Volatile Gateway" keys are in place, access is then granted. Upon one of two conditions, this "Random Volatile Gateway " key will be destroyed: a pre-programmed time-lapse or the first access/activation of the keys. The keys are only randomly generated upon successful identification of the client requesting access by the use of speaker-dependent voice verification technology.

Along with the key issuance, the system captures Caller ID number and I.P. address of the requesting client. This allows the system to log the access location and track what data has been compromised for system administrators. The combination of a voice-print, Caller ID and the I.P. address of the requesting machine allows a systems administrator to attach a face or identity to the requesting client.In application, a requesting client would log onto the secured server and be presented with an on-line form prompting them for their PIN# and an as yet unknown "Volatile Password".

To obtain the "Volatile Password", the client would be asked to call the IVR application on the Web server for identification. A caller dials into the IVR application (over the regular phone network) and gets prompted for a series of voice prints. These are recorded and carried to the spectral voiceprint analysis for verification against pre-registered voice patterns.

A comparison of the voice prints are made and the caller is either accepted or rejected. If accepted the system generates a random volatile passcode the caller will use to access the network (this can be a Web page, Internet or Intranet network).

Upon successful verification, the IVR application fires a random password generator and timer code. We then encrypt and write the PIN# and "Volatile Password" to the access table along with other I.P. client logging information. As the table is being written to, the IVR application verbalizes the "Random Volatile Password" to the client while they are still on the phone and notifies them that they have 3 minutes to log on.

The timed code then destroys the PIN# and "Volatile Password" combination after the pre-programmed time lapse and/or after first use. This method requires that an individual, voice authenticate every time they wish to log on. Though the PIN# and "Volatile Password" exists on the access table for a short time in an encrypted form, by the time that anyone with the resources required to break the encryption key can do so, the access table has been cleared of the captured or stolen keys through the time-fuse programming. This eliminates the possibility of "hacking".

Information from aborted transactions can be captured. This occurs when the caller simply makes a mistake (wrong phone number,) or their is an outright failure to authenticate . Citadel GateKeeper can capture Caller ID, find the associated address in a database and keep the voice-print of the "hacker" for prosecution.

As far as security systems go, this has huge appeal and potential. For any operation with a large employee or member base with turnover implications, the cost of set up and administrate traditional security methods is enormous. With "Citadel GateKeeper," you get a simple and inexpensive voice enrollment procedure working in minutes. You can test drive the enrollment aspect of the system by calling (512) 480-0918. After you have enrolled your voice-print, call back in to authenticate and receive your "random, volatile passcode."

Link to the iNTELiTRAK Website at www.intelitrak.com. Select menu item #6-secure demo application. In the dialog box, enter the last 6 digits of your social security number for the user name box, and enter the "random, volatile passcode" in the password box.

Logicom, Inc.

Web900

Logicom is a valueadded reseller, system integrator and developer of online products and utilities. In addition to the 900 service for Web sites, Logicom offers a line of addon extension software for 900 service system operators and Bulletin Board System (BBS) software, such as Worldgroup, Wildcat, and TBBS.

With its new Web900 service, companies now have a secure, nomaintenance solution for charging Web surfers to access their Web site content. Until now, only companies that were giving away information were able to tap into the Web's power. With Web900, anyone can charge for access to their Web site without worrying about startup costs or security issues.

Billing for the Web900 site is done via a 900 telephone number that is charged to the Web surfer's telephone bill. This solution offers Webmasters the advantages of no setup fees, ease of installation, and security. For visitors to the site, the Web900 method enables them to access the information they need online without the risks involved in giving out their credit card number or checking account information over the Internet.

A company can charge customers for accessing the entire Web site or only specific restricted pages. To implement feebased pages, the Webmaster simply assigns passwords to certain pages using normal server abilities. An information page with the appropriate disclaimers, a validation form, and a simple CGI program are also added to the Web site.

Currently, companies can charge in various increments between $2 and $30 for access to their Web sites. However, different dollar amounts can be worked out depending on the needs of a particular Web site.

Here's how it works: A Web surfer goes to your site and is prompted to call a 900 number on a form on the Web page. The form is similar in nature to the one pictured in Figure 6.4. The visitor then calls the 900 number and enters a code that identifies the system they are wishing to access. The caller is given a "redemption code" that acts as proof of being charged. The next and final step will have your customer entering the redemption code onto the form.

Figure 6.4 -- Logicom Web900 Billing Service Sample Form

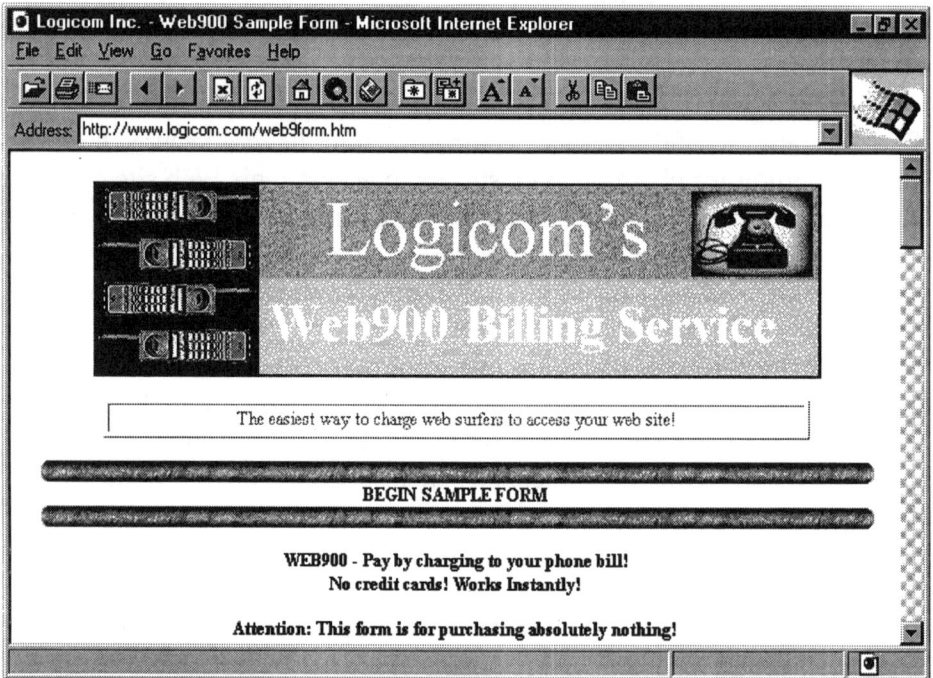

This code is entered into the validation form on the Web server and using the CGI program is matched against a small text file of valid codes.

Upon validation, the visitor is given the passwords to access the Web pages that were previously restricted. This foolproof process ensures that no confidential billing information or access codes are going across the Internet. A CGI application is runs in the background and the user's redemption code is verified against a text file full of codes that you've previously downloaded from the Logicom BBS via modem (not over the Internet for security purposes). Once the code has been verified, the CGI application will interact with your systems security and accounting mechanism. If you're unable to write CGI applications, you can hire Logicom to develop it for you. The company can be contracted to design the forms for you if needed.

Setup for Web900 is free. Once surfers start using Web900, you will receive checks on a monthly basis approximately 45 days after the end of the billing period. Logicom pays Web site content providers 80% of the call. The remaining 20% is used to cover administration fees and pay the phone company.

Here are the steps to enroll with Logicom. First, review their Sample Form and make sure you understand the basic concept (ww.logi-com.com/Web900.htm). You can modify Logicom's source code to suit your own needs. Next, you print out the service agreement, fill it out, and fax it back on 954-726-3748. Decide whether or not you need to use a CGI Script. If so, you'll be able to download the appropriate CGI Script, try it out, and get it working on your site with sample data. Finally, you e-mail Logicom and they will send your real redemption codes. That's it.

Periphonics Corporation

PeriWeb

Periphonics is a veteran in developing real-world, mission-critical, voice processing applications. They've been at it for 25 years. Yes, the industry is actually that old. The platforms are RISC-based VPS/sp and VPS/V AS systems, and stand-alone Sun workstations.

Their interactive voice response systems are installed in large government, commercial and enhanced service businesses. They've always been innovators, and now (like the smartest companies) they're jumping into Web-based call center integration and IVR.

PeriView. This package provides a suite of tools for VPS/is system administration and control. PeriView tools run from the PeriView Launcher Tool Bar or a "Tools" Menu button. With PeriView, you can launch the *Application Manager Tool.* It's used to assign, start and stop applications. The *Phone Line Monitor Tool* gives you pie and bar graphs showing line activity. The *Alarm Viewer* displays real-time and logged alarms. The *VPS Console Tool* is the VPS/is specific command line interface. In addition, there are tools for copying files across the VPS/is Network, scheduling tasks and doing reports. You can also launch the *PeriProducer* apps gen the *PeriStudio* graphical voice editor to record and manage prompts.

PeriProducer. This GUI-Based apps gen lets you create, test and monitor interactive applications for VPS/is systems. This is done with a set of building block icons. The icons represent basic functions. You can construct pretty sophisticated apps without being a programmer These building blocks are graphically arranged and connected in a flow sequence. You build apps in layers of increasing detail. This gives you a modular view of your work.

Periphonics emphasizes the use of pre-built components in their tool kit. New building blocks are formed by placing existing blocks in the construction area, connecting them together to indicate desired execution flow , and then "containing" them to create a new block. The result represents the combined functions of the contained blocks. Special containers can link to other applications or functions in UNIX.

PeriProducer applications carry their documentation with them. Textual notes and voice recordings can be added to any block. Blocks with either text or voice recording notes are graphically identified. You can access Oracle, Sybase and Informix databases with the dialog box fill-ins. You can also launch the PeriStudio package from within the apps gen.

PeriStudio. This graphical voice editor lets you create and edit speech output vocabularies for VPS/is systems. It's a graphical windows-based tool. You get iconic representations of common tape deck controls, pull-down menus, and online help screens. Visual depictions of audio waveforms make it easy to see the effects of editing voice files. You can cut and paste recordings and snip silence at the leading and trailing edge of prompts. You can run PeriStudio on a VPS/sp voice processing system, VRNA 2000 network management system or stand-alone Sun workstation.

The conventional mechanism for developing a voice response vocabulary is a time consuming, multi-step, repetitive operation. First, the vocabulary file is created. Then an entry within the vocabulary called an "element" is defined by specifying a name. Next, the audio source, either a prerecorded cassette tape, or voice provided through a microphone or telephone, is input and digitized by the editor . The digitized recording data is then associated with the named element. These steps are repeated for each element of the vocabulary until all recorded elements have been entered.

Periphonics developed a useful batch recording process. It saves time by eliminating some of the steps of sourcing, loading and tagging voice files. A cassette tape containing your vocabulary recordings provides sequencing. You prepare the recordings with an extra interval of silence between each element. During Batch Recording, PeriStudio detects the extended inter-element silence and automatically stops the digitization process, trims beginning and ending silence, saves the element, creates the next new element, and starts a new digitization process. The time consuming and repetitive steps of a manual process are eliminated.

IVR and Call Control. Periphonics computer telephony solutions use VPS systems along with PBX and ACD telephone switches, agent desktop positions and the Periphonics Computer Telephony Application Platform (C-T AP) CTI Server. You get call tracking, associated call data storage, PBX/ ACD interfaces, VPS, and agent connectivity. This includes "Call-VIEW" PC/ workstation software. You can use OS/2, UNIX, Windows 3.1 and X-Terminals on the OS side.

LANs supported include Novell NetWare, OS/2 LAN Server and UNIX TCP/IP. Switch links to Aspect, AT&T Definity, NEC, Northern Telecom Meridian and Rockwell are supported.

When the PBX or ACD answers an incoming call, it is directed to the VPS. The switch sends a message over the CTI link to the C-T AP server. If the IVR session senses a need for agent intervention, VPS sends a message to the C-T A P requesting a call transfer. The systems use the LAN for the message transfer. The C-T AP software and holds all the data associated with the call. It then sends a message to the PBX/ACD requesting the switch to transfer the call to the appropriate agent (or agent gate).

When the PBX/ACD is ready to actually deliver the call to an agent, it sends a message to the C-T AP identifying who is about to receive the call. C-T AP forms a message that including associated call data to the agents' PC or workstation.

The PCs Call-VIEW client software sees the message and displays a "Notice" window on the agents' screen. This window tells the agent about the call. Call-VIEW software also uses the associated data to form a request a screen pop from the agents' host. Call-View does this by automatically generating the appropriate keystrokes the host needs. There's a scripting tool you can use to store these keystrokes.

PeriWeb. PeriWeb supports Internet-based transaction processing. It works with Periphonics' RISC-based VPS/is, VPS/sp or VPS/V AS systems and stand-alone Sun workstations. You can use PeriWeb with PeriProducer to construct full-function transaction processing services. These apps can access both client-server and mainframe databases.

Building static HTML Web pages is relatively easy, but constructing Web services that perform transaction processing is not so straightforward. This because you have to capture and/or deliver of information unique to an individual or account.

Although IVR applications use the telephone as the primary input/output device, browsers can provide an alternate visual interface for many types of applications. PeriWeb makes this happen. A user of a browser "calls" an IVR application by clicking a hypertext link. PeriWeb "answers" the call and routes it to the application.

The application responds with the normal request to send a voice greeting. This is when PeriWeb translates this into a dynamic hypertext document and sends it to the user. User responses can then be entered through the browser via forms or clicks on displayed images.

Figure 6.5 -- Periphonics PeriWeb.

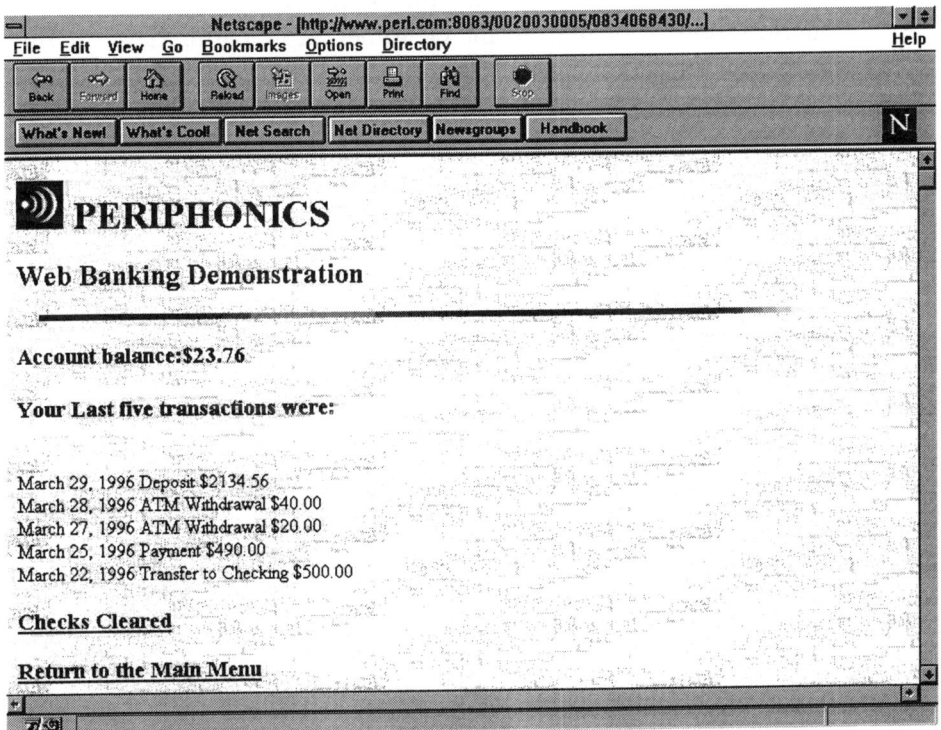

Figure 6.5 shows a NetScape browser screen being fed by PeriWeb. All the back-end transaction processing hooks to mainframes, databases and asynch hosts are part of traditional IVR systems. IVR platforms go to the trouble of dealing with voice prompts, telephony and interactive digit gathering over the phone. Web interaction is really just another "telephone call" transaction to PeriWeb. It's a natural extension to what Periphonics has been doing for a long time.

You can use PeriWeb to extend an IVR application with a hypertext translation table. This is used when the application is running with a Web browser. This dictionary acts like an alternate vocabulary to translate IVR output to Web documents. The IVR application is unchanged.

In addition, an application can be enhanced with WebHints. These make the presentation more appealing to the customer. Application data flowing in either direction can be encrypted for privacy. Encryption and key management are based on the Secure Socket Layer standard or the Secure-HTTP standard. Periphonics system pricing starts at $39,000.

Syntellect, Inc.

Web Access

Syntellect offers a broad range of interactive products and services. Syntellect's systems solutions include Interactive Voice Response and Predictive Dialing. Syntellect Interactive Services provides voice and data processing services for companies that prefer to outsource.

Syntellect is the parent company of Telecorp Systems, the leading provider of call processing systems and services to the cable television and newspaper industries. Home Ticket Intelligent ANI is the largest pay-per-view order processing service world-wide and is housed at Syntellect Interactive Services. Syntellect's new Web Access for the Internet enables IVR transactions via the WWW. The Web Access product is a software application tool.

Using Web Access through the Internet, end users will now be able to perform a variety of self-service applications such as home banking, student registration, catalog ordering, employee benefits and a host of other on-line interactive transactions.

Web Access was designed to expand the feature set of Syntellect's VocalPoint IVR, an open architecture Interactive Voice Response system. By using Web Access, VocalPoint provides connectivity between a Web server and a host computer or database. Syntellect's strategy is to provide interactive communication solutions that accommodate multiple communications devices.

Web Access takes IVR transactions from the simplicity of a telephone-based transaction to an Internet-based transaction. The company launched the solution due to their clients' desire to in turn satisfy their users' desire for high-level electronic access to information. Syntellect says its clients are looking for secure, reliable and easy ways to publish information and automate transactions.

Web Access provides security for sensitive account information by acting as a firewall between the Web server and the host computer or database. Host computer information not available through Web Access is inaccessible to the browser. By using account number, personal identification number and other identifying codes access is limited to authorized persons. Web Access emulates a virtual connection, this eliminating the need for users to reenter information (such as a PIN number) with each new request. The server recognizes each document returned to it from the browser.

Chapter Acknowledgments

My thanks to Joe Baranauskas, president of iNTELiTRAK Technologies, and a very bright gentleman. He's creating some of the best transaction security systems for the Internet. His new "Citadel GateKeeper" platform is what the industry needs to increase commerce and productivity on the Internet. Without security measures, IVR is a haven for hackers.

Chapter 7

Fax and the Internet

For the last decade, fax has held network managers hostage. They've been tied in *backwards-compatibility knots*. It happens every time they try to reduce their companies' fax phone bills. The result is spiraling, unchecked fax costs. Enter the Internet. Its rapid expansion has been quietly ushering us to a time when network managers will be free from this. With an installed base of over 100 million fax devices, we're on the cusp of a revolution in Internet fax. I asked Pete Davidson of Davidson Consulting to "unravel the Gordian knot" of Internet fax. The first part of this chapter manifests his wisdom. Pete is a fax industry guru. He spouts volumes on the subject and runs a thriving consulting practice as a result. Pete also contributed some great FAQ on how to buy interactive fax in my book: *1001 Computer Telephony Tips, Secrets and Shortcuts*.

Faster Fax And The Seven-Year Itch

Until now, there was a reason why network managers couldn't take unilateral action to reduce fax costs. It's the installed base of slow machines. Installing faster fax machines for their company just didn't work.

When fax machines first burst widely onto the office scene in the mid-1980s, the fastest fax machines transmitted at 9.6 Kbps (and the great majority still do). 14.4 Kbps fax machines were introduced in 1989. This promised to drive a rapid-growth replacement market. All this with faster transmission speed and improved compression. 14.4 machines could slash the cost to send a fax in half. But the fax machine installed base was a major obstacle.

Tens of millions of 9.6 Kbps fax machines were already in place. When 14.4 Kbps machines transmit to these slower units, they have to drop down to 9.6 and use the less efficient compression. Faster fax machines simply don't go fast when transmitting to slower machines. So network pay extra for faster fax machines without knowing how often they actually send faster.

Buying faster fax machines only reduces costs if other businesses install faster machines. Only network managers in large multi-site businesses had any interest in the early 1990s. And fax machine procurement was too dispersed to control. As a result, 14.4 Kbps fax machines have only gradually penetrated the marketplace. A full seven years after the first 14.4 Kbps machines appeared, less than one-third of all Fortune 500 machines use 14.4 Kbps devices (and fewer than 10% of SOHO fax machines).

Nonetheless, a new seven-year faster fax machine cycle is ready to begin as fax machine vendors, including JetFax (Menlo Park, Ca) and Pitney Bowes (Shelton, CT) have announced their intent to ship the first 28.8/33.6 Kbps fax machines. But the problem of slower machines has not gone away. Fax machine cost-cutting strategies remain elusive and limited.

Internet Fax
...and the Gordian Knot

A network manager's ability to respond to these concerns is analogous to the Greek myth of the Gordian knot. It was a huge, labyrinthine knot. The ends of the knot were hidden inside and couldn't be seen. As the prophecy goes: "whosoever unties the knot will rule Asia."

Countless aspirants labored at length to untangle it, but they all failed. Liken this to our frustrated network managers. They too, must somehow untangle the largely unknown patterns of fax traffic and capabilities to solve the dilemma. In the myth, the Gordian knot impasse was broken -- and the prophecy fulfilled by Alexander the Great. He dispensed with the seemingly infinite task of untangling the knot. Instead, he sliced it open with one swift swing of his sword. Alexander's action is analogous to Internet fax. The Internet can help you reduce fax phone bills regardless of receive-end fax machine speed. This is because the cost-cutting "sword" of Internet fax is not based on raw end-to-end throughput (the ends of the knot), but a ubiquitous bypass network.

Internet Fax and the Economy

"It's the economy, stupid." Dozens of vendors are emerging to provide one form or another of faxing over the Internet. Faxing over the Internet turns transforms a real-time (voice-like) phone call into a packetized data call. Faxes are simply put into a store and forward paradigm. The technology itself is unimportant. Users know faxes will be delivered within reasonable time periods. They also know error reports will flag undelivered faxes. They assume these transmissions will be given a secure and confidential ride across the Internet.

Besides these performance criteria, the critical issue economy. It just plain costs less to use the Internet. Consider the flat-rate model of the Internet versus the usage-rate model of the public phone networks. The potential for savings is promising. Multi-site businesses can place Internet fax servers on-site. They can fax from site to site without incurring any usage charges over and above their monthly Internet access fees. This can happen between sites not connected by private digital networks.

The average multi-site corporate fax machine generates intra-company charges in excess of $2,000 per year. Add another $1,000 if 10% go overseas. In a 1996 Pitney Bowes/Gallup study, I learned 48% of Fortune 500 faxes are sent to another site within the same company. The savings for *any* businesses are compelling.

Internet faxing can payback the cost of the fax machine in a year based on intra-company fax transmissions alone. According to a 1996 Pitney Bowes/Gallup study, telecom managers expect the average Fortune 500 annual fax phone bill for 1996 to increase by 12% to $18 million. In a joint effort with the same group of researchers, I discovered an explosion in fax costs expressed as a percentage of overall business telephone bills. It went from less than 1% in 1984 to between 30% and 40% in 1995.

As Internet Service Providers (ISPs) roll out Internet faxing services, even single-line fax machines and PC fax systems should be able to take advantage of huge cost savings. For instance, the first ISP to offer Internet faxing services, Concentric Network Corporation (Cupertino, CA), is providing domestic faxing for $9.95 per month for up 125 minutes (8 cents per minute) or $19.95 per month for up to 1,000 minutes (2 cents per minute). My guess is 75% of all fax machines in large and mid-sized businesses have monthly long-distance fax phone bills that amount to at least $40. When considering such a service, two rules of thumb merit attention:

1) The ideal services charge on the basis of fixed monthly rates. If Internet service providers charge usage rates suspiciously similar to your existing phone rates -- you can probably do better. You may find telecom resellers with phone rates lower than some Internet fax usage rates.

2) If usage services are levied for Internet faxing, they should be a magnitude less than current phone rates. For instance, if a business pays 10-cents-per-minute for traditional phone network faxing, then a 2-cent-per-minute rate merits a closer look, while an 8-cent-per-minute rate may neither be worth the trouble. Note that usage rates should only be levied for off-net Internet fax calls.

Internet Fax Limitations

Many early Internet fax systems and services have a curious limitation: you can only fax over the Internet if you use their software or browse to their Web page. This means you can only fax computer files, not paper documents, and only on their terms.

This is true of the Concentric service, which is based on a NetCentric Corporation (Cambridge, Ma) Internet fax router. The gist of the problem is not that the Concentric/NetCentric solution isn't potentially cost-effective, nor that it in anyway comes up short in terms of its advertised performance. Rather, the issue is that about 85% of all corporate fax transmissions still are initiated in the form of paper documents transmitted from standalone fax machines. For most companies, capturing the overwhelming majority of the potential savings from Internet faxing requires that fax machines be interfaced to the Internet fax server, too.

While NetCentric is promising fax machine support in a future release (scanner-based entry is an option), another early entrant in the marketplace, NetXchange (San Francisco, Ca), provides seamless integration with on-site fax machines. NetXchange also supports computer-based faxing. Their server can act as a platform for both private on-premises solutions and ISP-based services. You can integrate the two so ISP Internet fax services can be used as a virtual corporate fax "Intranet." This even addresses far-flung offices.

Internet fax is the sword to the Gordian knot. Network managers don't have to worry about backwards-compatibility with the fax installed base. The best solutions work with existing fax machines and computer fax systems transparently. You want Internet faxing that requires no change in worker habits. For the first time, network managers can proactively cut fax transmission costs – freed from their traditional shackles by the Internet.

American International Facsimile Products

HOST-FAX Production Fax Server

American International Facsimile Products (AIFP) owns the largest share of the production fax market, with over 400 installations in Fortune 2000 companies. AIFP customers include: Microsoft, 3M, Amoco Oil, Bank of America, Carnival Cruise Lines, John Deere, Federal Express, Harley-Davidson, Intel, PepsiCo and Walt Disney World.

Strategic partnerships include Oracle, Unisys, IBM, Dell Computer, Brooktrout, SunSoft and Attachmate. The fax software market can be broken down into two categories: production fax and ad hoc fax.

Production vs. Ad Hoc Faxing. Production fax software provides a high-volume, low-cost and real-time document delivery option for mainframe and mid-range system applications, replacing printing and mailing. These applications are typically batch-oriented, automating repetitive, mission-critical processes such as invoicing, purchasing, loan origination, etc. Generally, production fax software is tightly integrated with these host based applications, enabling high volume processing and transmission of dynamic documents (i.e., forms-based documents that contain variable data). With ad hoc faxing, the process required for a given document is not predefined; it usually involves relatively low-volume faxing from PC-based applications such as word processing, spreadsheets, etc. Typically, ad hoc faxing is used for routine office activities, such as document sharing and correspondence.

HOST-FAX 2.1 Production Fax Server. This is AIFP's flagship production fax server. It supports high-volume faxing of dynamic documents such as purchase orders, invoices and sales orders directly from mainframe and mid-range applications. HOST-FAX is based on AIFP's open, Unix-based fax technology. HOST-FAX 2.1 can process up to 2,880 faxes per hour - more than any other server.

Because the system is based on a dedicated server architecture, it does not use expensive host CPU cycles. HOST-FAX is also extremely scaleable, supporting one to 48 channels with the same server hardware platform and software. Standard fax boards (Brooktrout, et al.), PC hardware (IBM, Dell, et al.) and Posix-compliant SunSoft Interactive OS is at the heart of this platform. This allows AIFP to concentrate on their core expertise (rather than re-designing core technology to keep pace with technology advances).

Cross-platform enterprise support. Support for mainframe, mid-range and PC LAN Windows-based applications is available. Host support includes IBM; DEC VAX; Hewlett-Packard 3000 and 9000 systems; Sequent; and Unisys A, V, U6000, and 2200 systems.

You can access multiple hosts (whatever the topology) and multiple simultaneous sessions. Here is a run-down of the optional software modules for HOST-FAX:

INTERNETLINK. This is a messaging module. It allows HOST-FAX users to automatically deliver documents over the Internet using the MIME (Multi-purpose Internet Mail Extensions) format.

FAXMAIL. This gives customers a new way to handle inbound and outbound faxes - all from within CC:Mail or Lotus Notes. Any document you create in a Windows application can be faxed via CC:Mail or Notes.

HOST-FAX for 400. This native AS/400 client interface provides AS/400 users with the industry's most comprehensive set of production fax capabilities.

NET-LINK. PC LAN services for HOST-FAX are in this Windows-based application.

RESPONSE-FAX. This fax-on-demand module gives users touch-tone access to documents. The system automatically faxes back to them.

FAXWAY. This is a DID-based module for managing, viewing, and automatically routing high volume inbound faxes. It also routes e-mail.

Black Ice Software, Inc.

Internet Fax Server

Black Ice Software, Inc. is a provider of Fax Development Tool Kits, utilities and products for faxing and imaging applications in the Microsoft Windows environment. Black Ice's tool kits allow application developers to add raster image manipulation functions to windows applications.

The *Internet Fax Server* allows users to send or receive faxes through Internet.

The product's main components are: The *Internet Fax Server* and *SendFAX* client software for Microsoft Windows 3.1 x, Win95 and NT. In addition, a metering billing module is available. This allows user charge-back for local phone calls. The *Internet Fax Server* is scaleable and can be interconnected for up to 999 servers and expanded from 100 users to an unlimited number of users.

The product will be licensed in increments of 50, 100, 500, 1000 and unlimited users. Pricing starts at $1,000 for 50 users up to $10,000 for unlimited users.

The Internet Fax Server can use up to 255 ports with any Class 1, Class 2, or Class 2.0 fax modems, or with multi-channel modems from Brooktrout, or GammaLink. In addition, it is integrated with Microsoft Internet Server, Microsoft exchange and SNTP POP3 mail server.

With SendFAX, the user simply prints from any Windows 3.1X, Win95 or NT application to the SendFAX Driver: The users can then route the fax by selecting the destination fax number from the phone book. The fax will then be routed through an e-mail connection to the fax server like any other fax. The status will be reported back the same way as any other PC based fax software.

The Internet Fax Server sends the fax out on the local telephone exchange. The server can be interconnected dynamically to negotiate their hierarchy position in the network. The attached new server automatically handles all clients of previous servers.

Internet Fax Server is targeted at corporations with distributed offices around the world. Black Ice says you can bypass long distance telephone carriers for faxing and drastically reduce long-distance telephone rates. A typical fax page is transmitted in under 50 seconds, whereas the typical long distance call to Europe or Asia can cost more than $1.00 per minute. This means system cost can be recovered within a few days of operation.

Brooktrout Technology, Inc.

IP/FaxRouter

Brooktrout sells software and hardware products for telecommunications and networking environments. Brooktrout's fax, voice and telephony products include the TR Series and TruFax fax and voice processing boards and the QuadraFax imbedded fax and voice system. Their newest product, the IP/FaxRouter is an imbedded fax system for routing fax over IP networks, such as the Internet.

In addition, the company sells the Show N Tel development platform for voice, fax and telephone integrated applications. The platform is used by over 300 independent service bureaus and telecommunications companies. Users also include hundreds of small businesses and other organizations worldwide.

Along with GammaLink, Brooktrout pioneered the multi-channel fax board market. They were the first to combine fax and voice processing on a single board and the first to provide fax application development tools under UNIX and Windows NT.

The IP/FaxRouter is an Ethernet peripheral which allows facsimile traffic to be sent via TCP/IP Wide Area Networks. The primary benefit is efficiency as international faxing is measured in dollars per minute while fax over a WAN is pennies per minute or less. The system is invisible to users as standard fax numbers remain as the basic means to identify destinations. The IP/FaxRouter simply compares the fax numbers with IP addressing behind the scenes to route faxes over Frame Relay, ISDN, or even the Internet. Organizations with existing digital circuits can essentially achieve "fax for free" by routing fax traffic along with other data communications. Fax service providers can track usage with PIN number software.

Other features include store and forward, relay broadcast, and centralized management. The units can route fax traffic to worldwide destinations using a combination of data networks and telephone systems.

Companies like Abbott Labs are using the IP/FaxRouter to send and receive faxes among all their offices worldwide. Ditto for one of the world's largest clothing designers. These customers are eliminating charges of up to $6 a minute in their daily international fax communications. This only begins to illustrate the potential for a WAN fax solution.

The IP/FaxRouter can also be used to route faxes and deliver them locally, using standard telephony services., For system administrators, the IP/FaxRouter sits on an Ethernet LAN and manages fax traffic behind the scene. A Windows-based management package provides central (and simple) management and configuration facilities. All IP/FaxRouters on the IP network, regardless of their physical location can be managed from one PC. Fax senders and recipients continue to communicate via fax as they always have - the IP/FaxRouter does its work transparently.

Remote presence is a unique concept to take advantage of with the IP/FaxRouter. A built-in Auto-Route option will allow organizations to locate IP/FaxRouters anywhere in the world accepting local phone numbers for remote delivery. For example, customers of a particular company in the UK could send faxes with a local phone number in the UK. These faxes could actually be delivered to a site anywhere else in the world over a TCP/IP WAN. To the customer it appears that that company has a local site. The same could be used to "invisibly" deliver fax traffic from remote sites to a larger central server somewhere else. The API may be required to more elegantly deliver fax traffic over a LAN to make this issue a strong benefit.

The IP/FaxRouter provides low cost routing by looking at fax phone numbers and sending a fax over a wide area network if the destination phone number is associated with another router's IP address. The fax is sent from one IP/FaxRouter to another.

The IP/FaxRouter does not accomplish least cost routing. Least cost implies comparing destinations to tables which have line costs built-in. For example, a least cost routing implementation may dictate that fax from Brazil going to Germany first pass through the US.

The IP/Router can actually achieve some of the benefits of least cost routing through user dialing. For example, IP/FaxRouters may be installed in Brazil and the US. It may make sense for users in Brazil to dial into the US IP/FaxRouter. From there the fax would be sent via telephony to Europe. Least cost routing is achieved as a fax call from the US to Europe is much less than the same call made from Brazil.

The IP/FaxRouter can save thousands of dollars in telecommunication charges related to facsimile usage particularly with international applications. At a $5,995 list price, the small, stand alone network node can quickly pay for itself. Windows-based administration makes it easy to install with minimal on-going administration.

Figure 7.1 -- Brooktrout IP/FaxRouter

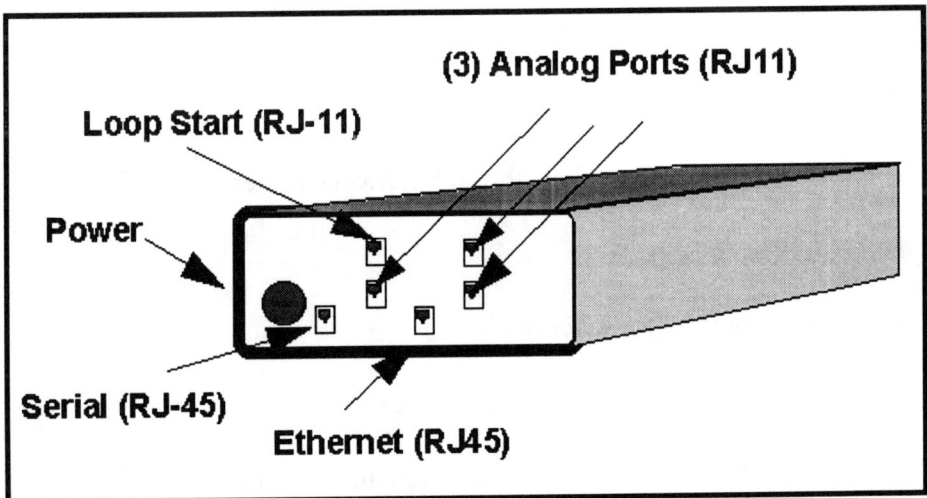

The Brooktrout IP/FaxRouter is a small network peripheral, approximately 2.5 by 7.2 by 11.8 inches with one Ethernet port (RJ-45), three analog modem ports (RJ-11), one fax loop start port, 425 megabyte disk storage and one serial port. This is illustrated in Figure 7.1. It moves fax data over the telephone and digital data lines using the standard international dialing plan as the basis for addressing. Routing tables reference these phone numbers and the IP address of each IP/FaxRouter. These tables are created automatically by the Windows-based Configuration and Network Management System (CNMS). This based on data entered by the system administrator. After these routing tables are downloaded to the fax routers they autonomously route faxes over the WAN based on destination phone numbers.

The IP/FaxRouter can operate with dial-up or dedicated wide area links. It will operate over any wide area network using the TCP/IP Protocol including the Internet, Frame Relay, T-1, ISDN, SMDS, etc. The system can be plugged into a PBX or directly connected to a PSTN. Remote sites can call into the IP/FaxRouter using its analog port number and then send a fax using secondary digits to identify the target fax machine. The following activity will occur when someone walks up to fax machine 1 and dials their fax destination number.

1) Fax sent using standard fax number

2) IP/FaxRouter determines IP route

3) Fax sent as TCP/IP packets through network router

4) Fax traverses IP net

5) Network router allows access

6) Fax received, IP/ FaxRouter determines route

7) Off-net delivery auto dials-out through analog ports

8) Fax sent through PBX to public telco service, fax delivered

Figure 7.2 -- IP/FaxRouter Topology

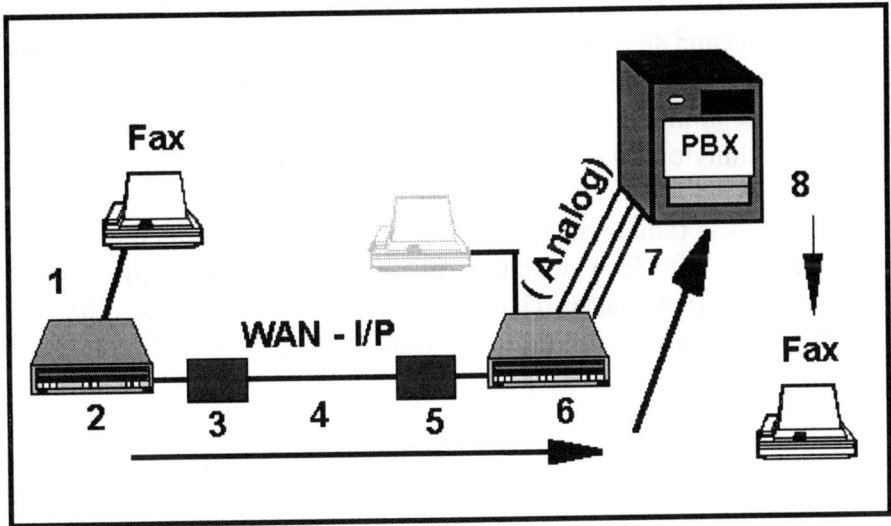

Figure 7.2 illustrates a basic configuration and highlights the key points of workflow. Network routers must be used for IP/FaxRouter to operate over a WAN. Routers use algorithms for choosing routes and convert a LAN signal to WAN. You can any router that supports 10baseT Ethernet II on the LAN side with TCP/IP protocols.

FaxSav Incorporated

FaxSav for Internet Services

FaxSav Incorporated (nee Digitran) is a privately held international facsimile services company. The company maintains a proprietary, fax-only network to provide customers with low-cost services for faxing. FaxSav recently activated its second Internet fax point of presence (POP) outside the U.S. This was done to broaden the service options available to users in the Pac Rim. By establishing a physical presence in Hong Kong, FaxSav is able to use the Internet to provide cost-savings to users of both its Internet-based desktop fax services and standard fax machines. The company is licensed by the Federal Communications Commission as an authorized telecommunications company.

This means the company has direct connection to long distance providers and both origin and destination numbers. At the heart of FaxSav's technology lie two, smart telecommunications switches, one located at 60 Hudson Street, the main telecommunications switching facility on the East Coast, and the other in Washington, D.C. at the main MCI facility.

Each switch is redundant in its processors, T-1 lines, Internet networks and power supplies. Each switch has two mirrored, Unix-based controllers. This means FaxSav can provide service without interruption. The switch is capable of storing Group III and IV files. This enables FaxSav to provide global store-and-forward broadcast fax services to its users.

In 1996, FaxSav connected its programmable switches to the World Wide Web. The Web-enabled suite enables users to send formatted and unformatted documents from their computer desktop to any international destination. From IP addressed Windows desktops, the user can merely select "print to FaxSav" from under his file menu. This sends any Windows as a fax through the FaxSav network via the Web. With the new E-mail Fax Access service, any e-mail message can be sent to any fax machine worldwide.

In a standard analog telecommunications call, the incoming scanned data bits are converted at the fax machine into standard fax modulated frequencies which are then delivered to the Unix-controlled switch. The switch then reroutes the tones to the destination fax machines over the best route. In the case of a data file arriving at the FaxSav switch from the Internet, FaxSav extracts key information that came with the file, including the sender's and destination's identity. It then converts the basic data file into the modulated frequencies before sending them to the destination fax machine.

This effectively gives every fax machine its own destination e-mail address: faxnumber@FaxSav.com. FaxSav has integrated the Internet into the fabric of its service platform and user options. The company launched it's PC-based *FaxSav for Internet Services* at the Networld + Interop show in Japan.

FaxSav for Internet lets users send faxes right from email or Windows applications over the Internet to the FaxSav network. The services combine the convenience end ease-of use of desktop fax software and cost- saving benefits of the FaxSav service.

Fax POP Network. For companies not yet connected to the Internet, FaxSav's multinational network allows low-cost delivery from fax machines to other fax machines using the Internet. Users address faxes to the desti- nation fax number. Faxes are then forwarded transparently through the POPs and switching nodes on the FaxSav network, eliminating costly PTT and international carrier service charges. The service uses multiple networks to dynamically select the best overall route for delivering each fax.

FaxSav For Internet. Besides bringing savings of the desktop, FaxSav for Internet extends FaxSav service to users outside the U.S. Faxes can be originated on PCs or scanners anywhere and delivered in the U.S. for fifteen cents per page. The Windows user can send any fax from his desktop, including scanned input, without first printing the file, picking up the output at the printer, dialing at the fax machine, and waiting to see if the fax actually goes through. Users can continue to use their preferred computer addressing mechanism or database. Beyond the simple convenience to the end user, the time saved on misfeeds alone is tremendous. It's as if the user hired an assistant to oversee his faxing.

FaxLauncher. This enables faxing within any Windows applications. you can send word processing, spreadsheet or graphic documents across the Internet to any fax machine.

FaxMailer. Email applications can be used to send a message as a fax to users who can't or do not wish to receive it as an e-mail.

FaxScan. This program allows users to send scanned documents over the Internet to fax machines worldwide, turning PCs into virtual fax machines. FaxSav provides RSA encryption for files sent from Windows desktops. Thus, any file delivered over the Internet will be readable only by individuals receiving the final fax, and not by any hacker that happens to sit on a line.

FaxSav provides significant review and notification of ongoing and completed faxes. Users receive notification of delivery at his preferred e-mail address. Before this, he had to wait at the fax machine to determine whether the fax had in fact been delivered. This saves substantial time in waiting and retrying fax delivery. Likewise, the user can visit the FaxSav Web site and monitor and review the delivery of all of his faxes.

Ibex Technologies, Inc.

FactsLine for the Web

Ibex Technologies, Inc. was first in allowing non-Web users access to Web pages by using a phone and fax machine. Ibex is a leader in traditional fax-on-demand. The company's FactsLine for the Web product will actually pull down a Web page, when requested by a caller, and render it into a fax image for transmission. FaxBack, another fax-on-demand company, also offers a fax-on-demand product integrated to the Web.

There are many methods of integrating the Internet, fax and voice, and many people become confused when discussing the various products (although some are not much more than ideas) on the market. The best way to analyze the ideas is to cut through the "cool" technology and figure out what, in simple terms, the benefits are. Then keep those benefits in mind when looking at the products.

Fax Delivery via the Web

Fax delivery or fax-on-demand via the Web differs from other voice/fax/Web products in that it is focused on document content and delivery, not store and forward messaging (voice, fax and e-mail messaging products), or Internet transport of voice or fax messages. There are normally three things that pop into a person's mind when fax-on-demand via the Web is mentioned.

Some think that this means that you can access Web pages via a telephone and a fax machine, while some believe that this means you can choose documents to be faxed by browsing and interacting with a Web site. Both are correct - it really depends what you are trying to accomplish and we'll describe both in detail.

A third type of person asks, "why would ever want to combine fax with the Web?" The answer to that is simple. Not everyone is on the Web. Davidson Consulting, an expert in the fax market, points out that there are 800 million people that have access to a phone and a fax machine, while only 30 million (and studies show they are predominantly younger males) are on the Web. If you want to reach a wide audience, then you can't ignore fax as a delivery medium.

Figure 7.3 -- Fax User Acceptance

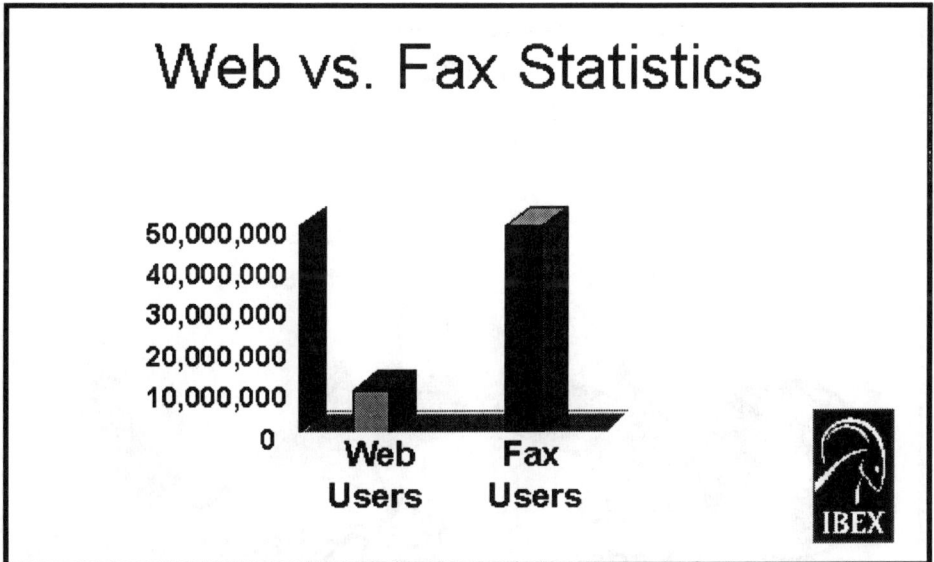

Web vs. Fax Statistics

50,000,000	
40,000,000	
30,000,000	
20,000,000	
10,000,000	
0	Web Users Fax Users

IBEX

Figure 7.4 -- Technology User Snapshot

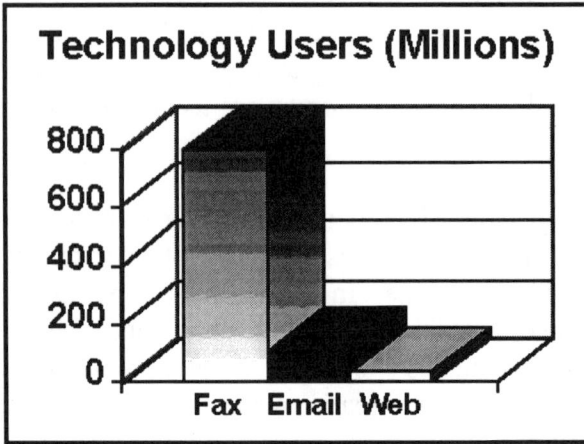

Figure 7.5 -- Fax-On-Demand & The Web

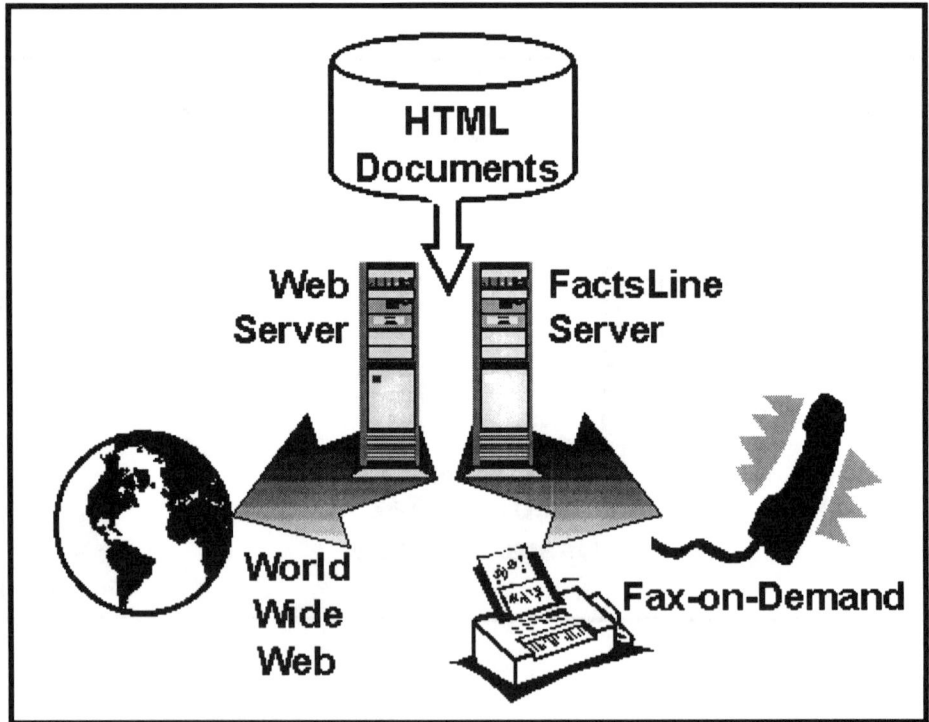

But the Web is big and more and more effort is going into getting Web sites up and running and authoring information on the Web. Companies are spending an awful lot of money to say they have a Web site, but the return on investment numbers are not yet there. Because of the ubiquitous reach of fax, many companies are allowing non-Web users fax access of Web pages to leverage their Internet investment and increase the ROI numbers.

The Ibex product uses Netscape browser technology so that the faxed page will look very much like it does when viewed in Netscape. In other words, newer Web features pioneered by Netscape such as text tables will appear on the faxed version just as they appear when view on the computer screen. The Ibex product also caches documents so they don't have to be retrieved from the Web by the Ibex server each time someone requests them.

Figure 7.6 -- Acquiring Images

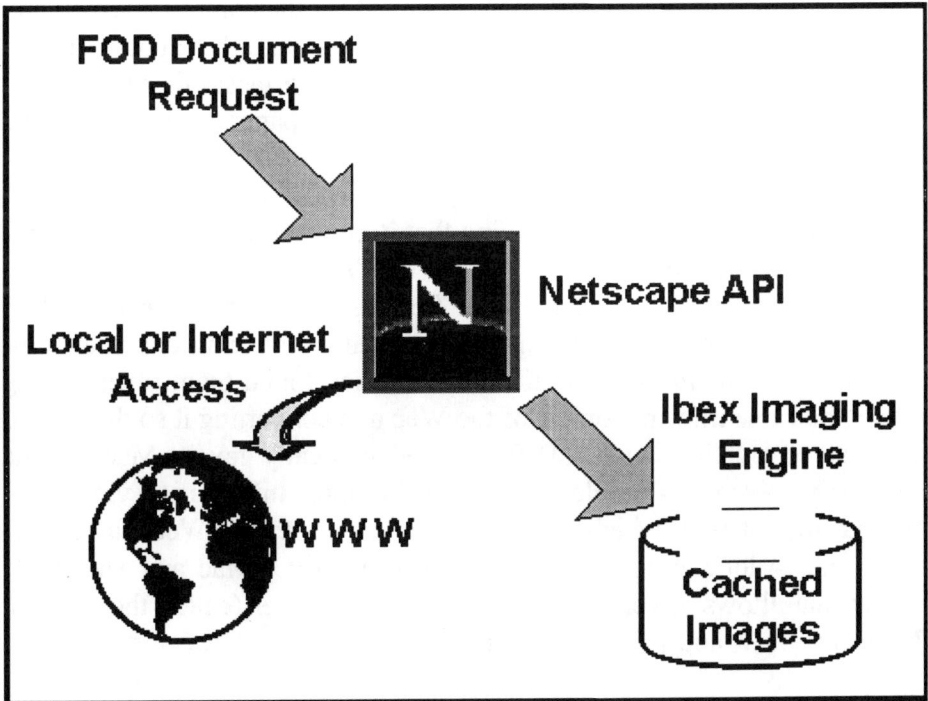

Fax-on-Demand and Web Issues

One issue is how someone using a phone can navigate through a Web page, and various companies have come up with different strategies on this. One company, Web-on-Call, actually reads the Web page to you over the phone with text-to-speech. FaxBack, another traditional fax-on-demand supplier, creates an index out of an actual Web page by placing small index numbers on the page next to any hot links. These index numbers are document numbers that can be entered on the phone when requesting a fax.

Ibex takes another approach by assuming that more than Web information will be available via phone and fax, and therefore creating a global index of documents. Some of the documents could be Web documents, some could be traditional fax documents, or some could come from other sources such as Lotus Notes or Adobe Acrobat.

Another issue is that Web pages are designed for the computer screen and not for the printed page. Fonts are generally larger and the layout is not as complex. Fax, on the other hand, is designed to be facsimile of a printed page, thus some Web pages don't look as good on paper as they did on the screen.

In fact, some companies are learning that it may not be a good idea to put documents directly on the Web (in the Web's HTML language) without putting them into a more traditional format first. One pioneer of Web technology is Macromedia. Macromedia starting authoring documents directly into HTML format, but after a while they found themselves having to take the same information off of the Web and converting it so they could still mail it, publish it via CD-ROM, and manually fax it. Macromedia eventually solved this problem by publishing most information via Adobe Acrobat format first, which then could be taken into the Web, fax-on-demand, etc. Adobe Acrobat is a cross platform (PC, Mac and Unix) file format that allows anyone with a free Acrobat viewer (called the Acrobat Reader) to view and print the document.

Since it more closely resembles a printed page with rich formatting, it is a great choice to be used for fax publishing, Web publishing and CD-ROM publishing. Some of the fax-on-demand vendors (e.g. Ibex) will use Acrobat files (sometimes called "PDF" files because of the .PDF file extension) and convert them on-the-fly into fax documents. You can get more information on Acrobat by calling the Adobe fax-on-demand system (206-628-5737)or by visiting their Web site, www.adobe.com.

This isn't to say that all Web documents should be in Acrobat format, but certainly highly formatted documents will look nicer when converted to traditionally hard-copy (via fax or print), and more and more companies are discovering this. Also, not all Web pages, whether in HTML format or Adobe Acrobat format, should be available via fax. Some Web pages, as you'll notice if you have spent any time on the Web, are mainly for navigation or to generate interest with flashy graphics. These pages are low on actual information content and generally don't translate well to fax.

Fax-Enabling A Web Site

Another aspect of fax delivery on the Web is being able to send a fax to someone by clicking a *fax button* on a Web site. Why would someone fax-enable their Web site? It allows non-Web documents (legacy documents) to be accessed via the Web. Older documents that have been scanned in or are in a format that is incompatible with the Web can stilled be accessed via the Web even if they can not be viewed on the Web. The user would select the document they wished, then they can fax them to themselves or forward the document to another party.

It separates information-gathering from information-consumption. It is a natural process to gather information first, then consume it by reading, analyzing and digesting it. The Web disrupts this process by forcing you to both gather and consume information at the same time. If you've spent time on the Web looking for information, you have probably noticed that you spend a lot of time quickly scanning pages for information, then moving on to the next prospect.

When you find something interesting, you have a dilemma. Do you stop and read it, perhaps losing your place in your search? Do you stop and print it out? Or do you merely select it to be faxed with the rest of your selections? It allows a company to have a central library of fax documents A list of faxable documents can be maintained on the Web site for internal employees, who can then send faxes by merely accessing the page. Thus no client software is needed except for a Web browser (and Internet access). This can be especially useful in companies with dispersed locations or in call center environments. A good example of this feature is located on Ibex's home page, www.ibex.com.

FIGURE 7.7 -- FAX-ON-DEMAND FROM WEB PAGE

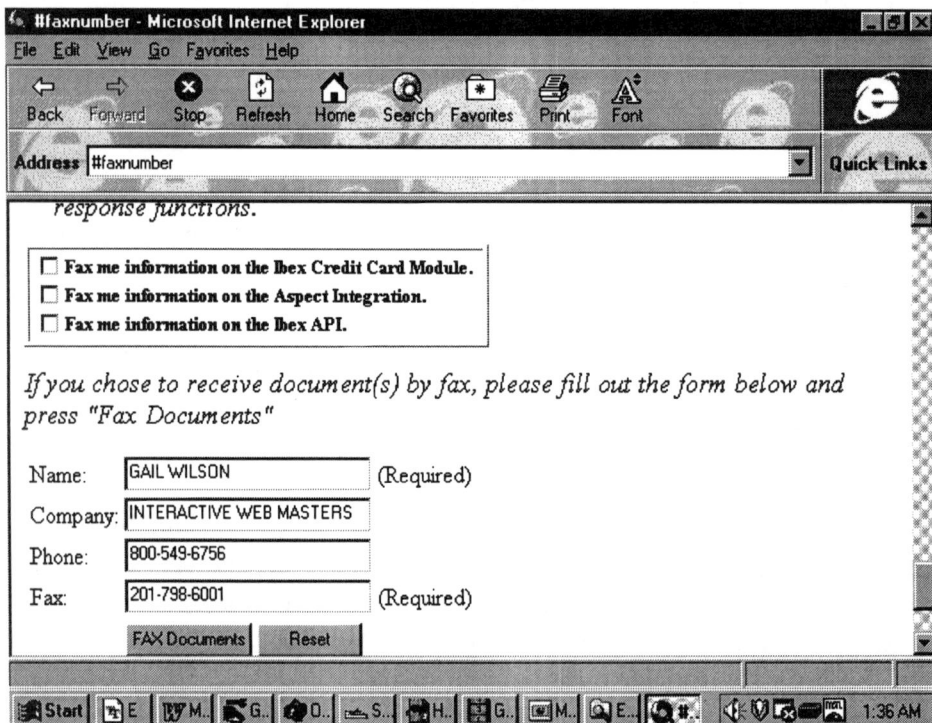

E-mail-On-Demand

Another interesting slant on fax-on-demand and how it integrates with the Internet is a e-mail-on-demand. Ibex's E-mail-On-Demand is an interactive e-mail system that allows users to request information via e-mail and receive it, within seconds, via e-mail or fax. E-mail-On-Demand goes beyond simple "Mailbots" or "Auto-responders" by providing menued access to a library of information and giving the user a choice of document formats. Rich text formats like Adobe Acrobat can be requested and sent via MIME e-mail or fax; while plain text formats can be universally sent to any e-mail system. When an initial e-mail is sent to the E-mail-On-Demand (EMOD) server, the server returns a catalog of documents which acts as a document order form. The e-mail user places an "x" next to the document(s) of interest and returns the e-mail. The Ibex EMOD server then retrieves the documents, in the appropriate format, and e-mails or faxes them to the user.

In the frenzy of "surfing" the net--jumping from page to page, link to link--users frequently find themselves passing up interesting information as they surf on to the next site. With E-mail-On-Demand there is no need to miss a thing. Users don't have to remember a phone number, a URL address, or take the time to load a Web browser to download the information. Users request information, on the spot, by using e-mail as an order form. A "Fax it to me" feature is available with the Ibex product which allows the e-mail user to request that the information be faxed instead of e-mailed.

NetPhonic Communications, Inc.

Web-On-Call Voice Browser

Web-On-Call Voice Browser, from NetPhonic Communications, Inc., is Web server software that joins Internet and telephony networks to provide universal access to information residing on Web servers. Designed for both Web surfers and non-surfers, Web-On-Call Voice Browser lets anyone obtain Web documents without a computer, Internet connection, or Web browsing software. Users need only a touch-tone phone, cellular phone or fax machine to obtain Web documents.

In order to 'telephone enable' Web sites, organizations install Web-On-Call Voice Browser, voice modems and analog telephone lines. Upon installation, the Web server is ready to answer telephone calls with, "Welcome to (Company Name) Voice Browser." Callers are prompted by simple touch-tone responses such as *"To find out general information about this site, press 1; to navigate to the document of your interest, press 2; to identify a document by its number, press 3...."* Once a caller reaches the destination document, he or she can request the information to be read over the phone, faxed back, sent as an e-mail attachment, or via postal mail.

Installed on the same computer as Web server software such as a Netscape server, Web-On-Call Voice Browser reads information stored in Web documents and transforms the content into various communication formats including audio over telephone, fax image, hard copy and word processing files attached to an e-mail message. Web-On-Call Voice Browser requires no training on the part of the end-user. Using widely known telephone response techniques and friendly prompts, callers find the interface natural and comfortable. As illustrated in Figure 7.8, telephone callers can access a variety of databases from the most ubiquitous data terminal in the world: the telephone.

Figure 7.8 -- Web On Call Voice Browser Access

The Net Without Membership. Although the Internet has become a key communication vehicle of the 90's, many have regarded Web browsing to be an advanced technology for the privileged or highly educated. Others think it is something for the latest personal computer platforms with graphical user interfaces. The truth is, most of the population is comfortable with and has easy access to traditional information-gathering means such as telephones and faxes.

Web-On-Call Voice Browser makes it possible for information providers to reach everyone, anywhere by leveraging organizations' investments already made in setting up Web servers and content. For those who are infrequent Net surfers, or do not have a computer or Internet connection, Web-On-Call Voice Browser provides a practical way to access Web documents. Once a Web Master or MIS professional installs Web-On-Call Voice Browser on a Web server, a phone call is all that is necessary for an end user to retrieve information.

Web Mobile. Experienced Net surfers can augment their Web experience by accessing the same information in a different way. Even the most frequent users of Web browsers can benefit from the mobility and quick connection benefits of Web-On-Call Voice Browser. For example, while traveling, meeting in a conference room or driving a car, all users need to do to access valuable Web information is make a phone call to a Web-On-Call Voice Browser-equipped site. Callers receive the same information they would have viewed using a browser. Instead of viewing the data on a monitor, they obtain information via audio, fax or electronic file in ASCII text or word processing-compatible format.

This built-in mobility allows anybody to take the entire resource of a Web server to the field, home or anywhere without carrying an office or laptop computer, or looking for a modem connection in an unfamiliar setting. Imagine yourself as a field sales person visiting a customer's factory site, a bank teller working at a counter, an executive waiting at an airport, or a branch office worker. Your productivity depends on a universal and reliable way to access most up-to-date information quickly wherever you are.

Web Spontaneous. Although Web browsing is a rewarding experience, the time invested in browsing for information can sometimes outweigh the benefits. When someone wants to look up timely and simple information quickly, e.g. stock quotes, account balances, the latest news update, Web surfing can be tedious and slow. For example, one can go through booting a computer, dialing a modem, getting an Internet connection, remembering the right URL, waiting for a busy Web site and finally, receiving graphical pages. Web-On-Call Voice Browser delivers ultimate spontaneity for quick information response. All users need is a split-second telephone dial tone.

Central Information Source. Individuals responsible for information fulfillment benefit from Web-On-Call Voice Browser because they no longer have to replicate and maintain the same content on multiple servers such as UNIX-based Web, OS/2-based Notes, DOS-based fax-on-demand, and Windows NT-based file retrieval servers. With Web-On-Call, Web documents are the single source of information regardless of the delivery paradigm.

This means less maintenance and better organization of information. Since there are no separate islands of information, there are no "out-of-sync data" problems. This also means more timely information delivery to anybody regardless of how users obtain information. Companies can realize an immediate investment pay-back based on saved time, less maintenance and fewer machines. They also get up-to-the minute information that is accessible to everyone through a Central Information Source.

Paradigm Advantages. While graphical browsers offer advantages such as eye-pleasing graphics and spatial organization of information (such as a spreadsheet), Web-On-Call Voice Browser provides a dimension no computer can replicate: rich audio including expression of emotion, control over pace, pitch, and ear-pleasing sounds.

Cost Savings. Organizations with automated information response systems are already experiencing large savings and increased levels of customer satisfaction. These benefits can be measured in terms of manpower savings, reduced office overhead, expanded hours, and real-time information delivery to any requesters. Some experience as much as 90% cost savings in fulfilling information and a dramatic increase in service responsiveness.

Without Web-On-Call Voice Browser, the initial investment required to realize such benefits are very high. In order to replicate the benefits of Web-On-Call Voice Browser, an organization needs to set up multiple servers running various operating systems to offer fax-on-demand, Audiotex, interactive voice response data retrieval, and file retrieval capabilities.

A combined cost of these servers can be tens of thousands of dollars at the outset. Other hidden costs of these systems are high overhead associated with maintaining multiple operating systems, separate software vendor relationships, disparate databases, incompatible computers, and personnel training.

Adding Web-On-Call Voice Browser to an existing Web server does not require the purchase of another computer or operating system. Web-On-Call Voice Browser costs substantially less than any single standalone server itself, let alone the combined cost of multiple systems.

Ease of Use and Installation

The Web-On-Call Voice Browser telephony user interface was designed for people who use phones; its systems administration features are designed for business people and computer administrators with no prior telephony background; and its database was designed for anybody who can design Web pages.

Unlike other telephony or voice server products, Web-On-Call Voice Browser does not require telecommunication knowledge. Anyone with modem knowledge can install and maintain the system. There are no special connection requirements with telephone companies, Internet service providers or PBX vendors.

To set up a Web-On-Call Voice Browser system, all that is needed is a Web server, regular analog or Centrex telephone lines, Web-On-Call Voice Browser compatible voice modems, and Web-On-Call Voice Browser software. System administration is performed using a graphical interface designed for GUI browsers and GUI systems administration.

Once the system is set up, any change to source Web documents are automatically reflected in audio, fax or e-mail deliveries. Alternately, administrators can use the 'Teleprompting' feature to create and maintain human voice recorded contents. If new content has not been recorded by a person, or if content changes frequently, a high accuracy text-to-speech technology will kick in for automatic synthesizing of audio content.

Security and Multi-language Support. Web-On-Call Voice Browser is designed to support both external and internal Web sites. For those internal sites requiring security, user ID and password protection are included with the system. Unlike the Internet's wide exposure for security breaches, callers to Web-On-Call Voice Browser system cannot break into key files on the Web server. Web-On-Call also recognizes any firewalls in place in existing sites.

For organizations that fulfill information requests from around the world and in different languages, Web-On-Call Voice Browser handles up to four language prompts simultaneously.

NetXchange Communications Ltd.

Internet Fax Exchange

NetXchange technology reduces associated fax costs by providing corporations and Internet Service Providers (ISPs) with the software to create a "virtual fax network" over the Internet. Its technology is designed for use by corporations, service providers, telcos, fax back/call back companies as well as VARs and software integrators.

The Internet Fax Exchange software solution from NetXchange Communications Ltd. is an advanced messaging platform. Service Providers can use it to implement high performance, costeffective fax services over their existing data communications infrastructure and the Internet. Standalone fax machines as well as any mobile, dialup and permanent Internet user can take advantage of this fax service.

Internet Fax Exchange runs on a Win NT server and automatically routes all fax traffic between the servers located on the global network. Operating over the Internet and private TCP/IP networks, faxes are delivered on a leastcost routing basis, depending on the volume of fax traffic and the global location of the Internet Fax Exchange servers. With Internet Fax Exchange installed on the global network, you reap the benefits of lower fax tariffs and gain sophisticated fax distribution services.

Internet Fax Exchange features a builtin Simple FaxTransport Protocol (SFTP), which creates a fax delivery infrastructure over the Internet. SFTP dynamically synchronizes between all other Fax Exchange servers in the network, eliminating the need for user intervention. Peertopeer transport of faxes is performed using a Dynamic Internet Bandwidth Allocation Protocol (DIBA) for Internet backbone communication. Servers automatically distribute the work load without user intervention. All servers are redundant and in the case of failure, the backup server automatically takes over all functions' assuring no loss of faxes, information or downtime.

Automatic Discovery. Internet Fax Exchange maps servers throughout the entire network for easy and dynamic system configuration. The addition or removal of a server from any location on the network is immediately discovered and faxes are routed accordingly.

Automatic LeastCost Routing. Based on the number dialed, optional preconfigured routing tables and local PSTN cost tables, the Internet Fax Exchange server determines the leastcost routing and transmits the fax via the most economical and efficient route.

System and Delivery Authentication. An encryption and authentication process assures system security by permitting the participation of only authorized servers and clients and assuring fax data integrity. The Internet Fax Exchange management system uses SNMP management. All Internet Fax Exchange servers in the organization can be managed from any station located on the Internet, running over standard HP OpenView platform. This provides integration with other network management applications.

A powerful SNMP agent (subagent) is located in each server. This agent implements a speciallydesigned MIB 11 extension that enable remote monitoring and control of the entire system from any point on the Internet. All server events are logged so that the Internet Fax Exchange manager can access a server at any time and obtain a complete history of that server's activities.

Figure 7.9 -- Internet Fax Exchange Detail Information

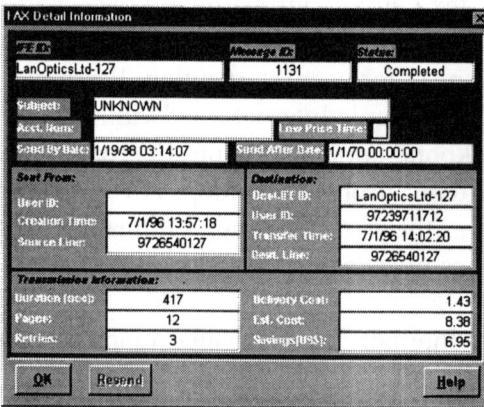

Based on the SNMP management platform, the Internet Fax Exchange interfaces with billing and accounting services. The application can perform account billing per client, account balancing for each branch office (or profit center), plus additional billing and accounting details can be customized based on a customer's requirements. Figure 7.9 shows the level of detail you get. This useful for forecasting service use and growth as well as for profitability calculations. System logs are recorded for each fax transaction on the network and a Call Data Record (CDR) is established for each individual transaction. This enables export of the relevant data for advanced billing capabilities and generation of user statistics using ODBC (Open Database Connection). Figure 7.10 shows a list of completed transactions that can be exported into any ODBC program.

Figure 7.10 -- Internet Fax Exchange Report

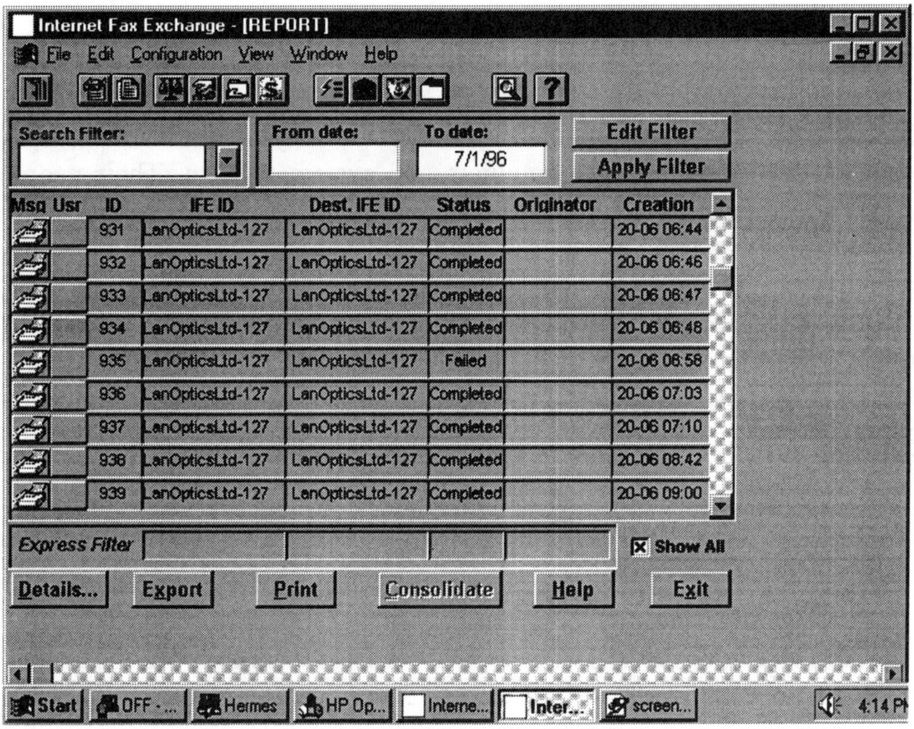

Internet Fax Exchange supports all types of fax clients. A dialup mobile Internet client can send a fax from a Windows application using the existing high speed, Internet connection, eliminating the need to establish a dedicated fax session. Standalone fax machines located on the client premises transmit faxes using standard procedures via the local PSTN to the local Internet Fax Exchange server. For large customers having a permanent Internet connection, an Internet Fax Exchange server is located on their private network. This server provides fax services to the PC's and fax machines on the local customer premises and routes all faxes out of the local area to the SP network.

Nice Systems, Inc.

NiceFax

Nice Systems, Inc. was founded by former military engineers with experience in digital recording, computers and systems design. Their people pioneered the development of highspeed data networking equipment using ATM technology. Nice is concentrating on developing telecommunication products for the digital logging market. The company's main product, NiceLog, has been sold to more than 150 companies worldwide. Additional products that the company offers include COMINT and NiceFix (a computerized system for detecting, locating and monitoring transmission sources).

Nice's voice logging systems are called NiceLog. The systems capture and record large volumes of voice data. This information is transmitted over multiple telephone or other communications lines. Users can retrieve and playback specific communications data. Until a few years ago, voice logging was based on analog reeltoreel technology. Analog technology limited users' ability to store and retrieve data effectively and efficiently and could not interface with digital computer and telecommunications networks. In the early 1990s, analog reeltoreel recorders were displaced by analog VHSbased products.

NiceLog can be used either as a stand alone unit or as part of a expandable and scaleable system comprised of several seamlessly integrated units. Each NiceLog unit can simultaneously record, monitor, archive and play back up to 120 channels, allowing for substantial space savings. NiceLog's open architecture provides a wide variety of connectivity options to both computer networks such as Novell, IPX and TCP/IP using DOS, Windows, NT and Unix . Telephone network interfaces the system uses are T1, E1, ISDN and analog trunks.

Nice has established a marketing arrangement with IPC' one of the largest CTI suppliers of switching equipment to trading rooms. In France, the company uses Etrali, which is a similar specialist. Nice has established alliances with Northern Telecom and Aspect Telecommunications. Both companies sell Nice's products through their own marketing channels. The affiliation with Nortel allows them to offer integrated services for telephone call centers using CTI technology.

Internet Fax Management

NiceFax integrates between existing fax machines and the LAN/WAN/Internet faxing scheme. NiceFax is designed to be a hub for all fax traffic of the organization regardless of the source and destination of the faxed document. The product stores and archives all faxes. It routes, redirects and resends faxes internally and externally. You can organize the documents in a database fashion permitting access to archived faxes from any authorized workstation across the LAN, WAN or the Internet. Administrators get a GUI interface as shown in figure 7.11.

Figure 7.11 — NiceFax User Configuration

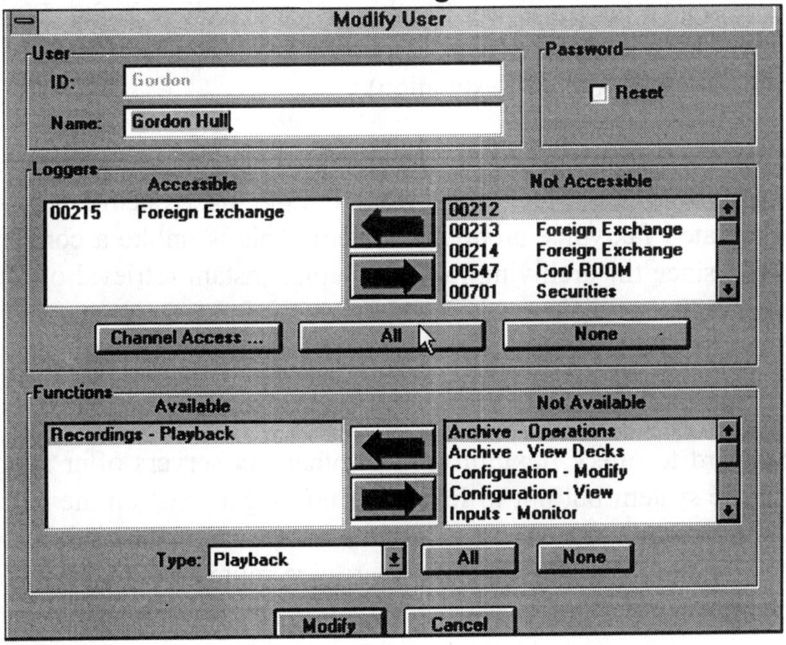

NiceFax eliminates the possibility of mislaying a fax and reduces the pileup of paper within an organization. The system provides a computerized archive of all faxes. No more timewasted searching through filing cabinets or concerns about lost orders. Authorized users have instant access to all incoming and outgoing faxes. Details of faxes, such as caller or transaction ID number, can also be linked to corporate databases, allowing crossreference and providing an allinclusive company database.

The main features exclusive to NiceFax include the ability to connect to standard fax machines. All other solutions are unable to log faxes sent and received by fax machines. The NiceFax feature of automatic archiving and retrieval is not offered by competitors since all others suggest to archive faxes on network server and from there to use standard archive means that have no connection to the fax server itself.

The Internet connectivity enables NiceFax users to access their documents from anywhere in the world. You can send faxes through a corporate NiceFax from anywhere in the world (the document will remain archived on corporate premises). The system will route outgoing faxes through least cost path. When you send a fax from your London office to a client in San-Francisco, the fax will be sent via the Internet to your Los Angeles office's NiceFax (and from there to your its destination).

The NiceFax system can be fully integrated with the NiceLog Digital Voice Logging System and NiceLog CLS (Call Logging System), providing a fully integrated fax/voice archiving system. This is unlike a conventional fax server, since the archiving facility enables instant retrieval of archived faxes. A number of different office tasks are performed automatically such as fax photocopying, distribution based on defined distribution list, storage for future reference and later day retrieval.

With regard to query flexibility, most other fax servers offer support to faxes in the system but not to faxes that no longer exist on the file server disk. As for security for fax transmission, in most cases this is limited. The user has the ability to see all faxes that were routed to him or that are in the system.

In all cases the fax will remain stored and archived in NiceFax as part of your document work-flow and management scheme. NiceFax starts at $3500 per port with minimum 8 port configuration. The product is compatible with most popular networks and protocols (Ethernet, Token Ring, TCP/IP, IPX, NetBios) and works on Win NT, Win95 and Windows 3.1 platforms.

SoftLinx, Inc.

Replix Enterprise Fax System

SoftLinx, Inc., delivers high performance fax messaging solutions for enterprise business communications. SoftLinx's fax messaging capabilities exploit World Wide Web, telephony, and electronic mail technology in a modular, standards-based, open architecture. SoftLinx's systems are installed in over 500 customer locations worldwide. Based on modular software architecture, Replix provides a full set of features and benefits for scaleable client-server messaging. This includes systems for a single location or multi-site global deployment over LANs, private WANs or the Internet.

Through internal development and strategic, SoftLinx also provides a range of horizontal and vertical industry business applications with fully integrated LAN and WAN fax capabilities. SoftLinx has integrated Replix into Electronic Mail, Groupware, Internet-fax, workflow applications, forms management and imaging solutions.

Replix Enterprise is a comprehensive network fax solution for Fortune 1000 companies. The Replix Enterprise Fax System scales from a small workgroup configuration to a large scale, multi-site enterprise-wide deployment. Multiple sites with heterogeneous Replix configurations work together in a seamless manner. The system provides World Wide Web (WWW) based administration, monitoring and configuration. High availability features such as "hot-pluggable" and fault-tolerant configurations provide uninterrupted system operation.

The server platform runs on Sun Sparc - Solaris 2.x and SunOS 4.x. you can also get HP 9000/700 or 800 (HP/UX), IBM RS/6000 (AIX) or IBM Power PC (AIX) versions. The Client Platform runs Win 3.x, 95 and NT. You can also run OS/2 Warp, Unix X/Motif and X-terminals.

Intelligent Modem Gateway. The IMG is a rack-mount Intel Pentium platform with "hot-pluggable" SCSI-2 hard drive, CD-ROM drive and Ethernet card. It supports 24 digital fax/voice channels and has T-1 connections.

Optional Modules and Upgrades. You can add fax-on-demand and set up fax mailboxes with remote retrieval as options. You can also get an e-mail interface for fax clients and least cost routing.

TAC Systems, Inc.

FAXfree On The Internet

TAC Systems has created a program that provides for ordinary fax while dramatically reducing or eliminating telephone fax charges. FAXfree On The Internet is an easy-to-use software program that allows Internet users to send faxes anywhere in the world at little or no cost. FAXfree lets you send e-mail with scanned images, charts, bar graphs, drawings, schematics and spreadsheets all within your documents via the Internet (free). A picture is worth a thousand words. The recipient doesn't even have to have a copy of FAXfree to receive faxes through their Internet email address.

The Win 95 Sender app must have an Internet connection through TCP/IP (dedicated or dial-up) lines. You also need a MAPI compatible service provider installed on your local machine. TAC Systems recommend using Microsoft Exchange for Windows 95 however Windows 95 provides MAPI compliant drivers for Microsoft Workgroup Mail and SMTP/POP3 MAPI service providers. Other MAPI drivers for messaging systems are currently being developed or have been completed for Windows95.

TAC Systems is working on Apple PowerShare, AT&T Easylink and Banyan Intelligent Messaging interfaces. The company is planning also to hook-up with HP's OpenMail, Lotus cc:Mail, Lotus Notes and MCI MAIL. High on the list of developments is connectivity to the Microsoft Exchange Server and Novell's MHS and GroupWise. Sytel and Octel integration are on the frontier.

There are a few limitations. The sender must have a TCP/IP based Internet connection. FAXFree will not work through Internet services provided by The Microsoft Network, CompuServe, American Online or other such third-party Internet gateways. The receiver is not restricted as to what service they use to access the Internet. If you can send someone an e-mail message, you can send them a fax via FAXFree regardless of the recipients Internet connection.

The recipient's mail system must be SMTP/POP3 compatible (i.e. Microsoft Exchange, PC Eudora or similar). You don't get least-cost routing with this version of the product.

Chapter Acknowledgments

My thanks to Pete Davidson of Davidson Consulting. His knowledge was a great help in the preparation of this chapter. If you need help with a computer-based fax project, you can reach him on 818-842-5117 in Burbank, California or davidsonco@aol.com.

Chapter 8

Web-Aware Call Centers

The beginning of this chapter is a discussion on how the Voice-Enabled Internet can be implemented using today's PBXs. In addition, a discussion on how the design of PBXs will evolve from their current form (predominantly voice switching) to become a multi-media communications server. This will have the most profound effect on call centers. I asked Dick Willson, Director Business Development for Securicor Telecoms, to outline this trend. Dick is an absolute expert on the subject and put much thought into the preparation of this data. Securicor is lucky to have him. After this, a roundup of Web-Aware call center products is presented.

PBX To MultiMedia Server Transformation

The voice-enabled Web is evidence that the "convergence" of technologies and markets is happening. The 'convergence' of technology is driven by the digitization of all media types - data, voice and video, and the availability of high bandwidth fiber optic transmission systems.

The convergence of computers and telephony otherwise known as Computer Telephony Integration (CTI) creates the platform to voice enable the Web. This is illustrated in Figure 8.1.

Figure 8.1 – Convergence of Circuit and Packet Switching

As a consequence of this process of digitization, markets (computing,

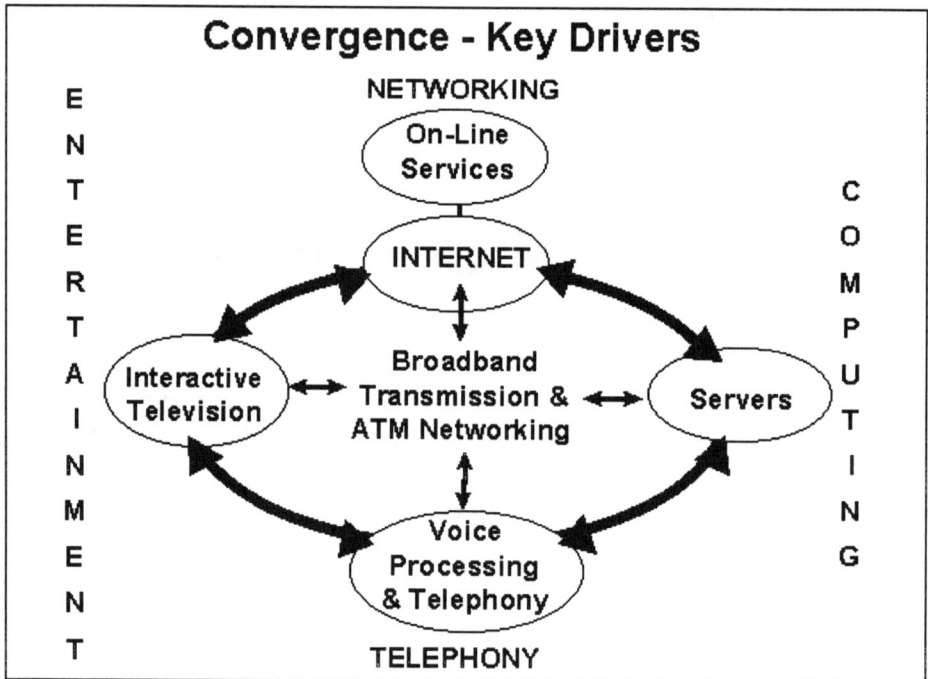

```
┌──────────────────────────────────────────────────────────────┐
│              Convergence - Key Drivers                         │
│   E                  NETWORKING                                │
│   N                 ┌─────────┐                                │
│   T                 │ On-Line │                          C     │
│   E                 │ Services│                                │
│   R            ┌────────────────┐                        O     │
│   T            │    INTERNET     │                       M     │
│   A   ┌──────────┐  Broadband   ┌─────────┐              P     │
│   I   │Interactive│ Transmission &│ Servers │             U     │
│       │Television │ ATM Networking│         │             T     │
│   N                                                      I     │
│   M                 ┌─────────┐                          N     │
│   E                 │  Voice  │                          G     │
│   N                 │Processing│                                │
│   T                 │& Telephony│                              │
│                      TELEPHONY                                 │
└──────────────────────────────────────────────────────────────┘
```

entertainment, data networking and telephony) that previously operated in isolation are being driven to work with each other to deliver these services to the customer via a single high digital pipe.

CTI Missing Links. Computer Telephony Integration (CTI) provides a networking platform for computer applications to *command and control* a telephony switch. The Computer Telephony market has just been born!

A lot more work is left to be done to get CTI products and services to 'real' customers. The initiatives taken by Microsoft and Novell to support Application Programmers Interfaces (APIs) for telephony has had its effect on the PBX manufacturers and the majority are retrofitting support for both Novell's Telephony Services API (TSAPI) and Microsoft's Windows Telephony API (TAPI).

Few, if any, PBXs are designed with an "open" architecture mind, the majority are still proprietary developments. It is technically possible to develop the same functionality using I/O boards within the IBM Personal Computer architecture we haven't yet been able to achieve the right price/performance ratio to create a mass market.

There are still a couple of missing links that need to be completed in order to enable Computer Telephony to become as ubiquitous as the Netscape browser is on the World Wide Web. The current spate of developments has not yet created a *control program*, the equivalent of MSDOS in telephony for *call routing*. We have good APIs (TSAPI & TAPI) for developing CTI software and we also have a comprehensive architecture now published by the Enterprise Computer Telephony Forum (ECTF) for applications that process multi-media streams (predominantly voice at the moment).

However one of the foundations for all these applications, telephony call routing, is still proprietary. We need a commonly accepted *call routing kernel* that will provide the basic PBX telephony facilities that we all use. Figure 8.2 shows the lack of cross-over between these two worlds. This kernel is akin to a *"telephony MSDOS"* providing basic call routing functions, implemented to run on all the popular multi-tasking operating systems - Microsoft Windows 95 and NT, IBM OS/2, Apple MacOS and UNIX.

The second missing link is the inability to easily interconnect PBXs and Key Systems from different manufacturers to create a larger network. In the Information Technology world Internet protocol technology is used to create large Intranets - the telephony industry does not have a readily available suite of networking software that is equivalent to TCP/IP.

Figure 8.2 – PC & PBX Function Comparison

Basic Functions

Function	PC Network	PBX Network
Control Program	MSDOS/ Windows	Real Time Executive/ Call Routing
Applications	MS Office	Telephony Features
Networking	Internet TCP/IP	DPNSS/ Q.Sig

The telephony industry does run the largest interconnected network in the world, the telephone network, but in reality the network is created by interconnecting a few "proprietary" national PTT or Regional Bell company networks, that are run by monopolies, to each other.

The Internet World Wide Web is built using technology that is readily available in the public domain and within the limitations of this technology it can carry multi-media information to be displayed on workstations and PCs. The technology was not originally designed to transport real time voice. With the advances in compression techniques, high speed computing, and a modest increase in bandwidth that is available to us today at an affordable cost, *voice over the Internet* is a demonstrable technology but cannot, as yet, be considered to be a reliable telephone service for business.

Estimating The Market. Before discussing the technology we should attempt to estimate the size of the individual computer networks and telephony markets. In 1995, it was estimated that there are 86,100 call center sites in Europe and the US. This according to a report by Ovum Ltd. called: *Computer Telephony integration, the Business Opportunity, 1995.*

The figure is expected to increase to 107,100 in 1996 and 191,500 by 2000. In 1995, 3.6 million seats were in use by call centers. In 1996, close to 4.3 million seats are expected and by the year 2000 6.76 million seats are expected to be operational.

Most companies have realized that call centers provide missioncritical operations since they are often the first and most important interface between a company and its customers. Therefore, growth in the callcenter segment is expected to be strong and digital voice logging will be an integrated part in the future.

I've gathered some of my own numbers for the UK below. This will help us gain some insight as to where the catalyst lies that will "fire up" the computer telephony market. Figures 8.3 and 8.4 show the difference between the number of systems installed (PBXs versus LANs).

Figure 8.3 – Telephone System Installed Base

Telephony System 20 - 200 extensions	No. of Systems
Installed base	40,000 systems
Annual market	10,000 systems
Value of Annual Market	£120M

This analysis confirms that in terms of revenue generated and the annual revenue growth the LAN industry dominates the customer premises network. The second observation that can be gleaned from these statistics is that *84% of UK businesses have employees.*

Figure 8.4 – NetWare Installed Base

LAN Networks	Units
NetWare base	294,000 units
Annual NetWare volume	34,000 units
Installed LAN Hub ports	730,000 ports
Annual Hub port volume	440,000 ports
Installed base NICs	2,000,000 units
Annual volume NICs	760,000 units
Value of Annual Market	£560M

Businesses that employ greater than 20 but less than 200 persons only account for account for 8% of business establishments. *The average number of PC clients per NetWare server is approximately 10.*

Due to the slow growth in the PBX market the mass market for Computer Telephony Systems is the addition of this functionality to the installed PBX base. The system should be targeted to work groups consisting of approximately 10 persons.

Local Area Network (LAN). For each desktop PC attached to a LAN, the telephone on the same desktop is attached to a PBX network. Generally the two networks operate independently but for wide area communications both networks connect to the same world-wide telephony network.

This is illustrated in Figure 8.5. As the telephony networks are upgraded to provide users with digital access via ISDN, (and ATM in the future), both customer premise networks, the LAN and the PABX will use the same ISDN digital technology for wide area communications.

Figure 8.5 - Typical LAN and PBX Topology

The CTI Market Gap. The use of separate networks for voice and data on customer premises has created separate and different distribution channels for LANs and PBXs, resulting in a *marketing gap* - the telephony channels does not have IT skills and the IT channel has little knowledge of telephony. To sell CTI products requires an investment in appropriate training to take place for each distribution channel.

Figure 8.6 - Novell Telephony Server (TSAPI)

IT companies Microsoft and Novell have recognized the business opportunity that exist in filling this market gap. Novell NetWare Telephony Server is a good example of how an IT software supplier has defined and supports an Applications Programmer Interface (API) in order to attracts third party application developers to create CTI software that is intended to create an additional demand for the basic Novell product - NetWare. A typical set-up is shown in Figure 8.6.

Microsoft has a similar strategy for Windows Telephony and develops and promotes its Telephony Applications Programmers Interface (TAPI). The creation of supported interfaces by some of the largest software companies Novell and Microsoft generates a market for Independent Software Providers (ISP) to create Computer Telephony Applications.

CTI Applications. A wide range of CTI software is now available, some of the functions provided by these applications are described below.

Voice Mail & Auto Attendant. Intercepts incoming call, routes call to desktop, if busy connects caller to voice mail.

Fax Mail. Creates individual Fax mail boxes and allows users to create and send Faxes from desktop.

Fax-on-Demand. Allows callers to access documents which are then transmitted as a Fax.

Unified Desktop Messaging. All the user's messages (voice, Fax and E-mail) are summarized at the desktop

Interactive Voice Response (IVR). Users may complete transactions by getting voice prompts and inputting data via the telephone keypad

Power Dialing. The application dial out directly from list created by database. System presents scripts to agent when call has reached a valid destination

Predictive Dialing. The applications mixes incoming and outgoing call to average the load for the agent

Text to Speech. The application is able to 'speak' the contents of a document e.g. e-mail.

Intelligent Call Distribution (ICD). Distributes incoming call to agents with "screen pops.'

Call Center. Distributes incoming calls to agent groups depending on agent's skills and/or type of incoming call.

Automatic Speech Recognition. (ASR) uses direct speech input.

Call Center Applications

Call Center applications (e.g. airline reservation systems, credit card authorization, telephone banking) using large telephony switches and main-frames have existed for many years. The CTI market opportunity now is to downsize Call Center applications and implement it using cheaper PC based technology thus enabling this technology to be used by smaller companies.

ISDN Data Communications

Because both customer premise networks, the LAN and the PBX, are connected to the same ISDN network the PBX can be used as the ISDN gateway for voice, data and video communications.

Sharing the common ISDN resources for voice, data and video calls reduces cost and increases the flexibility for the users.

World Wide Web Branch Exchange

I strongly believe that the CTI market need to be driven from the IT side. Hence my pre-occupation to find ways and means to install CTI enabling hardware/software into a LAN hub. To me voice enabling the Web is the creation of multi-media application where we need to use both the store and forward Internet technology and the synchronous telephony network. Some time in the future all networks become cell (ATM) based and all media streams will be carried by the same network. Even when we reach nirvana, applications will still have to manipulate each stream differently. Therefore everything we learn now will have use in the future.

The biggest potential for CTI is as an add-on to existing PBXs, just like how the voice processing market was created. The installed life for a PBX is about 7 years therefore any upgrade to provide CTI functionality is going to be a fork lift upgrade and is going to be expensive. Most CTI applications are not going to be enterprise wide but will be applied to specific depart-mental workgroups.

A small independent CTI add-on would be less costly and can be changed and upgraded as the functionality improves without touching the PBX. In fact, even Web-based call center development lends itself nicely to PBX add-ons.

Information available on a Web server is accessible by many clients but unlike a television service this information is not simultaneously broadcast to all viewers. Information on a Web server is selectively accessed by an individual client, and therefore this information is targeted to an *audience of one*. Similarly a telephone conversation is also one-to-one relationship.

The is a similarity between a client using a Web browser to access information on a Web server and a telephone conversation both one-to-one relationships.

Increasingly companies are publishing information electronically in Hyper Text Mark-up Language (HTML) format via the Internet. Therefore via a local call to an Internet Service Provider's node a user can "surf" the World Wide Web. Because the Internet is not operated by a single commercial organization it is not possible to request and maintain, for a given call, a specified end-to-end *quality of service*. The response time of the network will vary depending on the transaction load at the time of day resulting in variable and at times a very slow response for multi-media applications.

A business is known by many addresses. If we wish to communicate with a company by letter or actually visit the company, we would use its *geographic postal address* . If we are required to speak with a member of the company, we would use the published *telephone number*, and if we wished to look at the company's catalogue, we would in all probability visit the company's *Web site* electronically using a *Uniform Resource Locator (URL)*. Today each communication media uses a different network and a different method of addressing entities within that network. The voice enabled Web today will use a telephone number for voice communication and a Web address to login and access the company's Web pages.

To Voice enabling the Web we need to create a system where a software application is triggered by information received via the *Web server, and this will cause it to command and control the PBX using TSAP or TAPI*

This WebeX platform supports applications to be easily implemented that voice enable the Web. A typical application scenario would be the implementation of a Call Center. Here the incoming caller starts by logging into the Web server registering his/her name and giving the system the telephone number where he/she could be reached.

The system would allow the caller to browse pages on the Web server. Appropriate Web pages will have a telephone icon. The caller is invited to activate this icon if he/she requires help and wishes to speak to a call center agent. Activating this icon will cause the system to "find" a Call Center agent that has the right skills to respond to queries associated with information displayed on that particular Web page.

When the system has located an free Agent with the right skills, it will *screen pop* the same Web page that is currently being viewed by the caller on to the Call Center agent's PC and also makes an outgoing telephone call to the remote caller. When the caller accepts the call, the system connects the caller to the agent by ringing the agents telephone. The Agent answers the telephone, the Caller and the Call Center agent are now in conversation and are both viewing the same Web page. We have now *voice enabled the Web*. This is illustrated in Figure 8.7.

The ISDN network provides the user with a guaranteed n x 64 Kbps circuit depending on the number of simultaneous calls set-up between the source and destination locations. With an ISDN Basic Rate Interface (BRI) a user can get a maximum of two channels giving the user a maximum point-to-point bandwidth of 128 Kbps, with some data compression, it is possible to achieve a effective transfer rate of 400 Kbps. The actual transfer rate achieved now depends more on the processing power of the Web server and not on the communication network.

Figure 8.7 – Typical PBX to Web Topology

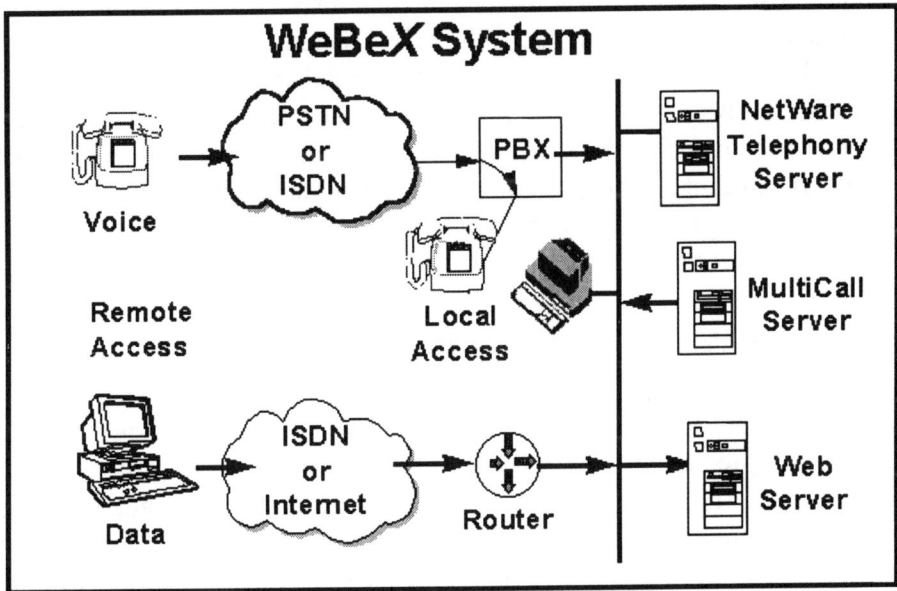

Providing direct ISDN access to a Web site will give multi-media Web pages a much better response. Obviously to achieve this the majority of call will be "long distance" ISDN calls. To achieve reliable verbal communication in business we accept the use of the long distance ISDN telephone calls. We can achieve the same quality of service for business information published as Web pages by using the ISDN network for point-to-point data communications.

Because the Web server will also be connected to the Internet via a gateway, the user would always have a choice; connect to the Web via a local call to the Internet Service Provider and accept a variable response, or connect via a long distant ISDN call at a guaranteed speed .

LAN Architecture for the Web

In all examples described the integration between Computer LAN networks and the voice network takes place at the *command and control* level - the two networks remain physically separate.

Most modern LANs are deployed using twisted pairs (Category 3 or 5) wiring in a star topology. The LAN usually consists of a backbone hub that is connected to distributed stackable hubs located in the individual work-groups. Due to the demands for additional bandwidth by multi-media applications, LANs are rapidly migrating from shared (bandwidth) media to switched (dedicated) bandwidth systems. The introduction of ATM technology will further accelerate this trend. Voice systems (PBXs) have always used a star wiring topology with fixed 64Kbps dedicated bandwidth allocated to each of the connected devices.

Computer Telephony & LAN Hubs

In the medium term, before the introduction of Asynchronous Transfer Mode (ATM) technology for wide area communications, all business premises will need to connect to ISDN services for both voice, data and video communications. Computer Telephony Integration exploits the control information delivered by ISDN supplementary services - Calling Line ID (CLI) and Direct Dial Inwards (DDI). This information is used by CTI applications located on the LAN to make decisions on how the incoming voice call is to be routed and what data is to be associated with the incoming call.

All business organizations require a telephone system. Not all organizations require a LAN. However when an end user wishes to add CTI applications it would be advantageous if the telephone system could be extended to include the LAN functionality and vice versa.

It is relatively straight forward to add the voice switching capability to a LAN hub as a separate independent function. The voice switch would integrate with the backbone hub for the routing of ISDN data and to support the command and control functions required by the CTI applications located on the LAN. *Separate physical wiring will be used to distribute the voice and data to the desktop.* Physical wiring that carries all forms of media streams (voice, data, video) only becomes viable when ATM technology is implemented in the workgroup switch and the desktop.

The integrating LAN functionality with an ISDN PBX creates a multi-media communications server today. This architecture can then evolve further to carry voice and data on the single wire to the desktop when ATM is introduced into the customer premises networks.

ATM/ISDN Gateway

Multi-media applications will force customers to migrate the site's existing LAN technology from shared media Ethernet, Token Ring and FDDI to ATM switched technology before Public Telecom Operators (PTO) are prepared to provide for general use, a cost effective ATM wide area access.. ISDN networks will remain the most cost effective means of wide area digital access for the foreseeable future. Multi-media communications across the wide area network will be via the ISDN network. Voice is the basic form of communications required by all business. Computer Telephony Integration allows computer applications to command and control the PBX as if it were a computer system peripheral. In addition to using information provided by the ISDN network about the incoming call, computer applications are able to route incoming calls to an appropriate destination using additional information from databases that is not accessible by a PBX.

The computer system can enhance the value of the call by simultaneously associating additional multi-media information with the incoming call in the form of a still or moving picture derived from a database. To achieve a consistent real-time response it will be necessary for the multi-media information to be delivered to users via a local network using ATM technology. For this reason it is appropriate for digital ISDN PBXs to implement an PBX/ATM gateway to local ATM networks.

Evolution of PABX Architecture

The notes below describes existing PBX architecture and proposed how this architecture will evolve to create an ISDN compatible customer premise multi-media switch.

V2 PABX Architecture. Existing digital PBX architecture consists of a N x N channel TDM switch module where each channel supports 64 Kbps of data that is compatible with the ISDN wide area network. The switch module interfaces with Input/Output (I/O) modules that support local devices and wide area communications. Each I/O module supports 30 x 64 Kbps channels and number of interfaces - ISDN access, Plain Old Telephones (POTs), Keyphones and a LAN interface. A customer's particular requirement is satisfied by installing the appropriate I/O interfaces. Software associated with the switch module implements many of the features associated with the PBX.

V3 PABX Architecture. Having recently completed a project that implemented a CTI link (PBX driver) to the NetWare Telephony Server has highlighted the fact that current PBX software architectures needs to be more "open" and flexible. Studies have been completed as to how this requirement is to be achieved.

The initial studies indicate that we are able to use the majority of the existing hardware and software implemented in the current I/O modules. The major changes will occur in the software that controls the switch module, this software implements "call routing" and produces many of the PBX "features" as seen by the user.

This software needs not only to be able to support software interfaces that will access the PBX via Novell TSAPI or Microsoft TAPI but also needs to expose additional application programmer's interface that allows developers with the right skills to implement PBX "features" appropriate to their own business requirements. From the software point of view the PBX will then behave more like a conventional real-time IT transaction processing system.

The customer could purchase a turn key PBX solution that will perform as soon as it is installed and commissioned but will also have the ability to customize the PBX to alter or add more features using standard software development techniques.

Figure 8.8 – Combined PBX and MultiMedia Router

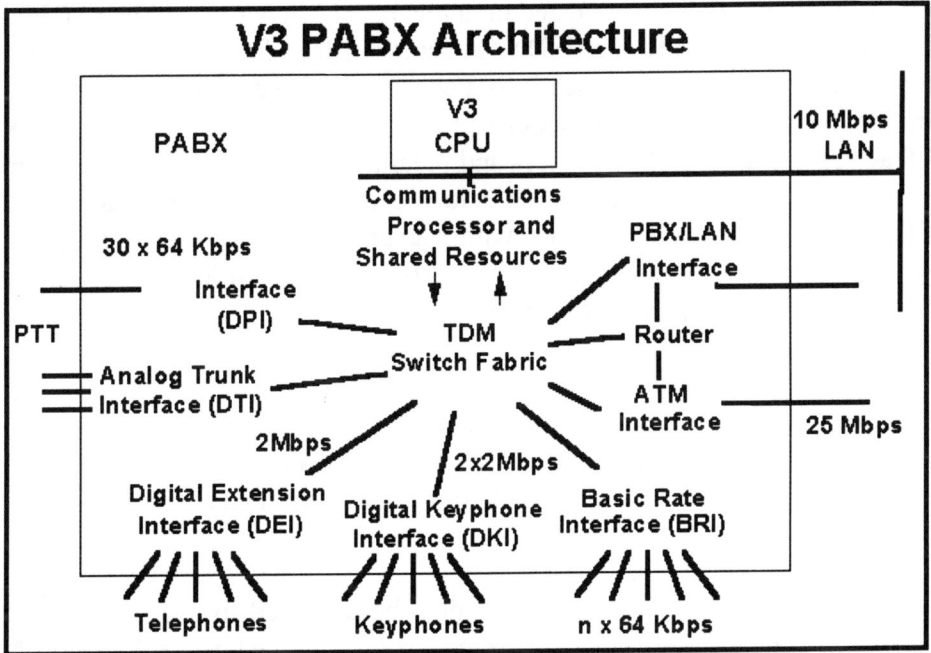

For this reason we intend to define a LAN based messaging interface between the PBX switching and signaling module and the higher layers of software that are necessary to implement "call routing" and PBX "features." This messaging interface will allow the PBX "call routing" and "features" software modules to be implemented in an IT environment (e.g. IBM OS/2, Microsoft Windows 95 or NT, NetWare or UNIX) using a programming language chosen by the customer. This is illustrated in figure 8.8.

ISDN/PABX/ATM Gateway

In the long term with the introduction of wide area access to ATM networks multi-media communications will become the norm. The features and functions provided by today's voice switch (PBX) will still be needed in the new networking environment.

PBX developers need to plan the migration of today's PBX "call routing" and "features" to the all ATM networks of the future. In the medium term multi-media workstations located on a local ATM network will be required to interface to the wide area ISDN, to access or transfer multi-media information to and from remote locations. For voice communications to and from the multi-media workstation requires the system to support the usual PBX "features". These ISDN interfaces and "features" are all available in current PBXs and can be made available to multi-media workstations via an PBX/ATM gateway. Not all users within an organization would be equipped with multi-media workstations and the system also need to support simple POTs interface attached to the ATM network.

The average installed life of a PBX is approximately seven years. It therefore may not be economic to upgrade the existing PBX hardware to interface to the local ATM network particularly if the multi-media application is only deployed in a specialized department within a corporate organization.

The planned ISDN/ATM gateway must be designed to use the existing telephony functions available via the legacy PBX. In the UK the ATM/ISDN gateway would use the Digital Private Networking Signaling System (DPNSS) protocol to interface with legacy PBX's.

Voice and Data Call Routing

In the medium term, the customer's private multi-media (Intranet) network will consist of both store and forward packet communications and isochronous circuit switched ISDN compatible digital channels. The private multi-media voice and data network needs a common call routing mechanism for both data and voice, this routing algorithm could be an extension of IP routing derived from standard Internet technology.

IP Router Software Architecture. The Internet Protocol (IP) is the most popular, open and generally accepted technology for routing datagrams in the IT world.

This protocol was developed to route data, encapsulated as packets (datagrams), over unreliable transmission circuits. Sophisticated routing algorithms have been developed over many years and the specifications are available in the public domain. Figure 8.9 shows how IP routers are being designed to handle circuit switched and packetized media streams.

Figure 8.9 -- IP Router Software Architecture

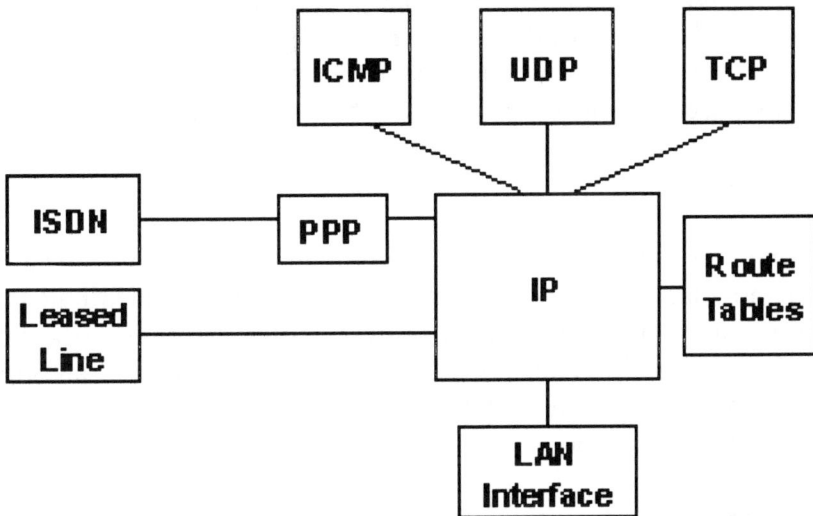

Routing IP Datagrams. IP datagrams are routed hop-by-hop using the destination network address. An important consideration when deciding the algorithm to use to route both ISDN data and voice calls across a customers private (Intranet) network that must support the existing IT environment and the emerging ATM customer premise switch.

TDM switches + IP Routers. To maintain the right quality of service for voice in the medium term, speech will not generally be packetized and transmitted as a stream of packets via an IP network. However, as the bandwidth of IP networks increase, and they migrate towards ATM technology with a guaranteed quality of service for individual virtual circuits, voice will eventually be carried end to end as a stream of packets.

In the medium term, the customer's private multi-media (Intranet) network will consist of both store and forward packet communications and separate switched digital ISDN calls. In the past, voice and data applications were not associated with each other and the therefore the supporting networks were developed independently of each other and used their own routing mechanisms. If multi-media applications are to used across a private network then the network needs a common routing mechanism for all media streams, this routing algorithm could be an extension of IP routing derived from the Internet. For media streams like voice and video calls that require synchronous end-to-end communications the IP routing algorithm would be extended to ensure that a isochronous channel is available at each hop in the route. If the circuit switched path cannot be completed hop by hop then insufficient resources are available to complete the synchronous path and a busy tone will be returned to the caller.

TDM Switches + IP Router. How IP router algorithms are implementation is flexible, in a large network the hardware and software is distributed and the routing algorithm is implement in each individual node. In a small network a single algorithm can be executed recursively, the routing algorithm is triggered as each circuit switched hop is completed using successive entries from a routing tables.

PABX Software Architecture. Traditional PABX software operates in a real-time environment and the software modules are triggered by telephony keyboard depressions or by incoming/outgoing call events. Due to the real-time constraints of the system, user programming of the system has been discouraged. Users however are not interested in writing application to interact at the low level with real-time events, but are definitely interested in developing new or additional PBX features that directly interface with and effect how their business is run. The PABX software architecture needs to be restructured such that the system will guarantee the execution of the low level real-time tasks and also make available a defined messaging interfaces for developers to access which will allow them to implement "new" PBX features.

Multi-Media Communications Server Software Architecture. In order to implement a multi-media communications server the PBX software architecture will be combined with IP routing software to create a combine voice/data multimedia communications server. Because ATM will support "classic" IP to provide a migration path for existing IT applications the routing software implemented as part of the PBX software can evolve as ATM networks evolve.

ISDN/PBX/ATM Gateway. The ISDN/PBX/ATM gateway implementation has many characteristics of the PBX/LAN (Ethernet) gateway that Securicor Telecoms is implementing for ISDN to LAN data communications. The experience gained in this development will be used to extend the functionality to transporting and switching voice over ATM. In the conventional PBX the telephony I/O interface for POTs and Keyphone behaves like a terminal (Telnet) server and services up to 30 devices. The ATM gateway will also act as a server to support the POTs or Keyphone functions located at each multi-media workstation. The workstation interface to support the telephone would therefore be a very simple hardware/software device.

ATM Multi-Media Communications. The longer term aim, when the ATM interface cost fall, we would create an all ATM based multi-media communications service that supports voice, data and video information streams. I/O will interface communications devices directly with the ATM switch and the PBX software would run on an IT application server.

PBX/ ATM Architecture. PBX software (PBX emulation) will be executed in an application server and the services will be delivered via devices interfaced to the ATM network. The ATM Workgroup Switch will have interfaces to PBXs and LANS, other ATM routers and IP links. Software will be built outside of the switch fabric in order to achieve hardware independence.

The Public Telecom Operators. Public Telecom Operators (PTO) need to migrate their existing Narrow band ISDN to Broadband (ATM based) ISDN service.

This migration will occur over many years and opportunities will arise to use the same interfaces and techniques developed for customer premises but applied on behalf of the PTO.

Current Network Services. The current telecom services provided by the PTOs appear to the user as separated distinct services. To provide more flexibility either the PTO and/or the customer equipment now available needs the "channels to be groomed" to provide the service the customer needs.

ATM Workgroups - Telco Solutions. Channel grooming can be applied by the PTO to create the services that the customer requires. The scenario assumes that the PTO will delay the introduction of ATM based B-ISDN. Both enterprise and workgroup ATM subnetworks will coordinate real-time media streams of any kind. All elements, as shown in Figure 8.10 will be weaved together. This distributed, client-server approach lends itself nicely to the idea of using legacy systems in the new model. And the opportunities for telephone, cable and ISP companies are tremendous. In time, the post, cable and IP network suppliers will become as one. ATM backbones and subnetworks are forcing the issue.

Figure 8.10 – Evolution of Integrated CPE

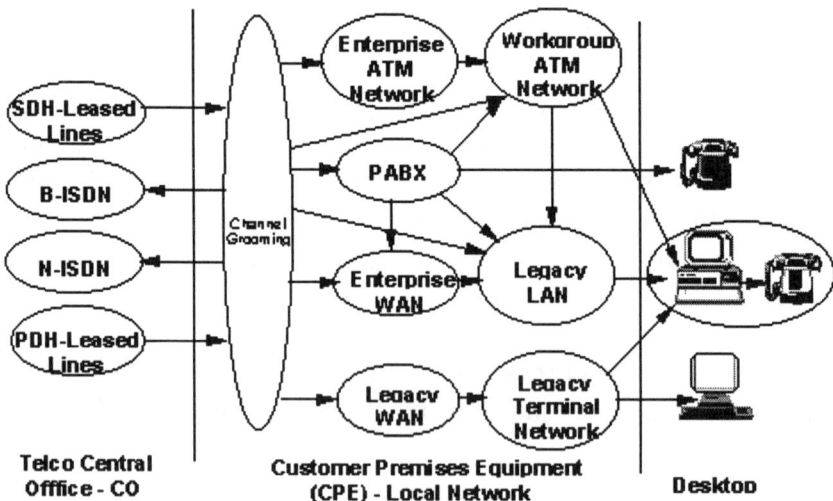

ATM Workgroup - Cable TV Solutions. The Cable TV organizations are now introducing telephony services to complement their TV service in the local loop. To compete with the established PTOs, Cable TV operators must provide more innovative services that their larger more established competitors. A prime opportunity for Cable TV operators would be to introduce a ATM service in the local loop operating at 25 Mbps for business users. All the interfaces and software developed for customer premise equipment previously discussed would be applicable when creating or interfacing to such a service. Carl Strathmeyer of Dialogic Corporation supplied us with a topology diagram for multimedia third party call control. It clearly expands n these precepts. Figure 8.11 shows how the software modules for communications control, media services and delivery services will be put together (yet acting as a cohesive whole).

Figure 8.11 – Multimedia Third Party Call Control

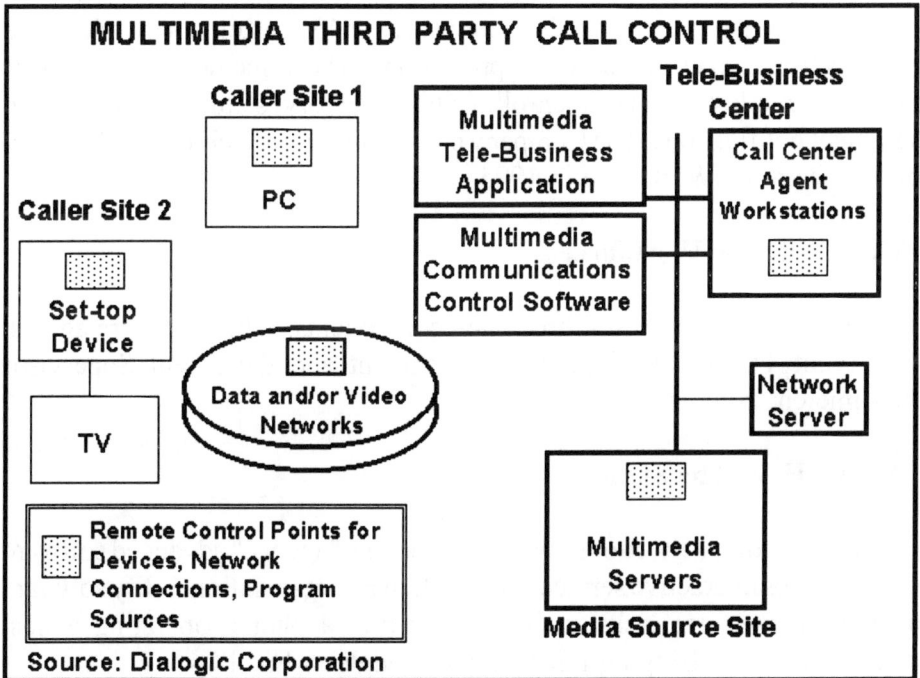

MULTIMEDIA THIRD PARTY CALL CONTROL

Source: Dialogic Corporation

Integrated Services ATM Networks. In the long term networks will evolve to provide an end-to-end ATM service. This will take many years to accomplish. In the intervening years there is a large business potential for suppliers who can quickly create multi-media communications using modular hardware and software for both PTO and customer networks as users migrate their application into the age of multi-media.

Edify Corporation

Page Call

Edify develops, markets and supports self-service software.

Their flagship offering is the Electronic Workforce (EW) package. It lets organizations provide automated customer and employees services through the Internet, private Intranets, Web browsers, telephones and electronic mail. Edify has licensed Electronic Workforce to over 450 customers for telephone and electronic mail self-service applications. These include bank account inquires, employee benefit enrollments, inventory status and automatic shipment notifications. The Company began shipping a Web-enabled version of its Electronic Workforce in 1995.

The Electronic Workforce

Electronic Workforce has three main components: Edify software agents, the Agent Trainer development environment and the Agent Supervisor run-time environment.

Agents Have The Skills

At the heart of the Electronic Workforce are the "agents," advanced software that provides interactive services on behalf of an organization. Edify software agents can perform tasks such as answering a phone, operating a host application or exchanging information through on-line PCs.

By defining the sequence of tasks agents will perform, you can quickly create robust interactive service applications that span across various media and back-office systems. Because our software agents are so flexible and multi-skilled, you can concentrate on creative valuable services, without the hassles of hard-coded system integration.

Agent Trainer

Edify's Agent Trainer is an object-oriented visual development environment. It lets you define and customize interactive service applications. A "point and click" interface lets you quickly build interactive services that *agents* will provide. Because all of the agent skills are represented in Agent Trainer as visual objects, you can create sophisticated applications without writing a single line of code. And to make development even easier, we've integrated a set of graphical tools, giving you everything you need to create services unique to your organization.

Agent Supervisor Orchestrates Service Delivery

Agent Supervisor is a run-time environment. It schedules software agents and assigns them to service applications built with Agent Trainer. Once agents and service applications are paired, Agent Supervisor manages all of the phone, fax, PC, host and network resources necessary for interactive service delivery. All of these resources are managed through an architecture that ensures reliability and security. With Agent Supervisor, you can deploy multiple interactive services, confident that they will be delivered through a secure run- time environment whose capacity scales to meet your needs.

Page Call

Page Call allows World Wide Web users to easily initiate a direct telephone link to customer service representatives in a call center at the touch of a button. With this technology, companies can extend their service offerings by making traditional call center service easily accessible to Web site users. Page Call combines Web applications with telephone service.

Page Call includes three service capabilities. The Call Me button appears on the Web user's computer screen and Page Pop and Page Shadow interact to help the customer service representative assist the user over the phone.

Call Me button. Appears on one or more of the company's Web pages and is activated by Web users who want customer service via telephone. Activation of the Call Me button automatically arranges for a call-back from an available customer service representative.

Page Pop. Technology which instantly "pops" the current page being viewed by the Web user and puts in on the agent's screen. In addition, customer information retrieved from the Web server or back office systems is displayed. This allows the customer service representative to more intelligently respond to the Web user's requests.

Page Shadow. Allows the customer service representative to track and view the Web user's movements from page to page within an interactive Web session.

A customer viewing a retailer's Web site may have questions about a particular item beyond the information given on a Web page. The customer simply activates a "Call Me" button on the screen. Page Call automatically sets up a telephone call to the customer and connects it to an available customer service representative. Page Call also provides the representative with specific customer information that can assist with the transaction. Page Shadow presents the same Web pages the customer is viewing onto the representative's computer screen in real time, as the customer moves from page to page. During the actual return phone call, the customer service representative has a computer screen with several windows of information: the Web pages being viewed by the customer, a screen providing current customer data (phone call, current request, etc.) with inventory status (of the item being requested) and a window displaying specific customer information (buying patterns, preferences, etc.). The transaction can be completed quickly and efficiently.

Page Call works with standard PBX and ACD protocols. Page Call solutions begins at $40,000.

Figure 8.12 -- Web-Initiated Teleservices

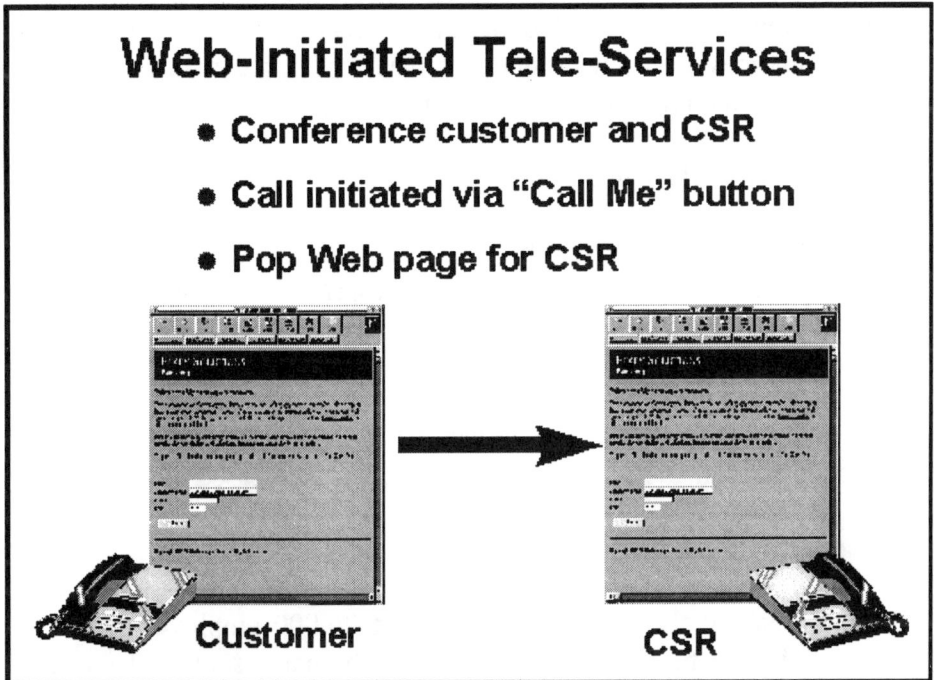

Web-Initiated Tele-Services

- Conference customer and CSR
- Call initiated via "Call Me" button
- Pop Web page for CSR

Customer   CSR

How it works (COMMERCE EXAMPLE)

1.A customer enters the merchant's Web server address into the Web browser (http://www.merchant.com).

2.The merchant's Web server presents a logon screen back to the customer that is displayed in their Web browser.

3.The customer enters their account number and PIN# and then clicks on the Submit button.

4.The Edify Electronic Workforce receives the logon request via the merchant's Web server and assigns a software agent. At this point, a session is established between the Edify server and the remote user.

5.The Edify software agent verifies the user's account information with the host computer and, if valid, dynamically creates a document containing a menu of choices (i.e. view product list, place order, order status, etc.), and then sends the document to the customer.

6.The customer selects the option they desire.

7.The Edify system receives the request (for order status), retrieves the customer's account information from the appropriate host database (pending orders, shipping instructions, etc.) creates a document containing that information, and sends it to the customer to be displayed in their Web browser.

8.When the customer has completed their transaction, they click on logoff, the session is terminated and the software agent is released

Human Resources at Unisys

Keeping track of the personnel records of 36,000 employees scattered across the globe is no small task. Even with a human resources department of 350, the Unisys Corporation found that updating employee records was an ongoing, costly challenge. Now, Unisys Corporation uses the World Wide Web to offer 24-hour self-service HR information to its employees.

HR staffers at the information technology company spent a large portion of their time answering routine questions, and manually entering employee data into legacy database systems. Lee Stivale, project director for HR systems, installed Edify's Electronic Workforce to leverage the Unisys Internet network. The new system integrates with existing servers and the employee database. This includes the Unisys' PeopleSoft HRMS, Oracle database applications, legacy systems and electronic mail systems.

All 36,000 employees now have instantaneous access to dynamic services 24 hours a day. This frees HR employees formerly bogged down with repetitive processes to solve higher-level problems and deliver a better level of service overall. The system allows worldwide access to self-service applications on virtually any type of PC -- no proprietary technology is needed. Most importantly, company employees can now take proactive control of their personnel information. No one in New York has to wait for Unisys offices to be open in Des Moine to get and work with their data. And since employees are now performing HR functions without assistance, the company is saving time and money.

New interactive voice response (IVR) applications developed with the Electronic Workforce's telephony capabilities will also give touch-tone access to the self-service HR applications to those employees who don't have PCs, or who prefer to access the solutions from home.

Visa Interactive Banking Services

Both Edify and Visa Interactive are promoting Edify's Web banking solutions to Visa member banks. These Web banking solutions include comprehensive bill payment services. Edify's Electronic Workforce is designed to provide financial institutions with an integrated service delivery software platform. The system automates financial services through the Web, telephone and personal financial managers. Edify connects to Visa Interactive processing centers via the Access Device Messaging Standard (ADMS) bill payment interface. Edify also plans to implement ADMS extensions that will tie into the VISA e-Pay system. Edify's support for e-Pay will allow consumers to electronically connect through their financial institutions to billing organizations and view and pay bills as part of a single transaction.

Intranet, WWW and Phone Access

Described by the company as "the killer application of the Internet," Edify is jubilant about its Electronic Workforce product.

Edify has a development and marketing agreement with SAP America, Inc. in which the two companies will work together to market self service solutions. The solutions are made up of SAP's R/3 enterprise business software and the Edify Electronic Workforce. These self service solutions will serve customers across all of SAP's enterprise. This includes manufacturing, financial services and human resources. Users can access the system via corporate Intranet, World Wide Web and telephone access.

The integration of Edify software, the Electronic Workforce, with the SAP R/3 system provides employees and customers a means to interact directly with SAP human resources, sales and distribution applications. This can be done with a choice of access devices including the Web, telephone, fax, e-mail and pagers.

Edify software communicates with SAP R/3 via SAP's Automation Interface. The Edify Electronic Workforce software maintains sessions with the Intelligent Terminal, a server that sits between the SAP Application Server and the Edify software. The Electronic Workforce will pull requested data out of SAP's Application Server via the Intelligent Terminal interface for distribution to client devices. The Intelligent Terminal acts as a simple data transmission bridge between Edify and the Application Server.

Lansys Ltd.

WebConnect and MultiCall

Lansys Ltd. Is the maker of the MultiCall for NetWare Telephony Services (TSAPI) system. MultiCall is a CTI server with a suite of applications including fax server and ACD functions. MultiCall was written in the Magic language and is resold by a number of Internet market-makers including NetCall, Securicor Telecoms and Venturian Software. WebConnect is an add-on product to the MultiCall TSAPI server. It lets customers initiate Call Center access through the Internet. Using a standard World Wide Web (WWW) browser.

Callers can connect to an organization's standard Web server from any PC either directly or through the Internet (depending on security requirements) and browse visually through all the available information.

"Telephone" icons are available at relevant points where the caller may wish to speak to someone in the organization. The caller clicks on the icon and is told to wait for a phone call (if the caller's phone number is not available in the organization's database he/she is prompted to enter it). The phone rings, and on the line is a specialist from the organization whose skills match the subject of the Web page from which the caller requested assistance. The specialist sees on his / her screen both information on the caller (in standard "screen pop" fashion) and the same Web page displayed on the caller's screen.

This lets specialists address the immediate needs of customers and help them navigate through the organization's Web pages. Additionally, the specialist may have access within the same application to all the organization's resources including databases, image banks and even audio recordings.

At any point during the conversation, it may be transferred to another specialist anywhere in the organization, carrying with it all previous call information. Thus the next specialist picks up exactly where the previous one left off, for a true "seamless" workflow.

WebConnect System Architecture

MultiCall provides intelligent, skill-based call routing services to any desk-top in the organization (both on and off site). The Web server is connected to the MultiCall CTI server through a data network (either Local Area Network - LAN, or Wide Area Network - WAN) as shown in Figure 8.13. When the caller clicks on the "telephone" icon, the Web server send a message to the CTI server with the caller's telephone number and Web page ID. The MultiCall software locates the next available specialist with the appropriate skill for this page and commands the PBX (through TSAPI) to set up a call between this specialist and the caller.

Figure 8.13 -- WebConnect System Architecture

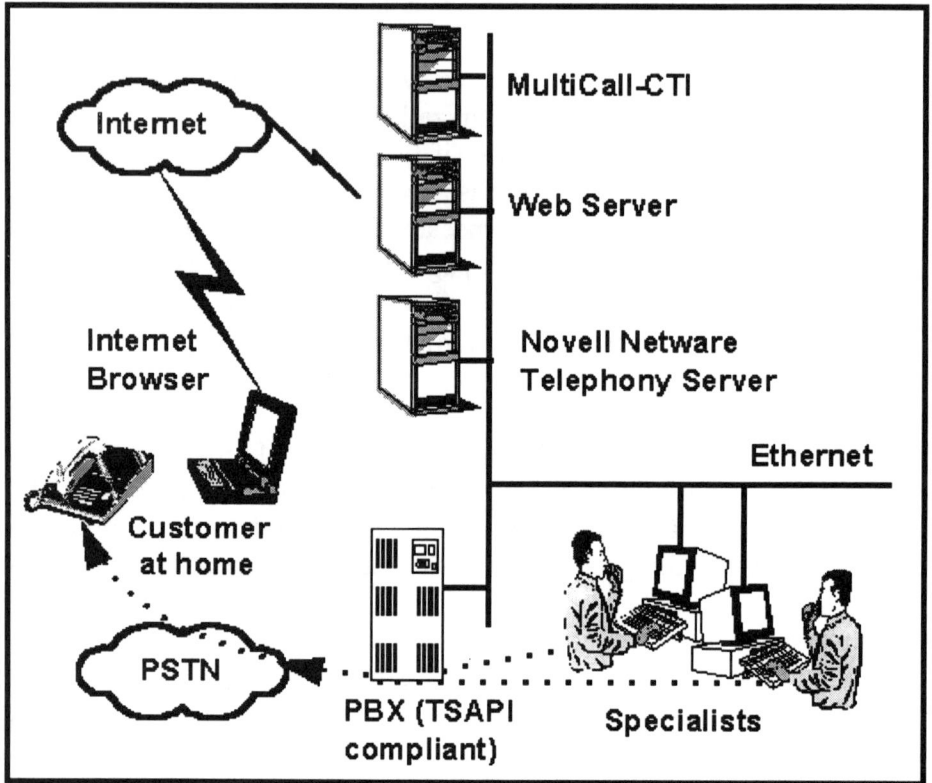

Simultaneously, the caller's ID and Web page ID are sent to the specialist's workstation, initiating a "screen pop" and a Web "page pop". Similarly, the call and information may be transferred to other specialists in the organization.

MultiCall

MultiCall is a computer telephony product. It handles just about everything you'd want to do in a call center. MultiCall also has Interactive Voice Response (IVR) capabilities and supports fax-on-demand, audiotex, voice mail and auto attendant.

MultiCall software is comprised of two key components:

MultiCall Generator. The generator is designed to allow programmers to develop advanced voice applications without being computer telephony experts. The menu-driven language is simple and powerful, and was specifically designed to be easy to learn.

MultiCall Runtime Engine. This is the program which runs the Voice Box hardware. It is multitasking and supports from 4 to 32 ports per each Voice Box Machine.

MultiCall Computer Telephone Integration

By utilizing caller ID, Computer Telephone Integration provides information about the incoming caller to the agent or representative taking the call. This facilitates better customer service by helping companies identify their caller's needs in advance and provide expedited service.

The call is routed to the staff member /members who are best suited to handle the request and the appropriate computer screen is automatically put on the representatives computer. If no one at the help desk is available, or if the call is after hours, the system has the ability to automatically provide the caller with information that is relevant to their request. This allows for applications such as intelligent call routing, intelligent call distribution, call pacing, adaptive predictive dialing, voice pops, screen pops and real-time call management.

MultiCall hardware requirements include:

Pentium PC. A regular PC with a BUS chassis that can easily hold an additional four voice cards and an additional network card.

MultiCall Voice Card. An OEM provided Card which is installed in the PC. A wide range of voice cards are available to support a number of different environments and worldwide phone systems. Supported cards include Rhetorex, Dialogic, and Acculab.

Rockwell Switching Systems Division

Spectrum Internet ACD

Rockwell's Switching Systems Division (SSD) is a leader in the design, manufacture, and service of call center technologies. SSD provides integrated call center solutions which address Total Transaction Call Processing (TTCP) utilizing automatic call distributors and Computer Telephony Integration (CTI), information collection and management, agent workstation applications, and integrated consulting services.

The Galaxy and Spectrum automatic call distributors are located in over 600 call center sites with 25-1200 service representatives per site handling a total of over 35 million calls per day. SSD customers are companies whose call centers are mission-critical, front-line businesses. The range of industries served includes: airlines, banking and financial, insurance, hospitality, retail, government, manufacturing, utilities, and service bureaus. SSD conducts business in Canada, United Kingdom, Japan, and South Africa.

Jon Anderson is the Product Marketing Manager for Rockwell's Internet ACD product. I asked him to outline the thrust (and his philosophy) on the merger between the Internet and the call center. He's very frank. And Rockwell is ardent in their position on the subject: "we invented it." This is his view of how the Internet ACD was hatched.

One of the largest costs involved in operating a call center today are the phone bills from long distance carriers. Imagine the ability to make calls worldwide for the price of a local call or less. Current consumer technology includes products which use the Internet as telephones. An Internet user pages a third party to join him in a conversation. It's as seamless as picking up the phone. Using the dead spaces in all transmissions, compressed sound is sent back and forth from microphones hooked up to each party's sound board.

Current technology is advanced enough to carry fully interactive conversations with simultaneous listening and talking. Sound quality is a bit murky, with audio sounding more like a 1950's trans-Atlantic call. But there are new products out claiming to address this issue (IBM). All achieved on a single phone line - no need for ISDN or 2 phone lines. Street pricing for these separate software products is about $50-60. Of course, you can also use the Web-telephony packages bundled in Netscape 3.0 and Explorer 3.0.

Internet Call Center Applications

If a call center were to utilize this technology, outbound calls could be placed worldwide for the price of the connection to a local Internet point. A CTI server and an ACD would manage the call traffic from the Internet much the same way they do PSTN calls today.

Outbound Calling. Host data, set up to fish from email or IP address, is used to set up a predictive dial Internet call. When the customer responds, host data and is passed to the Telephone Service Representative (TSR) and the connection made. Both parties are using local calling to achieve long distance conversations. *Caution:* any company thinking predictive dial campaigns on the Internet are a new channel, you're wrong. TSRs would only gain a sailor's vocabulary and no sales.

Inbound Application. The customer calls a Web site. If a TSR is available, a CTI application grabs the caller's email or IP address (similar to ANI) and pops the TSR's screen as the connection is made. If no TSR is available, a "Virtual VRU" may be used to keep the customer waiting for the next TSR or to get additional subscriber information. Also, just as applications are tagged by DNIS, Internet calls are tagged by home page address.

Callback around the Internet: This first generation technology allowed for a customer to request a callback from a home page owner around the Internet over the PSTN. The customer simply clicked on a "call me" button and after filling out a form, was called back.

This technology was invented by Rockwell International and a prototype was demonstrated for the first time in May 1995. The first commercial trial followed in September 1995. Many similar products were raced into production, but before a single user was up and running (beyond beta trials), the voice enabled Web became a reality, making this solution "all dressed up with nowhere to go." Figure 8.14 shows how the Rockwell Internet ACD fits in to this model.

Figure 8.14 -- Rockwell Internet ACD Access

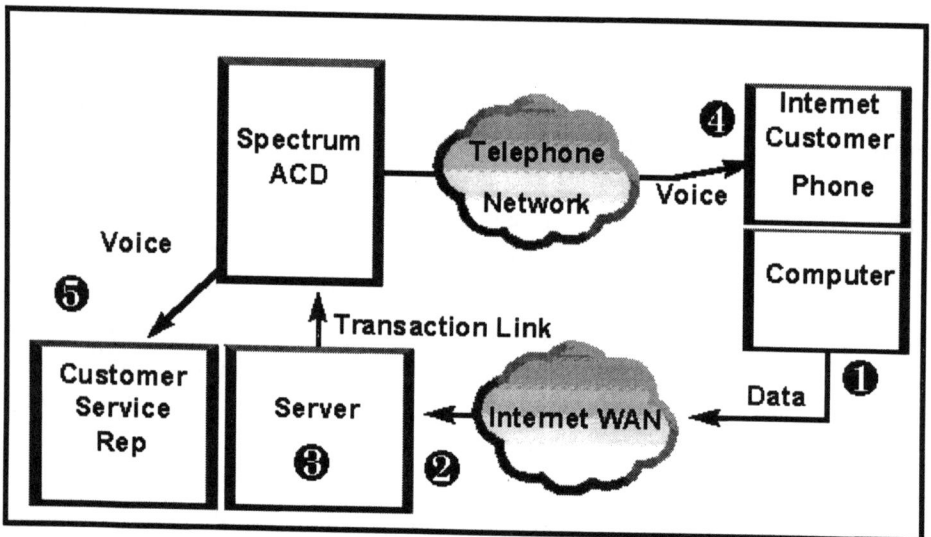

1. Caller activates "CALL ME" function
2. Internet home page sends request to IRU
3. IRU formats message into ACD call command
4. ACD dials to user's telephone number. On answer, the ACD connects a service representative

The drawback for this technology was that it needed the customer to have either ISDN or two phone lines to the house, otherwise, callbacks were not synchronous.

On the upside, it's allowed for more secure transmission of financial information by going around the seemingly insecure Internet. It also infected the call center industry with Internet hysteria. Like a broken strand of pearls, Internet conference flyers began littering corporate mail rooms. An Internet Guru was someone who knew that the difference between an "Internet" and an "Intranet" was a bit more than spelling.

Conversation through the Internet. The release of Netscape 3.0 and Microsoft's Explorer 3.0 remove the normal market shake-out which occurs between competing protocols. The two largest browsers have bundled the necessary protocols to conduct conversations *through* the Internet. The deal is done. A $30 microphone plugged into the sound board, and the consumer is ready.

Other capabilities beyond the standard call center morphs would be interactive whiteboarding where a customer or TSR can write on the screen for both to see. Technical support centers would eat this up. Also, the ability to send Web pages to a potential customer, not simply provide them with the address of the page, but pop their screen with it.

Real call center products are probably six months away from reality *(versus vapor)*. But the availability of product is only half the battle. Call centers are not ready for this. Hundreds of Internet conference flyers later, and the understanding is simply not there. Why?

Who maintains the call center? Who maintains the corporate Internet strategy? They are not the same groups of people and they do not communicate. Marketing knows the call center *just* answers the phones. The call center knows marketing as the people to ask when the right wine is required *(ah, an expense account)*. These new advances in call center technology which directly effect the entire Internet picture are unknown to the very people who control it. When I talk to Internet designers, they get gooey *(not GUI)* about the interactivity of the call center technology we have. These two sides of the corporate house are going to have to communicate before headway will be made.

Other Internet Developments. So far, the Internet hype in the call center industry has focused on the voice part of the transaction. The data side will be of equal value. Rockwell's CTI product, a workflow application generator for call centers, will soon be deployed on the Internet fully tied to back-office systems. The same forms *(order entry, loan applications, and subscription forms, etc.)* TSRs fill in today will be on the Internet for the customer to fill out themselves. And, unlike today, those forms will not be picked up and entered by a TSR later, but will be tied directly into the appropriate subsystems - truly untouched by human hands.

What's it mean? As the Internet becomes more entwined with our lives, a large portion of the call center workforce will be working from home, and the number of TSRs will be much smaller. Call centers in the high technology or business-to-business environments will feel it first. Draw an analogy from the banking industry. Twenty years ago, all transactions were handled by people. The advent of the Automatic Teller Machine (the first ATM) has almost cut out the need for a bank teller in most transactions. Some banks have even begun charging customers to see a teller!

Siemens Rolm Communications

Media Blending Technology

Siemens' Media Blending is a framework to integrate Web transactions or electronic commerce into the call center leveraging existing call center infrastructure. Media Blending illustrates how the Internet and voice network can be seamlessly integrated to provide better customer service.

According to Siemens, Media Blending offers many benefits to call centers. First, you can leverage existing call center infrastructure. This includes the Siemens Rolm 9751 ACD server, Siemens Rolm CallBridge and Siemens Rolm ResumeRouting (company's skills-based routing product). It acts as the single, central routing server for Media Blending applications.

Second, the idea behind of this technology is to give customers consistent service response in all media. Customers can use their phone, the Web or Intranets to navigate corporate information stores. This also optimizes the use of customer service staff and systems, since transactions are typically quicker with "over the shoulder" visual displays.

Lastly, most transactions are entered more accurately and with less frustration on both the customer and agent's part. Most of the typing is done by the Web-browsing customer. He or she can spell his or her name and type it in better than any agent. In addition, phone access offers a high level of security in conveying credit card information.

The Media Blending scenario explained below illustrates how a travel agency can integrate Web transactions into the call. The travel agency is called "Pleasure Travel". Pleasure Travel has implemented a travel service on the Web using Media Blending to serve its Web customers.

In the scenario a Web customer, Max Fiszer, is surfing the Web for a Caribbean cruise vacation. Max enters Pleasure Travel's home page and eyes its Western Caribbean cruise. He fills out an online reservation form and requests an agent to call him. Pleasure Travel's agent, Terri Johnson, calls Max immediately to help Max complete the cruise reservation. At the end Max gives his credit card number over the phone to book the reservation.

Media Blending Scenario

Max follows the *Cruise Reservation* link and views options for pleasure cruises, reservation and cruise ship information. He reads all the Caribbean cruise descriptions. Max is interested in reserving the Western Caribbean cruise. What he sees at this point is pictured in Figure 8.15. Max now fills out the online cruise reservation form by entering his name, phone number and address. This is illustrated in Figure 8.16. Max perceives the Internet to be insecure and doesn't want to enter his credit card number on-line. He would rather have a live agent call him back to give the credit card number over the phone.

Figure 8.15 -- Cruise Reservation and Ship Information

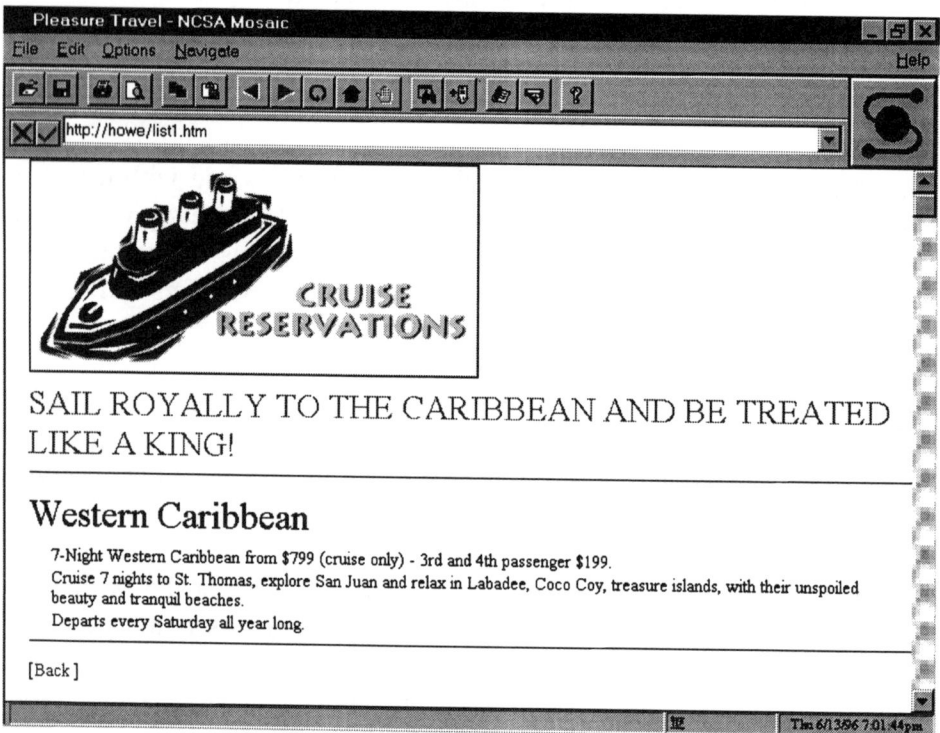

```
Pleasure Travel - NCSA Mosaic
File  Edit  Options  Navigate
                                                                    Help
```

CRUISE RESERVATIONS

SAIL ROYALLY TO THE CARIBBEAN AND BE TREATED
LIKE A KING!

Western Caribbean

7-Night Western Caribbean from $799 (cruise only) - 3rd and 4th passenger $199.
Cruise 7 nights to St. Thomas, explore San Juan and relax in Labadee, Coco Coy, treasure islands, with their unspoiled beauty and tranquil beaches.
Departs every Saturday all year long.

[Back]

Also Max has an additional question on the type of rooms available. Finally, Max clicks on the "Call Me" button. Max's "call me" request is sent to Pleasure Travel's Web server. The Web server passes the call request to ResumeRouting. ResumeRouting puts the call request into its queue. ResumeRouting sends Max a confirmation that his call request is received and queued.

At this point, ResumeRouting performs a skills-based routing and dynamically selects a group of agents who are qualified to serve him. All agents are busy, so ResumeRouting sends Max a *Call Status Update* with expected wait time. Now agent Terri Johnson becomes available. ResumeRouting routes Max's call to Terri by screen pop of Max's call information. Terri now knows Max's name, phone number, IP address and his questions.

Figure 8.16 -- Cruise Reservation Form

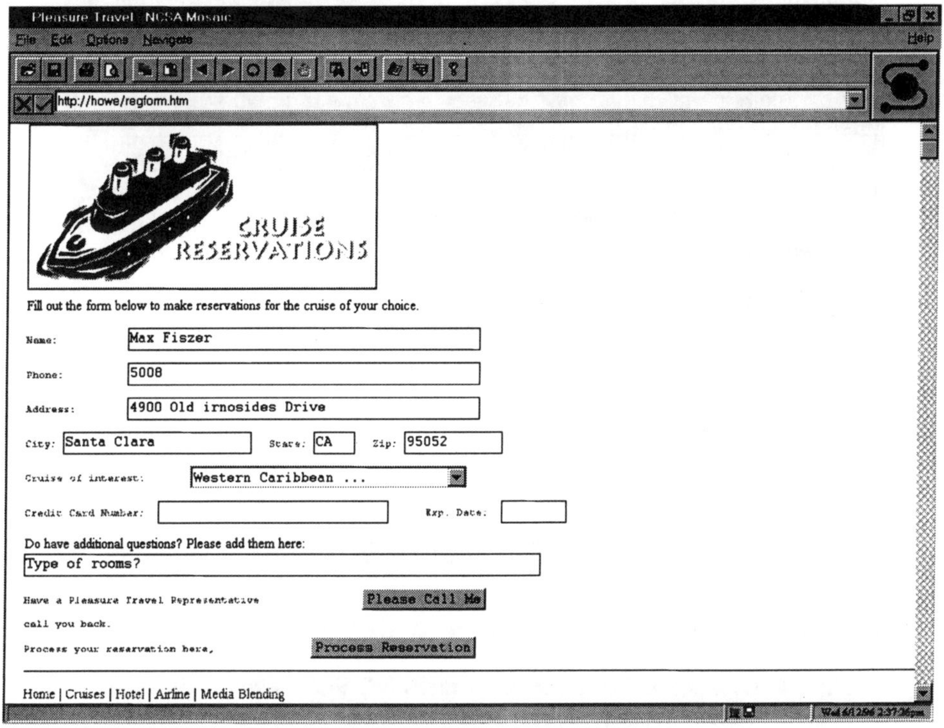

What she sees is illustrated in Figure 8.17. At the same time, Terri's agent interface automatically calls Max via a CTI link to establish a voice connection. Also Terri's agent interface transmits her Versit vCard to Max. Now Max's (regular) phone rings. He says "hello" and establishes a real-time call as he is connected to the agent. Also Max's Web browser receives Terri's Versit vCard with Terri's picture and business information as pictured in Figure 8.18. Now Max's browser changes to the agent's current Web page. Now the agent says: "Mr. Fiszer, I am Terri Johnson calling you from Pleasure Travel. I understand that you would like to take a Western Caribbean cruise and have a question on the type of rooms available. Let me answer your question on your Web browser. Let me sync up with your screen.

Figure 8.17. -- Call Confirmation Screen Pop

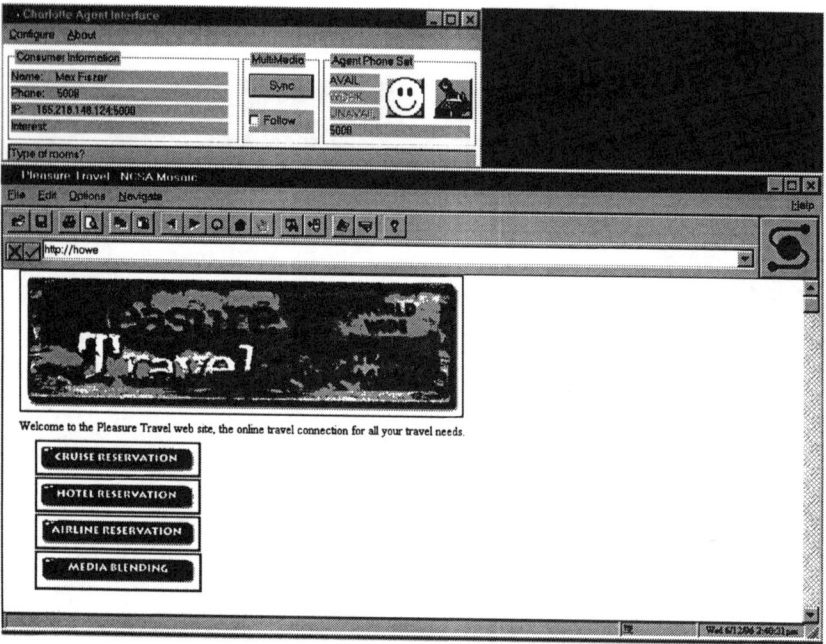

Figure 8.18 -- Customer Interface with Versit vCard

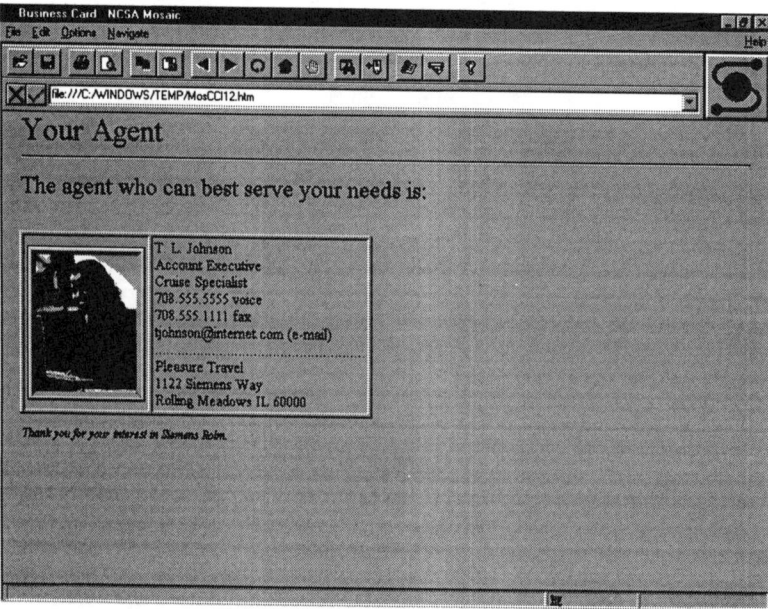

Now please follow me on your Web browser. I will lead your browser to the right Web page." Agent Terri surfs now to the right Web page with information on the type of rooms.

Max's browser now follows agent Terri's browser and displays the same Web page as the agent. Finally Max's browser displays the Web page with the type of rooms available as shown in Figure 8.19. After additional explanation on the phone, Max is completely satisfied with the Western Caribbean cruise and wants to book the reservation. Max now gives his credit card number (securely) over the phone and hangs up. Agent Terri confirms the booking and also hangs up top prepare for the next Web customer.

Figure 8.19 -- Room Availability Detail Screen

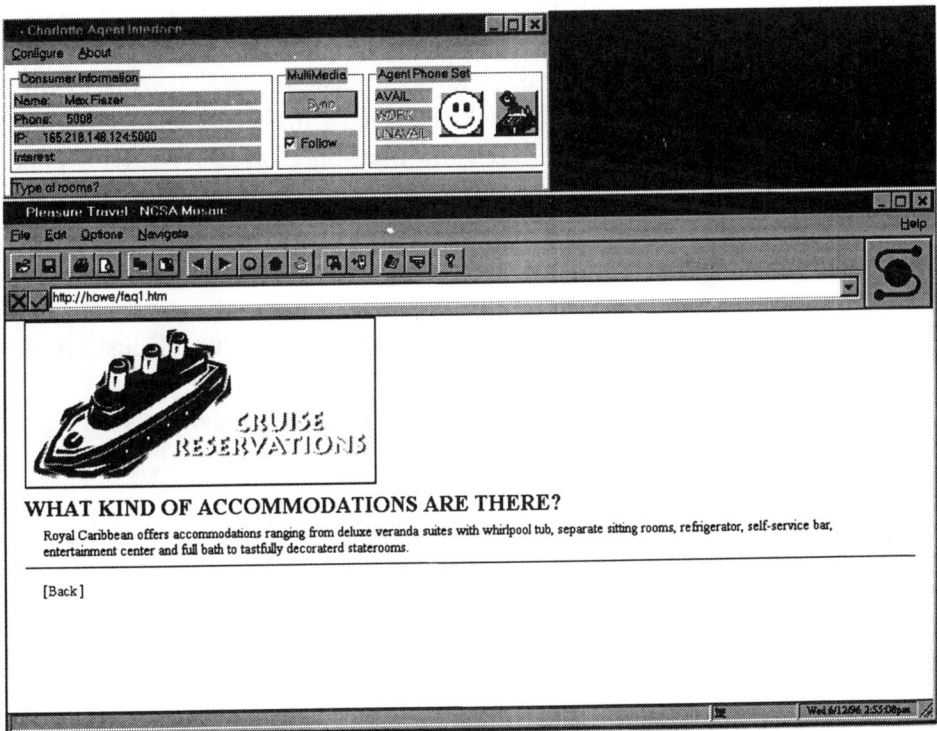

Spanlink Communications

WebCall

Spanlink has been delivering interactive communications solutions to businesses since 1988. That's a lifetime in this business. Back then, Computer Telephony was simply voice mail. Today it means voice processing, voice response, computer telephone integration, speech recognition, Internet integration and more. AT&T uses Spanlink's call center applications to improve customer service in most new AT&T Call Centers.

ExtraAgent for the Call Center allows callers to make choices based on their estimated wait in queue. It lets customers serve themselves rather than wait for an available representative. This shortens the overall call duration and reduces staffing costs through more efficient use of customer service personnel. The package can enhance caller services with broadcasts of general information, automated attendant and a Bulletin Board that menus of automated answers to routine questions. You can make ExtraAgent work with SmartLink -- Spanlink's CTI package. SmartLink's CTI feature streamlines call processing by passing caller information such as ANI, DNIS and ACD Status from your ACD to your voice processing applications: This enables you to do custom call routing, callback messaging and preview dialing. You can also:

Tailor announcements for a particular customer or group of customers.

Provide delay announcements and time estimates for callers waiting in the queue.

Use dynamic port allocation, which allows numerous applications to share one port.

SmartLink is available for integration with the Definity series (G1, G2, G3), System 75, 85 and Merlin Legend, as well as many Northern Telecom and Rolm models.

With *Custom Call Routing*, you can direct callers to particular queues or extensions. The routing can be based on the caller's number or dialed number, or information collected from the caller. Information about the caller may be sent to the extension along with the call. The feature enables specialists to service callers more efficiently.

Callback Messaging, together with anticipated delay announcements, helps flatten call peaks by providing a method for callers to request callbacks when agents are available. When a message is left, an ExtraAgent checks the queue status to determine if there are representatives available to receive callbacks. When the threshold is reached, the ExtraAgent automatically delivers a message to a representative. Callbacks may be launched automatically from telephone numbers provided by the caller.

Utilities for preview dialing provide access to ExtraAgent's callback features from managed outbound dialing lists. On an integrated or stand-alone basis, preview dialing may be used for telemarketing, collections or other outbound dialing campaigns. Data entry from file transfer or diskette is available.

The ExtraAgent package can be combined with additional Spanlink applications to offer callers fully automated transaction processing. This includes order entry, account information and service status. Regardless of the options selected, this package comes with speech recording and playback capabilities.

The ExtraAgent package greets callers with various announcements and voice prompts. These pre-recorded messages instruct callers to use their touch-tone phones to make selections and access the services they need. Depending on the options selected, callers can: listen to message while on hold, choose to be connected to an agent, or be automatically routed to a particular customer service group. And this package gives administrators touch-tone or screen-based access for easy updates to message and voice prompts.

On-Line Commerce Meets The Call Center. According to a Forrester Research / Yankee Group study, on-line purchases accounted for $240 Million in 1995. They say that will reach $6.9 Billion by the turn of the century. But Web users list security as a reason not to purchase on-line. This is one of the motivations behind Spanlink's WebCall product. WebCall allows customers who find you on the Internet's World Wide Web to ask to speak to a live agent from your Web page (without having a multi-media PC or a high speed Internet connection). WebCall makes use of your existing Call Center ACD and business computer systems.

A customer looking at your World Wide Web site wants to speak to a live agent to get more information or complete an electronic transaction. This customer clicks on a button which says "Talk to a Real Person." The customer is then presented with a form which asks for their phone number and up to fifteen additional pieces of information that you configure to your needs. After filling out the form, the customer presses the "Send" button.

Figure 8.20 – WebCall Wait Time

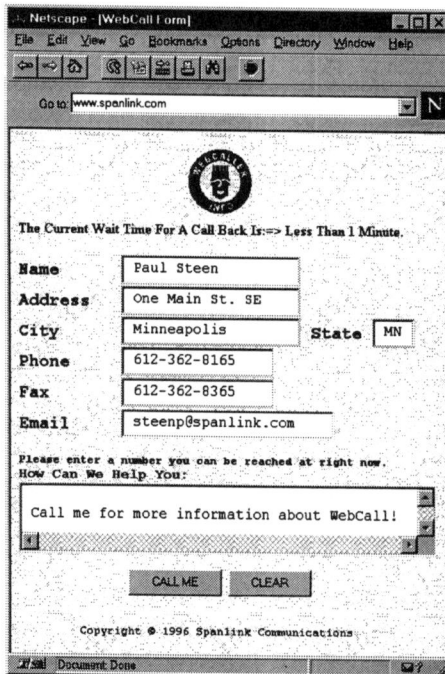

WebCall will give the customer an estimated wait time for call back and will queue the call for a live agent. This is illustrated in Figure 8.20. When the agent receives the call they will receive the caller information and be connected to the caller. Figure 8.21 shows what the agent sees after the Web-browsing customer enters order instructions.

Figure 8.21 – WebCall Agent Form

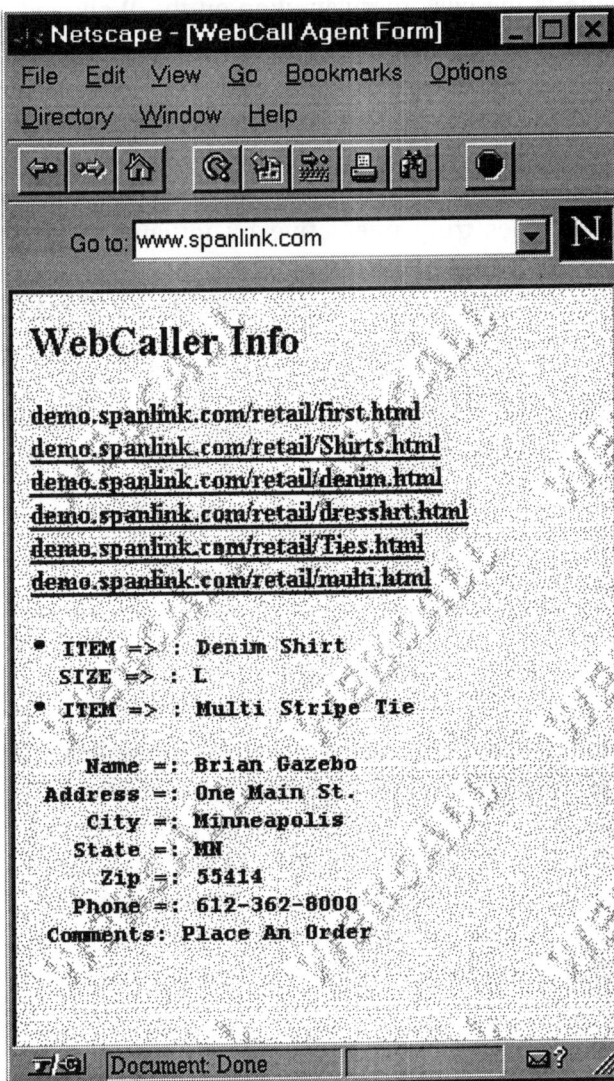

WebCall connects the Internet to existing call centers, so anonymous browsers become qualified customer opportunities. While this may increase the amount of traffic introduced to the call center, the integration of the elements makes things quicker. This combines the efficiency and cost savings of the Internet with personal service of a real person. It certainly gets around on-line security concerns.

The bottom line is the customer can *shop* on the Web, and *buy* over the telephone. This provides for secure credit card transactions by allowing customers to give information over the phone. It also offers upselling opportunities for service agents.

By linking you call center to a Web site, the process of ordering products over the Web becomes truly interactive by initiating a person-to-person interaction. This increases revenues for sales and marketing applications and does a better job of managing hold times. The end result is reducing costs *and* increasing service levels.

You need a Conversant version 5.0 system (for Definity, System 85, Northern Telecom and ROLM) and ExtraAgent Callback Messaging software to make it work.

Teknekron Infoswitch Corporation

Orchestra! and Rendezvous!

Teknekron Infoswitch Corporation provides integrated voice and data solutions for call centers. Teknekron sells the Series III ACD. This stand-alone switch can handle over 75,000 calls per busy hour. The Series III is based on an ISDN architecture and the Motorola 68030, 32-bit, VME microprocessor. It can handle 1,000 agents. The server side of their CT apps run on Sun SPARCstations. Teknekron says tells me their market research shows electronic commerce will have a major impact on call centers within the next few years.

With this in mind, Teknekron is focusing on making all of its products Internet/Intranet-aware. The Series III ACD is already Internet-aware, via a call back feature. When customers click on a call icon to select a live agent, the ACD will initiate a call-back. The performance management software, AutoQuality! and P&Q Review!, will have customized Web-access for either supervisors, quality managers, agents, or any combination thereof. Teknekron also is developing Web-aware CTI, IVR scripts and Internet voice technologies.

Orchestra! software controls call information (voice) from the telephone switch and data from host systems. This gets you simultaneous coordination of calls and data records. Agents can answer, route and control telephone calls as well as handle data transactions from a single workstation.

Orchestra! has a launch pad to spawn desktop applications, including network terminal emulators for mainframes, minicomputers or servers. You can execute other windows-based software programs like word processors, spreadsheets and e-mail. The product also gives you "soft phone" buttons on the screen. This lets you do call control, speed dial and automatic generation of wrap-up codes.

Rendezvous! coordinates the simultaneous delivery of telephone calls and customer host data to agent workstations. With it, you an do "screen pops" and customer call tracking without changing mainframe code.

The software uses Automatic Number Identification (ANI), Integrated Voice Response (IVR), or Dialed Number Identification Service (DNIS). This data is used to match incoming customer calls with the callers' account information in your customer database. Customer information is presented on the agent desktop in a screen pop along with the associated customer call. As shown Figure 8.22, agents get detailed customer transaction histories on their screens. Agents and supervisors can track how specific cases are being resolved. You can see how many times specific customers have called and what issues are outstanding.

Figure 8.22 -- Rendezvous! Call tracking

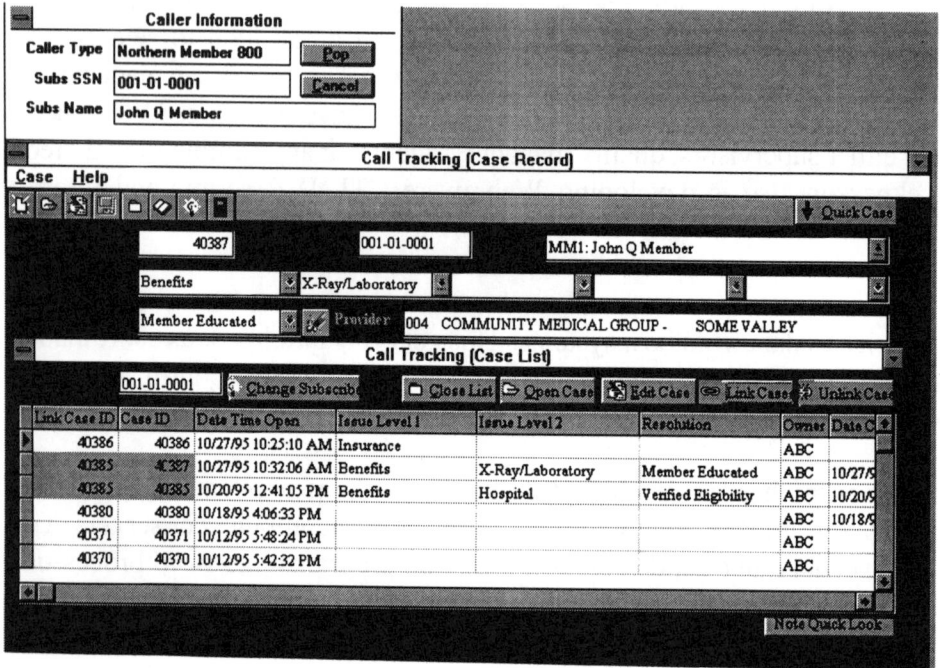

Caller Information		
Caller Type	Northern Member 800	**Pop**
Subs SSN	001-01-0001	**Cancel**
Subs Name	John Q Member	

Call Tracking (Case Record)

Case   Help

40387	001-01-0001	MM1: John Q Member

Benefits	X-Ray/Laboratory		

Member Educated	Provider	004 COMMUNITY MEDICAL GROUP - SOME VALLEY

Call Tracking (Case List)

001-01-0001   Change Subscriber   Close List   Open Case   Edit Case   Link Case   Unlink Case

Link Case ID	Case ID	Date Time Open	Issue Level 1	Issue Level 2	Resolution	Owner	Date C
40386	40386	10/27/95 10:25:10 AM	Insurance			ABC	
40385	40387	10/27/95 10:32:06 AM	Benefits	X-Ray/Laboratory	Member Educated	ABC	10/27/9
40385	40385	10/20/95 12:41:05 PM	Benefits	Hospital	Verified Eligibility	ABC	10/20/9
40380	40380	10/18/95 4:06:33 PM				ABC	10/18/9
40371	40371	10/12/95 5:48:24 PM				ABC	
40370	40370	10/12/95 5:42:32 PM				ABC	

Note Quick Look

During the call, agents can request additional customer data from the mainframe's database. You can transfer the call and associated customer data to another agent. You also get a Dynamic Data Exchange (DDE) application interface. This lets you share data with other DDE-compliant desktop apps. This is good for reducing data entry errors (it eliminates re-typing of data). Rendezvous! can automatically update screen pops with caller data received from VRUs. You can also get information from MS Word, Excel, and other programs into the Rendezvous! database.

If multiple customer records match the ANI, IVR, or DNIS information, all matching customer names are displayed in the screen pop. Agents can use this screen data to adjust customer records. If no customer information matches the caller id information, the agent is presented with an empty screen pop to add the new information. Teknekron calls this database enrichment or greening. It increases ANI "hits" on subsequent calls.

Figure 8.23 -- Orchestra! and Rendezvous agent screen

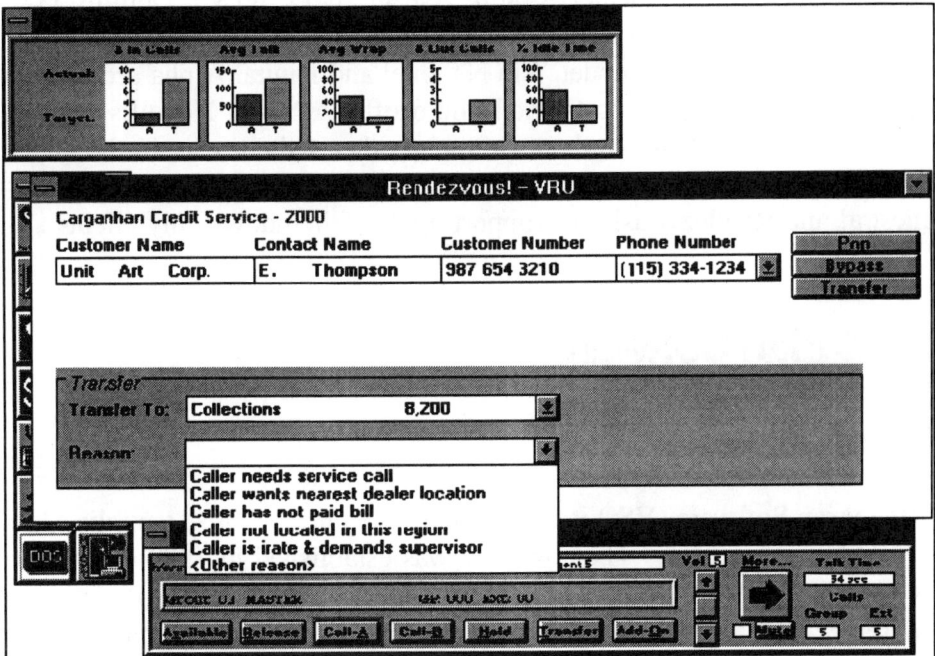

With Orchestra!, statistics can be displayed either numerically or graphically. All this in real time. This allows agents to monitor themselves and improve performance to meet the target levels visible on their screen as shown in Figure 8.23. The target performance stats include talk time, wrap-up time and number of calls handled on each agent screen. Rendezvous! manages screen pops, caller data and incoming calls at the agent PC workstation. All data can be transferred with the call to another agent.

The server part of Rendezvous runs on a Sun SPARCstation (AT&T and Northern Telecom switches require an NT server, as well) with Solaris 2.x. The client side runs under Win 3.x Win 95 and NT. These solutions sell for between $2,000 to $3,000 per agent seat, depending on call center size and configuration. In addition to support for their own Series III ACD/IEX Gateway, Teknekron bolts to many other switches. This due to their own efforts and an interface with Dialogic's CT-Connect call control server.

Dialogic's CT server supports major PBXs, ACDs and LANs. Compatible switches include the Alcatel A4400, Aspect ACD, AT&T Definity G-3, Ericsson MD110, Nortel Meridian 1, Rockwell Galaxy ACD and the Rolm CBX. CT-Connect runs under Win NT Intel and Digital Alpha processors. The server software supports Intel/Microsoft TAPI and Novell's TSAPI. CT-Connect is CSTA-compliant, so many other switches are in the queue for compliance testing. An entry-level CT-Connect configuration for Orchestra! and Rendezvous! will support up to 35 Windows-only clients.

Venturian Software

CyberCall

Venturian Software (VSI) is a division of Venturian Corp., a public Minnesota-based company. The company was established in 1993. Venturian is a Magic Software Enterprises Value-Added Dealer. Magic software is a table-based application development language. It is used to create client-server interop platforms. It serves as the back-end "data fetching" and integration environment for disparate platforms. Applications are written in Magic and then ported to UNIX, Windows, DOS and Novell environments.

Venturian serves as the authorized "Magic University" for the Israeli-based Magic Software Enterprises. Additional products include the DDF Wizard for Magic, a developer's tool created to assist Magic developers; and a Payroll Transfer Utility (PTU) for use by organizations that use a payroll service in conjunction with a variety of packaged accounting products. This positions them well for the call center and IVR markets, both of which require a lot of customization and integration. Among its customers are the Minnesota State Lottery, Prudential Select Insurance, K-Tel International, Norwest Bank, the University of Wisconsin and Napco Industries. Magic is the basis for a robust development environment. It was also the genesis of highly strategic technology access arrangements for Venturian.

In 1994, Venturian expanded into computer telephony by adding the MultiCall TSAPI (Novell Telephony Services) product developed by the Israeli-based Lansys Ltd. Early successes include an installation at American Express Financial Advisors.

MultiCall is an open computer telephony package written in Magic. It runs as a Novell NLM and handles call control, fax-on-demand and screen pops for call centers. NetCall Technologies Limited, UK are the designers of CyberCall, exclusively distributed by Venturian in the US. The initial prototype was a cooperative effort to demonstrate the concept of the Virtual Call Center and the potential *interactive* linking of the WWW with the PSTN voice network. I saw the prototype of CyberCall at the Olympia Conference Center in the UK last year and I was thoroughly impressed.

NetCall Technologies, Lansys Ltd., Securicor Telecoms and Origin UK were all present. Each company contributed to the live demo. NetCall Technologies created WeBX (CyberCall the U.S.) Web-aware client-server software. It's the piece that communicates between the CTI serve and the Web Server. Lansys Ltd. brought their NetWare Telephony Services expertise to the table (MultiCall as explained above). WebConnect is Lansys' own version of WeBX covered in this book.. Securicor Telecoms represented the switch element. They manufacture TSAPI-compatible PABXs and Key Systems. They are designers and manufacturers of Computer Telephony Integrated systems. They are also Resellers of NetCall's WeBX Product. Origin UK is a Global IT service supplier, software developer and systems integrator. They provide the ISP hook-ups and Web Server.

Based on the corroboration between these companies, Venturian was quick to strike up a distribution deal with NetCall for a U.S. offering of WeBX. The company already had great experiences with Magic software. They were already selling the MultiCall TSAPI solution. Venturian also had plenty of systems integration expertise, so the deal was a natural. All of the companies seem pleased with the arrangement. Venturian believes that growth in the area of Internet Call Center applications will outpace the dramatic growth forecast for the call center industry through 2001.

Says Ilan Sharon, VSI president: "Both call center and Internet implementation are strategic purchases that many mangers can recognize as key to customer satisfaction. Increased corporate recognition of the absolute necessity of these combined technologies will make them standards in the very near future."

CyberCall integrates the benefits of call center services with the power and reach of the World Wide Web. Utilizing the Internet as a means to intelligently route callers and information about them, agents and callers are linked in real-time by both phone and mirrored home page "screen pops." Agents that answer calls can be in one location or they can be home agents located anywhere in the world, making the "Virtual Call Center" a reality. CyberCall is platform independent, allowing Web page owners to set up a virtual call center without the expense of completely reinvesting in new hardware.

Appearing on the Web page as a button, browsers are able to place a call by simply clicking it. CyberCall, used in connection with a Web page automatically establishes a voice telephony link and home page screen pop between the user that is browsing the Web page and the owner of the Web page. Browser and agent are connected by voice and are viewing the same screen in real time.

The following outlines the key technologies that form the CyberCall system:

CyberCall Page Manager. Located at the Web page level, this contains the *HyperPhone Link*. The link passes telephony requests to CyberCall together with the page URL details. This links the requests contextually and determines the routing attributes.

CyberCall Site Manager. This Web Server Link module enables integration with a range of standard Web Servers -- supporting communications from customer Web browses and internal Web browses.

CyberCall Agent Manager. Associated with the Site Manager, this "Virtual Agent" module hold details of the capabilities and specialization of staff (internal & external), information on their skill sets, location and availability.

CyberCall ICD. Intelligent Call Distribution works with the call attributes from the *HyperPhone Link* and the resource profiles within Agent Manager, and integrates them with the company's telephone and IT networks to route the telephone call and the customer Web page to the right desktop.

CyberCall Tools

Two major tools compliment CyberCall modules. They can be used by Systems Integrators during the design and implementation of their platforms:

Telephony Server . Uses an open PBX API, such as Novell's TSAPI, to provide the necessary integration between the company's IT network and its telecommunications network.

CyberCall Environment. This is a logical systems structure which enables implementation within an existing systems structure. It will interface with end-user desktop applications such as Lotus Notes and provide API's & Libraries etc. to facilitate CyberCall's integration with databases such as Oracle and Informix. In addition, it will incorporate access and security controls.

CyberCall Applications

The CyberCall Web Virtual Call Center from Venturian Software is a promising entrant in Internet-based computer telephony. CyberCall delivers the virtual call center to the right desktop. You can link a customer anywhere in the world with your employee best skilled to resolve the issue. To better illustrate the power of the CyberCall environment it is good describe several scenarios.

Financial Services Company. "Anybank PLC" has implemented a *Virtual Call Center* using CyberCall and this is the contact point for their corporate customer service function. Anybank PLC is now able to accept customer contact from the following classes of customer.

Voice Only. The traditional customer contact

Data Only. A directed or casual Web browser contact

Hybrid. A Web browser contact with interactive voice support

Anybank PLC initially implemented the system across their high street branches and in phase two are opening up the service to the public at large. A customer makes contact with the CyberCall Call Center either via the Internet, or directly via an advertised Customer Line, using a PC equipped with a standard Web Browser (perhaps supplied by Anybank PLC).

Figure 8.24 – CyberCall-Based Home Page

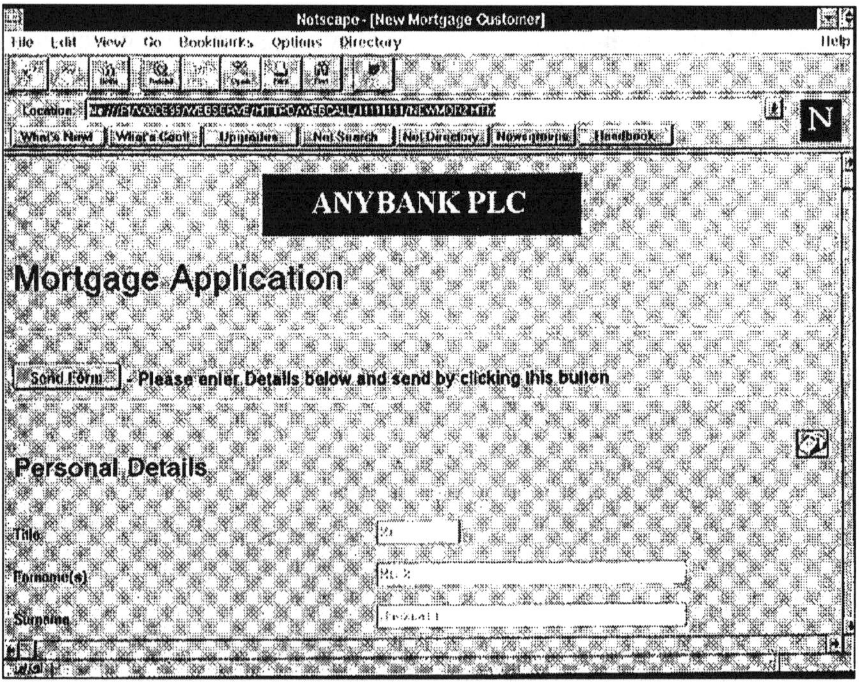

The customer is invited to log into CyberCall and investigate the Call Center's information resources. Once logged in (name, address etc.), the customer is provided with Anybank PLC's home page as illustrated in Figure 8.24. On subsequent contacts the customer can interact with his or her own home page, representing areas of interest and any on-going transactions. In our scenario, the customer is in the market for a mortgage and browses pages relevant to that subject. CyberCall can publish pages "on the fly" via its links with Anybank PLC's core IT systems. This way, product info, interest rates and sample quotes are up to the minute.

As with any good Web site, CyberCall provides the customer with Hy-perText Links to other pages connected with the chosen topic. *CyberCall goes one step further.* Within the Web pages published by Anybank PLC's new Call Center is CyberCall's unique *HyperPhone Link*.

Figure 8.25 – CyberCall Virtual Call Center Topology

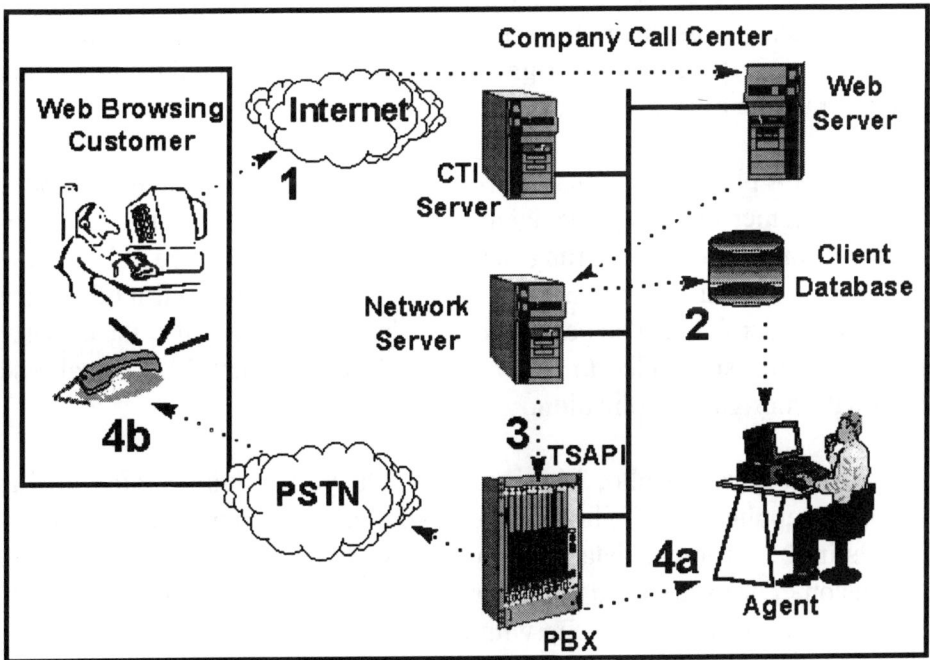

This is represented at key points throughout the information pages by a discrete telephone icon. Simply clicking on any of these, the customer is automatically placed in voice contact with the Virtual Call Center. The system will look for someone who has the capacity to assist with the topic that has been associated with that particular HyperPhone Link.

In this scenario, the customer has accessed a mortgage application form. It's populated with any customer information gleaned from the caller and combined with data found by CyberCall from Anybank PLC's core business systems. The customer has some difficulty selecting which Mortgage plan is best for him. He uses the HyperPhone Link associated with that section of the form. Detailed below are the steps the CyberCall system takes. This is illustrated in Figure 8.25.

CyberCall now locates a member of Anybank PLC's staff (a "Virtual Agent"). It locates one who has the skills to deal with the nature of this inquiry (mortgage, assurance linked etc. etc.). This inquiry profile is known by CyberCall from the information examined during the browse. Other factors such as customer geography and existing account contribute to CyberCall's selection of the right Anybank PLC person. Of course, that person must be available to take the call.

CyberCall "pops" the virtual agent's PC screen with the same Web page as the customer and rings the agent's phone to connect with the customer whose phone is also now rung. This is illustrated in Figure 8.26. If the customer is calling from home and does not have a dedicated modem line (or SVD modem), the Web page will have already requested that the browser be temporarily suspended to allow "Jane" from Anybank PLC to call and help with mortgage application.

The agent says: "Hello, Mr. Hucknall. Do you require advice on the mortgage application?" The agent can click an click icon for In progress details in the customer detail window. This causes the "mirrored side" of the customer browse screen to change. "Mr. Hucknall, I see from our records you currently have a mortgage with us."

Figure 8.26 -- CyberCall Mirrored Screen Pop

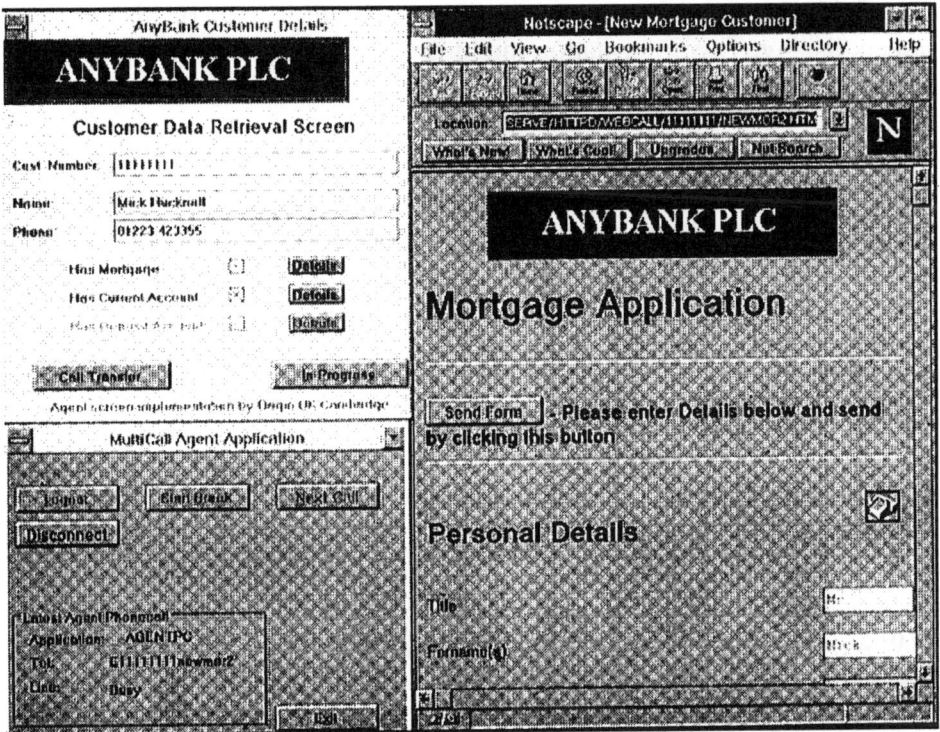

The agent can then click on the click on HyperText link for connected info. At this point, a salary statement appears on the agent's screen. "Good news, your employer has returned your salary statement."Mr. Hucknall says he needs more Information on repayment of mortgages abroad. Jane determines that another specialist would be better skilled to help with the query. Jane says, "Please hang up and our overseas repayment specialist will call you immediately." Both parties now hang up, and Jane clicks the transfer call button on the customer data retrieval screen. The transfer call window pops-up with a list box of departments to transfer the call to. From this list box, Jane selects the specialist type. CyberCall checks the location & availability of a new specialist and automatically connects the specialist to Mr. Hucknall.

CyberCall provides the new agents with the relevant information about this customer. So not only was the call transferred – so were the records. All of this is "published on-the-fly" to the agent as part of his/her Web screen display. This information might include savings account details or a document image.

At this point, the new specialist's screen populates as Mr. Hucknall's phone rings. When he answers, the new agent says: "Hello Mr. Hucknall, do you require information on repayment mortgages abroad?" In a few moments, Mr. Hucknall gets what he needs. Having assisted the customer with the application, CyberCall disconnects the telephone call and returns the customer to the appropriate Web page (other services, account balance, etc.).

IVR - Catalog Order Entry.

The integration of Web sites with an existing IVR system can provide companies with an additional convenient communication tool to reach potential clients. This helps to promote superior quality of service and support for their existing customer base. By using IVR along with the WWW, you can leverage the best attributes of both PC and phone-based customer service.

In this catalog order entry scenario, a customer calls to place a catalog order after normal customer service hours. He get the automatic attendant but hears the catalog has a Web site that takes orders 24 hours a day. The customer quickly surfs to the site and is prompted to log in (name, address, telephone number, etc.) Once logged in, the customer is given the option of browsing the on-line catalog, placing an order or checking order status.

The customer clicks the "placing an order" icon. An order screen pops in front of the customer. Filling in the item number size and color desired, the customer is prompted for payment method. After selecting one of the credit card payment options, the customer is prompted by the system to press the "HyperPhone Link". Figure 8.27 illustrates how this scenario is supported without a live agent. Instead, the IVR system acts as the virtual agent.

Figure 8.27 -- CyberCAll IVR as Virtual Agent

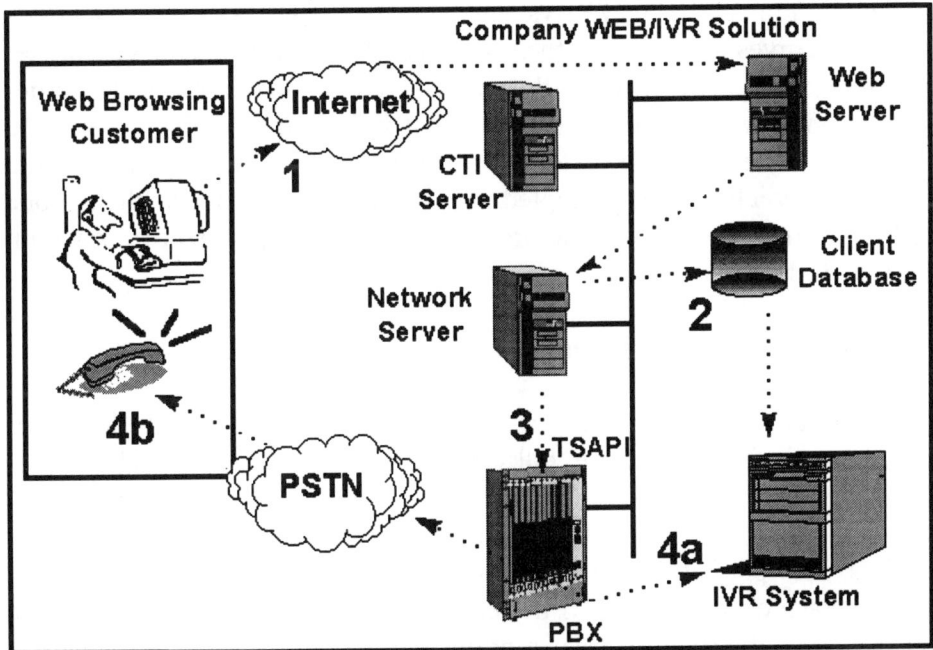

For security reasons, the credit card information will be collected over the phone. The customer clicks the icon and moments later their phone begins to ring. The prompt for IVR service has been routed through the catalog company's Web server. After collecting relevant information from the Web server and the customer database, the call has been linked to the IVR system.

Once the connection with the IVR system is made, a call from the IVR system is placed to the customer's home phone. The IVR system is now automatically linked to the customer through the telephone as well as through the Internet. The IVR system then confirms the information that the customer has already typed into the Web page by asking for key pad confirmation. After the system reads back the customer's name, address and order information the IVR system asks the customer to select a type of credit card by pressing the phone keypad (one for VISA, two for American Express, etc.).

After selecting a card, the customer is prompted to type in their card number and expiration date. The IVR system automatically checks for card authorization and gives the customer their order number. The customer's computer has an automatic screen pop of the confirmed order on the screen. The order form is complete except that the payment field is not on the screen. The IVR system then asks the customer if they would like written confirmation of the order via fax. After prompted, the customer presses one on their phone pad to confirm and a complete order form including payment information is faxed to him.

Chapter Acknowledgments

My thanks to Dick Willson, of Securicor Telecoms, Amy Anderson of Venturian Software and the folks at Lansys and NetCall Technologies Limited. Their relationship defines the meaning of global interoperability. This applies to their products and their recent corroboration to educate my readers. The project spanned three continents. They were cool, collected and a pleasure to deal with. If my experience with them is any indication, the Voice-Enabled Internet has a bright future.

Chapter 9

Help Desks and the Internet

The Internet presents a dizzying array of new terms and acronyms. Add to this an equally confusing technology like Artificial Intelligence (a chief discipline of help desk technology) and you've got more frustration than you can handle. For this reason, this chapter starts out answering some basic questions about how help desks are quickly becoming an "Enterprise Support Hub." Certainly, the vast information stores and ubiquitous access of the Internet are giving help desks a shot in the arm. I asked Frances Tischler, Ph.D., and Isidore Sobowski of Professional Help Desk to demystify this merger between the Web and help desks.

You will learn how the rise of Natural Intelligence is fueling even greater intelligence in computer telephony applications. We will cover Web-aware Help desks, automated help desk and workforce management issues. Isidore prepared an amazingly succinct yet informative run-down of natural intelligence, forward chaining, expert systems and neural nets.

Natural Intelligence in Help Desk Environments

Professionals in the field have long known that artificial intelligence was going to make its way out of the rarefied air of labs and smack into the business environment. Nowhere is this trend more useful than in help desk support; as PCs have proliferated for the last decade or so, organizations have seen the advent of the confused user. Thus sprang the help desk.

Help desks are interesting animals. People call them to get answers to such questions as, "My screen is blank, what should I do?" Given the complexity of today's PCs hardware and software there is truly a combinatorial explosion of things that can be wrong with someone's PC at any point in time.

The Antioch California school district needed this genre of solution when they found that they were supporting more than 500 computers at 17 sites throughout the Antioch area. They must not only maintain and repair their existing wide area network, but they must also train and support a user base composed of 40 percent administrators and 60 percent students on a variety of computer applications.

The October '94 issue of the *Client/Server Economics* Letter even goes so far as to say that help desks are a "killer app." And an article in that most respected of all computer rags, Computerworld, says that customer service software will be the next major wave of client-server applications. Writers Rosemary Cafasso and Julia King have found in their research that customer service needs are taking an ever higher priority in organization. Cafasso and King go on to say that help desk personnel are involved in many more functions, and in more areas of their business than ever, requiring software that allows them greater flexibility and wider access to other company systems. These help desk success stories do mount up. Satellite manufacturer Hughes Space and Communications Co. has signed a fiveyear outsourcing agreement for Electronic Data Systems Corp. to manage their LAN environment and provide help, desk support.

Color Tile of Fort Worth, Texas, is a leading home improvement retailer with over 770 stores and 4,600 employees. After going live with an automated help desk in the summer of 1991, they found that time spent per call to the help, desk was down from 10 minutes to 2.8 minutes The help desk is staffed by six operators who provide service seven days week and handle virtually every call that comes into Color Tile's corporate headquarters

And help desk productivity has lumped more than 40 percent at J C. Penney since help desk software was installed by the Plano, Texasbased department store chain approximately three years ago. Besides saving time, the use of the system has enabled the chain to reduce its number of help desk support teams from eight to three. This, in turn, has made possible the installation of an automated callrouting system that allows the user to select the team that's needed to help solve the problem.

Traditional help desk software acts as a type of call manager. It logs the caller, records his or her problem and its resolution. Where most help desk software fails is in its inability to provide a timely solution to all but the most simple problems. If a help desk is only as good as its "knowledge base," then most of today's help desks are truly in trouble since they rely solely on the expertise of the help desk analyst. And while even a great help desk analyst can solve some of the problems some of the time, it's statistically impossible for a human to solve all of the problems all of the time. That's where Natural Intelligence comes in. If call management functionality can be coupled With AI technology, then you have the possibility of a system that can only get smarter.

Natural Intelligence Defined

Simply put, natural intelligence is nothing less than providing software with the ability to think. It is the fusion of the branches of artificial intelligence with "record and calculate" capabilities to achieve new heights of capability. Today's customer service software merely records customer problems and attempts resolutions of problems by utilizing minor database searches. This is hardly an intelligent approach.

Figure 9.1 – Help Desk Cross-Disciplines

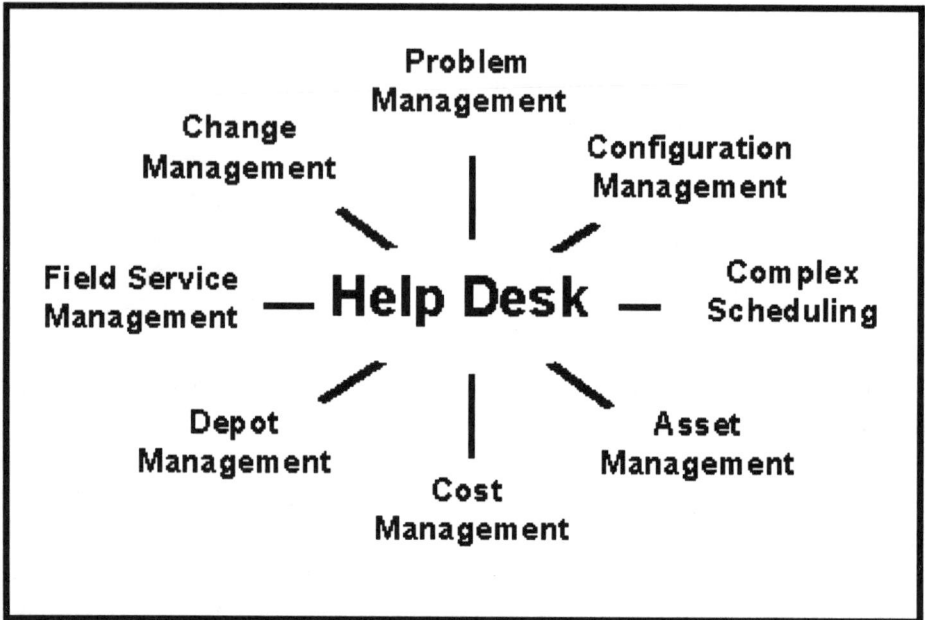

A naturally intelligent customer support module would serve to amplify the abilities of the support technician using the software. Software, up until now, has only been as intelligent as its most intelligent user. But naturally intelligent software could serve to "lead" the support technician through the steps necessary to solve his customer's problem. Naturally intelligent software, then, should be profoundly more intelligent than the most intelligent user. This is true because its embedded intelligence is a composite of the most expert of information with the most expert of analytical techniques. Natural intelligence, then, is the confluence of the branches of artificial intelligence with the capabilities of commercial software-whether that software be customer support, financial or word processing. While readers will readily understand the functional components of a commercial system (e.g., customer support consists, at a minimum, of call management, problem tracking and problem resolution capabilities), the AI aspect of natural intelligence requires some explanation.

Expert Systems Defined

What are expert systems really? Let's answer this by first explaining what they're not. They're not data base management systems. The database contains facts and figures. For example, it shows that John earns $26,000 a year and is 36 years old. It also shows that Pete earns $67,000 a year and is 45 years old. There's no knowledge here, just fact, all the facts and nothing but the facts.

Knowledge bases are different. For example, a human resources knowledge base might show that if the salary of the employee is greater than $25,000 then the job title is manager. It may also indicate that if someone is 35 years old or older then they are vested in the company's pension plan. This is knowledge in the form of rules. There's no facts or figures, just knowledge about how this department works.

The secret behind expert systems is the "expertise." Instead of capturing the data surrounding a securities trade, you capture the knowledge of why someone makes that trade. Instead of just capturing, data that describes a PC problem, you capture the knowledge that the help desk analyst uses in determining how to solve that problem. Just like databases were a better way to store data than just file systems, expert systems do a better job at storing and processing knowledge than do conventional systems.

Stored knowledge is easy to play back. A help desk analyst merely requests assistance and is immediately provided with a set of questions, procedures, and images that assists him or her in solving a given problem. Think of it as an expert-inabox. An expert that stores knowledge in a very particular way.

Rules are probably the easiest knowledgerecording structure to understand. Our lives are filled with decisions, so it's a natural to turn these into decision rules. A rule has two parts. A premise *IF IT'S COLD AND IT'S CREAMY*; and a conclusion: *THEN IT IS ICE CREAM*. Therefore, a rule is a conditional sentence starting with an *IF* and ending with a *THEN*. A rule, or production rule as it is sometimes called, stems from a decision.

Once rules or decision tables are code, there needs to be a mechanism to move around these rules picking and choosing the ones that are to be "fired." Expert systems do not operate in the same way traditional systems operate. Traditional systems execute one statement at a time, unless of course there is a branch statement.

Expert system rules execute according to a grand design called a control strategy which, controls the method of searching through the knowledge base. There are two major categories of searching: *forward chaining* and *backward chaining*.

Forward Chaining

In forward chaining we move from a set of assertions or facts to one or more possible outcomes. The way rule application works is that the system searches for a value where the conditions in the "if" part of the rule are matched in memory (deemed to be true). If so, then the "then" part is put Into working memory. Applying a forward chaining control strategy to a list of rules forces the execution of the rules from beginning to end. This is a sort of topdown reasoning approach. Here it reviews all known facts that were either entered at the very beginning of the system or became known as other rules triggered or fired.

After a rule is reviewed, if the premise is true then it is fired. In forward chaining every hit of available evidence is examined since the final goal is not predetermined. Suppose a CRT goes on the fritz. It just doesn't work. The screen is black. Well there can be many solutions to this problem. Perhaps the plug Is not plugged in. Perhaps the power is out. Perhaps the VGA board is bad. We go from an event (a bad screen) to one of many possible outcomes. Our forward chaining system would wind its way through rules that dealt with this topic trying to assist in figuring out what's wrong.

Backward Chaining

The opposite of forward chaining is backward chaining. This strategy operates from the perspective that you already possess an outcome and are searching for the conditions or circumstances that lead to that result. Here the system tries to determine a value for the goal by identifying rules that conclude a value for the goal. Then the system backs up and tries to determine if the IF clauses are true. Again an example can serve to enlighten you. This time we know we have a bad VGA board and we leaf through our rules to find out if a black screen is indeed symptomatic of this problem. Help desks employing an expert system stratagem are providing a powerful method for improving productivity and a superior method for providing customer support. How many times have customers called with a problem only to hang up, with no solution? If the reason for this dilemma is that it is simply not possible to maintain a consistently high level of expertise on a corporate help desk it is hard, often unrewarding work. As soon as an analyst reaches any level of experience, he or she opts for greener pastures. But an expert system-enabled help desk has the ability to capture the experience of senior level help desk analysts and maintain that level of experience long after that analyst jumps ship.

Figure 9.2 – Help Desk Pyramid of Expertise

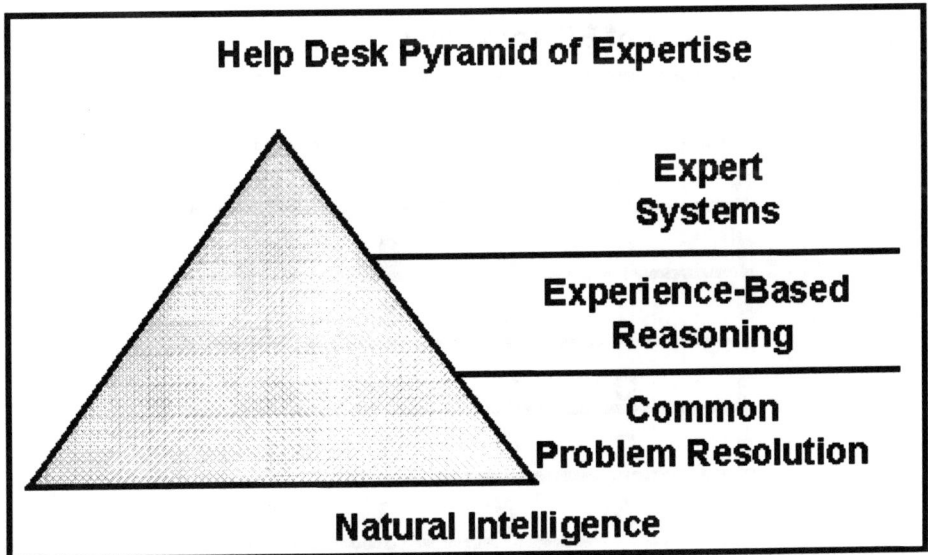

Help Desk Pyramid of Expertise

Expert Systems

Experience-Based Reasoning

Common Problem Resolution

Natural Intelligence

Neural Nets, Fuzzy Logic and Case Based Reasoning

Neural nets simulate a network of hundreds of parallel processing inter-connected units, shooting messages to each other at a rapidfire pace. The job of a neural net is to receive the input and respond.

This may first look like a task that can be handled as adequately by conventional means, but neural nets are computer programs with a difference. First, neural nets, and its sister paradigm *fuzzy logic*, have the capability of recognizing downgraded inputs. This capability is quite useful, it turns out, in dozens of commercial venues.

From handwriting recognition, to finding a solution to a problem when the variables offered as evidence are not quite in the database or expert system knowledge base (i.e. a user calls with a PC problem that has never been encountered before).

Neural nets are not easy to understand. The simplest explanation demonstrates how a neural net might understand a handwritten letter. Suppose that we represent a letter as a 5 by 7 matrix of binary values as shown in Figure 9.3.

Figure 9.3 – Matrix of Binary Values

0	0	1	0	0
0	1	0	1	0
1	0	0	0	1
1	1	1	1	1
1	0	0	0	1
1	0	0	0	1
1	0	0	0	1

The above matrix is a series of 35 ones and zeroes, therefore we have 35 input units. Each one represents one of the 35 positions in the matrix. The output of the analysis of each matrix would be an ASCII letter such as "A" or Z" (draw a line through the ones in the matrix above and see what you wind up with). Each ASCII letter is actually represented to the computer by an eight digit code. For example "A" would be 0100 0001. So what we have is input units and output units.

We also need middle units since it is these units that actually experience the activation that triggers a response in the output units. All units, like the neurons in the brain, are joined by connections. Each unit has an activation value of either 0 or 1. Input activity triggers a pattern of activation across the middle units, which causes some sort of pattern of activation in the output units a sort of a ripple effect.

Say a perfect letter "A" is handwritten into the system. Activation of the units produces a numeric score which is calculated as a result of a weight being multiplied by the activation that passes through the units as shown below in Figure 9.4.

Figure 9.4 -- Neural Net Numeric Scoring

0.001	0.977	0.002
	0.002	
0.015	0.009	0.011
	0.959	

Using the rule that any output above 0.9 is considered a 1 and any output less than 0.1 is considered a 0 then we get the correct ASII code for the letter "A": 0100 0001. Even if our handwritten letter "A" was less than perfect, that is even if one or more of the 35 input units was faulty, it would still be possible to produce the correct ASII code.

This is an example of what is known as a *backpropagation net* which is probably the most popular and certainly the simplest. It is also one of the neural net strategies that can learn by itself. Simply stated the input is inputted and the output is calculated. This output is then compared to the desired output. Next the real output of each unit is subtracted from the desired output and thus the net slightly adjusts itself towards correcting the error. This is a repetitive process that is performed until the net has learned a new set of connections that produce the correct output. If the letter is so poorly written as to be unrecognizable a more powerful net strategy could be employed to decipher even that.

Neural nets, casebased reasoning and fuzzy logic use intriguing statistical search, matching and retrieval techniques (similar to the example above) to sift through large amounts of data. The key, though, is the data. The more you have, the better the solution. It's not uncommon for users of this technique to refer to its "learning capabilities." That's because the quality of the solution that these technologies provide is directly proportional to the amount of information stored in the system (not unlike a human being). Compare this to a doctor, although possessed of a medical degree, one with 25 years of experience has more to base his/her decisions on than one directly out of medical schools. Experience really does count.

Although this genre Of AI is probably the most difficult to understand, it's the easiest to use. There's really no work on the part of the organization other than installing the software. and then using it. The more it's used the more it knows. Where the expert system helps the mote junior analyst give expert advice to users and thereby decrease the cost of running the help desk, fuzzy logic "guestimates" a solution to a difficult problem when there is no exact match. A realworld example illustrates how well this works.

Selling the likes of JellO Gelatin and Maxwell House Coffee to literally thousands of grocery stores requires some crafty maneuvering to remain competitive. Kraft Foods does this in a high-tech way. Armed with laptops, salespeople are not only mobile but are able to keep their information right at their fingertips.

To keep them that way required Caroline Summit to find an equally hightech way to manage her help desk. As manager of Kraft Foods' White Plains, NYbased Sales; Computer Help Line, Summit began a search through the dozens of help desk products on the market.

Summit needed something that would manage calls and problem resolutions. But many of the products on the market today do just that. So, how do you differentiate between so many products that do much the same thing?

The great differentiator, according to Summit, was intelligence. Kraft Foods didn't want anything that needed a heavily loaded database to begin with. What Summit and Kraft Foods wanted was a help desk system that sort of learned on its own. Most of Kraft Foods' problems are not exact replicas of problems that they had yesterday or the day before (there were variations on the theme). Kraft Foods wanted their help desk database to get smarter and smarter but didn't want to have to build it before they used it. They wanted it to grow and learn with them. They choose a fuzzy-logic based product. When a problem comes in that nobody knows the answer to they click on the fuzzy logic component which then makes suggestions as to what the answer might be (wilt percentage proximity to match). Summit recognizes the use of fuzzy logic in a help desk means the more problems she has the more adept at solving those problems her help desk becomes.

Natural Language Understanding Systems

That Kraft Foods so easily adapted to an AIinfused help desk was due to more than just the presence of fuzzy logic in the software. There also has to be a way for the software to interpret what the problem is.

Most software provides a rather rigid user interface. We enter data in hard to remember formats. How much better it would be to talk to the computer in our native tongue our natural language. So instead of pulldown menus, lists or radio buttons to indicate a flickering screen how about just typing "The user has a flickering screen"?

Natural language processing, yet another branch of artificial intelligence, enables people and computers to communicate on an equal footing. But it's hard work. Perhaps the biggest problem computer scientists working in this area have had to tackle is syntactic ambiguity. Especially in the English language. Many words can have more than one syntactic category. That is, some words can be used both as nouns and verbs. For example let's look at the sentence: *"WHY DON''T YOU GO OUTSIDE AND PLAY"*? The word play is used as a verb. In the following sentence, the word play is used as a noun: *"I ENJOYED THE BROADWAY PLAY."*

Along with syntactic ambiguity there is a host of other grammatical rules that must be factored into a natural language system. One of the harder to handle is pronominalization.

A example of how difficult it is for computers to understand the use of pronouns. is the following request: GIVE *ME A* REPORT ON DIRECTORS WHO *HAVE* SUBORDINATES *AND* THEIR SALARIES. Whose salaries do we want? The directors or their subordinates?

And added to all this confusion is the very human penchant for speaking ungrammatically. You know what you mean, your friends know what you mean, but does this computer understand PROFITS FOR LAST MONTHS SCREWDRIVERS?

People refer to the same thing in a multitude of ways. Keyword searching systems, a poor substitute for natural language, force users to memorize exact formats or the system refuses to give up the information. A robust natural language system should allow for this type of ambiguity when processing the following requests:

HOW MANY FIRMS SUBMMTED THEIR TAXES FOR 03/l3/95?

HOW MANY FIRMS SUBMITTED THEIR TAXES FOR 950313?

SHOW ME THE TAX RETURN OF FIRM 950313.

In The first two examples, the system needs to interpret the various formats of date. Easy as it looks, date and time are troublesome to all natural language systems, no matter how robust. In the last example we see that number again. Is 950313 a date, a tax identification number or what? It's obvious to us that we're referring to an identification number, but the natural language system must do some pretty fancy semantic interpretation to figure this one out.

Help desks with natural language front ends enable the organization to solve problems more quickly, without interference of rigid requirements which often serve to distort the meaning of the problem message itself.

Natural Intelligence Confluence

Using the example of help desk software, natural intelligence becomes quite easy to understand. Aside from the traditional functions of call management, a naturally intelligent help desk would enable the rapid resolution of customer problems, whether or not the information provided by the customer matched what was in the database.

When a call is forwarded to the help desk, the customer support technician or help desk analyst uses natural language processing to type one or more English sentences into the computer describing the problem. At that point, a naturally intelligent help desk syntactically and semantically parses the English input and then passes control to what can be referred to as an experiencebased processing module. Here it uses a combination of techniques such as fuzzy logic to "guestimate" a solution to a difficult problem.

For those occasions when the help desk analyst is required to provide a step-bystep detailed set of procedures to solve a problem (i.e., changing a board or installing a new memory chip), the decision tree/expert system component, coupled with its multimedia and visual capabilities, provides the optimum fit. Here the customer, as well as the customer support technician benefits from domain expertise unmatched in any of the other AI disciplines.

A Successful Help Desk Provides a shallow yet broad general knowledge. Opens and closes a large percentage (70-90 percent) of calls without the need of further assistance. Senior technical staff reserved for more l echnical requirements. Lower average time to diagnose and repair problems. More effective dispatching of field service crews. Intelligent Help Desks maintain deep knowledge of problems and solutions and use expert systems. Ability to rapidly search and sort information; use of heuristics. Ability to detect patterns, neural fuzzy and statistical methods. An intuitive user presentation; multimedia. Effective user interaction; voice synthesis and recognition.

G & R Data Group

WebDesk

G & R Data Group's WebDesk is a fully integrated World Wide Web based trouble ticketing and help desk system designed for system administrators. The reader is expected to have a general knowledge of UNIX system administration, basic UNIX commands and a conceptual understanding of how a World Wide Web server works.

WebDesk utilizes the World Wide Web (WWW) to provide an intuitive, easy to use interface to address the pressing administrative problem of handing a burgeoning load of system service requests. WebDesk acts as an electronic secretary, providing a buffer between users and system administrators, improving efficiency. WebDesk enables administrators to:

Accept help requests from users electronically

Evaluate requests according to problem severity, user level and machine type priorities let administrators fix urgent problems first, and justify delaying other requests

Distribute and receive help desk information painlessly over the Web

Queue requests by assigned priority

Generate audit trails

WebDesk enables end users to:

Submit requests via electronic mail from any location

Receive request confirmation electronic mail

Monitor the status of their request using a Web browser

See what priority their request was assigned

Avoid software training - they use standard Web browsers
and electronic mail

WebDesk is secure from a system perspective provided your WWW server daemon does not run as root. The documents and administrative activities inside the WebDesk product are secure as well. Access to administrative functions is password protected, and the WebDesk administration page is generated on the fly by WebDesk - it is not a static file and therefore cannot be bookmarked or linked to. Furthermore, the only users that have access to the WebDesk files without going through the WWW server are those accounts on the system that belong to the same group as the WWW server is running as. For this reason, we recommend creating a separate group for the WWW server to run under, for example WWW.

Here's a typical WebDesk Request Cycle:

1) A user has a problem. He/she sends electronic mail to the WebDesk system (generally helpdesk@company.com).

2) Shortly after sending mail to the WebDesk system, the user receives an email reply back from the system, indicating that the request was received successfully and provides a unique problem ID number.

3) The administrator, as part of his or her daily routine, uses a Web browser from any client on the network to enter the WebDesk system and evaluate the new requests.

4) The administrator must first enter an administration password and then click on "evaluate requests."

5) The administrator is presented with a list of all requests that need attention.

6) Using easy Web forms, the administrator clicks on three choices (User Level, Machine Type and Problem Severity) to rank the priority of the request.

7) The administrators may opt to click on the "trash" button which immediately moves the request to the archive area (no evaluation takes place).

8) Once a request has been ranked, it moves out of the "to be evaluated" queue and into a pending request queue.

9) The pending request queue is available to both administrators and end users so administrators can tackle the most pressing problems, and users can see the status of their request in the queue.

10) Once a request has been completed, the administrator completes the request by clicking on "complete request."

11) The request is removed from the pending request queue and physically moved to the archive area.

G & R is adding additional features such as a KBS evaluation mechanism, support for multiple administrators, etc. More information and a formal tour is available from: www.grdata.com/products/WebDesk. Beta testing is now in progress with an administrative password of alpha at: www.grdata.com:88/Webdesk/Webdesk.html.

Inference Corporation

CasePoint WebServer

Inference Corporation is a provider of strategic knowledge publishing, distribution and content management software. The company offers a family of CBR2 software products, a complete line of consulting, support and educational services, as well as pre-packaged knowledge. Inference has licensed its products to over 400 customers. This accounts for reaching more than 500,000 end users in over 22 countries.

CasePoint WebServer provides CBR search and retrieval facilities using any World Wide Web (WWW) browser. CasePoint WebServer is an interactive Web application that allows users to access quickly the answers or information they need. The product gives organizations a number of communication options for employees, customers and prospects over the World Wide Web. Organizations can use the Internet to provide on-demand information, such as technical support and product descriptions, directly to prospects and customers. CasePoint WebServer allows users to search and retrieve information by simply typing a description and interactively answering questions from any standard WWW browser. Organizations that have not set up Wide Area Networks (WAN) or connectivity to their Local Area Networks (LAN) can use CasePoint WebServer through "Intranet" access as a way for field employees to resolve problems, access policies and procedures or their technical documents through a common interface from anywhere in the world.

Inference customers can make existing case bases available through the World Wide Web to a wider audience of users and extend their customer service offerings to 7 x 24 hour coverage without significant increase in manpower costs. CasePoint WebServer uses HTML to provide the interface to the case base. You can customize screens to match a corporate Web style. In addition, centralized content management is part of the system. The product integrates with most standard Web server software. Organizations may wish to have CasePoint WebServer screens look and feel the same as the rest of their Web pages. The WebServer provides a text-based resource file which defines the user interface. The resource file can be customized to produce screens similar to the CasePoint appearance on other platforms, or a graphically enhanced screen matching other Web pages. Preferences are analogous to those under CasePoint.

CasePoint WebServer Architecture The CasePoint WebServer System (CPWSS) is organized into three main parts: The CasePoint Driver (CPD), CasePoint Server (CPS) and CasePoint Search Engine (CPSE). This is illustrated in Figure 9.5. The end user issues requests which are picked up by the HTTP server and passed on to the first of these three components, the CasePoint Driver.

Figure 9.5 -- CasePoint WebServer Architecture

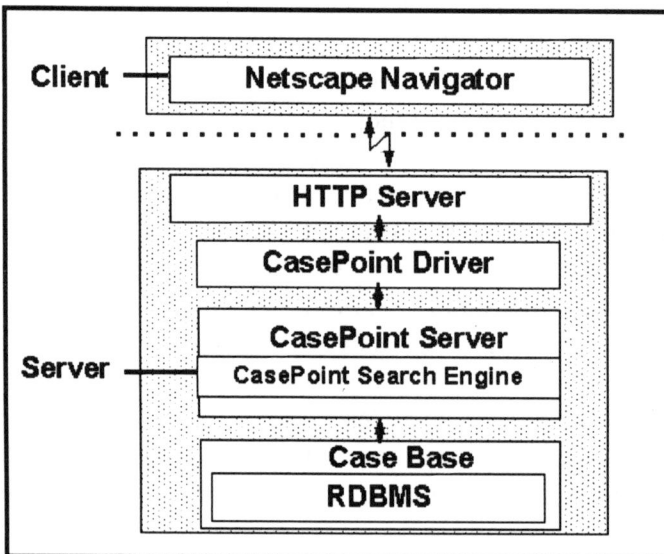

The CPD parses the string received from the HTTP server and calls the CPS to process it, using the RPC (Remote Procedure Call) mechanism. In turn, the CPS processes the parsed request, calling the CasePoint Search Engine to retrieve information or additional questions that will refine the search.

The CasePoint WebServer uses standard RPC facilities and is written to the CGI (Common Gateway Interface) specification. Security Application developers use the security built into their HTTP Server to prevent unauthorized access. Case bases can be stored in non-public directories to prevent unauthorized use. The WebServer has built-in security to allow the application developer to restrict access to a certain list of users or to a fixed maximum number of unique users.

CasePoint WebServer is currently available on Sun SPARC Solaris 2.X, with versions on HP-UX, OS/2 and Microsoft NT available in the near future. CasePoint WebServer supports the following popular databases: Oracle Sybase Microsoft SQL Server Informix DB2/2 RAIMA Data Manager(RDM)

CBR2 is a family of products and services for searching and retrieving unstructured information in front office applications. It is commonly used to serve the problem resolution and product recommendation needs of customer service call centers, help desks, human resources departments and telesales and telemarketing organizations. Inference's CBR2 products support a wide range of operating and deployment platforms, including file server, client/ server, speech-enabled server, Web server and embedded implementations.

Case-based reasoning (CBR) is a technology based on the observation that when someone solves a problem or looks for information, they often use similar past experiences as a basis for the new situation. CBR2 consists of a number of applications that help organizations to add new content and search through existing content.

KnowledgeBroker, Inc.

KnowledgeBases

KnowledgeBroker, Inc. (KBI) sells help desk "knowledge sets" called KnowledgeBases. They are prepackaged "plugandplay" problem resolution information. These can be imported into help desk systems like Remedy Corporation's Action Request System (AR System). KnowledgeBases provide staff with instant answers to questions users ask most about. This goes for software programs, communications packages and hardware.

KnowledgeBroker has its own 24hour multivendor support service called HelpNet. It answers over half a million support calls a year. KnowledgeBases are created from the records of these reallife problems and their solutions. Each KnowledgeBase covers multiple software versions, and a subscription service is available to keep them current.

Help desks are the focal point for answering user questions and solving user problems. Help desk personnel can't be experts at everything, so having access to systems with builtin "knowledge" is important. Finding and storing the knowledge is difficult. But now help desk managers can buy "knowledge sets." These sets are "knowledge engineered" by companies with expertise in both gathering knowledge and structuring it. Knowledge sets can be put on a diskette of frequently asked questions about hardware or software. The sets contain both questions and answers. This Q&A can be searched by help desk operators while on line with a user.

Integration Summary. An individual KnowledgeBase is a file with records on a specific topic. Each record contains a problem and a corresponding solution. In order to use a KnowledgeBase, it needs to be stored in a "solutions database" that can be queried by a help desk operator. You can get KnowledgeBases in many formats, including direct 'AR Export' format. The *arimport* tool is provided with the AR System for loading data in AR Export format into AR System templates.

Figure 9.6 – AR System KnowledgeBase Integration

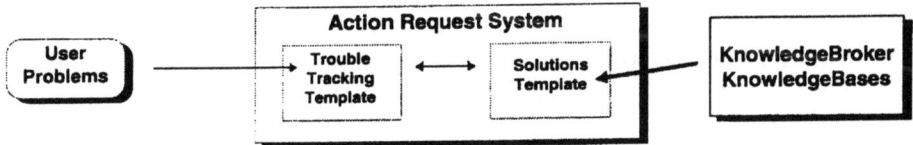

KBI provides an AR System template that can be used as the solutions database, or you can import the KnowledgeBase data into your own template. The template is linked to the primary trouble tracking template based on a keyword search. Once a user problem has been recorded in a trouble ticket, one or more keywords are specified.

This launches an AR System macro. A Query List of all matching KnowledgeBase records is displayed. You can scan the records to see which one contains a solution to the user's problem.

When a solution is found, the description of the solution can be copied to the open trouble ticket or additional notes can be added to the record. You can add your own knowledge records to the solutions database. All of the data in a KnowledgeBase is editable, so you can customize the data.

KnowledgeBases for the AR System are normally distributed over the Internet using FTP. Once you have purchased a KnowledgeBase, KBI gives you a password to download the KnowledgeBase. KnowledgeBases typically range in size from 400KB to 750KB, and can contain over 1000 records.

PHD

ClientView Internet Access

PHD 4.0 from Professional Help Desk can now be accessed from Web via the ClientView Internet Access module. It's compatible with Windows 95, NT and Windows for Workgroups. This is part of the company's vision of the *Virtual Help Desk*. In this model, you enter a description of your problem and have access to limitless domains of problem resolution. Your role becomes that of a Personal Information Manager. Help desk analysts also have ubiquitous access to the Web, so a virtual and dynamic engine of knowledge can be enabled.

Imagine your query being pored over by both Natural Language and other tools while a far-flung analyst looks "over your shoulder." This in addition to the automated help desk software. The Internet provides the access, transport and common interface. PHD supplies the search engine and Internet telephony tools. It's a killer concept: Once a user on the Web interfaces with the problem resolution engine (from anywhere), he or she can solve problems even without the help of help desk personnel. You could call it a self-navigation help desk. But if live help is needed, you have a co-pilot.

With the ClientView Internet Access module, you can create not only Virtual Agents on the Web, but you can merge computer telephony directly with the help desk software. This Internet integration software connects information from your Web site to your telephone system. This allows the help desk to respond to customer requests in real time. One of the best things about PHD's technology is that it's interactive. Help can come in the form of interactive (mirrored) screens between the help desk analyst and the user, or a telephone call can be outdialed automatically. This is enabled owing to PHD's CTI integration capabilities. Your PBX and servers can be linked via TSAPI, and ANI provides analysts with screen pops and instant access to information about callers. This can include including photos of callers, the subjects of previous calls and their solutions. This is illustrated in Figure 9.7.

Figure 9.7 -- ClientView Internet Access Topology

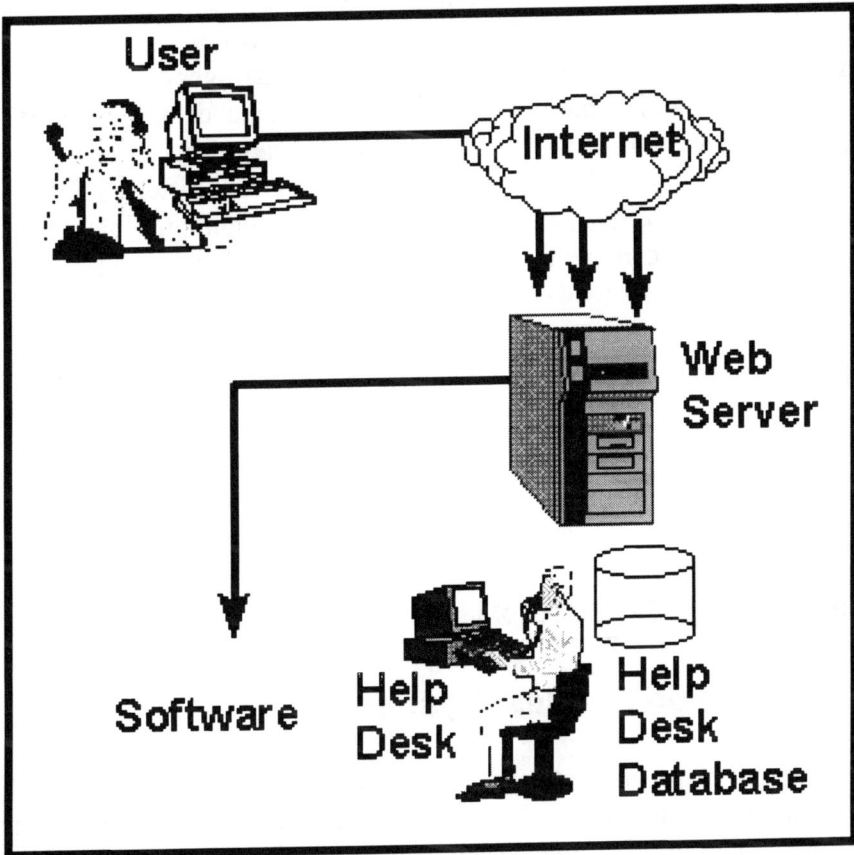

The folks at PHD are serious about help desks. They quote a Nolan Norton & Co. study wherein the cost of *not* having a help desk is between $6,000 and $15,000 a year per PC. This is the cost of lost productivity as PC users turn to other PC users for help. Implementation of a help desk by these organizations dramatically reduces these costs as well as boosts productivity. When the help desk is accurately dispatching calls, the entire workforce is more productive. This boosts profitability and also promotes employee satisfaction. Since the World Wide Web provides a universal and ubiquitous interface, the costs associated with help desks can be reduced dramatically. Frances Tischler of PHD has a good grasp on the issues of "untangling the Web" for help desks.

She says: "The Web market is evolving at lightning speed and the integration of the Internet to the help desk is streamlining access to both people and information. This Help-On-Demand system seamlessly provides access to knowledge and experience far beyond the resources of any single analyst or organization." At the core of PHD is "Natural Intelligence," a proprietary suite of methodologies that support a language-independent knowledgebase capable of providing answers and solutions. It can also learn on its own using the "Experience-Based Reasoning" system, an artificial intelligence technique similar to case-based reasoning (it uses quantitative statistics and fuzzy logic). PHD can create Analyst Groups so problems may be assigned to a group of analysts as well as individuals.

PHD can access ODBC-compliant databases such as Oracle, Sybase, SQL Server, dBase and Paradox and runs over Novel NetWare LANs and all networks supporting Windows. There is also a PHD Mail Server that lets end-users e-mail problems to the Help Desk from mobile and remote environments.

Remedy Corporation

ARWeb Action Request System

Remedy develops, markets and supports adaptable, client-server applications to automate support and business processes. Remedy's Action Request (AR) System is used primarily as an internal Help Desk application for tracking and resolving support requests and problems in PC, UNIX and NT computing environments. It has an adaptable workflow engine that allows customization without programming. The Action Request System is installed in over 2600 sites in 35 countries. ARWeb 1.1 is a major development for extending Help Desk offerings to the World Wide Web. Remedy significantly enhanced the features in its new version. In addition to eliminating the need for HTML programming, a feature available in the first release of ARWeb, version 1.1 provides update capabilities, allowing Web browser users to modify information in records that already exist in the AR System. It also extends ARWeb's existing security to include the Secure Sockets Layer (SSL) protocol.

Remedy allows customers to spread use of ARWeb across an entire enterprise cost-effectively. This is due to the company's practice of offering customers the ability to submit new entries and query the database for free.

ARWeb works with existing AR System applications and data to generate Web forms (schemas) and hyperlinks dynamically. This lets Help Desk managers focus on serving customers and improving business processes in the AR System, instead of constantly maintaining static Web pages. ARWeb also now adapts to support HTML 2.0 or greater browsers. When it detects an HTML 3.0-compatible browser, ARWeb 1.1 uses HTML tables to align fields and data precisely within forms. Administrators design forms only once, using the point-and-click Action Request System Administration Tool. ARWeb then renders each form to fit the capabilities of virtually any browser.

ARWeb also supports update transactions from Web browsers. This feature gives a broader range of user access to Help Desk applications. With the ability to update transactions via the Web, field technicians now can update information in existing requests from any location where they have Web browser access; end users can perform a range of actions such as authorize a change request and add new information to an existing trouble ticket; and in organizations that have adopted ISO 9000 processes, the submitter of a defect can use a Web browser to mark a request "closed" after the support team marks it as "fixed," creating a closed-loop system.

Doug Blair, ITS Help Desk Team Leader at the Motorola Cellular Infrastructure Group, said ARWeb 1.1 will streamline and extend their enterprise. "We support an extremely large, heterogeneous computing environment. About the only thing all systems have in common is a Web browser. The modify feature of ARWeb 1.1 gives service teams an easy way to update tickets, regardless of location or platform. With the previous release of ARWeb, our customers could submit tickets. Now they can add information to outstanding problem reports at their convenience and without significant training issues. The enhanced security features will allow us to make more sensitive information available to a wider audience within Motorola, which is important as we expand access to our client-server systems across the enterprise."

ARWeb is compatible with systems from Hewlett-Packard and Sun Microsystems. The new version also adds compatibility for systems from IBM. Customers may purchase ARWeb 1.1 directly from Remedy or through a list of Value-Added Resellers (VARs), System Integrators (SIs) and Original Equipment Manufacturers (OEMs). The US list price for the ARWeb server is $12,000. For users who need to modify transactions, floating licenses are available in five-packs for $2,000 per seat and a five-pack of fixed licenses is available at $800 per seat.

ARS ACD and Web Integration

ACD systems connect incoming calls to the agent who has been available the longest. ACDs can also put calls in a firstin, firstout queue until an agent becomes available. Now ACD manufacturers are working with companies like Edify, Spanlink and Venturian Software so Web-Based transactions can trigger Help Desk and ACD agent telephone calls.

ACDs are really special PBX telephone switches. They are a clearinghouse for telephone calls. ACDs queue incoming calls and send them on as support engineers and agents become available. Interactive voice response (IVR) can be used to get preliminary information from callers. his helps to route the call to a particular agent based on caller-supplied information. An ACD lets you have a single incoming contact number for the Help Desk and loadbalance the calls across the support staff. This is done without a live operator.

With conventional call centers, a prospective customer gets a printed catalog in the mail (expensive to produce), finds an item, then calls an 800-number (an expensive service) and bogs down an agent with questions.

Things are even worse with help desks. A recent survey by the market research firm Dataquest found that 85% of technical support calls made during peak hours received a busy signal, and more than half of all callers couldn't get through despite repeated dialings. Contrast that with: You surf up to a company's Web page, see something you want to order or need help with, but you really want to talk to a live agent on the phone.

You input your phone number, click on an icon and presto, the phone rings and you're talking with an agent ready to sell you a product or service and get your credit card number. Thus, the formerly expensive 800-number inbound call now becomes a free Internet request for callback.

This also eliminates inbound hold processing. Somebody awaiting callback (and activity) will be more tolerant of short delays than somebody glued to a phone. So your center requires less staff and is more tolerant of peak loading. Delayed callback requests gives you time to staff upcoming shifts appropriately.

Those systems that use the Internet as a help desk or as an adjunct to a call center also fall into two categories:

Delayed-access systems where you post your problem to the Web site and you get an e-mail later.

Real-time access systems where you fill out a form and get an answer from a database immediately (debit card or account number verification) or you do a keyword search through a block of text or you answer questions posed by an expert system or you simply become frustrated and connect with a live agent, either through the 'Net or over the phone.

The trend has been toward real-time access systems, since companies will try to distinguish themselves by providing the fastest customer service. A problem arises, though, when everybody loves your system and tries to use it in real-time at the *same* time. A fair amount of integration is required at the (traditional) call center. This takes not only an ACD, but connection to Computer-To-Switch Integration (CTI) links, help desk databases and Intranets.

One good example of this "back-end" call center interfacing is Prospect Software's Prospect CTI Server. The server works with Aspect Telecommunications' CallCenter ACD and Remedy's Action Request (AR) System help desk software.

The Aspect CallCenter is a highend ACD. The Prospect CTI Server and Client components let you integrate the AR System with the Aspect Call-Center. No custom code development is required. This is done with configuration definitions and AR System macro and workflow administration. The integration of an ACD into an AR System Help Desk gives callers easy access and allows the Help Desk to provide faster, more effective support.

As the scope of the Help Desk grows to cover more people, more questions and more functions, many companies are beginning to structure the operation like a highvolume customer care center. One of the standard components of most large external support environments is an automatic call distributor (ACD). Even internal Help Desks are integrating an ACD into their operations.

Figure 9.8 – ARS Aspect CallCenter Integration

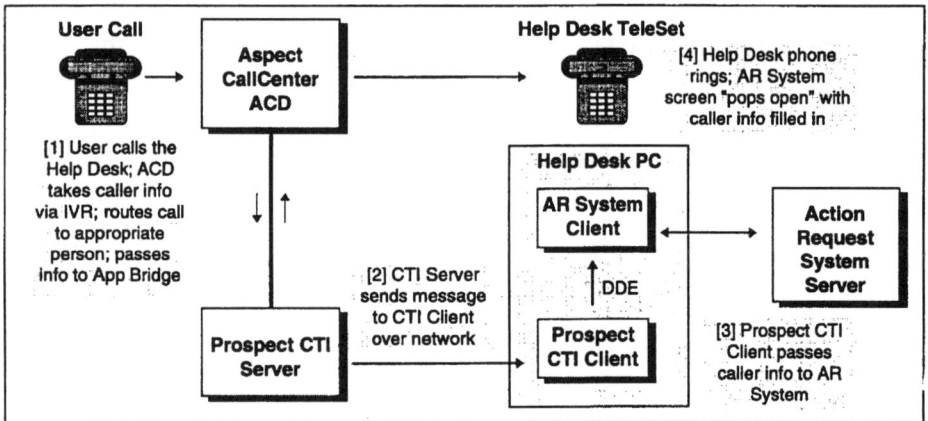

The Application Bridge is a computertelephony integration (CTI) solution. It supports a pointtopoint link with a computer host to tie the two systems together. Prospect Software developed a client-server implementation of an Application Bridge Interface. It allows an unlimited number of computer systems to integrate with an Aspect CallCenter as shown in Figure 9.8.

When a call comes into the Aspect CallCenter, the caller can supply information regarding their problem. This is done by interacting with the standard voice processing or the Agility IVR application. This information is passed as a message by the Aspect CallCenter through the Application Bridge to the Prospect CTI Server. The CTI Server determines which computer is related to the telephone where the call is going to be routed, and sends the information to the appropriate Prospect CTI Client. The CTI Client passes the information to the AR System client running on that computer, and the information is automatically filled in to an AR System trouble reporting screen for the support person. AR System workflow can also look up and display additional information.

Aspect CallCenter is an Automatic Call Distributor (ACD)./ It can handle up to 100,000 busy hour calls, faxes, and email. You can get CallCenter in both redundant and nonredundant configurations. It accommodates total nonblocking for up to 1,888 switched ports in configurations that can include up to 1,200 agents or 1,200 trunks. All models have the same base system software.

Each Aspect CallCenter system consists of a system controller, a switching subsystem, and a voice subsystem housed in a 6foot system cabinet and configured with one or more Aspect TeleSets (special Help Desk telephone sets), Management Workstations, and trunks to the public switched network. The system includes featurerich ACD software, an application language for creating call routing scenarios tailored to meet unique customer requirements, and an integrated voice prompting and voice storage and retrieval capability.

As an option, PC software applications from Aspect's CustomView. family allow you to customize the data, creating and running your own realtime status windows and historical reports. Aspect's EnterpriseAccess capabilities, which include CustomView, let the Aspect CallCenter be assigned an address on a company's Ethernet network. The Aspect CallCenter thus looks like a node on the LAN, and communicates with desktop PCs in a client-server arrangement.

The Prospect CTI Server is implemented as a client-server application. The CTI Server runs on a UNIX host (typically the AR System server) as a process named *ctisvrcc* (it is also available for Microsoft NT servers as *ctisvrcGexe)*. It communicates with the Aspect CallCenter via a TCP/IP socket connection. It communicates with CTI Clients running on support agent desktop computers using TCP/IP socket connections also. CTI Clients are available for UNIX workstations and MS Windows PCs.

On a UNIX workstation, the CTI Client is a daemon process *(ctidiard)*. On a PC, there is an executable application and a dynamically linked library (DLL) *(ctiddear.exe* and *ctiapiccdll)*.

On the Prospect UNIX client, configuration information for the communications between the Prospect client and the AR System is controlled by parameters on the command line. On PCs, a *ctiddear.ini* file performs the configuration functions, and the *ctiddear.exe* application communicates with the AR System. This gives the help desk administrator full control over the appearance of synchronized screens with AR System macros.

Unisys Corporation

I-Net Natural Language Assistant

UNISYS Corporation's Natural Language Understanding Group has launched their Solaris-based Natural Language Assistant (NLA). It's an expert software system for use with voice and text message response systems. I-Net is the term they use to describe the combined Intranet and Internet. Unisys works closely with Opus Systems, Periphonics and Quintus Corporation in the development of NL support for IVR and enhanced platforms. The company is forging relationships with many computer telephony developers. They want to be the "Natural Language" back-end to ASR and IVR systems worldwide. Unisys plans to work with makers of voice response and speech recognition products, 'Net application platform developers and call center vendors.

Natural Language Understanding goes beyond speech recognition. It provides a rules-based, context-sensitive model to engage in dialogue with a user. You can create applications that understand a verbal conversation over the telephone, or a typed message over the Internet.

Initial applications of NLU focused on understanding text documents for military use. From 1989 through 1991 Unisys began integrating its NLU technology with externally developed speech recognizers. Some of the vertical apps targeted for the technology:

Banking. Account balances, funds transfers, etc.

Insurance. Claims processing and policy Quotes.

Financial Services. Stock transactions and information requests.

Retail. Catalog orders and order servicing.

Manufacturing. Customer order input and status.

Public Utilities. Account and payment status.

Transportation. Pickup and shipment status, expediting data.

Health Care. Appointments and pre-visit screening.

Automated speech recognition (ASR) systems abound, but they are limited because most restrict caller responses. Saying "one" differs little from pressing "1" on a keypad. The problem is cumbersome structure of IVR dialog. NLA adds value to ASR by enabling a more natural dialog and by applying artificial intelligence to extract meaning from the ASR outputs. You can integrate NLA with continuous speech, speaker-independent ASR technology. By combining the Natural Language Assistant with speech recognition, you can create a natural conversation between callers and your system. NLA converts English language input (spoken words or stored text) into meaning, and then responds appropriately.

It can respond to many versions of the same statement, such as "I don't know" or I'm not sure" or "Let me have more information." It's not simply translating words into text but interpreting the meaning of words.

Conversational understanding and use of pronouns are handled nicely with this product. If you're asking about a mortgage, you might say: "I want it for 15 years." The system will say: "For an adjustable mortgage with a fifteen-year term, the current monthly payment is $656.98 at 9.5 percent." If you say: "How about 20 years?." NLA will say "For an adjustable mortgage with a 20-year term, the current monthly payment is $421.75 at 9.5 percent."

The system will even simplify complex statements. It interprets the question: "I want a thirty-year fixed-rate mortgage with three points." It answers: "The interest rate for that mortgage is 9.7 percent."

Keyboard/Text Recognition. NLA also accepts text-based input. In fact, it doesn't care if it's getting text from the Resource Manager (software) or voice or some other kind of textual input. This is good for network-based or kiosk-based services. Customers can phrase their questions in words instead of searching "point-and-click" screens or paging through complex hierarchical menus. Wherever customers interact with your business via a keyboard, NLA can be used. This applies to PCs or any other text input device.

This technology will be a boon to on-line service requests. Inquiries done via E-mail or Web site can be read by NLA. The queries can be routed, tracked, and escalated as necessary: "The roof is leaking in C building."

Unisys has been demonstrating their technology with a mortgage banking application. To do this, they put together their own front-end system to act as the telephone interface for the NLA demo. The speech recognizer runs a ASR from Lernout & Hauspie. They also use the Dialogic Antares open DSP board to run other algorithms. The L&H portion is running under Windows in a PC with an Opus Systems SPARCard. The UNIX part of the platform is running the run-time NL Assistant app and Resource Manager.

It's the Resource Manager's job is to aggregate all disparate PSTN/IVR voice input and ASCII text streams. These streams come from the Internet, PSTN and LAN connections. The Resource Manager is the front end to the Natural Language Engine. The engine does 3 things:

Parsing. Breaks-down text input into nouns, pronouns.

Semantic analysis. Interprets what's being said. This is beyond word spotting. It knows the difference between: "What is my checking account balance" versus "I want to balance my checking account."

Dialog management. It will understand the context of a conversation and how to respond.

Figure 9.9 -- NLA Translation Rules Generator

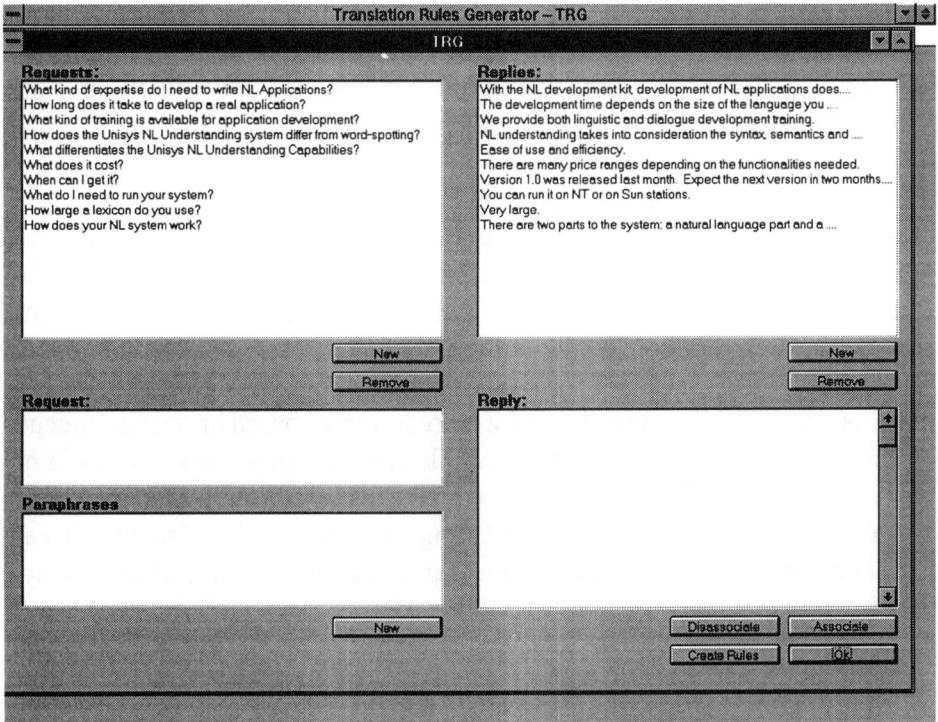

Figure 9.9 illustrates the Translation Rules Generator. NLA works with a Unisys tool kit so you can build custom language engines. For a "FAQ Finder" app to answer questions on a given topic, you first build a list of questions (the "corpus). The questions are mapped to replies. The tool kit then generates "translation rules" to map variations on each question (paraphrases) to the proper replies. These guys didn't skip grammar school.

The natural language engine was originally constructed to accept text input from a local keyboard, so keyboard based input across the I-net goes back to the origins of the NL Assistant's capability. It is perfectly suited for Web-based help desk environments. In fact, the engine does not care where the input comes from as long as it gets an ASCII text string.

For the last several years, the Natural Language Understanding Group at Unisys has been focused on the telephony market. They've invested a significant amount of effort to build an infrastructure to support a telephony/Internet environment. The group has enhanced the NLRM (Natural Language Resource Manager) to manage I-net sessions with the NL Assistant. They are preparing to launch a tool kit designed specifically to build request and response driven Internet applications.

A good application for this would be FAQs. Especially in situations where the information is not easy to access or find via point and click with a mouse. Right now one of the limiting characteristics of FAQ is that you have to be careful how big you FAQ database is, how many questions it houses and how big the answers are. People will only scroll through so much. With NL Assistant the FAQ database could be as large as needed, people type in their questions and the NL engine finds the correct answer based upon the concepts represented in the question. For example the way this works is: a dialog box is opened on the browser into which people can type their question. When the session is opened the NL engine tags the client so that it can maintain a session. Then releases the tag at the end of the session. Unisys sees a variety of uses for this capability:

1) Unlimited FAQ's. No need to scroll, just type the question.

2) Web Sites are getting so big it's difficult to find information. You could open a dialog box on a home page and let people type in a question. You can then redirect them to the proper page so they could go back to "point and click."

3) Provide information that does not lend itself naturally to point and click. For example suppose you were logged into your home banking system and wanted to know the minimum amount of money you had to keep in your checking account to avoid service charges. You type the question into a dialog box and get the answer, but it could be difficult to find the information by browsing the site. Where would you look?

5) One of the most interesting potentials for this capability is to create interactive advertisements. A very popular service/browser is the one being offered by PCN. They provide a significant amount of free service and flash advertisements across your screen. If you click on an ad sometimes you get redirected to a Webster. But imagine if you clicked on the ad and a dialog box opened up and asked "How can I help you?" The person could dialog with the ad to get the information they wanted. This provides the potential for interactive ads, a whole new way of selling. Just as easily, by using platforms from Venturian Software or Edify, you could route them to a live agent for a real-time telephone call.

A very recent development involves the use of speech recognition as a front end to the NL Assistant over the Internet. Since speech recognition is much better locally at a PC than it is over a telephone, and the NL Assistant requires simple text, the potential to build applications that use a local speech recognizer running on a PC is great. This would provide extremely high quality recognition since there's no loss of signal over the phone lines. This will allow people to talk to the applications executing on the server. Suppose a bank made their bank by phone services typically offered via an IVR available over the Internet. People could get their balance, review cleared checks, transfer funds, etc. You could potentially connect to the banks server, identify yourself with voice verification and ask: "What's my balance and did check 127 clear yet?"

Natural Language Assistant comes with the NL Resource Manager and the NL Engine. The Resource Manger handles connections to your IVR system or LAN. It comes with C libraries to connect to the IVR system. Each NL Engine handles 12 concurrent sessions. $6,000. Each Resource Manager handles multiple NL Engines. $1,000 per platform.

You can get an NL Assistant Developers Kit for $7,995. The development environment is Win NT. You get the toolkit, single-user NL Engine, and an Artificial Intelligence Prolog compiler. The NL Assistant run-time executes under SPARC Solaris and Sun OS and Intel Win NT. It's Sockets-based, so it can communicate with an OS/2 or other box over a LAN using the Resource Manager.

Chapter Acknowledgments

Special thanks go to Frances Tischler, Ph.D., and Isidore Sobowski of Professional Help Desk. Frances prepared and researched cross-over technologies between the help desk and the Web. Her efforts made this chapter possible. Isadore is Division Vice President of the Greenwich, CT-based Professional Help Desk (PHD). PHD is part of DSSI. A widely-known expert of artificial intelligence, Mr. Sobowski was the chief architect of the WinExpert, and expert system development tool and WinBrain, a neural net development tool. You can reach PHD directly on info@prohelpdesk.com.

Scott Miller of UNISYS' Natural Language Understanding Group was also very helpful in meeting several deadlines for the book. His mortgage quoting system / Natural Language demo is awesome. smiller@tr.unisys.com

Chapter 10

Audio and Video on the Net

The most likely path by which digital multimedia can succeed is through its use as a component in electronic commerce, or *tele-business*. The most prevalent form of tele-business technology now in use is the telephone, a relatively low-technology but universally-accepted medium for connecting buyers and sellers. The basic technology of the telephone has existed for over one hundred years, but its pervasive use as a medium for tele-business has only taken place over the last twenty years.

This was driven by a significant reduction in usage cost, innovative billing arrangements (800/900 numbers), and the evolution of call centers. These centers represent the restructuring of organizations and workflow around a cost-effective technology. And now we're doing it on the Internet. This is how Carl Srathmeyer, Director of Marketing at the Computer-Telephone Division of Dialogic Corporation explains where we are with multimedia. I thought it fitting to get his perspective. Formerly of Digital Equipment Corporation's CIT group, Carl has vast knowledge in systems integration, standards development and processes. He has a unique perspective: He makes computers and telephones talk to each other.

Multimedia - CTI Revisited

In the last decade, computer telephone integration (CTI) has accelerated the usage of telephone technology in commerce. It does this by coordinating the actions of telephone and data processing systems. CTI technology makes telephone-based business transactions more convenient, economical, accessible and reliable.

For example, voice response systems allow callers to hear data or generate transactions at all hours, without human assistance. If their call must be transferred to a representative, CTI technology informs the representative about the caller, speeding the transaction and improving the overall level of service.

Callers and service representatives must have a common set of reference materials that both can refer to during the call so that they can come to agreement on the transaction. In most circumstances, this material comprises either (1) a statement of account or documentation of a case, or (2) a catalog of some kind. Both items are typically sent from one party to the other in advance of the call via U.S. Mail.

The production and distribution of this material is expensive. The medium of the printed page limits the possible nature of communication. The logistics involved make it difficult to have timely reference materials on hand during a call. Some call centers have attempted to address these limitations through the creative use of facsimile technology (mostly business-to-business activities). This can solve the timeliness issue, but the limitations of the static printed page remain.

Real-time digital data in its various forms, especially digital multimedia, holds the promise of removing many of these restrictions. That's if it's distributed through a ubiquitous high-capacity transmission facility. If parties to a call could simultaneously refer to electronic soft-copy information, the range of possible telephone transactions would be considerably increased. For example:

Conferring with a real-time revisable model of a customer's account would be more useful than simply referring to a static statement. Adjustments to the account could be immediately reflected, discussed, and confirmed. Such a process would be similar to using a typical hotel in-room TV-based account review system, but with the added capability of being able to simultaneously review the account and discuss proposed changes with a representative who is viewing the same material. Such a facility applied to bank accounts would bring a whole new perspective to in-home telephone banking.

Jointly viewing a multimedia catalog with a sales representative would be a much more powerful sales experience than referring to separate copies of the same paper-based catalog. A multimedia catalog could contain elements such as videos of product usage, animations showing product design advantages, and intelligent rules for proper configuration. And while these could be distributed on CD-ROMs, timely updates would be difficult and expensive. Furthermore, many customers would probably prefer to discuss the material together with a sales representative rather than viewing it privately.

Like the earlier development of telephone-based commerce, there are several factors which must come together in order for the new digital multimedia technology to be adopted as an attractive tool for commerce. The first thing that comes to mind is the necessity for the technology of the basic transport and distribution network to be developed to the point where the digital multimedia medium is economical and ubiquitous.

The current products being researched and developed for the multimedia market are almost exclusively focused on point-to-point services and applications. They are either one-to-one connections, as in video-phones and Internet-phones, or one-to-many connections, as in video-on-demand. This situation is analogous to the state of the voice telephony systems prior to the introduction of Call Centers using Automatic Call Distribution (ACD) techniques and Computer Telephony Integration (CTI).

These call centers have led to the development and deployment of a whole new range of computer applications making sophisticated use of the voice telephony and available high bandwidth digital networks. However, it has taken almost a *decade* from the introduction of the first CTI links into telephone switches for the technology to become widely available and the corresponding call center industry to blossom. Building the corresponding capabilities into multimedia networks at the onset of their development will ensure a more rapid evolution of true interactive applications and business uses for this newly emerging technology.

A similar technology also needs to be developed for the multimedia networks currently being deployed to fully exploit their capabilities. This technology would be layered on top of the existing multimedia services, and allow applications to coordinate the use and operation of telephony, voice, data, video, and other multimedia services on behalf of the users. The research and development programs currently underway for multimedia services are focused on adding transaction capabilities to the network. We need to add a control and monitoring capability to these developing services, allowing applications to operate on behalf of the users of the multimedia network. This will enable businesses to fully exploit multimedia services by providing group-oriented multimedia capabilities.

As with the development of CTI technology, there is a need to architect and develop multimedia control and monitoring technology *prior to* the development of sophisticated applications. This enabling technology would facilitate a whole new range of applications utilizing telephony, video, voice, and data, further synchronizing their operation with the user's presentation and interaction. It is the control, monitoring, and synchronization of the multimedia environment that present *the key* technical challenges for this technology and make these and other future applications possible. [editors note: With any luck, the efforts of the IETF, IMTC, ITU and other standards bodies will pay off sooner than it did for CTI. The rest of this chapter concentrates on some of the market-makers in audio and video. These vendors sell products for private networks, IP networks and the public switched network. Some day, there will be one network. But for now, we count on these bright minds to make things work together "that weren't made to work together" – that is, computers and telephones.]

Automated Management Software

FreeVue

FreeVue from Automated Management Software (AMS) lets you transmit and receive audio and video in real time. This without expensive hardware. FreeVue transforms you PC into a mini radio or TV station (or at least a TV). AMS claims to have the first true Internet telecommunications network. By using the *FreeVue Telecommunications Network* and software, you can videoconference with other FreeVue users and watch live audio and video broadcasts over the Internet. With an inexpensive video camera like the QuickCam, you can videoconference with your friends and co-workers, or even start your own video broadcast channel.

FreeVue is a true communications network, allowing you to connect to other users or services simply by typing their name, without complicated IP addresses or host names. FreeVue will tell you if the person or service you are trying to call is busy or unavailable, and will soon allow you to leave "Video Mail" for users who are not at their computers.

You can also receive calls when you are not at your PC but are using FreeVue on another machine. This is achieved by entering a "handle" on the machine you are using. FreeVue will log you in as yourself. Anyone trying to call you will now be directed to this computer. It doesn't matter where you are or even what service you are connected to the Internet through - you will receive your calls. FreeVue should work with any Video for Windows compatible card that has a grayscale palette mode and offers 160x120 resolution. These include Video Blaster SE100, Reveal TV300, Connectix QuickCam and the Creative Labs FS-200. You should try it with a 28.8 modem to get 10 frames per second. At slower speeds, things get a bit jumpy. You also need a sound card and a 386 or better PC.

FreeVue does on the fly encoding of video without hardware. Xing Technologies achieves better performance on their Unix-based MPEG encoding platform they sell for $10,000. But the picture is realistic, because the image is dynamically updated.

When you start the software for the first time, you will see the settings screen, where you are prompted for your handle, and for a password. The handle that you enter here is the one you will be logged into the network under. If you have registered on the network, you should enter the handle you registered and the password the network gave you when you registered. This will verify that you are who you say you are when FreeVue logs you onto the network.

To find the current active users (people who are logged into FreeVue right now), go to the User Directory, and choose List Active Users. You will see a list of the handles of users who are logged in and who you can call. If you want the name of a person whose handle is on the list, use the White Pages (also in the user directory) to look them up by their handle. When you make a call with FreeVue, you are routed to a proprietary (non-TCP/IP) and invisible server that's always live. No "meet me reflector" servers are used.

Connectix

VideoPhone

Connectix VideoPhone has been shipping since October of 1995, and version 1.1 has been available since February 1996. Users of Version 1.0 can download the updater for free from the Connectix Web site and online services such as AOL and CompuServe. It's probably the least expensive ($149) commercial package that does high-quality black-and-white video conferencing over the Internet (besides TCP/IP, VideoPhone can also work over IPX networks, ISDN and DSVD analog modems). VideoPhone is bundled with a shared whiteboard application, Future Labs' TalkShow, that lets you share and annotate data files from any Windows application. The "slide tray" ability lets you display a PowerPoint, Freelance or Harvard Graphics slide show directly as a shared document. Although there's a cheaper software-only version available if you already own a video camera (or any standard Video for Windows device), it's tough to beat Connectix's $99 6-bit grayscale QuickCam digital camera that comes with the full VideoPhone package.

QuickCam plugs into your PC parallel port, drawing power from the keyboard port via a pass-through adapter plug. A color version of the camera will soon be available for an additional $100.

Figure 10.1 -- Connectix VideoPhone In Action

To call another user with the Connectix VideoPhone over the Internet (or other network) you select "Call" from the File menu and then pick the person you want to call from the built-in address book. When you're connected, you see the other person as illustrated in figure 10.1.

You can plug in NTSC cameras, videotape recorders or TV tuners as input if you've got a video card such as the Intel Smart Video Recorder Pro, Logitech Movie-man, MediaVision Pro Movie Studio, Creative Labs VideoBlaster and VideoSpigot or Miro D1. Anyone can broadcast a signal and those using this software can view the broadcast. You can also place a call from the Viewer to other Connectix VideoPhone users as well. For example, a remote user may call a site and view video and hear sound. Also, the Viewer can communicate with another Viewer or a Connectix Video-Phone user and have an audio conference (this is essentially a free Internet Phone!)

If you already have a NetWare or TCP/IP based network, you probably have the connection you need to begin videoconferencing. You can adjust both the bandwidth and the frame rates used by VideoPhone. There's also full duplex audio.

Other bundled software includes QuickPick, an image capture utility and multicast broadcast support so you can audio broadcast to an unlimited number of phones. You can also distribute the video software to as many people as you like so you can do video broadcasting.

Registered users will receive an enhanced movie recorder -- if you've got SMTP/MIME mail, you'll be able to send video messages to other Video-Phone users.

VideoPhone needs at least a 486DX2-50, 8 MB RAM, a display card capable of 256 or more colors, Windows 3.1, Windows for Workgroups 3.11 or Windows 95, a Sound board (Any WAV device, e.g. Soundblaster), TCP/IP communications software (Microsoft MS/TCP-32 recommended) or Novell's IPX communications software.

Users of the Connectix VideoPhone and the Connectix VideoPhone Viewer for Windows can now directly locate and contact each other over the Internet, using a directory created by Four11 Corporation. It's a free and complete directory of Connectix VideoPhone and Connectix VideoPhone Viewer addresses.

Lucent Technologies

AVP-III Videoconferencing

Lucent Technologies sells standards-compliant video-conferencing gear since it introduced its first-generation AVP videoconferencing chip set for H.320 videoconferencing in 1992. The company has demonstrated interop with other vendors' systems for H.324 videoconferencing.

Lucent Technologies was formed as the result of AT&T's restructuring into three separate, publicly held companies. Its Microelectronics Group designs and manufactures integrated circuits, optoelectronic components, power systems and printed circuit boards for the data networking and telecommunications industries. Lucent Technologies also offers public and private networks, communications systems and software, and consumer and business telephone systems. Bell Laboratories is the research and development arm of the new company.

The Microelectronics Group of Lucent Technologies announced that its new AVP videoconferencing solution can achieve a complete H.324-compliant audio and video interoperability with videoconferencing solutions from two other vendors. One thing Lucent Technologies knows how to do is connect communications systems together (One would hope so, after 100 years of it). Using ordinary phone lines, Lucent Technologies executed a successful two-way video and audio telephone call with a Pentium processor-based PC with an Intel Video Phone with ProShare technology. Lucent Technologies also completed a two-way audio/video call with a PC using host-based videoconferencing software distributed by PictureTel Corp. under license from Vivo Software Inc.

The H.324 communications protocol software developed by Lucent Technologies comes with the AVP-III device. In addition, Lucent also supplies its H.320 communications protocol software (the international standard for videoconferencing over ISDN lines) to users of the AVP-III device. This software enables H.320 interoperability as well.

Progressive Networks

RealAudio

Audio broadcasting and real-time audio on demand is another related area that seems to be growing rapidly on the Internet. Progressive is a new company founded by Rob Glaser, formerly vice president of Multimedia and Consumer Systems at Microsoft. The major investor is Mitchell Kapor, founder of Lotus Development Corp. and the Electronic Frontier Foundation. RealAudio Player 2.0 brings live and on-demand audio to your desktop over Internet connections of 14.4 Kbps and faster.

The RealAudio system lets you and your multimedia PC browse and play back audio or audio-based multimedia content on demand via voice-grade phone lines over the Internet with the immediacy of an audiotex or cassette player system. The user interface is illustrated in figure 10.2.

Figure 10.2 -- RealAudio Player

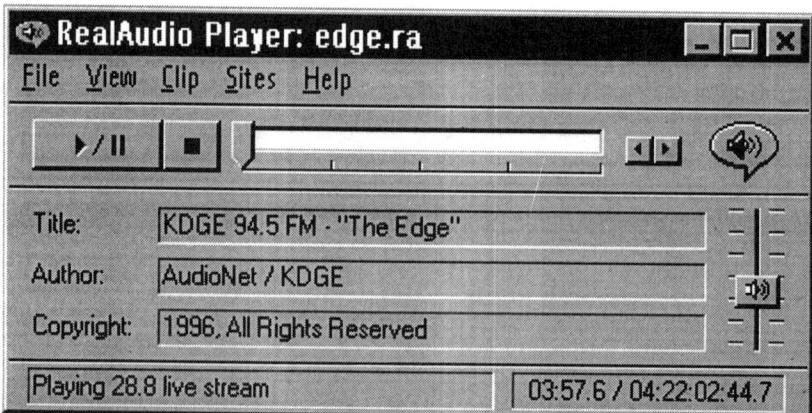

Providers of entertainment, information and news can now deliver audio-on-demand services that can be accessed and played back immediately at any time of day or night.

Clients and servers can maintain a two-directional, real-time communication flow that users can control with cassette-like functions such as *start*, *stop*, *forward* and *rewind*.

There are actually three RealAudio products: RealAudio Player for consumers, RealAudio Studio for content creators and RealAudio Server for on-line audio publishers.

Since its introduction in April 1995, over 700,000 RealAudio Players have been downloaded from the RealAudio Web site on www.RealAudio.com. More than 150 Web sites on the Internet offer RealAudio content. A UNIX server with a T-1 line can maintain up to 100 simultaneous audio connections.

Progressive Networks' first two content partners were the American Broadcasting Co. (ABC) and National Public Radio (NPR). Other Web site providers producing audio entertainment and news using RealAudio are Metaverse, HotWired, GNN, PBS, RadioNetHuman / Factor, Voice of America, Radio Yesteryear and former-MTV VJ Adam Curry's On Ramp.

These Internet "radio stations" should cause a few folks to faint over at the FCC, since conventional through-the-atmosphere radio stations normally have to pay the government a $200,000 broadcast license for a medium-sized market, many times what it costs to set up a Progressive Networks audio server.

And while other companies are spending a fortune trying to pry off a piece of the $78 billion television and movie industry using expensive video on demand schemes, the Internet is a potential $240 billion market waiting to be tapped. The RealAudio Player Corporate Licensing Program allows corporations to license the RealAudio Player for use as part of a RealAudio Intranet Solution and for use over the Internet.

The RealAudio Player is designed to work in all Windows environments. The following table explains which hardware is required for specific Windows operating systems. Note that different hardware is required for playing 14.4 and 28.8 files.

My Webmaster, Freddie Golino (he helped a lot with this book) became an instant Internet radio star from his home in the Bronx. He was surfing the Internet and stared his RealAudio Player. He went to the RealAudio home page. To view their "TV Guide" on what's happening real-time on the 'Net. Freddie choose Radio Stations. He clicked on radio station 94.5 FM KDGE in Texas and he was hyperlinked to their home page.

Within seconds, KDGE's broadcast is coming through Freddie's PC speakers. It's was clear, though not in stereo. He called KDGE's request line to suggest some music. The DJ asked where Freddie was calling from. He tells them he's calling from New York and the Internet. They make him say, "This is Freddie from New York and I'm listening to the EDGE via AudioNet." Instant stardom. You can download RealAudio System Version 2.0 from the RealAudio home page. You'll find versions for PCs running Windows 3.1, Windows 95, Windows NT and for 68040-based Macintoshes or PowerPC. It requires a 14.4 Kbps modem or better.

Quest Interactive Media

Visual Agent

Quest Interactive Media (Richardson, TX -- 214-231-4313) announced a patent pending for interactive remote control of a network of cameras and sound equipment over the Internet using TCP/IP protocols. A product called Visual Agent using this technology will provide an "images on demand" system. Besides TCP/IP, Visual Agent can also be configured to work over standard phone lines or ISDN circuits. It has a view module for displaying and enhancing images, navigation tools, a database and archival system, a communication program, system security and monitoring, and a database reports generator.

There is also a "transactional imaging" function that lets users access a remote camera and selectively capture images of events as they occur or over a specified time sequence, with each image automatically "tagged" as it is captured and stored in a database. Quest is now working with one of the largest software development companies in the central station alarm business to integrate Visual Agent into their new Windows NT platform and to design the CTI interface for the platform's Nortel Meridian One switch. Quest is also designing all of the system's TAPI and TSAPI functionality.

Smith Micro Software, Inc.

AudioVision

Smith Micro provides communication software for personal computers. The Company offers a range of software products for use on the Windows 95, Windows NT, Windows, DOS, OS/2 and Macintosh operating systems. The Company markets its products worldwide through a network of OEMs and retail distributors.

AudioVision, its new Plain Old Telephone Service (POTS) based video teleconferencing software product. AudioVision is designed to be enjoyed by those at home in addition to being a useful tool at the office. The software has a suggested retail price of $149.95 and can achieve an average of 12-15 frames per second. One of the unique features included in AudioVision is the capability to record video email that can be sent over the Internet. AudioVision and Smith Micro's OEM video teleconferencing product VideoLink, target the rapidly evolving personal computer-based video teleconferencing market. The recipient of the video mail can play the message directly from their personal computer even if they are not an AudioVision owner because a viewer is imbedded in the video mail message. What you see is illustrated in Figure 10.3. AudioVision owners can also use their Video/Voice Mail answering machine function to save and later play back the video/voice message from another AudioVision user.

Figure 10.3 -- Smith Micro's AudioVision

Just recently my friend, Harry Newton, received his first video mail from David Glass, an engineer at Smith Micro. He says the sound was fine, but the video is not great. But the overall effect is awesome. Great potential as a sales tool. Sending video clips cheap to his family. David says that with AudioVision, a capture card, and a reasonable video telephone connection, you can see 10-15 frames per second of video. "It can climb to 20 fps or higher if you know the tricks, but we're not into naming only the *tricks* speeds. VMail speeds can be 20-25 fps, depending on the CPU speed and the picture quality levels. Digital cameras are in the 7-10 fps range."

While a video conference is going on, the participants can send and receive data files, high resolution photos, modify video and audio quality parameters on both their own and remote personal computer, increase the picture size and even record the conference while it is taking place.

AudioVision was developed with the same advanced technology that corporate boardroom videoconferencing systems use but made much more affordable. The video is compressed in the H.261 ITU standard format, so you have control over the picture quality vs. speed trade offs.

You need a high end 486 based multimedia PC with a minimum of a 14.4 kbps modem over POTS. AudioVision also fully supports ISDN lines as well. It supports digital cameras that plug into the personal computer's parallel port or analog cameras and regular camcorders that plug into a video capture card installed in the personal computer. VideoLink, the OEM version video teleconferencing product, is currently available for modem, digital and analog camera, and personal computer manufacturers to bundle along with their hardware.

VDONet

VDOLive and VDOPhone

VDONet sells two browser-based products called VDOLive and VDO-Phone. Both offer "streaming" video. Steaming video is a means to expand and display images before the entire download is complete. Given the right amount of power, modem speed and memory, you get pretty close to real time. You can visit the VDONet Home page to download evaluation copies, view live broadcasts and browse the VDOPhone Directory to see a list of other (active) users on www.vdo.net. When video begins to transmit in your direction, you get a small window in which the video feed appears after an eight to twelve second wait. VDONet provides both a client and broadcast version of the software. They are called the *Player* and *Personal Server*, respectively. You can broadcast sound on the personal server.

CBS News, CNBC, PBS and others are using the technology to provide live broadcasts to an expanded audience over the Internet. Companies like Packard Bell are beginning to bundle the software with their PCs. VDONet is also working on an ActiveX control for Microsoft's Internet Explorer. VDOPhone is a Netscape plug-in and runs under Win 95. It works like CU-SeeMe and CoolTalk. The software itself may be downloaded for free along with tools.

Vosaic Corporation

Vosaic plugin

Vosaic is a joint venture between the University of Illinois and Digital Video Communications. Vosaic is streaming video and audio for the World Wide Web. The technology was invented in the Department of Computer Science at the University by members of the Systems Research Group. Vosaic Corp. holds an exclusive worldwide license from the University of Illinois to distribute and further the use of real time video on the Internet.

Streaming video and audio is "instant" and allows users to view videos that are larger than local disk storage. The VDP protocol is an adaptive protocol that is "net friendly" and uses only available bandwidth. Real time streaming of video means you don't have to wait for the whole video to be downloaded before being able to watch it. Vosaic's Video Datagram Protocol intelligently adapts to the available network bandwidth and CPU power on your machine, providing the best possible video transmission under the circumstances. A full set of control buttons enable you to play and stop, and even fast forward or rewind through the video. Detachable video windows let you expand the image to any size you want. Video hyperlinks embedded within the video stream make objects within the video itself clickable (click on a video hyperlink to go off to another related page). The Video Mosaic client integrates time video and audio into hypertext documents.

Vosaic's Video Datagram Protocol (VDP) efficiently transmits continuous media over the Internet. The video server manages large stores of video and audio files. Tools are provided for building your own video database. Video and audio is fully integrated into HTML. Video is no longer an external data type on the Web. Audio can be used as background music. Embedded hyperlinks are allowed within the video stream, and moving objects in the video stream are clickable and lead to other documents. New network protocols are used to transmit video and audio over the Internet. The protocol adapts what it sends to the available bandwidth between the server and the client.

The software is organized as a plug in to Netscape and Spyglass browsers. Using Direct X, the video may be detached from the browser and scaled or viewed full screen. Fast forward and rewind video controls are accessed through the mouse and popup menus. PC, Macintosh and Unix versions of Vosaic are available. The *Vosaic plugin* uses standard techniques for audio compression running over IP. It adjusts its data rates to accommodate other users, while maintaining the best possible delivery of video and audio compressed with MPEG1, MPEG2, half rate GSM audio, and H.263. *Vosaic video browser* is integrated as a plug-in into the Netscape and Spyglass Web browsers. *Vosaic video server* is available for the Windows 95 and NT platforms, the Macintosh Power PC platform, as well as for various flavors of Unix. The design team is busy developing tools to help build video databases on PC, Mac, and UNIX platforms. They are also improving the network transmission protocol and creating a database interface at the server. Look also for a Java interface and multicast extensions.

White Pine Software

Enhanced CUSeeMe

White Pine Software a developer of video conferencing and desktop connectivity software. They licensed Voxware's ToolVox technology, including the RT24 codec, for use in its video conferencing software. This will enable White Pine's Enhanced CUSeeMe to operate at low bandwidth and provide persontoperson connections for telephone and video conferencing.

Enhanced CU-SeeMe is White Pine's desktop video conferencing software for real time person-to-person or group conferencing. You can use CU-SeeMe over the Internet or any TCP/IP network giving you the power to communicate globally without expensive hardware. This software only solution runs on both Windows and Macintosh computers offering full-color video, audio, chat window, and white board communications. You can participate in 'Live over the Internet' conferences, broadcasts or chats. CU-SeeMe can be launched directly from Web pages with your favorite Web browser. All of this and more over your 28.8k modem, ISDN link or better. For audio-only telephony use, CU-SeeMe works effectively over a 14.4k modem.

White Pine's Enhanced CU-SeeMe is the leading desktop video conferencing software solution providing group conferencing over the Internet or other TCP-IP networks. Whether you are an instructor conducting a training a class, a business manager communicating to a customer or someone wanting to speak with a friend, Enhanced CU-SeeMe is a simple, software-only solution. Return to Table of Contents

Enhanced CU-SeeMe uses a unique protocol to manage, receive and rebroadcast video and audio data. The protocol was developed specifically for TCP/IP networks and the Internet. It is capable of running over ISDN networks with TCP/IP network support. Person-to-person, group conferencing, and large audience broadcasting over TCP/IP networks are all possible with CU-SeeMe technology - with little or no added cost for making connections.

CU-SeeMe achieves low bandwidth Internet connections through software only algorithms that reduce data transmission and save you money. It does not require expensive hardware compression/decompression (codec) boards. SLIP and PPP modem connections are supported; however it is recommended that you use a 28.8k modem connection or better. CU-SeeMe is compatible with video codec and audio standards on both Windows and Macintosh systems, providing versatility and compatibility for the future.

CU-SeeMe can be used with most video boards that support Video for Windows. Similarly, CU-SeeMe supports Apple's QuickTime to display video for Macintosh computers. CU-SeeMe was developed as a free video-conferencing program (under copyright of Cornell University and its collaborators) available to anyone with a Macintosh (16 gray scale) or Windows (256 color card / monitor) and an Internet connection. With CU-SeeMe you can videoconference with another site located anywhere in the world or -- with a "reflector" server -- up to eight "windows" to other "parties" may participate in a CU-SeeMe conference on your computer screen.

A number of universities, non-profit and private organizations, led by Cornell, have formed the CU-SeeMe Consortium to support further innovation, development and dissemination of CU-SeeMe. For more information contact Martyne Hallgren, executive director, CU-SeeMe Consortium at 607-254-8324 or e-mail m.hallgren@cornell.edu.

CU-SeeMe was originally a video program without audio, used in long distance learning applications. After students began doing primitive sign language to try to communicate over the video channel, it was decided to add the Maven audio routines to the package, yielding full-blown video-conferencing capabilities.

Sound quality is good, but it may be degraded at 14.4 Kbps. Viewing images is impossible at 14.4 Kbps and slow at 28.8 Kbps, but pure audio conferencing without images will work okay. Images can be sent with a camera available for $99. CU-SeeMe for audio conference users can either connect directly to each other (point-to-point) or they can enter a multiperson conference at a "reflector," which is a computer (Sun SPARC) running a Unix program.

The CU-SeeMe Reflector idea was developed out of necessity, there being no support in the Macintosh TCP/IP facilities for multicast. You need to use a CU-SeeMe reflector to have a multiparty conference using CU-SeeMe on the Internet. CU-SeeMe reflectors can send multicast but not receive.

Also, CU-SeeMe probably offers good compatibility with other applications, across Windows, Mac and the Web. The CU-SeeMe web page is http://cu-seeme.cornell.edu/.

Xing Technology

Streamworks

Xing (pronounced "ZING") is a pioneer in digital compression software. The produce standards-based solutions for creating, delivering, and playing digital audio and video. StreamWorks customers include NBC, Reuters, Bloomberg, Capitol Records, Cnet, Sportsline USA, Telcom Finland, and Sumitomo. The company recently demonstrated its version 2.0 of Stream-Works. The product is used for creating, delivering, and playing live and on-demand audio and video for the Internet and corporate intranets . Using a technology called streaming, StreamWorks enables audio and video playback over a network without any wait for file download.

Streamworks allows users to view and hear video programming in real-time without having to download large files to their computer before viewing. High fidelity audio can also be "streamed" to 'Net users providing near CD quality sound through computers having audio cards and ISDN connections to the Internet. Lesser "AM" quality sound is heard over systems having 14.4 Kbps and 28.8 Kbps modems.

StreamWorks 2.0 includes a Netscape Navigator plug-in interface, and additional server capabilities through StreamWorks Server plusPACKs. A redesigned interface for StreamWorks 2.0 Player makes it easier for non-technical users to play content from the Internet, whether they are connected by modem, ISDN, or high-speed link. Version 2.0 increases the degree of integration between StreamWorks and the Web. Web browsers such as Netscape Navigator and Microsoft Internet Explorer are now the primary method for browsing and selecting audio and video content.

A new Netscape Navigator plug-in enables in-line playing, where a content provider can place the StreamWorks audio or video window within a standard HTML web page. "The new interface for StreamWorks 2.0 puts even more power in the hands of content producers.

StreamWorks Server is the center of Xing's Internet broadcast solution, the place where audio and video streams are routed and coordinated.

StreamWorks Server Thinning plusPACK adds on-the-fly bitrate scaling and stream thinning, enabling a content provider to deliver a single source at multiple data rates. For example, a 1.5 megabit per second source file could be delivered simultaneously at 1.5 megabits per second, ISDN, and modem rates.

StreamWorks Server Propagation plusPACK adds the ability to deliver live StreamWorks feeds across multiple servers. This increases potential audience size, while economizing impact on network traffic and bandwidth requirements. Deployed across the network, StreamWorks Servers with the propagation plusPACK give broadcasters the capability to reach millions of Internet users from a single originating feed.

StreamWorks Server LIVEfile plusPACK enables streaming of virtual live feeds (simulated live broadcasts) from pre-recorded files, providing the appearance and features of a live feed without the cost of live encoding hardware.

StreamWorks Transmitter remains the only product available for creating and delivering live MPEG audio and video streams over the Internet. This includes baseball games to concerts to live news coverage.

Figure 10.4 illustrates a page from Xing's Web site. You can visit the company's home page and jump to live feeds using the Streamworks technology. Digitcom Multimedia Corporation and KWHY-TV, Los Angeles, have launched Channel 22's daily business and financial news onto the Internet (www.digitcom.com). KWHY's Webcast is available to desktop computers connected to the Internet using Streamworks software.

Figure 10.4 -- Xing Technology Live Feed "Jump Site"

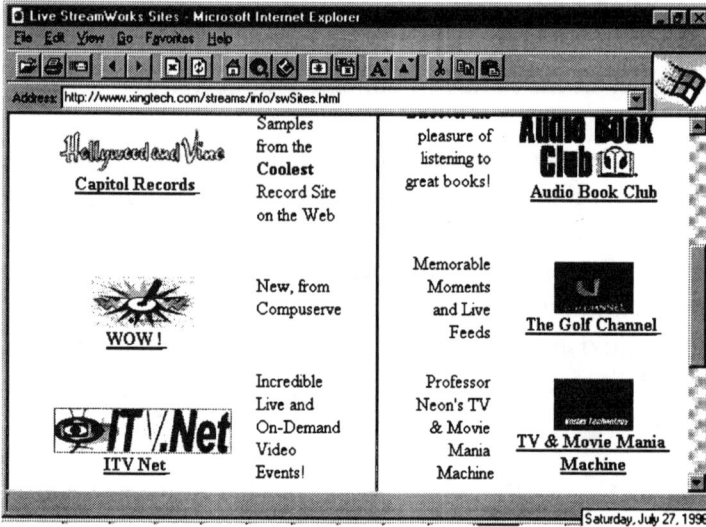

KWHY's business news and analysis programming is on the Web from 6 AM to 2:30 PM PST, Monday through Friday, making it the first regularly scheduled television programming on the Internet. Optimal viewing is achieved by those accessing the Internet with ISDN modems that operate at 112 Kbps second, but 28.8 Kbps and 14.4 Kbps modems can listen to and view the video at a "stop-action" two- to three-frames per second.

Chapter Acknowledgments

Many thanks to Carl Strathmeyer of Dialogic's Computer Telephone Division. I ask him frequently for his opinions and he always shares them. Portions of the chapter opening are Copyright (c) 1996 Dialogic Corporation - and published with permission.

Freddie Golino, our Webmaster at Flatiron Publishing, and Richard Grigonis, our Technical Editor were invaluable resources for helping with all the test drives. Extra praise to Freddie for the "radio star" anecdote.

Chapter 11

Internet Telephony

In February 1995 when VocalTec, Ltd. launched Internet Phone, it hit a nerve with people who were on the Internet, especially those who used the Internet's chat services like IRC (Internet Relay Chat). Internet Phone quickly became the most popular Internet telephony software product in use during 1995. During the first week Internet Phone was on the net, over 40,000 people downloaded an evaluation copy.

The April 22, 1996 issue of Business Week estimates that over 1.5 million copies of Internet Telephony software has been downloaded. While this may be close to the actual number of total copies distributed, it does not reflect the actual number of weekly users of these products.

Most Internet telephony users are hobbyists. These are the same people on CB or Ham radio. They enjoy speaking with strangers, sometimes hours at a time. The quality of a two way Internet Phone conversation over the Internet is not as good as a regular telephone line, and the service is not as reliable as the local phone company. But this software allows us to use the Internet to make virtually free phone calls. Naturally, this attracts a lot of media attention... others call it hype.

Now corporations have started to consider implementing *Voice On the Net* (VON) technologies over their corporate networks. Other companies have evaluated Internet telephony software to bypass their long distance carriers. The quality and reliability of this technology need to improve before businesses embrace IT products wholeheartedly. Before the end of 1997 many corporations will be using these products on their own leased circuits and Intranets.

Internet Telephony Principles

Internet telephony is based on both voice processing and data communications principles. Today's PCs are often equipped with multimedia sound systems, enabling them to record the human voice through a microphone and store it for later playback. This is achieved by digitizing the voice and storing it as data. We use voice modems, computer telephony cards and other devices to do this.

Internet Telephony products take this voice digitization capability several steps further. First, the digitized voice is sent as data over the Internet like an e-mail message is sent. Just as e-mail messages require addressing, so do IT-based telephone calls.

Second, the digitization processes happens in real time. Instead of storing the voice on the PCs hard disk, it is sent directly from RAM over the SLPP or PPP Internet connection. This process happens in reverse on the other end (at the called party location). Since the general idea is to pass digitized files over an IP-like network, there are also applications for doing this on private networks in you business (LANs and WANs). Most of these products use UDP and TCP protocols.

There are a variety of schemes for digitizing, compressing and routing the calls. Depending on the equipment and sped of modem you are using, these calls can be made as "full duplex" calls. This means both parties can speak simultaneously without delay. Half duplex communication is like a CB radio, wherein one party must stop transmitting momentarily to allow the other party to speak.

Although most Internet telephony products do not interoperate, the industry is mobilizing behind some popular IETF (Internet Engineering Task Force) and ITU (International Telecommunications Union) standards. Some companies are hedging their bets by promoting their own proprietary implementations as a standard. Others, like Microsoft and Intel and pushing ITU standards. Most IT enthusiasts insist on a Pentium processor with at least 16 megs of RAM and a 28.8 modem. It's also a good idea to have a headset with a built-in microphone. This cuts down on background noise and makers it easier to hear, as well. There are several ways IT products make a connection. Perhaps the most popular is the "meet me" approach. This requires both parties to consciously log on to a IT host and choose one another from a list of connected parties.

A more sophisticated approach is to use a system (like NetSpeak's WebPhone) wherein both parties enter an IP address for the other caller. This is roughly equivalent to entering someone's phone number when you make a regular telephone call. Some IT software will log on to a global server automatically and perform registry operations. Registry servers are used as a beacon to find the people you are looking for and then dial them. What's really exciting is to apply this global registry approach to Internet/PSTN gateways. These systems act as protocol converts, keeping the callers transparent from details of transmission. In this case IT software acts as a proxy for your POTS-initiated telephone call. The called party may answer with their IT/PC or with a regular phone depending on how the call is routed.

VON Coalition

The initial reaction to this technology by major telephone companies has been passive. But in March of 1996 a small trade group called the Americas Carriers Telecommunication Association (ACTA, representing 130 technology-challenged long distance phone companies) filled a petition with the FCC. ACTA asked the FCC to regulate content on the Internet and to ban the sale and use of Internet telephony software products.

Within two weeks of the ACTA filing, the VON Coalition was formed, and Jeff Pulver was named Chairman. Two others have contributed significantly to the efforts of the coalition. The are Sandy Combs as the Director of the Coalition and Bruce Jacobs, acting as VON Coalition counsel. Things happen fast on the Internet. In less than two weeks, the VON Coalition quickly became *the* Trade association for this industry. This due to the support of hobbyists and makers of VON technology.

VON Mission

Part of the VON Coalition's sustaining mission is to proactively provide updates on the state of the industry to consumers and as well as the trade media. The Coalition has started to reach out to various business and non-profits, and has provided a voice to be heard at numerous trade conferences. The members want to educate consumers and the media by monitoring and supporting present and newly developed *audio, multimedia, telephony, video*, and *voice* technologies that are specifically designed and manufactured for the Global Internet community.

Says Coalition Chairman Jeff Pulver: "We act as the key industry advocate in the fight against regulation." The VON coalition approach has been to keep an open and ongoing relationship with the FCC, and maintain contact with foreign regulatory agencies.

Within four days of the March 4, 1996 ACTA petition, the original founding members of the VON Coalition had joined. The coalition convinced the FCC to establish a mailbox for people to directly e-mail the agency with their comments on the ACTA petition. This was a first for the FCC. The VON Coalition Home page (www.von.org) also helps to educate the media on the importance of Internet telephony and it's continued growth. The Coalition held the first "Common Ground" meeting in NYC on May 9th, 1996 we. This brought together a group of industry representatives from the regulatory, technology, and businesses sides of VON and related technologies. This was the first time a formal group gathered to discuss the issues at hand. Booz-Allen Hamilton, Cascade, IBM MCI, Microsoft Netscape, NetSpeak, ,VocalTec and VoxWare were there.

The group discussed standards, market segmentation, growth and the techno-economics of mass market penetration. At issue, of course was VON's positioning with the traditional telecom industry. To be predatory or cooperative with the infrastructure and status quo? If ACTA was successful, the Internet would no longer be the place which showcases enabling and emerging technologies. However, in the end of June, 1996 it looks like the efforts and actions of the VON Coalition and others in response to the ACTA petition has not gone unnoticed by FCC Chairman Reed Hundt.

In a speech delivered on behalf of Reed Hundt, Chairman of the FCC, at the INET '96 Conference in Montreal, Blair Levin, FCC Chief of Staff commented: "the right answer at this time is *not* to place restrictions on software providers... or to subject Internet telephony to the same rules that apply to conventional circuit-switched voice carriers".

After reviewing the entire text of the speech on-line from the FCC web site (www.fcc.gov), it seems that Chairman Reed Hundt agrees with the majority of the points raised in the VON Coalition lead Joint Filing of Reply Comments dated June 10th, 1996. The complete text of the June 10th filing can be found on www.von.org/reply.html

While this speech by Reed Hundt indicates his current position on the ACTA situation, it doesn't mean that a change of politics in Washington, D.C. could not change the position of the FCC. The VON Coalition will continue to closely monitor this situation and situations similar to it around the world. Common Ground meetings will be held every four to six months.

ACTA Internet Phone Petition

On March 8, 1996, the Commission issued a routine public notice inviting comment on a petition filed by America's Carriers Telecommunication Association (ACTA) seeking a declamatory ruling, special relief, and institution of a rulemaking proceeding dealing with Internet telephony and with FCC regulation of the Internet. On March 25, 1996, the Bureau issued a second public notice clarifying the issues upon which comment in being requested, and extending the comment deadlines. An unofficial copy of the Petition is now available online.

The VON Coalition has a fact sheet on how to file formal comments with the FCC. Informal comments in this proceeding may also be filed via electronic mail at rm8775@fcc.gov. All filings on the ACTA Petition should reference RM No. 8775. Comments are due May 8, 1996, and reply comments are due June 8, 1996. Please contact Kevin Werbach (kwerbach@fcc.gov) if you have specific questions about this proceeding. 1996 VON Coalition. All rights reserved. Toll Free - 1.888.4VON INFO (see the end of this chapter for acknowledgments on the VON Coalition, its chief members and contact information).

Internet Telephony Market Assessment

Internet telephony (IT) is currently a specialty market. Based on recent technological advances and standards activity, IT has the potential to rapidly become mainstream. Response by long distance carriers, RBOCs, cable, and computer companies and the evolution of telecommunications deregulation are external influences that will affect the IT market. This according to Mark Winther, analyst for IDC in his 1996 - 1999 Internet telephony Market Assessment.

Winther says the estimated number of active IT users was 500,000 by the end of 1995. Of active users, VocalTec had the lion's share of the market at 94%. Active users are characterized as individuals who use the product on a routine basis, rather than the number who purchased or downloaded an IT product tried it, and are no longer using the product.IDC projects the IT market will grow to 16 million users of all types by the end of 1999. Internet telephony market revenue at the end of 1995 is estimated at $3.5 million. IDC forecasts this market to reach $560 million by the end of 1999. This forecast could change substantially in the 1997 period, based on several factors outlined in this report.The primary uses of Internet telephony in 1995 were for consumer long distance calls, Internet chat groups, and some modest business experimentation in Intranet applications. Potential future applications include interactive electronic commerce, intraenterprise connectivity, and collaborative computing.

Before IT can reach mainstream usage, three critical factors for success are apparent. The first is "ease of connectivity," namely, for anyone connected to the Internet to dial another party direct, whether or not the other party is on the Internet. Second, an open set of standards are required, independent of which IT software product is used. Third, IT efforts must include ubiquitous telephony features available today, coupled with valueadded features and options that serve as a means for competitive differentiation and market segmentation.

The barriers to entry in the IT market are relatively modest. New entrants will either license the technology or serve as a valueadded distribution channel. Basic research and development in voice and compression techniques will continue to pace the need for capital investment. Only a few companies will engage in the basic R&D necessary for new IT product innovation. Smaller companies will be forced to license their patents, form alliances with one or more of the major telecommunications, entertainment, or information technology players, or be absorbed.

Advances in voice and data compression technologies, coupled with differentiated communications features, will drive the fundamentals for this market. Patents, copyrights, and licensing will be prime considerations, with "first to market" a secondary consideration. OEM relationships with major computer telephony companies and VARs will be essential by 1997. Due to the low selling price of product, methods of marketing, promotion, and distribution will represent fundamental cost structure challenges. Finally, customer satisfaction and support will be crucial in the creation of a broad customer base. Additional features and options, targeted at specific market segments, will be needed to sustain repeat sales and profitability.

Client To Client Voice Communications

IT products allow clienttoclient voice communications via the Internet. Most Internet telephony products require the same vendor's software to be used on both ends of a connection. So far, that has put Internet telephony more in the category of a cool trick than an upandcoming business tool.

The lack of vendor interoperability is being addressed through consortia formed to adopt standardsbased communications. Initiatives are under way to allow Internet users to dial into a switch and place an outbound call to any telephone, thereby broadening the appeal and applicability of IT.

The Internet, and specifically the World Wide Web (WWW), continues to evolve, promising new commercial and social opportunities. While the promise remains, suppliers of Internetenabled product services and solutions are seeking ways to improve their value proposition to customers; companies that have invested in general "brochureware" Web sites are demanding more specific applications that produce direct and measurable results. By linking the $700 billion global telephony market with the embryonic Internet market, IT extends the value proposition. Furthermore, by seamlessly connecting realtime voice communications with the Internet's rich text/graphic/image communications, critical applications such as electronic commerce, enterprise communications, and collaborative computing are significantly enhanced.

Any commercial opportunities that are highly dependent on the use of the Internet need a hard reality check. There is mounting evidence that the Internet as a viable commercial outlet will require companies to invest for the long term. One fact stands out: The Internet and its various embodiments continue to be too expensive and too confusing for the typical individual or business user. However, the recent addition of gateways by the online commercial services has eased this confusion somewhat.

In addition, there are as many different estimates of the number of users on the Internet and how they are using it as there are companies that conduct polls and surveys. Factual information is sparse due to the newness of the Internet telephony market and products. The prospects of major changes in IT products could quickly result in mainstream usage. However, mainstream adoption will depend on several factors external to the IT market, such as the recent petition by the telephony trade group America's Carriers Telecommunication Association (ACTA) requesting the FCC to prohibit any future sales of IT products.

IT Market Forecast Assumptions

IDC projects the IT market to grow from 500,000 active users at the end of 1995 to 5 million users at the end of 1997. By 1999, we project 16 million IT users. Figure 11.1 presents IDC's forecast of IT business and consumer users through 1999. Figure 11.2 presents IDC's forecast of end user spending on IT software. Key assumptions in these forecasts include the following:

Worldwide Internet Telephony Active Users, 1995–1999 (000)

	1995	1996	1997	1998	1999	1995-1999 CAGR (%)
Consumer	475	1,500	2,500	4,000	6,000	89
Business	25	500	2,500	6,000	10,000	347
Total	500	2,000	5,000	10,000	16,000	138

Source: International Data Corporation, 1996

Figure 11.1 -- IT Business And Consumer Users

Worldwide End-User Spending on Internet Telephony Software, 1995–1999 ($M)

	1995	1996	1997	1998	1999	1995-1999 CAGR (%)
User spending	3.5	70.0	175.0	350.0	560.0	256

Estimated average revenue per unit over the projected time frame is $35.00.
Source: International Data Corporation, 1996

Figure 11.2 -- EndUser Spending On IT Software.

The projections represent a conservative forecast. Growth could increase dramatically, depending on response from long distance carriers, RBOCs, and cable companies. Assuming a positive response by these companies, penetration could reach 50% of WWW users, or 63 million, by 1999.

At the end of 1996, the number of IT users will represent 6% of WWW users worldwide. By the end of 1999, the number will be 12 % of WWW users worldwide. The forecast of end user spending on IT software is based on today's market price ranges and on the typical price trends for desktop software. The current list price range for the most widely used commercial IT software is $69 (VocalTec Internet Phone) to $49 (Quarterdeck Webtalk). Our assumption is that most users have obtained software for $35 after package discounts, special promotions, and the like.

IDC's 1995 market value estimate of $3.5 million is based on a series of data points. First, 1995 was the startup year for IT, so a lot of products were downloaded for free or deployed as beta tests with "friendly" customers. Second, revenues from market leader VocalTec were posted at just under $2.5 million for the year. After consideration of channel costs and discounts, IDC estimated enduser expenditures on VocalTec's Internet Phone software at well over $3 million in 1995.

The 1996 to 1999 forecast analysis assumes an average $35 expenditure per user from 1996 throughout the forecast period, based on typical desktop software price trending. The software price trend model goes as follows: The basic price for today's product will decline as the market grows and as economies of scale enable vendors to maintain profitability. The price decline will be offset by three types of product upgrades:

- Improvements for quality and reliability

- Enhancements with additional telephony features (voice mail, call forwarding, multicasting/conferencing calls)

- Changes required to comply with standards when they are set

The added features will minimize price erosion, with the result of a constant price point of $35.

Internet Telephony Forecast Methodology

IDC developed these forecasts through application of existing IDC Internet forecasts and analyses, combined with specific data collection activities relating to the Internet telephony market. This process included interviews with the following Internet telephony players:

- All current vendors of Internet telephony products

- Potential vendors of Internet telephony products

- Leading Internet technology vendors

- Online/Internet service providers

- Desktop software distribution companies

Research activity also included searching all secondary sources, including relevant Web sites. usenet groups, mailing lists, and the business   trade press.

Internet Telephony Market Segments

IT software is distributed through multiple channels, including software retail channels, software preloaded into PCs and modems, software down-loaded from the Web, and software distribution through online and Internet service providers (ISPs).

Based on discussions with IT vendors and distributors, IDC estimates the split of distribution channels for 1995 shown in Figure 11.3. The percentages represent the number of products sold through or to a given segment. Retail areas that have successfully sold IT products to small businesses are business supply and PC specialty stores such as OfficeMax.

Figure 11.3 -- Split Of IT Distribution Channels

The channel of Web downloading and online service/ISP distribution has not proven to be a significant direct channel in the market to date. For

1995 Distribution Channels for IT Products

Channel	% of IT Sales	Market Segment
Software retail (Egghead, Circuit City)	35	Individuals and small business
Corporate/VARs	10	Corporate intranet applications
OEM (bundled with modems, PCs)	55	Individuals

Source: International Data Corporation, 1996

example, America Online (AOL), which has offered VocalTec's Internet Phone product to its members since early December 1995, reports a little over 1,000 downloads per month through February 1996. It is probable that the download channel is used to trial products, with purchase made subsequently through the retail channel. Generally, the current use of IT software can be characterized as novel and/or experimental. The economics of placing long distance calls for far less cost than telephony rates is the most obvious appeal. IT is being used by early adopters, who are typically users with annual family incomes over $70,000.

The primary consumer home market usage is for placing long distance calls to contact relatives, friends, and acquaintances. On a more exploratory basis, social contacts are pursued through chat mode (IRC) and point-to-point initiated phone calls.

Experience to date suggests that businesses are essentially experimenting with IT software for making long distance calls and inhouse Intranet applications. Quality, reliability, and the lack of standards are currently the main inhibitors for true business usage.

Internet Telephony Competition

A growing number of companies are selling software programs that enable a computer to transmit voice conversations. Four vendors' products form the core of existing IT systems. These include Camelot Corp.'s Digiphone, VocalTec's Internet Phone, Quarterdeck's WebTalk, and NetSpeak's WebPhone. Many other companies have built or are planning to build IT functions into their products. These include the following:

Vendors of collaborative computing and desktop connectivity such as InSoft's CoolTalk, White Pine Software's Enhanced CUSeeMe video conferencing software

Developers of digital speech processing technologies such as VoxWare's ToolVox for the Web and Dialogic, which has joined with VocalTec to develop the Internet Phone Telephony Gateway server

IDT, an Internet service provider and a provider of discounted international calling services to U.S. businesses, has developed a software technology called Net2Phone; which allows anyone to dial into the IDT switch through the Internet and place outbound calls from the United States—cheaper than international calling rates

Leading Internet technology companies, including Netscape, Microsoft, and IBM, are paying close attention to IT by initiating standards for vendor interoperability and by introducing IT features on their existing Internet client and server software portfolios. Microsoft's NetMeeting and Intel's Internet Phone are examples. The new entrants and the large Internet companies are likely to have a major impact on the nearterm and longterm direction of the IT market. It is unclear how the actions of large companies, namely IBM, Microsoft, and Netscape, will alter the competitive structures and market shares that currently exist in the IT market. However, their impact is expected to be significant. This is reflected in IDC's marketshare projections, in which several products are expected to be either discontinued or absorbed through acquisition into other companies.

As an example of the acquisition impact, Netscape has already announced the acquisition of InSoft and an equity investment in VoxWare.

Internet Telephony Success Factors

The IT participants are hoping that, by gaining market share, their product will become the de facto standard. This is normally a reasonable expectation; however, interoperability across platforms and products will be essential if IT is to capture a mass market. The driving factors are reliability and efficiency for businesses and ease of use for consumers.

Internet Telephony Connectivity

IT needs to be refined to the extent that the technology is transparent to the user. In essence, this translates to IT being as simple as picking up the telephone and connecting to another party, regardless of where the other person is or what equipment that person is using. A common platform interface is required to mask proprietary front ends and to ensure interconnection ubiquity across the Internet and company Internist. For business-to-business and business-to-consumer applications, this is a critical requirement.

Internet Telephony Standards Cooperation

In January 1996, Netscape Communications Corp. announced Netscape LiveMedia, a standards-based framework for bringing realtime audio and video to the Netscape open software platform. The LiveMedia framework is intended to enable easier access to new Internet applications such as audio and video on demand, realtime video conferencing, and Internet telephony. Eleven companies announced plans to support Netscape LiveMedia, which is based on open standards and interfaces that will enable Netscape and third-party, realtime audio and video products to interoperate, including Progressive Networks, Adobe Systems, Digital Equipment Corp., Macromedia, NetSpeak, OnLive!, Precept, Silicon Graphics Inc., VDOnet, VocalTec, VoxWare, and Xing. IBM, as part of its Statement of Direction, plans to form a similar standards consortium.

In March 1996, Microsoft and Intel jointly announced an "open platform" intended to standardize video, voice, and data communications over the Internet. To date, 100 companies have joined in this effort, including information technology, multimedia, telecommunications, and network equipment vendors.

Basic Telephony Plus

To ensure mainstream acceptance, basic telephony features are considered essential. Such capabilities include call waiting, voice messaging, and call forwarding. Again, the availability of this type of functionality will pace acceptance by business and the consumer.

Additional valueadded features and options offered by IT companies will be key to competitive differentiation. Wireless and remote location features within IT applications should serve to motivate the marketplace.

Internet Telephony Future

Consumer market segment applications include the following:

Interactive entertainment games. The entertainment/gaming industry attracts a wide and varied audience. Interactive games could be enhanced with realtime dialogue occurring between one or more players; this enhancement would be possible on commercial services and the Internet.

Customer service. This type of realtime activity could compete with current 800 number productpurchase calls. The consumer would have the added advantage of discussion with a live operator or with a voice messaging system to check prices, product features, and other pertinent information before purchase. Service applications and realtime problem solving present similar types of opportunities. Education and distance learning. Realtime, multicast interaction between teacher and students would further enable the distance learning market that is currently text and email based.

Business market segment applications consist of the following:

Interactive electronic commerce. Companies big and small are pursuing online shopping and commercial transactions. The IT scenario could permit live interaction with an operator or interaction with voice messaging systems while viewing the product(s) and placing orders online. The enabling factor would be live operator interchange for questions, clarifications, and special requests.

Intranet and businesstobusiness applications. The use of IT applications could encompass two major business opportunities— namely, within the enterprise (intranet) and businesstobusiness communications. Netscape indicates that 80% of its 1995 revenue stream of $80.7 million, or approximately $64 million, was derived from intranet site licenses for internal business communications. Connectivity to both public and private networks makes this a particularly attractive opportunity.

Collaborative computing. IT, coupled with video conferencing, suggests an economical means for shared activity within companies. Examples such as whiteboarding, document sharing, and other typical interoffice tasks would be enhanced by live interaction among personnel. whether at local desktops or in remote locations.

Internet telephony is currently a specialty market. Based on recent technological advancements and standards activities, IT has significant potential to rapidly become mainstream.

Ease of connectivity, coupled with interoperability standards, are the prime requirements for IT to capture a mainstream market. Additional valueadded features and capabilities, coupled with basic telephony functions. will be the key product differentiators.

The economics of a competitive IT industry suggest the need for alliances with major players and product licensing through a variety of channels beyond retail.

OEM relationships with major computer/telephony companies and VARs will be essential. The costs associated with narrow market segmentation may constrain a company's ability to gain market share or realize a profit.

Response by long distance carriers, RBOCs, cable, and computer companies, as well as the evolution of telecommunications deregulation, are external influences that will also affect the IT market. Governmental regulatory issues are still to be resolved (portions Copyrighted 1996 International Data Corporation. See end of chapter for acknowledgments).

Camelot

DigiPhone
...and E-PHONE (aka NetPhone)

DigiPhone is from Third Planet Publishing, a subsidiary of Camelot. DigiPhone is definitely a commercial Windows program, not a freebie. It's $89.95. DigiPhone was originally known as the Personal Internet Companion Kit. Another version, DigiPhone Deluxe, includes a Web browser, e-mail, telnet, FTP, voice messaging and Caller ID, all for $149.95. Both versions use a proprietary compression scheme.

Inside the Digiphone box you'll find two 3.5 inch floppies, a CD-ROM disc, an owners manual and a DigiPhone Security Access Card at the back of the manual.

You'll need Windows 3.x, a Winsock 1.1 compliant protocol stack (if you decide not to use the "DigiSocket" software that comes on one of the floppies) and at least a 33MHz 386DX or a 33MHz 486DX (recommended), plus the usual full or half duplex sound card, mic and speakers.

At least a 9.6 Kbps modem connection is required, a 14.4Kbps modem is recommended, but the best connection would be a direct TCP/IP network connection.

Third Planet Publishing has created the DigiPhone Global Directory, a worldwide DigiPhone users directory that is updated daily and is available either by e-mail or on the DigiPhone Web Page.

If you know the e-mail address of the person you're going to call:

Click on the DigiSocket icon or start another Winsock 1.1 Compliant Protocol Stack program.

Click on the Remote Site field on the main menu.

Enter in the e-mail address of the person you're calling.

Press the Call button. The other person will see your e-mail address on their screen. If they wish to answer your call they will click on an "accept" button, otherwise they can click on "reject." If you hear your party answer, start talking.

With the half-duplex option you must press the Talk button when you want to talk, and the Stop Talking button when you are done talking.

Click on the Hang Up button when you're finished. The Call button will change to say Hang Up while your call is active.

If you don't know the e-mail address of the person you're going to call, you will first have to click on Directories, then Global Directory, then perform a search of the directory via e-mail. When the requested information arrives in your e-mail, you cut and paste the numbers into your currently active personal DigiPhone book for future use as shown in Figure 11.4.

That's because DigiPhone was structured to be a real software-based telephone system using direct-connection technology (DCT). It doesn't rely on IRC servers, or chat lines, or special connections sites which may or may not be operational when you want to make your call.

Figure 11.4 -- Camelot's DigiPhone Book

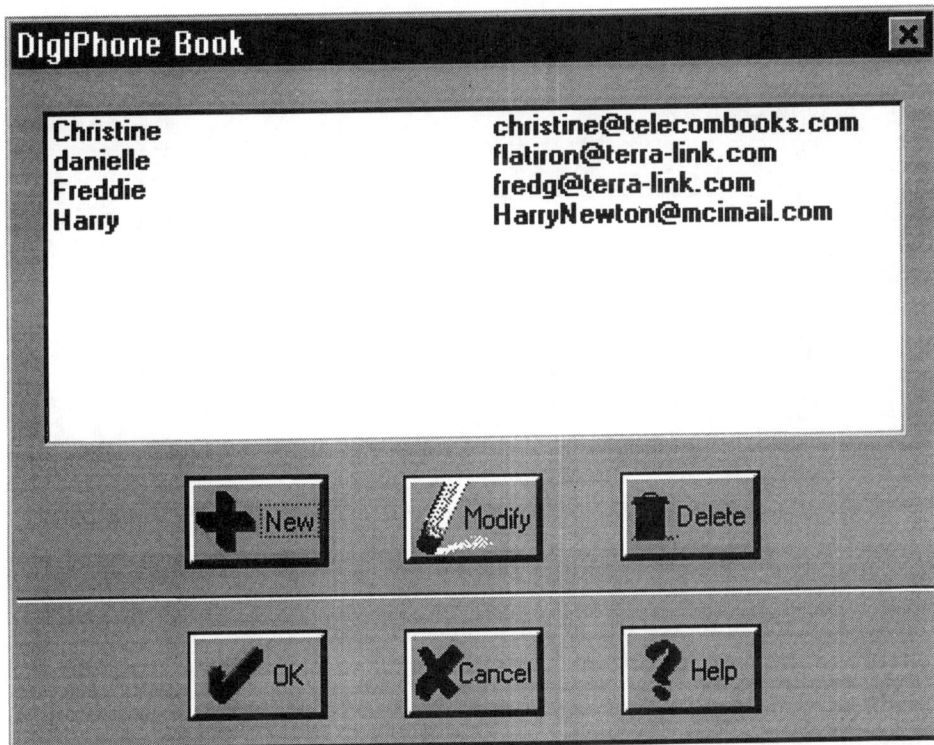

And it works, straight out of the box, because we've equipped DigiPhone with full-duplexing sound card drivers specifically written for the most popular full-duplexing sound cards on the market today, including the Sound Blaster 16. Have a look at our list of tested sound cards and you'll probably discover that the one you already own works with DigiPhone. And even if your card isn't full-duplexing, chances are you can still use DigiPhone in half-duplex mode.

You can buy DigiPhone at many retail outlets: APlus Software (Canada), Aventure Electroniq (Canada), Best Buy, Babbage's, Club Biz (Canada), CompUSA, Egghead Software, Elek-Tek, Fry's Electronics, FutureShop, Hastings, J&R Computer World, London Drug (Canada), MediaPlay, MicroCenter, Mr. CD-ROM and Software Etc.

Figure 11.5 -- DigiPhone Deluxe Interface

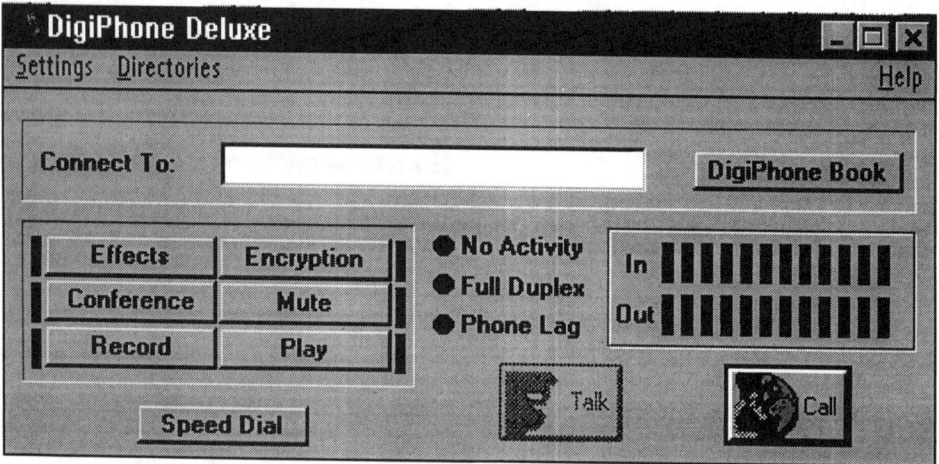

DigiPhone's main screen is made up of the Information Bar, Main Menu Bar, and Main Screen Area as illustrated in Figure 11.5. The top-most bar is used for displaying call information such as second party's name and the length of time connected to them. Also located on the upper right are three indicator lights, showing connection status, duplex mode status and phone lag status. Just below you can see the talk button -- if you have a half duplex sound card you will have to click on this just before you speak each time. But this is a full duplex connection. At the top, there are three drop-down choices on the main menu bar. These are Settings (connection settings and the VOX level, or the amount of silence recorded by DigiPhone before it automatically turns off the microphone), Directories (Global and Personal Directories) and the Help file.

E-PHONE (aka NetPhone)

NetPhone version 1.2.3 from the Electric Magic Company (bought by Camelot) was a full duplex phone program for Internet audioconferencing. It ran on any Macintosh from a IIsi to the fastest Power Mac -- with a IIci or faster you could use GSM audio compression.

NetPhone was bought first by New Paradigm Software (New York, NY -- 212-557-0933) who renamed it "e-phone" and announced both a Windows version and the program's integration into their Copernicus product. New Paradigm sold the rights to e-phone to Camelot who also owns the DigiPhone, which is PC based.

E-phone runs in the background and listens for incoming calls. To answer a call you launch the main application. E-phone tells you the name of the person calling, their IP address and their host name. You can have multiple call windows open at once so there are no busy signals.

E-phone can work with the Netscape Navigator browser which provides a convenient way to connect to "NetPubs" (informal discussion groups). It also supports the CSVD and vat protocols, letting you talk to CU-SeeMe users (and reflectors) and UNIX workstations.

And since your Mac's IP address may be assigned dynamically each time you start a SLIP/PPP connection, you may actually need NetPub for others to call you. If you are both connected to the same NetPub you can call them by double clicking their name in the NetPub list.

Unlike the bandwidth hungry competing Mac program Maven, e-phone performs only about 10,000 samples per second, allowing a conversation to pass through a 14.4 Kbps modem with bandwidth to spare.

Extensive testing revealed that e-phone and SLIP / PPP driver software when used together need at least a 68020 running at 20MHz. Running e-phone on the slower Mac LC and LCII's with their 16MHz 68020/68030 processors results in the computer becoming unresponsive to mouse clicks, unless your TCP/IP connection is made over Ethernet or LocalTalk, in which case everything will be okay.

However, if your e-phone audio is breaking up and you're using a 68030 or 68020-based Mac, check the "This is a slow machine" box in the program's preferences dialog box. It will give you the good or bad news.

Another source of sluggish performance is the Express Modem, as found in the Duo model. Apple says that the Express Modem's driver software uses up to a whopping 30% of a 33MHz 68030 processor's cycles. Between the modem software and e-phone, there's not much processing power left over for, say, displaying menus. If it makes you feel any better, other software will also creep along when working in conjunction with the Express Modem.

Also, the "limited" Apple Sound Chip was a cost saving measure Apple used resulting in machines that can either play sound or record it, but not both simultaneously. Thus, only half duplex mode is available on Macs having this chip, such as the PowerBook 1xx, Duos, Mac LC series and equivalent Performa models. With these machines you must enable "Push to Talk" in the "e-phone" menu.

Another caveat involves Quadra AV machines with GeoPort modems. The Quadra 840AV and 660AV's DSP chip emulates a 14.4 Kbps modem, but the same chip is also used to digitize the audio -- you can either record sound from the microphone or use the GeoPort modem, but not both at the same time, which means that other people won't be able to hear you even though you can hear them. AplePhone, which is included with the GeoPort software, can do both simultaneously because it includes custom driver software which unfortunately is not available to other applications.

Firewalls. If you're using e-phone in a corporate setting and your Mac is behind a firewall, the firewall will have to be reconfigured for you to call out. E-phone uses UDP ports 3456 and 3457. It embeds the IP address of the sending machine in each packet, so your network administrator must configure your firewall to retransmit packets on these ports to your machine.

e-phone costs $75 per copy or $125 for two copies. The demo is free. If you already have an earlier version of e-phone, simply download the 1.2.3 demo package from www.emagic.com and enter your registration code to unlock it. The demo version limits calls to 90 seconds. If you're using System Software 7.1 or earlier, you'll need Sound Manager 3.x, downloadable from Apple's FTP site.

FreeTel Communications

FreeTel

FreeTel Communications says the Internet is revolutionizing the way people can interact with one another. They also believe Internet telephony can change how business is conducted. If you run a business, FreeTel urges you to include a special Web link in your Web page that enables their users to call you at the click of a mouse. The link is of the form:

A HREF="FreeTel:John Doe"Call John Doe via FreeTel/A

When the user is running both Netscape Navigator and FreeTel, clicking on such a link will place a FreeTel call to "John Doe". Just change "John Doe" to whatever name you desire.

If you include such a link, the company wants you to include a link their home page (www.freetel.com) so users can download the free software. If you are a business, and you expect to receive a large volume of incoming FreeTel calls, the company will sell you a special server for this purpose.

FreeTel has a Business Sponsorship Program. It is a means to develop a unique means of delivering your marketing message to the Internet community. As FreeTel users are speaking with one another, small graphical images, delivered via the Internet, are periodically displayed on their screens. Unlike TV or radio commercials, they neither intrude nor interfere with the use of the product.

Unlike magazine or Web advertising, they do not require action on the part of the user to cause them to appear. This is similar to what NetSpeak does with their WebPhone.

When a user is intrigued by your advertisement, he can mouse-click on it, and be taken to your Web page. He can even call you via FreeTel if you have elected to receive incoming FreeTel calls via the Internet.

GMD Fokus

NEVOT

The Institute for Open Communication Systems FOKUS is an institute of the GMD and is working in research areas described through the Open Application and Intercommunications Model (OAI). FOKUS has about 180 employees and is located in the center of the city of Berlin in Germany. Nevot (Network Voice Terminal) is a free program providing voice communications using unicast, simulated multicast or IP multicast and employing either the vat or RTP protocols. It requires a high-end OS and platform such as SunOS 4.1, Solaris 2, Irix and HP/UX. It's part of the experimental SPOKES conferencing system that lets you create flexible multimedia applications from independent components. It consists of three modules:

Nevot/Nevotd is the audio engine (or audio media agent). It gets audio samples from the workstation and sends them as packets on attached networks. It also receives packets and plays the audio samples on the workstation sound card. Each running instance of Nevot can handle one or more audio conferences. Unlike Nevot, Nevotd has no graphical user interface, but has the same telecom functions. Icc is a manual conference controller that establishes conferences and then displays participants. Each instance of Icc handles one conference. Pmm is the message replicator. If a system doesn't support local multicast, the message replicator is used to distribute messages between the conference controller and the media agents. There is always one running instance of Pmm per host.

IBM

Internet Connection Phone

In February 1996, International Business Machines Corp. entered the Internet multimedia communications business. Their Internet telephony software is called the Internet Connection Phone.

IBM's software was demonstrated at Germany's CeBit conference and Los Angeles' Computer Telephony Expo '96 in March 1996. IBM's plan to for the technology is to bundle it with modems and distribute it through ISPs.

The technology is based on Simultaneous Video and Data (SVD) capabilities. SVD technology enables a computer user to combine a voice conversation and data transmission at the same time. The phone would use the GSM transmission standard. The product is bundled as part of OS2/Warp. Additional distribution is planned via the Internet and several other product platforms.

IBM is also pursuing IT standards through a consortium approach. The goal is to reach consensus on telephony application interfaces and other network characteristics in order to enable ubiquity and interoperability across platforms. IBM Global Network was quick to point out their support of industry standards such as H.323 and the efforts of Intel to build standards-based Internet products. Implementation of H.323 standards will enable the Intel Internet Phone, IBM's Internet Connection Phone, Microsoft's Net-Meeting and similar products to interoperate.

Other incarnations of voice transfer technology have problems with echoes and lost packets that lead to transmissions with lots of break up. IBM modified the GSM compression/decompression (codec) algorithm (the European cellular telephony standard) in such a way as to suppress echoes and to better control the loss of packets. The new algorithm compresses 8-Khz 16 bit voice samples to 9400 bits per second (bps) leading to clear, near echoless conversations. IBM researchers continue to integrate other standard codecs such as G.723 and wide-band coders into the improved framework as they become available. The goal is to support a full H.323 network videoconferencing standard. Internet Connection Phone takes full advantage of IBM's MWave technology -- the technology that more efficiently processes multimedia and audio data -- whenever it can. A computer that has an MWave installed can offload the Internet Connection Phone's compute intensive compression and decompression. This way the computer can do other tasks more effectively while Internet Connection Phone is working.

Internet Connection Phone requirements are a 486 /DX66 or Pentium PC, minimum 33 MHZ, 8MG RAM (recommended) and MWave digital signal processor. The DSPs are built into IBM's multimedia PC's and Thinkpads, and available for other PC's as an add-in card. You also need a microphone and speaker (or headphones) connected to the MWave.

Intel

Intel Internet Phone

The H.323 compliant Internet Phone is an applet for PCs running Win 95. It's designed to work with other upcoming standards-based communications software from Microsoft and others. It was announced on July 24, 1996 amidst much fanfare. The company calls it "the world's first standards-based audio-web phone." Storm EasyPhoto Net is an Internet Phone companion application. You can exchange photos, play interactive games while speaking to other players and do data conferencing with it. They made a beta version of the applet available free of charge at their Web site: www.in-tel.wm/iaweb/cpc.

Internet Phone manifests the March 1995 Microsoft technology exchange agreement with Intel. The companies intend is to make H.323 and T.120 standards-based communication on the Internet commonplace. These steps, combined with the Internet Phone announcement, show that Intel is serious about their Internet and seamless communication model they call the "Connected PC." Future versions of Microsoft NetMeeting will support H.323 for universal interoperability with products from Intel and other vendors. In fact, Microsoft is swapping Intel their respective implementations of T.12 and H.323.

Figure 11.6 is a blow-up of the Internet Phone user interface. It's pretty sleek and has many controls. During set up, you can define what directory service you wish to use. This lets you quickly find other registered users anywhere. It even has a "speed dial" button and remembers up to twenty previously dialed numbers.

Figure 11.6 – Intel Internet Phone User Interface

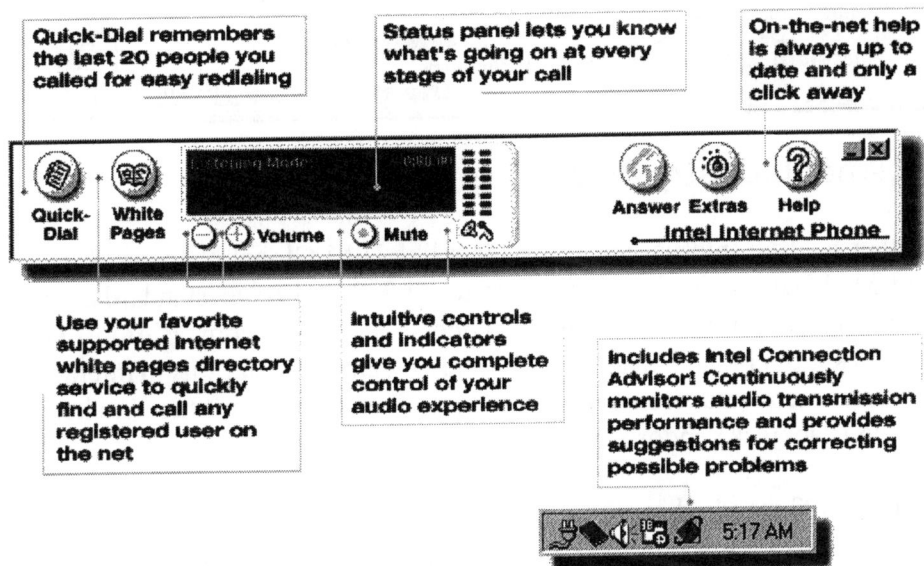

Quick-Dial remembers the last 20 people you called for easy redialing

Status panel lets you know what's going on at every stage of your call

On-the-net help is always up to date and only a click away

Quick-Dial | White Pages | Volume | Mute | Answer | Extras | Help
Intel Internet Phone

Use your favorite supported Internet white pages directory service to quickly find and call any registered user on the net

Intuitive controls and indicators give you complete control of your audio experience

Includes Intel Connection Advisor! Continuously monitors audio transmission performance and provides suggestions for correcting possible problems

5:17 AM

Intel Connection Advisor

This application; a smart utility that monitors your PC's connection to the Internet, alerts you to possible problems, and provides tips for corrective action. Figure 11.7 shows how the applet gives you processor overhead, quality settings and audio activity levels. You can adjust the levels, which in turn can reduce the amount of power the phone is using. This is useful if you establish several communications streams and wish to allocate more juice to one session.

Figure 11.7 -- The Intel Connection Advisor

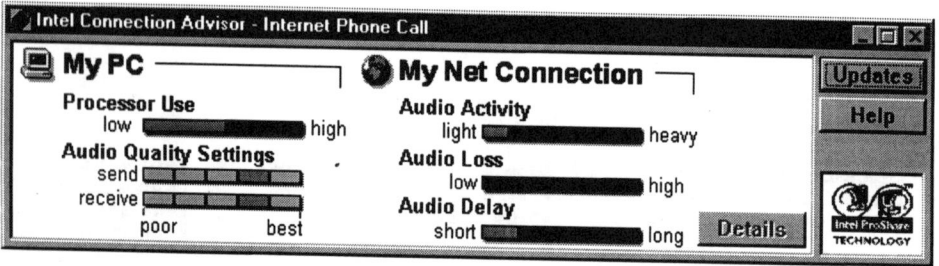

Internet Industry Standards Support

Other leading Internet market-makers like IBM Global Network, Lucent, and MCI have voiced their support for H.323 and other standards, along with Internet Directory Service providers Coordinate.com, Bigfoot, DoubleClick, Four11, and WhoWhere?. Internet game vendors Virgin Interactive Entertainment (makers of Subspace) and Sierra On-Line, Inc. (makers of Hoyle Blackjack) endorse support for H.323 standard.

The H.323 standard came out of an effort from the International Telecommunications Union (ITU). H.323 gives Intel's Internet Phone better audio quality than proprietary Internet phone solutions. It uses the G.723 audio codec ,which offers excellent audio quality. I used the pre-launch version and was impressed with it. You'll need a 90 Mhz Pentium processor-based system or higher and a full duplex sound card. A microphone for voice input , 5 MB free disk space and 16 MB RAM. Internet Phone uses the Windows 95 operating system, Microsoft Internet Explorer 2.0 or higher or Netscape Navigator 2.0 or higher.

Internet Directory Service
...Provider Support

Jeff Pulver, chairman of the VON Coalition says he's excited that the companies are using standards to solve two fundamental problems:

1. how to find people on the Internet, and

2. how to get connected with them using standards-based communications technology.

The Internet Phone has a clean-looking user interface. It snaps into the bottom edge of the your web browser. This is illustrated in Figure 11.8. Here, you can see how the applet uses Microsoft's User Location Service (ULS) technology to locate other Internet phone users through existing Internet Directory Services.

Figure 11.8 – Automatic Domain Search

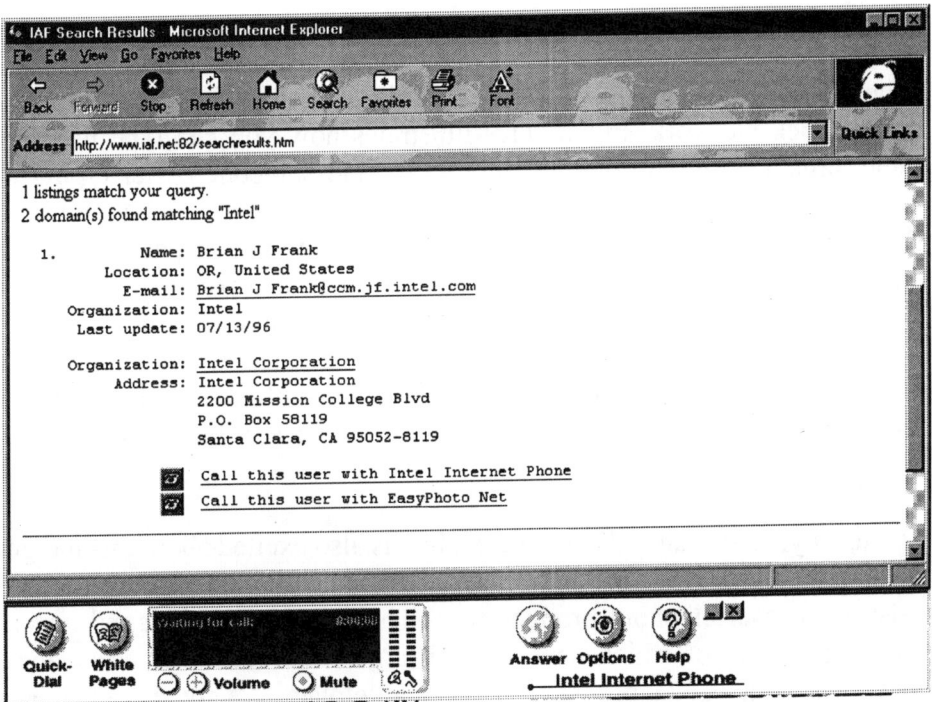

These directory services provide an easy way to find other Internet phone users. Once connected via an Internet phone on a multimedia PC, users can talk to each other over the Internet while using other Internet applications.

Intel's Web phone is also the first to work with white page directory services such as Bigfoot, Four11, Internet Address Finder, Switchboard, and WhoWhere?. Registering with white pages directories makes it easy for people to find and call you. Look up a name, click on the Intel Internet Phone hyperlink, and the phone rings.

Bigfoot Directory, Inc. offers a global e-mail directory service to Intel's Internet Phone subscribers by providing international access to Intel Internet Phone numbers. You can also protect your privacy by maintaining an unlisted Intel Internet Phone number. This gives you control over who reaches you. Coordinate.com, the Internet Division of Banyon Systems offers *Switchboard*. Coordinate says it enables people to quickly find and rendezvous with family and friends, via postal mail, e- mail or telephone. Intel's Internet Phone lets these reunions happen instantly via the Internet.

The *Internet Address Finder* site, is part of the DoubleClick Corporation's DoubleClick Network. Figure 11.9 illustrates how you can type in a last name, organization and domain address to find someone. After typing in the data, the program coordinates with Internet Phone to make a real time phone call. This assumes a match occurs and the called party has their Internet Phone turned on. Four11 Corporation is also part of the Internet Phone launch team. Their president, Michael Santullo, said the H.323 standard complements Four11's goal of making Internet communications technologies universal and accessible to people of all skill and experience levels. Judging from how easy it is to use his service, it looks like they are reaching that goal quickly.

Ashu Roy, chairman of WhoWhere?, Inc. is also excited about this merger of directory and real-time phone services on the Internet. This because existing Internet telephony products rely on proprietary protocols and custom directories, both of which have limited large-scale consumer acceptance. Roy says with H.323 products in the marketplace, "a much richer user experience is possible." There will be others. This is the beginning of an absolute revolution in communications.

Figure 11.9 -- Internet Address Finder

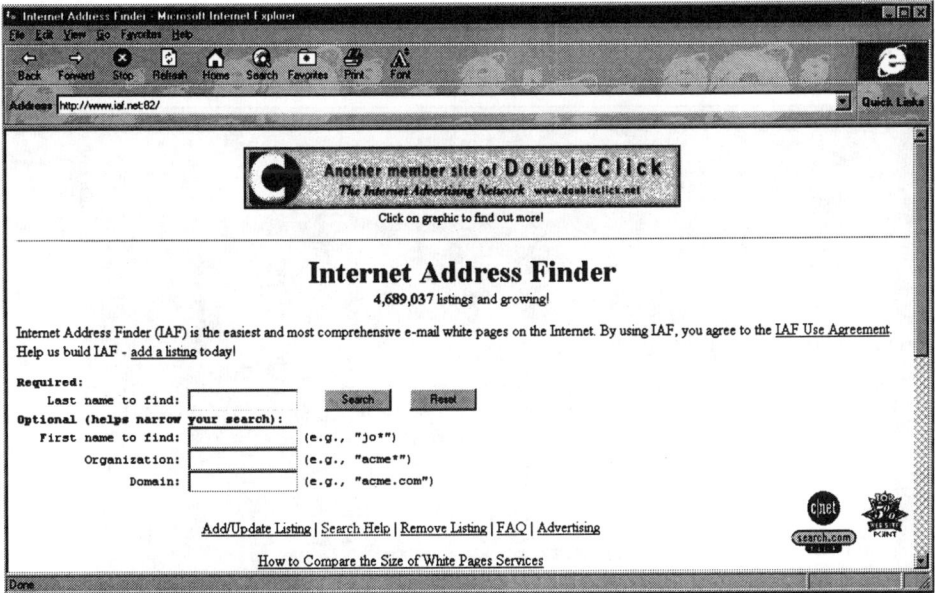

Internet Game Vendor Support

Intel's Internet voice technology is an excellent enhancement to multiplayer games, such as *Hoyle Blackjack* from Sierra On-Line. It also works with other interactive games like *Subspace* from Virgin Interactive Entertainment. Both games provide a real-time, graphical view of multiparty game participation. The Holyle Blackjack game, for instance lets you join gaming rooms to partner with your fellow players. By using the Intel Internet Phone, you can speak with one of the other participants while you play. Ditto for Subspace. In this game, you guide a spaceship through a maze and do battle with dozens of other players. The Subspace server sends data streams out to all the players which in turn are used by your Subspace client application to re-map your screen. The display is very hi-res and the action is absolutely real-time. You can shout: "Hey look out behind you" to a fellow player in this game.

Figure 11.10 shows how Tim Dowling of Intel set up his partners to play Hoyle Blackjack. You can see how the Internet Phone applet is running in the background.

Figure 11.10 – Internet Phone and Interactive Games

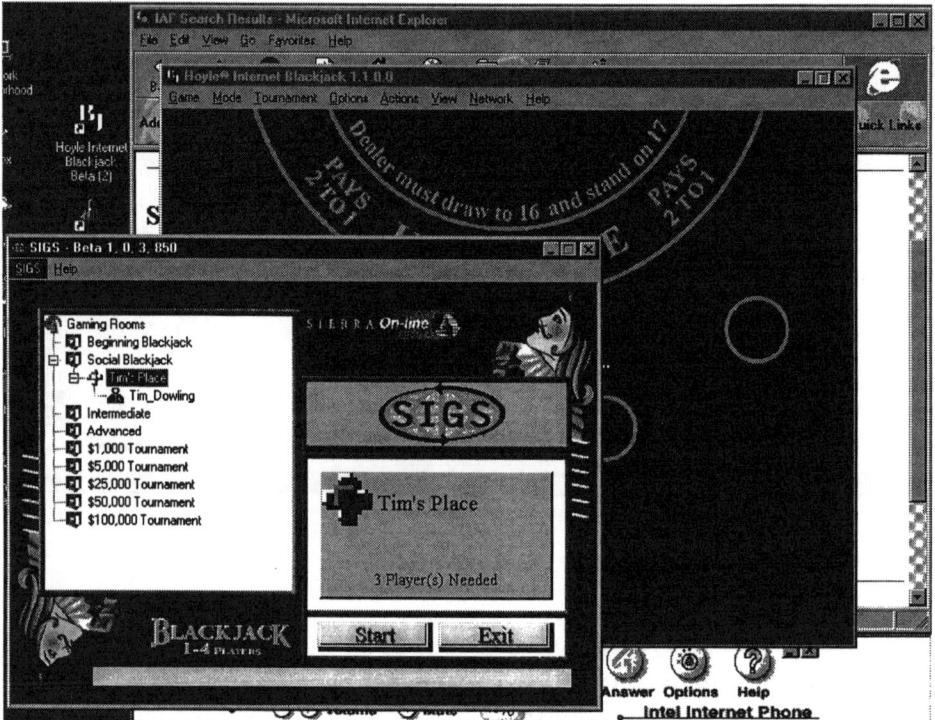

IPC Peripherals

CyberChat Card

CyberChat from IPC Peripherals is a 16-bit full-duplex stereo sound card for Internet telephony. The package includes a headset with built-in speaker and microphone and software and a registration code to allow for the installation of VocalTec's Internet Phone software.

The hardware / software combination digitizes your voice signals into data packets and then sends them across the Internet so you can have a long distance phone conversation for the price of a local call.

Interestingly, since CyberChat doesn't have a modem on board, it costs less than competing products -- it's $129.95. This also allows CyberChat to be shipped internationally without have to undergo country-by-country approval for modem use. CyberChat is compatible with most PC-compatible 14.4 or 28.8K fax / modems.

To use the CyberChat card, you'll need at least a 25MHz 486SX, 8MB RAM, Windows 3.1, an Internet Winsock 1.1 compatible TCP/IP stack, a 14.4 Kbps or 28.8 Kbps connection to an Internet Service Provider that allows a SLIP or PPP account, and a 14.4 Kbps or 28.8 Kbps fax / modem (28.8Kbps recommended for full duplex). CyberChat includes drivers for Windows 3.1, Windows 95 and supports such audio standards as Sound Blaster, Adlib and Windows Sound System.

Marin Software Partners

John Walker's

Speak Freely

Speak Freely is a network phone application for Windows and UNIX written in Switzerland by John Walker, the founder of Autodesk. It's free and considered by many to be one of the best apps of its kind.

Speak Freely is a program for 80x86 Windows machines and a variety of Unix workstations. It lets you talk to other people across a local network or the Internet. Optional party-line support and data compression are available, using the algorithm employed by GSM digital cellular telephones to reduce bandwidth requirements to 1700 characters per second. Sound packets can be encrypted with IDEA, DES, a binary key supplied in a file, or any combination.

Speak Freely cooperates with a copy of PGP installed on your computer to automatically exchange session keys with users on your public keyring. Windows and Unix machines can intercommunicate, and Speak Freely can communicate with other Internet voice programs which support RTP or VAT protocol. The program includes voice mail, multicasting conference support for those few existing Winsock implementations which support it (Windows 95's built-in Winsock does), full or half duplex modes and encryption.

You'll need Windows 3.1 or above running in 386 Enhanced Mode, a sound input/output card loaded with the Windows Multimedia driver, a microphone and speaker(s). It's compatible with a network interface having a TCP/IP Winsock driver.

Speak Freely usually has excellent sound quality, but it needs a high-end 486 or Pentium processor. Using a 14.4 Kbps or slower modem with GSM and a slow computer will degrade sound quality. Walker believes that although high speed modems are available and affordable, serial port hardware and software drivers in most Windows machines simply cannot operate at the speeds required. Code to support modem connections is included in Speak Freely, but unless you have special serial port hardware (such as fast UART 16550A chips with 16 byte FIFO buffers) and Windows drivers that take advantage of it, dealing with modem connections may become frustrating.

If your connection isn't fast enough to support real-time voice data, three different forms of compression (Simple, GSM and ADPCM) may allow you to converse anyway, assuming your computer is fast enough to handle the compression algorithms in real-time. You can select an appropriate compression mode and evaluate both your computer and network's performance by clicking on the "Loop-back" option, which forces the computer at the other end of the connection to immediately retransmit every packet of sound it receives back to your computer. If it sounds bad, try a different compression algorithm. In order to use loop-back, your audio input/output hardware needs to be full-duplex.

For secure communications, Speak Freely provides three different kinds of encryption: the Data Encryption Standard (DES), the same highly-secure patented International Data Encryption Algorithm (IDEA) that PGP uses to encrypt message bodies and/or a key file.

The current version (Release 5.3) of Speak Freely isn't compatible with other software except for Speak Freely for Unix, which currently works with Sun and Silicon Graphics workstations. Version 6.0 will be compatible with the VAT / RTP standard for establishing calls and will include DVI4 and L16 compression as well as a user directory accessible from both within the application and on the Web.

To give Speak Freely a try, download the speakfb.zip executable program archive (for Windows): www.fourmilab.ch/netfone/windows/speakfb.zip; for Unix: www.fourmilab.ch/netfone/unix/speak_freely-5.3.tar.gz

Complete source code is available in the archive's speakfs.zip file. Programming wizards who want to hack the source code will need Visual C / C++ 1.52 (no C++ features are used) to compile. Speak Freely is still under development. If you try this software and something goes wrong, please e-mail John Walker a report at kelvin@fourmilab.ch

Massachusetts Institute of Technology

Philip Zimmermann's

PGPfone

The Pretty Good Privacy Phone (PGPfone) is a free program from Philip Zimmermann that turns your desktop or notebook computer into a secure telephone. It uses speech compression and strong cryptography protocols to give you real-time secure telephone conversation (full duplex only) via a modem-to-modem connection.

It is currently only available in beta form for Macs (MIT has been distributing PGPfone version 1.0b4 since August 25, 1995), but a Windows 95/NT version will be out soon.

To run PGPfone you'll need a reliable fast modem -- at least 14.4 Kbps V.32bis (28.8 Kbps V.34 recommended) and a Mac with at least a 25MHz 68LC040 processor (PowerPC recommended), running System 7.1 or above, Thread Manager 2.0.1 and Sound Manager 3.0. These are available from Apple's FTP sites.

When the PC version is finally released, you'll need a multimedia PC running Windows 95 or NT, with at least a 66 MHz 486 CPU (Pentium recommended), sound card, microphone and speakers or headphones.

To install PGPfone on the Mac, just unpack it from its self-extracting archive, which creates a folder caller PGPfone. In this folder you'll find the PGPfone executable program, the PGPfone Owner's Manual and a small README file. Running PGPfone for the first time will create a "PGPfone Preferences" file and "PGPfone Keycache" file, which PGPfone places in the Preferences folder in the System Folder.

PGPfone has some user preferences that can be set in some dialog boxes within PGPfone. To get started quickly, use as many default settings as possible. PGPfone's creator Philip Zimmermann is the same fellow who brought us the "pretty good" PGP encryption scheme. In fact, after he first developed and released PGP for free in 1991, Zimmermann came come under criminal investigation by US Customs for PGP's spread overseas, with risk of criminal prosecution and other unpleasantness. Fortunately, that the government seems to have relented in its efforts to send Zimmermann to crypto limbo.

PGPfone version 1.0 uses the Diffie-Hellman algorithm for key exchange, biometric signatures (your voice) to authenticate the key exchange, triple-DES or Blowfish for encrypting the voice stream, and GSM for speech compression -- none of which we find particularly interesting, though the US government obviously thinks otherwise.

Anonymous FTP users should get the file /pub/PGPfone/README from net-dist.mit.edu which contains instructions on how to download PGPfone. Web users can get PGPfone itself from web.mit.edu/network/pgpfone/.

It's recommended that you leave PGPfone's encryption algorithm set to "Blowfish," which is much faster than the triple Data Encryption Standard (DES) algorithm and just as strong, perhaps stronger. Triple DES is so slow that only PowerPCs can handle it. You should also set your preferred Diffie-Hellman prime to 1024 bits.

Microsoft

NetMeeting

NetMeeting 1.0 enables real-time voice and data communications over the Internet. This includes the ability for two or more people to share applications, transfer files, view and illustrate a shared whiteboard, and chat— all over standard connections. For example, on an intranet, you can have a voice connection over the office phone system and a data connection over the LAN.

Data conferencing features of Microsoft NetMeeting work with a 14,400 bps or better modem connection, IPX networks, and TCP/IP networks such as corporate LANs and the Internet. Real-time voice is designed for TCP/IP networks only.

It's 100% software. Download it for free. Go to www.microsoft.com and click on the "NetMeeting" banner (or www.microsoft.com/ie/conf).

NetMeeting adheres to major international standards from both the International Telecommunications Union (ITU) and the Internet Engineering Taskforce (IETF). Get details and a list of conferencing products and services compatible with NetMeeting from a recent press release.

User Location Service provides a way to find other people to communicate with on the Internet. You can even find out who is currently logged in. We logged on to the Internet and used the NetMeeting server to get a directory of who was "on line." You get "on line" by logging into the Internet with NetMeeting. Your ID is automatically dropped into the directory. While you're on line, you're available to "speak" to anyone else who logs on.

Which means you can call your nearest and dearest to log on *now.* Or send them a fax or email telling them when to log on. Or simply schedule a time when everyone will be on line. The possibilities on your own Intranet are great. With your own highspeed (more predictable) system (say one using T1 lines), you can have a voice connection over the office phone system and a data connection / multipoint data conferencing over the LAN. Application Sharing lets you share a program running on one computer with other people in a conference.

Because Microsoft NetMeeting handles this feature transparently, it works with existing Windowsbased programs. You can share a Microsoft Word document with three coworkers. Each person now sees an image of your program on his or her computer. You can review the document together and each can take turns editing. Your colleagues do not need a copy of the program or the file. But they do need a copy of NetMeeting, which presently only runs under Win95 (but soon will under NT and on Macintoshes, according to Microsoft).

Sharing Apps On Line is illustrated in Figure 11.11. NetMeeting lets you scroll for open apps and pick one to share with your partner. You can switch app control between partners. We tried PowerPoint. A little slow (28.8 connections) but it works. Here I logged on to the Internet using Internet Explorer 3.0 via the Microsoft Network. I launched NetMeeting after logging-in. Freddie used a PPP connection from Terra-Link Corp. (New York, NY -- 212-929-6500) and launched NetMeeting with Win 95's built-in TCP/IP stack (no browser). NetMeeting automatically finds the conference server. You pick from a windowed list of conferees to call. If you're called, the "phone" rings on your PC. You just click on the pop-up "accept" button to answer.

Figure 11.11 -- NetMeeting Application Sharing

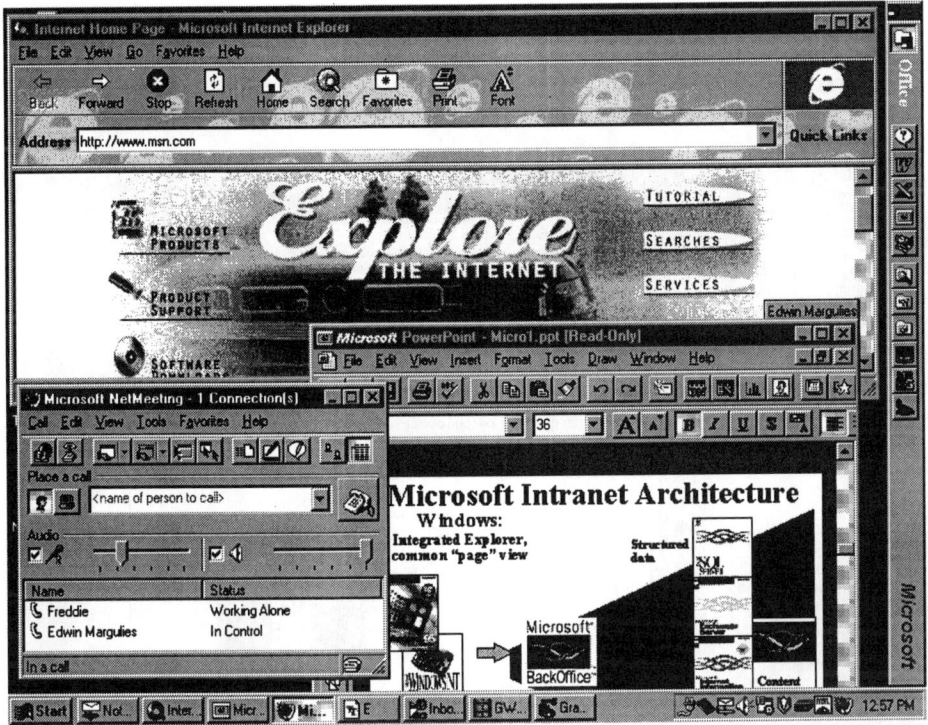

Real-time Voice enables you to talk to another person over the Internet and can be used in conjunction with the other data and conferencing features.

Whiteboard is a multi-page, multi-user drawing program you can use to sketch an organization chart, draw a diagram, type action items, and perform similar tasks. You can point out your co-workers' errors by using a remote pointer or highlighting tool, or take a "snapshot" of a window and then paste the graphic on a page as shown in Figure 11.12. You can share your ideas on the fly with other NetMeeting conferees. You can even ID yourself as a "host" for a multi-party conference. Here, the whiteboard is a scratch pad for a drawing I made on line for Freddie. You can use the menu bar to create text and graphics.

Paste stuff from your clipboard, too. All this while you're speaking with the other party. Anyone in the conference can jump-in and join the fun. It's a communal on line etch-a-sketch. If you prefer to do your drawing off-line, you can send a file instead.

Figure 11.12 -- Whiteboarding with NetMeeting.

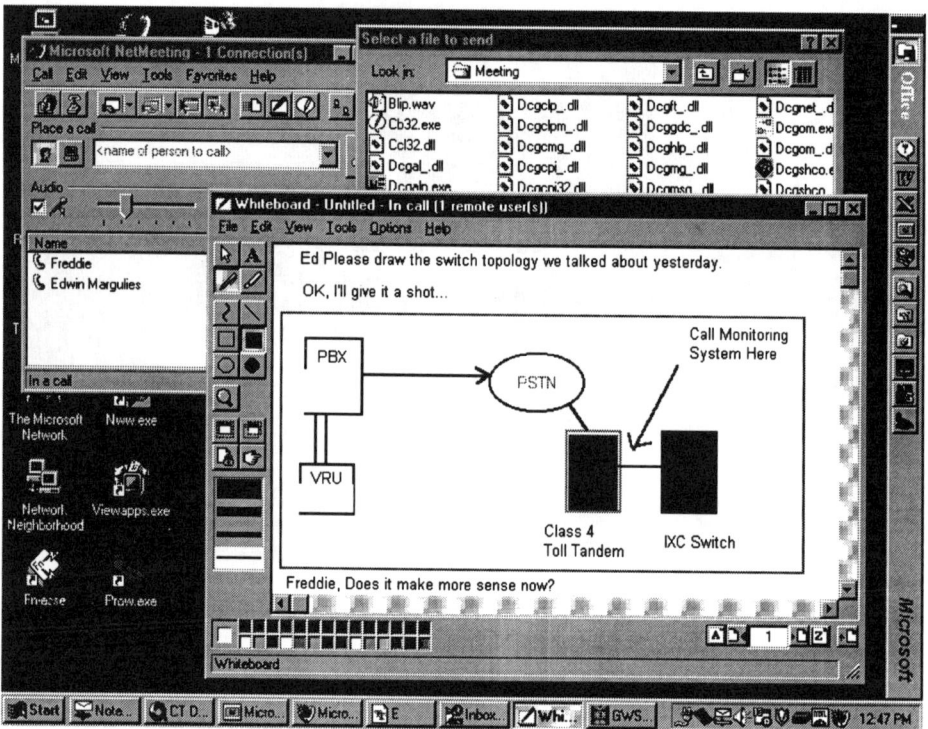

File Transfer enables you to send a file to all the participants in a conference by dragging it into the Microsoft NetMeeting window. The file transfer occurs in the background as everyone continues sharing programs, using the whiteboard, and chatting.

Chat lets you record meeting minutes and action items or carry on a conversation with fellow conference participants. Figure 11.13 shows how Freddie and I were talking, while typing stuff in a chat box (background) and sharing a spreadsheet all at once.

For full duplex conversation (both of you speaking at the same time) you need full duplex sound hardware and a 28.8 connection. But even with full duplex, the tell-tale "Citizens Band" feel is still there with a 500ms or better delay. Full Duplex is kind of moot when there's a delay. You can use NetMeeting for "better than CB" communications. It's useful still to speak over your spreadsheet numbers and change them on line. For more confidential stuff, you can use the chat box instead of speaking. Handy.

Figure 11.13 -- NetMeeting's Chat Feature

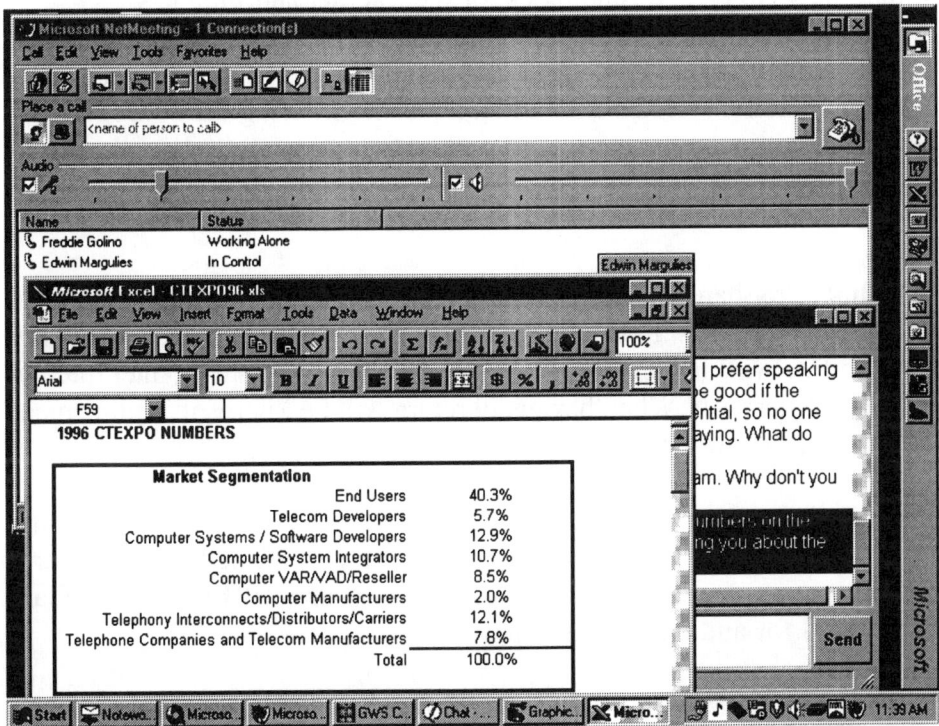

We asked Microsoft's Charles Fitzgerald what he liked about NetMeeting. His comments: It's fun. (That it is.) Ease of use. (True.) Multi-person application sharing (flawlessly). White board (works well). File transfer (yes). Chat (online email, works fine). Multipoint data conferencing (yes). His most important points were that it's "standards based."

With standards come what the industry calls interoperability (connect to other packages and equipment) and extensibility (it becomes a platform on which you and I can build on and add things to). At the NetMeeting announcement, Microsoft had 20+ companies announce products and services that are interoperable with NetMeeting.

These included bridges (VideoServer, Accord), conferencing services (MCI), interactive white boards (Liveworks) and videoconferencing (Intel, PictureTel and Creative Labs). Then, in a joint statement with Intel Corp., Microsoft announced a set of communications standards under the umbrella of their new ActiveX technologies for the Internet and Intranets.

The communications implementation includes International Telecommunications Union (ITU) standards and Internet Engineering Task Force (IETF) specifications, including the T.120 standard for data conferencing, the H.323 standard for audio and video conferencing, and the RTP/RTCP and RSVP specifications.

The Intel ProShare PCbased conferencing Platform will also integrate the ActiveX components. Recently, Microsoft and Intel agreed to a technology transfer. Intel will transfer its H.323 implementation (from its Intel Internet Phone) to Microsoft. What they get in return will be Microsoft's implementation of T.120 (inside NetMeeting).

Microsoft is really pushing its ITU standards-based ActiveX Conferencing. It uses T.120 for data conferencing. T.120 is a part of the H.323 standard, and in future implementations, ActiveX Conferencing will be fully compliant with H.323 for audio and video as well.

Microsoft will target the Windows 95 and Windows NT platforms first. Microsoft will then work to ensure that conferencing will be supported on the Macintosh, OS/2, and UNIX. Because ActiveX conferencing is based on standards, it can also interoperate with products that adhere to the standards.

Netscape/InSoft, Inc.

CoolTalk for the Internet

Netscape offers a full line of open software to enable electronic commerce and secure information exchange on the Internet and private TCP/IP-based networks. All Netscape products are compatible with other HTTP-based clients and servers.

Netscape's clients, servers, Commercial Applications, and tools combine to form the Netscape Applications Platform, a processor- and operating system-independent foundation for developing and deploying live online applications. These apps are targeted for the enterprise and across the Internet. These live online applications incorporate text, images, multimedia content, application logic, and scripting capabilities into distributed programs.

Netscape acquired InSoft Inc., a maker of TCP/IP based audio and video conferencing technology. In addition, it has a licensing arrangement with VoxWare Inc. VoxWare has a proprietary speech compression technology for the Internet. These acquisitions fuel Netscape's LiveMedia architecture. They plan to deliver real-time, streaming audio and video files to Netscape's client and server product line. The company is targeting two-way audio and video communications from within the browser.

Netscape stated that the InSoft product line would be integrated into its existing software architecture (CoolTalk for the Internet was announced in January, 1996). InSoft's core expertise is in high-speed local area network (LAN) solutions, so they know a lot about traffic. CoolTalk came out of their efforts to build a platform for IP-based audio and video using low bit-rate technology. Netscape Navigator allows you to access every type of file on the Internet. When the browser encounters a sound, image, or video file, it hands off the data to other programs, called helper applications, to run or display the file.

Most of these helper apps are shareware or freeware that can be found at various archive sites around the world; you can configure them in the Helper Applications dialog box found under Preferences in the Options menu. CoolTalk runs in this environment.

CoolTalk provides realtime, fullduplex audio conferencing and data collaboration capabilities. The data collaboration supports a chat tool for text conferencing and a "whiteboard" for graphical conferencing. Whiteboarding can be used simultaneously with audio conferencing. The CoolTalk user interface is elegantly simple. You get a small window as depicted in Figure 11.14. You can raise and lower the volume controls easily, and the display for the mic and speaker look like "electronic LEDs." $49.95 through InSoft direct.

Figure 11.14 – CoolTalk User Interface

Netscape's LiveMedia standards are based on the Internet Realtime Transport Protocol (RTP), RFC number 1889, and other open audio/video standards such as MPEG, H.261, and GSM. Netscape plans to publish the LiveMedia standards on the Internet and to license key components. Netscape will offer real-time APIs that will talk to its browser and servers. In addition, LiveMedia will be built in modular fashion that lets other vendors plug-in different pieces, such as better quality codecs.

NetSpeak

WebPhone

WebPhone by NetSpeak (nee ITEL)is a Windows program providing real-time full duplex conversations over the Internet or any TCP/IP based network. WebPhone uses patent-pending calling mechanisms which allow users to establish point-to-point connections using only a party's e-mail address. It supports Caller ID, can handle four lines for multiple conversations, employs GSM compression and the DSP Group's TrueSpeech audio codecs. It has a voice mail system which allows voice mail to be delivered to off-line parties.

The package also has conversation muting, call holding, a calling directory, integrated directory assistance, and the best-looking multimedia help system we've ever seen.

Perhaps the most striking aspect of WebPhone is its aesthetic graphical user interface. WebPhone actually looks and "feels" like a phone. Its animated, flip-down audio control pad, spot-lighted neon LED indicators and three-dimensional controls make it look more like an exercise in industrial design than simply a piece of telecom software. To run WebPhone, you'll need a 33MHz 486 running Windows 3.1 or higher, 4MB or more of RAM, and MCI compliant sound card (duplex preferred), Winsock 1.1 or higher compliant sockets library, a 14.4 Kbps or faster modem, a VGA card capable of displaying 256 or more colors and 5 MB or more of hard disk space.

WebPhone will be available on the Web for an introductory price of $49.95.
You can get the beta software on: www.netspeak.com.

Figure 11.15 -- NetSpeak WebPhone Client Interface

NetSpeak's WebPhone has a main screen that looks like a cellular phone
as pictured in Figure 11.15. You can use the number keypad either as
speed-dial buttons or to manually input numeric IP addresses. At right are
the four Line buttons, one for each line. The LED color on each button
indicates that line's call status. You can toggle a Line button to answer an
incoming call or take a call off hold. Point the cursor to and click the right
mouse button on a Line button to display the information about the party
on that line.

You may playback voice mail or WAV files to a party on a line by dragging a v-mail message from the v-mail messages dialog box or dragging a .WAV file from the File Manager or Windows Explorer and dropping it onto the Line button. See the Internet Gateway and Platforms Products roundup for an explanation of how WebPhone is part of an advanced virtual circuit switching model for a global business system.

Quarterdeck

WebTalk

Quarterdeck Corporation develops software products in four strategic business areas: Utilities, Internet Solutions, Internet Services, and Communications. The company also offers an entire line of Internet tools for corporate, small business and individual users This includes WebCompass and Web-Talk, the later being Quarterdeck's first communications product. WebTalk is an impressive Internet phone package. The program comes on a CD-ROM and there's a free LabTec mic bundled with the well-written documentation.

WebTalk works over an ordinary, analog phone line. The only things you will need besides a 50MHz 486DX PC and Windows 3.X or Windows 95 are a 14.4 Kbps or higher modem, a 16-bit full duplex or half duplex sound card and speakers (or a headset). Multimedia PCs should already have everything you need to get you going.

One nicety is the map with a line connecting the two geographical locations of the callers as shown in Figure 11.16. WebTalk supports full-duplex transmission but also works with half-duplex sound cards, using its internal VOX technology to emulate full-duplex quality. The WebTalk Server Network, a critical WebTalk component, provides a directory of other on-line callers and lists Virtual Meeting Places where users can locate callers with common interests. The WebTalk Server Network is designed to create a community of WebTalk users with members located across the globe.

Figure 11.16 -- Quarterdeck WebTalk

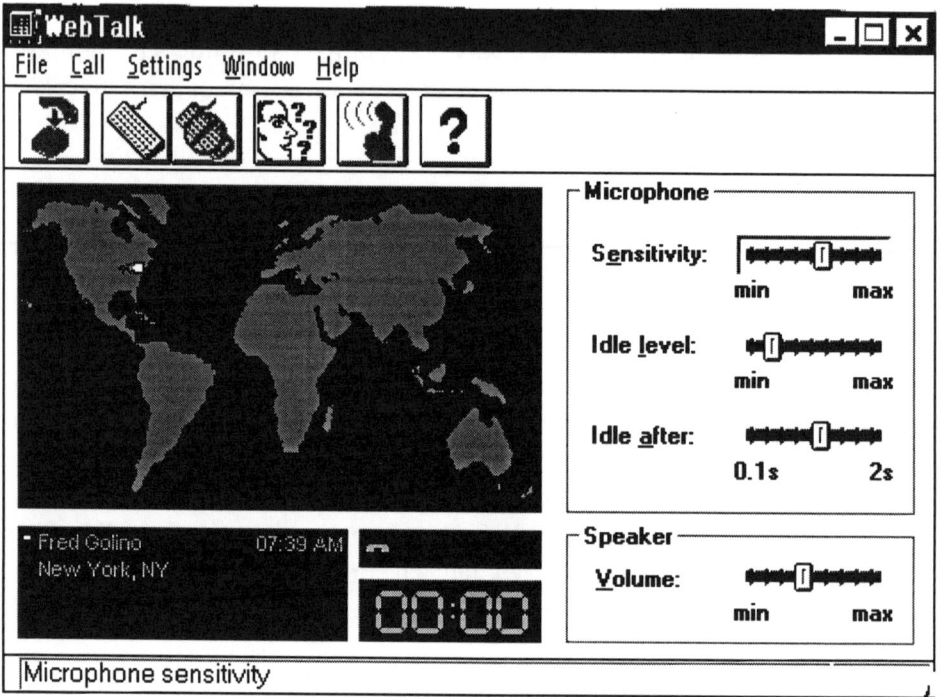

The Connect and Play Location Manager gives you the option to sign-up with your choice of the leading Internet providers (NetCom, Cerfnet, Portal, PSINet, UUNET, etc.) if you don't have one yet. Quarterdeck WebTalk includes a free bonus license for a friend, so you can be up and talking as soon as possible.

As a nice extra touch, every Quarterdeck WebTalk license includes Quarterdeck's version of the Mosaic Web browser, so while you are talking on WebTalk, you can still browse the Net. Quarterdeck now bundles JABRA Corp's new JABRA PC earpiece/microphone combination with WebTalk. The combination of these products provides you with a comfortable, quality audio Internet solution. You can download a free trialware version at www.quarterdeck.com.

Silver Soft

SoftFone

SoftFone 2.2 is described by its makers as "a software phone for the Internet." You can download an evaluation copy (279,589 bytes) of SoftFone on www.pak.net/softfone.htm . With a full duplex sound card, you can talk while you are listening, but it's still not as good as a real telephone conversation. As shown in Figure 11.17, the user interface looks like a cassette deck. All the controls you need for most operations are built-in to the app. List price: $50. It still needs some further development to enhance its sound quality, however, Silver Soft has created some useful features:

Figure 11.17 -- Silver Soft's SoftFone

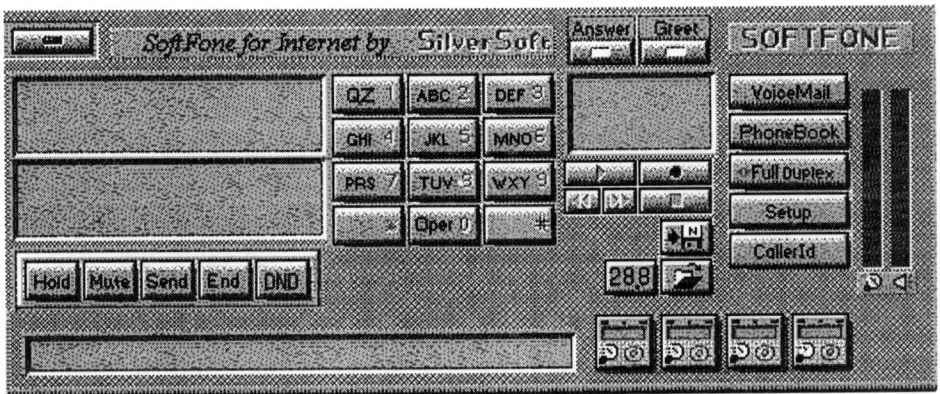

Built-in Answering machine. You can cue SoftFone as a voice messaging system. If you are not on line or don't wish to take calls, the software will store incoming conversations.

Voice Activation. A built-in vox software circuit idles the line if your aren't speaking.

Mute and hold for Privacy. You can put calls on hold or mute them so the other party can't hear you.

Telescape Communications

TS Intercom

TS Intercom is the first of a family of Internet telephony products from Telescape Communications. Telescape recently announced a licensing agreement with DSP Group of Santa Clara, California to license DSP Group's TrueSpeech compression technology for their Internet telephony products. TrueSpeech is an integral component of Microsoft's Windows 95 and Windows NT operating systems and will enable TS Intercom to be fully inter-operable with applications built upon these platforms. TrueSpeech has been adopted for use by several major companies including Microsoft, Intel, Creative Labs, US Robotics, Sony, Sharp, Panasonic and Siemens.

With TS Intercom you can show and view graphics files of yourself or anything else while talking to someone online. You can send each other any computer file such as a spreadsheet document, digital pictures, programs or what-not, while talking to someone on-line. A connection speed of 28.8 Kbps is recommended for simultaneous data and voice exchange.

Instead of fumbling with IRC chat channels, TS Intercom uses your Internet e-mail address: Normally, every Internet TCP/IP connection has a unique phone-number-like identifier called an IP address (such as 123.456.789.0). If everyone who wanted to use TS Intercom had permanent Internet connections with permanent IP addresses, they could simply enter each other's IP addresses, connect and start talking. This can be done and it's a way of using TS Intercom over TCP/IP LANs and WANs for an enterprise-wide teleconferencing solution. Unfortunately, most IP addresses are not permanent: Many people connect to the Internet by dialing into an Internet Service Provider who sells Internet accounts -- a new IP address is assigned to you every time you dial in, so your exact Internet location becomes a moving target, depending on which line or port you happen to connect to.

TS Intercom instead relies on e-mail addresses (which don't change very often) to connect two parties. When TS Intercom is started (this should be done after connecting to the Internet), it automatically registers your current e-mail address, TS Intercom's status (whether it's In Use, Ready or Not Connected) and your current IP address with Telescape's Global Operator.

Like a real live operator, the Global Operator tracks all this information, using it to connect two parties together by sending each person the current IP address of the other one. This ensures the best possible connection since the packets of voice information are transported directly between the two IP addresses, not through an intermediate destination. There's a phone book included to help you keep track of other TS Intercom enthusiasts.

Figure 11.18 -- TS Intercom Configuration

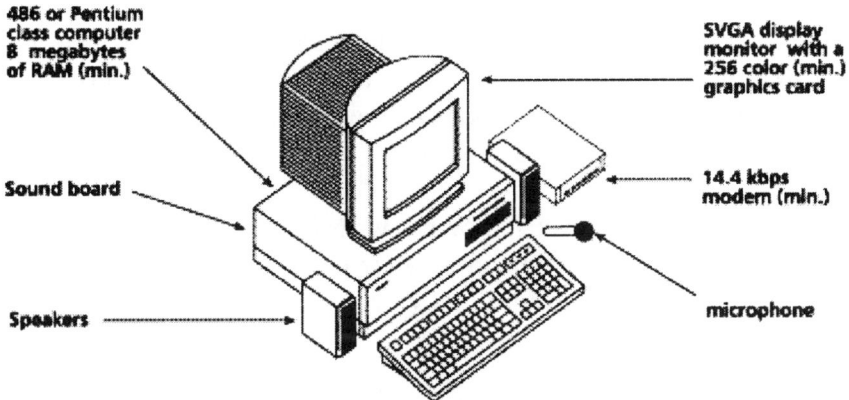

TS Intercom needs a 33 MHz 486-based personal computer with 4 MB RAM (Pentium 75 MHz system or better with 8 MB RAM recommended), Windows 3.1, Windows for Workgroups 3.11, Windows 95 or Windows NT 3.5x (NT version coming soon), 8-bit color VGA display (640 x 480 with 256 colors), an MPC II compliant audio card (SoundBlaster or compatible), and a v.32bis 14.4 Kbps modem (v.34 bis 28.8 Kbps modem recommended), microphone and speakers for your audio card.

You can do dial-up or direct connect Internet access with Trumpet or Microsoft Winsock. TS Intercom also supports Ethernet, ATM, FDDI, frame relay, ISDN or SDMS networks running the TCP/IP protocol for LAN support.

You can download TS Intercom at no charge from Telescape's Web site at: www.telescape.com. Please e-mail any problems and bug reports to support@telescape.com. For general info, e-mail info@telescape.com. The Viewport function in Telescape's TS Intercom lets you display a visual signature, photograph or any graphic file to whomever you're talking to over the Internet.

Tribal Voice

POWWOW

Tribal Voice is an Internet communications software development company. PowWow is a Windows program for the Internet allowing up to seven people to chat via typing or voice, send and receive files, view JPEG pictures and cruise the Web together as a group.

PowWow needs a Windows 3.1, Windows NT or Windows 95 PC with a TCP/IP and Internet connection. A 33MHz or faster 486DX, a 28.8 Kbps or faster Internet connection and Windows compatible sound card are needed for voice chatting.

A Web browser is required for cruising the web together. PowWow works with Netscape Navigator 1.1N or later (16-bit and 32-bit versions) and Microsoft Internet Explorer Version 4.40.308 or later for Microsoft Windows 95. PowWow is not available for the MacIntosh, Unix or OS/2 Presentation Manager (native mode) operating systems. You can, however, try running it inside a Windows emulator on Mac or Unix equipment, such as SoftWindows for Power Macintosh 2.0 from Insignia Solutions (www.insignia.com).

Perhaps the most philosophical of all Internet experts, the folks at Tribal Voice put a lot of psychic energy into their mission. They say Tribal Voice "was created to facilitate the propagation of cybertribes within the realm of cyberspace. PowWow is the tool that provides the means of communication and shared experiences that are necessary for the formation of tribes. The Journey provides the shared world view that is necessary to hold a tribe together. Tribes were the first social structures to emerge in the path to civilization. They are still among the most effective social structures that allow a sense of community while maintaining harmony with the world that surrounds them. As cyberspace becomes more of an extension of the mind, real-world paradigms will gradually take hold here. A paradigm of social structure must be the first step."

To find other users to "have a PowWow with" or add yourself to a list so that others may chat with you, go to the Tribal Voice PowWow White Pages server on the Web at: www.tribal.com/wpsearch.htm.

University of Illinois

Charlie Kline's

Maven

Maven was the first Internet audioconferencing program for the Macintosh, developed by Charlie Kline at the University of Illinois. It runs in either full or half duplex. Maven wants 16 Kbps of bandwidth -- too much for a 14.4 Kbps modem -- but it will run at a bare minimum of 13 Kbps. Besides other Macs running Maven, you can also talk to Unix workstations running VAT. It's free. You can find the software on the Internet at ftp://sun-site.unc.edu/pub/packages/infosystems/maven
(University of North Carolina at Chapel Hill) and
ftp://ftp.univie.ac.at/systems/mac/info-mac/comm/tcp (
Vienna University, Vienna, Austria). To get on the mailing list, send e-mail to listserv@cnidr.org. In the body of e-mail message
type: subscribe maven *Your Name.*

University of North Carolina

MTALK

MTALK is a free, experimental voice system for Linux -- a shareware version of UNIX. It uses a remarkably low bandwidth (about 1 Kbps) and runs on a Linux workstation with a Sound Blaster compatible sound card.

The software's at: ftp://sunsite.unc.edu/pub/Linux/apps/sound/talk/. Source code is situated at: ftp://sunsite.unc.edu/pub/Linux/apps/sound/talk/. E-mail contact: misch@elara.fsag.de

VocalTec Inc.

VocalTec Internet Phone

Internet Phone by VocalTec lets you have direct real-time conversations with other Internet users anywhere in the world for the price of a local Internet connection. It lets you only to speak to one person at a time -- no conferencing capabilities yet.

How do you find other Internet Phone users? When you log onto the Internet the software lets you connect to the Internet Relay Chat (IRC) network by clicking on one of the IRC servers available in a dialog box. This provides you with a phonebook-like, dynamically-updated list of users currently online and equipped for a voice conversation, as well as a list of topics of conversation.

You can also create your own topics and wait for others to notice them and give you a call. To place a call, you click on a user name and an Internet Phone rings on their end. The person clicks at the other end and picks up to begin the conversation. If the person isn't at home, the program records the last six people that you called or those who tried calling you.

In terms of privacy, Internet Phone lets you set up "private topics" that only you and your family, friends or business associates can use. These topics are "unlisted," accessible only by the users that know about them.

In this way you can have discreet conversations, without getting calls from all other on-line users. When you only use private topics, your name does not appear on the global list of on-line users. Only users that know where to look can reach you.

To further enhance security, the Internet Phone sends and receives audio directly from the other user, without going through the Internet Phone server (which is used only to let users locate each other) making calls hard to trace.

The Internet Phone uses a voice compression algorithm to minimize bandwidth usage to about 7.7 Kbps of raw audio data. By adding VocalTec's voice compression VC Card, you can reduce bandwidth consumption to about 6.72 Kbps of raw data.

Figure 11.19 -- VocalTec Internet Phone

VocalTec's Internet Phone has 10 Quick-Dial buttons that store the names of people whom you call the most. A Quick Tour and Pop-Up Tips are included to help you start your conversation immediately. Audio fidelity is obviously not quite up to the best POTS connections, but future generations of this product may give long-distance carriers the creeps. The Internet Phone needs at least a 486SX running at 25MHz with 8MB RAM, Windows 3.1, a Windows compatible sound card, microphone, speaker and an Internet Winsock 1.1 compatible TCP/IP connection -- the minimum being a 14.4 Kbps modem SLIP or PPP connection. Winsock drivers successfully tested with Internet Phone include Microsoft's TCP/IP, NetManage's Chameleon and the Trumpet Winsock driver.

For full duplex audio you'll need at least a 486 PC running at 50MHz and either two standard Windows compatible sound cards or a full duplex sound card such as the Gravis Ultrasound Plug & Play ($149) and Ultrasound Plug & Play Pro ($199) from Advanced Gravis Computer Technology (Bellingham, WA -- 604-431-5020), the ASB 16 Audio System (seven models ranging from $60 to $180) by AdLib Multimedia (Quebec, Canada -- 418-522-6100) or the OfficeF/X package (Version I is $239, a 28.8Kbps Version II is $299) from Spectrum Signal Processing (British Columbia, Canada -- 604-421-5422).

The Spectrum OfficeF/X package includes the Spectrum Switchboard, a phone answering and control system, with unlimited voice mailboxes, remote retrieval of messages, caller ID, full-duplex speakerphone, conversation recording, contact manager, etc.

Recently VocalTec announced it will bundle the Internet Phone with the SoundXchange audio appliance by InterActive (www.iact.com) which connects to a sound card installed in a PC to give hands-free audio or uses its exclusive handset for immediate privacy. The kits costs about $100. To try a free trial copy of Internet Phone software that will run for 60 seconds, you can FTP an evaluation version from ftp.vocaltec.com with user name ftp or download it from their Web page on www.vocaltec.com. Internet Phone is $99 for software only, $349 with speakerphone and a sound card.

VocalTec supplies the Internet phone software bundled with PhoneWorks ($299) by Connectware. PhoneWorks' companion program, Cruiser ($199), supports MAPI and the Microsoft Exchange Client in Windows 95, so Cruiser can send messages over Internet using the Exchange Client. Using the two products together you should be able to forward voice mail over the Internet too. The Internet Wave or IWave is also VocalTec's. It's an Internet "broadcast-quality digital audio broadcaster" enabling radio stations to go "on-air" online with both speech and music.

Voxware

Televox IT

Voxware, Inc., is a developer and marketer of proprietary digital speech processing technologies. Their products voice in computing, Internet and communications applications. According to Voxware, the Voxware RT24 codec (compressor/decompressor) has an encoding algorithm that enables highquality speech at 2400 bps. Other features include "handsfree" operation, caller ID, call blocking, automated login/logout, and userdefined address groups. In March 1996, Voxware introduced Televox IT software. Televox is a serverbased Internet phone system that supports realtime, fullduplex audio, file transfers, and textbased chat.

Voxware acquired the assets of K & F Software, (dba CyberScience), including rights to the company's CyberPhone product. The acquisition happened one week after the announcement that Netscape Communications Corporation licensed elements of Voxware's ToolVox technology, including the RT24 codec, for the Netscape LiveMedia framework.

The agreement establishes ToolVox as the Netscape-endorsed technology for low-bandwidth speech transmission with Netscape Navigator. The agreement also includes plans for Voxware to develop a variety of future Internet telephony applications, based on Netscape LiveMedia specifications, that interoperate with Netscape Navigator and other LiveMedia-compatible products.

In February 1996, White Pine Software, a developer of video conferencing and desktop connectivity software, announced that it had licensed Voxware's ToolVox technology, including the RT24 codec, for use in its Enhanced CUSeeMe video conferencing software. This will enable White Pine's Enhanced CUSeeMe to operate at low bandwidth functionality and provide persontoperson connections for telephone and video conferencing.

Despite their proprietary leanings, Michael Goldstein, president and CEO, said this when asked by Intel to support the launch of their standards-based Internet Phone: "Establishment of open interoperability standards, such as H.323, are critical to the long-term growth of Internet telephony. Voxware is committed to this goal, which benefits the industry as a whole and creates a platform for innovation. We fully support Intel's newest contribution in this area and look forward to working closely with Intel, and others, to demonstrate and promote full interoperability among products in this important market."

ToolVox For The Web

Voxware introduced *ToolVox for the Web* in January 1996. ToolVox consists of both an authoring tool and a player and makes it simple for virtually anyone to add highquality voice to World Wide Web pages. ToolVox makes it simple for Web authors to add high-quality voice clips to Web pages. Based on Voxware's revolutionary MetaVoice technology, ToolVox delivers 53:1 compression ratios. That's more than three times smaller file sizes than first-generation "real-time" Internet voice products. ToolVox has two components:

ToolVox Player. The ToolVox Player lets you hear sound files when you access Web sites that include VOX files. It works as a "helper" application that can be used with virtually any Web browser. Through the ToolVox Player interface, users also can speed up or slow down playback by up to a factor of 2, without changing the pitch or character of the original voice. This enables users to slow down playback for enhanced comprehension, or to speed it up for scanning purposes.

When used with Netscape Navigator 2.0, the Player becomes a Netscape plug-in, which allows it to manage data streams in cooperation with the HTTP/HTML servers and to automatically play voice.

ToolVox Encoder. The ToolVox Encoder compresses input voice files to 8 kHz at 2400 bps. Voice files at other sampling rates are automatically downsampled to 8 kHz before being compressed into VOX files that are ready to be embedded into any HTML document. ToolVox runs on any standard HTML server and does not require installation of special server software. There is no license fee, no matter how many users are listening. With ToolVox, Webmasters can set up their home page to automatically play a welcome message. Politicians can offer sound bites to voters. Comedians can deliver punch lines to their fans. And users can listen to voice clips while waiting for graphics and text files to finish downloading.

Chapter Acknowledgments

Sandy Combs, Director of the VON Coalition compiled an appendix of FCC Filings Timelines and Associated URLs. Jeff Pulver is the Chairman of the VON Coalition, a Wall Street computer network administrator and a worldwide authority of Internet telephony. His interest in Internet telephony grew out of a fondness for HAM radio and started as a hobby. Mr. Pulver contributed significantly to the research and editorial comments for this chapter. For more information regarding Internet telephony technology: www.von.com. For more information regarding upcoming VON Coalition meetings: e-mail conference-info@pulver.com.

FCC Common Carrier Bureau website www.fcc.gov/Bureaus/Common_Carrier/WWW/hottopic.html#acta

Portions of Mark Winther's Internet Telephony Market Assessment,1996 - 1999, an IDC White Paper called *The World Wide Web Phones Home* is (c) 1996 by International Data Corporation and used by permission.

Chapter 12

Voice-Enabled
Internet Standards

Internet telephones were a long time coming. But the phenomenon isn't new. Our Internet ancestors have been transmitting audio over IP and ST-II Internet protocols since the early 70's. They used special-purpose hardware and low-bit-rate coders like LPC (Linear Predictive Coding). The Information Sciences Institute at the University of Southern California was one of the pioneers. They built a PSTN/Packet Voice Gateway card fifteen years ago. The Switched Telephone Network Interface (STNI) card was Z-80 based. It used PCM encoding and a POTS circuit to front-end a DARPA 3Mbps wideband packet satellite network.

Stephen Casner of Precept Software, Inc. and now member of the IETF Audio/Video Transport Working Group, was enthused to share this little jewel with me. Mr. Casner had a hand in preparing the February, 1983 ISI draft for this project called *Providing Telephone Line Access to a Packet Voice Network*. The abstract talks about the hardware built for the project:

"The STNI (Switched Telephone Network Interface) card is designed to provide an interface between the commercial telephone network and a Packet Voice Terminal, developed by the M.l.T. Lincoln Laboratory." I thought it would be a fitting tribute to all those involved in this and other projects to give you a peak at our past (and future). Figure 12.1 shows a typical STNI call. The voice terminal handled the packet network protocol and a digital connection to the network. The STNI card would answer calls from the public telephone system, present a dial tone, and accept digits from the caller. The live voice call would then be introduced into the digital packet voice network. Calls to the switched telephone network could also originate in the packet network; the users would route them to an STNI card and tell it to dial the distant phone number. Once in progress, the STNI performed the analog and digital conversions on the call. The device also did sound and silence detection as a means of optimizing bandwidth.

The looping arrows in the drawing show the path of a typical call originating at any telephone. The process start by dialing into an STNI card, transmitting up across the wideband network, down to an STNI at another network site and then on to the distant telephone.

Figure 12.1 -- Early Internet Telephony Gateway

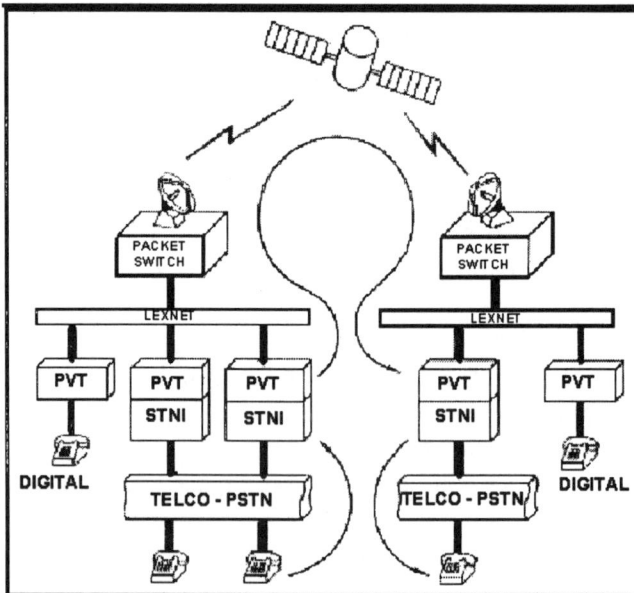

Sun Microsystems popularized doing voice over packet networks when they put a mu-law audio codec in their SPARCstation 1. Vt and vtalk (early Internet Telephony software) were bundled with Sun workstations five years ago. Standards for doing audio and video over IP networks has come a long way.

Now, many Internet Telephony programs are free, experimental or shareware. Others are part of fledgling companies out to create their own pseudo-phone network running on top of the 'Net. At first glance the idea seems terrific. For example, an international call from South Africa costs as much as $5 per minute. In fact there's no such thing in South Africa as a free phone call anywhere -- even a local call costs about 12 cents per five minutes. Internet phone competition would doubtless force prices down, even where the telephony infrastructure is government controlled (as it is in South Africa and most places around the world).

The staff at Computer Telephony Magazine and some of our editorial contributors came up with a little checklist for our readers. Richard Grigonis and Harry Netwon deserve praise here. Same for our guest columnist Jeff Pulver, chairman of the VON consortium. Not all of this is completely unknown territory, as the rest of this chapter attests. The standards are out there. And now the big companies with the big bucks (Intel, Microsoft, Lucent, et. al.) are helping to push standards through faster than I've ever seen.

Standards Upkeep

Can the Internet expand fast enough to keep up with such an additional digital load? And what will the backlash from governments and telcos be? Keeping all this in mind, let's set sail into the Internet...

1. Information Highway Potholes. A decent digitized phone conversation needs 8,000 bytes per second of bandwidth. Your average 14.4 Kbps modem and a good Serial Line Internet Protocol (SLIP) or Point to Point (PPP) Internet connection can deliver 1,800 bytes per second.

Expensive solution: Get a bigger bandwidth pipe into the 'Net like a 128 Kbps ISDN BRI or a direct network connection. At those rates, you'll be able to transmit right from your networked or standalone PC. And you won't need to worry about compression or encryption (though if you don't, you will have to worry about eavesdropping).

Cheaper (and more popular) solution: Keep your analog modem, but compress the audio information before transmission and then expand it at the other end.

2. Compression Tactics. Some Internet telephony packages such as Speak Freely let you use different kinds of compression based on the speed of your computer and network connection. Some examples:

"Simple compression" (Speak Freely's term) discards every other sample and thereby halves the data rate to 4,000 bytes per second, placing it within the throughput abilities of a 64 Kbps connection. On the receiving end, the samples are synthesized by averaging adjacent samples.

Simple compression needs little CPU time but it degrades sound quality -- high frequency overtones are lost and weird sampling aliasing occurs. Still, voices are generally intelligible and it's better than enduring random pauses and clipped off sounds.

The compression scheme used by the European Global System Mobile (GSM) digital cell phone standard is one of the best, reducing the data bandwidth requirement by about a factor of five -- from 8,000 bytes per second to 1,650 with little degradation of voice-grade audio. It makes 28.8 Kbps and maybe even 14.4 Kbps modem connections okay to use.

Unfortunately GSM is so computationally intense (and GSM encoding requires twice the computation as decoding) that Internet telephony can only be done in real time with at least a fast 486, Pentium or P6. A nice computational compromise is Adaptive Differential Pulse Code Modulation (ADPCM).

Its compression algorithm halves the data rate to 4,000 bytes per second, just like Simple Compression, but the loss in fidelity for voice-grade audio is hardly detectable.

ADPCM needs more computation than Simple Compression but much less than GSM. If your computer is too slow for GSM and the compression achieved by ADPCM is adequate for your network connection, this is a good choice.

Proprietary algorithms (such as CyberScience's CyberPhone software that squeezes speech into a 2.4 Kbps pipe) may give you better performance, but then it's up to the maker to sort out compatibility issues. CyberScience was recently bought by Voxware, Inc. and their technology was folded-in to VoxWare's TeleVox product.

Nice compression side effect: If you're concerned about eavesdropping, compression reduces encryption processing overhead since there's less data to encrypt.

3. Dealing With Gridlock. Intelligible audio requires not only adequate bandwidth (data rate) but consistent delivery time. The latter collapses as sound packets are delayed by a sudden increase of other data traffic on your LAN, WAN or the Internet itself.

Internet telephony operates "between the cracks" on the 'Net. Unlike file transfers, these products attempt to use a continuous amount of bandwidth -- if it's not available, then the audio is "dropped." Even on a well-configured system, delays normally seem to be in the range of .01 to .05 -- so you'll get some breaks and pauses in conversations.

Again the "weak link" in the Internet telephony chain are the on-ramps. Some Internet service providers are oversubscribed and their servers don't have enough bandwidth to support times of peak customer usage.

Your reputable Internet service provider (or your company's Internet server) should strive to maintain some decent bandwidth and we should all pray that the Internet backbone itself will continue to do so too.

And in any case, it's really the cost of the call (or lack thereof) that's propelling this market. It's funny how acceptable its choppy, fuzzy audio quality becomes when you realize you're not paying long-distance charges.

4. Standards. Some packages were designed from the start for a broad base of users: For example, the CyberPhone program was built to connect with as many different kinds of computers, platforms and software as possible.

However it's clear that Internet telephony needs some official committees and standards. Real standards plus a new generation of compression algorithms and the proliferation of Pentiums, ISDN or 28.8 Kbps or 33.6 Kbps modems could make the telcos and LD carriers pretty nervous about Internet telephony -- if they aren't already.

Some of the few real "standards" that exist in this field are the nonproprietary protocols some developers use. As long as you and whoever you're talking to on the Internet are using the same connection schemes and compression types, both of you can be using different software and even different kinds of computers.

This shouldn't seem so strange since, after all, in the data communications world, a Mac and a PC can send ASCII files to each other via something like the XMODEM protocol.

Standard protocol and / or compression methods include: GSM, CVSD, ADPCM, the Real Time Protocol (RPT) and UNIX VAT.

The two standards emerging for establishing connections, VAT and RTP, happen to be compatible with each other. VAT was the first Internet voice conferencing program and other applications mimic its method of establishing a call. Programs using RTP use the same connection procedure but have more functions to control call quality. Applications conforming to the RTP / VAT standard include Maven, e-phone, VAT, Nevot and soon Speak Freely. GSM seems on the way to becoming the compression standard and is supported by Maven, e-phone, Speak Freely, Nevot and others.

Unfortunately there are slight variations between the compression algorithms that may cause compatibility problems depending on what software you are using. Furthermore, if you're using a commercial product with a proprietary compression system, then you're obviously restricted to talking with people running the same kind of software.

5. The Bare Essentials. Besides whatever software package you've selected, you will need an Internet connection, the cheapest being a SLIP or PPP connection dialed up from your modem, which should run at least at 14.4 Kbps, preferably 28.8 Kbps or higher.

You'll also need a computer with at least a 25MHz processor, a PC sound card (Macintoshes already have sound onboard), speakers and a microphone which plugs into the sound card. Most Macintoshes have mic jacks -- if yours doesn't you'll need a serial mic like the MacRecorder or Sound Advantage.

6. Full or Half Duplex? Most Internet telephony applications support both full and half duplex modes.

A full duplex conversation is like a regular phone call -- both you and the other party can speak and hear at the same time. With half duplex only one person can speak at a time. To maintain order, a half duplex-based application usually forces you to press a button to speak.

Sound cards support either full or half duplex. Most new Macs and UNIX stations come with full duplex sound cards, but most PCs don't.

7. Splurge on a headset. If the audio quality sounds like its coming out of a speakerphone, use a headset. Audio compression introduces distortions into the sound made worse by small speakers. Headsets put the sound right in your ear, bypassing your room's reverberation and background noise.

More importantly, if you want to converse in full duplex mode, both parties really should use headsets instead of speakers, otherwise audio feedback between the speakers and the microphones can make your voices echo back and forth.

8. Multicasting is coming. Multicasting lets you send packets to several users for conferencing.

Multicasting tries to compensate for slow access lines and wasted bandwidth by allowing a computer to send one data stream to many computers. "Unicast" in contrast requires one computer to send information to only one other computer at a time.

Prodigy uses simple multicasting, with frequently requested files replicated on servers all over the US instead of just in Prodigy's home system in White Plains, NY.

Some Windows Sockets packages support "IP Multicasting," allowing the creation of conference groups where individual hosts can join and leave at will. A multicast conference is far more efficient than sending all recipients duplicate messages since Internet packet replication is done as close as possible to the recipient (MBONE is discussed later on in the chapter).

There are a lot of important or emerging/proposed standards. They are not all here. It's all happening very fast. They are listed in are listed in alphabetical order by their most common name.

Cyber Radio 1

John Selbie's

Cyber Radio 1 is the distribution name of the live Internet audio broadcast system that John Selbie (a graduate student at the University of Florida -- jselbie@cis.ufl.edu) wrote under UNIX for the 40,000 watt Georgia Tech student radio station, WREK Atlanta 91.1 FM. WREK has been using this system under the name WREK-NET. Trying to compress audio and video using software (in real time) requires significant amounts of CPU power. At the same time, the novice Internet users are wanting to watch television on their computer using their 14.4 modem. Progressive Networks (RealAudio), StreamWorks, and others offer such services.

The result, according to John Selbie is poor quality, "but it fills the demand."

CR1 uses UDP to transmit audio data from a server that can handle multiple clients. CR1 was written in the Fall of 1994 - before RealAudio came onto the scene. CR1 has superior sound quality and requires little CPU time, but at the cost of network resources. CR1 is also primarily for UNIX, but a Windows client exists as well. The program set is free and comes with the C source code, which is fairly easy to understand.

Cyber Radio 1 is intended for radio stations to broadcast their sound on. It is especially hoped that other computer hackers that work in college radio will attempt to use it and perhaps improve it.

Cyber Radio 1 is a client-server system. The server continually reads digital data from an audio device and multiplexes it out to any number of connected clients. Connected clients in turn, receive the digital audio data to play out of their audio device.

The Cyber Radio 1 system has been tested to work with any Sun Sparc, PCs running Linux or BSD with a sound card. The client program runs on any SGI workstation as well, thanks to the audio programming of Ian Smith. It's reported that it should work on HP/UX workstations too. It could potentially work on NeXT machines and other systems with minimal hacking. Someone by now may have also hacked a Windows version.

Cyber Radio 1 is distributed under the GNU General Public License. The GNU GPL gives everyone the right to have access to the source code, the right to modify and redistribute it under the terms of the GNU GPL. Although not as sophisticated as CU-SeeMe, RealAudio or other 'Net audio software, the sound quality of CR1 is claimed to be better suited for music than other packages and uses minimal CPU and network resources. Neither Cu-SeeMe nor VAT provide source code. There is neither source code availability nor any UNIX version of RealAudio. Thus, Cyber Radio 1 is ideal for those wanting to put together something for UNIX platforms.

Cyber Radio 1 has been written in C and will compile on any UNIX system. After downloading the package, read the installations instructions on how to build it into a network audio broadcast system: www.cis.ufl.edu/~jselbie/cr1.html

H.323

(ITU)

The ITU (International Telecommunications Union) H.323 recommendation is an internationally agreed-upon specification which defines how PCs interoperate to share audio and video streams over computer networks, including intranets and the public Internet.

This includes the low bandwidth G.723 audio codec. This sophisticated audio compression/decompression algorithm assures the best possible audio. Communications software products that are H.323-compliant provide you with a greater assurance of interoperability.

The driving force behind the H.323 effort is quite simple; to assure that communications products offered by different vendors work well together (i.e. that they interoperate). Intel has been and will continue to be instrumental in the definition, development, and marketplace diffusion of H.323 technology. H.323-compliant applications and infrastructure on the Internet represent the foundation for a new class of PC-based people-to-people communications capability.

H.323 Overview

Recommendation H.323 describes terminals, equipment, and services for multimedia communication over Local Area Networks (LAN) which do not provide a guaranteed Quality of Service. H.323 terminals and equipment may carry real-time voice, data, and video, or any combination, including videotelephony.

The LAN over which H.323 terminals communicate, may be a single segment or ring, or it may be multiple segments with complex topologies. It should be noted that operation of H.323 terminals over multiple LAN segments (including the Internet) may result in variable performance. The possible means by which quality of service might be assured on such types of LANs/internetworks is beyond the scope of the H.323 recommendation.

H.323 terminals may be integrated into personal computers or implemented in stand-alone devices such as videotelephones. Support for voice is mandatory, while data and video are optional, but if supported, the ability to use a specified common mode of operation is required, so that all terminals supporting that media type can interwork. H.323 allows more than one channel of each type to be in use. Other Recommendations in the H.323 series include H.225.0 packet and synchronization, H.245 control, H.261 and H.263 video codecs, G.711, G.722, G.728, G.729, and G.723 audio codecs, and the T.120 series of multimedia communications protocols.

H.323 makes use of the logical channel signaling procedures of Recommendation H.245, in which the content of each logical channel is described when the channel is opened. Procedures are provided for expression of receiver and transmitter capabilities, so transmissions are limited to what receivers can decode, and so that receivers may request a particular desired mode from transmitters. Since the procedures of H.245 are also used by Recommendation H.310 for ATM networks, Recommendation H.324 for GSTN, and V.70, interworking with these systems should not require H.242 to H.245 translation as would be the case for H.320 systems.

H.323 terminals may be used in multipoint configurations, and may interwork with H.310 terminals on B-ISDN, H.320 terminals on N-ISDN, H.321 terminals on B-ISDN, H.322 terminals on Guaranteed Quality of Service LANs, H.324 terminals on GSTN and wireless networks, and V.70 terminals on GSTN. Software from Intel and others, which take advantage of H.323, will allow you to share audio and video data with others at the click of a button in ways that were not previously possible.

The Intel Internet Phone, based on H.323's communications capabilities for the Internet, indeed does sound "pretty good." Call it an inside joke.

Figure 12.2 -- H.320 Interop With Other Standards

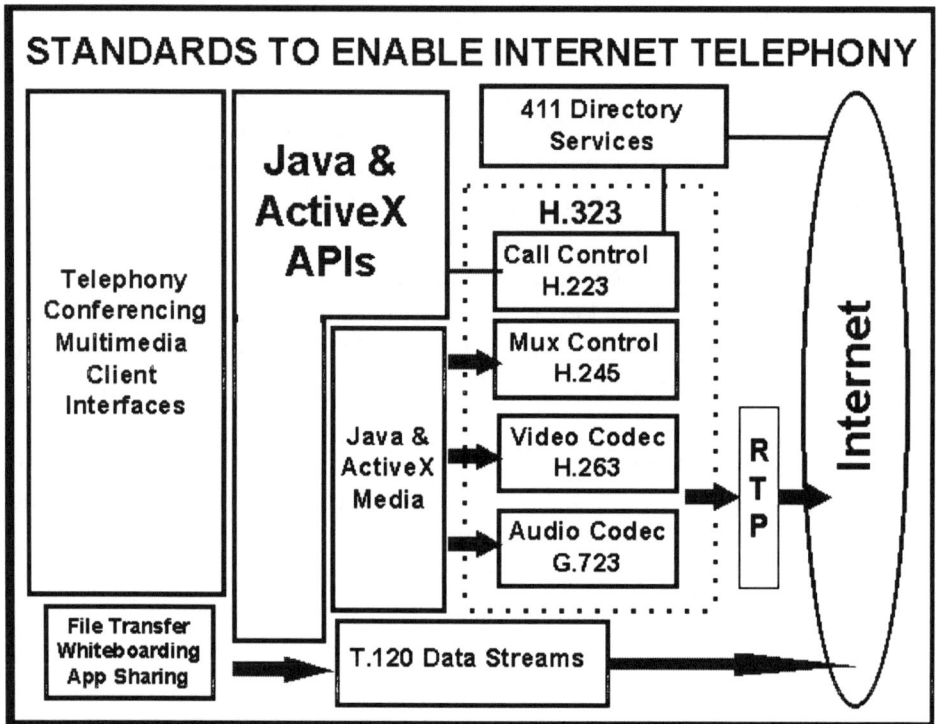

Various standards are driving Internet Telephony, thanks to the ITU (International Telecommunications Union) and IETF (Internet Engineering Task Force) effort. Both Microsoft's NetMeeting product and Intel's Internet Phone use these standards. The giants are swapping licenses. Microsoft will incorporate Intel's H.323 multimedia elements into NetMeeting. This buys them better voice quality and call control. Intel wants Microsoft's T.120-based data stream handler. It lets them transfer files and do whiteboarding while you talk. Both companies advocate the merger of ActiveX and Java Applets to build multimedia applications as illustrated in figure 12.2.

Intranets Vs. Groupware

I asked Richard Grigonis, the Technical Editor at *Computer Telephony Magazine* to tell us about Intranets and Groupware. He knows about these things. He knows all the vendors and has done zillions of test drives. Here's what he's learned.

Web technology is the new information exchange standard not only out on the Internet but within the enterprise too -- the corporate "Intranet." With their cost savings, easy access to up-to-date information, minimal training, single-data source, cheap links to outside sources and easy management, Intranets (and "Intrawebs") have benefits far beyond those of traditional "unconnected" collaborative-groupware systems.

Intranets use web server and browser technology and other Internet emerging standards to share data on Internet-like networks within an organization (the "intraprise") rather than just for external connection to the Internet.

Traditionally, companies used hard copy material such as price lists, sales guides, catalogs, status reports, annual reports, phone books, job postings, newsletters, employee handbooks and training manuals for internal and external use. This mountain of printed material involves design time, type-setting, printing, distribution and mailing / shipping costs.

All this is further complicated in a large organization if certain groups require special access to confidential data. Also, each geographical region may have a unique database containing status reports and marketing / financial data shared with the home office.

Now consider that 18% of business information is generally outdated every 30 days -- resulting in more revising, typesetting, printing, distribution, etc.

The situation screams for a cheaper and more efficient alternative to corporate communications -- the Intranet. The main advantages of the Intranet paradigm are:

1. Multiplatform Functionality. Web browsers exist for all client platforms (PC, Mac, UNIX, etc.) and they're either free or cost very little.

2. Cheap Connectivity. The Web lets you centralize your data. A local call to an Internet on-ramp can ultimately connect you anywhere -- including a connected Intranet.

3. Universal Interface. Internal and external information resources are accessed via a single GUI environment -- the browser -- which will become the common app for sharing information.

One theory is that Windows will become more and more transparent as people boot up into the interface used for e-mail, applications and just about everything else, which would presumably be Netscape's. In the future, unless you're an MIS director who knows your company's system inside and out, you won't be able to tell by looking at your PC screen whether you're on the Internet or an Intranet.

4. Open Systems. The Web technology standards such as HTML, Java, JavaScript (an extension of LiveScript) and Microsoft's upcoming VB Script will gain quick acceptance. HTML, TCP/IP and CGI have already spread rapidly. Open APIs, Frames and Inline Plugins will enable Web browsers to be the front-end for all corporate activities.

5. Scalability. Web-type Intranet apps are scaleable in size and complexity just as they are on the Internet. Custom applications relying on middleware and desktop "suites" are less scaleable and manageable and don't integrate well with future systems.

6. Separating Form from Content. Web servers are managed by "content creators" (marketing staff for example) instead of MIS staff. This lowers development costs and enhances productivity by letting the technical folks focus on running computers rather than deciding what color a Web form should be.

7. Cheap Development. A Web server can be had for $10,000 or less. Learning HTML Web page markup code or a third-party Web-page generator is a cinch.

8. Security. This can range from standard firewalls to other kinds of customized security levels, such as restricting information to and from designated departments.

With the same products that enable "cybermalls" on the public Internet, internal Web applications can securely post corporate finance information, place purchase orders, distribute billing. A secure Web site offers many advantages for both internal and external exchange of highly confidential material. For example, your finance department in New York can share information with another department in Tokyo.

9. PaperLess Office. Web interfaces bring us closer to the Holy Grail of the paperless office. The Web keeps employees updated and eliminates paper processing and routing for things like job postings, telephone directories, price lists and holiday / vacation day balances.

10. Forced Literacy. Web pages force you to read and input words.

But what about Groupware? Your first reaction to all of this may be something like: "But isn't the Intranet just another name for Groupware? Can't I do that with Lotus Notes?"

While Lotus Notes impresses everyone as the "Rolls Royce" of premium groupware platforms, not every organization needs or can afford Notes. It's expensive. It takes major technical expertise to get it going and to keep it going and to integrate your applications with it.

The bottom line is that the Internet / Intranet is cheaper and more flexible than "collaborative" computing solutions like Lotus Notes. Expensive, sophisticated, commercial groupware products will have trouble competing with the lowly Web browser.

According to a study by the International Data Corporation, the average corporate Lotus Notes implementation costs $245,000, with a payback period of over two years. Web applications, however, can be fully developed and deployed for $10,000.

Intranet software sales are already rising, from $142 million in 1995 to a predicted $1.2 billion in 1997, according to Zona Research as reported in the November 7, 1995 Wall Street Journal. And while Lotus Notes has three-million users, Intranets already handle about 15 million people.

Because of the ease in programming in HTML or other open-standard Web languages (or using Web-page generator add-ons for Microsoft Word and WordPerfect), existing corporate "content" is easily ported over to a Web environment: It takes less than $1,000 to "program" a Web site. Contrast that with multiples of $10,000 for Lotus sites and training IS professionals.

A Web server can be easily integrated into an existing LAN or WAN. For example, Purveyor WebServer from Process Software (Framingham, MA -- 800-722-7770) uses an API to connect to ODBC-compliant databases, giving you drag-and-drop access to them -- a feature only recently supported by Notes Release 4.

Lotus Notes and similar groupware computing solutions are generally internal applications relying upon a proprietary database structure. When they do connect to remote databases over conventional telecom lines it's done essentially just to replicate data at another location.

A Web server, on the other hand, eliminates database replication by letting users tap into the Internet's cheap worldwide network to connect to the server from any platform, at any location. This eliminates the kind of expensive line charges of conventional phone line connections ($25 to $80 per month per user, in the case of AT&T's Notes Network). For companies with existing Internet connections, the incremental cost is virtually zero.

Unlike Notes, the Intranet will let you do real-time, on-demand data distribution over a LAN, WAN or the Internet. And the same Web server that does internal information sharing within your company can also be used for external marketing on the Internet's World Wide Web.

From the client side, those Windows-based browsers give you the easiest integration with scads of other Windows apps, such as e-mail, fax, voice mail, unified messaging, calendaring, videoconferencing and embedding / hot links via OLE.

As a single interface to many information sources, a Windows-based Web browser is cost-effective, highly efficient and very easy to use. Some commercial browsers cost from $20 to $40 per user -- many are available as freeware.

As for adding multimedia applications, Video for Lotus Notes is a one-way (no conferencing) expensive deal: $2,700 for the server license and $120 per client. On the World Wide Web, of course, you can download and use free and/or inexpensive packages such as CU-SeeMe, WebTalk, Internet Phone, etc.

Not surprisingly, the Wall Street Journal reported recently that IBM may have severely overpaid for Lotus Notes because many companies have already invested in Intranets, using Netscape as the browser interface of choice.

Lotus then sprang into action. First, it lowered prices. It lowered the desktop client software from $155 to a more Web-browser-like $69. The basic server program went from $275 to $495, with a 1,000 user package going for $2,295.

Then it began to marry Lotus Notes to Internet protocols and standards so a Notes server can also function as a Web server, allow Web browsers as alternative clients. Lotus Notes Version 4, released on January 10th, even has its own Web browser.

Notes clients will continue to use the native Notes protocol to exploit the Notes compound document object store, and Web browsers will leverage Notes' native HTTP protocol and native HTML document format.

As Lotus itself explains: "Just as Notes clients use the Notes server to provide a central access point for all corporate data (e.g., mail, Notes workflow applications, access to relational data, access to desktop applications) the Notes client extends all of its services to exploit information on Web servers. That is, the Notes client now applies its entire set of functionality, disconnected use, client/server messaging, rich text, security, workflow applications, discussion databases and document libraries to information published in HTML format on HTTP servers."

There are other ways of leveraging your Notes investment on the Internet / Intranet, with products such as Lotus InterNotes Publisher, a Windows NT package that converts Notes documents into Web HTML documents. It transforms Notes document links into Hypertext links, preserves attachments to Notes documents that can then be downloaded from a Web browser, converts Notes tables into HTML tables, and converts bitmaps in Notes documents into GIF files.

Interestingly, Netscape Communications, makers of the world's most popular Web browser, recently decided to purchase Collabra Software, a leading developer of collaborative messaging software. The intent is to work Collabra workgroup functionality into the Netscape Navigator and other products. Their Collabra Share 2.0 product has received an Editors' Choice from PC Magazine in the Group Discussion category, surpassing five other group conferencing products tested -- among them Lotus Notes.

A few sharp, new companies have already jumped into the Intranet / Intraweb development frontier: Attachmate (Bellevue, WA -- 206-644-4010), Frontier Technologies (Mequon, WI -- 414-241-4555), Hummingbird Communications (Mountain View, CA -- 415-917-7300), JSB (Scotts Valley, CA -- 408-438-8300), Mustang Software (Bakersfield, CA -- 805-873-2500) and Process Software (Framingham, MA -- 800-722-7770).

IP Multicasting

Steve Deering's

This abstract is from the Network Working Group RFC 1112 *Host Extensions for IP Multicasting* memorandum in August, 1989. Steve Deering (Stanford University Computer Science Department) was the author. This description of multicating is one of the best I've seen. Thanks also to John Selbie, who consumed the document and also created his own multicasting system (CYBER RADIO 1).

IP multicasting is the transmission of an IP datagram to a "host group", a set of zero or more hosts identified by a single IP destination address. A multicast datagram is delivered to all members of its destination host group with the same "best-efforts" reliability as regular unicast IP datagrams, i.e., the datagram is not guaranteed to arrive intact at all members of the destination group or in the same order relative to other datagrams.

The membership of a host group is dynamic; that is, hosts may join and leave groups at any time. There is no restriction on the location or number of members in a host group. A host may be a member of more than one group at a time. A host need not be a member of a group to send datagrams to it.

A host group may be permanent or transient. A permanent group has a well-known, administratively assigned IP address. It is the address, not the membership of the group, that is permanent; at any time a permanent group may have any number of members, even zero. Those IP multicast addresses that are not reserved for permanent groups are available for dynamic assignment to transient groups which exist only as long as they have members.

Internetwork forwarding of IP multicast datagrams is handled by "multicast routers" which may be co-resident with, or separate from, Internet gateways. A host transmits an IP multicast datagram as a local network multicast which reaches all immediately-neighboring members of the destination host group.

If the datagram has an IP time-to-live greater than 1, the multicast router(s) attached to the local network take responsibility for forwarding it towards all other networks that have members of the destination group. On those other member networks that are reachable within the IP time-to-live, an attached multicast router completes delivery by transmitting the datagram as a local multicast.

Extensions are required of a host IP implementation to support IP multicasting, where a "host" is any Internet host or gateway other than those acting as multicast routers. The algorithms and protocols used within and between multicast routers are transparent to hosts and will be specified in separate documents.

JavaScript

Sun Microsystems

JavaScript is a new scripting language announced by Netscape and Sun Microsystems. It's built into Netscape Navigator 2.0. JavaScript is a simplified scripting shell built around Sun's recently-released Java language. Java adds to Web pages programmable functions such as interactive elements, animation, video, audio and continually updated windows with things like weather and traffic reports, stock market tickers or what-not. Java works by creating a "virtual computer" inside your PC (regardless of the operating system it's downloaded into) that can run any Java program or "applet" that comes in over the 'Net.

You can download the Java 1.0 programming environment from java.sun.com. The current release runs on Windows 95 and NT, Solaris on SPARC platforms and a Mac OS 7.5 version is expected soon. JavaScript will let non-programmers take advantage of many Java features without actually having to learn Java's sophisticated, object-oriented syntax. Scripts written in JavaScript are embedded into your HTML Web pages.

JavaScript adds a sort of client / server flavor to the Web: Normally, when you input something into a Web form it's first transmitted to the Server, verified and sent back. With JavaScript, however, the client application verifies input and it can be transmitted later. Entire programs can be run on the local client.

Since JavaScript is meant to be easier to understand than Java itself, some Java features are not supported in JavaScript. Examples of JavaScript and Java applications and applets can be found at Netscape's JavaScript page at www.netscape.com/comprod/products/ navigator/version_2.0/script/index.html, and Gamelan (pronounced "Gah' mah lonn") at www.gamelan.com.

The only browsers that can view this stuff are Sun's HotJava browser for UNIX and Netscape's Navigator 2.0 for Windows 95. Versions of Navigator 2.0 should also be ready as you read this for the Macintosh, UNIX, Windows 3.1 and Windows NT.

MBONE

This stands for Multicast Backbone. It's a circa 1992 IETF (Internet Engineering Task Force) effort originated as a way for members to keep in touch via videoconferencing. It's roots are from earlier ARPA DARTnet experiments. MBONE Supports multicast audio and video across the Internet. It provides one-to-many and many-to-many network delivery services for apps like videoconferencing and audio. It also supports simultaneous communication between several hosts.

MBONE is an experimental quasi-public "virtual" multimedia network allowing you to do real-time audio and videoconferences and broadcast to many users simultaneously. Besides conferencing, MBONE can create Internet broadcast services so you can hear live radio or video broadcasts over the 'Net.

The video requires around 150 Kbps of bandwidth, restricting MBONE usage to users of powerful UNIX workstations with T-1 links, although sound-only users can get by with 56 Kbps access.

MBONE networks are comprised of "mrouters." An MBONE network uses a public-domain multicast routing protocol called the Distant Vector Multicast Routing Protocol (DVMRP). Companies such as Silicon Graphics and Sun Microsystems offer commercial versions of DVMRP and are developing tools for distributed and audio whiteboards.

There are now over 1,500 networks handling MBONE traffic. In fact, some think that the MBONE / Internet combination will one day compete with commercial radio, cable TV and the phone company. But the current Internet backbone of T-3 lines can handle only about 100 real-time MBONE video connections at once. But bandwidth is a quickly fading issue. The proliferation of ATM networks will help.

NVP Network Voice Protocol

NVP had its roots in the mid-seventies. This description is in NSC NOTE 68 authored by Danny Cohen, ISI January 29, 1976. The major objective of ARPA's Network Secure Communications (NSC) project was to develop and demonstrate the feasibility of secure, high-quality, low-bandwidth, real-time, full-duplex (two-way) digital voice communications over packet-switched computer communications networks.

This kind of communication is a very high priority military goal for all levels of command and control activities. ARPA's NSC project will supply digitized speech which can be secured by existing encryption devices. The major goal of this research is demonstrate a digital high-quality, low-bandwidth, secure voice handling capability as part of the general military requirement for worldwide secure voice communication. The development at ISI of the Network Voice Protocol was important to that effort.

NVP was implemented first in December 1973. It has been used for both local and transnet real-time voice communication over the ARPANET. Here are a few of the "Internet Telephony Pioneers":

Information Sciences Institute, for LPC and CVSD, with a PDP-11/45 and an SPS-41.

Lincoln Laboratory, for LPC and CVSD, with a TX2 and the Lincoln FDP, and with a PDP-11/45 and the LDVT.

Culler-Harrison, Inc., for LPC, with the Culler-Harrison MP32A and AP-90.

Stanford Research Institute, for LPC, with a PDP-11/40 and an SPS-41.

The NVP's success in bridging the differences between the above systems is due mainly the cooperation of many people in the ARPA-NSC community, including Jim Forgie (Lincoln Laboratory), Mike McCammon (Culler-Harrison), Steve Casner (ISI) and Paul Raveling (ISI), who participated heavily in the definition of the control protocol; and John Markel (Speech Communications Research Laboratory), John Makhoul (Bolt Beranek & Newman, Inc.) and Randy Cole (ISI), who participated in the definition of the data protocol. Many other people have contributed to the NVP-based effort, in both software and hardware support.

RealAudio Client-Server Streaming

This is an abstract developed by Progressive Networks. It positions RealAudio against HTTP. To get more information on this, see: www.RealAudio.com. As audio-on-demand over the Internet nears ubiquity, a variety of technical approaches are coming to the fore. When Progressive Networks began developing RealAudio in early 1994, we spent a substantial amount of time investigating and prototyping a range of approaches before settling on a generalized Client-Server system.

In our development process, we learned what would work and would not work under the real-world conditions of the net. The following summarizes what we learned.

The Problem. The Internet is a fantastically scaleable packet-switched network, but was not designed to handle isochronous (continuous time-based) information. As a result, to get a system such as RealAudio to work reliably and consistently in the real world, engineering design decisions need to be made very carefully.

Under the hood, the net has two basic ways it can send data -- reliably, and hopefully as fast as it can (the TCP protocol), or as fast as possible, but without guaranteed reliability (the UDP protocol). UDP does not "guarantee" packet delivery; instead it provides a stream of audio packets without significant delay, but at the cost of occasional lost packets. TCP is more reliable, but at the cost of what are on occasion substantial delays when the protocol "retransmits" information from the server to the client and waits for its receipt to be acknowledged. Neither method gives the user either guaranteed throughput rates or guaranteed minimum latency periods, although UDP is generally superior in both of these regards.

Time-based streams are often very long -- a 30 minute news program, for instance. Yet often users only want part of a program -- the part 15 minutes into the program when the sports reporter presents the latest scores. Information sharing protocols on the Internet such as FTP and HTTP are designed for one-way continuous transmission and have no concept of bi-directional communication between the client and the server that would allow the client to ask the server for only a particular portion of the file, say the 15th through 20th minutes.

Possible Solutions. There are a range of possible solutions to the problem of delivering time-based information such as RealAudio over the net. Web servers are one possible solution. They're already ubiquitous and commonly available. Web Servers use the HTTP protocol, which in turn sends information using TCP.

Web browsers, particularly commercial-grade browsers such as Netscape, begin presenting some of the information to the user before it has all arrived, thereby shortening presentation delays.

Unfortunately, when web servers are used to send time-based data such as audio that gets rapidly "consumed" by the listener, the TCP "delay" problem can really bog things down. Even a 2 or 3 percent re-transmission rate can bring even a low bitrate audio data stream over a standard modem (say 8 kilobits/second over a 14.4 modem) to a grinding halt. This problem is less commonly observed over high bandwidth communication paths such as T1 lines, but for the content publisher that wants to make audio available to people gaining access to the net through standard phone lines and 14.4 or 28.8 modems, this issue is a significant problem.

A second problem with Web Servers is that, because the HTTP protocol is designed for one-way continuous transmission, it does not allow for a user friendly implementation of such desirable features as "fast forward," "rewind", and "seek" to a particular part of the program. Consumers are used to having these features as part of how they listen to recorded material via their VCRs and CD players, and users will reasonably expect the same features to work over the Internet.

A third problem with Web Servers is that they were designed to deliver large blocks of data to a client as quickly as possible but handle a small number of concurrent accesses. A large scale Web Server is often configured to support around 100 or fewer concurrent connections. This means that a high capacity, expensive server is need to deliver even 100 streams of audio.

An additional problem is that a Web Server approach is inefficient in using network bandwidth. A Web server would typically try to send the whole file as fast as possible -- whether it be a 10 second audio clip or a 2 hour program. However, since in the real world listeners generally listen to relatively short segments -- we have found that the average length per listen is about 4 minutes, even when the source material is an hour or longer -- this often results in wasted bandwidth and transmission time.

There is a strong need to avoid this problem by controlling the delivery rate of time based media.

RealAudio

... Solution To HTTP

For the above reasons, Progressive Networks found in its field tests in late 1994 and early 1995 that Web servers are not an appropriate vehicle for delivery of audio or other time-based media. As a result, we created the RealAudio protocol and the RealAudio client-server architecture. A key underlying technology was a new protocol for time-based media that supported bi-directional communication between clients and servers, which enables RealAudio users to pause, fast forward, rewind, and skip to particular tracks or particular sections quickly and reliably.

While the RealAudio system and protocol support both the TCP and UDP protocols, we've found that in the vast majority of the cases the results are much better when the audio is delivered via UDP, which results in a continuous presentation a very high percentage of the time. To get around the problem of occasional packet loss, Progressive Networks developed a sophisticated loss correction system that in essence minimizes the impact of any given lost packet and enables the client to "recreate" the missing pieces of the signal. This system works very well under normal lossless conditions, degrades gracefully when packet loss is in the 2-5% range, and even works acceptably when packet loss is as high as 8-10%. From a user standpoint, access to RealAudio programs is typically via a standard Web link, albeit a magical one. The user clicks on these links and after a second or two of start-up they play, with no further delays. And because the RealAudio Server runs on nearly all of the platforms that popular Web servers run on, a RealAudio Server and a Web Server can be run as separate processes on the same physical hardware. Because the RealAudio Server is more efficient at sending time-based data than a Web server -- it just sends the information the user needs plus a little extra for buffering -- this configuration supports a higher level of overall usage than a Web server alone.

And when it's time to scale up and add hardware, it's easier to scale up by moving the RealAudio server to a different physical machine without having to restructure and split the Web site. This scalability enables support of hundreds, thousands, and soon, even hundreds of thousands of simultaneous listeners.

Web servers are designed to deliver large blocks a data as quickly, by contrast the RealAudio Server was designed to deliver streaming data in a paced fashion. This is conservative of system resources and commodity level computers such as a standard Pentium 100 PC can easily deliver several hundred concurrent streams.

Consumers want access to live programming on the Internet. A Web Server based solution has no way of delivering the dynamic data that a live broadcast requires. This requires a client/server architecture, such as the RealAudio System, that is designed to send such a dynamic stream. The nature of live programs encourages a large audience and thus scalability of the system is a key aspect of any product that addresses this market.

The appropriateness and scalability of the technical underpinnings of the RealAudio approach have been proven out since its introduction. Hundreds of thousands of RealAudio users enjoy global access to live and on-demand RealAudio content that's deployed in hundreds of server sites around the globe.

RSVP

Resource Reservation Setup Protocol.

Description of RSVP Working Group: RSVP is a resource reservation setup protocol for the Internet. Its major features include: (1) the use of ''soft state'' in the routers, (2) receiver-controlled reservation requests, (3) flexible control over sharing of reservations and forwarding of subflows, and (4) the use of IP multicast for data distribution.

The primary purpose of this working group is to evolve the RSVP specification and to introduce it into the Internet standards track. The working group will also serve as a meeting place and forum for those developing and experimenting with RSVP implementations.

RSVP was a DARPA/ITO-funded effort by ISI to develop and standardize an Internet protocol for installing and maintaining resource reservations in the network. The RSVP protocol is part of a larger effort to enhance the current Internet architecture with support for Quality of Service flows.

The RSVP project has specified Version 1 of RSVP and the Internet Engineering Task Force (IETF) has reached consensus to submit this version as an Internet Proposed Standard. The project has also developed and distributed an implementation of RSVP and coordinated interoperability demonstrations with several vendors. This RSVP project focused on incorporating RSVP into the Internet Multicast Backbone (MBONE), designing and implementing a pre-registration agent, specifying and prototyping an enhanced RSVP version 2, and developing a routing support architecture. For Archives go to ftp://ftp.isi.edu/rsvp/rsvp.mail.

RTP

Real-Time Transport Protocol

RTP is a thin protocol providing support for applications with real-time properties, including timing reconstruction, loss detection, security and content identification. RTCP provides support for real-time conferencing for large groups within an Internet, including source identification and support for gateways (like audio and video bridges) and multicast-to-unicast translators. RTP can be used without RTCP if desired. While UDP/IP is its initial target networking environment, efforts have been made to make RTP transport-independent so that it could be used, say, over CLNP, IPX or other protocols. RTP is currently also in experimental use directly over AAL5/ATM.

RTP does not address the issue of resource reservation or quality of service control; instead, it relies on resource reservation protocols such as RSVP. Other applications, such as real-time control and distributed simulation, are also targets.

This an abbreviated abstract of the January, 1996 RTP memorandum. This is based on discussions within the IETF Audio/Video Transport working group chaired by Stephen Casner. The current protocol has its origins in the Network Voice Protocol and the Packet Video Protocol (Danny Cohen and Randy Cole) and the protocol implemented by the vat application (Van Jacobson and Steve McCanne). Christian Huitema provided ideas for the random identifier generator. I would like to thank the authors for their insights and cooperation: Henning Schulzrinne of GMD Fokus, Hardenbergplatz 2 D-10623, Berlin, Germany, schulzrinne@fokus.gmd.de and Stephen L. Casner, Precept Software, Inc., 21580 Stevens Creek Boulevard, Suite 207, Cupertino, CA 95014, casner@precept.com and Ron Frederick of the Xerox Palo Alto Research Center, 3333 Coyote Hill Road, Palo Alto, CA 94304, frederic@parc.xerox.com and finally Van Jacobson, MS 46a-1121 Lawrence Berkeley National Laboratory, Berkeley, CA 94720, van@ee.lbl.gov.

RTP provides end-to-end network transport functions suitable for applications transmitting real-time data, such as audio, video or simulation data, over multicast or unicast network services. RTP does not address resource reservation and does not guarantee quality-of- service for real-time services. The data transport is augmented by a control protocol (RTCP) to allow monitoring of the data delivery in a manner scalable to large multicast networks, and to provide minimal control and identification functionality. RTP and RTCP are designed to be independent of the underlying transport and network layers. The protocol supports the use of RTP-level translators and mixers.

Note that RTP itself does not provide any mechanism to ensure timely delivery or provide other quality-of-service guarantees, but relies on lower-layer services to do so.

It does not guarantee delivery or prevent out-of-order delivery, nor does it assume that the underlying network is reliable and delivers packets in sequence. The sequence numbers included in RTP allow the receiver to reconstruct the sender's packet sequence, but sequence numbers might also be used to determine the proper location of a packet, for example in video decoding, without necessarily decoding packets in sequence.

While RTP is primarily designed to satisfy the needs of multi- participant multimedia conferences, it is not limited to that particular application. Storage of continuous data, interactive distributed simulation, active badge, and control and measurement applications may also find RTP applicable.

RTP consists of two closely-linked parts:

1) the real-time transport protocol (RTP), to carry data that has real-time properties.

2) the RTP control protocol (RTCP), to monitor the quality of service and to convey information about the participants in an on-going session. The latter aspect of RTCP may be sufficient for "loosely controlled" sessions, i.e., where there is no explicit membership control and set-up, but it is not necessarily intended to support all of an application's control communication requirements. This functionality may be fully or partially subsumed by a separate session control protocol. RTP represents a new style of protocol following the principles of application level framing and integrated layer processing proposed by Clark and Tennenhouse. That is, RTP is intended to be malleable to provide the information required by a particular application and will often be integrated into the application processing rather than being implemented as a separate layer. RTP is a protocol framework that is deliberately not complete. Unlike conventional protocols in which additional functions might be accommodated by making the protocol more general or by adding an option mechanism that would require parsing, RTP is intended to be tailored through modifications and/or additions to the headers as needed.

Several RTP applications, both experimental and commercial, have already been implemented from draft specifications. These applications include audio and video tools along with diagnostic tools such as traffic monitors. Users of these tools number in the thousands. However, the current Internet cannot yet support the full potential demand for real-time services. High-bandwidth services using RTP, such as video, can potentially seriously degrade the quality of service of other network services. Thus, implementers should take appropriate precautions to limit accidental bandwidth usage. Application documentation should clearly outline the limitations and possible operational impact of high-bandwidth real- time services on the Internet and other network services.

RTP Use Scenarios

The following sections describe some aspects of the use of RTP. The examples were chosen to illustrate the basic operation of applications using RTP, not to limit what RTP may be used for. In these examples, RTP is carried on top of IP and UDP, and follows the conventions established by the profile for audio and video specified in the companion Internet-Draft draft-ietf-avt-profile.

Simple Multicast Audio Conference. A working group of the IETF meets to discuss the latest protocol draft, using the IP multicast services of the Internet for voice communications. Through some allocation mechanism the working group chair obtains a multicast group address and pair of ports. One port is used for audio data, and the other is used for control (RTCP) packets. This address and port information is distributed to the intended participants. If privacy is desired, the data and control packets may be encrypted, in which case an encryption key must also be generated and distributed. The exact details of these allocation and distribution mechanisms are beyond the scope of RTP. The audio conferencing application used by each conference participant sends audio data in small chunks of, say, 20 ms duration. Each chunk of audio data is preceded by an RTP header; RTP header and data are in turn contained in a UDP packet.

The RTP header indicates what type of audio encoding (such as PCM, ADPCM or LPC) is contained in each packet so that senders can change the encoding during a conference, for example, to accommodate a new participant that is connected through a low-bandwidth link or react to indications of network congestion.

The Internet, like other packet networks, occasionally loses and reorders packets and delays them by variable amounts of time. To cope with these impairments, the RTP header contains timing information and a sequence number that allow the receivers to reconstruct the timing produced by the source, so that in this example, chunks of audio are contiguously played out the speaker every 20 ms. This timing reconstruction is performed separately for each source of RTP packets in the conference. The sequence number can also be used by the receiver to estimate how many packets are being lost.

Since members of the working group join and leave during the conference, it is useful to know who is participating at any moment and how well they are receiving the audio data. For that purpose, each instance of the audio application in the conference periodically multicasts a reception report plus the name of its user on the RTCP (control) port. The reception report indicates how well the current speaker is being received and may be used to control adaptive encodings. In addition to the user name, other identifying information may also be included subject to control bandwidth limits. A site sends the RTCP BYE packet when it leaves the conference.

Audio and Video Conference. If both audio and video media are used in a conference, they are transmitted as separate RTP sessions RTCP packets are transmitted for each medium using two different UDP port pairs and/or multicast addresses. There is no direct coupling at the RTP level between the audio and video sessions, except that a user participating in both sessions should use the same distinguished (canonical) name in the RTCP packets for both so that the sessions can be associated. One motivation for this separation is to allow some participants in the conference to receive only one medium if they choose.

Despite the separation, synchronized playback of a source's audio and video can be achieved using timing information carried in the RTCP packets for both sessions.

Mixers and Translators. So far, we have assumed that all sites want to receive media data in the same format. However, this may not always be appropriate. Consider the case where participants in one area are connected through a low-speed link to the majority of the conference participants who enjoy high-speed network access. Instead of forcing everyone to use a lower-bandwidth, reduced-quality audio encoding, an RTP-level relay called a mixer may be placed near the low-bandwidth area. This mixer resynchronizes incoming audio packets to reconstruct the constant 20 ms spacing generated by the sender, mixes these reconstructed audio streams into a single stream, translates the audio encoding to a lower-bandwidth one and forwards the lower- bandwidth packet stream across the low-speed link. These packets might be unicast to a single recipient or multicast on a different address to multiple recipients. The RTP header includes a means for mixers to identify the sources that contributed to a mixed packet so that correct talker indication can be provided at the receivers.

Some of the intended participants in the audio conference may be connected with high bandwidth links but might not be directly reachable via IP multicast. For example, they might be behind an application-level firewall that will not let any IP packets pass. For these sites, mixing may not be necessary, in which case another type of RTP-level relay called a translator may be used. Two translators are installed, one on either side of the firewall, with the outside one funneling all multicast packets received through a secure connection to the translator inside the firewall. The translator inside the firewall sends them again as multicast packets to a multicast group restricted to the site's internal network.

Mixers and translators may be designed for a variety of purposes. An example is a video mixer that scales the images of individual people in separate video streams and composites them into one video stream to simulate a group scene.

Other examples of translation include the connection of a group of hosts speaking only IP/UDP to a group of hosts that understand only ST-II, or the packet-by-packet encoding translation of video streams from individual sources without resynchronization or mixing.

RTP Definitions

RTP payload. The data transported by RTP in a packet, for example audio samples or compressed video data. The payload format and interpretation are beyond the scope of this document.

RTP packet. A data packet consisting of the fixed RTP header, a possibly empty list of contributing sources (see below), and the payload data. Some underlying protocols may require an encapsulation of the RTP packet to be defined. Typically one packet of the underlying protocol contains a single RTP packet, but several RTP packets may be contained if permitted by the encapsulation method.

RTCP packet. A control packet consisting of a fixed header part similar to that of RTP data packets, followed by structured elements that vary depending upon the RTCP packet type. Typically, multiple RTCP packets are sent together as a compound RTCP packet in a single packet of the underlying protocol; this is enabled by the length field in the fixed header of each RTCP packet.

Port. The "abstraction that transport protocols use to distinguish among multiple destinations within a given host computer. TCP/IP protocols identify ports using small positive integers." The transport selectors (TSEL) used by the OSI transport layer are equivalent to ports. RTP depends upon the lower-layer protocol to provide some mechanism such as ports to multiplex the RTP and RTCP packets of a session.

Transport address. The combination of a network address and port that identifies a transport-level endpoint, for example an IP address and a UDP port. Packets are transmitted from a source transport address to a destination transport address.

RTP session. The association among a set of participants communicating with RTP. For each participant, the session is defined by a particular pair of destination transport addresses (one network address plus a port pair for RTP and RTCP). The destination transport address pair may be common for all participants, as in the case of IP multicast, or may be different for each, as in the case of individual unicast network addresses plus a common port pair. In a multimedia session, each medium is carried in a separate RTP session with its own RTCP packets. The multiple RTP sessions are distinguished by different port number pairs and/or different multicast addresses.

Synchronization source (SSRC). The source of a stream of RTP packets, identified by a 32-bit numeric SSRC identifier carried in the RTP header so as not to be dependent upon the network address. All packets from a synchronization source form part of the same timing and sequence number space, so a receiver groups packets by synchronization source for playback. Examples of synchronization sources include the sender of a stream of packets derived from a signal source such as a microphone or a camera, or an RTP mixer (see below). A synchronization source may change its data format, e.g., audio encoding, over time. The SSRC identifier is a randomly chosen value meant to be globally unique within a particular RTP session. A participant need not use the same SSRC identifier for all the RTP sessions in a multimedia session; the binding of the SSRC identifiers is provided through RTCP. If a participant generates multiple streams in one RTP session, for example from separate video cameras, each must be identified as a different SSRC.

Contributing source (CSRC). A source of a stream of RTP packets that has contributed to the combined stream produced by an RTP mixer. The mixer inserts a list of the SSRC identifiers of the sources that contributed to the generation of a particular packet into the RTP header of that packet. This list is called the CSRC list. An example application is audio conferencing where a mixer indicates all the talkers whose speech was combined to produce the outgoing packet, allowing the receiver to indicate the current talker, even though all the audio packets contain the same SSRC identifier (that of the mixer).

End system. An application that generates the content to be sent in RTP packets and/or consumes the content of received RTP packets. An end system can act as one or more synchronization sources in a particular RTP session, but typically only one.

Mixer. An intermediate system that receives RTP packets from one or more sources, possibly changes the data format, combines the packets in some manner and then forwards a new RTP packet. Since the timing among multiple input sources will not generally be synchronized, the mixer will make timing adjustments among the streams and generate its own timing for the combined stream. Thus, all data packets originating from a mixer will be identified as having the mixer as their synchronization source.

Translator. An intermediate system that forwards RTP packets with their synchronization source identifier intact. Examples of translators include devices that convert encodings without mixing, replicators from multicast to unicast, and application- level filters in firewalls.

Monitor. An application that receives RTCP packets sent by participants in an RTP session, in particular the reception reports, and estimates the current quality of service for distribution monitoring, fault diagnosis and long-term statistics. The monitor function is likely to be built into the application(s) participating in the session, but may also be a separate application that does not otherwise participate and does not send or receive the RTP data packets. These are called third party monitors.

Non-RTP means. Protocols and mechanisms that may be needed in addition to RTP to provide a usable service. In particular, for multimedia conferences, a conference control application may distribute multicast addresses and keys for encryption, negotiate the encryption algorithm to be used, and define dynamic mappings between RTP payload type values and the payload formats they represent for formats that do not have a predefined payload type value. For simple applications, electronic mail or a conference database may also be used. The specification of such protocols and mechanisms is outside the scope of this document.

RTP Byte Order, Alignment, and Time Format

All integer fields are carried in network byte order, that is, most significant byte (octet) first. This byte order is commonly known as big-endian. Unless otherwise noted, numeric constants are in decimal (base 10). All header data is aligned to its natural length, i.e., 16-bit fields are aligned on even offsets, 32-bit fields are aligned at offsets divisible by four, etc. Octets designated as padding have the value zero.

Wallclock time (absolute time) is represented using the timestamp format of the Network Time Protocol (NTP), which is in seconds relative to 0h UTC on 1 January 1900. The full resolution NTP timestamp is a 64-bit unsigned fixed-point number with the integer part in the first 32 bits and the fractional part in the last 32 bits. In some fields where a more compact representation is appropriate, only the middle 32 bits are used; that is, the low 16 bits of the integer part and the high 16 bits of the fractional part. The high 16 bits of the integer part must be determined independently.

RTP Data Transfer Protocol

RTP Fixed Header Fields. The RTP header has the format illustrated in Figure 12.3.

Figure 12.3- RTP Fixed Header Fields

```
0 1 2 3 0 1 2 3 4 5 6 7 8 9 0 1 2 3 4 5 6 7 8 9 0 1 2 3 4 5 6 7 8 9 0 1
+-+-+-+-+-+-+-+-+-+-+-+-+-+-+-+-+-+-+-+-+-+-+-+-+-+-+-+-+-+-+-+-+
|V=2|P|X| CC |M| PT | sequence number | +-+-+-+-+-+-+-+-+-+-+-+-
+-+-+-+-+-+-+-+-+-+-+-+-+-+-+-+-+-+-+-+-+-+-+-+ | timestamp | +-+-+-+-+-
+-+-+-+-+-+-+-+-+-+-+-+-+-+-+-+-+-+-+-+-+-+-+-+-+-+-+-+-+ |
synchronization source (SSRC) identifier |
+=+=+=+=+=+=+=+=+=+=+=+=+=+=+=+=+=+=+=+=+=+=+=+=+=+=+=+=+
=+=+=+=+=+=+ | contributing source (CSRC) identifiers | | .... | +-
+-+-+-+-+-+-+-+-+-+-+-+-+-+-+-+-+-+-+-+-+-+-+-+-+-+-+-+-+
```

The first twelve octets are present in every RTP packet, while the list of CSRC identifiers is present only when inserted by a mixer. The fields have the following meaning:

version (V). 2 bits This field identifies the version of RTP. The version defined by this specification is two (2). (The value 1 is used by the first draft version of RTP and the value 0 is used by the protocol initially implemented in the "vat" audio tool.)

padding (P). 1 bit If the padding bit is set, the packet contains one or more additional padding octets at the end which are not part of the

payload. The last octet of the padding contains a count of how many padding octets should be ignored. Padding may be needed by some encryption algorithms with fixed block sizes or for carrying several RTP packets in a lower-layer protocol data unit.

extension (X). 1 bit If the extension bit is set, the fixed header is followed by exactly one header extension.

CSRC count (CC). 4 bits The CSRC count contains the number of CSRC identifiers that follow the fixed header.

marker (M). 1 bit The interpretation of the marker is defined by a profile. It is intended to allow significant events such as frame boundaries to be marked in the packet stream. A profile may define additional marker bits or specify that there is no marker bit by changing the number of bits in the payload type field.

payload type (PT). 7 bits This field identifies the format of the RTP payload and determines its interpretation by the application. A profile specifies a default static mapping of payload type codes to payload formats. Additional payload type codes may be defined dynamically through non-RTP means.

An initial set of default mappings for audio and video is specified in the companion profile Internet-Draft draft-ietf-avt-profile, and may be extended in future editions of the Assigned Numbers RFC An RTP sender emits a single RTP payload type at any given time; this field is not intended for multiplexing separate media streams.

sequence number. 16 bits The sequence number increments by one for each RTP data packet sent, and may be used by the receiver to detect packet loss and to restore packet sequence. The initial value of the sequence number is random (unpredictable) to make known-plaintext attacks on encryption more difficult, even if the source itself does not encrypt, because the packets may flow through a translator that does.

timestamp: 32 bits. The timestamp reflects the sampling instant of the first octet in the RTP data packet. The sampling instant must be derived from a clock that increments monotonically and linearly in time to allow synchronization and jitter calculations. The resolution of the clock must be sufficient for the desired synchronization accuracy and for measuring packet arrival jitter (one tick per video frame is typically not sufficient). The clock frequency is dependent on the format of data carried as payload and is specified statically in the profile or payload format specification that defines the format, or may be specified dynamically for payload formats defined through non-RTP means. If RTP packets are generated periodically, the nominal sampling instant as determined from the sampling clock is to be used, not a reading of the system clock. As an example, for fixed-rate audio the timestamp clock would likely increment by one for each sampling period. If an audio application reads blocks covering 160 sampling periods from the input device, the timestamp would be increased by 160 for each such block, regardless of whether the block is transmitted in a packet or dropped as silent.

The initial value of the timestamp is random, as for the sequence number. Several consecutive RTP packets may have equal timestamps if they are (logically) generated at once, e.g., belong to the same video frame.

Consecutive RTP packets may contain timestamps that are not monotonic if the data is not transmitted in the order it was sampled, as in the case of MPEG interpolated video frames. (The sequence numbers of the packets as transmitted will still be monotonic.)

SSRC: 32 bits. The SSRC field identifies the synchronization source. This identifier is chosen randomly, with the intent that no two synchronization sources within the same RTP session will have the same SSRC identifier. Although the probability of multiple sources choosing the same identifier is low, all RTP implementations must be prepared to detect and resolve collisions. If a source changes its source transport address, it must also choose a new SSRC identifier to avoid being interpreted as a looped source.

CSRC list. 0 to 15 items, 32 bits each The CSRC list identifies the contributing sources for the payload contained in this packet. The number of identifiers is given by the CC field. If there are more than 15 contributing sources, only 15 may be identified. CSRC identifiers are inserted by mixers, using the SSRC identifiers of contributing sources. For example, for audio packets the SSRC identifiers of all sources that were mixed together to create a packet are listed, allowing correct talker indication at the receiver.

Multiplexing RTP Sessions

For efficient protocol processing, the number of multiplexing points should be minimized In RTP, multiplexing is provided by the destination transport address (network address and port number) which define an RTP session. For example, in a teleconference composed of audio and video media encoded separately, each medium should be carried in a separate RTP session with its own destination transport address. It is not intended that the audio and video be carried in a single RTP session and demultiplexed based on the payload type or SSRC fields.

A detailed description of the RTP protocol which is beyond the scope of this abbreviated abstract is available on the GMD Fokus home page: www.fokus.gmd.de/

T.120

International Multimedia Teleconferencing Consortium

(Courtesy International Multimedia Teleconferencing Consortium (IMTC). The goals of the IMTC are to promote the awareness and adoption of ITU teleconferencing standards, including T.120 and H.32x. The IMTC provides a forum for interoperability testing and helps to define Application Programming Interfaces (APIs). DataBeam's co-founder and chief technical officer, C. J. "Neil" Starkey, serves as the president of the IMTC. Previously, Starkey served for six years as chairman of the ITU study group that defined T.120.)

The T.120 standard contains a series of communication and application protocols and services that provide support for real-time, multi-point data communications. These multi-point facilities are important building blocks for a whole new range of collaborative applications including desktop data conferencing, multi-user applications, and multi-player gaming.

Broad in scope, T.120 is a comprehensive specification that solves several problems that have historically slowed market growth for applications of this nature. Perhaps most importantly, T.120 resolves complex technological issues in a manner that is acceptable to both the computing and telecommunications industries.

Established by the International Telecommunications Union (ITU), T.120 is a family of open standards that was defined by leading data communication practitioners in the industry. Over 100 key international vendors, including Apple, AT&T, BritishTelecom, Cisco Systems, Intel, MCI, Microsoft, and PictureTel have committed to implementing T.120-based products and services. While T.120 has emerged as a critical element in the data communications landscape, the only information that currently exists on the topic is a weighty and complicated set of standards documents. This primer attempts to bridge this information gap by summarizing T.120's major benefits, fundamental architectural elements, and core capabilities.

Key Benefits of T.120

So why all the excitement about T.120? The bottom line is that it provides exceptional benefits to end users, vendors, and developers tasked with implementing real-time applications. The following list is a high-level overview of the major benefits associated with the T.120 standard:

T.120 Multi-point Data Delivery. T.120 provides an elegant abstraction for developers to create and manage a multi-point domain with ease. From an application perspective, data is seamlessly delivered to multiple parties in "real-time."

T.120 Interoperability. T.120 provides a means for endpoint applications from multiple vendors to interoperate. It also specifies how applications may interoperate with (or through) a variety of network bridging products and services that also supportT.120.

T.120 Reliable Data Delivery. Error-corrected data delivery ensures that all endpoints will receive each data transmission. An application can even specify that each endpoint must receive data packets from multiple senders in the exact same order.

T.120 Network Transparency. Applications are completely shielded from the underlying data transport mechanism being used. Whether the transport is a high-speed LAN or a simple dial-up modem, the application developer is only concerned with a single, consistent set of application services.

T.120 Network Independence. The T.120 standard supports a broad range of transport options, including the Public Switched Telephone Networks(PSTN or POTS), Integrated Switched Digital Net-works(ISDN), Packet Switched Digital Networks (PSDN),Circuit Switched Digital Networks (CSDN), and popular local area network protocols (TCP/IP and IPX).Furthermore, these vastly different network transports, operating at different speeds, can easily co-exist in the same multi-point conference.

T.120 Platform Independence. Because the T.120 standard is completely free from any platform dependencies, it will readily take advantage of the inevitable advances in computing technology. In fact, DataBeam's customers have already ported the T.120 source code easily from Windows to a variety of environments including OS/2, MAC/OS, several versions of UNIX, and other proprietary real-time operating systems.

T.120 Support for Varied Topologies. Multi-point conferences can be set up with virtually no limitation on network topology. Star topologies, with a single Multi-point Control Unit (MCU) will be common early on. The standard also supports a wide variety of other topologies ranging from those with multiple, cascaded MCUs to topologies as simple as a daisy-chain. In complex multi-point conferences, topology may have a significant impact on efficiency and performance.

T.120 Application Independence. Although the driving market force behind T.120 was teleconferencing, its designers purposely sought to satisfy a much broader range of application needs. Today, T.120provides a generic, real-time communications facility that can be used by many different applications including interactive gaming, virtual reality and simulations, real-time subscription news feeds, and process control applications.

T.120. Scalability. T.120 is defined to be easily scalable from simple PC-based architectures to complex multi-processor environments characterized by their high performance. Resources for T.120 applications are plentiful, with practical limits imposed only by the confines of the specific platform running the software.

T.120. Co-existence with Other Standards. T.120 was designed to work alone or within the larger context of other ITU standards such as the H.32x family of video conferencing standards. T.120 also supports and cross-references other important ITU standards such as V.series modems.

T.120 Extendability. The T.120 standard can be freely extended to include a variety of new capabilities such as support for new transport stacks (like ATM or Frame Relay), improved security measures, and new application-level protocols.

T.120 Architectural Overview

The T.120 architecture relies on a multi-layered approach with defined protocols and service definitions between layers. Each layer presumes the existence of all layers below. The lower level layers (T.121, T.122, T.123, T.124, and T.125) specify an application-independent mechanism for providing multi-point data communication services to any application that can use these facilities. The upper level layers (T.126 and T.127) define protocols for specific conferencing applications, such as shared whiteboarding and multi-point file transfer. Applications using these standardized protocols can coexist in the same conference with applications using proprietary protocols. In fact, a single application may even use a mix of standardized and non-standardized protocols. This is illustrated in Figure 12.4.

Figure 12.4- T.120 Multi-Layered Architecture

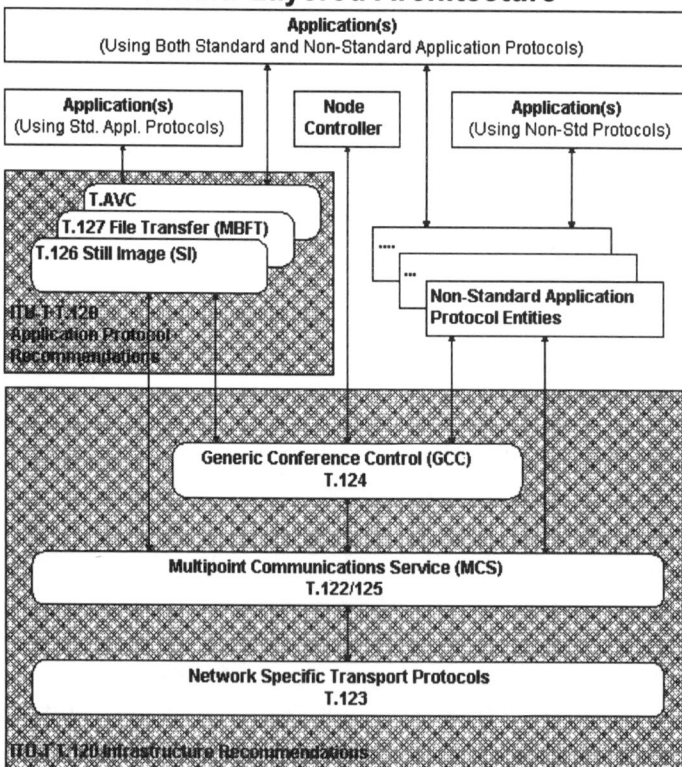

T.120 Component Overview

T.123 Transport Stacks. T.120 applications expect the underlying transport to provide reliable delivery of its Protocol Data Units (PDUs) and to
segment and sequence that data. T.123 specifies transport profiles for each
of the following:

- Public Switched Telephone Networks (PSTN)

- Integrated Switched Digital Networks (ISDN)

- Circuit Switched Digital Networks (CSDN)_

- Packet Switched Digital Networks (PSDN)

- Novell Netware IPX (via reference profile)

- TCP/IP (via reference profile)

The T.123 layer presents a uniform OSI transport interface and services
(X.214/X.224) to the MCS layer above. It includes built-in error correction
facilities so application developers do not have to rely on special hardware
facilities to perform this function.

In a given computing environment, a transport stack typically plugs into
a local facility that provides an interface to the specific transport connection.
For example, in the Windows environment, DataBeam's transport stacks
plug into COMM.DRV for modem communications, WINSOCK.DLL for
TCP/IP communications, and NWIPXSPX. DLL for Novell IPX communication support. In 1996, the ITU is expected to adopt extensions to support
important new transport facilities, such as Asynchronous Transfer Mode
(ATM) and H.324 POTS videophone. It is necessary to note that developers
can easily produce a proprietary transport stack (supporting, for example,
AppleTalk) that transparently uses the services above T.123.

An important function of MCUs or T.120-enabled bridges, routers, or gateways is to provide transparent interworking across different network boundaries.

T.122, T.125 Multi-point Communication Services (MCS). MCS defines the multi-point services available to the developer, while T.125 specifies the data transmission protocol. Together they form MCS, the multi-point "engine" of the T.120 conference. MCS relies on T.123 to deliver the data. (Use of MCS is entirely independent of the actual T.123 transport stack(s) that is loaded.)

MCS is a powerful tool that can be used to solve virtually any multi-point application design requirement. MCS is an elegant abstraction of a complex organism. Learning to use MCS effectively is the key to successfully developing real-time applications.

How MCS Works. In a conference, multiple endpoints (or MCS nodes) are logically connected together to form what T.120 refers to as a domain. Domains generally equate to the concept of a conference. An application may actually be attached to multiple domains simultaneously. For example, the chairperson of a large online conference may simultaneously monitor information being discussed among several activity groups. If the chairperson wanted to bring two of these groups together to share ideas, the conference provider could use the sophisticated domain merge facility to accomplish this request.

In a T.120 conference, nodes connect up-ward to a Multi-point Control Unit (MCU).The MCU model in T.120 provides a reliable approach that works in both public and private networks. Multiple MCUs may be easily chained together in a single domain. Each domain has a single top provider or MCU that houses the information base that is critical to the conference. If the top provider either fails or leaves a conference, the conference is terminated. If a lower level MCU (i.e., not the top provider) fails, only the nodes on the tree below that MCU are dropped from the conference. Because all nodes contain MCS they are all potentially "MCUs."

One of the critical features of the T.120 approach is the ability to direct data. This capability allows applications to communicate efficiently. MCS applications direct data within a domain via the use of channels. An application can choose to use multiple channels simultaneously for whatever purposes it needs (for example, separating annotation and file transfer operations). Application instances choose to obtain information by subscribing to whichever channel(s) contains the desired data. These channel assignments can be dynamically changed during the life of the conference.

It is up to the application developer to deter-mine how to use channels within an application. For example, an application may send control information along a single channel and application data along a series of channels that may vary depending upon the type of data being sent. The application developer may also take advantage of the MCS concept of private channels to direct data to a discrete subset of a given conference.

Data may be sent with one of four priority levels. MCS applications may also specify that data is routed along the quickest path of delivery using the standard send command. If the application uses the uniform send command, it ensures that data from multiple senders will arrive at all destinations in the same order. Uniform data always travels all the way up the tree to the top provider.

There are no constraints on the size of the data sent from an application to MCS. Segmentation of data is automatically per-formed on behalf of the application. However, it is the application's responsibility to reassemble the data upon receiving it by monitoring flags provided when the data is delivered.

Tokens are the last major facility provided by MCS. Services are provided to grab, pass, inhibit, release, and query tokens. Token resources may be used as either exclusive (i.e., locking) or non-exclusive entities.

Tokens can be used by an application in a number of ways. For example, an application may specify that only the holder of a specific token (i.e., the conductor)may send information in the conference.

Another popular use of tokens is to coordinate tasks within a domain. For example, suppose a teacher wants to be sure that every student in a distance learning session answered a particular question before displaying the answer. Each node in the underlying application inhibits a specific token after receiving the request to answer the question. The token is released by each node when an answer is provided. In the background, the teacher's application continuously polls the state of the token. When all nodes have released the token, the application presents the teacher with a visual cue that the class is ready for the answer.

T.124 Generic Conference Control (GCC). Generic Conference Control provides a comprehensive set of facilities for establishing and managing the multi-point conference. It is with GCC that we first see features that are specific to the electronic conference.

At the heart of GCC is an important information base about the state of the various conferences it may be servicing. One node, which may be the MCU itself, serves as the top provider for GCC information. Any actions or requests from lower GCC nodes ultimately filter up to this top provider.

Using mechanisms in GCC, applications create conferences, join conferences, and invite others to conferences. As endpoints join and leave conferences, the information base in GCC is updated and can be used to automatically notify all endpoints when these actions occur. GCC also knows who is the top provider for the conference. However, GCC does not contain detailed topology information about the means by which nodes from lower branches are connected to the conference.

T.121 Generic Application Template (GAT). This standard provides a template for T.120 resource management that developers should use as a guide for building application protocols. This template is mandatory for standardized application protocols and is highly recommended for non-standard application protocols to ensure consistency and reduce the potential for unforeseen interaction between different protocol implementations.

Within the T.121 model, GAT defines a generic Application Resource Manager (ARM). This entity manages GCC and MCS resources on behalf of the application protocol-specific functionality defined as an Application Service Element (ASE). Simply put, GAT provides a consistent model for managing T.120 resources required by the application to which the developer adds application-specific functionality.

T.126 Still Image Exchange and Annotation (SI). T.126 defines a protocol for viewing and annotating still images transmitted between two or more applications. This capability is often referred to as document conferencing or shared whiteboarding.

An important benefit of T.126 is that it readily shares visual information between applications that are running on dramatically different platforms. For example, a Windows-based desktop application could easily interoperate with a collaboration program running on a PowerMac. Similarly, a group-oriented conferencing system, without a PC-style interface, could share data with multiple users running common PC desktop software.

T.126 is designed to provide a minimum set of capabilities required to share information between disparate applications. Because T.126 is simply a protocol, it does not provide any of the API-level structures that allow application developers to easily incorporate shared whiteboarding into an application. These types of facilities can only be found in toolkit-level implementations of the standard (such as DataBeam's Shared Whiteboard Application Toolkit, known as SWAT).

T.127 Multi-point Binary File Transfer. T.127 specifies a means for applications to transmit files between multiple endpoints in a conference. Files can be transferred to all participants in the conference or to a specified subset of the conference. Multiple file transfer operations may occur simultaneously in any given conference and developers can specify priority levels for the file delivery. Finally, T.127 provides options for compressing files before delivering the data.

T.120 Node Controller. The Node Controller manages defined GCC Service Access Points (SAPs). This gives the node flexibility in responding to GCC events. Most of these GCC events relate to establishing conferences, adding/removing nodes from a conference, and breaking down and distributing information. The Node Controller's primary responsibility is to translate these events and respond appropriately.

T.120 and T.130 Standards Ratification

The Recommendations for the core multi-point communications infrastructure components (T.122, T.123, T.124 and T.125) were ratified by the ITU between March of 1993 and March of 1995. The first of the application standards (T.126 andT.127) were approved in March of 1995. An overview of the T.120 series was approved in February of 1996 as Recommendation T.120. T.121 (GAT) was also approved at that time.

The existing ratified standards are being actively discussed for possible amendments and extensions. This commonly occurs when implementation and interoperability issues arise. Work is also progressing on a new series of application standards (T.130-T.133, formerly T.128) that specifies the way in which T.120 data channels are used for control of real-time media streams.

The first of these are pending approval for early 1997. Work is also underway on T.120/30 series standards for reservation systems protocols (known as T.RES; no numbers yet assigned) between clients, reservation systems, and MCUs.

More than 100 multi-national companies have pledged their support for the T.120standard and more are being added to this list every week. Public supporters of T.120include international market leaders such as Apple, AT&T, British Telecom, Cisco Systems, Deutsche Telecom, IBM, Intel, MCI, Microsoft, Motorola, PictureTel, and DataBeam.

T.120 Information Sources:

DataBeam Corporation
info@databeam.com
www.databeam.com

International Telecommunications Union (ITU)
sales@itu.ch
www.itu.ch

International Multimedia Teleconferencing Consortium, Inc. (IMTC)
dkamlani@imtc.fabrik.com
www.imtc.org/imtc

UMP

Unified Messaging Protocol

Enhanced Systems, Inc.

Enhanced Systems, Inc. has developed a set of *Unified Messaging Protocol (UMP)* extensions to the ESMTP and POP3 protocols that have been placed in the public domain. UMP makes existing protocols message-type independent, and enables the sending, receiving, and storage of messages between dissimilar equipment.

Any UMP-compliant application can communicate with any other UMP-compliant application, anywhere in the world. UMP allows servers of various types to communicate over TCP/IP, and allows users to access any type of message with a single user interface.

The primary protocols for Internet messaging are Post Office Protocol (POP3), Simple Mail Transfer Protocol (SMTP), and Extended SMTP (ESMTP). These protocols make possible the sending and receiving of e-mail through any combination of compliant clients and servers.

SMTP is the method for delivering e-mail to a message system, and specifies how a client mail application should send generic text mail. When a client attaches to an SMTP server to send a message, it specifies the "From," "To," and "Date/Time" fields in the message header, then sends the message data. ESMTP extends that function by adding the ability to deliver a binary file (with MIME encoding) as an e-mail attachment.

POP3 complements SMTP's send function by providing the means for message retrieval. POP3 allows a user's workstation to access mail from a mailbox server (mail drop). It assumes mail has been delivered to the mailbox server via SMTP, and performs a simple passthrough of whole messages from a mailbox server to a client workstation.

These protocols combine to perform the necessary functions of sending, storage, and retrieval necessary to make e-mail operable, and the universal adoption of SMTP/ESMTP and POP3 has resulted in an exceptional degree of interoperability among Internet-related e-mail applications. Internet e-mail has become thoroughly homogeneous, even among products developed by different vendors.

While existing protocols work extremely well for text-based messaging, they are limited to that function. Created specifically to meet the needs of e-mail, SMTP and POP3 cannot currently support *unified messaging*.

If users are to retrieve all message types from a single source, they will need certain conveniences. For example, they will need to know which messages are voice mail, which are fax, and which are e-mail, and will need the ability to select messages by type.

When delivering messages, they will expect the functionality provided by traditional messaging systems, such as marking voice mail urgent, private, or forwarded. And when managing messages, they will need the ability to identify status (new, saved, deleted, read or unread) and to assign messages to folder.

These needs cannot be met with current e-mail protocols, which assume every message is generic e-mail. SMTP does not specify headers to include information beyond To, From, and Date/Time, so messages cannot be identified by type, status, etc. While ESMTP accommodates the attachment of files, it does not specify the type of file attached. POP3 does not analyze message headers, so that even if further intelligence were included in SMTP and ESMTP, a POP3 the client system would not be able to support user conveniences required of unified messaging -- for example, the user would not be able to retrieve FAX messages specifically or distinguish between read and unread messages.

The sending and receiving of such diverse message types as voice, fax, and e-mail through a single server will require the creation and widespread adoption of extensions to these protocols if unified messaging is to become a reality over the Internet -- just as extensions to SMTP were necessary for the attachment of files to text messages. Such protocol extensions have already been developed, implemented, and tested by Enhanced Systems, Inc. (ESI), an established manufacturer of voice processing systems.

In late 1995, ESI announced an important step in unified messaging over the Internet with a new product called @once. @once is a unified messaging server, operating on Windows NT, that enables the sending, receiving, and management of e-mail, voice mail, faxes, and pages over the World Wide Web from a single source. Remote and mobile users can retrieve and manage e-mail, voice mail, fax messages, and pages, all in a single connection through a standard Web browser, from anywhere in the world.

A key to the development of @once was the creation of the Unified Messaging Protocol (UMP) extensions to ESMTP and POP3. UMP allows @once to communicate with ESI's own voice mail system and with other @once servers over the Internet.

UMP also supports interconnectivity between applications from any manufacturer who wishes to participate in open, messaging by adopting it.

UMP can be implemented on any type of system; it is not specific to UNIX, DOS, OS/2, or Windows. If implemented by third-parties according to its specification, UMP will also allow those third-party products to exchange unified messages over the Internet, independent of any ESI-specific products. And because the protocol runs over TCP/IP, two UMP-compliant servers in different locations can communicate directly through the World Wide Web, essentially using the Internet as a long-distance carrier.

UMP Interoperability

UMP extensions to ESMTP and POP3 enable unified messaging by supporting multiple message types, and by providing the means for management of those various types according to their typical usage. UMP leaves all POP3 and ESMTP commands, headers, and specifications intact. Extensions consist of additions to ESMTP headers, and new POP3 commands.

Extensions to *POP3 commands* include commands necessary to allow clients to filter messages by type or status, to update header fields in message management, and to differentiate between UMP and non-UMP systems.

Extensions to *ESMTP headers* allow for precise identification of the message type, status, and management. For example, the header includes such information as the message's type (voice, fax, e-mail, etc.), status (new, saved, deleted, etc.), and the folder to which it belongs, along with other items necessary for proper message handling in a unified messaging environment.

Further extensions to ESMTP include the ability for the server to assign values to the extended SMTP headers and assure they appear first in the message header list. A UMP-compliant server, when accessing a message, first identifies the messaging system, then the user, and finally, the message content. The message headers are relatively small compared to the size of the message data. When retrieving a message, a UMP-compatible client system can retrieve just the headers, which minimizes overhead when a user checks messages or selects messages for retrieval. The entire message is retrieved only when the user specifically requests it.

At the beginning of a transmission, a UMP-compatible server identifies to the client system what types of messages it supports, and then sends the correct message type. The actual message delivery occurs as usual for ESMTP, except that more specific header information is sent. Message retrieval occurs as for POP3, but UMP's additional header information allows different message types to be targeted.

By bringing together unified messaging and the World Wide Web, UMP helps make possible applications that represent potentially enormous cost-savings, simplified usage, and highly increased messaging efficiency for organizations whose employees are not all co-located, and those who conduct significant messaging with partners, suppliers, and customers over wide geographic distribution.

For LAN-based unified messaging, UMP can make possible the advantages of simplified usage and increased efficiency for organizations who are seeking to streamline communications among the corporate, LAN-based user community.

In the interest of promoting open communications between message servers of all types, ESI has placed UMP in the public domain. A UMP specification is available for product developers who need complete details on UMP. To receive a copy, please fax a request to Enhanced Systems at 770-242-1630, or send e-mail to mittel@esisys.com.

VAT

Vat was the first Internet audio conferencing program. It needs to run on a high-end UNIX machine such as a Sun SPARCstation, Silicon Graphics and the DECstation 5000. Both the VAT and VAT-like RTP standards for establishing a call on the Internet are quickly becoming the dominant standards, allowing users of different applications to communicate.

Get the free software at: ftp://cs.ucl.ac.uk/mice/videoconference/vat/

VIC

Steven McCanne's

The Video Conferencing tool (VIC) is a real-time UNIX multimedia application for video conferencing over the Internet.

VIC started out as a research vehicle for exploring packet video and multimedia conferencing as part of Steven McCanne's dissertation research at UC Berkeley. VIC continues as an active research project by the Network Research Group at the Lawrence Berkeley National Laboratory in collaboration with the University of California.

Although VIC can be run point-to-point using standard unicast IP addresses, it's intended for multiparty conferencing. To do this, your system must support IP Multicast and, ideally, your network should be connected to the IP Multicast Backbone (MBONE). Calls are established via RTP.

VIC has a flexible and extensible architecture to support heterogeneous environments and configurations. In high bandwidth settings, for example, multi-megabit full-motion JPEG streams can be sourced using hardware assisted compression, while in low bandwidth environments like the Internet, aggressive low bit-rate coding can be carried out in software.

VIC provides only the video portion of a multimedia conference -- audio, whiteboard and session control tools are implemented as separate applications: Their audio tool is called VAT, their whiteboard tool WB, and their session directory tool is SD.

VIC viewing windows can "follow the speaker." Using cues from VAT, VIC will switch the viewing window to whomever is speaking. More than one window can be configured this way, which causes the most recent set of speakers to be displayed.VIC also allows graphics to be composited on top of the captured video. Overlays can be downloaded and manipulated across the "Conference Bus" allowing a "production team" to enhance a broadcast with on-the-fly titles, credits, logos, etc.

Video streams can be displayed simultaneously on a workstation display and on an external video output port, allowing you to render a single stream to a full-sized NTSC/PAL analog video signal that you can run on a large external monitor or video projector. Free source code and pre-compiled binaries are available via anonymous ftp. Contact the developers via e-mail at vic@ee.lbl.gov.

Visual Basic Script

Microsoft

Microsoft announced Visual Basic Script (VB Script), an Internet Web scripting language that's essentially a cross-platform subset of Visual Basic. It's part of the Microsoft Internet platform and will be licensed at no cost to Internet application, browser and tool developers.

VB Script allows developers to build Web pages that can respond to questions and queries, ask questions, check user data, calculate expressions, link to other applications, and connect to OLE controls, 3-D animations and even "applets" created using the Java language from Sun.

Just as Visual Basic (the complete development environment) made it easier to develop Windows-based applications, and Visual Basic for Applications did the same for Microsoft Office-based applications, so the VB Script subset is optimized to ease Internet application development (but it's still compatible with the other VB products).

Also either VB Script or Visual Basic 4.0 can be used to extend the Microsoft Internet Information Server (code-named Gibraltar). This will allow developers to create business object extensions to Web applications and help integrate them into existing corporate systems.

As soon all the VB Script language specs are defined, we'll run a tutorial on how it all works and how it can be CT-tweaked.

VPIM

Voice Profile for Internet Mail Protocol

The Voice Profile for Internet Mail (VPIM) is a standards based digital protocol for the sending and receiving of voice messages. This protocol is a profile of existing Internet messaging standards such as SMTP and MIME in the context of traditional voice-primary messaging.

The VPIM protocol specification is freely available on the Internet. FTP:\\ds.internic.net\rfcs\rfc1911.txt. The author of this abstract is Greg Vaudreuil of Octel 214-733-2723. The PR agency which handles VPIM is MC Communications (214-480-8383).

VPIM Digital Networking

Digital networking provides a voice messaging service through the use of digital leased lines such as frame relay or switched digital services such as ISDN. Digital technology provides reduced costs for higher volumes of messages and may provide increased voice fidelity to and from destinations with analog or highly compressed PSTN trunks.

Digital protocols can provide a range of features including traditional voice messaging with urgent, private, and read receipt, real-time directory services, and full multimedia email integration.

Digital protocols provide for the inexpensive sending of high message volumes through two mechanisms. Digital protocols typically compress the voice data in half, permitting sending in half the time over a digital telephone line. Additionally, because digital links may be of a higher bandwidth than a digital telephone line, messages may be sent much faster. Use of a typical T1 speed link is capable of sending messages up to 50 times faster than is possible with analog networking. A single T1 speed link can be used to send up to 2000 messages per hour using a typical digital networking protocol.

VPIM provides a standards based voice networking protocol using proven Internet email technology and TCP/IP data networking. The foundation technology is well understood and there are commercial implementations widely available on most operating systems.

It is expected that the standard will be rapidly adopted by the industry for the corporate and CPE markets. The standard is rapidly reaching completion. It is documented and available for implementation as experimental Internet standard, RFC 1911. It will become a standard document soon after there are multiple interoperable implementations publicly demonstrated.

VPIM provides the following features:

B7 Urgent and private indications. These are defined identically to the X.400 based AMIS-Digital protocol.

B7 Spoken Name. The senders spoken name is sent with each message.

B7 Fax. Fax is one of several optional body parts that can be sent with a bi-lateral agreement.

B7 Unlimited Message Length. There are practical limits to the size of a voice message, but these are imposed by the messaging systems themselves and not by the protocol.

Systems may negotiate the maximum message length at the time of message delivery. B7 Unlimited Number of Recipients. The number of recipients per message is not pre-defined.

B7 Remote Defined Errors. In addition to an extended set of error codes to indicate the reason for a message failure, VPIM provides the ability for the system sending a return message to include a voiced descriptive error phrase. This is particularly useful in environments such as OcteLink where users expect a detailed description of the error and how to avoid it in the future.

VPIM has several missing functions:

B7 Directory Synchronization. There is no mechanism for directory synchronization capability beyond the simple transport of the text and spoken name with each message.

B7 Read Receipt. There is no provisions in the current Internet mail standards for requesting or providing a read receipt confirmation. Work is underway to provide this feature in a later version.

VPIM has been known by several names throughout the development process. It has been known as the Voice Profile for MIME and more generally as SMTP/MIME. The VPIM protocol specification is freely available on the Internet. FTP:\\ds.internic.net\rfcs\rfc1911.txt The availability of the protocol on specific voice processing platforms can be found from the vendor.

WINSOCK

Most of these PC-based Internet Telephony applications need to use the Microsoft Windows Socket standard or "WinSock." WinSock is the standard Windows-to-TCP/IP programming interface, usually coming in the form of a Dynamic Link Library (DLL) file called WINSOCK.DLL supplied with most TCP/IP packages.

Winsock enables WWW browsers, FTP clients, email packages, and word processors talk to the Internet. WinSock was born at Interop in 1991. Led by Martin Hall, the group defined a common way for MS Windows applications to talk to TCP/IP. Thousands of applications have been written to WinSock. WinSock has played a instrumental role in the growth and use of the Internet, groupware, video-conferencing, email, and other communications technologies for MS Windows.

The WinSock specifications are produced by the WinSock Group - a loose coalition of vendors made up of developers and technologists from around the world who work together to define, refine and extend this popular interface definition. The Windows Sockets Forum, a coalition including Microsoft, Intel, Motorola and Sun Microsystems, has completed work on version 2.0 of the WinSock specification.

The WINSOCK.DLL is now divided into two layers, the WinSock API for applications programmers and a service provider interface translator for converting the WinSock API into a multiple network transport access protocol. Version 1.1 of WinSock addresses only connectivity over TCP/IP.

WinSock 2 is a more universal API. It extends to IPX/SPX, AppleTalk, Digital DECnet, NetBEUI, Vines IP, ATM networks, wireless communications and telephony-based protocols. Also, "shared sockets" let you multitask communications. WinSock 2 will enable a single application to access multiple network types (TCP/IP, IPX/SPX, DECnet, ISDN, ATM, etc.). It will also increase the speed of networked applications.

XTL & JavaTel

Sun Microsystems

"The Network is the Computer" is Sun Microsystems' battle cry. For computer telephony, this means you can put Open Systems Interconnection philosophy to meaningful work. The tenets of Sun's OSI religion are RISC microprocessors (SPARC/UltraSPARC), and the UNIX operating system. Add to this the Internet protocol (TCP/IP), NFS-based network computing and Java. Sun says these are the ultimate foundation for linking commercial IT enterprise networks (Intranets) and telephony domains. This plays well with mission critical buyers like telephone companies and enhanced services folks. Until Java, hints of Sun Microsystems, Inc. in computer telephony were just that. Mostly tucked away in private-label OEM agreements. All of this at the "high end" of computer telephony.

But add the new Java technology to the mix and you've got the makings of global domination. And you thought that was reserved for Microsoft. According to Doug Ehrenreich, Sun's biggest CT evangelist: "A new breed of computer and telephony technology suppliers are adopting Open Systems Interconnect principles. Internet protocols, browsers and digital packet networks are changing the rules of the game for Network Computing." And now the most serious vendors are taking this idea to heart.

Every vendor we've interviewed has weaved the Internet, the Web and Intranets into their overall CT vision. In tandem with their VARs and integrators, Sun is clearly giving Microsoft a run for their money in high end computer telephony. NT does not dominate the central office. UNIX comes much closer. And Sun servers support over 30% of all Internet servers world wide. Sun's knowledge of electronic messaging and the Internet are a perfect fit for the new breed of network-based CT solutions.

Sun likens the state of computer telephony to network computing for LANs and WANs in the mid 80's. The opportunity to link data and CT services with a common call management method is here. CT is now one of many regular components under Sun's network computing umbrella. The company fancies itself as navigator in your quest to integrate CT into the enterprise.

The reasons for Sun's increased focus on computer telephony is simple. As companies rely more on their information systems to provide competitive advantage, the network is pivotal. You need it to communicate with both an internal and external constituency. Companies cannot afford complex architectures to bridge voice and data services over the long run. TCP/IP and network computing will be the control network for the enterprise. Over time voice and data technologies will merge over one network. this will begin within the enterprise and finally spread into the public network. This when protocols are abstracted into software components. Microsoft would have to agree. Why else would their Internet Explorer 3.0 interface be proposed as the new desktop GUI for access to all applications (net or not).

Sun in Computer Telephony

CT is the final frontier for Sun. They've got a pretty good handle on computing in general. Their product line starts with low end servers and desktops and ends with a full line of enterprise servers. Applications and operating system don't change from server to server. So as your applications expand and require more computing power to run, Sun has a solution. Hardware components in the servers are common. This means you can move disk drives from server to server. You can even get NEBS (Telco-approved) Sparc servers from other companies, too. Sun is known for its ability to churn-out good, competitive platforms and still OEM its technology to other vendors.

Sun's CT Tool Box

These APIs leverage Sun's overall network computing model. Sun calls the suite "teleservices" products.. They are SunXTL (est. 1994) and the new JavaTel (part of the Java API suite). Sun's key to enabling CT on client devices is one of abstraction. With SunXTL and JavaTel, you can develop apps independent of topology, telephony interface, or phone system. Ideally, an application will be written once, so it works with various wiring con-figurations and any telephony gear. SunXTL enables CTI screen pop, 3rd party call control, fax servers, messaging, voice response and Internet services. The JavaTel toolkit provides a framework for the first party (desk-top, client device) and the third party (call center) telephony apps. The toolkit provides extensions so you can add your own functions. JavaTel runs on hardware configurations wherever the Java run-time can be used.

SunXTL

SunXTL allows multiple desktop/device applications to share telephone interfaces. Multiple applications can cooperate in managing and individual call without sacrificing data integrity or security. One application can create or receive a call and pass it to another application for voice processing. SunXTL allows, but does not require, a single "call manager" application to own all calls and impose a user or site-defined policy on call treatment.

If this sounds familiar, it should be. The ECTF's S.100 specification borrows heavily from these XTL precepts.

With SunXTL, there's no constraint on content or format of the data stream. The stream is delivered to an app for interpretation. SunXTL works equally well for audio/voice, fax, video, TCP/IP, or other data communications protocols (i.e. PBX interfaces). Sun positions it as the future control API for establishing multimedia connections on WANs.

Figure 12.5 -- SunXTL with JavaTel

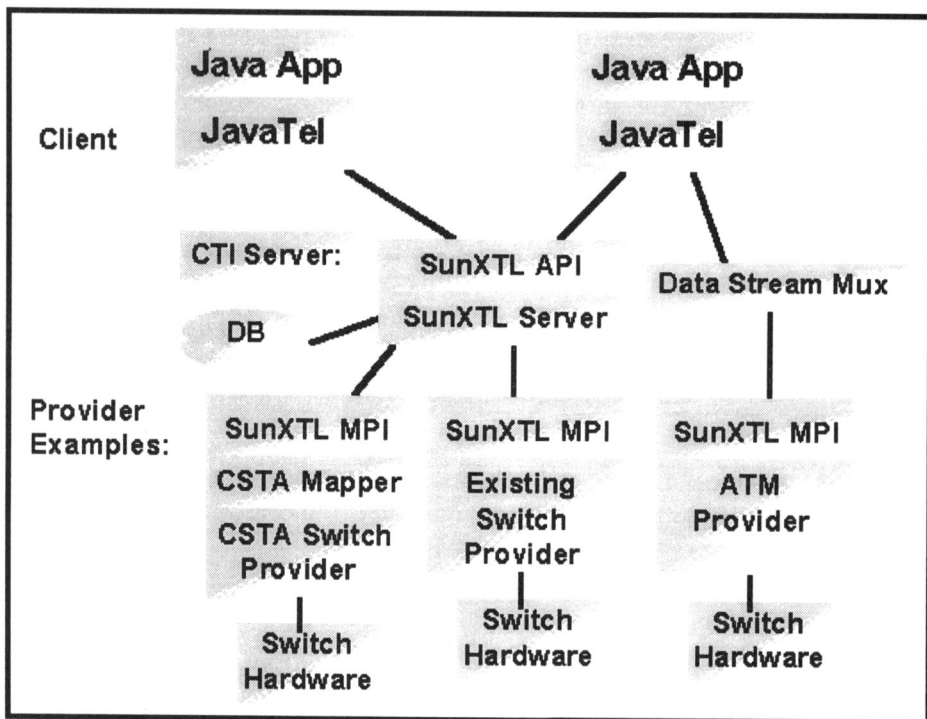

SunXTL with JavaTel is shown in Figure 12.5. With SunXTL, applications use the SunXTL API, providers of SunXTL services, and the SunXTL libraries and system services.

The details of the system services are hidden from applications and providers by the API and Media Platform Interface (MPI) libraries. The system services include a "message" passing server, a data stream multiplexor streams driver, a provider configuration database, and a tool for administration of that database.

Java

Java offers a "go anywhere" API. It's built to run on all platforms. Develop to Java and you get all of the platforms instead of porting to each one separately. CT vendors need an easy and cheap way to do 3rd party call control and screen pop interfaces. Java appletes promise to handle differing desktops easily by interpreting the application for the target environment. Same interface, same look and feel from a MAC, to a PC, to a SUN. The JavaTel toolkit was created by Sun to add this same portability to CT application development. Microsoft was quick to write a white paper positioning their ActiveX (COM) technology as a "friendly cohabitant" to Java. This is one indication that Java should be taken seriously.

Java Chip

The Java Chip is an imbedded processor. It allows application-specific tasks to run on a user-by-user basis. The chip itself is bundled as part of common terminals. These terminals can be workstations, telephones or any user device. The Java Chip will let desktops interface with network based applications on an as-need basis. This mirrors Sun's overall philosophy of Network Computing: "The Network is the Computer" or the network is everything outside of your device. The idea is to drive down cost and increase performance. Most apps don't require all of the CPU power all of the time. Most desktop applications are word processing, spread sheet and data base access. Only complex applications with real time modeling require 100% of the available CPU cycles on the desktop.

Java Chips promise to deliver performance on demand. If every application is available on the network on as need basis, every one can use it. This versus single user copies or licenses for advanced apps. This re-defines the run-time license for network users. Now instead of expensive software packages, individual Java Chip-enabled apps allow you to run program s "network based" and only pay for a transaction fee or right to use fee.

Already companies like Northern Telecom are building Java Chips into their phones. The possibilities are endless. You'll be able to get Caller-ID appletes imbedded in your home phones. Screen-pop Java Chips for your workstation. Universal messaging Java chips for your laptop. The plan is to do this at a fraction today's cost while using the latest and greatest release. It's kind of an imbedded point-of-use Flash ROM.

Sun's platform lets you mix and match available system, network and client components. Client devices like desktops, Kiosks, Internet terminals, phones and PDAs are accessed by any enterprise app. These can be any Java device using Java chipsets or devices using Java APIs. Network mediation includes CTI services and call management. This to handle network interface cards for voice/audio, fax and text-to-speech. All CTI and PBX interfaces, ISDN,T1/E1,ATM, serial and modem links are included. All CT-aware enterprise apps use servers configured to support CT requests and call management services. To do this, the Solaris OS handles MP (Multiprocessing), MT (Multithreading) and HA (High Availability).

Pushing CT into mainstream enterprise applications is becoming much easier. The industry is moving towards Sun's idea of distributed network computing model. Just three years ago, these ideas were considered "far off in the future." What brought much of this into focus is Sun's program: Customer Management Solutions (CMS). It's part "let's go Sun, let's go open" and part roll-up-your-sleeves VAR partnerships. Sun touts 65 partners in CMS. Not all are CT experts, but many are (see the roundup in this article). These CMS partners have targeted financial service companies, banking institutions, telecommunications companies, retail companies, government and educational institutions.

They go in and analyze the overall information flow in a company. The inevitable outcome is telephone-based transactions can be improved.

Figure 12.6 -- Dialogic's Java Call Center Vision

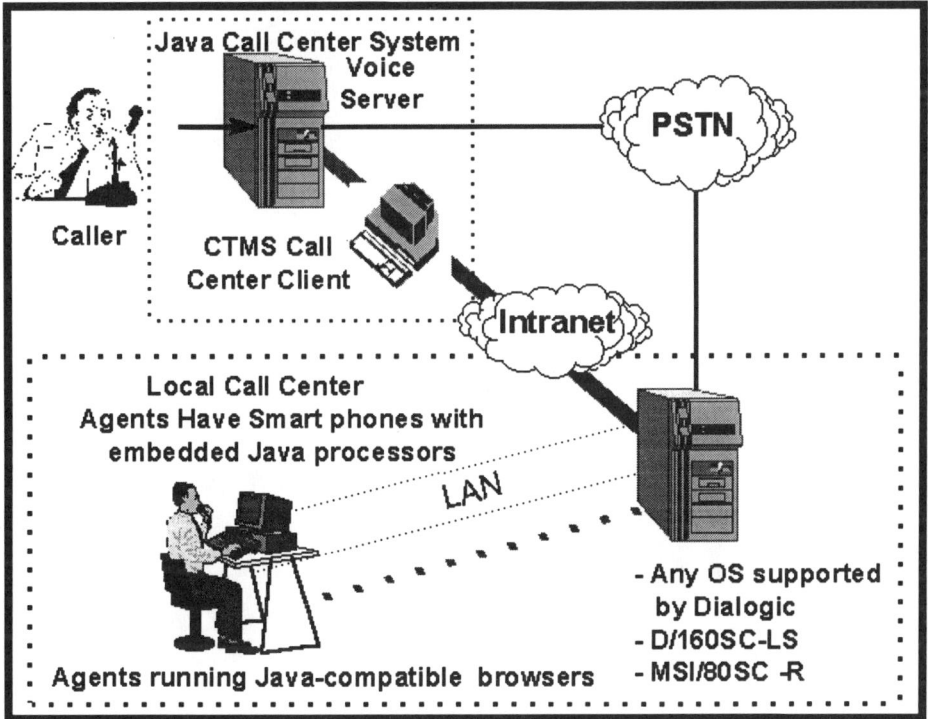

Figure 12.6 illustrates how an Intranet-based customer service call center (Java Call Center) takes a customer call. An IVR system using Java telephony extensions greets the customer. The call is routed via a drop and insert over the PSTN to the Local Call Center. The Java customer data servlete 'pushes' the appropriate customer data information over the Intranet to a smart phone with an embedded Java chip. Or the call could go to an MSI (Modular Station Interface) agent running any Java compatible Internet browser, or Hot Java applet. Java applications can be deployed on Windows NT in the voice processing server or under any OS supported by Java on a Dialogic CTMS client, including NC, Mac, NT, AIX, UnixWare, NetWare.

Appendix A

Recommended Resources and Bibliography

The publications cited here offer a comprehensive and detailed understanding of the subjects covered in this book. The publisher would like to acknowledge the authors of copyrighted material for the permissions granted to use portions of their work as solicited by the research staff.

Great Books on Computer Telephony:

1001 Computer Telephony Tips, Secrets and Shortcuts,
Edwin Margulies, Flatiron Publishing, Inc., 1996.

236 Killer Voice Processing Applications,
Edwin Margulies, Flatiron Publishing, Inc., 1995.

Basic Book of Information Networking,
Motorola Codex, Motorola University Press, 1992.

Basic Book of ISDN,
Motorola Codex, Motorola University Press, 1992.

Client Server Computer Telephony,
Edwin Margulies, Flatiron Publishing, Inc., 1994.

Complete Traffic Engineering Handbook,
Jerry Harder, Flatiron Publishing, Inc., 1992.

Computer Based Fax Processing,
Maury Kauffman, Flatiron Publishing, Inc., 1994.

Computer Telephony on the Sun Platform,
Patrick Kane, Flatiron Publishing, Inc., 1996.

Customers: Arriving With a History and Leaving With an Experience,
Andrew Waite, Flatiron Publishing, Inc., 1996.

Customer Service Over the Phone,
Stephen Coscia, Flatiron Publishing, Inc., 1995.

Handbook of Telecommunications,
James Harry Green, Flatiron Publishing, Inc., 1993.

International CallBack Book,
Gene Retske, Flatiron Publishing, Inc., 1995.

Local & Long Distance Billing Practices,
M. Brosnan & J. Messina, Flatiron Publishing, Inc., 1993.

Newton's Telecom Dictionary - 11th edition,
Harry Newton, Flatiron Publishing, Inc., 1996.

PC Telephony,
Bob Edgar, Flatiron Publishing, Inc., 1995.

Predictive Dialing Fundamentals,
Aleksander Szlam, Flatiron Publishing, Inc., 1996

Reference Manual for Telecommunications Engineering,
Roger L. Freeman, John Wiley & Sons, publisher.

SCSA - Signal Computing System Architecure - 2nd Edition
Edwin Margulies, Flatiron Publishing, Inc., 1996.

Speech Recognition,
Pete Foster, Flatiron Publishing, Inc., 1993.

Telecommunications Management,
Harry Green, Flatiron Publishing, Inc., 1993.

The MVIP Book,
GO-MVIP, Flatiron Publishing, Inc., 1995.

Telephony For Computer Professionals,
Jane Laino, Flatiron Publishing, Inc., 1994.

Testing Computer Telephony Systems and Networks,
Steve Gladstone, Flatiron Publishing, Inc., 1994.

The Guide to T-1 Networking,
Bill Flanagan, Flatiron Publishing, Inc., 1990.

Understanding Computer Telephony,
Carlton Carden, Flatiron Publishing, Inc., 1996.

Understanding Data Communications,
G. Friend & J. Fike, Flatiron Publishing, Inc., 1993.

Understanding Telephone Electronics,
J. Fike, Flatiron Publishing, Inc., 1993.

Visual Basic Telephony,
Krisztina Holly & Chris Brookins, Flatiron Publishing, Inc., 1995.

Voice Processing,
Walt Tetschner, Artech House, 1991.

Glossary

10Base2
IEEE standard for baseband Ethernet at 10 Mbps over coaxial cable to a maximum distance of 185 meters. Also known as Thin Ethernet.

10Base-T
IEEE standard for operating Ethernet LANs on twisted pair wiring that appears like telephone cabling. Sometimes old cabling will not work.

A

A & B Bits
Bits used in digital environments to convey signaling information. A bit value of one generally corresponds to loop current flowing in an analog environment. A bit zero corresponds to no loop current, i.e. to no connection. Other signals are made by changing bit values. For example, a flash-hook is set by briefly setting the A bit to zero.

A & B Leads
Additional leads used typically with a channel bank two-wire E&M interface to connect certain types of PBXs (also used to return talk battery to the PBX).

A & B Signaling
Procedure used in most T-1 transmission links where one bit, robbed from each of the 24 subchannels in every sixth frame, is used for carrying dialing and control information. A type of in-band signaling used in T-1 transmission, A and B signaling reduces the available user bandwidth from 1.544 to 1.536 Mbps. See also PRI.

A4

Basic Group 3 standard defined for the scanning and printing of a page 215 mm (8.5 in) wide. An A5 page is 151 mm (5.9 in) wide, and the A6 is 107 mm (4.2 in) wide.

A LAW

The PCM coding and companding standard used in Europe. See A LAW ENCODING and E-1.

A LAW Encoding

The method of encoding sampled audio waveforms used in the 2048K bit 30 channel PCM primary system, widely used outside North America. See E-1.

Access Tandem

A special type of local phone company central office. It's designed to provide equal access for all the long distance carriers in that area.

Activity Report

Provides a record of transmission time, date, size of the file, recipient's telephone number, transmission success or failure, the sender's name, and other pertinent information. This is a valuable management tool to get an overview of a company's fax traffic and costs.

A/D

Analog to digital conversion.

Adaptive Pulse Code Modulation

A way of encoding analog voice signals into digital signals by adaptively predicting future encodings by looking at the immediate past. The adaptive part of this method reduces the number of bits per second that another rival and more common method called PCM (Pulse Code Modulation) requires to encode voice. Adaptive PCM is not especially common because, even though it reduces the number of bits required to encode voice, the electronics to do it are expensive. See also PULSE CODE MODULATION.

ADC
Analog-to-Digital Converter.

Administrable Service Provider
A service provider which supports administrable services (e.g., SCR).

ADPCM
Adaptive Differential Pulse Code Modulation. A speech coding method which calculates the difference between two consecutive speech samples in standard PCM coded voice signals. This calculation is encoded using as adaptive filter and therefore, is transmitted at a lower rate than the standard 64 Kbps technique.

Typically, ADPCM allows an analog voice conversation to be carried within a 32k-kbit/s digital channel; 3 or 4 bits are used to describe each sample, which represents the difference between two adjacent samples. Sampling is done 8,000 times a second.

ADSI
Analog Display Services Interface. ADSI is a Bellcore standard defining a protocol on the flow of information between something (a switch, a server, a voice mail system, a service bureau) and a subscriber's telephone, PC, data terminal or other communicating device with a screen. The simple idea of ADSI is to add words to, and therefore a modicum of simplicity of use to a system that usually uses only touch tones.

Imagine a normal voice mail system. You call it. It answers with a voice menu. Push 1 to listen to your messages, 2 to erase them, 3 to store them, 4 to forward them, etc. It's confusing. You have to remember which is which. ADSI is designed to solve that. It's designed to send to your phone's screen the choices in words that you're hearing.

You then have the choice of responding to what you hear or what you see. Your response is the same -- a touch-tone button. ADSI's signaling is DTMF and standard Bell 202 modem signals from the service to your 202-modem equipped phone. From the phone to the service it's only touch-tone.

With ADSI, you don't hear the modem signaling because every time the service gets ready to send you information, it first sends a "mute" tone. ADSI works on every phone line in the world.

Advisory Tones
Signals such as dial tone, busy, ringing, fast-busy, call-waiting, camp-on-- and all the other tones which your telephone system uses to tell you that something is happening or about to happen.

AEB
Analog Expansion Bus. Dialogic's name for the analog electrical connection between its network interface modules and its analog resource modules. This bus is now "open." Technical specifications are available, thus enabling outsiders to make their own resource modules and/or network interface modules. The AEB interfaces DTI/124 and D/4x voice response component boards which fit in an AT-expansion slot of a PC. See also PEB, which is the more modern digital PCM expansion bus. See also SCSA, which is Dialogic's latest standard.

AGC
Automatic Gain Control. There are two electronic ways you can control the recording of something -- Manual or Automatic Gain Control (AGC). AGC is an electronic circuit in tape recorders, speakerphones, and other voice devices which is used to maintain volume. AGC is not always a brilliant idea, since AGC will attempt to produce a constant volume level.

This means it will try to equalize all sounds -- the volume of your voice, and, when you stop talking, the circuit static and/or general room noise which you undoubtedly do not want amplified. Sometimes it's better to have quiet, when you want quiet. Manual Gain Control is preferred in professional applications.

Alerting Signal
A ringing signal put on subscriber access lines to indicate there's an incoming call.

Algorithm

A set of ordered steps for solving a problem, such as a mathematical formula or instructions in a program. In the context of speech coding, it refers to the mathematical methods used to compress speech. Unique speech-coding algorithms are patentable. Specific implementations of an algorithm in the form of computer programs are also subject to copyright protection.

All Trunks Busy

When a user tries to make an outside call through a telephone system and receives a "fast" busy signal (twice as many signals as a normal busy in the same amount of time), he is usually experiencing the joy of All Trunks Busy. No trunks are available to handle that call.

The trunks are all being used at that time for other calls or are out of service. These days, many long distance companies are replacing a "fast" busy signal with a recording that might say something like, "I'm sorry. All circuits are busy. Please try your call later."

AMIS

See AUDIO MESSAGING INTERCHANGE SPECIFICATION. AMIS is a standard for networking voice mail systems.

Amplitude

The distance between high or low points of a waveform or signal. Also referred to as the wave "height."

Amplitude Distortion

The difference between the output wave shape and the input wave shape.

Amplitude Equalizer

A corrective network that is designed to modify the amplitude characteristics of a circuit or system over a desired frequency range. Such devices may be fixed, manually adjustable, or automatic.

Amplitude Modulation

Also called AM, it's a method of adding information to an electronic signal in which the signal is varied by its height to impose information on it.

"Modulation" is the term given to imposing information on an electrical signal. The information being carried causes the amplitude (height of the sine wave) to vary. In the case of LANs, the change in the signal is registered by the receiving device as a 1 or a 0. A combination of these conveys different information, such as words, numbers or punctuation marks.

AMX

Analog Matrix Switch. A Dialogic product. An 8 x 8 analog crosspoint switch on a board used for sharing resources among AEB-based products and for connecting to phones and external audio devices.

Analog

Comes from the word "analogous," which means "similar to." In telephone transmission, the signal being transmitted -- voice, video, or image -- is "analogous" to the original signal. In other words, if you speak into a microphone and see your voice on an oscilloscope and you take the same voice as it is transmitted on the phone line and ran that signal into the oscilloscope, the two signals would look essentially the same. The only difference is that the electrically transmitted signal (the one over the phone line) is at a higher frequency. In correct English usage, "analog" is mean-ingless as a word by itself. But in telecommunications, analog means telephone transmission and/or switching which is not digital. See ANALOG TRANSMISSION.

Analog Bridge

A circuit which allows a normal two-person voice conversation to be extended to include a third person -- without degrading the quality of the call. Digital bridges work better.

Analog/Digital Converter

An A/D Converter. Pronounced: "A to D Converter." A device which converts an analog signal to a digital signal.

Analog Facsimile

Facsimile which can transmit and receive grey shadings -- not just black and white. "Analog" facsimile is usually transmitted digitally.

But it's called analog because of its ability to transmit what appear to be continuous shades of grey.

Analog Transmission

A way of sending signals -- voice, video, data -- in which the transmitted signal is analogous to the original signal. In other words, if you spoke into a microphone and saw your voice on an oscilloscope and you took the same voice as it was transmitted on the phone line and threw that signal onto the oscilloscope, the two signals would look essentially the same. The only difference between them is that the electrically transmitted signal would be at a higher frequency.

ANI

Automatic Number Identification. A phone call arrives at your home or office. At the front of the phone call is a series of digits which tell you the phone number calling you. These digits may arrive in analog or digital form. They may arrive as touch-tone digits inside the phone call. They may arrive in a digital form on a separate circuit.

Whichever way they arrive, you will need some equipment to decipher the digits AND do "something" with them. That "something" might be throwing them in a database and bringing up your customer's record on a screen in front of your telephone agent as he answers the phone. "Good morning, Mr. Smith." Some large users say they could save as much as 20 seconds on the average IN-WATS call if they knew early on the phone number of the person calling them. They wouldn't need to ask their regular customers for their address, phone number, credit card number, etc.

Announcement Service

Allows a phone user to hear a recording when he dials a certain number. Could be an answering machine. Could be a voice response system. Could also be a solid-state digital announcer. Or a voice response system.

ANSI

American National Standards Institute. A standards- setting, non-government organization which develops and publishes standards for voluntary use in the U.S.

Answer Detect

The use of a digital signal processing technique to determine the presence of voice energy on a telephone line. It is used with call (answer) supervision, to identify an answered line. It is beginning to be used with computerized dialing equipment in business to consumer calling. This technique eliminates the need for a telephone representative to constantly monitor call set-up progress on each telephone line in the event a call is answered. See ANSWER SUPERVISION.

Answer Supervision

Follow this scenario: I call you long distance. My central office must know when you answer your phone, so my central office or long distance phone company can start billing me for the call. It works like this: when you, the called party, answer your phone, your central office sends a signal back to my central office (the originating CO). This tells my central office to start billing me for the call. This signal is called Answer Supervision.

Before the Divestiture of the Bell System in early 1984, most of the nation's long distance companies -- with the exception of AT&T -- did not receive Answer Supervision. They did not know precisely when the called party answered. So they started their billing cycle after some time -- 20 or 30 seconds after the caller completed dialing. These long distance companies presumed that after this time, some one will have answered and the call will be in progress (and they therefore start timing and billing for the call). Without Answer Supervision, their billing of calls is inaccurate. With the Divestiture of the Bell System, and the introduction of Equal Access, long distance companies now receive true Answer Supervision. See also SOFT-WARE SUPERVISION.

Anti Aliasing

A computer imaging term. A blending effect that smoothes sharp contrasts between two regions of different colors.

Properly done, this eliminates the jagged edges of text or colored objects. Used in voice processing, anti-aliasing usually refers to the process of removing spurious frequencies from waveforms produced by converting digital signals back to analog.

API

See Application Program Interface.

Application Class

A group of client applications that perform similar services, such as voice messaging or fax-back services.

Application Profile

A description of the kinds of resources and services required by a client application (or an application class). An application profile is defined once for an instance of an application; then system services such as the SCR will be able to fulfill the needs of the application without the application having to state its needs explicitly.

Application Programming Interface. "Hooks" into software. A set of standard software interrupts, calls, and data formats that application programs use to initiate contact with network services, mainframe communications programs, or other program-to-program communications. For example, applications use APIs to call services that transport data across a network. A set of formalized software calls and routines that can be referenced by an application program to access underlying network services.

Standardization of APIs at various layers of a communications protocol stack provides a uniform way to write applications. NetBIOS is an early example of a network API. Also, applications use APIs to call services that transport data across a network. See also WINDOWS TELEPHONY.

Application

A software program that carries out some useful task. Database managers, spreadsheets, communications packages, graphics programs, and word processors are all applications.

Applications Generator

Basically, software that writes software. Applications generators are software tools that, in response to your input, write software code which a computer can understand. Applications generators have two major benefits:

First, they save time. An applications generator is perfect for demonstrating a quick, though not complete, programming application.

Second, they can often be used by non-programmers. Applications generators are often used in programming voice processors. Applications generators come in many flavors. They may be general purpose tools. Or they may provide support for specific application segments such as: connecting voice response units to mainframe databases; voice messaging system development; audiotex system development, etc.

One of applications generators' biggest advantages is that their ability to translate user specified screens and menus into programming code. In essence you produce the screen or menu using an interface as simple as a word processor. Then the applications generator translates that screen into programming code in a language, such as the widely-used "C." Once translated into C, a programmer proficient in C could go through the code and "improve" on it.

Applications Processor
A special purpose computer which attaches to a telephone system and allows the telephone system (and the people using it) to do different "applications" things, like voice mail, interactive voice response, etc. We think AT&T invented the term Applications Processor.

Appli/COM
See T.611.

Apps Gens
See APPLICATIONS GENERATORS.

ASCII
American Standard Code for Information Interchange. ASCII Character Set A character set consisting only of the characters included in the original 128-character ASCII standard.

ASP
See Administrable Service Provider

Asynchronous Communication

A method of data communication in which the transmission of bits of data is not synchronized by a clock signal but is accomplished by sending the bits one after another, with a start bit and a stop bit to mark the beginning and end of the data unit. The two communicating devices must be set to the same speed-called the baud rate. Asynchronous communication normally is used for transmission speeds under 19,200 baud. Because of the lower communication speeds, normal telephone lines can be used for asynchronous communication.

Asynchronous Request

A request where the client does not wait for completion of the request, but does intend to accept results later. Contrast with synchronous request.

AT WORK Protocol

Microsoft's integration protocol for linking peripheral office equipment, including telephony services, to Windows applications.

Audio

Sound you hear which may be converted to electrical signals for transmission. A human being who hasn't had his ears blown by listening to a Sony Walkman or a ghetto blaster can hear sounds from about 15 to 20,000 hertz.

Audio Frequencies

Those frequencies which the human ear can detect (usually in the range of 15 to 20,000 hertz). Only those from 300 to 3,000 hertz are transmitted through the phone. Which is why the phone doesn't sound "Hi-Fi."

Audio Menu

Options spoken by a voice processing system. The user can choose what he wants done by simply choosing a menu option -- hitting a touch-tone on his phone, or speaking a word or two. There are basically two ways of organizing computer or voice processing software -- menu-driven and non-menu driven. Menu-driven programs are easier for users to use. But they can only present as many options as can be reasonably spoken in a few seconds.

Audio menus are typically played to callers in automated attendant/voice messaging, voice response and transaction processing applications. See also MENU.

Audio Messaging Interface Specification (AMIS)

Issued in February 1990, AMIS is a series of standards aimed at addressing the problem of how voice messaging systems produced by different vendors can network or inter-network. Before AMIS, systems from different vendors could not exchange voice messages. AMIS deals only with the interaction between two systems for the purpose of exchange voice messages. It does not describe the user interface to a voice messaging system, specify how to implement AMIS in a particular systems or limit the features a vendor may implement. AMIS is really two specifications. One, called AMIS-Digital, is based on completely digital interaction between two voice messaging systems. All the control information and the voice message itself, is conveyed between systems in digital form. By contrast, the AMIS-Analog specification calls for the use of DTMF tones to convey control information and transmission of the message itself is in analog form. AMIS was discussed in detail in the October 1990 issue of Business Communications Review. AMIS specifications are available from Hartfield Associates, Boulder CO. 303-442-5395.

Audio Response Unit (ARU)

A device which translates computer output into spoken voice. Let's say you dialed up a computer and it said "If you want the weather in Chicago, push button "123," then it would give you the weather. But that weather would be "spoken" by an audio response unit.

Audiotex

A generic term for voice response equipment and services. Audiotex may be passive or interactive. In "passive," the classic applications fall into "Jokes, Scopes and Soaps." Dial a number, hear the joke of the day.

Dial a number, hear your horoscope. Dial a number, hear what's happening on your latest TV soap. In its interactive form, Audiotex is basically another term for Interactive Voice Response. You call a phone number.

A machine answers. It presents you several options, "Push 1 for information on Plays, Push 2 for information on movies, Push 3 for information on Museums." If you push 2, the machine may come back, "Push 1 for movies on the south side of town, Push 2 for movies on the north side of town, etc." Or it says, "To hear your present bank balance, touch-tone your bank account number in now." See also INTERACTIVE VOICE RESPONSE.

Auto Fax Tone

Also called CNG, or Calling Tone. This tone is the sound produced by virtually all Group 3 fax machines when they dial another fax machine. CNG is a medium pitch tone (1100 Hz) that lasts 1/2 second and repeats every 3 1/2 seconds. A FAX machine will produce CNG for about 45 seconds after its dials. See also CNG.

Automatic Cover Letter

Allows the user to automatically attach a cover letter to the document being sent. This is especially convenient when sending material such as spreadsheets, for example.

Automatic Redial

Provides for the automatic redialing of a voice, data, or fax number in the event the receiving line is busy or an error occurred in sending the data. Some products allow the user to specify the redial attempts and correct specific errors to be used when redialing.

Automatic Routing

Allows incoming fax documents to be automatically routed to the addressed individual on a LAN or centralized system. Current technology provides several methods of accomplishing this using various techniques.

Automated Attendant

A specialized form of an Interactive Voice Response system. An IVR connected to a PBX. When a call comes in, this device answers it, and says something like: "Thanks for calling the ABC Company. If you know the extension number you'd like, push-button that extension now and you'll be transferred. If you don't know it, push button "0" (zero) and the live operator will come on. Or wait a few seconds and the operator will come on, anyway."

Sometimes the automated attendant might give you other options -- like "dial 3" for a directory. Automated attendants are sometimes connected also to voice mail systems ("I'm not here. Leave a message for me."). Some people react well to automated attendants. Others don't.

A good rule: Before you spring an automated attendant on your people/customers/subscribers, etc., let them know. Train them a little. They'll then perceive the automated attendant device a lot more positively. Tip: When you reach an automated attendant and don't know the extension number, dial the person's last name on your touch-tone pad. Better automated attendants will recognize the name and translate it into the extension number.

Automatic Call Distributor (ACD)

A specialized phone system used for handling many incoming calls. Typically used by airlines, rent-a-car companies, hotels, etc. An ACD has four functions. First, it will recognize and answer an incoming call. Second, it will look in its database for instructions on what to do with that call. Third, based on that database's instructions, it will send the call to a recording that "somebody will be with you soon, please don't hang up!" Fourth, it will send the call to one operator of a group of operators -- as soon as that operator has completed their previous call, and/or the caller has heard the canned message.

The term Automatic Call Distributor comes from distributing the incoming calls in some logical pattern to a group of operators. That pattern might be Uniform (to distribute the work uniformly). It also might be Top-down. Distributing calls logically is the function most people associate with an ACD. But it's not the most important. Much more important is the management information which the ACD produces. This information typically is of two sorts -- 1: The arrival of incoming calls (when, how many, which lines, from where, etc.) and 2: How many callers were put on hold, told to wait and didn't. This is called information on ABANDONED CALLS. This information is very important for staffing, for buying lines from the phone company and also for figuring what level of service to provide to the customer. And what different levels of service (how long for people to answer the phone) might cost.

Automatic Call Distributors are now combined with Interactive Voice Response Systems and ANI (automatic number identification) to give much effective and faster handling of incoming customer calls.

Automatic Call Sequencer

ACS. A device for handling incoming calls. Typically it performs three functions. 1. It answers an incoming call, gives the caller a message, and puts them on "Hold." 2. It signals the agent (the person who will answer the call) which call on which line to answer. Typically, the call which it signals to be answered is the call which has been on "hold" the longest. 3. It provides management information, such as how many abandoned calls there were, how long the longest person was kept on hold, how long the average "on hold" was, etc.

Automatic Callback

When a caller dials another internal extension and finds it busy, the caller dials some digits on his phone or presses a special "automatic callback" button. When the person he's calling hangs up, the phone system rings his number and the number of the original caller and the phone system automatically connects the two together. This feature saves a lot of time by automatically retrying the call until the extension is free.

Automatic Calling Unit

ACU. A device that places a telephone call on behalf of a computer.

Automatic Circuit Assurance

ACA is a PBX feature that helps you find bad trunks. The PBX keeps records of calls of very short and very long duration. If these calls exceed a certain parameter, the attendant is notified. The logic is that a lot of very short calls or one very long call may suggest that a trunk is hung, broken or out of order. The attendant can then physically dial into that trunk and check it.

Automatic Number Identification

ANI. Equipment at your central office which recognizes the telephone number of the person making the call so that information about the call can be sent to the call accounting (i.e. billing) system.

B

Backbone
The part of a communications network which carries network traffic between access devices.

Backplane
The high-speed communications line which individual components of a modern electronic system are connected to. For example, all the extensions of a PBX are connected to line cards (circuit boards), which slide into the PBX's cage. At the rear of the PBX cage, there is a connector. Each of these connectors is plugged into the PBX's Backplane. Also called a Backplane Bus. This backplane bus is typically very high speed, since it carries many conversations, much address information and considerable signaling. These days, the backplane bus is typically a time division multiplexed line -- somewhat like a train with many cars, each of which represent a time slice of another conversation. The backplane's capacity determines the overall capacity of the switch.

Baseboard
A Dialogic voice processing board without any daughterboards attached.

Battery
1. Term used to reference the DC power source of a telephone system.
   Often called "Talk Battery." 2. Storage battery used with central office switching systems and PBXs serving locations which cannot tolerate outages. Batteries serve the following purposes: Act as a filter across the generator or power rectifier output to smooth out the current and reduce noise; provide a cushion against periodic overloads exceeding the generator/rectifier capacity; supply emergency power for a limited time in event of commercial power failure.

Baud

The number of changes in signal state (switching) per second in a signal sent by a modem. A baud may contain four or more bits. Sometimes confused with BPS, the bits per second transmitted on the channel.

Baud Rate

The transmission rate of a communications channel. Technically, baud rate refers to the maximum number of changes (switching) that can occur per second in the electrical state of a communications circuit. Under the RS-232C communications protocol, 300 baud is likely to equal 300 bps, but at higher baud rates the number of bits per second transmitted is actually higher than the baud rate because one change can represent more than one bit of data. For example, 1,200 bps is usually sent at 600 baud by sending two bits of information with each change in the electrical state of the circuit.

BISDN

Broadband ISDN (Integrated Services Digital Network) Also see ISDN.

Bit

Binary digit, the smallest amount of information in a binary system, a 0 or 1 condition.

BIT RATE

The number of bits that a communications channel can transmit in a fixed time interval, typically measured in kilobits (1000 bits) per second (kbps). Uncompressed, telephone-quality speech is 64 kbps. It is made up of 8,000 samples every second, with each sample being 8 bits. CD-quality voice requires approximately 706 Kbps (44,100 samples every second with each sample being composed of 16 bits).

Board

An SCSA definition. Any hardware module that controls its own physical interface to the SCbus or SCxbus. From a programming point of view, a board is an addressable system component that contains resources.

Bong

A tone that long distance carriers and value added carriers make in order to signal you that they now require additional action on your part -- usually dialing more digits.

BPS

Bits per second.

Broadcasting

This procedure allows the user to send a voice message, data file, or fax document to a group of people or companies. Groups can be temporarily or permanently stored in the telephone directories for repeated broadcasting.

Busy

In use. "Off-hook". There are slow busies and fast busies. Slow busies are when the phone at the other end is busy or off-hook. They happen 60 times a minute. Fast busies (120 times a minute) occur when the network is congested with too many calls. Your distant party may or may not be busy, but you'll never know because you never got that far.

Byte

A group of 8 bits, making up a single memory location. Most computers cannot address a bit, they can only address bytes.

C

C

The most common programming language in the voice processing industry. C operates under MS-DOS or UNIX, and other operating systems. It is very powerful and is becoming a standard also for programming telecom switches, PBX and central office.

Cadence

In voice processing, cadence is used to refer to the pattern of tones and silence intervals generated by a given audio signal. Examples are busy and ringing tones.

A typical cadence pattern is the US ringing tone, which is one second of tone followed by three seconds of silence. Some other countries, such as the UK, use a double ring, which as two short tones within about a second, followed by a little over two seconds of silence.

Call

Two or more parties connected together for the purpose of communication. A party may be either a person or a client application, each respectively directing a group or telephone terminal equipment (phone, fax, etc.)

Call Center

A place where calls are answered and calls are made. A call center will typically have lots of people (also called agents), an automatic call distributor, a computer for order-entry and lookup on customers' orders. A Call Center could also have a predictive dialer for making lots of calls quickly. The term "call center" is broadening. It now includes help desks and service lines.

Call Control

The establishment and control of telephone links. This involves answering, originating, transferring, conferencing, and terminating telephone calls, and monitoring their status. The electronic signaling functions that control the setting up, monitoring and tearing down of telephone calls. The electronic signaling functions that control the setting up, monitoring, and tearing down of telephone calls. First-party call control is the view of directly controlling a telephone set; third-party call control takes the view of controlling the call through a switch (PBX) in a centralized fashion. Generally third-party call control also refers to the control of Other functions that relate to the switch at large, such as ACD queuing, etc.

Call Processing

Call processing is setting up, connecting, transferring, disconnecting, etc. a phone call. Call processing does not affect the content -- voice or otherwise -- of the conversation. That process is called "voice processing." And that is a broader concept, encompassing everything from compression, storage, editing to recognition.

Call Progress Tone

A tone sent from the telephone switch to tell the caller of the progress of the call. Examples of the common ones are dial tone, busy tone, ringback tone, error tone, re-order, etc. Some phone systems provide additional tones, such as confirmation, splash tone, or a reminder tone to indicate that a feature is in use, such as confirmation, hold reminder, hold, intercept tones.

Caller ID

Signals that identify the telephone number of the calling party; these signals are sent along the telephone line at the start of the call. Not all telephone network connections support caller ID signaling. In a more general sense, caller ID can be obtained by prompting the caller for an identity code.

Calling Party Identification

A new service being tested in some local areas which tells the person being called which number is calling them. They can then decide to answer or not answer the call. See ANI, which stands for Automatic Number Identification.

CALLPATH

IBM's announced telephone system link to IBM's computers. See CALLPATH SERVICES ARCHITECTURE.

CALLPATH CICS

Enabling software that connects your telephone systems with your IBM 370 or 390 (i.e. the mainframe version of CallPath/400, which works on the AS/400 platform).

CALLPATH Host

IBM and ROLM's CICS-based integrated voice and data applications platform which links to ROLM's 9751 PBX. See CALLPATH SERVICES ARCHITECTURE.

CALLPATH Services Architecture

CSA. IBM's program for integrating voice and data technologies. It is both a strategy and set of open architecture commands and interfaces for integrating voice and database technologies.

The idea is that with CallPath a call will arrive at a computer terminal simultaneously with the database record of the caller. And such call and database record can be transferred simultaneously to an expert, a supervisor, etc. The first implementation is CallPath/400 which works with the IBM AS/400 minicomputer. CallPath CICS works with IBM mainframes. See OPEN APPLICATION INTERFACE and DIRECTTALK.

Carrier Frequency
The frequency of a carrier wave.

Carrier Wave
A wave having at least one characteristic that may be varied from a known reference value by modulation.

CAS
Communicating Applications Specification. A high-level API (application programming interface) developed by Intel and DCA that was introduced in 1988. CAS enables software developers to integrate fax capability and other communication functions into their applications.

CBF
Computer-Based Fax.

CBR
Case-based reasoning.

CCITT
Comite Consultatif Internationale de Telegraphique et Telephonique (Consultative Committee for International Telephone and Telegraph - CCITT). Now called the International Telecommunications Union (ITU), the world standards-setting organization. See aslo Telecommunication Standardization Sector.

CED
Called Station Identification. A 2,100-Hz tone with which a fax machine answers a call.

Central Office (CO)

Telephone company facility where subscribers' lines are joined to switching equipment for connecting other subscribers to each other, locally and long distance.

Centrex

Centrex is a business telephone service offered by a local telephone company from a local central office. Centrex is basically single line telephone service delivered to individual desks (the same as you get at your house) with features, i.e. "bells and whistles," added. Those "bells and whistles" include intercom, call forwarding, call transfer, toll restrict, least cost routing and call hold (on single line phones).

Centrex is known by many names among operating phone companies, including Centron and Cenpac. Centrex comes in two variations -- CO and CU. CO means the Centrex service is provided by the Central Office. CU means the central office is on the customer's premises.

CFR

Confirmation to Receive frame.

Channel

1. An SCSA definition. A transmission path on the SCbus or SCxbus Data Bus that transmits data between two end points. 2. Typically what you rent from the telephone company. A voice-grade transmission facility with defined frequency response, gain and bandwidth. Also, a path of communication, either electrical or electromagnetic, between two or more points. Also called a circuit, facility, line, link or path.

Channel Bank

A multiplexer. A device which puts many slow speed voice or data conversations onto one high-speed link and controls the flow of those "conversations." Typically the device that sits between a digital circuit -- say a T-1 -- and a couple of dozen voice grade lines coming out of a PBX. One side of the channel bank will be connections for terminating two pairs of wires or a coaxial cable -- those bringing the T-1 carrier in.

On the other side are connections for terminating multiple tip and ring single line analog phone lines or several digital data streams. Sometimes you need channel banks. Sometimes, you don't. For example, if you're shipping a bundle of voice conversations from one digital PBX to another across town in a T-1 format -- and both PBXs recognize the signal -- then you will probably not need a channel bank.

You'll need a Channel Service Unit (CSU). If one, or both, of the PBXs is analog, then you will need a channel bank at the end of the transmission path whose PBX won't take a digital signal. See CHANNEL SERVICE UNIT and T-1.

Channel Service Unit
CSU. A device used to connect a digital phone line (T-1 or less) coming in from the phone company to either a multiplexer, channel bank or directly to another device producing a digital signal, e.g. a digital PBX, or data communications device. A CSU performs certain line-conditioning, and equalization functions, and responds to loopback commands sent from the central office. A channel service unit is also called a Data Service Unit. See CSU.

CIG
Calling Subscriber Identification. A frame that gives the caller's telephone number.

CGI
Common Gateway Interface

CLASS
1. Custom Local Area Signaling Services. It is based on the availability of channel interoffice signaling. Class consists of number-translation services, such as call-forwarding and caller identification, available within a local exchange of Local Access and Transport Area (LATA). CLASS is a service mark of Bellcore. Some of the phone services which Bellcore promotes for CLASS are Automatic Callback, Automatic Recall, Calling Number Delivery, Customer Originated Trace, Distinctive Ringing/Call Waiting, Selective Call Forwarding and Selective Call Rejection.

See also CALLING LINE IDENTIFICATION. 2. In an object-oriented programming environment, a class defines the data content of a specific type of object, the code that manipulates it, and the public and private programming interfaces to that code.

Class 1
The Class 1 interface is an extension of the EIA/TIA's (Electronics Industry Association and the Telecommunications Industry Association) specification for fax communication, known as Group III. Class I is a series of Hayes AT commands that can be used by software to control fax boards. In Class 1, both the T.30 (the data packet creation and decision making necessary for call setup) and ECM/BFT (error-correction mode/binary file transfer) are done by the computer. A specification being developed (fall of 1991) Class 2, will allow the modem to handle these functions in hardware. Industry analysts believe Class 2 will be the standard for the long haul, but approval is slow. Even so, some modem makers will shortly deliver data/fax modems. See also CLASS 1 OFFICE.

Clear Channel
A channel which is used exclusively for data transmission, with no bandwidth required for administrative messages such as signaling or synchronization. All SCbus data channels are clear.

Client
The requesting communication element in a distributed computing system. Clients send requests to servers across a network and wait for indication from the server that the request is complete. Any object that uses the resources of another object.

Client Application
Any computer program making use of the processing resources of another program.

Client Operating System
Operating System running on the client.

Client-server

A software architecture which splits operation between two component programs and their respective communication elements: the client and the server. Client elements make requests of servers. Servers process the requests and often return processed data to the client.

CNG

Also called Auto Fax Tone, or Calling Tone. This tone is the sound produced by virtually all fax machines when they dial another fax machine.

CNG is a medium tch tone (1100 Hz) that lasts 1/2 second and repeats every 3 1/2 seconds. A fax machine will produce CNG for about 45 seconds after it dials. The CNG tone is useful for owners of fax/phone/modem switches. Such switches answer an incoming call. If they hear a CNG tone, they will transfer the call to a fax machine. If they don't, they'll transfer the call to a phone, answering machine or perhaps a modem. Depends on how they're set up.

CO

Central Office. In North America, a CO is that location which houses a switch to serve local telephone subscribers. Sometimes the words "central office" are confused with the switch itself. In Europe and abroad, the words "central office" are not known. The more common words are "public exchange." But those words tend to refer more to the switch itself, rather than the site, as in North America. See also CENTRAL OFFICE or PUBLIC EXCHANGE.

CO Lines

These are the lines connecting your office to your local telephone company's Central Office which in turn connects you to the nationwide telephone system.

Compression

Reducing the representation of the information, without losing the information itself. Reducing the bandwidth or bits necessary to encode information. Compression saves transmission time and storage requirements on storage devices such as hard disks, tape devices, and floppy disks.

Compression Algorithm
The arithmetic formulae which convert a signal into a smaller bandwidth or fewer bits.

COMPRESSION RATIO
Measurement of compressed data. For example, a file compressed to 1/4th its original size can be expressed as 4:1. In telecommunications, compression ratio also refers to the amount of bandwidth-reduction achieved. For example, 4:1 compression of a 64 kbps channel is 16 kbps.

CO Simulator
A desktop device which pretends to act like a mini-central office. The smallest version will consist of two lines and two RJ-11 jacks. Plug a phone into both jacks. Pick up one phone. You hear dial tone. Dial or touch-tone two or three digits. Bingo, the second phone rings.

You pick up the second phone. You can have a conversation with yourself or with a machine -- like a voice processing system. Most central office simulators can simulate normal on-hook, off-hook, dialing, answering, speaking, etc. Some now can simulate caller ID features -- including number of person calling.

Compiler
A computer program used to convert symbols meaningful to a human into codes meaningful to a computer. For example, taking instructions written in a "higher" level language such as C, BASIC, COBOL or ALGOL and converting them into machine code which can be read and acted upon by a computer.

Compression Algorithm
The arithmetic formulae which convert a signal into smaller bandwidth or few bits.

Computer-Aided Dialing
Another term for Predictive Dialing. See PREDICTIVE DIALING.

Computer Telephony

Computer telephony represents the cooperative merger between telephony and data communications. It is a form of telecommunication that concentrates on the movement of both encoded and voice-related information from one point to another for the purpose of automating transactions between machines and humans, or between machines.

Interactive voice response, voice mail, and every type of host computer-to-switch integration scheme are examples of computer telephony. Because computer telephony requires both computers and telephones to work cooperatively, data processing is employed. Computer Telephony is a $3.5 billion, 30%-a year growth industry, with many areas growing at over 100% a year. Computer Telephony has two basic goals:

to please customers and to enhance corporate productivity.

In order to please customers, developers of this technology must orchestrate a broad range of technologies, each of which is changing and growing more powerful every minute. The top disciplines being attacked by computer telephony are:

1. Messaging. This includes voice, fax and electronic mail, fax routers, paging and unified messaging (also called integrated or mixed media messaging). We use it to control our fax blasters, fax servers and Internet Web-vectored phones.

2. Real-time Connectivity. This means handling both inbound and outbound call calls. Your automated attendant and "predictive" or "preview" dialing system are the most used in this area. Today, "follow me" numbers, video, audio and text-based conferencing, "PBX in a PC," and collaborative computing are gaining acceptance. Real-time connectivity is at work when you use one number calling and when calls are routed with the help of LAN-based call director programs like Phonetastic or CallWare.

3. Transaction Processing and Information Access via the Phone. We live in a world of self-navigation over the phone.

Every day, we encounter Interactive Voice Response, Audiotex, and Other means to gain customer access to enterprise data. This is the classic "giving data a voice," model. You encounter it when you order documents over the phone with a fax on demand system or when you shop on the World Wide Web. Transactions as simple as hearing the time or weather over the phone are included.

4. Adding Intelligence to Phone Calls. When a "screen pop" of customer records collides at an agent's desk coincident with inbound or outbound phone calls - intelligence is added. This includes mirrored Web page "pops," smart agents, skills-based call routing and virtual (geographically distributed) call centers.

Companies like GeoTel, Lansys, Teloquent and Edify really shine in this area. These folks are pioneering the concept of computer telephony groupware, smart help desks and "AIN" (intelligent network-based) computer telephony services.

5. Core Technologies. There are dozens of them. We use voice recognition, text-to-speech, applications generators (of all varieties -- GUI to forms-based to script-based), VoiceView, DSVD, computer-based fax routing /binary file transfer, USB (Universal Serial Bus), GeoPort, video and audio compression, call progress, dial pulse recognition, Caller ID and ANI, digital network interfaces (T-1, E-1, ISDN BRI and PRI, SS7, frame relay and ATM), voice modems, client-server telephony, logical modem interfaces, multi-PC telephony synchronization and coordination software, the Internet, the Web and the "Intranet." We owe most of the recent advances in these technologies to DSPs (Digital Signal Processors). With DSPs, we can manipulate, crunch, analyze, decode, reformat and in general do just about anything we want with LAN,WAN, or POTS phone line transmissions. DSP algorithms are on the lowest level of the computer telephony food chain - but the most fundamental building block we have.

Conference Bridge
A telecommunications facility or service which permits callers from several diverse locations to be connected together for a conference call.

The conference bridge contains electronics for amplifying and balancing the conference call so everyone can hear each other and speak to each other. The conference call's progress is monitored through the bridge in order to produce a high quality voice conference and to maintain decent quality as people enter or leave the conference.

Configuration Manager

A service which manages configuration information and controls system startup.

Connection

A TDM data path between two Resources or two Groups. It connects the inputs and outputs of the two Resources, and may be unidirectional (simplex) if either of the Resources has only an input or an output; Otherwise it is bi-directional (dual simplex). It usually has a bandwidth that is a multiple of a DS0 (64kbit) channel. Inter-group connections are made between the Primary Resource of each Resource Group.

Cover Page

The cover page is the first page of a fax message. It generally includes a header, typically the sender company's logo; the recipient's name and fax telephone number; the sender's fax and voice telephone numbers; the system's date and time; a message; and a footer.

CPE

Customer Provided Equipment, or Customer Premise Equipment. Originally it referred to equipment on the customer's premises which had been bought from a vendor who was not the local phone company. Now it simply refers to telephone equipment -- key systems, PBXs, answering machines, etc. -- which reside on the customer's premises. "Premises" might be anything from an office to a factory to home.

CPU

The Central Processing Unit. The computing part of a computer. The "brain" of the computer. It manipulates data and processes instructions coming from software or a human operator. See CENTRAL PROCESSING UNIT.

CRP
Command repeat.

CSI (CSID)
Called Subscriber Identification. An identifier whose coding format contains a number, usually the telephone number from the remote terminal used in fax.

CSTA
Computer Supported Telecommunications Applications. This is a set of API calls agreed upon by the ECMA.

CSU
Channel Service Unit. Also called a Data Service Unit. A device to terminate a digital channel on a customer's premises. It performs certain line-conditioning, and equalization functions, and responds to loopback commands sent from the central office.

A CSU sits between the digital line coming in from the central office and devices such as channel banks or data communications devices. See CHANNEL SERVICE UNIT.

CTI
Computer Telephone Integration. Basically a polite term for connecting a computer to a telephone switch and having the computer issue the switch commands to move calls around. The most classic application for CTI is in call centers. Picture this: A call comes in. That call carries some form of caller ID -- either ANI or Class Caller ID. The switch "hears" the calling number, strips it off, sends it to the computer. The computer does a lookup, sends back the switch instructions on what to do with the call. The switch follows orders. It might send the call to a specialized agent or maybe just to the agent the caller dealt with last time.

Customer Premises Equipment
CPE. Terminal equipment, supplied by either the telephone common carrier or by a competitive supplier, which is connected to the nationwide telephone network and resides on the customer's premises.

CVSD

Continuously Variable Slope Delta modulation. A method for coding analog voice signals into digital signals.

D

D/A

Digital to analog conversion.

DAA

Data Access Arrangement. A device required to hook up CPE (Customer Provided Equipment), usually modems and other data equipment, to the telephone network.

Database

A data file and its associated index files. (Occasionally the term is used to refer to multiple data files, each with its own index files.)

Data File

The file used to store the data portion of a database. Data files are usually given the .DBF extension when using any of the xBASE family of database managers.

Database Handle

See Handle.

Data Communications

This is a form of telecommunications that concentrates on the movement of encoded information from one point to another. This information is readable by machines, such as modems, computers, and fax machines as opposed to telephony, which is "readable" by the human ear.

Data Stream

A continuous flow of call processing data.

dB

Decibel. A unit of measure of signal strength, usually the relation between a transmitted signal and a standard signal source. Therefore, 6 dB of loss would mean that there is 6 dB difference between what arrives down a communications circuit, and what was transmitted by a standard signal generator.

DBMS

Database Management System. An inclusive term for a database format and its management and development software tools.

DCN

Disconnect frame. Indicates the fax call is done. The sender transmits it before hanging up; it does not wait for a response.

DCS

Digital Command Signal. Signal sent when the caller is transmitting, which tells the answerer how to receive the fax. Modem, speed, image width, image encoding, and page length are all included in this frame.

DDS

Digital Dataphone Service

Device Driver

A piece of software that expands MS-DOS's ability to work with peripherals. The routines that make peripherals (a mouse, a RAM disk, a print spooler) work. They may be part of another program (many applications include device drivers for printers) or separate programs.

DOS comes with two device drivers: ANSI.SYS and VDISK.SYS. These are things DOS is not used to. The first is to expand the capabilities of the keyboard. The second is used to carve a RAM disk out of the 640K of RAM that MS-DOS can address. In short, device drivers can be used to expand the abilities of DOS. They are loaded from your CONFIG.SYS file when you boot up the computer. Some network operating systems run as device drivers.

They do this to get loaded before anything else so they can get the memory space they want. By being loaded as a device driver they are able to tell DOS how to operate certain "network" things, like virtual drives, shared printers, spoolers, print queues and so on. See DRIVER and VOICE DRIVER.

Dial-It 900 Service

A special one-way mass calling service that allows prospects, customers and others to reach you from anywhere across the country. In contrast to 800-service, the caller pays the 900 charge. The caller generally pays one charge for the first minute, with a lesser charge for each additional minute. DIAL-IT 900 Service is a great way to involve your customers and prospects in a promotion! Premium Billing lets you select a rate above standard DIAL-IT 900 rates. The long distance carriers (through their deals with local phone companies) handle the billing. You, the information provider, may split the revenues with the long distance provider. International DIAL-IT 900 service is currently available from a growing number of countries.

Dial Pulsing

A means of signaling consisting of regular momentary interruptions of a direct or alternating current at the sending end in which the number of interruptions corresponds to the value of the digit or character. In short, the old style of rotary dialing. Dial the number "five" and you'll hear five "clicks." See DIAL SPEED and DTMF.

Dial Speed

The number of pulses that a rotary dial can send in a given period of time, typically 10 pulses per second. A Hayes modem with a communications package, like Crosstalk, can send 20 pulses a second.

Dial Tone

The sound you hear when you pick up a telephone. Dial tone is a signal (350 + 440 Hz) from your local telephone company to you that it is alive and ready to receive the number you dial. If you have a PBX, dial tone will typically be provided by the PBX. Dial tone does not come from God or the telephone instrument on your desk. It comes from the switch to which your phone is connected to.

Dictation Access and Control

A telephone system feature which allows a user to dial a dictation machine and use that machine (giving it instructions by push button) as if that machine were in his office. Typically the material on that dictation machine is taken off by one or several typists out of a centralized word processing pool and word processed into letters, reports, legal briefs, etc.

Telephone suppliers usually don't supply the dictation equipment. Newer telephone dictation machinery is, in reality, a specialized application of voice processing equipment. See VOICE PROCESSING.

DID

Direct Inward Dialing. You can dial inside a company directly without going through the attendant. This feature used to be an exclusive feature of Centrex but it can now be provided by virtually all modern PBXs and some modern hybrids.

DID Trunks

DID trunks are employed to reduce the number of channels between the PBX and the telephone company central office. DID trunks are one-way trunks. A PBX perceives the DID trunk as one of its single-line telephones and can interpret four-digit dialing.

Digital Facsimile

A form of fax in which densities of the original are sampled and quantized as a digital signal for processing, transmission, or storage.

Digital Recording

A system of recording in which musical information is converted into a series of pulses that are translated into a binary code intelligible to computer circuits, and stored on magnetic tape of magnetic discs. Also called PCM - Pulse Code Modulation.

Digital Signal Processor (DSP)

A specialized digital microprocessor that performs calculations on digitized signals that were originally analog and then sends the results on.

The big advantage of DSP lies in the programmability of digital micro-processors. DSPs can be used for compression of voice signals to as few as 4,800 bps. DSPs are an integral part of all voice processing systems and facsimile machines.

Digital Transmission
The use of a binary code to represent information. Analog signals, like voice or data, are encoded digitally by sampling the signal many times a second and assigning a number to each sampling. Unlike an analog signal which picks up noise along the way, a digital signal can be reproduced precisely.

Digital Trunk
Generic name for a telephone connection for which uses digital rather than analog transmission. Common examples are T-1 in North America and E-1 in Europe.

Digital-To-Analog Conversion
A circuit that accepts digital signals and converts them into analog signals. A modem typically has such a circuit. It also has other circuits, such as those doing with signaling. See MODEM.

Digital Voice Coding
Technology by which linear audio (voice) samples are collected and then compressed using an encoding algorithm. Typically used to store voice data for future decoding.

Digitize
Converting an analog or continuous signal into a series of ones and zeros, i.e. into a digital format.

Digitized Voice
Analog voice signals represented in digital form. There are many ways of digitizing voice. See Pulse Code Modulation for the most common.

Direct Inward Dialing

DID. The ability for a caller outside a company to call an internal extension without having to pass through an operator or attendant. In large PBX systems, the dialed digits are passed down the line from the CO (central office). The PBX then completes the call. Direct Inward Dialing is often proposed as Centrex's major feature. But automated attendants (a specialized form of interactive voice response systems) also provide a similar service.

DIRECT TALK

A family of IBM voice processing products introduced in the summer of 1991. According to IBM, its IBM CallPath DirectTalk product line lets businesses automate routine operations and also provide callers with easy access to many kinds of information over the telephone -- at any hour of the day and with greater accuracy. Businesses can raise the level of service they provide and do it with fewer people and with greater efficiency.

DIS

Digital identification signal.

Disconnect Supervision

The change in electrical state from off-hook to on-hook. This indicates that the transmission connection is no longer needed.

DMX

Digital Matrix Switch. Dialogic board that provides digital switching among four PEB spans -- for a maximum of 96 channels.

DNIS

Dialed Number Identification Service. DNIS is a feature of 800 lines. Let's say you subscribe to several 800 numbers. You use one line for testing your advertisements on TV stations in Phoenix; another line for testing your advertisements on TV stations in Chicago; and yet another for Milwaukee. Now you get an automatic call distributor and you terminate all the lines in one group on your ACD. You do that because it's cheaper to man and run one group of incoming lines.

One queue is more efficient than several small ones, etc. You have all your people answering all the calls. You now need to know which calls are coming from where. So your long distance carrier sends you the call's DNIS -- the numbers the person dialed to reach you. Those DNIS digits might come to you in many ways, depending on the technical arrangement you have with your long distance company. In-band or out-of-band. ISDN or data channel, etc. Make sure you understand the difference between DNIS and ANI. DNIS tells you the number your caller called. ANI is the number your caller called from.

DOMAIN
Internet name of a computer on the 'Net. Flatiron Publishing's domain name is FlatironPublishing.com.

DOS
Disk Operating System. As in MS-DOS, which stands for MicroSoft Disk Operating System. DOS is the software that organizes how a computer reads, writes and reacts with its disks -- floppy or hard -- and talks to its various input/output devices, including keyboards, screens, serial and parallel ports, printers, modems, etc.

DPI
Dots per inch. A measure of output device resolution. The number of dots a printer can place in a horizontal inch.

Driver
Also called a Device Driver. A piece of software which lets applications software tell a computer's various parts what to do. Those parts might be everything from Dialogic boards to laser printers.

Drop And Insert
That process wherein a part of the information carried in a transmission system is demodulated (dropped) at an intermediate point and different information is entered (inserted) for subsequent transmission.

Dry T-1
T-1 with an unpowered interface.

DS-0

Digital Service, level 0. It is 64,000 bps, the worldwide standard speed for digitizing one voice conversation. There are 24 DS- channels in a DS-1.

DS-1

Digital Service, level 1. It is 1.544 megabits per second in North America, 2.048 Mbps elsewhere. Why there's no consistency is one of those wonderful questions. The 1.544 standard is an old Bell System standard. The 2.048 standard is a ITU standard. Standard for 1.544 per second is 24 voice conversations. Standard for 2.048 is 30 conversations.

DSP

Display System Protocol or Digital Signal Processor. A Digital Signal Processor is a specialized computer chip designed to perform speedy and complex operations on digitized waveforms. Useful in processing sound and video.

DTC

1. Digital Trunk Controller. 2. Digital transmit command.

DTMF

Dual Tone Multi Frequency. A fancy term for describing push button or touch-tone dialing (touch-tone is a former trademark of AT&T).

In DTMF, when you touch a button on a push button dial, it makes a tone, which is actually the combination of two tones, one high frequency and one low frequency. Thus the name Dual Tone Multi Frequency. In U.S. telephony, there are actually two types of DTMF signaling -- one that is used on normal business or home push button/touchtone phones, and one that is used for signaling within the telephone network itself. When you go into a central office, look for the testboard. There you'll see what looks like a standard touch-tone pad.

Next to the pad there'll be a small toggle switch that allows you to choose the sounds the touch-tone pad will make -- either normal touch-tone dialing or the network version. The eight possible tones that comprise the DTMF signaling system were specially selected to easily pass through the telephone network without attenuation and with minimum interaction with each other.

Since these tones fall within the frequency range of the human voice, additional considerations were added to prevent the human voice from inadvertently imitating or "falsing" DTMF signaling digits. One way this was done to break the tones into two groups, a high frequency group and a low frequency group. A valid DTMF tone has only one tone in each group. Here is a table of the DTMF digits with their respective frequencies. One Hertz (abbreviated Hz.) is one cycle per second of frequency.

	Low frequency	High frequency
1	697 Hz.	1209 Hz.
2	697	1336
3	697	1477
4	770	1209
5	770	1336
6	770	1477
7	852	1209
8	852	1336
9	852	1477
0	941	1336
*	941	1209
#	941	1477

There are four other digits defined in the DTMF system and usable for specialized applications that cannot be generated by standard telephones. They are:

Digit	Low frequency	High frequency
A	697 Hz	1633 Hz.
B	770	1633
C	852	1633
D	941	1633

DTMF Cut-Through
The capability of a voice response system to receive DTMF tones while the voice synthesizer is delivering information, i.e. during speech playback.

This capability of DTMF cut-through saves the user waiting until the machine has played the whole message (which typically is a menu with options).

The user can simply touch-tone his response anytime during the message -- when he first hears his selection number, when the message first starts, etc. When the voice processor hears the touch-toned selection (i.e. the DTMF cut-through), it stops speaking and jumps to the chosen selection. For example, the machine starts to say, "If you know the person you're calling, touch-tone his extension in now.." But before you hear the "If you know" you push button in 230, which you know is Joe's extension. Bingo, the message stops and Joe's extension starts ringing.

Dumb Switch

A slang word for a telecommunications switch that contains only basic switching software and relies on instructions sent it by an outside computer. Those instructions are typically fed the "dumb" switch through a cable from the computer to one or more RS-232 serial ports which the dumb switch sports. The switch makes no demands on what type of computer it talks to, but simply insists that it be able to feed the computer questions and promptly receive responses in a form that it (the switch) can understand. Plain ASCII is OK. For example, the dumb switch might signal the computer, "A call is coming in on port 23, what do I do now?" The computer might reply:

"Answer it and transfer it to extension 23." Or it might say "answer it and put it on hold," or "answer it, put it on hold and play it recording number three."

In essence, a dumb switch is anything but. It is in reality an empty cage containing whatever network interface cards the user has chosen. Each of these network interface cards is designed to "talk" to one type of telephone line. That line might be a T-1 line. It might be a normal tip and ring loop start line. It might be a tie trunk with E&M signaling. The card may handle one or many lines, but always of the same type. The card knows how to answer a call or pulse out a call on that particular type of line. It has all the telephony smarts.

What it lacks is the intelligence of what to do with the calls. That is provided by the outside computer. Well, almost. Most "dumb" switches do contain rudimentary intelligence -- a small computer and some memory.

That computer is usually programmed to handle "default" calls -- and to handle calls should the link to the outside computer fail, or the outside computer itself fail. Dumb switches come in flavors all the way from residing in their own cabinet to being printed circuit cards which reside in one or more of the personal computer's slots.

Dumb switches are programmed to do "specialized" telecom applications, for example emergency 911, added value 800 services, cellular switching, automatic call distributors, predictive dialers, etc. They can, of course, be programmed to be "normal" PBXs. The question increasingly being asked is "If I want to program a specialized telecom application should I use a dumb switch or should I use an open PBX?" And the answer is "It depends." Depends on what you want to do. Depends on what software is available, etc. See also OAI.

E

800 Service
See 800 SERVICE, spelled as EIGHT HUNDRED SERVICE.

E & M Leads
The pair of wires carrying signals between trunk equipment and a separate signaling equipment unit. The "M" lead transmits a ground or battery conditions to the signaling equipment. The "E" lead receives open or ground signals from the signaling equipment. These leads are also known as Ear and Mouth Leads. The Ear lead typically means to receive and the Mouth lead typically means to transmit.

Changes of voltage on these leads convey such information as seizure of circuit, recognition of seizure, release of circuit, dialed digits, etc. In the old days it was the PBX operators who originated trunk calls by asking the long distance carrier for free trunks using their mouth or M lead.

If the carrier had a free trunk, the PBX heard about it through its ear or E lead. See also E & M SIGNALING.

E & M Signaling

In telephony, an arrangement that uses separate leads, called respectively the "E" lead and "M" lead, for signaling and supervisory purposes. The near end signals the far end by applying -48 volts dc (vdc) to the "M" lead, which results in a ground being applied to the far end's "E" lead. When -48 vdc is applied to the far end "M" lead, the near-end "E" lead is grounded. The "E" originally stood for "ear," i.e., when the near-end "E" lead was grounded, the far end was calling and "wanted your ear."

The "M" originally stood for "mouth," because when the near-end wanted to call (i.e., speak to) the far end, -48 vdc was applied to that lead. When a PBX wishes to connect to another PBX directly or to a remote PBX or extension telephone over a leased voice grade line, a channel on T-1, the PBX uses a special line interface which is quite different from that which it uses to interface to the phones it's attached directly to (i.e. with in-building wires).

The basic reason for the difference between a normal extension interface and the long distance interface is that the signaling requirements differ -- even if the voice signal parameters such as level and two-wire, 4-wire remain the same.

When dealing with tie lines or trunks it is costly, inefficient and too slow for a PBX to do what an extension telephone would do, i.e. go off hook, wait for dial tone, dial, wait for ringing to stop, etc. The E&M tie trunk interface device is the closest thing there is to a standard that exists in the PBX, T-1 multiplexer, voice digitizer telco world. But even then it comes in at least five different flavors. See E & M LEADS.

Eight Hundred Service

800-Service. A generic and common (and not trademarked) term for AT&T's, MCI's, US Sprint's and the Bell operating companies' IN-WATS service. All these IN-WATS services have "800" as their "area code."

Dialing an 800-number is free to the person making the call. The call is billed to the person or company being called.

The telephone company suppliers of 800 services use various ways to configure and bill their 800-services. One way: you can buy an 800 line which will ring on your normal phone line. You'll only pay per call, but you won't receive any incoming call if you're making an outgoing one. (You can even terminate an 800 number on your cellular phone.) For other 800 services you might pay a flat monthly rate plus "so-much" (i.e. timed usage) per call. That timed usage may include some calculation for the distance the incoming call traveled. 800-Service is now available for calls from Canada and some countries in Europe.

More and more long distance companies are introducing 800-service. 800 Service works like this: You're somewhere in North America. You dial 1-800 and seven digits. Your local central office sees the "1" and recognizes the call as long distance. It ships that call to a bigger central office (or perhaps processes the call itself). At that central office it's processed, a machine will recognize the 800 "area code" and examine the next three digits. Those three digits will tell which long distance carrier to ship the call to. Each long distance company has been assigned specific 800 three digit "exchanges." For example, MCI has the exchange 999. AT&T has the exchange 542. If you want a phone number beginning with 800-999, then you must subscribe to MCI 800 service. If you want a phone number beginning with 800-542, you must subscribe to AT&T 800 service.

Once the 800-call is "passed off" to whichever carrier it belongs to, that carrier sends the call to a switch attached to a huge "translation" database. The call arrives at the switch. The database says the call 800-NNN-XXXX is really 212-555-1234, and sends the 800 line to that number.

As a real-life example, Flatiron Publishing, publishers of this book, has an 800 number, namely 800-LIBRARY (or 800-542-7279). When you call that number, the following number -- 212-206-6870 -- in New York City rings. Dialing 800-542-7279 is effectively the same as dialing 212-206-6870, except that if you dial 212-206-6870 you'll pay. If you dial 800-542-7279, I'll pay.

Because 800 long distance service is essentially a database lookup and translation telephone service, there are endless "800 services" you can create.

E-1

Another name given to the CEPT digital telephony format devised by the ITU that carries data at the rate of 2.048 Mbps (DS-1 level). CEPT format consists of 30 voice channels, one signaling channel, and one framing (synchronization) channel. Since robbed-bit signaling is not used (as it is for T-1 in North America) all 8 bits per channel are used to code the waveshape sample. E-1 is the European version of North American T-1, though T-1 is 1.544 Mbps. See T-1.

Echo

A wave reflected or otherwise returned with sufficient magnitude and delay to be perceived. This is an effect sometimes experienced with long distance calls. It is usually associated with relatively long round-trip delay in the four-wire portion of the circuit so that the unwanted sound is perceived as being separate in time from the wanted one. The phenomenon of echo primarily affects the talker and not the listener. Ghosts on a television picture are a type of echo.

Echo Canceller

The echo suppressor used on circuits with long transmission time. It attenuates the direction of transmission which is not active so that any echoes that are fed into a circuit do not return to the starting point and cause confusion. Echo cancellation stops a received signal from being transmitted back to its origin by constructing a signal closely approximating the echo component and subtracting this from the locally transmitted signal. This avoids double-talking problems. ECM Error Correction Mode. Encapsulated data within HDLC frames providing the receiver with an opportunity to check for, and request retransmission of garbled data.

ECMA

European Computer Manufacturers Association. An independent standards group of computer and PBX manufacturers. Their standards are recognized internationally.

EDI

Electronic Data Interchange. A series of standards providing automated computer-to-computer exchange of business documents (structured business data, editable documents, or electronic transactions such as invoices, purchase order, etc.) between different companies and computers over telephone lines.

E-Mail

Electronic mail. A popular application on both LANs and WANs which provides communication among users. There is a variety of systems which vary considerably in their level of sophistication. E-mail services can include simple message handling as well as complex file sharing.

E-Mail Fax Gateways

With an E-mail fax gateway, all E-mail users can send and receive faxes from within the company's E-mail package. Because the fax messaging is integrated directly into the mail system, fax users have virtually no new software to learn and can take advantage of E-mail features.

This includes workgroup distribution lists, attaching graphics files to text messages, support for different user operating systems on the network, and instant notification of received messages. With an E-mail fax gateway, it is possible to send the same message to both mail users and fax recipients.

Electronic Mail Integration

Integrating computer fax and E-mail technology allows the user to send and receive fax documents using a company's E-mail program. The most popular method uses MHS for Novell networks.;

Electronic Voice Mail

A system which stores messages spoken by a user usually over a telephone, which can be retrieved by the intended recipient when that person next calls into the system. Also called Voice Mail, it operates just like a touch-tone controlled answering machine.

Email-to-fax

Conversion of electronic mail (ASCII text) into fax image format, suitable for sending to a fax machine.

Emulate

To imitate a computer or computer system by a combination of hardware and software that allows programs written for one computer or terminal to run on another. The most common data terminal is a DEC VT-100. Our communications program, Crosstalk, allows us to "emulate" a DEC-VT100 on our IBM PCs and PC clones.

EOM

End of Message frame. A frame from the sender indicating that the message is done, and that Phase B can be repeated. See also EOP.

EOP

End of Procedure frame. A frame indicating that the sender wants to end the call.

ESP

Enhanced Service Provider. A vendor who adds value to telephone lines using his own provided software and hardware. Also called an IP, or Information Provider. An example of an ESP is a public voice mail box provider or a database provider, say one giving the latest airline fares. An ESP is an American term, unknown in Europe, where they're most called VANs, or Value Added Networks. See also INFORMATION PROVIDER.

Ethernet

A LAN used for connecting computers, printers, workstations, terminals, etc., within the same building. Ethernet operates over twisted pair wire and over coaxial cable at speeds up to 10 Mbps.

Event

An unsolicited, asynchronous signal from a device or device driver that reports on a change in the status of the device.

Events are generally attention-getting messages, allowing a process to know when a task is complete or when an external event occurs. A message that reports on a change in the status of an object.

Expansion Slots

In a computer there are card slots for adding accessories such as voice processing interface cards, internal modems, extra drivers, hard disks, monitor adapters, hard disk drivers, etc.

Most modern PBXs are actually cabinets with nothing but expansion slots. And into these slots we fit trunk cards, line cards, console cards, etc. Some phone systems have "universal" slots, meaning you can put any card in any slot. Some phone systems have dedicated expansion slots, meaning that they expect only a certain card in that slot.

Extensibility

This means that it's easy to add new technologies without re-inventing the wheel.

F

Facsimile

Facsimile, or fax, equipment allows information (written, typed, or graphic) to be transmitted through the switched telephone system and printed at the other end. The sending fax scans the material to be sent, digitizing it into binary bits and sending those through a modem to the receiving fax, which essentially reverses the process and outputs it through a printer.

Fast Busy

A busy signal which sounds at twice the normal rate (120 interruptions/minute vs. 60/minute). A "fast busy" signal indicates all trunks are busy.

Fax

Abbreviation for facsimile.

Fax Activity Records

Much of the power and flexibility in GammaFax comes from the Queue Manager. This is a set of programs and files that operate in the background while the user works with GammaFax or other application programs in the foreground. As the Queue Manager handles fax activity, it updates three detailed activity logs that provide the status of each task: the pending log for tasks still being processed; the received log for incoming faxes; and the sent log for outgoing faxes.

Fax-Back

You go to your fax machine. You dial a voice response unit. It says "Punch in 23 if you want to receive the latest specs on our new XYZ machine. Now when you are ready, hit the 'start' button on your fax machine and hang up." A few seconds later, your fax machine disgorges paper containing the latest specs on the XYZ machine. Welcome to "fax-back."

FaxBIOS

API used for in-application faxing. Developed by WordPerfect Corp.; and Everex Systems, Inc.;

Fax Board

A specialized synchronous modem designed to transmit and receive facsimile documents. Many also allow for binary synchronous file transfer, and V.22 bis communication.

Fax Mailbox

Companies can send facsimiles of documents to be stored for later retrieval to a fax mailbox -- a cousin to a voice mailbox. Travelers can check their fax mailboxes and have the faxes sent to convenient locations, like a hotel front desk.

Fax Server

In a LAN, a PC or a self-contained unit that has fax circuitry accessible to all the network's workstations. The server receives requests for fax services and manages them so that they are answered in an orderly, sequential manner. It is used to send and receive faxes by any network user, sharing the common resource of one or more fax boards.

Depending on application, a fax server may have a specialized interactive voice response system that routes faxes to a fax machine the user designates by touch-tone numbers. The receiving unit may be the user's or one designated by him.

FCC Registration Number

A number assigned to specific telephone equipment registered with the FCC, as set forth in FCC docket 19528, part 68. The presence of this number affixed to a device indicates that the FCC has approved it as being a compatible device for direct connection to telephone line facilities.

Field

A component of a record. Fields may contain either numeric, string, or date values. Fields are numbered starting with 0 as the first field.

FIREWALL

Hardware and\or software which limits the exposure of a computer or group of computers to an attack from an external location. Routers and other internetworking devices use their access control capabilities to build firewalls that can, for example, keep fault from propagating throughout the entire internet.

Firmware

Programs kept in semi-permanent storage, such as various types of read-only memory. These programs can be altered, but with difficulty.

Firmware is used in conjunction with hardware and software. It also shares the characteristics of both. Firmware is usually stored on PROMS (Programmable Read Only Memory) or EPROMs (Electrical PROMS).

Firmware contains software which is so constantly called upon by a computer or phone system that it is "burned" into a chip, thereby becoming Firmware. The computer program is written into the PROM electrically at higher than usual voltage, causing the bits to "retain" the pattern as it is "burned in". Firmware is non-volatile. It will not be "forgotten" when the power is shut off. Hand-held calculators contain firmware with instructions for doing their various mathematical operations.

First Party Call Control

See call control.

Flash

Quickly depressing and releasing the plunger in or the actual handset-cradle to create a signal to a PBX or Centrex that special instructions will follow such as transferring the call to another extension.

Flash Hook

A brief on-hook period. A common use of the flash-hook is in the residential call waiting feature. A new call comes in while a conversation is in progress.

The central office, however, doesn't give the caller a busy signal. The caller hears ringing and the called party, who's having a conversation, hears a special "beep" tone. If he or she chooses, the called party can quickly push the hook-switch on their telephone, sending what the industry calls a "flash hook." The central office puts the original caller on hold and the new dial tone, allowing a three-way conference or call transfer.

Flowchart

A graphic or diagram which shows how a complex operation, e.g. programming, takes place. The flowchart breaks that operation down into its smallest, and easiest-to-understand events.

FOD

Fax On Demand. Dial up a number. hear an voice response unit say, "Would you like a timetable?" You say "Yes." It says put in your fax number. You punch in your fax number and bingo, your fax machine starts receiving a fax of the timetable.

FORMANT

A point of excitation, or high energy, in a speech waveform caused by resonance in the human vocal tract. Formants are responsible for the unique timbre of each individual's voice.

Frame

A group of data bits in a specific format, with a flag at each end to indicate the beginning and end of the frame. The defined format enables network equipment to recognize the meaning and purpose of specific bits.

Frame (Data)

A set of time slots which are grouped together for synchronization purposes. For example, as with SCSA, the number of time slots in each frame depends on the SCbus or SCxbus Data Bus data rate. Each frame has a fixed period of 125us. Frames are delineated by the timing signal FSYNC.

Frame (Message)

A data link layer frame the encapsulates control and signaling data transmitted on the SCbus or SCxbus Message Bus. The form of a Message Bus frame is fully compliant with ISO HDLC UI (Unnumbered Information) Frame specifications.

Frame Relay

Frame relay switching is a form of fast packet switching, but uses smaller packets and requires less error checking than traditional forms of packet switching. Like traditional X.25 packet networks, frame relay networks use bandwidth only when there is traffic to send.

Frequency

The number of complete oscillations per second of an electromagnetic wave.

FREQUENCY DOMAIN

Waveforms, such as speech signals, are typically viewed in the time domain, i.e. as power levels or voltages varying over time. The 19th century French mathematician Fourier demonstrated an algorithm called "Fast Fourier Transform," or FFT, which can express any complex waveform over a fixed interval as the sum of a series of sine waves of different energy levels. Analyzing signals in the frequency domain has proven an extremely powerful technique with diverse applications, including filtering, recognition, and speech modeling.

Frequency Response

The variation (dB) in relative strength between frequencies in a given frequency band, usually the voice frequency band of an analog telephone line.

FTT

Failure-to-train signal.

FTP

File Transfer Protocol. Software that can transfer files from one computer to another across the 'Net.

Full Duplex

A communications protocol in which the communications channel can send and receive signals at the same time.

FSK

Frequency Shift Keying. A modulation technique for translating 1s and 0s into something that can be carried over telephone lines, like sounds. A 1 will be assigned a certain frequency of tone, and a 0 another tone. The transmission of the bits keys the sounds to shift from one frequency to the other.

G

G.711

ITU (International Telecommunications Union) standard for audio codecs. Provides encoding at 64 kilobits per second (mu-law and A-law).

G.723

ITU standard for audio codecs. This standard is for compressed digital audio over POTS lines -- Plain Old Telephone Lines. It is the voice part of H.324.

GIF

Graphic Interchange Format. A popular graphics file format used on the Web. It's sort of compressed. JPEG is another.

Glare

Glare occurs when both ends of a telephone line or trunk are seized at the same time for different purposes or by different users. Most embarrassing.

GOPHER

A menued interface to Internet files.

Ground Start

A way of signaling on subscriber trunks in which one side of the two wire trunk (typically the "Ring" conductor of the Tip and Ring) is momentarily grounded to get dial tone. There are two types of switched trunks one can typically lease from a local phone company -- ground start and loop start. PBXs work best on ground start trunks, though many will work -- albeit intermittently -- on both types. Normal single line phones and key systems typically work on loop start lines. You must be careful to order the correct type of trunk from your local phone company and correctly install your telephone system at your end -- so that they both match. A ground start trunk initiates an out-going trunk seizure by applying a maximum local resistance of 550 ohms to the tip conductor. See LOOP START.

Group

An associated set of one or more Resource Objects. Groups encapsulate the functionality of the Resource Objects that are associated with them. Resource Objects within a Group have defined connectivity. The Group provides three services to the application: implicit management of connectivity between group members; representation of a single entity to the applications (group ID); and reservation of all physical resources (CPU, memory, time slots) required to provide the application with exclusive use of configured resources.

Group1

Analog fax equipment, according to Recommendation T.2 of the ITU.

It sends an ISO A4 or (U.S. letter size) 8.5 x 11- inch page in six minutes over a voice-grade telephone line using frequency modulation with 1,300 Hz corresponding to white and 2,100 Hz to black of the original. Because North American six-minute equipment uses a different modulation scheme, it is not compatible with Group 1 equipment.

Group2

Analog facsimile equipment, according to Recommendation T.3 of the ITU. It sends an A4 or 8.5 x 11-inch page in three minutes over a voice-grade telephone line using 2,100-Hz AM-PM- VSB.

Group3

A digital high-speed fax standard for reliable transmission over ordinary telephone lines. Based on ITU Recommendation T.4.

Group4

ITU fax standard primarily designed to work with ISDN. Written before a real machine was made, it is generally considered difficult to implement. Although it offers a transmission rate of about five seconds per page, it requires an ISDN or leased line. Currently, there is no way to use it over ordinary voice grade telephone lines, and equipment from different manufacturers cannot interface.

GSM

GSM stands for Groupe Speciale Mobile, now known as Global System for Mobile Communications, is the standard digital cellular phone service you will find in Europe and Japan. GSM actually is a set of ETSI standards specifying the infrastructure for a digital cellular service. To ensure interoperability between countries, these standards address much of the network wireless infrastructure, including the radio interface (900 MHz), switching, signaling, and intelligent network. An 1,800 MHz version, DCS1800, has been defined to facilitate implementation in some countries, particularly the UK. Since GSM is limited to technical standards, an association of GSM operators called the Memorandum of Understanding (MoU) ensures service interoperability, allowing subscribers to roam across networks.

GSM has gained widespread acceptance in several parts of the world, most notably Europe, with deployment in 52 countries by mid year '94. GSM subscriber data is carried on a Subscriber Identity Module (SIM) or "smartcard" which is inserted into the phone to get it going. As a result, the subscriber potentially has the option of either SIM card mobility or terminal mobility across multiple networks.

One of GSM's major problem is that people wearing hearing aids can't use GSM cell phones, because GSM phones produce unpleasant high-pitched squealing the closer they get to the cell phone.

GSM technical Characteristics: Receiver frequency: 935.2 -- 959.8 MHz. Transmitter frequency: 890.2 -- 914.8 MHz. Access method: mixed TDMA & FDMA with optional frequency hopping. Security: Optional radio interface encryption. Carrier frequency division: 200 KHz. Users per carrier frequency: 8. Speech bit rate (transfer rate): full rate (13 kbps) or half rate. Total bit rate: 21 Kbps. Bandwidth per channel: 25 KHz

H

H.221
ITU standard for ISDN conferencing. Defines frame structure for 64 to 1,920 kilobits per second channels in audiovisual teleservices. Related ITU standards are H.223 (multiplexing), H.245 (controlling), and H.261 for video codecs.

H.261
ITU standard for video encoding. It was the watershed standard (1990) that made it possible for video codecs from different makers to successfully communicate with each other.

H.263
ITU standard for video encoding. Improvements on H.261.

H.320
The most common family of ITU-T videoconferencing standards for transmitting audio and video over circuit-switched digital networks (primarily ISDN).

H.323
ITU standard for taking the H.320 video standard and running it over LANs and IP networks (e.g. the Internet). It defines the bridge between LAN-based terminal, equipment and services to systems connected to circuit-switched networks.

H.324
ITU standard for taking the H.320 standard to transmit audio and video over analog lines. Uses 28.8 kilobits per second (V.34) modems. Uses H.263 video compression algorithm and G.723 voice compression algorithm. Uses H.223 and H.245 multiplexing and control protocols.

Half Duplex
A communications protocol in which the communications channel can handle only one signal at a time. The two stations alternate their transmissions.

Handle
A string of characters (alphabetic, numeric, or any combination including the underscore), userdefined in the database configuration file, used by Pro/Found to reference database and index files.

Handoff
The change of ownership of a Group (and therefore, typically, a call) from one session to another. For example, if a call center application discovers that a caller wishes to access a technical support Audiotex database, it hands off the call to an application servicing that database.

Handshaking
An exchange of signals between the fax transmitter and the fax receiver to verify that transmission can proceed, determine which specifications will be used, and to verify reception of the documents sent.

HDLC

High-Level Data-Link Control Standard. It always contains a frame called the Digital Identification Signal (DIS), which describes the standard ITU features of the machine. It can also contain two other frames: a Non-Standard Facilities (NSF) frame, which tells the caller about vendor-specific features, and, usually, a Called Subscriber Identification (CSI) frame, which contains the answerer's telephone number.

High Level Languages

Essentially any of the computer languages whose code is not unique to the hardware or architecture of a particular computer. High level languages are more like human language than the machine language which computers talk. High level languages translate human instructions into the machine language computers can understand, but which humans don't have to (in order to tell the computer what to do).

Computer languages such as C, BASIC, FORTRAN, COBOL and Pascal are high level languages. They are a number of levels (at a High Level) away from the actual bit manipulation (machine language, also called "bit twiddling" by the Hackers).

HIVR

Host Interactive Voice Response. Tying a voice response unit into a mainframe computer which has lots of data. Applications which can be produced include bank-by-phone, reservations-by-phone, etc.

Hook Flash

See FLASH

Hookswitch

Also called SWITCHHOOK. It's typically the place on your telephone instrument where you lay your handset. When you lift the handset, you are said to be going "off hook." When you place your handset back, you are said to be "on hook." When you lift the handset (i.e. go off hook) you are, in effect, signaling your central office that you'd like to make a call, or that you have answered the incoming ringing call.

Host Computer

A computer attached to a network providing primarily services such as computation, data base access or special programs of special programming languages. The central computer in a time-sharing operation.

Host Interactive Voice Response

Voice Response system communicating with a host computer See HIVR.

Host Processor

Same as HOST COMPUTER.

Hot Key

Refers to TSR utilities in DOS or filters in a Windows environment that allow users to fax without leaving their present application. The ability to send a fax from within an application is one of the most important features of computer fax technology.

HTML

HyperText Markup Language. The formatting language of the World Wide Web. HTML is how you actually "write" or "program" Web pages. It's a primitive language, really. Everything is in ASCII. You put codes in to define fonts, layout, embed graphics and hypertext links.

HTTP

Hypertext Transfer Protocol is the transport protocol in transmitting hypertext documents around the Internet.

Huffman Encoding

A popular lossless data compression algorithm that replaces frequently occurring data strings with shorter codes. Some implementations include tables that predetermine what codes will be generated from a particular string. Other versions of the algorithm build the code table from the data stream during processing. Huffman encoding is often used in image compression. (Q.v., Modified Huffman Code.)

Hunt

Refers to the progress of a call reaching a group of lines. The call will try the first line of the group. If that line is busy, it will try the second line, then it will hunt to the third, etc. See also HUNT GROUP.

Hunt Group

A series of telephone lines organized in such a way that if the first line is busy the next line is hunted and so on until a free line is found. Often this arrangement is used on a group of incoming lines. Hunt groups may start with one trunk and hunt downwards. They may start randomly and hunt in clockwise circles. They may start randomly and hunt in counter-clockwise circles.

Inter-Tel uses the terms "Linear, Distributed and Terminal" to refer to different types of hunt groups. In data communications, a hunt group is a set of links which provides a common resource and which is assigned a single hunt group designation. A user requesting that designation may then be connected to any member of the hunt group. Hunt group members may also receive calls by station address.

Hyperchannel

A data path on the SCbus or SCxbus Data Bus made up of more than one time slot. By bundling time slots into a hyperchannel, data paths with a bandwidth greater than 64 Kbps can be created.

HYPERTEXT

A method of writing and displaying text that allows the text to be linked to something else. Click on it. Go elsewhere. Hypertext can contain photos, audio and video.

I

ICFA

International Computer Facsimile Association. Formed in 1991, its members include the leading companies in the computer and communications industries.

Idle

A state of the SCbus or SCxbus Message Bus where no information is being transmitted and the bus line is pulled high.

IGMP

Internet Group Management Protocol. IGMP is used by IP hosts to report their host group memberships to any immediately-neighboring multicast routers. IGMP is an asymmetric protocol and is specified here from the point of view of a host, rather than a multicast router. (IGMP may also be used, symmetrically or asymmetrically, between multicast routers. GMP is a integral part of IP.

In-Band Signaling

Signaling made up of tones which pass within the voice frequency band, and are carried along the same circuit as the talk path that is being established by the signals. Virtually all signaling -- request for service, dialing, disconnect, etc. -- in the U.S. today is in-band signaling.

Most of that signaling is MF -- multi-frequency dialing. The more modern form of signaling is out-of-band.

Indexed Database

A database indexed on a key field. Indexing allows for rapid retrieval of records through an index field.

Index Field

The field to be used when indexing a database.

Index File

An (optional) file used for indexing the data in a database. Index files are usually given extensions which identify them as index files. For example, when using dBASE III+, the index files are given the NDX extension.

Index Handle

See Handle.

IndexOrder Retrieval

Implies a sequence in which records are read from the database in an order based on the contents of each record's index field.

Information Center Mailboxes

A voice bulletin board on a voice mail system. Here's their explanation: Multiple callers can access, directly or indirectly, recorded announcements containing information that would otherwise have been given live by employees. Callers are frequently "outside" users of the system. One type of "listen only" mailbox simply plays the messages to the callers. This technology, sometimes known as audiotex, makes it possible to create a verbal database so callers can select which information they want to hear.

Another type of Information Center Mailbox prompts callers to reply to announcements. Callers wanting further information can be given the opportunity to leave their names and phone numbers after listening to a product description. They can also be transferred to a designated employee who can immediately take an order. If desired, a password can be required before confidential or controlled access information can be heard.

Information Provider

A business or person providing information to the public for money. The information is typically selected by the caller through touch tones, delivered using voice processing equipment, and transmitted over tariffed phone lines, e.g., 900, 976, 970. Typically, billing for information providers' services is done by a local or long distance phone company.

Sometimes the revenues for the service are split by the information provider and the phone company. Sometimes the phone company simply bills a per minute or flat charge. A typical "information provider" is American Express, which provides a service -- 1-900-WEATHER. By dialing that number you can touch-tone in city names and find out temperatures, weather forecasts, etc. Calling 1-900-WEATHER costs several dollars a minute.

Interactive Voice Response

IVR. Picture a standard personal computer.

You enter information through the keyboard. You see the results of your work on your screen. With interactive voice response, the keyboard, (or data entry device) becomes the touch-tone pad of a telephone (either local, but most likely remote) and the screen (the output device) becomes a voice synthesizer which electronically converts the computer's output (what you'd normally see on the screen) into spoken words.

You call a phone number. A machine answers. It presents you with several options, "Push 1 for information on Plays, Push 2 for information on movies, Push 3 for information on Museums." If you push 2, the machine may come back, "Push 1 for movies on the south side of town, Push 2 for movies on the north side of town, etc." That's a very simple interactive voice response (also called Voice Processing) application.

There are literally thousands of others. A bank might say "Thanks for calling the XYZ Bank, if you'd like your balance, punch in your account number now." A cable TV company might say "Thanks for calling ABC TV, if you'd like to see tonight's feature movie, push 1. $5.00 will be billed to your account." There are applications for Interactive Voice Response in every industry, in every company. Hint: Think customer!

What can we do to make our customers' lives easier? Can we help them find our nearest store? Can we tell them where to get the stuff we sell them repaired? Would they like to know where the order is they placed a week ago?

Intercept Service

A service of the local phone in which a phone call is redirected by an operator or a recording to another phone number or a message. Intercept could also be sold to companies who have moved and would like to retain a recording and/or a phone advertisement for many months after they've moved.

Interconnect Companies

Companies which sell, install and maintain telephone systems for end users, typically businesses.

Inter-LATA

Telecommunications services that originate in one and terminate in another Local Access and Transport Area (LATA). Under provisions of Divestiture, the Bell operating companies cannot provide Inter-LATA service, but can provide Intra-LATA service.

Some LATAs are very large. So some "local" phone companies provide the equivalent of long distance service. And some of these phone companies have different pricing packages. Some of these packages are cheap, but not highly-publicized. See also LATA.

INTERNET

Internet is a computer network which joins many government and university and private computers together over phone lines (mostly T-1s and T-3s). In 1995 the Government Accounting Office (GAO) said that Internet linked 59,000 networks, 2.2 million computers and 15 million users in 92 countries. Internet traces its origins to a network set up in 1969 by the Defense Department. In 1991 it was running off $20 million a year in federal subsidies and managed by the National Science Foundation. An IBM/MCI venture known as Advanced Network and Services manages a network called NSFnet, which connects hundreds of research centers and universities. NSFnet also manages links to dozens of other countries. All these networks are collectively known as Internet. NSFnet was founded by the National Science Foundation, a Federal Government agency and is composed of leased telephone lines that link special computers called routers, which transmit packages of data to three million users in 33 countries. See various INTERNET definitions following.

INTERNET ADDRESS

A unique, 32-bit identifier for a specific TCP/IP host on a network. Also called an Internet Protocol or IP address. IP addresses are normally printed in dotted decimal form, such as 128.127.50.224.

INTERNET GATEWAY

Internet gateways are devices which typically sit on a local area network and handle all the translations between IPX traffic on your LAN

(IPX is the NetWare protocol) and the TCP/IP traffic on the Internet. TCP/IP is the protocol used on the Internet.

INTERNET GROUP NAME
In Microsoft networking, a name registered by the domain controller that contains a list of the specific addresses of computers that have registered the name. The name has a 16th character ending in 0x1C.

INTERNET MIB SUBTREE
A tree-shaped data structure in which network devices on a local area network and their attributes can be identified within the confines of a network management scheme. The name of an object or attribute is derived from its location on this tree. For example, an object in MIB-I might be named 1.2.1.1.1.0. the first 1 indicates the object is on the Internet. The 2 denotes that it falls within the Management category. The second 1 shows the object is part of the first fully defined MIB, known as MIB-I. The third 1 indicates which of the eight object groups is being referenced. And the fourth 1 is a textual description of the network component. The O indicates there is only one object instance. An object instance links a particular object to a specific node on the network. The numbering system is infinitely extendible to accommodate additions to this base identification scheme. This common naming structure permits equipment from a variety of vendors to be managed by a single management station that uses SNMP. The four main categories of the tree are Directory, Management, Experimental and Private/Enterprises.

INTERNET NUMBER
The dotted-quad address used to specify a certain system. The Internet number for cs.widener.edu is 147.31.130. A resolver is used to translate between hostnames and Internet addresses.

INTERNET PACKET EXCHANGE IPX
Novell NetWare's native LAN communications protocol, used to move data between server and/or workstation programs running on different network nodes.

INTERNET PROTOCOL

IP. Part of the TCP/IP family of protocols describing software that tracks the Internet address of nodes, routes outgoing message, and recognizes incoming messages. Used in gateways to connect networks at OSI network Level 3 and above.

INTERNET PROTOCOL SUITE

A suite of network protocols which have been adopted as the main de facto protocols for LANs.

INTERNET RELAY CHAT IRC

Sort of like CB radio, but run on the Internet, and far more confusing than CB radio.

INTERNET SERVER

An Internet server is a device which users on the Internet access to get services. Such services might be electronic mail, news, a Web page, etc. A company will have one or more Internet servers attached to the Internet when it wants to deliver services to people on the Internet. Such Internet servers could be called e-mail servers, FTP servers, News servers and World Wide Web servers. Internet servers most commonly run on Unix. But Microsoft Windows NT is increasingly gaining popularity.

INTRANET

An Internet-like network within an organization. Intranets use web server and browser technology and other Internet emerging standards to share data on Internet-like networks within an organization (the "intraprise") rather than just for external connection to the Internet.

IP MULTICASTING

The transmission of an IP datagram to a "host group", a set of zero or more hosts identified by a single IP destination address. A multicast datagram is delivered to all members of its destination host group with the same "best-efforts" reliability as regular unicast IP datagrams, i.e., the datagram is not guaranteed to arrive intact at all members of the destination group or in the same order relative to other datagrams.

IPX

Internet Packet eXchange. A lowlevel network communications protocol used by Novell networks. In most networks, IPX is supplemented and extended by SPX.

ISDN

Integrated Services Digital Network. A collection of standards which define interfaces for, and operation of, digital switching equipment, developed by carriers, equipment manufacturers, and international standards organizations. It is intended to form the basis for the next generation telephone network and is currently being implemented by carriers throughout the world. Instead of one analog telephone line, there would be two 64 kbps bearer lines and one 16 Kbps data line. Each bearer line could carry voice, video, data, images or combinations of these. As the name implies, it would be a point-to-point digital system. BISDN stands for Broadband Integrated Services Digital Network. It is a packet switching technique which uses packets of fixed length, resulting in lower processing overhead and higher speeds. Also known as cell switching and ATM.

ISO

The International Standards Organization in Paris, devoted to developing standards for international and national data communications. The U.S. representative to the ISO is ANSI.

ISP

Internet Service Provider. This company rents lines into the Internet and typically sells dial-up service to you and me. Sometimes, an ISP will let a company put up its Web page on ISP equipment.

ITU

International Telecommunications Union, the world standards-setting organization. Formerly the Comite Consultatif Internationale de Telegraphique et Telephonique (Consultative Committee for International Telephone and Telegraph - CCITT). See Telecommunication Standardization Sector.

IVR

Interactive Voice Response.

IXC

InterExchange Channel, or InterExchange Carrier -- as contrasted to the LEC -- the Local Exchange Carrier, a new word for a local phone company. InterExchange Carriers used to be called "Other Common Carriers," except that didn't include AT&T. Now, AT&T, MCI, Sprint and all the Other Common Carriers are called InterExchange Carriers.

K

KBPS

Kilobits per second. It is a bandwidth equal to 1000 bits.

L

LAN

Local Area Network. A short distance network (typically within a building or campus) used to link together computers and peripheral devices under some form of standard control. See RING and ETHERNET.

LATA

Local Access and Transport Area; one of 161 local telephone service areas in the United States.

As a result of the Bell divestiture that now distinguishes local from long-distance service, switched calls with both endpoints within the LATA (intraLATA) are generally the sole responsibility of the local telephone company, while calls that cross outside the LATA (interLATA) are passed on to an interexchange carrier.

LEC

Local Exchange Company. The local phone companies, which can be either a Bell Operating Company (BOC) or an independent (e.g. GTE) which provides local transmission services. Prior to divestiture, the LECs were called telephone companies or telcos.

Line
See Channel.

Line Powered
Telephone equipment that is powered solely by the CO talk battery supplied in a standard phone line.

Local Loop
The physical wires that run from the subscriber's telephone set, or PBX or key telephone system, to the telephone company central office. Increasingly, the local loop now goes from the main distribution frame in the basement to the phone company. And the subscriber is responsible for getting his/her wires from the box in the basement to his phone system.

Local Mode
A client-server application with both the client User Function and server modules running on a single PC. (See also Distributed Mode.)

Loop
1. Typically a complete electrical circuit. 2. The loop is also the pair of wires that winds its way from the central office to the telephone set or system at the customer's office, home or factory, i.e. "premises" in telephones. 3. In computer software. A loop repeats a series of instructions many times until some prestated event has happened or until some test has been passed.

Loop Current Detection
When a voice, modem, or fax resource seizes the line (i.e., completes the connection between tip-and-ring terminals of the telephone cable), current flows from the positive battery supply in the telephone central office, through the twisted pair in the loop, through the board, and back to the central office negative terminal where it is detected, showing that this telephone line is off hook. The fax board also detects the loop current and can detect problems such as disconnects, shutting down the connection or a busy signal, making it wait and redial.

Loop Start

You "start" (seize) a phone line or trunk by giving it a supervisory signal. That signal is typically taking your phone off hook. There are two ways you can do that -- ground start or loop start. With loop start, you seize a line by bridging through a resistance the tip and ring (both wires) of your telephone line.

Loop Timing

A way of synchronizing a circuit that works by taking a synchronizing clock signal from incoming digital pulses.

Lossless Compression Coding

Coding designed not to lose any data when compressing or restoring an image.

Low Level Language

A programming language that uses symbols -- one step away from the machine language of a computer. Low level computer languages such as Assembler and C which actually manipulate the bits in computer registers. Higher level languages such as Basic and Fortran will take care of the piddling details of doing specific functions when you give it a broad command like "PRINT". In a lower level language, you must provide all the details of instruction necessary in the code (program) to perform the operation. It is possible to do this by calling standard routines, but still takes up the programmers' time in deciding which routines, and keeping the registers straight as he designs the program.

M

MAE

Metropolitan Area Ethernet. This is a basically a fiber-optic data ring around the city. It is used to inexpensively connect companies and offices to this citywide network.

Mailbox

Messages belonging to a single owner in a voice mail system. Today, these will be recorded voice messages, but increasingly mailboxes will include E-mail and fax documents.

MAPI

Messaging Application Programming Interface. Developed by Microsoft.

MBONE

Multicast Backbone. Circa 1992 IETF (Internet Engineering Task Force) effort. Came out of earlier ARPA DARTnet experiments. Supports multicast audio and video across the Internet. Provides one-to-many and many-to-many network delivery services for apps like videoconferencing and audio. Supports simultaneous communication between several hosts.

MCA

Micro Channel Architecture.

MCF

Message Confirmation Frame. Confirmation by the receiver that it is ready to receive the next fax page, starting Phase C again.

Media Processing

The processing of transactions during a telephone call; these transactions may include fax operations, speech recognition and synthesis, Touch Tone recognition, voice and fax store-and-forward messaging, and the conversion of messages from one format to another (such as from text to voice, or from fax to text).

Menu

Options displayed on a computer terminal screen or spoken by a voice processing system. The user can choose what he wants done by simply choosing a menu option -- either typing it on the computer keyboard, hitting a touch tone on his phone, or speaking a word or two. There are basically two ways of organizing computer or voice processing software -- menu-driven and non-menu driven.

Menu-driven programs are easier for users to use. But they can only present as many options as can be reasonably crammed on a screen or spoken in a few seconds. Non-menu driven screens can allow more any alternatives. But they're much more complex and frightening.

It's the difference between receiving a bland "A" or "C" prompt on the screen -- as in MS-DOS and receiving a menu of "Press A if you want Word Processing," "Press B if you want Spread Sheet," etc. It's very easy to write menus in MS-DOS using BATch files. See also AUDIO MENUS.

Message
The transport container for SCSA requests, replies and events. Assumes a set of conventions for directing the delivery of the message to the proper entity, either a client or service provider. See also SCSA Message Protocol.

Method
The specific implementation of an operation for a class; code that can be executed in response to a request.

Micro Channel
A proprietary 32-bit bus developed by IBM for its PS/2 family of computers' internal expansion cards. Also offered by Tandy and other vendors.

Microcode
Programmed instructions that typically are unalterable. Usually synonymous with firmware and programmable read-only-memory (PROM).

MIDI
Musical Instrument Digital Interface. The standard protocol for the interchange of musical information between musical instruments, synthesizers, and computers.

Mini/Mainframe Fax Servers
Many mini/mainframe fax servers function in the same way as LAN fax servers: users can send and receive faxes from their terminals, saving both time and money while they increase the quality of their fax transmissions.

By being on the same computer system as an organization's data, mini/mainframe servers can provide an EDI-like component for large, vertical applications such as accounting or purchase order systems, broadening the electronic reach of these programs to any recipient with a fax machine.

Modem

Acronym for MOdulator/DEmodulator. Equipment that converts digital signals to analog signals and vice-versa. Modems are used to send data signals (digital) over the telephone network, which is usually analog. A modem modulates binary signals into tones that can be carried over the telephone network. At the other end, the demodulator part of the modem converts the tones back to binary code.

Modified Huffman Code (MH)

A one-dimensional data compression technique that compresses data in an horizontal direction only and does not allow transmission of redundant data. Huffman encoding is a lossless data compression algorithm that replaces frequently occurring data strings with shorter codes. Often used in image compression.

Modified READ (MR)

Relative Element Address Differentiation code. A two-dimensional compression technique for fax machines that handles the data compression of the vertical line and that concentrates on space between the lines and within given characters.

Modified Modified READ (MMR)

A two-dimensional coding scheme for Group 4 fax, but now finding use with Group 3 machines.

Modulation

The process of varying some characteristic of the electrical carrier wave as the information to be transmitted on that carrier wave varies. Three types of modulation are commonly used for communications, Amplitude Modulation, Frequency Modulation, and Phase Modulation. And there are variations on these themes called Phase Shift Keying (PSK) and Quadrature Amplitude Modulation (QAM).

MPS
Multi-Page Signal. A frame sent if the sender has more pages to transmit.

MSI
Modular Station Interface. A Dialogic board that interfaces analog phones to SCbus and PEB-based products.

MTBF
Mean Time Between Failure. The length of time a user may reasonably expect a device or system to work before an incapacitating fault occurs.

MTTR
Mean Time to Repair. The average time required to return a failed device or system to service.

Multiplexer
Electronic equipment which allows two or more signals to pass over one communications circuit. That "circuit' may be a phone line, a microwave circuit, a through-the air TV signal. That circuit may be analog or digital. There are many multiplexing techniques to accommodate both.

MVIP
Multi-Vendor Integration Protocol. A standard for digital switching technology that permits the design of sophisticated applications such as voice, fax, speech recognition, and others. The technology was developed by Mitel, and the standard was proposed by Natural Microsystems.

N

NAP
Network Applications Platform (Unisys, Blue Bell, PA, term). A public telephone network service with the ability to send and receive voice messages and facsimile documents.

NetBIOS

The Network Basic Input Output System. An IBM-developed standard for network communication. Most nonIBM networks require a NetBIOS compatibility module or utility to use NetBIOS communication and protocols. (See also SPX.)

Network

1. Networks are common in our lives. Think about trains and phones. A networks ties things together. Computer networks connect all types of computers and computer-related things together -- terminals, printers, modems, door entry sensors, temperature monitors, etc. The networks we're most familiar with are long distance ones, like phones and trains.

But there are also Local Area Networks (LANs), which exist within a limited geographic area -- like the few hundred feet of a small office, or they can span an entire building, or even touch a "campus," such as a university, or industrial park. There are also Metropolitan Area Networks (MANs). See LAN.

Network Board

A board device designed to act as an interface between a computer-based signal processing system and a telephone network.

Network Fax Servers

A network fax server allows users to send faxes from their network workstations. Many fax servers allow the faxing of documents from the applications that created them, leaving users free to continue with their work. Incoming faxes can be directed back to your workstation as well.

Different fax server products offer different ways of handling incoming faxes, but most use one of the following: the fax can be received by an operator who forwards it to the proper workstation, a fax extension can be assigned to particular workstations for touch-tone routing, or there can be a direct fax telephone line accessed through a Direct Inward Dial (DID) line.

Network Interface

The point of inter-connection between Telephone Company communications facilities and terminal equipment, protective apparatus or wiring at a subscriber's premises. The network interface or demarcation point is located on the subscriber's side of the Telephone Company's protector.

Network Interface Module

Electronic circuitry connecting a workstation (typically a personal computer) to the telephone network. Network interface modules come in as many flavors as there are ways of connecting to the telephone network -- from simple loop start phone lines to complex primary rate interfaces (PRI) on ISDN. Usually, the network interface module slides into one of the expansion slots inside a personal computer. The card transmits and receives messages from the resource modules connected to the telephone network.

NNX/NXX

A three-digit code to identify the central office in which N is any digit 2 to 9 and X is any digit. The first three digits of a North American telephone number. Originally only NNX codes were used. Now subscriber dials 1+ in making a direct distance dialed toll call and the code may be NXX. Area codes are also being changed to NXX codes.

Node

1. A point of connection into a network. In LANs, it is a device on the network. In packet switched networks, it is one of the many packet switches that form the network's backbone. 2. An independent SCSA unit in a distributed processing SCSA network (MNA - Multinode Architecture) consisting of one or more resource and/or network boards, and one or more SCxbus adapter boards. Communication between nodes take place via the SCxbus. From a device programming point of view, a node is simply an addressable system unit which contains boards connected by an SCbus.

Noise

Unwanted electrical signals introduced into telephone lines by circuit components or natural disturbances that tend to degrade the line's performance.

NonIndexed
A database which is not indexed on a key field.

Novell Telephony Services (TSAPI)
Novell's telephony server product, providing a single standard client-server call control interface (including an API for programmers) to many of the diverse PBX systems on the market today.

NSC
Non-Standard Facilities Command. A response to the called fax DIS response.

NSF
Non-Standard Facilities.

NSS
Non-Standard Facilities Setup command, a response to an NSF frame.

NVP
Network Voice Protocol. Circa 1973 ARPANET protocol. Old voice protocol. Used to support real-time voice over the ARPANET. Both LPC and CVSD encoding schemes were successfully implemented by Culler-Harrison, Inc., the Information Sciences Institute, Lincoln Laboratory and Stanford Research Institute.

O

OAI
Open Application Interface. Basically an opening in a telephone system that lets you link a computer to that phone system and lets the computer command the phone system to answer, delay, switch, hold etc. calls. The term is also called PHI -- as in PBX-Host-Interface. The term OAI was first used by PBX makers, NEC and InteCom. And now the term has become somewhat generic, like all good things. Essentially every manufacturer of phone systems is evolving towards open application interfaces of their own.

OA&M

Operations, Administration and Maintenance. This term refers to PBX management.

Octet

The ITU standard term for byte.

Off-Hook

When the handset is lifted from its cradle it's Off-Hook. Lifting the hookswitch alerts the central office that the user wants the phone to do something like dial a call. A dial tone is a sign saying "Give me an order." The term "off-hook" originated when the early handsets were actually suspended from a metal hook on the phone.

When the handset is removed from its hook or its cradle (in modern phones), it completes the electrical loop, thus signaling the central office that it wishes dial tone. Some leased line channels work by lifting the handset, signaling the central office at the other end which rings the phone at the other end. Some phones have autodialers in them. Lifting the phone signals the phone to dial that one number. An example is a phone without a dial at an airport, which automatically dials the local taxi company. All this by simply lifting the handset at one end -- going "off-hook."

Off-Hook Signal

In telephone switching, a signal indicating seizure, request for service, or a busy condition.

One-Dimensional Coding

A data compression scheme that considers each scan line as being unique, without referencing it to a previous scan line. One-dimensional coding operates horizontally only.

On-Hook

When the phone handset is resting in its cradle. The phone is not connected to any particular line. Only the bell is active, i.e. it will ring if a call comes in. See ON-HOOK DIALING and OFF-HOOK.

On-Hook Dialing

Allows a caller to dial a call without lifting his handset. After dialing, the caller can listen to the progress of the call over the phone's built-in speaker. When you hear the called person answer, you can pick up the handset and speak or you can talk hands-free in the direction of your phone, if it's a speakerphone. Critical: Many phones have speakers for hands-free listening.

Not all phones with speakers are speakerphones -- i.e. have microphones, which allow you to speak, also.

Operator Services

Any of a variety of telephone services which need the assistance of an operator. For example, such services typically include collect calls, third-party billed calls, person-to-person calls.

Out-Of-Band Signaling

Signaling that is separated from the channel carrying the information -- the voice, data, video, etc. Typically the separation is accomplished by a filter. The signaling includes dialing and other supervisory signals. Out-band-band hardware signaling takes place on its own data path, without the necessity of "bit robbing" or other methods of mixing signals into a data stream.

P

Packet

A bundle of data, usually in binary form, organized in a specific way for transmission.

Packet Switching

Sending data in packets through a network to a remote location. The data are subdivided into individual packets of data, each with a unique identification and individual destination address. This way each packet can take a different route and may arrive in a different order than it was shipped. The packet ID allows the reassembling of data in the proper sequence. This is an efficient way to move digital data. Although it has been used with fax messages, is not yet useful for voice.

PABX (PBX)

Private Automatic Branch Exchange. Originally, PBX was the word for a switch inside a private business (as against one serving the public). PBX means a Private Branch Exchange. Such a "PBX" was typically a manual device, requiring operator assistance to complete a call.

Then the PBX went "modern" (i.e. automatic) and no operator was needed any longer to complete outgoing calls. You could dial "9." Thus it became a "PABX." Now all PABXs are modern. And a PABX is now commonly referred to as a "PBX." Some manufacturers have tried to make their PBX appear different by calling it something else.

Siemens/Rolm calls theirs the "CBX" (Computerized Branch Exchange). Some others call theirs the "EPABX" (the Electronic Private Automatic Branch Exchange. Then there are the special ones, like SRX's SRX, NEC's IMS (Information Management System), etc.

PAGE

A chunk of information, such as a document or a file, on the Web. You write them in HTML code. They can contain graphics, audio and video.

PAM

Pulse Amplitude Modulation. The process of representing a continuous analog signal (a voice conversation) with a series of discrete analog samples. This concept is based on the information theory which suggests that the signal can be accurately recreated from a sufficient sample. Why bother? Sampling allows several signals to then be combined on a channel that otherwise would only carry one telephone conversation.) PAM was used as part of a method of switching phones calls in several PBXs. It is not a truly "digital" switching system. PAM is the basis of PCM, pulse code modulation. See PCM.

Part 68 Requirements (Registration)

Specifications established by the FCC as the minimum acceptable protection which communications equipment must provide the telephone network. Meeting these requirements does not certify that equipment performs any task. Equipment which is sold for connection to the public network in the US must conform to Part 68.

PBX (PABX)

Private Branch eXchange. A private (i.e. you, as against the phone company owns it), branch (meaning it is a small phone company central office), exchange (a central office was originally called a public exchange, or simply an exchange). In other words, a PBX is a small version of the phone company's larger central switching office.

A PBX is also called a Private Automatic Branch Exchange, though that has now become an obsolete term. In the very old days, you called the operator to make an external call. Then later someone made a phone system that you simply dialed nine (or another digit -- in Europe it's often zero), got a second dial tone and dialed some more digits to dial out, locally or long distance. So, the early name of Private Branch Exchange (which needed an operator) became Private AUTOMATIC Branch Exchange (which didn't need an operator). Now, all PBXs are automatic. And now they're all called PBXs, except overseas where they still have PBXs that are not automatic.

PCM

Pulse Code Modulation. PCM is a method of taking an analog voice signal and encoding it into a digital bit stream. First, the amplitude of the voice conversation is sampled. This is called PAM, Pulse Amplitude Modulation. This PAM sample is then coded into a binary (digital) number. This digital number consists of zeros and ones. It can then be switched and transmitted digitally. There are three basic advantages to PCM voice. They are the three basic advantages of digital switching and transmission.

First, it is less expensive to switch and transmit a digital signal. Second, by making an analog voice signal into a digital signal, you can interleave it with other digital signals -- such as those from computers or facsimile machines. Third, a voice signal which is switched and transmitted end-to-end in a digital format will usually come through "cleaner," i.e. have less noise, than one transmitted and switched in analog. The reason is simple: An electrical signal loses strength over a distance. It must then be amplified. In analog transmission, everything is amplified, including the noise and static the signal has collected along the way.

In digital transmission, the signal is "regenerated," i.e. put back together again, by comparing the incoming signal to a logical question: Is it a one or a zero? Then, the signal is regenerated, then it is "amplified and sent along its way. PCM refers to a technique of digitization. It does not refer to a universally accepted standard of digitizing voice. The most common PCM method is to sample a voice conversation at 8000 times a seconds. The theory is that if the sampling is at least twice the highest frequency on the channel, then the result sounds OK. Thus, the highest frequency on a voice phone line is 4,000 Hertz. So one must sample it at 8,000 times a second. Many PCM digital voice conversations are typically put on one communications channel. In North America, the most typical channel is called the T-1 (also spelled T1). It places 24 voice conversations on two pairs of copper wires (one for receiving and one for transmitting). It contains 8000 frames each of 8 bits of 24 voice channels plus one framing (synchronizing bit) bit which equals 1,544,000 bits per second. i.e. 8000 x (8 x 24 + 1) equals 1.544 megabits.

Europe uses a different scheme for multiplexing voice conversations. It is based not on 24 voice channels, but on 32 channels. This scheme keeps two of the 32 channels for control and actually transmits 30 voice conversations at a data rate of 2,048,000 bits per second. The European system is calculated as 8 bits x 32 channels x 8000 frames per second. European PCM multiplexing is not compatible with North American multiplexing.

The two systems cannot be directly connected. Some PBXs in the U.S. conform to the U.S. standard only. Some (very few) conform to both. Both the European and North American T-1 "standards" have now been accepted as ISDN "standards." In addition to PCM, there are many other ways of digitally encoding voice. PCM remains the most common. See E-I, T-1 and VOICE COMPRESSION.

PCM-30
Short name of international 2.048 Mbps T-1 (also known as E1) service derived from the fact that 30 channels are available for 64 Kbps digitized voice each using pulse code modulation (PCM).

PEB

PCM Expansion Bus. Dialogic's name for the digital electrical connection between its network interface modules and its resource modules. This bus is now "open." Technical specifications are available, thus enabling outsiders to create their own resource modules and/or network interface modules. See also AEB, which is Dialogic's Analog Expansion Bus.

Pel

Picture Element. A pel contains only black and white information, no grey shading.

Personal Identification Number

PIN number. 1. An AT&T term meaning the last four digits of your AT&T, MCI Bell operating company Credit Card -- the card you use for making long distance numbers. 2. Some banks and financial institutions issue credit cards for machine, teller-less banking. These machines, called Automated Teller Machines, ask you for a password consisting of several numbers or characters. These are not on your credit card. These numbers or characters, called PIN numbers, are designed to make sure the right person is using your card. It's not a good idea to use your birthday as you PIN number.

Phase A

In a fax machine's call process, the call establishment, when the transmitting and receiving units connect over the telephone line, recognizing one another as fax machines. This is the start of the handshaking procedure.

Phase B

In a fax machine's call process, the pre-message procedure, where the answering machine identifies itself, describing its capabilities in a burst of digital information packed in frames conforming to the HDLC standard.

Phase C

In a fax machine's call process, the fax transmission portion of the operation. This step consists of two parts-C1 and C2-which take place simultaneously. Phase C1 deals with synchronization, line monitoring, and problem detection. Phase C2 includes data transmission.

Phase D

In a fax machine's call process, this phase begins once a page has been transmitted. Both the sender and receiver revert to using HDLC packets as during Phase B. If the sender has further pages to transmit, it sends an MPS frame, and the receiver replies with an MCF and Phase C recommences for the following page.

Phase E

In a fax machine's call process, the call release portion. The side that transmitted last sends a DCN frame and hangs up without awaiting a response.

Phonemail

A ROLM term for Voice Mail. Rolm's PhoneMail is a voice messaging system that provides (1.) telephone answering (with the user's own greeting), (2.) the capability to store and forward voice messages, and (3.) the capability to turn on a message waiting light or message on the recipient's phone. PhoneMail can be used positively -- to speed the flow of information. It can also be used negatively -- to allow the user to "hide behind" the system and avoid the outside world and anyone in the outside world who might actually want to buy something. See also VOICE MAIL.

PIN

Procedure interrupt negative.

PIN Number

Personal Identification Number. A group of characters entered as a secret code to gain access to a computer system, such as the one that completes long distance calls. See PERSONAL IDENTIFICATION NUMBER.

Pixel

Picture Element. The smallest area of an original sampled and represented by an electrical signal. A pixel has more than two levels of greyscale information.

Phone Book

This is a special file for fax telephone numbers and other transmission information for people with whom the user regularly communicates. It has Category and Class fields to organize contacts into groups and subgroups. With the Phone Book it is not necessary to type numbers and names each time a fax is sent. It can be used to send to a single number or to more than one fax number broadcasting purposes.

PIP

Procedure interrupt positive.

Playback

Retrieval, decoding and transmission of encoded data.

Player

A resource object that plays TVM data. The audio data can come from a voice or audio encoded file, or from text that has passed through a text-to-speech service. The output of a player can be analog audio, TDD, ADSI, etc.

Polling

Refers to some form of data or fax network arrangement whereby a central computer or fax machine/board very quickly asks each remote location in turn whether they want to send some information. The purpose is to give each user or remote data terminal an opportunity to transmit and receive information on a circuit or using facilities which are being shared. Polling is typically used in a multipoint or multidrop line. It is done mostly to save money on telephone lines.

POP

Post Office Protocol. A system on the Internet you can use to get your e-mail. You use a mail server to get the mail and then download it to your computer.

Pop-Up

See Hot Key.

Port

An entrance to or exit from a network, the physical or electrical interface through which one gains access. The interface between a process or a program and a communications or transmission facility. A point in the computer or telephone system where data may be accessed. Peripherals are connected to ports.

Portability

This means that application software can be dragged across different computing platforms and operating systems. With the TAO spec, developers can write an application that will run on a PC, Alpha Server or Tandem host. SCSA's operating-system-independent APIs give developers a uniform method for supporting multiple operating systems.

PostScript

A page description language for PCs, which is standard for many graphics and desktop publishing applications. It allows the creation of elaborate documents. Other applications such as spreadsheets, word processors, and databases rarely require this sophistication.

POTS

Plain Old Telephone Service. The basic service supplying standard single line telephones, telephone lines and access to the public switched network. Nothing fancy. No added features. Just receive and place calls. Nothing like Call Waiting or Call Forwarding. They are not POTS services. Pronounced POTS, like in pots and pans.

POINT-TO-POINT PROTOCOL

PPP. An implementation of TCP/IP which is intended for transmission using telephone lines. PPP is a new standard which supersedes SLIP.

Predictive Dialer

See PREDICTIVE DIALING.

Predictive Dialing

An automated method of making many outbound calls without people and then passing answered calls to a person as the calls are answered.

Here's the story: Imagine a bunch of operators having to call a bunch of people. Those calls may be for collections. They may be for employee call-ups. They may be for alumnae fund raising. When it's done manual, here's how it works: Before each call operators spend time reviewing paper records or computer terminal screens, selecting the person to be called, finding the phone number, dialing the numbers, listening to rings, listening to phone company intercepts, busy signals and answering machines.

Operators also spend time updating the records after each call. Predictive dialing automates this process, with the computer choosing the person to be called and dialing the number and only passing it to an operator when a real live human being answers. There are enormous productivity gains made by screening out answering machines, busy signals, network busy signals, non-completed calls, operator intercepts etc. The result is productivity increases of 300% to 600%.

According to generally accepted industry lore, a well-run manual dialing center can get its people talking on the phone for 25 minutes an hour. With a predictive dialer you can get them on the phone making sales, collecting money, etc. for 55 minutes an hour. It's a major productivity gain. True predictive dialing should not be confused with automated dialing.

True predictive dialing has complex mathematical algorithms that consider, in real time, the number of available telephone lines, the number of available operators, the probability of getting no answer, a busy signal, a disconnected number, operator intercept or an answering machine, the time between calls required for maximum operator efficiency, the length of an average conversation and the average length of time the operators need to enter the relevant data. Some predictive dialing systems constantly adjust the dialing rate by monitoring changes in all these factors. Some people don't like the term "predictive dialing," since they think it's getting "a bad rap" in Washington, DC by being associated with junk phone calls. As a result some e people would prefer to call it Computer Aided Dialing.

Preview Dialing
Preview dialing is a term used to describe an automatic dialer.

Preview dialing is also called "screen dialing" or "cursor dialing." Typically the prospect's account information and/or phone number appears on the screen BEFORE the call is made. Thus the agent can "preview" the number, the screen, the customer. If the agent wants to make the call, the agent hits a key, such as "Enter" and the computer dials the number.

In some preview dialing equipment, the agent must hit a key if he/she DOESN'T want the number dialed. Contrast preview dialing with Predictive Dialing where the computer makes all the dialing decisions and presents the calls to the agent only after they are connected. Predictive dialing is a lot faster than preview dialing. See PREDICTIVE DIALING.

PRI
See PRIMARY RATE INTERFACE.

PRI-EOM
Procedure interrupt-end of message.

PRI-EOP
Procedure interrupt-end of procedures.

PRI-MPS
Procedure interrupt-multipage signal.

Primary Rate Interface
PRI. The ISDN equivalent of a T-1 circuit. The Primary Rate Interface (that which is delivered to the customer's premises) provides 23B+D (in North America) or 30B+D (in Europe) running at 1.544 megabits per second and 2.048 megabits per second, respectively. There is another ISDN interface. It's called the Basic Rate Interface. It delivers 2B+D over either one or two pairs. In ISDN, the "B" stands for Bearer, which is 64,000 bits per second, which can carry PCM-digitized voice or data.

Primary Resource
The main resource around which a Group is constructed. Typically, the primary resource will be an interface to the telephone network, but it may also be a switch port.

Printed Circuit Board

PCB. Flat material (fiberglass/epoxy) on which electronic components mount. A PCB also provides electrical pathways, called traces, that connect components. Printed circuit boards are what PBXs and computers are made of these days.

Be careful when you're replacing PCBs. They're usually very sensitive to static electricity. Handle them only when you're attached to a static electricity strap that is properly grounded. Lay them down only on a surface you're sure is static electricity free. And don't touch the components on PCBs whatever you do.

Printer Emulation

Enables the mimicking of a printer-generated document. This way, the outgoing fax will look as if it has come from the printer attached to a computer. This can include full formatting, as well as letterhead, signature, and different graphic images.

Private Branch Exchange

PBX. Term used now interchangeably with PABX. See PABX.

PROCESSING POWER

The number of computations that a computer, microprocessor, or digital signal processor can complete in a fixed time interval. May be measured in MIPS (millions of instructions per second) or MFlops. Typical low-end DSP chips provide up to 10 MFlops; high-end chips 30 or more.

Program Logic

The particular sequence of instructions in a program.

Programming Language

A language used by a programmer to develop instructions for the computer. It is translated into machine language by language software called assemblers, compilers and interpreters. Each programming language has its own grammar and syntax.

Prompts

1. Recorded instructions delivered by voice processing units. Prompts may include MENUS or other information that is played each time you get into the system. 2. Messages from the computer instructing the user on how to use the system. See MENU and AUDIO MENU.

Prosody

Intonation. In text to speech, prosody refers to how natural it sounds -- the ups and downs of the sentence.

Protocol

A specified set of rules, procedures, or conventions, relating to format and timing of data transmission between two devices. A standard procedure that two data devices must accept and use to be able to understand each other.

PSK

Phase Shift Keying. A method of modulating the phase of a signal to carry information.

PSTN

Public Switched Telephone Network. An abbreviation used by the ITU.

PTT

Post Telephone & Telegraph Administration. The PTTs, usually controlled by their governments, provide telephone and telecommunications services in most countries.

Pulse Amplitude Modulation

PAM. A technique for placing binary information on a carrier to transmit that information. PAM is a technique for analog multiplexing.

The amplitude of the information being modulated controls the amplitude of the modulated pulses. Samples of each input voltage are placed between voltage samples from other channels. The cycle is repeated fast enough so the sampling rate of any one channel is more than twice the highest frequency transmitted. See also PAM and PCM.

Pulse Code Modulation

PCM. The most common and most important method in North America in which a telephone system samples a voice signal and converts that sample into an equivalent digital code. PCM is a digital modulation method that encodes a Pulse Amplitude Modulated (PAM) signal into a PCM signal. See PCM and T-1.

Pulse Density

In T-1, since "O"s are represented by no pulse and "1"s by alternating pulses, pulse density refers to the number of no pulse ("O") periods allowed before a pulse ("1") must occur. Typically, no more than 15 no pulse periods ("O"s) are allowed before a pulse ("1") must occur.

Pulse Dialing

One or two types of dialing that uses rotary pulses to generate the telephone number.

Pulse Dispersion

The spreading out of pulses as they travel along an optical fiber.

Pulse Duration Modulation

PDM. That form of modulation in which the duration of the pulse is varied in accordance with some characteristic of the modulating signal.

Pulse Link Repeater

A signaling set that interconnects the E and M leads of two circuits. In E & M signaling, a device that interfaces the signal paths of concatenated trunk circuits. Such a device responds to a ground on the "E" lead of one trunk by applying -48Vdc to the "M" lead of the connecting trunk, and vice versa. This function is a built-in, switch-selectable option in some commercially available carrier channel units.

Pulse Overshoot

In T-1, the amount of signal voltage that can remain at the trailing end of a pulse. It can be no more than 10-30% of the pulse amplitude. Also called afterkick.

Pulse-Position Modulation

PPM. That form of modulation in which the positions in time of the pulses are varied in accordance with some characteristic of the modulating signals, without modifying the pulse width.

Pulse Repetition Frequency

PRF. In radar, the number of pulses that occur each second. Not to be confused with transmission frequency which is determined by the rate at which cycles are repeated within the transmitted pulse.

Pulse Stuffing

When timing signals on digital circuits get out of whack, some method of allowing mismatches must be provided. In time division multiplexing, this is called pulse stuffing. One stream of data has bits added to it so its final rate is the same as the master clock.

Pulse Train

The resulting electronic impulses that transmit encoded information.

Pulse Width

In T-1, refers to the width (at half amplitude) of the bipolar pulse (typically 324 + or -45 nsec).

PVC

Permanent Virtual Circuit

Q

QAM

Quadrature Amplitude Modulation. A modulation technique that uses variations in signal amplitude, allowing data-encoded symbols to be represented as any of 16 or 32 different states. Some QAM modems allow dial-up data rates of up to 9,600 bps.

QUANTIZATION

Breaking down into discrete values for the purposes of sampling or transmission. In speech-compression algorithms, quantization is the art and science of encoding a set of model parameters about a speech signal with as few bits of information as possible.

Quantize

The process of encoding a PAM signal (Pulse Amplitude Signal) into a PCM signal (Pulse Code Modulation). See QUANTIZING and QUANTIZATION.

Quantizing

The second stage of pulse code modulation (PCM). The waveform samples obtained from each communication channel are measured to obtain a discrete value of amplitude. These quantized values are converted to a binary code and transmitted to a distant location to reconstruct the original waveform. See QUANTIZATION.

Quantization

Take an analog voice signal, sample it and put numbers on those samples. That's called quantization. Here's an explanation from Understanding Telephone Electronics: "A circuit called a quantizer takes in the analog signal and produces an equivalent number.

Threshold levels are established and numbers are assigned to the analog samples as their amplitudes fall within the bands formed by the threshold numbers. (For example, everything within the range 1000.05 and 1000.06 Hz is given the number 14568.) The assigned number in most costs is an approximation rather than a true value because the true value would require many more bits (i.e. more threshold limits) in the binary code...

This approximation causes an error which is the difference between the approximate number and the true sample. This quantization error adds noise to the signal, called quantization noise, which is heard in the telephone as hissing.

Quantization noise can be reduced by making the threshold bands narrower...However, providing more intervals requires more bits in the binary code. Therefore, more bandwidth is needed. There is a tradeoff between small quantizing intervals (higher bandwidth, lower noise), and fewer intervals (lower bandwidth, higher noise).

Quantization Noise
Signal errors which result from the process of digitizing (and therefore ascribing finite quantities to) a continuously variable signal. See QUANTIZATION.

Queuing
The act of stacking or holding calls to be handled by a specific person, trunk, or trunk group.

R

RAM
Random Access Memory. The primary memory in a computer. Memory that can be overwritten with new information. The random access part of the name comes from the fact that the next bit of information in RAM can be located-no matter where it is-in an equal amount of time, making access to it considerably faster than to information in other storage media, such as a hard disk.

Raster Scanning
The method of scanning in which the scanning spot moves along a network of parallel lines, either from side to side or top to bottom.

Real Time
A voice telephone conversation is conducted in Real Time. That is, there is no perceived delay in the transmission of the voice message or in the response to it. This concept often applies to interaction between a computer and a terminal. See also REAL TIME CAPACITY.

In data processing or data communications, real time means the data is processed the moment it enters a computer, as opposed to BATCH processing where the information enters the system, is stored and is operated on a later time.

Record

An entry in a database. Records contain fields. Records may be retrieved in either recordorder or keyorder. The sampling, encoding and storage of data.

RecordOrder Retrieval

Implies a sequence in which records are read from the database in the order in which they were added to the database.

Record Storage Buffer (RSB)

A storage area allocated within the Pro/Found User Function which is used to store the last record read from a database. The contents of the record storage buffer can be moved into registers on a fieldbyfield basis. Each AP line has its own RSB.

Reference Line

The first scanning line in memory. The location of each black pixel of this line is kept in memory for the next scanned line. Depending on the compression technique used, more or fewer scan lines are necessary.

Registration Number (FCC Part 68)

Approval number given to telephone equipment to certify that a particular device passes the tests defined in Part 68 of the FCC Rules. These tests certify the phone won't cause any harm to the public network. They do not attest to the commercial value of the product, nor whether it will (or won't) sell.

Relational Database

A database composed of multiple table files, linked or related by the contents of a single "key" field duplicated in each.

Remote Diagnostics

You own a phone system. You have a service company. There's some problem with it. Instead of sending a technician out, your service company dials your PBX from a data terminal or PC and "asks" your PBX in computerese what's wrong with it. If it isn't too broken, it will come back and give you some indication. This is called remote diagnostics.

Remotely-hosted

The Client and the Server are different (i.e., the application is on a different physical box than the service provider).

Remote Programming

Dial your phone system with your friendly personal computer, modem and a communications software package and you can change the telephone system's programming remotely. This feature is great for companies with telephone systems in many locations. They can all be run from one central point. This feature is also great. You may want some changes made on your system. It's obviously a lot cheaper for your vendor to make those changes from his office than having to visit yours. It's also a lot faster. See REMOTE DIAGNOSTICS.

Reply

An event which is a service providers response to a synchronous or asynchronous request.

Request

A request for service from an object to a service provider.

Resolution

A measure of capability to delineate picture detail.

Resolution Levels

Provides for high- and low-resolution levels (ITU Group 3 standard is most popular) up to 400 dots per inch. Most computer fax products allow users to select which resolution meets their needs.

Resource

The abstraction of a standardized vendor-independent interface of a physical device used for call processing as seen by the Application. All Resources have common methods across all implementations. Examples of Resources are voice store and forward, fax send and receive, text to speech conversion, voice recognition, etc. Resources are assumed to have at a minimum one input or output of circuit switched TDM on the internal switch fabric of the system. Resources are shared among multiple applications. Once a Resource has been allocated to an application it is locked from the use of any Other application until freed. It is assumed that applications specify at some level their resource requirements to the server prior to accessing them.

This may either be through explicitly attaching them to a Group, or having the server implicitly allocate them based on usage.

Resource Class

A set of methods (in object-oriented terms, a class) for controlling resource instances (or a resource). May be abbreviated as just "class."

Resource Module

A Dialogic term referring to devices which perform specific voice processing functions, such as voice compression, voice recognition, facsimile transmission and reception and conversion of computer text to spoken words over the phone. Resource modules are typically connected to the telephone network through devices known as "network interface modules."

Resource Object

An instance of a Resource Class.

Resource Unit

An entity that communicates directly with a resource device. From the client application's point of view, it is the Resource Unit that provides services such as voice store-and-forward, fax send and receive, etc.

Ring

1. As in Tip and Ring. One of the two wires (the two are Tip and Ring) needed to set up a telephone connection.

2. Also a reference to the ringing of the telephone set. 3. The design of a Local Area Network (LAN) in which the wiring loops from one workstation to another, forming a circle (thus, the term "ring"). In a ring LAN, data is sent from workstation to workstation around the loop in the same direction. Each workstation (which is usually a PC) acts as a repeater by re-sending messages to the next PC in the ring. The more PC's, the slower the LAN.

Network control is distributed in a ring network. Since the message passes through each PC, loss of one PC may disable the entire network. However, most ring LANs have a way of recovering very fast should one PC die or be turned off. If it dies, you can remove it physically from the network. If it's off, the network senses that and the token ignores that machine. In some token LANs, the LAN will close around a dead workstation and join the two workstations on either side together. If you lose the PC doing the control functions, another PC will jump in and take over. This is how the IBM Token- Passing Ring works.

Ringing Voltage
In addition to talk battery, a Central Office provides ringing signaling. Ring Voltage is generally 70 to 90 volts at 17 Hz to 20 Hz.

RJ-11
RJ-11 is a six conductor modular jack that is typically wired for four conductors (i.e. four wires). Occasionally it is wired for only two conductors -- especially if you're only wiring up for tip and ring. The RJ-11 jack (also called plug) is the most common telephone jack in the world.

The RJ-11 is typically used for connecting telephone instruments, modems and fax machines to a female RJ-22 jack on the wall or in the floor. That jack in turn is connected to twisted wire coming in from "the network" -- which might be a PBX or the local telephone company central office. RJ-22 wirings typically flat. None of its conductors (i.e. wires) are twisted. You cannot use flat cable for high-speed data communications, like local area networks. See also RJ-22 and RJ-45.

RJ-14

A jack that looks and is exactly like the standard RJ-11 that you see on every single line telephone. Whereas the RJ-11 defines one line -- with the two center, red and green, conductors being tip and ring, the RJ-14 defines two phone lines. One of the lines is the "normal" RJ-11 line -- the red and green center conductors. The second line

RJ-45

The RJ-45 is the 8-pin connector used for data transmission over standard telephone wire. That wire could be flat or twisted. And it's very important that you know what you're working with. You can easily use flat wire for serial data communications up to 19.2 Kbps.

If you wish to connect to a 10BaseT local area network, which you also do with a RJ-45, you must use twisted wire. You can typically tell the difference by looking at the cable. If it's flat grey satin (like a typical phone wire, only bigger) than it's probably untwisted. If it's circular, then it's probably twisted and therefore good for LANs. RJ-45 connectors come into two varieties -- keyed and non-keyed. Keyed means that the male RJ-45 plug has a small, square bump on its end and the female RJ-45 plug is shaped to accommodate the plug. A keyed RJ-45 plug will not fit into a female, non-keyed (i.e. normal) RJ-45. See RJ-11 and RJ-22.

Robbed-Bit Signaling

This explanation from Gary Maier of Dianatel: ISDN is the key to future sophisticated telephone network services with its dynamic, highly configurable T-1 connection (also called PRI connection). Since T-1 is a common method of carrying 24 telephone circuits, many wonder about the uses for ISDN, especially when they learn ISDN signaling requires an entire voice channel, reducing today's T-1 from 24 voice channels to 23.

But the popular signaling mechanism of "robbed bit" signaling in T-1 has serious limitations. Robbed bit signaling typically uses bits known as the A and B bits. These bits are sent by each side of a T-1 termination and are buried in the voice data of each voice channel in the T-1 circuit. Hence the term "robbed bit" as the bits are stolen from the voice data.

Since the bits are stolen so infrequently, the voice quality is not compromised by much. But the available signaling combinations are limited to ringing, hang up, wink, and pulse digit dialing. In fact, the limitations are obvious when one recognizes DNIS and ANI information are sent as DTMF tones. This introduces a problem: time.

Each DTMF tone requires at least 100 milliseconds to send, which in a DNIS and ANI situation with 20 DTMFs will take at least two full seconds. There is also a margin for error in transmission or detection, resulting in DNIS or ANI failures. With the explosion of telephone related services, the telephone companies are turning to ISDN PRI to provide the more complicated and exact signaling required for new services. ISDN employs a more robust method of signaling. ISDN uses a T-1 circuit as 23 voice channels and one signaling channel.

The term 23B plus D refers to 23 bearer (voice) channels and 1 Data (signaling) channel. The data channel carries the signaling information at a rate of 64 kilobits per second. This speed is many times greater than some of the most powerful modems available. Because of this high speed, telephone calls can be placed more quickly, and because of the protocol used, DNIS or ANI transmission failures are impossible.

Additionally, since no bits are "robbed" from the voice channels, the voice quality is better than that of Robbed Bit signaling on today's T-1 circuits. Also, computer modems and high speed faxes can use the voice channel for sending digital data instead of the traditional analog bit "noise." Therefore, ISDN PRI offers the end user countless new service capabilities. One channel could be used for faxing, another for modem data, several for video, another for a LAN and the remainder for voice. Suddenly, the average T-1 circuit becomes a pipeline for all communications! Increasingly long distance carriers are using ISDN PRI to provide inbound 800 calls with ANI and DNIS and re-routing skills. Dianatel makes some of the most sophisticated ISDN interface equipment around.

Rotary Dial
The circular telephone dial. As it returns to its normal position (after being turned) it opens and closes the electrical loop sent by the central office.

Thus it generates pulses for each digit dialed. You can hear the "clicks". The number "seven," for example consists of seven "opens and closes," or seven clicks. You can dial on a rotary phone without using the rotary dial. Simply depress the switch hook quickly, allowing pauses in between to signify that you're about to send a new digit. It's a good party trick.

Routing
The process of selecting the correct path for a message.

RS-232
A set of standards specifying various electrical and mechanical characteristics for interfaces between computers, terminals, and modems. It applies to synchronous and asynchronous binary data transmission.

RSB
See Record Storage Buffer.

RSVP
ReSerVation Protocol. Circa 1993 resource reservation protocol, as contrasted with simple set-up and tear down controls. RSVP is based on receiver-oriented simplex control. It uses "reservation styles" to control the aggregation of reservations in real-time multipoint-to-multipoint apps. RSVP uses a soft-state approach in maintaining receiver-initiated resource reservations. Allows for decoupling the routing and reservation elements of transactions.

RTC
See Runtime Control.

RTN
Retrain negative.

RTCP
1. Real Time Conferencing Protocol. Supports real-time conferencing for large groups on the Internet. It has source identification and support for audio and video bridges/gateways. Supports multicast-to-unicast translators. 2. Retrain positive.

RTP

Real Time Protocol. Supports transport of real-time data like interactive voice and video over packet switched networks. A thin protocol providing support for content identification, timing reconstruction, loss detection and security. The ARPA DARTnet transcontinental IP network experiments lead to RTPs popularity. Now championed by the Audio/Video Transport (AVT) Working Group. AVT is part of the IETF (Internet Engineering Task Force). RTP does not do resource reservation or quality of service control. It relies on resource reservation protocols like RSVP.

Runtime Control

The mechanism by which one Resource Object can influence the behavior of another. Typically used for things such as terminating conditions and speed/volume control. Runtime Control is often abbreviated RTC.

S

Sampling Rate

The number of times per second that an analog signal is measured and converted to a binary number -- the purpose being to convert the analog signal to a digital analog. The most common digital signal -- PCM -- samples 8,000 times a minute.

Scalability

This is "Forklift Upgrade" shark repellent. It means you can expand the application code to handle more lines without having to trash your existing investment in the hardware. The SCSA application model can accommodate system expansion without requiring changes to application code. Applications are insulated from the underlying hardware implementation. Developers can add or subtract resources in a system without affecting the application.

Scanner

A device used to input graphic images in digital form. A fax machine's scanner determines the brightness of a document's pixels for transmission.

Scheduled Transmission

A feature allowing the user to schedule a fax transmission at a specific date or time in the future. Key benefits are convenience and cost savings. Scheduling jobs at a period of low telephone rates can have immediate considerable savings.

SCR

See SCSA Call Router

SCSA

Signal Computing System Architecture. A new standard for the telecom/voice processing/computing industry announced by Dialogic in early Spring 1993. SCSA incorporates virtually every other standard in PC-based switching -- including the most popular ones, Mitel's ST-Bus, MVIP, Siemens PCM Highway, AEB and PEB.

SCSA Call Router

A system service of SCSA which provides the basic necessities of inbound and outbound call processing and call sharing to client applications, without those applications needing to be aware of the underlying telephony interface operations.

SCSA Message Protocol

The open communications protocol by which entities communicate with one another in an SCSA system. The SCSA Message Protocol (SMP) is independent of the transport layers it is built upon, computer hardware, operating system, network topology (or lack thereof), and technology vendor. All SCSA-compliant AIAs will translate the functions called by client applications (via the API) into SMP messages; these are transmitted to service providers regardless of their location. Therefore, applications written to the API will be portable from one call-processing environment to another.

SCSA Server

A collection of service providers (objects) which in the aggregate implement the minimum set of services required for SCSA system conformance.

The assumption is that these services are at a minimum provided to remote-hosted client applications via common transports such as LANs, but may also be provided to client applications which are hosted on the SCSA server itself (see Self-hosted). Note that this is a logical image which may be implemented through multiple nodes (machines).

SDK
Software Development Kit

SDLC
Synchronous Data-Link Control.

Secondary Resource
Any resource that is attached to a Group after the Group has been created around a primary resource.

Self-hosted
The Client and the Server are on the same computer platform. A server with one or more self-hosted applications may be a standalone unit which is not connected to any Other system.

Server
A communications element providing a service such as shared access to a file system, a printer or an E-mail system to LAN users. Usually a combination of hardware and software. A process in a distributed computing system that provides a service in response to requests from clients.

Server Module
A module within a client-server architecture system that provides resources or resource management for one or more client modules. Server modules may be located on the same system as the client AP (Local Mode), or on a separate resource server PC linked via a network (Distributed Mode).

Server Operating System
Operating System running on the SCSA Server.

Service Control Points

SCPs. The local versions of the national SMS/800 number database. SCPs contain the intelligence to screen the full ten digits of an 800 number and route calls to the appropriate, customer-designated long distance carrier.

Service Provider

An addressable entity providing application and administrative support to the client environment by responding to client requests and maintaining the operational integrity of the server.

Service Provider Interface

The message presentation format required by, and used by, the service provider in delivering SPM information. Contrast with Service Provider Messages.

Service Provider Messages

The message information required by, and provided by, the service provider in order to perform its functions in the environment in which it is installed. Contrast with SCSA Message Protocol Interface

SFC

See Switch Fabric Controller

SHELL ACCOUNTS

Text-based-only interfaces controlled by the host servers which normally don't allow for the use of graphic Web browsers.

Sidetone

A part of the design of a telephone handset which allows you hear your own voice while talking on the telephone. The idea of doing this is to give you a little feedback that the telephone you're speaking on is working. Too much sidetone becomes an echo and is bad. Too little sidetone makes the channel unerring.

Signal Errors

Signal errors indicate the return status of a Do/Change function. Despite the name, signal errors do not always indicate an error condition.

If a signal error is encountered and the k command line option specifies a Level to go to, the application will continue from the specified Level.

Signaling
Pertains to the transmission of electrical signals to and from the user's premises and the telephone company central office. Examples of central office signals to the user's premises are ringing (audible alerting) signals, dial tone, speech signals, etc.

Signals from the user's telephone include off-hook (request for service), dialing (network control signaling), speech to the distant party, on-hook (disconnect signal), etc.

Signal-To-Noise Ratio
The ratio of the usable signal being transmitted to the noise or undesired signal. Usually expressed in decibels. This ratio is a measure of the quality of a transmission.

Signal Processing Component
An atomic bundle of signal processing functionality which can be allocated to a single group. It can be capable of supporting the functionality of one or more resources or a simple coder.

Signal Processing Element
That part of a Signal Processing Component which is associated with a single Resource.

Signal Processing Platform
This is a software component that supports a specific hardware package. This is typically an executable program and may control one or more instances of the vendor-specific hardware package. Each SPP may support several different types of signal processing functionality clustered into SPCs.

SIR (ASR)
Speaker Independent Recognition. See SPEAKER INDEPENDENT RECOGNITION.

SIT Tones

1. Standard Information Tones. These are tones sent out by a central office to a pay phone to indicate that the dialed call has been answered by the distant phone, etc. 2. Special Information Tones. These are tones for identifying network provided announcements. Here's Bellcore's explanation: Automated detection devices cannot distinguish recorded voice from live voice answer unless a machine-detectable signal is included with the recorded announcement.

The ITU, which specifies signals that may be applied to international circuits, has defined Special Information Tones for identifying network provided announcement. The SIT used to precede machine-generated announcements also alerts the calling customer that a machine-generated announcement follows. Since SIT consists of a sequence of three precisely defined tones, SIT can be machine-detected, and therefore machine-generated announcements preceded by a SIT can be classified.

Many SIT encodings have been defined including: Vacant Code (VC), Intercept (IC), Reorder (RO) and No Circuit (NC). With the exception of some small Stored Program Control Systems (SPCSs) and some customer negotiated announcements, Bell operating companies in North America now precede appropriate announcements with encoded SITs to detect and classify announcements.

SLIP

Serial Line IP; a protocol that allows a computer to use the Internet protocols (and become a full-fledged Internet member) with a standard telephone line and a high-speed modem. SLIP is being superseded by PPP, but still is commonly used. A software technique for connecting a computer to the 'Net. With SLIP you can dial up an ISP that offers SLIP to place yourself directly on the 'Net. You are no longer just a terminal. You can telnet and FTP to other computers and pull their files directly back to your computer, not to the ISP's computer. Other 'Net surfers with SLIP can do the same to you.

SMP

See SCSA Message Protocol.

SMS/800

The national database Service Management System that will retain all 800 records. This database provides long distance carriers a single interface for 800 number reservations and record maintenance. Developed by Bellcore, the database has been in use by various Regional Bell Operating Companies (RBOCs) since 1988. The FCC has mandated that a neutral third party administer the database.

SMTP

Simple Mail Transfer Protocol. Internet mail is routed using this software protocol.

Software Supervision

"Answer Supervision" is knowing when the person at the other end answers the phone. The main reason for wanting to know this is so that a phone company can start billing the call. There are two ways of doing answer supervision. You can get it from the nation's phone system, i.e. the distant office signals back across the country when the called person picks up the phone. Or you can fake it with "software supervision."

Essentially this means there's electronics which "listens" to the call. If it "hears" voice or something like voice, it assumes the conversation has started and it's time to start billing the call. Software supervision is not accurate.

But when you haven't got access to real answer supervision (for whatever reason) it's better than the previous alternative, which was "timeout." In timeout answer supervision, the carrier simply assumed the call had begun after a certain number of seconds -- like 30 -- had elapsed with the calling person hanging up. This meant, for example, if you called Grandma and she wasn't there, but you left it ringing, 'cause you knew she took time to answer the phone, then you'd be charged for the call -- even though she didn't answer phone! See also ANSWER SUPERVISION.

Source Code

A computer program which can be translated by another program into a program that will run on a particular computer. The program which finally runs on that computer is known as the object code.

Span

1. Refers to that portion of a high speed digital system than connects a C.O. (Central Office) to C.O. or terminal office to terminal office. 2. Also called a T-Span Line. A repeatered outside plant four-wire, two twisted-pair transmission line.

Span Line

A T-1 link.

Speaker Independent (Voice) Recognition (ASR)

SIR. Technologies for the automated conversion of speech to accurate and meaningful textual information (typically ASCII). SIR is typically used to accept input from callers to voice processors where the callers are using rotary dial phones instead of touch-tone -- Dual Tone Multi-Frequency (DTMF) -- phones. SIR can substitute for the numbers on the DTMF keypad and can add the benefit of a few basic voice commands, e.g., Yes, No, Help, etc.

Because computer processing demands are formidable with speaker independent recognition, accurate speaker independent products are created with limited vocabularies. In contrast, trainable or speaker dependent recognizers can feature larger vocabularies at lower prices. SIR has been slowly gaining acceptance in telephone applications.

SIR is increasingly used in automated operator assistance applications. SIR will see increased use as system builders respond to pressures to provide voice processing functions to the enormous rotary phone installed base domestically and abroad.

SPC

See Signal Processing Component

SPC Allocation Service

A service which allocates SPCs to Groups

SPCAS

See SPC Allocation Service

SPE

See Signal Processing Element

SPECTRAL ENERGIES

The energy intensity of a waveform at specific frequencies, as analyzed by an FFT. See "Frequency Domain."

Speech Concatenation

A term used in voice processing for economical digitized speech playback that uses independently recorded files of phrases or file segments linked together under application program control to produce a customized response in natural sounding language. For example, order status, bank balances, bus schedules or lottery results, etc.

Concatenation is done for speed and economy. It lends itself to limited and structured vocabularies that are best stored in RAM (Random Access Memory) or speedily accessible from disk. Concatenation does not replace Text-To-Speech (TTS) as a method of getting the voice processor to deliver its responses. Concatenation, however, can be an excellent complement to TTS when a voice application demands broad, real time vocabulary production. See TEXT-TO-SPEECH.

Speech Synthesis

See TEXT-TO-SPEECH.

SPI

See Service Provider Interface.

SPM

See Service Provider Messages.

Spooler

A program that controls spooling. Spooling, a term mostly associated with printers, stands for Simultaneous Peripheral Operations On Line. Spooling, temporarily stores programs or program outputs on magnetic tape, RAM, or disks for output or processing.

On a LAN, a printer is controlled by a spooler. The spooler places each print request on the LAN in the print queue and prints it when it reaches the top of the queue.

SPP
See Signal Processing Platform

Springboard
Dialogic's term for a general purpose computing engine designed for a wide range of powerful voice processing applications. It contains Motorola 5600x DSPs (Digital Signal Processors) and Intel 80xxx microprocessors. It allows Dialogic's Technology Partners to extend D/12x functions. The Antares Open DSP board is based on this technology.

SPX
Sequenced Packet eXchange. A connectionoriented session protocol for network data exchange that uses the IPX (Internetwork Packet Exchange) communication protocol. (See also NetBIOS.)

Standards
Agreed principles of protocol. Standards are set by committees working under various trade and international organizations. RS standards, such as RS-232-C are set by the EIA, the Electronics Industries Association. ANSI standards for data communications are from the X committee.

Standards from ANSI would look like X3.4-1967, which is the standard for the ASCII code. The ITU does not put out standards, but rather publishes recommendations, owing to the international personalities involved.

V series recommendations refer to data transmission over the telephone network, while X series recommendations, such as X.25, refer to data transmission over public data networks.

State
The instantaneous properties of an object that characterize that object's current condition.

State Machine Programming

To control multiple telephone lines in a single voice processing program, a new program structure is required. Dialogic calls this technique state machine programming. Computer Science called state machines "Deterministic Finite State Automata."

Station

A dumb word for a telephone. Also called an instrument, or a telephone instrument. An extension station is one connected "behind" a PBX or key system. In other words, the PBX or key system is between the station and the telephone central office. We tried to remove the word "station" from this dictionary, but failed. We suspect the word comes from the very old days when the telephone industry was regulated by the Interstate Commerce Commission, (the ICC) which also regulated the railroad industry.

Station Adapters

Cables and interface assemblies for connecting Dialogic network interface and switching products to telephones or analog telephone lines.

Station Set

Another word for a common desk telephone.

Store And Forward

In communications systems when a message is transmitted to some intermediate relay point and stored temporarily. Later the message is sent the rest of the way. Not very convenient for voice conversations, but useful for telex type, and other one way transmissions of messages. Telephone answering machines, as well as voice mailboxes are considered forms of Store and Forward message switching.

Supervised Transfer

A call transfer made by an automatic device such as voice response unit which attempts to determine the result of the transfer -- answered, busy, ring no answer -- by analyzing call progress tones on the time.

Supervision

Supervision of a phone call is detecting when a called party has picked up his phone and when that party has hung up. Supervision is used primarily for billing purposes. Not all long distance carriers have supervision capability. It depends on how "equal accessed" they have chosen to be. See ANSWER SUPERVISION and SOFTWARE SUPERVISION.

SVC

Switched Virtual Connections

Switch

A mechanical, electrical or electronic device which opens or closes circuits, completes or breaks an electrical path, or selects paths or circuits.

Switch Domain

A single instance of a particular technology-specific connection type.

Switched Network

A network providing switched communications service; that is, the network is shared among many users, any of whom may establish communication between desired points when required.

Switch Fabric

The facility for connecting any two (or more) transmitting or receiving Service Providers.

Switch Fabric Controller

A technology-specific, replaceable ASP within the SCSA server. The SFC is designed to support both the internal connectivity within the group and multiparty call processing not directly addressed by the Group.

Switchhook

A switchhook was originally an electrical "switch" connected to the "hook" on which the handset (or receiver) was placed when the telephone was not in use.

Switch Hook Flash

A signaling technique whereby the signal is originated by momentarily depressing the switch hook.

Switch Port

A resource that allows a Group to communicate with anOther Group. All Groups implicitly possess a Switch Port as a secondary resource, but in order to use it, the application must explicitly connect the Switch Ports of two Groups.

Synchronous Request

A request where the client blocks until the completion of the request. Contrast with asynchronous request .

Synthesized Voice

Human speech approximated by a computer device that concatenates basic speech parts (or phonemes) together.

System Service Provider

An entity that provides system-wide services, such as session management and security, and the allocation and tracking of resources and groups.

System Vendor

A provider of a complete SCSA server.

T

T-1

Also spelled T1. A digital transmission link with a capacity of 1.544 Mbps (1,544,000 bits per second). T1 uses two pairs of normal twisted wires, the same as you'd find in your house. T1 normally can handle 24 voice conversations, each one digitized at 64 Kbps. But, with more advanced digital voice encoding techniques, it can handle more voice channels. T1 is a standard for digital transmission in North America. It is usually provided by the phone company and used for connecting networks across remote distances.

Bridges and routers are used to connect LANs over T1 networks. There are faster services available, such as T2 and T4, but these are not used much. T1 links can often be connected directly to new PBXs and many new forms of short-haul transmission, such as short-haul microwave systems. It is not compatible with T1 outside the United States and Canada. In Europe T-1 is called E-1 or E1. Outside of the United States and Canada, the "T-1" line bit rate is usually 2,048,000 bits per second. Japan, France and West Germany impose slight variations that make their formats unique. Only one element remains constant -- the DS-0. The 64 kilobit per channel is universal. Most often it represents a PCM voice signal sampled at 8,000 times per second. However, the form of PCM encoding differs between T-1 (mu-law) and E-1 (A-law companding).

According to Bill Flanagan's book, the differences are not so great that a multiplexer cannot convert between them. Conversion of E-1 to T-1 involves both the compression law and the signaling format. At the higher rate of 2,048,000, 32 time slots are defined at the CEPT interface, but two are used for signaling and other housekeeping chores.

Typically 30 channels are left for user information -- voice, video, data, etc. CEPT is the Conference of European Postal and Telecommunications administrations. Standards-setting body whose membership includes European Post, Telephone, and Telegraphy Authorities (PTTs). For a full explanation of T1 see Bill Flanagan's book The Guide to T-1 Networking.

T.120
The most important transmission protocol standard for document conferencing over transmission media ranging from analog phone lines to the Internet. It's Network independent (Internet, PSTN, LAN, ISDN). T.120 does conference control, application and data sharing. It's for documents and files what H.320 is to video. Creating products based on the both standards is what Intel (Internet Phone) and Microsoft (NetMeeting) are doing.

T.122
ITU standard for multipoint communication service for audiographic conferencing.

T.123
ITU standard for protocol stacks in audiographic teleconferencing.

T.124
ITU standard for generic T.120 conference control.

T.125
ITU standard for the T.120 Multipoint Communication Service Protocol Specification.

T.126
ITU standard for T.120 Multipoint Still Image and Annotation Protocol.

T.127
ITU standard for T.120-based Multipoint Binary File Transfer.

T.128
ITU standard for Audio Visual Control for Multipoint Multimedia Systems.

T2
A digital transmission link with a capacity of 6.312 Mbps. T2 can handle at least 96 voice messages.

T3
A digital transmission link with a capacity of 44.736 Mbps. T3 can handle 672 voice messages simultaneously. T3 runs on fiber optic cable.

T.4
ITU recommendation for Group 3 machines, using T.30 and various V series standards. It also describes compression methods (Modified Huffman and Modified READ).

T.6
ITU recommendation for Group 4 machines. It defines the facsimile coding schemes and their associated coding control functions for black and white images.

T.30

ITU recommendation. This handshake protocol describes the overall procedure for establishing and managing communication between two fax
machines. It covers five phases of operation: call setup, pre-message procedure (selecting the communication mode), message transmission (including phasing and synchronization), post-message procedure (EOM and
confirmation), and call release.

T.35

ITU recommendation proposing a procedure for the allocation of ITU
members' country or area codes for non-standard facilities in telematic
services.

T.611

Also known as Appli/COM. A messaging standard proposed by France
and Germany, defining a programmable communication interface (PCI) for
Group 3 fax, Group 4 fax, teletext, and telex service.

Table

See data file.

Table-Driven

Describing a logical computer process, widespread in the operation of
communications devices and networks, where a user-entered variable (e.g.
a password) is matched against an array of predefined values (a table of
acceptable passwords) and checked for access, authorization, etc.

A frequently used process in least cost routing, in network routing, in
access security, and in modem operation.

Tag

Some database formats use individual DOS files for each index. Others,
such as dBASE IV and FoxPro, combine multiple indexes into a single file.
Each such index within the index file is known as a tag. Two parameters
are required to access a tag within an index file: the name and extension of
the index file, and the name of the desired tag within it.

Talk Battery

The DC voltage supplied by the central office to the subscriber's loop to operate the carbon transmitter in the handset.

Talk Path

The tip and ring conductors of a telephone circuit.

Talk-Off

Talk-off is one hazard of in-band signaling. Talk-off occurs when your voice has enough 2600 Hz energy to activate the 2600 Hz tone- detecting circuits in the central office. The 2600 Hz tone is used for in-band signaling.

TAO

See TELEPHONY APPLICATION OBJECT FRAMEWORK

TAPI

See Windows Telephony API

TCF

Training Check Frame. Last step in a series of signals called a training sequence, designed to let the receiver adjust to line conditions.

TCP

Transmission Control Protocol. ARPAnet-developed transport layer protocol. Corresponds to OSI layers 4 and 5, transport and session. TCP is a transport layer, connection-oriented, end-to-end protocol. It provides reliable, sequenced, and unduplicated delivery of bytes to a remote or local user. TCP provides reliable byte stream communication between pairs of processes in hosts attached to interconnected networks. It is the portion of the TCP/IP protocol suite that governs the exchange of sequential data. See also TCP/IP.

TCP/IP

Transmission Control Protocol/Internet Protocol. A set of protocols developed by the DOD to link dissimilar computers across many kinds of networks. Including unreliable ones and connected to dissimilar LANs.

Developed in the 1970s by the U.S. Department of Defense's Advanced Research Projects Agency (DARPA) as a military standard protocol, its assurance of multi vendor connectivity has made it popular among commercial users. Consequently, TCP/IP now is supported by many manufacturers of minicomputers, personal computers, mainframes, technical workstations and data communications equipment. It is also the protocol commonly used over Ethernet (as well as X.25) networks and the Internet. It has been implemented on everything from PC LANs to minis and mainframes. Although committed to an eventual migration to an OSI architecture, TCP/IP currently divides networking functionality into only four layers:

A Network Interface Layer that corresponds to the OSI Physical and Data Link Layers. This layer manages the exchange of data between a device and the network to which it is attached and routes data between devices on the same network.

An Internet Layer which corresponds to the OSI network layer. The Internet Protocol (IP) subset of the TCP/IP suite runs at this layer. IP provides the addressing needed to allow routers to forward packets across a multiple LAN inter network. In IEEE terms, it provides connectionless datagram service, which means it attempts to deliver every packet, but has no provision for retransmitting lost or damaged packets. IP leaves such error correction, if required, to higher level protocols, such as TCP.

IP addresses are 32 bits in length and have two parts: the Network Identifier (Net ID) and the Host Identifier (Host ID). Assigned by a central authority, the Net ID specifies the address, unique across the Internet, for each network or related group of networks. Assigned by the local network administrator, the Host ID specifies a particular host, station or node within a given network and need only be unique within that network.

A Transport Layer, which corresponds to the OSI Transport Layer. The Transmission Control Protocol (TCP) subset runs at this layer. TCP provides end-to-end connectivity between data source and destination with detection of, and recovery from, lost, duplicated, or corrupted packets – thus offering the error control lacking in lower level IP routing.

In TCP, message blocks from applications are divided into smaller segments, each with a sequence number that indicates the order of the segment within the block. The destination device examines the message segments and, when a complete sequence of segments is received, sends an acknowledgement (ACK) to the source, containing the number of the next byte expected at the destination.

An Application Layer, which corresponds to the session, presentation and application layers of the OSI model. This layer manages the function required by the user programs and includes protocols for remote log-in (Telnet), file transfer (FTP), and electronic mail (SMTP).

TDM
Time-division multiplex. This is the means whereby a single electric circuit may be used by multiple devices: use of the circuit is divided into "time slots" which are allocated to the contending devices in a rotating fashion. Each device gets exclusive use of the circuit for the duration of its time slot.

Telco
The local telephone company. Often a term of endearment.

Telecommunications
Telecommunications, or telecom for short, is the transmission or reception of signals, images, sounds, or intelligence of any nature by wire, radio, light pulse, or electromagnetic system. That just about covers virtually any means of transmission, regardless of source, channel, or media type. Telephony and data communications are subsets of telecommunications that are specific to computer-type transmissions and telephone-type transmissions, respectively.

Telefax
European term for fax.

Telecommunication Standardization Sector (TSS)
One of four permanent parts of the International Telecommunications Union (ITU), based in Geneva, Switzerland.

It issues recommendations for standards applying to modems, packet switched interfaces, V.24 connectors, etc. Although it has no power of enforcement, the standards it recommends are generally accepted and adopted by industry. Until March 1, 1993, the TSS was known as the ITU (see above).

Telecopier
European term for fax.

Telemarketing
Marketing and sales conducted via the telephone. There are two sides to telemarketing -- incoming and outgoing. Incoming telemarketing is largely run through 800 toll-free IN-WATS numbers and local FX (foreign exchange) lines. Outgoing telemarketing is organized over OUT-WATS lines. Everything from computers to clothes is now sold over the phone.

An expanding range of telecom gadgetry is being developed to automate telemarketing -- including automated outbound dialers, voice processing technology, and automatic call distributors.

The tone recognition, voice detection and transaction Audiotex and transaction processing capabilities of voice processing gear can be used to enhance all telemarketing applications.

Telephone Manager
Apple's telephony API for the Macintosh environment.

Telephony
Taken from Greek root words meaning "far sound," telephony is the discipline of converting or transmitting voice or other signals over a distance, and then re-converting them to an audible sound at the far end.

Telephony Application Object (TAO) Framework
TAO is the software part of the Signal Computing System Architecture (SCSA). The TAO Framework is made up of four components:

1) A set of standard SCSA Application Programming Interfaces (SCSA APIs) that defines the way client and server applications access the Message Protocol to communicate with server resources and system services. 2) The Message Protocol that defines a standard way for passing messages among applications, system resources, and system services. 3) A set of core System Services that includes resource management, runtime control, switching, event and error handling, configuration management, session management, and security. 4) A set of Service Provider Interfaces (SPIs) that defines the way System Services and Resources (the Service Providers) access the Message Protocol. Other key features of the SCSA Telephony Application Object Framework are: It is an open software architecture; It is designed specifically for multiple application client server environments, where multiple distributed applications use the same server resources; It has sophisticated application management capabilities; It facilitates both simple and complex application development; Its core system services and technology-specific resource APIs are interoperable; It is object-oriented and operating system and hardware independent.

Telephony Database Transactions
The use of telephony terminal equipment (phone and/or fax) as input/output devices to operate on a computer database.

Telephony Interface Control
A Telephony Interface Control resource is any resource that interfaces with the telephone network (public or private). This is usually claimed as the primary member of a group.

Telephony Service Provider
(TSP); a software encapsulation of all the services provided by a particular network interface device or line device. A line device may be a single POTS bearer channel or it may be several bearer channels; for example, a single E1 span with 30 network channels of 64 Kb/s bandwidth. The TSP is provided be the vendor who has developed a network interface device for SCSA.

Telephony Server

A server software program that allows client applications to take advantage of call control hardware remotely. See Novell Telephony Server for an example.

Telephony Workgroup

A group of people with a common telecomputing requirement: for example, a technical support group might need an application that automatically links incoming calls to client records on a database.

TELNET

A program that lets you log into other computers on the Internet.

Terminal Emulation

A microcomputer or personal computer mimics, pretends to be (i.e. emulates) a data terminal. It does this with special printed circuit boards inserted into its motherboard and/or special software.

Text-To-Speech (Speech Synthesis)

TTS. Technologies for converting textual (ASCII) information into synthetic speech output. This technology is used in voice processing applications that require the production of broad, unrelated and unpredictable vocabularies, e.g., products in a catalog, names and addresses, etc.

This technology is appropriately used when system design constraints prevent the more efficient use of speech concatenation alone. See SPEECH CONCATENATION.

Third party Call Control

See Call Control.

TIFF

Tagged Image File Format. TIFF provides a way of storing and exchanging digital image data. Current TIFF specifications support three main types of image data: black-and-white data, halftones or dithered data, greyscale data and, more recently, color.

TIMBRE
The quality of tone distinctive to a particular voice

Time-Varying Media
Time-varying media, such as audio data (as opposed to space-varying media, such as image data).

Tip & Ring
An old fashioned way of saying "plus" and "minus," or ground and positive in electrical circuits. Tip and Ring are telephony terms. They derive their names from the operator's cordboard plug. The tip wire was connected to the tip of the plug, and the ring wire was connected to the slip ring around the jack. A third conductor on some jacks was called the sleeve. That's it. Nothing more sinister. Nothing more interesting.

Tone
An audio signal consisting of one or more superimposed amplitude modulated frequencies with a distinct cadence and duration.

Tone Dial
A push button telephone dial that makes a different sound (in fact, a combination of two tones) for each number pushed. The correct name for tone dial is "Dual Tone MultiFrequency" (DTMF). This is because each button generates two tones, one from a "high" group of frequencies -- 1209, 1136, 1477 and 1633 Hz -- and one from a "low" group of frequencies -- 697, 770, 852 and 841 Hz.

The frequencies and the keyboard, or tone dial, layout have been internationally standardized, but the tolerances on individual frequencies vary between countries.

This makes it more difficult to take a touch-tone phone overseas than a rotary phone. You can "dial" a number faster on a tone dial than on a rotary dial, but you make more mistakes on a tone dial and have to redial more often. Some people actually find rotary dials to be, on average, faster for them. The design of all tone dials is stupid. Deliberately so.

They were deliberately designed to be the exact opposite (i.e. upside down) of the standard calculator pad, now incorporated into virtually all computer keyboards. The reason for the dumb phone design was to slow the user's dialing down to the speed Bell central offices of early touch tone vintage could take. Today, central offices can accept tone dialing at high speed. But sadly, no one in North America makes a phone with a sensible, calculator pad or computer keyboard dial. On some telephone/computer workstations you can dial using the calculator pad on the keyboard. This is a breakthrough. It a lot faster to use this pad. The keys are larger, more sensibly laid out and can actually be touch-typed (like touch-typing on a keyboard.) Nobody, but nobody can "touch-type" a conventional telephone tone pad. A tone dial on a telephone can provide access to various special interactive voice response services and features -- from ordering your groceries over the phone to inquiring into the prices of your (hopefully) rising stocks.

Tone Set
A collection of tones which are customarily used as a set for the purposes of call setup and teardown (e.g., DTMF, R1 MF, R2 MF). In the case of DTMF, the tone set can also be used by the Client Application during the conversation portion of a call.

Touch Tone
A term coined by AT&T for Tone Dialing.

TSP
See Telephony Service Provider.

TTS
Text-To-Speech. A term used in voice processing. See TEXT-TO-SPEECH.

Trellis Coding
A method of forward error correction used in certain high-speed modems where each signal element is assigned a coded binary value representing that element's phase and amplitude. It allows the receiving modem to determine, based on the value of the preceding signal, whether or not a given signal element is received in error.

Trellis Code Modulation (TCM)

A version of quadrature amplitude modulation (QAM) that enables relatively high bit rate signals to be used on ordinary voice-grade circuits. When used as a modem modulation technique in which algorithms are used to predict the best fit between the incoming signal and a large set of possible combinations of amplitude and phase changes. TCM provides for transmission speeds of 14.4 Mbps and above on single voice-grade telephone lines.

Trunk

A communication line between two switching systems. The term switching systems typically includes equipment in a telephone company's central office and PBXs. A tie trunk connects PBXs. Central office trunks connect a PBX to the switching system at the central office.

TSI

Transmitting Subscriber Information. A frame that may be sent by the caller, with the caller's telephone number (may be used to screen calls).

T-Span

A telephone circuit or cable through which a T-carrier runs. See T-1.

TSR

Terminate and Stay Resident. A term for loading a software program in a DOS computer in which the program loads into RAM and is always ready for running at the touch of a combination of keys.

TTI

Transmit Terminal Identification. The telephone number and words on top of a received fax document, identifying its point of origin. This information does not originate with the telephone company, but with the sender, who programs it into the fax.

TVM

See Time-Varying Media.

TVM Object
An encapsulation of an atomic piece of time-varying media. This encapsulation may be the data itself or a reference to the data.

Twisted Pair
Two insulated copper wires twisted around each other to reduce induction (thus interference) from one wire to the other. The twists, or lays, are varied in length to reduce the potential for signal interference between pairs. Several sets of twisted pair wires may be enclosed in a single cable.

In cables greater than 25 pairs, the twisted pairs are grouped and bound together in a common cable sheath. Twisted pair cable is the most common type of transmission media. It is the normal cabling from a central office to your home or office, or from your PBX to your office phone. Twisted pair wiring comes in various thicknesses. As a general rule, the thicker the cable is, the better the quality of the conversation.
And the longer cable can be and still get acceptable conversation quality. However, the thicker it is, the more it costs.

Two-Dimensional Coding
A data compression scheme that uses the previous scan line as a reference when scanning a subsequent line. Because an image has a high degree of correlation vertically as well as horizontally, two-dimensional coding schemes work only with variable increments between one line and the next, permitting higher data compression.

Two-Wire Circuit
A transmission circuit composed of two wires -- signal and ground -- used to both send and receive information. In contrast, a four wire circuit consists of two pairs. One pair is used to send. One pair is used to receive. All trunk circuits -- long distance circuits -- are four wire. A four wire circuit costs more but delivers better reception. All local loop circuits -- those coming from a Class 5 central office to the subscriber's phone system -- are two wire, unless you ask for a four-wire circuit and pay a little more.

U

UDP

User Datagram Protocol. A TCP/IP protocol describing how messages reach application programs within a destination computer. This protocol is normally bundled with IP-layer software. UDP is a transport layer, connectionless mode protocol, providing a (potentially unreliable, unsequenced, and/or duplicated) datagram mode of communication for delivery of packets to a remote or local user.

UDP/IP

User Datagram Protocol/Internet Protocol. See UDP.

Unified Messaging

A telecomputing application that treats incoming and outgoing electronic mail, voice messages, and fax messages together. A mixed-media messaging control mechanism.

UNIX

An immensely powerful and complex operating system for computers. UNIX is developed, marketed, championed and trademarked by AT&T. UNIX is very powerful and very complex to use. Because of its power it needs a computer with a large amount of RAM memory.

It has been extensively used in universities, and is only now emerging onto the business scene. UNIX allows a computer to handle multiple users and multiple programs simultaneously. It works on many different computers. This means you can often take applications software which runs on UNIX and often move it -- with little changing -- to a bigger, different computer. Or to a smaller, different computer. This process of moving programs to other computers is known as "porting." UNIX was developed in 1969 by Ken Thompson of AT&T Bell Laboratories.

URL

Uniform Resource Locator. The address of a page on the Internet. Our URL is ComputerTelephony.com. By employing URLs, you can locate pages on the Web.

UUNET

A nonprofit organization that runs a large 'Net site linking the UUCP mail network with the 'Net. It contains a large, useful FTP archive.

V

V.17

ITU recommendation for simplex modulation technique for use in extended Group 3 facsimile applications only. Provides 7,200, 9,600, 12,000, and 14,400 bps trellis-coded modulation.

V.21

ITU recommendation for 300 bps duplex modems for use on the switched telephone network. V.21 modulation is used in a half-duplex mode for Group 3 fax negotiation and control procedures.

V.22

ITU recommendation for 1,200 bps duplex modems for use on the switched telephone network and on leased lines.

V.22bis

ITU recommendation for 2,400 bps duplex modems for use on the switched telephone network. V.22bis also provides for 1,200 bps operation for V.22 compatibility.

V.27ter

ITU recommendation for 2.4/4.8-kbps/s modem for use on the switched telephone network. Half-duplex only. It defines the modulation scheme for Group 3 facsimile for image transfer at 2,400 and 4,800 bps.

V.29

ITU recommendation for 9,600 bps modem for use on point- to-point leased circuits. This is the modulation technique used in Group 3 fax for image transfer at 7,200 and 9,600 bps. V.29 uses a carrier frequency of 1,700 Hz which is varied in both phase and amplitude. V.29 can be full duplex on four-wire leased circuits, or half duplex on two-wire and dial-up circuits.

V.32

ITU recommendation for 9,600 bps two-wire full duplex modem operating on regular dial-up lines or two-wire leased lines. V.32 also provides fallback operation at 4,800 bps.

V.32bis

ITU recommendation for full-duplex transmission on two-wire leased and dial-up lines at 4,800, 7,200, 9,600, 12,000, and 14,400 bps. Provides backward compatibility with V.32. It includes a rapid change renegotiation feature for quick and smooth rate changes when line conditions change.

V.33

ITU recommendation for 14.4 kbps and 1.2 kbps modem for use on four-wire leased lines.

V.42

ITU recommendation, primarily concerned with error correction and compression for modems. The protocol is designed to detect errors in transmission and recover with a retransmission.

Vari-A-Bill

A new 900 service of AT&T whereby the call's price varies depending on certain events -- the caller punching out some tones on his phone, or a service technician coming on line, etc.

Visual Voice Mail

An application displaying and controlling voice messages on a desktop computer. Usually associated with unified messaging.

VOCODER

A family of voice-coding technologies for speech compression that are based on an underlying model of human speech. For example, many vocoders recognize voiced and unvoiced phonemes and code them differently. Voxware's MetaVoice technology is a new type of vocoder.

Voice Board

Also called a voice card or speech card. A Voice Board is an IBM PC- or AT-compatible expansion card which can perform voice processing functions. A voice board has several important characteristics: It has a computer bus connection. It has a telephone line interface.

It typically has a voice bus connection. And it supports one of several operating systems, e.g. MS-DOS, UNIX. At a minimum, a voice board will usually include support for going on and off-hook (answering, initiating and terminating a call); notification of call termination (hang-up detection); sending flash hook; and dialing digits (touch-tone and rotary). See VRU.

Voice Circuit

The typical analog telephone channel coming into your house or office. It has a bandwidth between 300 Hz and 3000 Hz. This is not sufficient for high fidelity voice transmission. You'd probably need at least 10,000 Hz. But it's sufficient to recognize and understand the person on the other end.

Voice Data

Encoded audio data.

Voice Digitization

The conversion of an analog voice signal into binary (digital) bits for storage or transmission.

Voice Driver

A Dialogic product that comes for MS-DOS, OS/2 and UNIX. In MS-DOS, it is a terminate and stay resident (TSR) program which acts as a central server for MS-DOS based applications. It provides all of the services required to support installable device drivers for each hardware component and for the application. See also DEVICE DRIVER.

Voice Frequency

VF. An audio frequency in the range essential for transmission of speech. Typically from about 300 Hz to 3000 Hz.

Voice Integration

Allows computer fax solutions to be store and forward hubs for both image as well as voice communication. Many of these products work on PC-based systems and offer all the capabilities of a message center.

Voice Mail

A specialized form of Interactive Voice Response. Includes Voice Messaging and Automated Attendant systems. Denotes customer premise or central office systems that are aimed at automating and enhancing message taking and ATTENDANT console styled services. See VOICE MAIL SYSTEM.

Voice Mail System

A device to record, store and retrieve voice messages. There are two types of voice mail devices -- those which are "stand alone" and those which profess some integration with the user's phone system. A stand alone voice mail is not dissimilar to a collection of single person answering machines, with several added features; you can instruct the machines (voice mail boxes) to forward messages amongst themselves; you can organize to allocate your friends and business acquaintances their own mail boxes so they can dial, leave messages, pick up messages from you, pass messages to you, etc; you can also edit messages, add comments and deliver messages to a mailbox at a pre-arranged time. In addition, messages can be tagged "urgent" or "non-urgent" or stored for future listening. The range of voice mail options varies among manufacturers.

An integrated voice mail system includes these features. First, it will tell you if you have any messages. It does this by lighting a light on your phone, and/or putting a message on your phone's alpha-numeric display. Second, if your phone rings for a certain number of rings (which number you set), the phone will transfer your caller automatically to your voice mail box, which will answer the phone, deliver a little "I am away" message and then receive and record the caller's message.

Voice Message Service

A service typically over dial up phone lines which provides the ability for a phone user to access a voice mail system and leave a message for a particular phone user. See VOICE MAIL SYSTEM.

Voice Messaging

Recording, storing, playing back and distributing phone messages. New York Telephone has an interesting way of looking at voice messaging.

NYTel sees it as four distinct areas: 1. Voice Mail, where messages can be retrieved and played back at any time from a user's "voice mailbox"; 2. Call Answering, which routes calls made to a busy/no answer extension into a voice mailbox; 3. Call Processing, which lets callers route themselves among destinations via their touch-tone phones; and 4. Information Mailbox, which stores general recorded information for callers to hear.

Voice Processing

1) Term which applies to all forms of technology used for the digitization, decoding, storage, or manipulation of the human voice. 2) Form of Computer Telephony which uses interactive voice response elements and/or call processing elements in order to interconnect computer-based information to telephone callers. See also INTERACTIVE VOICE RESPONSE.

Voice Recognition

The ability of a machine (obviously a computer) to understand human speech.

Voice Response Unit

VRU. Another term for INTERACTIVE VOICE RESPONSE. Think of a Voice Response Unit as a voice computer. Where a computer has a keyboard for entering information, an IVR uses remote touch-tone telephones.

Where a computer has a screen for showing the results, an IVR uses a digitized synthesized voice to "read" the screen to the distant caller. An IVR can do whatever a computer can, from looking up train timetables to moving calls around an automatic call distributor (ACD).

The only limitation on an IVR is that you can't present as many alternatives on a phone as you can on a screen. The caller's brain simply won't remember more than a few. With IVR, you have to present the menus in smaller chunks. See TELECOMPUTING; VOICE BOARD.

Voice Store And Forward

Voice mail. A PBX service that allows voice messages to be stored digitally in secondary storage and retrieved remotely by dialing access and identification codes. See VOICE MAIL SYSTEM.

Voice Switched

A device which responds to voice. When the device hears a voice, it turns on and transmits it, while muting the receive side. The most common voice-switched device is the common desk speakerphone.

With voice switching, it's easy to hog a circuit. Just keep making a noise. Watch out for voice hogging. If you're calling someone and waiting for them by listening in on your speakerphone, mute your speakerphone. This way you'll hear them when they answer.

VRU

See Voice Response Unit.

VS&F

Voice Store and Forward. Voice is digitally encoded, sent to large storage devices and later forwarded to the recipient. See VOICE MAIL.

W

WAN

Wide Area Network. A network using common carrier-provided lines that cover an extended geographical area. WANs are data networks typically extending a LAN outside the building, over telephone common carrier lines to link to other LANs in remote buildings or other geographic areas.

WATS

Wide Area Telecommunications Service. WATS is basically discounted toll service. It is provided by all long distance and local phone companies. AT&T started WATS but forgot to trademark the name, so now every supplier uses it as a generic name. There are two types of WATS services -- in and out WATS, i.e. those WATS lines that allow you to dial out and those which allow you to receive incoming calls (the typical 800 line service). You subscribe to in and out-WATS services separately. In the old days you needed separate in and out lines to handle the in and out WATS services. But these days you can choose to have in and out WATS on the same line. This is not particularly brilliant traffic engineering, since you can't receive an incoming 800 call if you're making an outgoing call.

WEB BROWSER

Client software used to view information on Web servers. Can display graphics. Netscape is the most popular, accounting for an alleged 75% of all browsers out there.

WEB SERVER

A server dedicated to storing data (such as Web pages in HTML format) and distributing it on the World Wide Web. There were an estimated 6,000 Web servers at the beginning of 1994. Today there are around 200,000

WHOIS

A command on some systems that reveals the actual user's name, based on that person's username.

Windows Telephony API

Microsoft's standard call control programming interface for the Windows environment. Microsoft and Intel introduced Windows Telephony as a concept in the Spring of 1993.

The announcement included a joint specification that has three elements: 1. An API, Application Programming Interface for applications developers. 2. A SPI, Service Provider Interface for service providers and network interface cards. 3. Windows DLL, software code to be incorporated into Microsoft Windows. It now ships with every copy of Windows 95.

Wink

A momentary interruption in SF (single frequency) tone indicating the distant central office is ready to receive the digits you just dialed.

Wink Operation

A timed, off-hook signal, normally of 140 ms, which indicates the availability of an incoming register for receiving digital information from the calling office.

Wink Release

On most modern central offices when the person or device at the other end hangs up, your local central office will send you a single frequency tone. That tone is called wink release. Such a tone can be used to alert a data device that the device at the other end has hung up. (Remember it can't tell by just listening -- like you and me.) When a data device hears a wink release, it usually takes it as a signal to hang up also.

Wink Start

Short duration off-hook signal. See Wink Operation.

WinSock

Windows Sockets or WinSock is API for Microsoft Windows and TCP/IP. It's how WWW browsers, FTP clients, email packages, and word processors talk to the Internet. WinSock was born at Interop in 1991. Led by Martin Hall, the group defined a common way for MS Windows applications to talk to TCP/IP. Thousands of applications have been written to WinSock. WinSock has played a instrumental role in the growth and use of the Internet, groupware, video-conferencing, email, and other communications technologies for MS Windows. The WinSock specifications are produced by the WinSock Group - a loose coalition of vendors made up of developers and technologists from around the world who work together to define, refine and extend this popular interface definition.

WOSA

Windows Open Architecture. Developed by Microsoft.

WWW

World Wide Web. A vast, worldwide hypermedia system consisting of a network of networks that allows you to browse through information on hundreds of thousands of databases. WWW is the multimedia-enabled layer of the Internet.

X

X.5

ITU recommendation on digital data communication networks and services, dealing with interfaces.

X.25

Possibly one of the most important international standards ever recommended by the ITU. From the beginning, it has provided a common reference point by which mainframe computers, word processors, minicomputers, VDUs, microcomputers, and varied equipment from different manufacturers can operate together over a packet switched network.

X.25 defines the interface between a public data network and a packet-mode user device. Typically used to connect WANs, packet switching breaks network data into smaller packets and sends them from point to point through interconnected switches. X stands for packet switched network.

X.38

ITU recommendation for the access of Group 3 facsimile equipment to the Facsimile Packet Assembly/Disassembly (FPAD) facility in public data networks situated in the same country.

X.39

ITU recommendation for the exchange of control information and user data between a Facsimile Packet Assembly/Disassembly (FAPD) facility and a packet mode data terminal equipment (DTE) or another pad, for international internetworking.

X.400

ITU recommendations for the transmission of electronic text and graphic mail between unlike computers, terminals, and computer networks. Briefly, X.400 describes how mail messages are encoded, and X.25 sets up how they are transmitted.

X.500

The ITU standard defining directory services, most commonly for E-mail systems. It provides for common naming and addressing in the networks of large-scale enterprises.

xBASE

The collective term for all database management systems using dBASE-compatible (.DBF format) data files, with a variety of enhancements and differing index formats (e.g., dBASE III+, dBASE IV, FoxBASE, FoxPro, Clipper).

XENIX

Microsoft trade name for a 16-bit microcomputer operating system derived from AT&T Bell Labs' UNIX.

Yellow Alarm

A T-1 alarm signal sent back toward the source of a failed transmit circuit in a DS-1 2-way transmission path. A yellow sends 0's (zeros) in bit two of all time slots. See also T-1.

Yellow Pages

A directory of telephone numbers classified by type of business. It was printed on yellow paper throughout most of the twentieth century until it was obsoleted in the late 1990s by dial-up yellow page directories operated by voice processing systems and in the early 21st century by electronic directories delivered on disposable laser disks. As a concession to history, the laser disks are now painted bright yellow. Actually, yellow pages remain one of the phone companies' most lucrative sources of revenues. Advertising rates are not cheap. There is now competition. There are many "Yellow Pages" directories, since AT&T never trademarked the term "Yellow Pages." Some "yellow page" directories are better value than others.

And some are more legitimate than others. Some actually never get printed or, if they are printed, are not printed in great quantity and are not distributed as widely as their sales literature implies. Many businesses have been suckered into paying money for listings and advertisements in directories that never appeared. This fictitious directory scam also has happened with "telex" and "fax" directories. This "scam" is fraud by mail and is heavily stomped upon by the US Postal Service. As a result, many fake directories (especially the telex ones) are "published" abroad.

Zero Code Suppression

The insertion of a "one" bit to prevent the transmission of eight or more consecutive "zero" bits. Used primarily with digital T1 and related telephone-company facilities which require a minimum "ones density" keep the individual subchannels of a multiplexed, high-speed facility active. Several different schemes are currently employed to accomplish this. Proposals for a standard are being evaluated by the ITU. See also ZERO SUPPRESSION.

ZeroFill

A traditional fax device is mechanical. It must reset its printer and advance the page as it prints each scan line it receives. If the receiving machine's printing capability is slower than the transmitting machine's data sending capability, the transmitting machine adds fill bits (also called zero fill) to pad out the span of send time, giving the slower remote machine the additional time it needs to reset prior to receiving the next scan line.

Zip Tone

Short burst of dial tone to an ACD agent headset indicating a call is being connected to the agent console.

Appendix C

Experts of the Voice-Enabled Internet

Active Voice Corporation
2901 Third Avenue
Seattle WA 98121
206-441-4700
206-441-4784 (fax)
www.activevoice.com

Advantage KBS
1 Ethel Rd. Suite 106B
Edison, NJ 08817
908-287-2236
908-287-3193 (fax)
www.akbs.com

American International
Facsimile Products (AIFP)
5560 SW 107th
Beaverton, OR 97005
800-600-4329
503-520-5458 (fax)
www.aifp.com

American Network Systems, Inc.
4615 Industrial Street, Suite 1G
Simi Valley, CA 93063
805-579-8898
805-579-9552 (fax)

Applied Voice Technology, Inc.
11410 NE 122nd Way Box 97025
Kirkland, WA 98083
206-820-6000
206-820-4040 (fax)
www.appliedvoice.com

Aspect Telecommunications
1730 Fox Drive
San Jose, CA 95131-2312
408-441-2200
408-441-2260 (fax)
www.aspect.com

Aum Tech, Inc.
201 Concourse Blvd. Suite 104
Glen Allen, VA 23060
804-967-9035
804-967-9039 (fax)

Automated Management Software
FreeVue Telecommunications Network
415-896-1330
www.freevue.com

Black Ice Software, Inc.
292 Rte 101
Amherst, NH 03031
603-673-1019
603-672-4112 (fax)

Boardwatch Magazine
8500 W. Bowles Ave., Suite 210
Littleton, CO 80123
303-933-8724
303-933-2939 (fax)
www.boardwatch.com

Bonzi Software
Paso Robles, CA
805-238-5798 (fax)
www.bonzi.com
info@bonzi.com

Brooktrout Technology
144 Gould Street
Needham MA 02194
617-449-4100
617-449-9009 (fax)
www.brooktrout.com

Call Center Magazine
12 West 21 Street
New York, NY 10010
212-691-8215
212-691-1191 (fax)
www.flatironpublishing.com

CallWare Technologies, Inc.
2323 Foothill Dr.
Salt Lake City, UT 84109
801-486-9922
801-486-8294 (fax)
www.callware.com

Camelot
17770 Preston Rd.
Dallas, TX 75252
214-713-2607
214-733-0574 (fax)

Centigram Communications Corporation
91 E Tasman Dr.
San Jose, CA 95134
408-428-3837
408-944-0250 (fax)
www.centigram.com.

Computer Telephony Magazine
12 West 21 Street
New York, NY 10010
212-691-8215
212-691-1191 (fax)
www.flatironpublishing.com

Connectix
2655 Campus Dr. Suite 100
San Mateo, CA 94403
415-571-5100
415-571-5195 (fax)
www.connectix.com

Cyber Radio 1
t-johns@microsoft.com

DataBeam Corporation
3191 Nicholasville Road
Lexington, KY 40503
606-245-3500
606-245-3528 (fax)
info@databeam.com
www.databeam.com

Davidson Consulting
530 N. Lamer Street,
Burbank, CA 91506
818-842-5117
818-842-5488 (fax)
davidsonco@aol.com

Dialogic Corporation
1515 Route 10
Parsippany, NJ 07054
201-993-3000
201-631-9631 (fax)
www.dialogic.com

Digital Sound Corporation
6307 Carpinteria Ave.
Carpinteria, CA 93013
805-566-2000
805-684-2848 (fax)

Edify Corporation
2840 San Tomas Expressway
Santa Clara, CA 95051
408-982-2000
408-982-0777 (fax)
www.edify.com

Enhanced Systems, Inc.
6961 Peachtree Industrial Blvd.
Norcross, GA 30092
770-662-1504
770 242 1630 (fax)
www.esisys.com

FaxSav, Inc. (nee Digitran)
Edison, NJ
800-828-7115
908-906-2000 (fax)
www.faxsav.com

FreeTel Communications, Inc.
540 N. Santa Cruz Ave. Suite 290
Los Gatos, CA 95030
408-358-6385 (fax)
www.freetel.com

G & R Data Group, Inc.
Atlanta, Georgia
404-876-4257
404-733-6838 (fax)
www.grdata.com

GMD Fokus
Hardenbergplatz 2
D-10623 Berlin Germany
49-30-25499-182
49-30-25499-202 (fax)
http://www.fokus.gmd.de/

HTI Voice Solutions
333 Turnpike Rd.
Southborough, MA 01772
508-485-8400

Ibex Technologies, Inc.
550 Main Street # G
Placerville, CA 95667
916-939-8888
916-621-2004 (fax)
www.ibex.com

IBM Corp.
3039 Cornwallis Rd.
RTP, NC 27709
919-254-7452
919-254-4913 Fax
www.hursley.ibm.com/dtmail

Inference
100 Rowland Way
Novato, CA 94945
415-899-0100
415-899-9080 (fax)
www.inference.com

Intel Corporation
Jones Farm Facility
2111 NE 25th Avenue
Hillsboro, OR 97124-5961
503-696-8080
800-697-5611 (fax)
www.intel.com

iNTELiTRAK Technologies, Inc.
PO Box 203102
Austin, Texas 78720-3102
512-480-2211
512-473-3680 (fax)
www.intelitrak.com

Intelligent Visual Computing (IVC)
a Division of Imonics Corp.
2205 Candun Dr. Suite C
Apex, NC 27502
919-363-0292
www.ivc.com

International Data Corporation
5 Speen Street
Framingham, MA 01701
508-872-8200
508-935-4015 (fax)

International Multimedia
Teleconferencing Consortium, Inc.
111 Deerwood Road, Suite 372
San Ramon, CA 94583
510-743-4455
510-743-9011 (fax)
www.imtc.org/imtc

International Telecommunications Union
Sales Service Place des Nations CH-1211
Genve 20 Switzerland
41-22-730-6141
41-22-730-5194 (fax)
www.itu.ch

IPC Peripherals, Inc.
48041 Fremont Blvd.
Fremont, CA 94538
510-354-0800
510-354-0808 (fax)
www.ipcp.us.com

Jabra Corporation
9191 Town Centre Drive, Suite 330
San Diego, CA 92122
619-622-0764
619-622-0353 (fax)
www.jabra.com

KnowledgeBroker, Inc.
1430 Valwood Dr., Suite 130
Carrolton, TX 75006
214-488-2494
214-488-2470 (fax)
www.kbi.com

Lansys Ltd.
7 Abba Hillel Street
Ramat Gan 52522 Israel
972-3-575-6633
972-3-575-6967 (fax)
multcall@netvision.net.il

Latitude Communications
2121 Tasman Drive
Santa Clara, California 95054
408-988-7200
408-988-6520 (fax)
www.latitude.com

LINKON Corporation
North American Sales Office
354 Lynn St.
Harringtom Park, NJ 07640
201-768-4397
201-767-9159 (fax)

Logicom, Inc.
5701 Pine Island Road, Suite 300
Tamarac, Florida 33321
954-726-3868
954-726-3748 (fax)
www.logicom.com/web900.htm

Lucent Technologies
211 Mt. Airy Road Room 2E402
Basking Ridge, NJ 07920
908-953-8605
908-953-2486 (fax)
www.lucent.com

Marin Software Partners
Neuchâtel, Switzerland
www.fourmilab.ch/netfone/windows/speakfb.zip

MediaGate
2059 Camden Ave. #121
San Jose, CA 95124
408-559-0897
408-559-8307 (fax)

Microsoft
1 Microsoft Way,
Redmond WA 98052-6399
206-936-7611
206-936-7329 (fax)
www.microsoft.com

MIT
Massachusetts Institute of Technology
77 Massachusetts Ave.
Cambridge, MA 02139
617-253-1000
http://web.mit.edu/

Natural MicroSystems
8 Erie Drive
Natick MA 01760-1339
508-650-1300
508-650-1350 (fax)
www.nmss.com

NetCall Technologies Limited
10 Harding Way
St Ives, Huntington
Cambbridgehire PE17 4WR U.K.
44-1480-495300
44-1480-496717 (fax)

NetPhonic Communications
1580 W. El Camino Real
Mountain View, CA 94040
415-962-1111
415-962-1370 (fax)
www.netphonic.com

Netspeak Corporation
902 Clint Moore Rd.
Boca Raton, FL 33487
407-997-4001
407-997-2401 (fax)
www.netspeak.com

NetWatch, Inc.
2 Brookbridge Rd.
Great Neck NY 11021
516-487-1424
516-829-1624 (fax)
www.von.com

NetXchange Communications Ltd.
225 Bush, Suite 1625
San Francisco, CA 94104
415-346-4131
415-346-2430 (fax)

Nice Systems, Inc.
150 Broadway, Suite 1200
New york, NY 10038
212-267-3545
212-267-3669 (fax)

Novell
2275 Trade Zone Blvd.
San Jose, CA 95131
408-434-2300
408-577-5920 (fax)
www.novell.com

Octel Communications Corporation
1001 Murphy Ranch Road
Milpitas, CA 95035
408-321-2000
408-321-2100 (fax)
www.octel.com

Periphonics Corporation
4000 Veterans Memorial Hwy
Bohemia, NY 11716
516-467-0500
516-737-8520 (fax)
www.peri.com

Precept Software, Inc.
21580 Stevens Creek Boulevard, Suite 207
Cupertino, CA 95014
casner@precept.com

Precision Systems, Inc.
11800 30th Court N.
St Petersburg, FL 33716
813-572-9300
813-573-9193 (fax)
www.talkpsi.com

Professional Help Desk
800 Summer St. Suite 500
Stanford, CT 06901
203-869-4433
203-356-7900 (fax)

Progressive Networks
616 1st Avde Suite 701
Seattle, WA 98104
206-447-0567
206-223-8221 (fax)
www.RealAudio.com

Prospect Software, Inc.
1737 N. First Street, Suite 240
San Jose, CA 95112
408-451-2451
408-451-2454 (fax)
prospect@netcom.com

Quarterdeck Corporation
13160 Mindanao Way
Marina del Rey, CA 90292
310-309-3700
www.quarterdeck.com

Quest Interactive Media, Inc.
2060 North Collins Blvd. Suite 130
Richardson, TX 75081
214-231-4313
214-231-6159 (fax)

Remedy Corporation
1505 Salado Drive
Mountain View, CA 94043
415-903-5200
415-903-9001 (fax)
www.remedy.com

Rockwell Switching Systems
1431 Opus Place
Downers Grove, IL 60515
708-960-8000
708-960-8165 (fax)
www.rockwell.com

Securicor Telecoms
Oasis Park
Stanton Harcourt Road
Eynsham
Oxfordshire, OX8 1TQ
44-1865-883177
44-1865-883199 (fax)
100125.762@compuserve.com

ShadowTel Communications Corporation
Mississauga Ontario
905-890-4921
www.twg.on.ca

Siemens Rolm Communications, Inc.
4900 Old Ironsides Dr.
P.O. Box 58075
Santa Clara, CA 95054
408-492-2000
408-492-2160 (fax)
www.rolm.com

Silversoft
softfone@silver.com.pk
www.pak.net/softfone.htm

Smith Micro Software, Inc.
51 Columbia
Aliso Viejo, CA 92656
714-362-5800
714-362-2300 (fax)
www.smithmicro.com

SoftLinx, Inc.
234 Littleton Road
Westford, MA 01886 USA
508-392-0001
508-392-9009 (fax)
www.softlinx.com

Spanlink Communications
1 Main St. SE 4th Floor
Minneapolis, MN 55414
612-362-8000
612-362-8300 (fax)
www.spanlink.com

Stardust Technologies, Inc.
1901 S. Bascom Ave, Suite 333
Campbell, CA 95008
408-879-8080
408-879-8081 (fax)
www.stardust.com

Stylus Product Group
Artisoft, Inc.
201 Broadway
Cambridge MA 02139-1955
617-621-9545
617-621-7862 (fax)
www.stylus.com

Sun Microsystems
2550 Garcia, Mailstop UMPK10-107
Mountain View, CA 94043-1100
http://java.sun.com

Syntellect Inc.
1000 Holcomb Woods Parkway
Building 410A
Roswell, Georgia 30076-2585
770-587-0700
770-587-0589 (Fax)
www.syntellect.com

TAC Systems, Inc.
1035 Putman Drive Suite A
Huntsville, AL 35816-1822
205-721-1976
205-721-0242 (fax)

Teknekron Infoswitch Corporation
4425 Cambridge Road
Fort Worth, TX 76155
817-267-3025
817-571-9464 (fax)
www.teknekron.com

TELECONNECT Magazine
12 West 21 Street
New York, NY 10010
212-691-8215
212-691-1191 (fax)
www.flatironpublishing.com

Telescape Communications
1965 West 4th Avenue, Suite 101
Vancouver, BC V6J 1M8
604-738-2500
604-469-5589 (fax)
info@telescape.com

Telinet
3000 Northwoods Parkay
Norcross, GA 30071
770-242-0492
www.telinet.com

Tribal Voice
627 West Midland Avenue
Woodland Park, CO 80863-1100
603-886-9050
719 687-0716 (fax)
www.tribal.com

Trumpet Software International
21660 East Copley Drive Suite 340
Diamond Bar, CA 91765
909-861-4400
909-861-0215 (fax)
www.trumpet.com

UNISYS Corporation
Natural Language Understanding Group
2476 Swedesford Rd.
Paoli, PA 19301
610-648-6000
610-695-5636 (fax)
www.unisys.com

University of Illinois
1200 West Harrison Street
Chicago, IL 60680
312-996-4350
www.uiuc.edu/

University of North Carolina
Chapel Hill, NC 27599
919-962-2211
http://www.unc.edu/

VDONet
www.vdo.net

Venturian Software
1300 Second Street South
Hopkins, Minn. 55343
612-931-2500
612-931-2459 (fax)
www.venturian.com

Virtuosity
520 Washington Blvd. Suite 908
Marina Del Rey, CA 90292
310-574-0574
310-306-2795 (fax)
www.virtuosity.com

VocalTec, Inc.
157 Veterans Dr.
Northvale, NJ 07647
201-768-9400
201-768-8893 (fax)
www.vocaltec.com

Vosaic Corporation
Digital Video Communications
www.vosaic.com

Voxware, Inc.
172 Tamarack Circle
Skillman, NJ 08858
609-497-1212
609-497-2490 (fax)

White Pine Software, Inc.
40 Simon Street
Nashua, NH 03060-3043
603-886-9050
603-886-9051 (fax)
www.wpinw.com

Xing Technology Corp.
1540 West Branch Street
Arroyo Grande, CA 93420
805-473-0145
www.xingtech.com

INDEX

C

D

J

K

R

S

W

X